Overview

Gadar literally means "Rebellion"/"Revolt"/"Mutiny," and Sikh Gadar Lehar means "Sikh Revolutionary Movement." Historical truth is hard to come by because typically history is written by the victors and not by those who make history. The hard fact is that over 85% of the Gadarites were Sikh males in North America. The Sikh Faith clearly was a guiding inspiration in starting the revolution from North American soil. It is awe inspiring that a handful of Sikhs created fear in the British Empire, and a case titled "War against the King" was filed against them. Vedic Indian writers from day one have purposely skewed, ignored, or outright lied about the overwhelmingly noble role of the Sikhs, versus the cunningly ignoble role of the few Vedics in the Gadar movement. For centuries Brahmanism has always had a patronizing attitude with extreme prejudice against the minorities, including the Sikh Faith. Sikh theology destroys the very edifice of the foundational postulates of the Hindu Varna concept. The Sikh teachings stand firmly for women's rights, equality of all, democracy, freedom, justice, liberty, for universalistic, humanistic values, and is completely against any form of tyranny, classism, casteism which denigrates humans. Vedic and left-leaning historians project Veer Savarkar and Lala Hardyal as the founders of this movement, which is contrary to the historical fact as noted by various writers in this book. Setting the record straight for posterity is not just important for the future generations of Sikh Americans, but for all Americans to know the unbiased, untainted, historical fact, so that the nearly a century of half-truths cooked up by mostly Vedic and other Indian nationalist writers can be rectified. Further, the Indian National Congress failed to pass any resolution honoring the Gadarites. Most attacks were on Sikh identity, and British consulates offices in North America worked against the immigrants and even tried to move them to British Honduras. The Gadarite dream of equality in independent India must be honored by implementing Supreme Court Justice Venkatachelliah's 2002 commission recommendation on changing Article 25 B, so that Buddhists, Jains, and Sikhs become "equal citizens" on truly secular ground in India. Indian diaspora, rather than paying lip service, must work together on the Gadarite dream of secular India like the US. Papers included in this book establish the historical record of the Gadar movement accurately. I am fortunate that my maternal grandfather Ram Singh Sarkaria was a student at UC, Berkley, CA, during this period which refreshes my memory of many stories I heard from my grandmother (Naniji).

Kavneet Singh Pannu

SIKH GADAR LEHAR
1907-1918

Edited by Jasbir Singh Mann MD & Satnam Singh Johal

Published By
Shri Guru Granth Sahib Foundation
1771 W. Romneya Drive, Suite E,
Anaheim, 92801 Tel 714-758-8553 Fax 714-758-1485
Email; sggsfca@gmail.com
Web page www.globalsikhstudies.net

The contributors themselves, not editors and the publishers, are responsible for the views expressed by them in their articles. The contributors have spelt the word *Gadar* differently as *Ghadar* or *Ghadr* and *Gadaris* as *Ghadaris, Ghadarites, Ghadrites* and *Gadrites*, etc. The learned reader may find this discrepancy in the spellings though each means the same thing. That is, *Gadar*, etc., for the mutiny/rebellion/revolt against the King, and *Gadaris*, etc., for heroes who participated in it.

ISBN 978-0-9862987-9-0

Dedicated to the members of Khalsa Diwan Society, Vancouver, B.C., Canada, and Pacific Coast Khalsa Diwan Society, Stockton, California, USA, who were the pioneers of Gadar Movement, 1907 to 1918.

Contents

The Canadian Sikh Study and Teaching Society 1

Preface 3

Introduction. 11

The Indian Mutiny of 1857 and The Sikhs 15
By Dr. Ganda Singh *15*

Life and Times of Sant Teja Singh: 1906–1912 37
By Dr. Sukhmander Singh. *37*

Reevaluating the Origin and Inspiration of "Sikh Gadar 1907–1918" 53
By Jasbir Singh Mann MD, California. *53*

Effect of the Sacrificial Traditions of Sikh Heritage
on the Journalism of Ghadar Movement 123
By Dr. Gurvinder Singh Dhaliwal. *123*

Central Role of Gurdwaras in Ghadri Movement 133
By Rajwinder Singh Rahi *133*

Perspectives On The Ghadr Movement 153
By Dr. Gurdarshan Singh Dhillon. *153*

Relevance of Sikh Ideology for the Ghadar Movement. 169
By Dr. J.S. Grewal Former VC GNDU. *169*

Sikh Pioneers in North America and the Crisis of Leadership 175
By Dr. Amrik Singh *175*

Gadaris, Gadar Party, and Anglo-Vedic Games of the British 197
By Dr. Amrik Singh *197*

The Surveillance of Indian Nationalists in North America, 1908–1918 .. 221
By Dr. Hugh Johnston.. *221*

The Komagata Maru Episode and the Ghadar Party 247
By Dr. Hugh Johnston.. *247*

Social and Political Lives of Early Sikh Settlers
in California: 1897–1946...................................... 265
By Dr. Bruce La Brack *265*

Social and Political Lives of Punjabi Settlers
of the Columbia River, Oregon 1910–1920 277
By Johana Ogden *277*

The 1907 Bellingham Riot and Anti-Asian Hostilities
in the Pacific Northwest 303
By Dr. Paul Englesberg *303*

The Ghadar Movement: Its Aims and Objectives and the
Effect of this Movement on the Tragedy of Komagata Maru.......... 339
By Dr. Puran Singh. *339*

Bhai Mewa Singh Lopoke – The Immortal Martyr of Canada......... 353
By Sohan Singh Pooni *353*

Pen-profiles of the Renowned Ghadarites of Canada and America..... 367
By Sohan Singh Pooni *367*

Bhai Randhir Singh: An Uncommon Personality.................. 391
By Dr. Balwant Singh Dhillon. *391*

Life and Times of Pakher Singh Gill:
A Panjabi Californian in the Early Twentieth Century.............. 397
By Dr. Nirmal S. Mann, MD................................... *397*

Role of Gadrites in Babbar Akali Movement and
India's Freedom Struggle 411
By Dr. Baljeet Singh Sahi and Dr. Gurcharan Singh Aulkh.......... *411*

Ghadar Movement: Its Origin and Impact on Jallianwala
Bagh Massacre and Indian Freedom Struggle. 437
By Dr. Tarlochan Singh Nahal *437*

Gadar Lehar and Lala Har Dayal: Life, Activities, & Ideology. 471
By Jatinder Singh Hundal. *471*

Fresh Look at Ram Chandra Bhardwaj and
Vinayak Damodar Savarkar. 499
By Jasbir Singh Mann MD, California. *499*

It Takes a Massacre: The Sikhs are Really Americans Now. 519
By Dr. Harold A. Gould. *519*

Ghadar Movement: Role of Media and Literature 523
By Dr. Gurmel S. Sidhu, Professor. *523*

Appendices. 547

Brief Bio with Photos of Contributors 557

Index 565

The Canadian Sikh Study and Teaching Society

The Canadian Sikh Study and Teaching Society, in association with the Shri Guru Granth Sahib foundation in Anaheim, California, organized the international conference on the Sikh Gadhar Lehar 1907–1918 on March 16, 2013, at the India Banquet Hall in Surrey, BC. The conference was hosted in the memory of the Sikh Gadar Lehar, which was launched to secure independence for India. The main objective of this conference was to discuss the origin and source of the inspiration of Gadar Lehar in North America. Well-known scholars from North America participated in the conference and delivered their well-researched lectures on the Gadhar movement. The audience was impressed with their research and presentations.

The Canadian Sikh Study and Teaching Society was formed in 1987 under the guidance of Dr. Gurbakhash Singh Gill (former Dean PAU Ludhiana) and the late Giani Harbhajan Singh, a great preacher (Kathwachick). The society was registered as a nonprofit organization in 1988. Its main objective is to educate us as well as our youth about Sikh religion, history, and culture.

The society started teaching Punjabi language classes in Burnaby, Richmond, Surrey, and Vancouver and also started summer youth camps for children. The society also published numerous books about the Sikh faith for children and adults. Another major project of the society was to run Gurbani classes. The classes were taught by Giani Harbhajan Singh, and hundreds of Sikhs took advantage of his scholarly way of teaching and learning Gurbani. The Society has organized numerous academic and religious conferences on an international level, and many scholars from India, UK, USA, and Canada participated to deliver their philosophical lectures.

In 2011, the Canadian Sikh Study and Teaching Society also started a free homework club to assist local students from grade 4 to 12 with their homework every Saturday. Dedicated volunteers with college and university backgrounds help students in English, history, math, science, and other projects.

The Canadian Sikh Study and Teaching Society would like to extend our sincere gratitude to our supporters and generous donors who helped make the conference a success. We would also like to thank the Gurdwara Akali Singh Sikh Society for publishing this book. Without their generous support, it may not have been possible.

Finally, the Canadian Sikh study and Teaching Society is grateful to all the scholars who accepted our invitation to participate in the Sikh Gadar Lehar conference.

Satnam Singh Johal, President

Preface

The idea for the Sikh Gadar Lehar 1907–1918 international conference held in March, 2013, in Surrey, British Columbia, Canada, came during discussions between Satnam Singh Johal, President of The Canadian Sikh Study and Teaching Society, and Dr. Jasbir Singh Mann of the Shri Guru Granth Sahib Foundation, Anaheim, California. Further discussions were held among Pritam Singh Aulakh, Dr. Pooran Singh Gill, Jasbir Singh Gandham, Harvindar Singh Parmar, Dr. Amrik Singh, Dr. Gurmel Singh Sidhu, Jatinder Singh Hundal, Dr. Baljit Singh Sahi, and Raminderjit Singh Sekhon. As the movement had started from the Pacific Northwest, a need was felt to hold such a conference in British Columbia, after two successful and well-attended centennial Sikh conferences for the Pacific Coast Khalsa Diwan Society (Sikh Temple Stockton) held on September 22nd and Sept 30th, 2012, at the University of the Pacific, Stockton, California. Papers presented in both of these conferences confirmed that the Gadar of 1914–15 was a historic movement by Sikh migrants who returned to Punjab/India from North America to overthrow the colonial British rule. The Gadari Babas took inspiration and guidance from both the Sikh ideology and history of Sikh armed revolution. But, in spite of a preponderance of evidence, after India got independence, the majority of national historians presents the Gadar movement of Sikh pioneers from the Indian state's perspective, as if Sikh Gadaris abandoned the Sikh values and totally adopted the Indian/Hindu nationalist values. History shows that it all started from the Pacific Northwest from 1907 onwards as soon as the Pacific Coast Khalsa Diwan Vancouver was established between 1906 and1908. Literature produced by national historians has suppressed the role of Sikh ideology, Sikh temples (Gurdwaras), Sikh priests, Professor Teja Singh, and the good relations of the Gadari Babas with the Sikh Leage, SGPC, and Sri Akal Takhat, and their participation in Sikh affairs. In his book *India as I Knew It*, Sir Michael O'Dwyer, the lieutenant governor of Punjab from 1912 to 1919, calls it the "Sikh Gadar Conspiracy" (O'Dwyer, 190–210). As British literature and government records per O'Dwyer call the 1907–1918 period of this movement "Sikh Gadar Conspiracy," it is therefore correct to label this movement "SIKH GADAR LEHAR 1907–1918."

The movement was launched from Sikh Gurudwaras and the Guru Granth Sahib's social, secular, and egalitarian teachings along with its direct interpretation, since its compilation in 1604, and the Nash doctrine of Guru Gobind Singh, since the creation of Khalsa in 1699; thereby, promoting equality, denouncing the caste system (Varan dharam ashram), etc., were the real inspirations of the majority of Sikh participants. Data shows that more than 85% of these immigrants were male Sikhs, and this movement did not involve repudiation of their religious faith; instead, their faith strengthened their involvement in the Sikh Gadar revolution. That is why they went back to India to fight for the cause. Between 1907 and 1918, their religious conscience was their guiding force, and that's why the movement was non-sectarian and non-racial. From 1905 to 1913 in Europe, Shyamaji Krishna Varma's Arya Smaj philosophy, Veer Savarkar and Abhinava Bharat's philosophy, and Bhikaiji Cama and Sardar Singh Rana's Social Democratic philosophy were tried. But inspiration behind their thought processes could not produce any mass international movement in Europe for the freedom of India, as compared to the West Coast of North America where the movement was finally produced and action taken through Sikh inspiration.

Sikhs were loyal for the complete independence from British India and were also loyal to their belief in Sikhism. In their writing, national historians ignore the role played by several Hindustan freedom societies, multiple constitutional struggles, and propaganda from northwest America against joining military in India, as well as their explosive schemes and their publication and distribution of seven newspapers prior to 1907–1912. Evidence shows that Germans have connections with Indian revolutionaries since 1909. Bernhardi, a German general in 1911, thought that the Hindu population of Bengal and Pan-islamists would create danger for British. But he was proved wrong. It was only Sikhs from Punjab in North America who created such danger for the British from 1907 onwards. December 31, 1913, German Consulate Franz Bopp was in meeting with Gadrites in Sacramento. From 1913 onwards, German money only facilitated the struggle by making the travels of Gadarites easy. Additionally, within six months of German help, the Gadar literature found easy placement in many countries, such as in Egypt, South Africa, Fiji, Canada, British East Africa, British Guiana, Philippines, Hong Kong, Thailand, Burma, Dutch, East Indies, etc. On March 6th, 1914, a German newspaper talks of organized enterprise in California for the purpose of providing India with arms and explosives. But no serious attempt was made by the Germans or Gadarite leaders to send any money or arms to the Gadaries in Punjab prior to February 19th, 1915, when the Gadar had collapsed due to lack of funds and arms. Later on, German Ambassador Bernstorff referred to the Hindu plot in his memoirs as "an absolute wild-goose chase," whereas, years later, German military attaché Von Papen wrote in his own memoirs that "he never really expected Germany to successfully export revolution to India, but rather create a diversion of British effort."

Germany wanted to become superpower but soon realized that America's resources might well be the key to the victory of the World War I as all the ammunition and arms were supplied from the US. Therefore, they sabotaged the American ammunition factories and Canadian Pacific railways to achieve their goals. The British had two objectives before them: (1) how to reduce German-Americans' influence in American society and (2) how to induce the US into the First World War. The British needed many collaborators who could bring inside information of the Germans' decision-making leadership and who could provoke the US to jump into the War. It appears that the Hindu leaders of Arya Samaj and Abhinava Bharat had larger goals in the background of securing the Indian subcontinent for Hindus. This is proved by evidence of Savarkar's promotion of Hindutva from 1923 onwards and the political statement of Lala Hardyal in 1925. Sikhs' real value lay in creating danger for the British and thereby increasing the bargaining power of their leaders. Sarvarkar's radicalism, Gadar rhetoric of Lala Har Dayal, and the anti-British tone of Ram Chandra compelled many patriots to jump into the Gadar, but evidence shows all three of them surrendered to the British. What motivated them? It appears their idea was to secure the Indian subcontinent for Hindu civilization, which would win back all those who had converted to other faiths? The British knew this aspect, and, therefore, they appeared to have used many Hindu radicals and anarchists to identify the rebellious elements mostly among Sikhs but also among Hindus and Muslims who followed the same path. However, most Sikhs who joined the Gadar Movement were fully conversant with Sikh martyrdom tradition, and their primary source of inspiration was Sikh martyrdom tradition and khalsa revolution. On this movement, Don K. Digan writes, "great surprise to find that a large proportion of the political files of the American Department of the British Foreign Office—nearly half of the bound volumes for 1916—relate to the Indian seditionist problem." The British used the sacrifices of Sikhs as their evidence for use of (USA) land by Gadrites to push the United States into World War I.

National historians are either silent or they misrepresent the true role played by Lala Hardial and his mentor Savarkar for promotion of Hindu nationalism. The Stockton conferences in September of 2012 and the Surrey conference in March of 2013 were held to present the true historical evidence. Based on evidence, our emphasis is to present before the readers that, between 1907 and 1918, the Sikh inspiration of the majority of participants played a substantial role in the Indian freedom movement from North America. The Sikh participants in the Sikh Gadar Lehar of 1907–1918 were loyal to the movement for independence from British India and were also "loyal Sikhs." They never abandoned their Sikh values. It was not a Sikh religious movement. It is very unfortunate that left-leaning writers are now misrepresenting the historical evidence and are misleading their readers by comparing it with the Sikh movement of the last century. Communist influence in the Gadar movement is a late phenomenon, after 1922–1927 as is clearly supported by their own writings of Sohan Singh Josh and Rattan Singh Ajnala. Values of equality, goodness, civil liberties, social reforms, universal human freedom, independence, and religious freedom as ingrained in SGGS were known to the Sikhs from 1604 AD till the **Khalsa Revolution** of 1699 AD. The **French Revolution** is a later period of social and political upheaval from 1789 to 1799. Therefore, the French Revolution had no influence on this movement. Moreover, none of the French political thinkers showed any marked concern for the lower classes as compared to the Sikh revolution of 1604–1699, which was not only an egalitarian social revolution but was plebeian (for low class) as well. The Mexican Revolution began in 1910, ended dictatorship in Mexico, and established a constitutional republic.

Recording correct history, opinions, and experiences is an important component for exposing our heritage and history to the North American generations, especially the younger North American (Sikhs) generation who may not visit India in future. But, many of them will see portraits of their great grandparents with turbans in their drawing rooms and may have some

Preface

queries. If they read the right books, only then will know about the true contributions of the Sikh pioneers of North America for the "WAR AGAINST THE KING" independence movement from British India in 1914–1915. What exactly happened? Why did the Sikh pioneers go back to India in 1914 with no money and no arms to fight an armed revolution to liberate India? Their leaders promised them that they would get money and arms when they reached India. Did they fail in their inspiration derived from the following stanza: "If you desire to play the game of love with me, and then step onto my Path with your head in palm of your hand? When you place your feet on this Path, Then give your head, and do not blame/find imperfection with anyone/pay any attention to the public opinion." Or did their leaders fail? Did the pioneer Sikhs ever dream in 1914 that their future generations would have to go by the explanations in the Constitution Article 25 B, Hindu marriage Act 1955, Hindu Adoption Act 1956, Hindu minority guardianship Act 1956, Hindu succession Act 1956, and Hindu undivided family tax Act 1955, wherein "Hindus shall be construed as including a reference to persons professing the Sikh, Jain, or Buddhist religion"? Explanation II of Article 25 of the Constitution unnecessarily and illegally clubs Sikhs with Hindus and others for authorizing the state to pass laws for throwing religious places of those religions to all belonging to that religion, while Sikh religious places are open to everyone even the non-Sikhs. Therefore, it appears inclusion of Sikhs in Exp. II was a mischievous ploy rather than plain ignorance. The Anand Marriage Act of 1909 continues to be applicable since then. Some Sikhs misconstrue that the Anand Marriage Act ceased to be applicable to the Sikhs when the Hindu Marriage Act came into force in 1955. Similarly, others think that the Hindu Marriage Act ceased to apply to the Sikhs after amendment of the Anand Marriage Act in 2012. It may be clarified that both continue to be applicable to Sikhs to date. While the Anand Marriage Act regards the ceremonial (and now registration) aspect of the marriage, the Hindu Marriage Act deals with validity, divorce, maintenance, etc. The 2012 amendment of the Anand Marriage Act is yet to become applicable (October 2013) as State Government has not framed the necessary rules as required by the amendment. Sikhs in India feel that the titles of the four acts should be amended either by omitting the word "Hindu" or by adding the words "Buddhist, Jain, and Sikh." The latter option of adding the names of three religions is in accordance with the recommendation of the Constitution Review Commission to amend article 25(2)(b) of the Constitution against which similar grouse is being expressed by the Sikhs and others. In 2002, the Government of India instituted a Constitutional Review Committee headed by Justice Venkata Chaliah for recommending amendments to the Constitution of India. The Constitution Review Committee thoroughly studied the issue and accepted the just and logical demand of the Sikhs to amend Article 25. The Constitution Review Committee recommended the deletion of explanation II of Article 25, which is the controversial portion of Article 25. This recommendation for amending Article 25 has been lying with the Prime Minister's Office for about a decade. Check the following for details; http://www.lawmin.nic.in/ncrwc/finalreport.htm. The Commission, without going into the larger issue on which the contention is based, is of the opinion that the purpose of the representations would be served if Explanation II to article 25 is omitted and sub-clause (b) of clause (2) of that article is reworded as follows: "(b) providing for social welfare and reform or the throwing open of Hindu, Sikh, Jain or Buddhist religious institutions of a public character to all classes and sections of these religions." By rewording clause (b) and deleting Explanation II, Sikhism, Jainism, and Buddhism will become independent religions legally per the Constitution and will have equal recognition and equal representation. The Dream of Gadarites 100 years ago was the "Secular United States of India, like the United States of America." Why are nationalist and left-leaning writers silent about the shattered dreams of Gadari Babas? The papers presented highlight the evidence ignored so far by many national historians. The papers project the authentic role played by the Sikh pioneers between 1907 and 1918 for the independence of India.

Evidence shows that Ram Chandra became materialistic and was a British spy as reported by Hari Singh Usman. Savarkar's nationalism was Hindutva, for which the BJP government honored him by renaming the Port Blair Airport in the Andaman Islands the Veer Savarkar Airport in 2002 and by putting his portrait alone in parliament in 2003. BJP honored followers of Hindutva; Congress honored the followers of Gandhi and his non-violence. Meanwhile, the sacrifices of all who fought for independence from British India between 1907 and 1918 from North America were ignored. Finally, thanks to Dr. Manmohan Singh who at least officially acknowledged Gadar Movement as part of India's freedom movement in 1913.

I am thankful to many speakers who presented their papers at centennial Sikh conferences held at the Universty of the Pacific, Stockton, California, in 2012 and again accepted our request to speak in March 2013 at the Surrey, BC,

Preface

conference. We are also thankful to the many other scholars who could not attend the Surrey conference, including Dr. Sukhmandar Singh, Dr. Bruce La Brack, Dr. Harold A. Gould, Dr. Tarlochan Singh Nahal, Dr. Balwant Singh Dhillon, Dr. Nirmal Singh Mann, Dr. Gurdarshan Singh Dhillon, Dr. Jagtar Singh Grewal, and Rajwinder Singh Rahi. Their scholarly work on Sikh pioneers and the Gadar movement for inclusion in this volume is highly appreciated. We are also thankful to the late Dr. Ganda Singh for his evidence-based paper (1969) which has been specially included in this volume for clarification of readers and which concludes ". . . it would be a travesty of truth to describe the revolt of 1857 as a national war of independence."

Equally, we express our thanks to Gursagar Singh and Kavneet Singh Pannu for their invaluable guidance and help involving the publication of this volume. Our thanks are also due to Pritam Singh Aulakh, Dr. Baljit Singh Sahi, Balwant Singh Dhillon, Dr. Gurmel Singh Sidhu, Dr. Sarabjinder Singh, Dr. Kashmir Singh, Dr. Kulwinder Singh Bajwa, Sohan Singh Pooni, Dr. Sukhmandar Singh, and Raminderjit Singh Sekhon for their valuable suggestions. We also take the opportunity to thank the Canadian Sikh Study and Teaching Society, Gurdwara Akali Singh Sikh Society, and Sikh Sangat of BC who liberally funded the conference and offered generous hospitality to the scholars and other participants. I am thankful to my family, especially my wife, Dr. Satinder Kaur Mann, for her loving support and never-ending faith in me and my Sikh community projects.

Jasbir Singh Mann, MD
President, Shri Guru Granth Sahib Foundation
Anaheim, California

Introduction

Gadar Lehar 1907 - 1918
Movement to free India from the British Rule

The Canadian Sikh Study and Teaching Society of Vancouver, Canada, along with the Federation of Sikh Societies of Canada, arranged an international conference at the India Banquet Hall in Surrey, BC, on March 16, 2013, where speakers from Bellingham, Washington; Astoria, Oregon; six speakers from California, USA; and four from Vancouver, Canada, read their papers. This conference was held to commemorate the 100th anniversary of the very brave and selfless souls who started the Gadar Lehar, a revolutionary movement in 1907. This movement was originally started in Vancouver in 1907 and was followed by the opening of an office in San Francisco, USA, in 1913.

This book attempts to recognize the hundreds of Sikhs, Hindus, and Muslims whose efforts and sacrifices have been ignored by history or have been misquoted by the historians. The papers in this book provide information based on well-researched historical evidence to prove that the Gadar movement had the major impact in awakening, educating, and readying the public in India to fight for independence from the British. It's a captivating look into the political, social, legal, and economic environment in Punjab, India, and here in the West Coast of North America that brought about and motivated these people, the vast majority of whom were Sikhs, to endeavor to end rule in India of one of the most powerful empires—the British. How could these people, who were limited in resources and rights, organize such a vast revolutionary movement and spread their message? What challenges did they face in trying to have their voices heard? With Canada being a colony of Great Britain, what role did the Canadian government and officials play in preventing their work?

The proceedings in this book provide answers to all these questions. According to information provided by these papers and supported by historical evidence, the major players were mostly the farmers and army personnel from Punjab, who were driven out from their homes, in search for better life, mainly because of the social, economic, political, and justicial treatment they received under British rule. More than 85% of them were the Sikhs from Punjab. Out of these, more than two dozen who joined the movement from outside India were tried and hanged in India by the British Rulers, while hundreds of others were jailed to rot for life, some in the Andaman Islands and others in many jails across India. This book provides an insight into the movement and activities of these revolutionaries in the different countries where they migrated, such as Singapore, Malaya (present day Malaysia), Thailand, Shanghai (China), Japan, etc. In addition, they had also started to migrate to the West Coast of North America in the later part of the 19th century.

The reader can see how, in contradiction to Queen Victoria's Proclamation of 1858 in Council to the princes, chiefs, and people of India, these migrants of North America were treated with hostilities by the government officials and faced racial discrimination. The British Government completely ignored this, and, instead of helping them, it tried to block their migration to the West Coast of North America. It did not end there; it tried even to move them to British Honduras. From this book, the reader will be surprised to discover why the British did this.

All this has become part of North American history, and the schools in Whatcom County and Bellingham, USA, have already included this as part of their schools' curriculum. The readers will also get to read the proclamations issued by the Mayor of Bellingham and the Whatcom County Executive recognizing what took place in 1907 and in 1913.

Papers included in this book not only set the historical record of the Gadar movement straight while recognizing the major players in the Gadar movement, but they also prove that the Gadar movement was started originally in 1907 in Vancouver, Canada, and then moved to San Francisco in 1913. Second and furure generations of immigrants from India will find this historical record in North America as part of their proud heritage connected with the independence of India.

I would highly recommend that everyone read this book, because it not only informs the reader on a very interesting and little known part of Indian history while they were living in North America, but it also enables the reader to truly imagine how these Gadrites covered the span of so many countries where they had established effective centers to carry out their revolutionary activities and were able to network so effectively with all of the different groups in different countries with such limited resources. It's also inspiring to see how the Sikh Gadrites were able to use the social and political media to spread their message. They were able to publish weekly and monthly papers and pamphlets in Punjabi, Urdu, Gujarati, and English from America and Canada, which were disseminated to all their centers across the world. Poetry was as an integral part of these publications for the Gadar movement and played a frontal role in conveying the message of the revolt. The message was vehemently preached through popular versification by employing images and motifs relating to heroes and martyrs of the movement who were influenced by none else but the teachings of Guru Granth Sahib and the tradition of Martyrdom in Sikhism for the cause of righteousness.

Pritam Singh Aulakh, Vancouver

The Indian Mutiny of 1857 and The Sikhs

Ganda Singh

1969
GURDWARA PARBANDHAK COMMITTEE
SISGANJ, CHANDNI CHOWK
DELHI

Introductory

The first part of the this paper on *the Indian Mutiny of 1857 and the Sikhs* was written for the Indian Freedom Struggle Centenary (1857–1957) Souvenir Committee, New Delhi, and was published in the *Tribune*, Ambala, on August 15, 1957. I had been asked by the Secretary to the Committee in his letter No. AL/722 of June 13, 1957, to rebut, if I could, the charge that the "Indian Struggle for freedom (1857) failed as the Sikhs betrayed and sided with the British."

For some time, the Indian people had been fed on the writings of the self-glorifying political propagandists, calling this uprising the First War of Indian Independence. And they were taken aback by the truthful statements contained in this paper. To them, objective history was not palatable enough, nor was it easy for them to digest. The result was a number of letters that appeared in the *Tribune* during August and September 1957. Some of them raised points which, I felt, needed clarification for those who had not studied the subject from firsthand sources and had depended for their knowledge on non-historical literature. For them was written the second part of the paper which was published in the same journal on October 6, 1957.

It is a great pity that in a spirit of misguided patriotism our countrymen—even the educated ones —are not unoften carried away by self-glorifying emotions, against which the venerable Acharya Kriplani cautioned them at the State History Congress at Bhopal in January 1968, with particular reference to the "Sepoy Mutiny of 1857, which has been glorified into the First War of Indian Independence. According to him it was nothing but an attempt by the old order to get back their kingdoms and principalities." And it is a lamentable fact "that the motives of some of the principal actors [in the drama of Mutiny] were not free from suspicion." "But historical research and writing in India," to quote the editor of the *Tribune,* from his editorial of January 16, 1968, "has seldom been able to surmount what it falsely regards to be its patriotic duty even at the cost of objective scholarship." The late Maulana Abul Kalam Azad, one of the leading most fighters for the freedom of India in the twentieth century, writes in his foreword to *Eighteen Fifty-seven* by Dr. Surendra Nath Sen, published by the Publication Division of the Government of India:

> *Some Indians have written on the struggle in the early years of the century. If truth is to be told, we have to admit that the books they have written are not history but mere political propaganda. These authors wanted to represent the uprising as a planned war of independence organized by the nobility of India against British Government. [p. viii]*

But the conception of India as a whole as one unified country and of its people as one solid nation, for whose independence they could combine together and fight to the last, was yet in embryo in 1857 and was not familiar to the Indian mind. It was, in fact, propounded by the sponsors and leaders of the Indian National Congress some three decades later when a beginning came to be made for the emotional integration of the people under its banner.

Dr. Romesh C. Majumdar, the author of the *History of the Freedom Movement in India,* volume I, tells us on the basis of his life-long researches in the history of the country that:

I thought it necessary . . . to counteract the current view that the outbreak of 1857 was the first national war of independence. I have tried to show, with the help of details given, that it was neither "first," nor "National" nor "a war of independence." [Preface, xvii, 258. Cf. The Tribune, January 31, 1968]

The Mutiny failed, as described in the following pages, not because the Sikhs, the people of the Panjab, or of any other province kept themselves aloof from it or sided with the British, but because there was no patriotic and national sentiment, either among its prompters or soldiers, to back it and also because there were no selfless leaders, no general plan, and no central organization to guide it, nor was there any unity of command and competent generalship to direct its military operations and to watch and arrest the augmentation and successful progress of the British Indian Army.

The paper places before its readers a number of historical facts based on the research of India's leading historians of international fame and unimpeachable integrity, and their impartial verdict is that it would be a travesty of truth to describe the revolt of 1857 as a national war of independence.

Patiala,
October 21, 1968.   GANDA SINGH

THE INDIAN MUTINY OF 1857 AND THE SIKHS
PART I

UNDESERVED PRAISE

The Mutiny at Meerut on May 10, 1857, which later became widespread and developed into a revolt in some parts of the UP and neighboring territories, has been called by some writers "the Indian War of Independence." This view, however, has not been accepted by the most recent research of well-known Indian historians of international fame. The full-throated praise showered by some of our modern political leaders on the sepoy mutineers and their so-called leaders have all been undeserved. And equally, if not more, undeserved have been the censures and charges of betrayal and treachery levelled against those who did not espouse their cause or were opposed to their activities. The worst sufferers in the latter case have been the people of the Punjab, particularly the Sikhs. This is because of the intensive propaganda of some politicians who do not appear to care much for historical truth.

FALSE ALLEGATIONS

Some people say that the "Indian Struggle for Freedom (1857) failed because the Sikhs betrayed their comrades and sided with the British." The charge of "betrayal" against the Sikhs could be justified only if they "had given up," or "had been disloyal to, or had violated allegiance to" a cause, person, or trust they had at any time befriended or owned. As history knows, the Sikhs were never at any time privy to, or took up the cause of, the mutiny of 1857. They had never been taken into confidence. They had neither been consulted nor invited. The Poorbia sepoys, as the soldiers of the Bengal army were then, and are still, called in the Punjab, had not the moral courage to approach the Sikhs for cooperation and assistance against the British as they had themselves helped the British destroy the independent kingdom of the Punjab in 1845–46 and reduce it to British subjection in 1848–49. As such, there was not much love lost between the Poorbia sepoys and the people of the Punjab. The offensive airs of the Poorbia garrison in the Punjab had been particularly galling to the martial Sikhs. Their behavior towards the civil population during their first march in 1846 from the theatre of war to the capital of Lahore, and during the British occupation of the country before and after the annexation, had caused such deep wounds in the hearts of the people as could not be healed in so short a period.

NOTHING NATIONAL ABOUT MUTINY

The Sikhs could not volunteer to help these erstwhile enemies of the Punjab, nor could they, for obvious reasons, espouse the cause of the Mughal Emperor, Bahadur Shah II, whom the mutineers had raised to the throne. For over two centuries, the Sikhs had fought against the Mughal tyranny, and they could not now be persuaded to support an alliance which might have resulted in its re-establishment. Moreover, as the mutiny later turned out to be, there appeared to be nothing national or patriotic in it to appeal to the noble sentiments of the Sikhs to attract them to the side of the mutineers.

The wrath of the mutineers was mostly directed against the Christians, who had interfered with their religion. A large number of unsuspecting Englishmen and their women and children were indiscriminately murdered in Meerut, Delhi, and other places. The first man to be killed in Delhi was an Indian Christian, Dr. Chamanlal, who was standing in front of his dispensary. Their next victims were banias and Mahajans, whose shops they plundered, and account books and debt-bonds they burnt and destroyed. Beyond this, there was no planned or organized scheme or effort on their part either to subvert the rule of the East India Company or to weaken the administrative hold of the British over the country.

Moreover, the mutiny was exclusively confined to the Poorbia sepoys of the Bengal army.

Territorially, too, it was limited to the UP and its neighborhood, while the remaining 80% of India was practically unaffected by it. Even in the UP, there were a number of pockets which remained undisturbed. The reason for this lack of interest in, and sympathy with, and, in many cases, active opposition to, the continuance and progress of the sepoy mutiny was the absence of any common cause, any planned scheme, any unity of interests.

The early activities of the sepoys in Delhi and its neighborhood were repugnant not only to the civil population of the country but also to the non-Poorbia soldiers, the Rajputs, the Marathas, the Madrasis, the Garhwalls, the Gorkhas, the Dogras, the Punjabi Muslims, the Sikhs, and the Pathans who could not associate themselves with the murderers of innocent women and children and the despoilers of their own countrymen.

RELIGIOUS RIOT

The mutiny at best was a religious riot of the Hindu and Muslim soldiers of the UP against the indiscreet but, perhaps, unintentioned callousness of some British military officers, who happened to be careless about the religious sentiments of Hindus and Muslims, offended by greased cartridges. With passions inflamed, and a number of murders committed in Meerut and Delhi, the sepoys could not retrace their steps. They were then joined by a large number of hooligans set free from jails, and of professional dacoits and plunderers from the criminal tribes of the neighboring areas.

BAHADUR SHAH A PUPPET KING

It is true that the Mughal Emperor, Bahadur Shah, had been proclaimed king, in whose name they professed to have risen in defense of Hinduism and Islam. But in practice, this was nothing more than a mere pretense to seek a cover for their crimes and misdeeds. His authority, they openly flouted, and his orders, they publicly disobeyed. They insulted him to his very face and treated him insolently in his own palace. Such behavior as this was certainly not becoming of the faithful and devoted soldiers towards the king whom they had themselves raised to the throne. But, in truth, they had done so only to use him as a handy tool. If he were not to be useful to them, they had no hesitation in renouncing him. "The sepoys at Delhi refused to fight unless they were paid their salaries, and that on an adequate scale—a demand which is hardly in consonance with the spirit which should guide a fighter in a war of independence" [RCM, 233].

The king himself was only a victim of circumstances. He had no hand either in organizing or encouraging the mutiny. He might have been glad within his heart to see the English humbled, but he was too old to plan or lead an insurrection. In fact, he had no knowledge of the rising of the sepoys till they had actually arrived at the palace gates and called upon him to assume command. He pleaded infirmity and poverty, but the sepoys would hear nothing of the sort. He was in a dilemma. He sent a fast camel rider to Agra to inform the Lieutenant-Governor of the mutiny in Meerut and of the arrival of the mutineers in Delhi.

TREACHEROUS AND UNRELIABLE MUTINEERS

Finding himself helpless before the increasing violence of the armed sepoys, violating the sanctity of the palace itself, the old king quailed before them. In fear, he issued the proclamations desired by the sepoys and outwardly espoused their cause. Within a week, the indisciplined sepoys disregarded the king's authority and refused to be commanded by his nominee, Bakht Khan, and transferred their allegiance to Prince Abu Bakr whom, on May 17, they elected as their king in place of the old emperor. The king's confidant, Ahsanulla, then complained that "the mutineers were a treacherous, bloodthirsty class on whom no dependence could be placed."

BAHADUR SHAH AND HIS FAMILY SEEK TO ASSIST THE BRITISH

The king himself had no faith in the sepoys or in the success of the mutiny. He, therefore, entered into secret negotiations with the British and offered to have the gates of the fort and the city of Delhi opened to them if they guaranteed his life, pension, and privileges. These negotiations came to nothing, it is true, but they "show Bahadur Shah in the true color so far as his attitude to the mutiny or the War of Independence is concerned" [RCM, 123].

The principal queen, Zinat Mahal, on her own part, offered to assist the British if her son, Jawan Bakht, was recognized as successor to the old emperor to the exclusion of other princes. The Mughal princes, too, were not sincere and faithful to the mutineers. They, as well, offered their services to the British in the occupation of Delhi on condition of favor being shown to them [SNS, 95-96]. "During the brief term of their authority," the princes "occupied themselves in feathering their nests" with the loot of the city, and then "their only anxiety was to save their skin as best they could" [SNS, 109]. All this leaves no doubt "that Bahadur Shah and his family betrayed the cause not only of the mutineers, of whom he was the nominal head, but also of the whole country" [RCM, 124].

DOUBLE ROLE OF THE RULING CHIEFS

Raja Nahar Singh of Ballabhgarh, Nawab Abdur Rahman Khan of Jhajjar, and Rao Tula Ram of Rewari, who were supposed to have identified themselves with the king and the mutineers, were playing a double game and negotiating with the British for a settlement. Their double dealings, however, did not succeed with the British who treated them as other mutineers and hanged them [SNS, 91, 111].

SELFISH MOTIVES OF LEADERS OF MUTINY

About the other prominent leaders of the sepoys, the less said the better. In the words of Maulana Abul Kalam Azad, supported by the evidence adduced in recent research in mutiny records, "with a few honorable exceptions—of whom the most distinguished were Ahmadullah and Tantya Tope—most of the leaders who took part in the struggle did so for personal reasons. They did not rise against the British till their personal interests had been damaged. Even after the revolt had begun, Nana Sahib declared that if Dalhousie's decisions were reversed and his own demands met, he would be willing to come to terms."

RANI OF JHANSI A VICTIM OF CIRCUMSTANCES

The Rani of Jhansi had her own grievances [SNS, XV]. There is nothing on record to say that she had any hand in planning, instigating, or organizing the mutiny of sepoys at Jhansi. In fact, she informed the British that she had been ill-treated by the mutineers and forced to pay money, and she asked for their help to maintain order. Believing in her innocence, the Commissioner of Saugor division nominated her to rule in Jhansi till the British could re-establish their administration. When the British changed their attitude and suspected her of complicity in the mutiny, she sent pathetic appeals to the authorities pleading her innocence and professing her loyalty to the British. If she had succeeded in dispelling the suspicions of the British, she would have gone to their side. But when, at last, she found that the British held her responsible for the mutiny and massacre at Jhansi, she preferred to fight. And it may be said to her credit and glory that she died heroically in the battlefield [RCM, 155].

TANTYA TOPE A FUGITIVE

Tantya Tope was neither an organizer nor a leader of the mutineers, but only a follower of Nana Sahib, to whom he was devotedly attached. But luck did not favor him. He was driven from place to place and could not find even a single Maratha village across the Narbada to give him shelter. He had, therefore, to fly to the forests where he was betrayed to the British by a professed rebel friend, Raja Man Singh of Narwar, a feudatory of Sindhia.

HINDU-MUSLIM CONFLICT

The mutiny having broken out all of a sudden, and nobody having an idea of the turn it would take, there was no understanding between the Hindus and Muslims. Whereas, in the chaos and confusion that followed the arrival of the Meerut sepoys at Delhi, a number of Muslims were oppressed and their homes plundered, and a regular *jehad* was proclaimed against the Hindus by Muslims in a number of places. Some clever adventurers found in the mutiny an opportunity for the revival of an Islamic kingdom and used the cover of religion for their anti-Hindu activities. The green flag of holy war was not unoften displayed in Delhi. It was hoisted in Bareilly, Bijnor, Moradabad, and many other places where the Hindus were plundered and massacred. This estranged the feelings between the Hindus and Muslims. As fellow sufferers, the Hindus in many places took the side of the English, protected their lives and property, and prayed for their victory. "It was generally held," says Dr. Sen, "that as the Hindus were as a community well disposed towards the British and the Muslims as a community were hostile, the Hindus should be exempted from any penalty. Some Hindus of the trading classes were allowed to return [to the city of Delhi] . . . It was ultimately realized that disaffection towards the British government was not the monopoly of any particular community, and there were exceptions in both . . . It was, therefore, decided that every citizen who desired to return should pay a fine, but there should be a discrimination in the rate on a communal basis. Whereas the Muslim had to pay a fine equivalent to 25 per cent of the value of his real property, the Hindu was required to pay 15 per cent less."

RIVAL FACTIONS

A close and critical study of the mutiny records reveals a very sad story of "everyone for himself and no one for the country." The Mughal Emperor, the proclaimed head of the mutiny, the Queen and the princes, and other leaders of the revolt all pulled in their own directions and played a double game to secure their ends and interests. The sepoys of Oudh fought for the restoration of their own king. Nana Sahib and the Rani of Jhansi pressed their own claims. A number of smaller adventurers, not inspired by any patriotic impulse, sprang up to exploit the opportunity offered by the mutiny. Khan Bahadur Khan, a grandson of Hafiz Rahmat Khan, set himself up as Viceroy or Naib Nazim of Rohilkhand. The Banjaras of Saharanpur set up a king of their own. The Gujjars had different rajas in different areas, Fatua being proclaimed as the king of the Gujjars. One Devi Singh proclaimed himself king of fourteen villages in the Mathura district. Similarly, one Mahimaji Wadi, a dacoit, and Belsare, a Maratha Brahman, were attracted to the rebel camp to improve their fortunes.

MUTINEERS IN FACT ANTI-NATIONALISTS

The idea of Indian nationalism and of fighting for the independence of India was a thing unknown both to the so-called leaders of the mutiny and to the Poorbia sepoys who had been instrumental during the past hundred years in the destruction of the independence of the various Indian independent kingdoms. The Marathas, the Mysorians, the Malabaris, the Rajputs, the Gurkhas, the Pathans, the Sikhs, and the Assamese had all been reduced to dust with their help, and never had the Poorbias raised their little finger in protest, much less in their defense. This was not a very creditable record for attracting the non-Poorbias to their side.

The people of the Punjab were the worst and the most recent sufferers at their hands. In addition to the Poorbia sepoys who fought against them under the British in 1845–46 and 1848–49, it was the Poorbia soldiers of fortune, Tej Singh and Lal Singh, the Commander-in-Chief and Prime Minister of the Punjab, who had entered into secret agreements with the British and had betrayed the Sikhs in the first Anglo-Sikh War. Again, it was mostly with the help of the Poorbia regiments and Poorbia civilian subordinate officials that the Punjab was being held under British subjection in 1857 when the mutiny took place. As such, the people of the Punjab, particularly the Sikhs, could not have looked upon them as worthy of their support in a cause which threatened them with the re-establishment of Mughal tyranny of the seventeenth and eighteenth centuries.

SIKHS THE LAST DEFENDERS OF INDIAN LIBERTY

The Sikhs, says Dr. Majumdar, "were the last defenders of the liberty of India." But "the sepoys [Poorbias] . . . had not the least scruple to fight the Sikhs." "We have not the least evidence to show that the Indian leaders like Nana Sahib and others raised their little finger to help the cause of the Sikhs." "It is difficult to resist the conclusion," he continues, "that the attitude and activities of the sepoys in 1849 certainly did not correspond to the patriotic fervor with which they are supposed to be endowed in 1857" [RCM, 233-34].

CONDUCT OF MUTINEERS

Moreover, the conduct of the mutineers and their leaders in Meerut, Delhi, and other places was not such as to give others the impression of the insurrection being anything like national or of common interest and benefit to the people of the country at large. The discriminate massacres of Indian Christians on the basis of their religion and of unsuspecting Englishmen, and their innocent women and children, were the worst type of bloodthirstiness that sent throughout the country a thrill of horror and hatred against the mutineers and alienated the sympathies of their prospective friends. And when Bahadur Shah wrote to Indian princes on behalf of the mutineers, nobody took any serious notice of his letters, and some of them resolutely refused to identify themselves with the unscrupulous rebels.

INDIAN ARMY STOOD ALOOF

Although the movement had begun as a military mutiny of the Bengal Army, that army itself did not as a whole join it, but a large section of it actively fought on the side of the government to suppress it. The Madras and Bombay armies took no part in it. The mutiny could not, as such, be called a general mutiny of the Indian Army.

HISTORICAL MISINTERPRETATION

With the sepoys not having the overthrow of the East India Company's rule as their objective and the leaders being positively selfish and treacherous playing a double game, it is a cruel misinterpretation of history to call it a war of Indian independence. And it would be the height of injustice to accuse for its failure those who happened not to join this aimless, planless, and leaderless uprising. The Punjabis were not alone in not joining the revolt. They could not have joined it for reasons that have been stated above at some length. The Bengalis, the Marathas, the Madrasis, and the Malabaris, whose love for the independence of India has been in no way less than that of anyone else in the country, took no part in it. The Rajputs, the Jats, the Dogras, and the Garhwalis kept studiedly aloof. The educated communities of Bengal and Madras openly condemned the rising and denounced the mutiny and the mutineers [SNS, 407–08].

The cooperation of the Sikhs with the mutineers could not have made much difference, nor could it have contributed much to their success. There were the Punjabi Musalmans, the Bahawalpuri Daudpotras, the Baluchis, and the Frontier Pathans who were deadly opposed to the mutineers.

The strength of the East India Company's rule in India depended mostly on the naval power of England. The rising in the Punjab could not have placed any obstacles in the way of their reinforcements from the West. A few more murders of Englishmen in the Punjab or even in a military defeat of the British in that province could not have ended the rule of the Company in India and freed her from the British yoke.

NOTED HISTORIAN'S VERDICT

"The Sepoy Mutiny was not a fight for freedom," says Sir Jadunath Sarkar. "It was not a rising of the people for political self-determination, but a conspiracy of mercenary soldiers (only of the North Indian army) to prevent the cunning destruction of their religion by defiling their bodies with pig's lard and cow's fat which were used in lubricating the paper parcels of catridges . . ."

> *A number of dispossessed dynasts, both Hindu and Muslim, exploited the well-founded caste-suspicions of the sepoys and made these simple folk their cat's-paw in a gamble for recovering their thrones. The last scions of the Delhi Mughals or the Oudh Nawabs and the Peshwa, can by no ingenuity be called fighters for Indian freedom. [Hindusthan Standard, Puja Annual, 1956, p. 22]*

NO NOBLE SENTIMENT

The mutiny of 1857 failed not because the Sikhs, or the people of the Punjab or of any other state or province, did not join it, but because it had no noble sentiment behind it, no plan to guide it, and no sincere leader to see it through. "The failure of the outbreak," according to Dr. Majumdar, "may also be attributed to the fact that neither the leaders nor the sepoys and masses were inspired by any high ideal. The lofty sentiments of patriotism and nationalism, with which they are credited, did not appear to have any basis in fact. As a matter of fact, such ideas were not yet familiar to Indian minds." "In the light of the available evidence, we are forced to the conclusion," says Maulana Abul Kalam Azad, "that the uprising of 1857 was not the result of careful planning, nor were there any masterminds behind it" ISNS, x]. "As I read about the events of 1857, I am forced to the conclusion," he continues, "that the Indian national character had sunk very low. The leaders of the revolt could never agree. They were mutually jealous and continually intrigued against one another ... In fact these personal jealousies and intrigues were largely responsible for the Indian defeat" [*Ibid.* XV].

PART II
CONTROVERSIAL POINTS CLEARED

HISTORY takes no cognizance of the sentiments of people coming a century after the event, twisting and molding it, mixing politics with history, to give it the color and appearance which never belonged to it.

My conclusions are based on facts which have not so for been controverted by anyone. They are not only my conclusions. They are also the conclusions of the greatest living authorities on the history of India—Dr. Sir Jadunath Sarkar, Dr. Romesh C. Mazumdar, and Dr. Surendranath Sen. They are scholars of international fame and are acknowledged as the leading educationists of India. They have been the Vice-Chancellors of the universities of Calcutta, Dacca, and Delhi. Their conclusions have not only been accepted but also supported by the late Maulana Abul Kalam Azad, the Education Minister of the Government of India, and other men of sound learning and judgment.

One of my critics thinks that I have "derisively" referred to the soldiers of the Bengal Army as "Poorbia." Not at all. If he were to refer to contemporary records of the Central and provincial governments and to the regimental histories of the then Bengal Army, he would find the words "Poorbia" and "Hindoostanee" then commonly used for men from beyond the Jamuna. [See MacMunn's *The Armies of India*, the *Punjab Mutiny Reports*, and *Regimental History of the 54th Sikhs*]. And in the Punjab, the word "Poorbia" was more commonly used than "Hindoostanee," as it continues to the present day, and there is no derision attached to it.

MURDER PLOT

According to regimental records, there was only one Sikh Regiment at Dehra Ismail Khan when the Mutiny broke out at Meerut on May 10, 1857, and that was the 3rd Sikh Infantry. Although it carried a Sikh name, it was not completely Sikh in its composition. Like the other three Sikh regiments, it had 50% Punjabi Muslims from Jhelum and Rawalpindi, Pathans from across the Indus, Dogras from the Shivalaks, and Hindoostanees (Poorbias) from the other side of the Jamuna. It was among the last named Hindoostanee sepoys of the 3rd Sikh Infantry (and not among the Sikhs, the Punjabi Musalmans, or the Dogras) that the plot to murder British officers was discovered. To quote from the regimental history:

> *In July it came to the notice of the Commanding Officer that some of the Hindoostanees had been talking in a very mutinous and insubordinate manner regarding the disturbances in Hindoostan, and all efforts failing to discover the ring leaders, he determined to disarm the whole, which was accordingly done . . . They consisted of 4 native officers, 12 Havildars, 26 Naiks, 60 Privates. [Historical Records of 3rd Sikhs, pp. 10–11]*

This is supported by the *Punjab Mutiny Report* by R. Montgomery, pp. 67–68, paragraphs 107–08.

Another conspiracy reported at Dera Ismail Khan was amongst the 39th Native Infantry composed exclusively of the Poorbia sepoys who had quietly surrendered their arms.

The argument that "the democratic press of the various European countries hailed the 1857 uprising as a National revolt of the Indian people" carries no weight with a man of history. It was nothing more than political propaganda of the jealous anti-British European countries against England.

PUNJABIS DID NOT LACK PATRIOTISM

It is true that the Punjabis were not devoid of patriotic fervor. I would be the last man to say that. But what they could not believe was that the Poorbia soldiers, who had been the most devoted henchmen of the British for a hundred years, who had helped the British subjugate the Marathas, the Rajputs, the Jats, the Gurkhas, the Pathans, and the Sikhs, and were garrisoning the Punjab for the British even during the Mutiny, could have turned patriots overnight. Such a movement for which the various martial fraternities of Indian people had not been consulted and taken into confidence, and which was openly denounced by the people of Bengal and Madras, and was not joined by the people of Maharashtra, Bombay, Gujrat, Sindh, and Rajasthan, could not, according to the Punjabis, be a national movement. The Poorbias alone did not constitute the Indian nation, nor was nationalism the name of whatever they did, whether it was the indiscriminate murder of innocent women and children, the plunder and spoliation of their own countrymen, or secret negotiations with the British to further their personal interests.

HINDU-MUSLIM UNITY LACKING

There is no denying the fact that there was then no understanding between the Hindus and Muslims. It is true that the majority of the Poorbia soldiers were high-caste Hindus, and they sought shelter under the banner of the Mughal emperor who was raised to throne. The emperor was practically a helpless puppet in the hands of his sons and of Muslim lieutenants, who had all the power and authority in their own hands. The efforts at Hindu-Muslim unity were mostly one-way traffic. Having broken with the government, and not supported by either Hindu Rajput, Maratha, Dogra, and Gurkha princes or the people, the Hindu sepoys were left with no alternative other than following the Muslim leaders who saw in the success of the mutiny the revival of Muslim rule in the country. Emperor Bahadur Shah favored them with the prohibition of cow slaughter in Delhi on the occasion of Id, and Khan Bahadur Khan of Bareilly also offered to prohibit cow killing not for Hindu-Muslim unity or for respect for Hindu sentiments, but only as a bargain, for killing Englishmen. "If the Hindus will come forward to slay the English," said he, "the Mohammedans will from that very day put a stop to the slaughter of cows" [SNS, 93]. This needs no comments.

MUSLIM FANATICISM

The unfurling of the Green Flag of holy *jihad* and the plunder and massacre of Hindus in Delhi, Bareilly, Bijnor, Moradabad, and other places were certainly not the symbols of Hindu-Muslim unity. Nor was the Muslim attempt to hoist the Green Flag on the Hindu temple of Bisheshwar at Benaras the result of friendly regard for the Hindus.

"The communal hatred," says Dr. Majumdar, "led to ugly communal riots in many parts of UP. The Green Flag was hoisted, and bloody wars were fought between Hindus and Muslims in Bareilly, Bijnor, Moradabad, and other places where the Muslims shouted for the revival of Muslim kingdom" [pp. 230–31].

On the authority of the *Bidrohe Bengali* of Durgadas Bandyopadhyaya, an eyewitness. Dr. Majumdar tells us: "The demon of communalism also raised its head. The Muslims spat over the Hindus and openly defiled their houses by sprinkling them with cows' blood and placing cows' bones within the compounds. Concrete instances are given where Hindu sepoys came into clash with Muslim hooligans and a complete riot ensued. The Hindus oppressed by the Muslims were depressed at the success of the mutiny and daily offered prayers to God for the return of the English" [RCM, 177].

This was the foretaste of the feared revival of Muslim rule. One shudders to think of what would have actually followed it.

In spite of this all, if some people wish to live in a state of hallucination and believe that there was a complete friendly understanding and great communal harmony between Muslims and Hindus at all stages in the Mutiny, they are most welcome to do so, but they should not expect a student of history to be one with them. Past history has to be recorded as it was and not as we wish it to be presented a century afterwards. It cannot be written to order, or molded and remolded according to changing times.

MUTINEERS WORSE THAN PLUNDERERS

That the mutineers behaved worse than bands of plunderers and professional dacoits is proved by a large number of petitions submitted to Emperor Bahadur Shah, and his instructions and orders issued thereon to the military and police authorities. According to the evidence on record, the mutineers took the law into their own hands and helped themselves with whatever they wished to take away. The bad examples set by the Mughal princes and rebel leaders encouraged the soldiers to enter any house in and outside the city of Delhi and billet themselves on whomsoever they liked. There is nothing on record to support the argument advanced to defend or to explain away the conduct of the mutineers that "the rebels harmed only those [Indians] who either refused to give supplies to them or were suspected of being in league with the British."

The Emperor forwarded the petitions of helpless sufferers to Prince Mirza Mughal for affording protection. But finding that his orders were not obeyed, the Emperor wrote to his son, Mirza Mughal, on June 18: "It is surprising that, up to the present time, no arrangements should have been made . . . It is the business of the Army to protect, and not to desolate and plunder." On the 19th of June, the residents of Jaisinghpura and Paharganj complained that "the Troops of the State . . . oppressing the shopkeepers forcibly take away their wares, without the payment of prices, and also, entering the dwelling houses . . . forcibly carry away all such articles . . . that they can lay hands on, and wound with fire-arms and swords those who may supplicate their forbearance" [TB, 11, 12].

In his order of June 27, the Emperor wrote to Princes Mughal and Khair Sultan: "Not a day has elapsed since the arrival of the army, and its taking up quarters in the city, that petitions from the towns-people have not been submitted, representing the excesses committed by numerous Infantry sepoys . . . You, our sons, are directed to take all proper steps to prevent the men of the Army from plundering and desolating the City" [TB. 14].

Syed Abdulla, priest of the shrine of Hazrat Sheikh Muhammad Chishti, petitioned on June 29 that "the whole of the autumnal crop of sugarcane, churee, etc. . . . has been totally devastated, and more than this, the very implements of agriculture such as ploughs, woodwork on wells, have all been carried away in plunder by soldiers" [TB. 15].

Similarly, petitions from all types of people, rich and poor, Hindus and Muslims, came in from all quarters of the capital and from towns and rural areas, complaining against the depredations of the mutineers. In his orders to Prince Mughal, the Emperor tells him "that Troopers of Cavalry come from Jodhpur have picquetted their horses in front of the shops and have taken possession of a number of them," and that the rebel Gujjars of Aliganj, Mallanji, Hasangarh, and Alapur "are now engaged in highway robbery and in plundering the country" [TB. 21, 22].

BAHADUR SHAH DISGUSTED

But who cared for the wishes and orders of Bahadur Shah, a helpless puppet in the hands of the mutineers? They only meant to use his name to have their own way. And, when they found that his wishes clashed with their own, they just ignored him. Openly disobeyed and insulted by the mutineers, Emperor Bahadur Shah, in disgust, threatened to abdicate, leave the capital, and commit suicide, as is evident from his memorandum of August 9, 1857, addressed to the officers of the Army at Delhi.

He says:

> *If you are not disposed to comply with these requests, let me be conveyed, in safety, to the Khwaja Sahib. I shall there sit and employ myself in the occupation of a mujavir (sweeper) and, if this even is not acceded to, I shall relinquish every concern, and go away. Let those who think they can detain me attempt to do so. Not having been killed by the hands of English, I shall be killed by yours. Further, the oppression that is at present inflicted on the people, it is inflicted on me. It is incumbent on you all to take measures to prevent it. Or let me have my answer, and I shall swallow a diamond and kill myself. [TB. 35]*

Even this had no effect, and there was no improvement in the attitude and conduct of the mutineers. Emperor Bahadur Shah, therefore, resolved to discard the world, to adopt the garb of a faqir and go to the shrine of Khwaja Kutb-ud-Din, and thence proceed to the holy city of Mecca [TB, 39–40]. One can hardly imagine the agony and mental torture to which the helpless Emperor was subjected by the misbehavior of the mutineers and their leaders.

The following extracts from the order of Bahadur Shah addressed to his son, Mirza Mughal, speak volumes for themselves and leave no ground for any further comments on the point under discussion:

> *Repeated injunctions have been issued prohibiting plunder and aggression in the city, but all to no purpose; for although ten days have now elapsed, the same evils are prevailing to the present time . . . [Regiments of Infantry] have thoroughly desolated several of the bazaars. Moreover without reference to night or day, they enter and plunder the houses of inhabitants on false pleas . . . They force locks*

and shop-doors, and they forcibly loose the horses of cavalry and take them off. . . . A notification, under special seal was issued publicly proclaiming that courts of justice had been established in the city, and prohibiting acts of violence on the part of soldiery. Even this had no effect . . . They now clamorously demand allowances daily, and above all, daily take allowance for more men than are present . . . Under these circumstances, how is it to be believed that these people can have the welfare of the state at heart, or that they cherish and desire to yield subjection and obedience to the royal authority? . . . Wearied and helpless, we have now resolved on making a vow to pass the remainder of our days in service acceptable to God, . . . assuming the garb of a religious mendicant to proceed first and stay at the shrine of Saint Khwaja Sahib, and, after making necessary arrangements for the journey, to go eventually to Mecca. [TB, 220–223]

Men such as these who would observe no discipline, recognize no authority, and obey no orders, even of the supreme head of the State, and who would indulge in cold-blooded murders of women and children, despoil their own countrymen, and rob their own exchequer by fraud and dishonesty, are a disgrace to any movement and cannot, in truth, be hailed as champions of a national cause.

BRITISH ATROCITIES

It is being said that "there is ample evidence to prove that the atrocities committed by the Britishers exceeded those committed by the rebels in all respects." Admitted. Nobody would justify and acclaim the British atrocities—not even the Britishers. They deserve our strongest condemnation. They were the result of revengeful madness. But the atrocities committed by the Britishers, later, in retaliation, do not justify those committed by the rebels who began the Mutiny with cold-blooded butchery in Meerut and Delhi. And to acclaim and celebrate activities which had no moral or religious justification is not becoming of a nation with a rich heritage as India has.

It would have been more in the larger interests of the country to have allowed these painful memories to be quietly forgotten. Who does not know that in violent movements and bloody revolutions the national character of the people not unoften sinks very low? That is why Mahatma Gandhi studiedly avoided the introduction of violence in his movements. And if he were alive, I am sure, he would not have permitted the celebration of the centenary of the Mutiny. I have nothing but pity for those who can, even after a century, extol the bloodthirsty murderers of innocent women and children. For, if murder is the worst of crimes for the purpose of history, those who promote or defend it, before or after, share in proportion the guilt of the crime. May the Lord, in his boundless mercy, give light and guidance to his erring people.

TREACHERY OF RAJA NAHAR SINGH AND RAO TULA RAM

About Raja Nahar Singh and Rao Tula Ram, in whose memory a memorial is being raised in the Punjab for their supposed sacrifice in the Mutiny, the less said the better. They were both playing a double game to secure and further their personal interests. "These Chiefs," says Dr. Surendranath Sen, "were supposed to have closely identified themselves with the King's cause, but they were secretly negotiating for a settlement with the English, even before the British had succeeded in achieving any notable success against the sepoys" [*Eighteen Fifty-Seven* pp. 91–92].

If memorials are being raised in honor of them, this is being done by politicians and not by historians.

The Sikhs, according to one calculation, formed hardly 10% of the population in the Punjab at the time of Mutiny, and the remaining 90% of the Punjabis were Hindus and Muslims. One may ask, if the Sikhs had, for some reasons, kept aloof from the mutineers, why did not the Hindus and Muslims of the Punjab join them? The 90% majority could have easily ignored the 10% or brushed them aside. In the all-India calculation, the Sikhs would hardly be 1%, and they could not have successfully opposed the 99% majority of the Hindus and Muslims, if they were all united and there was complete harmony amongst them, as claimed by a writer.

The truth is that not only did the people of the Punjab, the Hindus, the Muslims, and the Sikhs keep aloof from the mutineers, but the people of Bengal, Madras, Maharashtra, Gujarat, Sindh, Rajasthan, Jammu and Kashmir, and the North-Western Frontier Province also did not join them. Some of them actually opposed them. Not only this. Out of the three

Presidency Armies—Bengal, Madras and Bombay—it was only a part of the Bengal Army that had mutinied. The other parts fought on the side of the British Government to suppress it. The Madras and Bombay armies remained quiet and loyal. Evidently, the Poorbia soldiers had failed to win the sympathies of their own class of people in the south and south-west as in the west and north-west.

HOLLOW CRIES

Surely, there was, then, something fundamentally wrong with the Mutiny and its leaders that kept the majority of the Indian people and army away from them.

In the first place, the movement had nothing national or patriotic about it. The idea of India being one nation had yet to grow in the country. The conduct of the mutineers and their leaders in Delhi, Meerut, and other places was not such as to convey to others the impression of the mutiny being anything like national or of common interest and benefit.

The cry of *din* and *dharma,* raised by the mutineers and Emperor Bahadur Shah, carried no weight with the people at large. Beyond this, there was no common popular aim to appeal to, and attract, the people.

The past record of the Poorbia soldiers was not creditable enough to win the confidence of the non-Poorbias. Then, there was no plan for the mutiny on an all-India basis. The non-Poorbias had not been consulted nor invited.

And, lastly, the mutineers failed to produce from among themselves, or win over from amongst the people, sincere and selfless leaders who could command respect and obedience.

There was no mutual understanding between the Hindus and Muslims, and between the various social, economic, and geographic fraternities of the country for a joint effort against the British. The exhibition of bloodthirstiness in the murder of women and children sent throughout the country a thrill of horror and hatred against the mutinous sepoys and alienated the sympathies of their probable friends.

All this put together was responsible for the failure of the Mutiny of 1857.

REFERENCES

SNS.　　Surendranath Sen, *Eighteen Fifty-Seven*. Publication Division, Government of India, New Delhi, 1957.

PGR. MR.　*Punjab Government Records, Mutiny Reports*.

RCM.　　R. C. Majumdar. *Sepoy Mutiny and Revolt of 1857*. Firma K. L. Mukhopadhyay, Calcutta, 1957.

　　　　—*History of the Freedom Movement in India* Firma, K. L. Mukhopadhyay, Calcutta, 1962, three Vols.

TB.　　　*The Trial of Muhammad Bahadur Shah* (ex-king of Delhi), ed. H.L.O.G. Garett. Punjab Government, 1932.

TC.　　　Tara Chand. *History of the Freedom Movement in India*, Publication Division, Government of India, 1961, 1967, two Vols.

Life and Times of Sant Teja Singh: 1906-1912

Dr. Sukhmander Singh

Abstract

Much has been written about the life of Sant Teja Singh, who was born in 1877 and passed away at the age of 88 years. He made outstanding contributions for the cause of spreading the glorious teachings of Guru Nanak all across the world throughout his life. But this paper will restrict presentation of his works during the period of 1906 through 1912. This period was full of intense activities for young Teja Singh in England, Canada, and America. He was only 29 years of age in 1906. A young, brilliant but a dedicated Sikh, he did pioneering works in educating Americans and Canadians about Sikhism and establishing Gurdwaras in Victoria (Canada) and Stockton (California). This paper will describe the state of affairs that existed from 1906 to 1912. The paper will present how the combination of a young scholarly person like Teja Singh, spiritually enlightened souls like Baba Vasakha Singh and Baba Jawala Singh, and a revolutionary person like Baba Sohan Singh Bhakna would make an everlasting imprint on the pages of history of the Sikhs in America and for the freedom of India. They drew their strength and inspiration from their Sikh faith, thereby providing a springboard for the rise of Gaddar movement.The paper will attempt to show that a neglect of the above noted lesson with regard to the cooperation between the educated Sikh youths and the elderly persons managing the Gurdwaras, has bogged down the progress of the Sikh image in modern times in Western countries. Certain examples and suggestions are made in the context of current pursuit of scholarship on Sikhism through Sikh chairs and otherwise and the current management styles of Gurdwaras in USA.

Keyword: Academic studies at London, Cambridge, Columbia and Harvard Universities, Teja Singh's Fights for Justice in Canada. First Gurdwaras in Victoria, London & Stockton, Groundwork for Nationalist Movement for Gaddar.

Introduction

Although the focus of this paper is to examine the life and times of Sant Teja Singh for the period of only 6 years, from 1906 through 1912, a brief look into his life up to 1906 is given first. Born in 1977, he attained his BA at the age of 19, his LLB degree in 1900 at the age of 23, and an MA in 1901. He became vice principal of Khalsa College in 1904 at the unprecedented young age of 27, a brilliant and remarkable achievement. At Khalsa College, he started as a wholly materialistic, non-religious, and disbelieving person. But a deep spiritual transformation took place in Teja Singh's life in 1905 after meeting Sant Attar Singh who persuaded him to go for higher education. Sant Atar Singh valued education and wanted to establish schools, to provide spiritual as well as western-style science education.

England (1906-1908): Studies at University of London and Cambridge University

Young, 29-year-old Teja Singh arrived in London on 24th of August, 1906. He had his wife and two children with him. Three other Sikhs also accompanied him and reached London at the same time. It is interesting to note that these four young Sikhs did not choose to do minimal types of jobs, but straight way embarked upon their pursuit for education in the subjects of science and technology. Teja Singh joined the University of London for his Doctor of Science degree, Dharam Singh enrolled for electrical training in a London college, Amar Singh joined for textile and clothing in Manchester, and Hari Singh joined Edenburgh University. Alas, such pursuits are mostly missing among today's arrivals.

Analysis:
In those days (1906), Britishers knew about Sikhs and their turbans, yet universities like Cambridge would not allow students to wear turbans. This was Teja Singh's first fight for justice for Sikhs. He left London University after one term and joined Cambridge University where he successfully defended the right to wear turbans. Thus, he was the first ever Sikh with turban at Cambridge. It may be noted that, at Cambridge, he enrolled for the Science Tripose Degree and took subjects of physics, chemistry, and zoology. For a one-hour lecture for these subjects there were three hours of laboratory. The significance of science and technology for progress was recognized by Teja Singh so early. But these days, although there are many acadmies/organizations in Punjab/USA to recognize achievements of Sikhs in literature/culture/language, there is none to acknowledge their achievements in science, engineering, and medicine. Remember, Kartar Singh Sarabha enrolled himself in chemistry, and Dalip Singh Saund did his Ph.D in mathematics at UC Berkeley. From 1906 through 1908, he completed five terms at Cambridge University. Only one more term was needed. But before completing the 6th term, he left for New York to join Columbia University where he won a scholarship for teachers-training studies.

USA (Columbia University 1908) and Impact of Teja Singh's Lectures

While at Columbia University, Teja's grasp of Indian life and the teachings of Guru Nanak was acknowledged not only by his teachers at Columbia but the general public also. During one of his classes at Columbia, he disagreed with his teacher's description of Kipling's character. Teja Singh explained the reason for his disagreement in such a scholarly way that the teacher asked Teja Singh to give a public lecture on Indian society. The teacher took upon himself to advertise and to invite people to listen to Teja Singh. It is said that about 10,000 people gathered for his lecture. Teja Singh's thorough knowledge and eloquence impressed everyone. But his deep unshakable inner peace as Gursikh, while explaining the teachings of Guru Nanak, was the most moving experience for the audience, who consisted of professors, students, press reporters, and social scholars. Many of the audiences developed reverence for Guru Nanak and the Sikh faith and requested Teja Singh to give weekly discourses to about 100 persons initially, but it doubled in a short time (1).

Analysis:
The fact that the first two lectures of Teja Singh were widely covered by the newspapers throughout America is testimony to the universal appeal of Guru Nanak's teachings and the clarity and the earnest way Teja Singh presented these to the American audience. How many of Teja Singh's like are there among us these days? Kathakaars may be quite learned, yet, because of their lack of command in English, they cannot help much. Then there are Sikh chairs, but their scholars are too obsessed with history as to how and when it came about. That may be fine, but to keep splitting hairs on this for over 15 years with good amounts of financial resources is beyond comprehension. As such, their spiritless research has created more fog than clarity regarding the Sikh philosophy/faith. Granted, and it is appreciable, that their chairs have taught Sikhism/Sikh studies to many of their students, yet their scholarly presentation can often be dry and lack that appeal which a truly learned and dedicated Sikh can make to the American audience. Is that one of the reasons that we the Sikhs remain misunderstood? An average American still does not know who Sikhs are and what their religion is. Thanks to CNN that, after the tragic event in Wisconsin, has done a great job in portraying the right image of Sikhs and Sikh values to Americans.

The news about Teja Singh's landmark lectures in New York reached the Western Shores of Canada where Sikhs were suffering because of the general ignorance about them, and they were thinking to invite a learned person from India to explain them and their faith to Canadians.

Vancouver (Summer of 1908): Teja Singh's First Visit to Canada

As soon as Canadian Sikhs learned about Teja Singh's lectures from a Canadian well wisher of Sikhs who had read the news of the two lectures given in New York, they made an immediate and urgent request for Teja Singh to come to Vancouver. This was a time of summer vacation in 1908 at Columbia University, so Teja Singh hurried to reach Vancouver. This was his first visit. Teja Singh delivered lectures on the teaching of Guru Nanak and endeared himself with the Sikhs living in British Columbia. At the end of summer vacation, he returned to Columbia University to finish his studies. His return to New York delighted many of his American admirers who requested him to resume his weekly discourses on the teaching of Guru Nanak. One of the American admirers named T.C. Crawford became deeply and spiritually attached to Sikh faith and also to Teja Singh. He would visit Teja Singh daily to discuss spiritual matters and even started his daily meditation. As the fate would have it, one early morning Crawford came and made an urgent request to Teja Singh to raise $15,000 to help him save his share in a gold mine in Jacksonville, California. Mr. T.C. Crawford appeared very distressed. Teja Singh could not see a devotee of Guru Nanak in trouble. So he decided to return to Vancouver area to seek funds from fellow Sikhs (2). This was in December 1908.

Teja Singh's Second Visit to Vancouver and His Stand Against Injustice (December 1908)

This was indeed a drastic decision for Teja Singh to interrupt his studies for such a difficult mission. But somehow there were the inner callings of the Sikhs of Canada, who were to be shipped like sheep to Honduras by the Canadian government on the pretext that the Sikhs are mostly unemployed, unclean people and that they are public charge. Honduras in those days was a land infested with yellow fever, and there were no job opportunities. This misfortune was looming over Sikhs, and they needed some learned and capable person who could save them from their misery by presenting a true picture of Sikhs and their faith. The arrival of Teja Singh was a fortunate coincidence. The Sikhs were overjoyed to see him and requested him for help. Teja Singh delivered a couple of lectures within the first week of his arrival. These lectures were so powerful and full of profound wisdom about Sikh faith that many of the Canadians became keenly interested to know more about Guru Nanak's teachings. Some of Teja Singh's lectures were also published in the newspapers. Since Teja Singh had lectured at Columbia University, he was now popularly known as Professor Teja Singh. This was during the first week of December 1908, and Teja Singh was only 31 years of age. He was considered no match against Mr. J.B. Harkin, a government commissioner, and a well-seasoned elderly Governor Swayne who were to tell the Sikhs to move to Honduras (3, 5 & 7). But Teja Singh, though relatively much younger than these powerful officials, defended the Canadian Sikhs by forcefully discussing against the racial injustice for Sikhs.

> *Later speaking at the O'Brien Hall, in Vancouver, Professor Teja Singh, vehemently pleaded for sympathy of the white brethren in Canada over his fellow citizens. He said that: If India's rights are not granted, as prophesied by an English officer in India years ago, that will cause a direct warfare. At the outset, I appeal to our white brethren here to help us in our efforts to prevent the movement from being carried out. It is alleged that we are to be shipped out of the country because there is no work here. No, this is not true. It is a safe estimate that about seventy percent of them are working. (The Vancouver Daily Province)*

It was reported that Teja Singh spoke in perfect English and that the audience warmly applauded his speech many times.

He presented such a genuine description of the Sikhs and the Sikh faith in the context of world history and historic events that a Vancouver newspaper published an article with the headline "Mystery and Power of Teja Singh." A few quotes from this newspaper are as follows:

> *"There was no jingoism (boast) in his two hour address. He spoke calmly and dispassionately quoting historical authorities. . . . The professor showed himself to be a man of profound erudition with a marvelous grasp of the principles of European civilization and intimate knowledge of oriental philosophy. He expounded the principles of truepolitical economy. . . . White men and white women are remembered among his warmest admirers"* (6).

> *"The newspaper further writes that in appearance he is quite distinguished. He wears European attire, his head being surrounded by a large turban. A glossy black beard knotted at the end. He looks like a man who is terribly earnest"* (6).

Besides being a learned and spiritual person, Teja Singh was a remarkable planner and organizer. He successfully organized the Sikhs to purchase 250 acres of land near Eagle Harbour for $25,000 to establish a Sikh colony and

Life and Times of Sant Teja Singh: 1906–1912

Sikh university (4). He also persuaded Sikhs to register Guru Nanak Mining and Trust Co. and to buy one-fourth share of Gold Mine in Jacksville, California, by collecting $15,000 and sending this amount to Crawford. All this built a good image and a firm position of Sikh community in Canada. The strong financial strength of Sikhs became a public knowledge, and there was no reason for them to become a public charge. Thus, the Canadian government's propaganda against Sikhs was exposed, and it became worldwide news, including in India. Sikhs were now enjoying a good political image and a comfortable life. Their financial position was sound and improving (1).

Analysis:
Now, we all know what follows when Sikhs become too rich and Sikhi becomes poor; they fight with each other. This was perhaps the first and the last time a land of this much size (250 acres) was bought by Sikhs together to develop and to set up a university. Crawford was very keen for Sikhs to have a Sikh university on this land, and that the profit from the Guru Nanak Mining Company could be used for the purpose, and to spread/preach the mission of Guru Nanak. But the mutual bickerings and fights among Sikhs resulted in selling that piece of land which would have been worth billions of dollars now (8). Sikhs also withdrew their shares from the mining company. A somewhat similar story, but on a smaller scale, happened in Berkeley, California, in the early seventies. A two-story apartment building located only two blocks from the University of California, Berkeley, at the crossing of Alliston Way and Roosevelt Street was bought by Stockton Gurdwara members. This was done soon after the establishment of Stockton Gurdwara and to help Berkeley students stay free for their education. It was named Khalsa Club. Later, after several decades and due to the lack of maintenance and students opting to stay in other places, it got infested with rats and spiders and finally got torn down by the city of Berkeley. In 1969 and the early 1970s, we came to know of it when a friend of ours rented an apartment just across the corner where the Khalsa Club apartment used to be. I was studying at UC Berkeley at that time, and we decided to clean up the lot. We worked very hard for several weeks with shovels, picks, and bins and cleared most of the debris out of the lot. We planned to request the Stockton Committee to build a memorial there. Somehow, for some reason or the other, our team members were not all there in the early 1970s. I was on transfer to Houston and then to Alaska. In 1974–76, we learned that the land had been sold by the Stockton

Gurdwara Committee. What a shortsightedness born either out of ignorance or due to mutual bickering/fighting which often would not let our members have visions beyond these fightings/jealousies. The exact date and price at which this piece of land was sold can be found out from the city records.

Reaching Out to Sikhs on the Western Coast

Victoria: In order to reach out to Sikhs on the western coast of the USA, Professor Teja Singh undertook visits to Victoria, Seattle, Portland, Oregon, and California. His first stop in Victoria happened to be in a house where his host and other Sikhs were drinking alcohol. Unperturbed, Teja Singh decided to stay there for the night. The next morning, when he addressed them in his uncanny yet profoundly dedicated way to be the jewels of Guru and not a blot, about 15–20 Sikhs decided to take Amrit, which was administrated to them the same day. Such was the power and influence of this deeply devoted Sikh of Guru. Upon Teja Singh's suggestion, a plot was purchased to build the first ever Gurdwara in Victoria. Every Sikh gave one month's salary to pay for construction. Real estate agent Robert W. Clark's wife arranged public lectures by Teja Singh in a city hall. The impact of Teja Singh's lectures was such that many Europeans loved the Sikh doctrines. Mrs. Clark printed 10,000 copies of pamphlets written by Teja Singh on Guru Nanak and Guru Gobind Singh. She sent these pamphlets far and wide to cities across Canada, America, and Europe. As usual, none of these pamphlets were saved by Sikhs, and the efforts to find copies of these pamphlets have not been successful. It would have been great to know in what inspiring way Teja Singh wrote and spoke.

California (1909): Accompanied by a few Sikhs of Canada, Teja Singh undertook a mission to visit Sikhs on the western coast of America for the purpose of helping them and to administer Amrit. Lectures were given in Seattle, Portland, and California to Sikhs, and many of them took Amrit. This was his first visit to California. When this group of Canadian Sikhs, including Teja Singh, returned from America and narrated stories of the Sikhs of California's enthusiasm in taking Amrit, many more Canadian Sikhs got into the Khalsa fold. Again, an urgent request came from Sikhs in Pleasanton, California. Teja Singh with his group of Sikhs reached them after a brief stop over in Porland, Oregon. This second visit turned out to be short but equally successful, and the group returned to Vancouver.

Teja Singh's Legislative, Organizational, and Constitutional Skills

As such, a need was felt to form an organization of Sikhs. Professor Teja Singh formulated the bylaws and other rules of the organization, which was named Khalsa Diwan Society. This society was formally registered in Vancouver, BC. This was in 1906. Later in 1912, at the time of starting the Stockton Gurdwara in 1912, Teja Singh prepared bylaws for the Pacific Coast Khalsa Diwan Society and got it registered on May 27th, 1912. His vision was far reaching. The name Pacific Coast was purposely used to allow this as an umbrella body to facilitate establishing more Gurdwaras without forming another set of bylaws. Unfortunately, we did not see it, and now we have many names, sometime after a community name that built the Gurdwara. Anyway, here is the opening statement of the articles of incorporation:

> *That we, the under-signed persons, all residents of the State of California, and members of the Sikh faith, do hereby voluntarily associate ourselves together for incorporating under the laws of the State of California and in pursuance of the purposes for which we have been elected as hereinafter set out, a religious corporation, not for profit and without capital stock, and we do hereby certify. (11)*

It demonstrates the able guidance and skill of Teja Singh in drafting these. These articles of incorporation were signed by Teja Singh, as President, and Tara Singh, as Secretary.

Teja Singh's Constitutional Fight for Justice for Families of Immigrants

Teja Singh joined UC Berkeley for his Doctor of Literature degree, and his plan was to build a Gurdwara at Berkeley also. But he had hardly settled at Berkeley when another urgent letter came from Vancouver.

This was to help Indians in British Columbia resolve a rule by the government of Canada, according to which their families could not come from India to join them unless they came on one direct voyage from India, which was not possible. Upon consultation with California Sikhs and after registering the Pacific Coast Khalsa Diwan Society to facilitate further opening of Gurdwaras in California, Teja Singh reached Vancouver along with his family. A meeting was called and three persons, Dr. Sunder Singh, Mr. L.W. Hall (priest), and Teja Singh, were deputed to go to Ottawa to request the immigration ministry to modify the rule. In spite of a very persuasive presentation, the ministry denied the demand. Roman Catholic priest Mr. L.W. Hall congratulated Teja Singh for smartly neutralizing each and every argument put forward by the ministry, and requested Teja Singh to deliver a public lecture to explain their position to the public. A large public hall was arranged, and an audience of about 10,000 came in. Teja Singh explained the history of great empires' falling when they denied justice to their people. The British Empire could face the same fate. Teja Singh's mastery of the fall of Greek, Roman, and the Mughal empires was remarkable, and several people agreed with the demand. Later, Maharaja Bhopinder Singh of Patiala got it approved during an Empire Conference in London. The delegation returned to Vancouver empty handed but made significant inroads to the legislative and constitutional rights of Indians in Canada. At a meeting at the Sikh Temple, they drafted the cable as below:

> *"Khalsa Diwan Society and United India League, Vancouver, implore your office to stop deportation ordered by the Dominion Government of two Sikh ladies and their children under wrong interpretation of immigration laws. This is a gross breach of Imperial unity by attack on Sikh homes."*

London and Back to Vancouver (1910)

Meanwhile, as mentioned earlier, tensions and mutual bickering among Sikhs were becoming more common. Teja Singh thought of fulfilling the promise of Sant Attar Singh to set up Gurdwara in England. So he left Vancouver for London via New York and reached London with his family.

Upon reaching London, Teja Singh sent letters to Sikh students across England to get together in London for the purposes of seting up of a Gurdwara in London. However, it had only been two weeks since his arrival in London when Teja Singh received an urgent request with prepaid tickets to come back to Vancouver to resolve a deepening crisis. Teja Singh left his family in London and returned to Vancouver to find that misappropriation of accounts was being blamed on him. A complete auditing of all the accounts by an impartial body revealed no misuse or misappropriation. Teja Singh's honor was vindicated, and he returned to London.

Analysis:
Now 100 years later, Gurdwara accounts remain the main source of division and fighting among Sikhs even today. There are examples of good record keeping by responsible persons. But there are also lousy/sloppy/opportunistic persons keeping doubtful records. This seems to be becoming quite common these days, resulting in wastage of money and time of our community on lawsuits. It's during a climate of distrust and infighting that Sikhs have often missed golden opportunities in their lives. Selling off the 250 acres of land and shares in the mining company happened under these circumstances when Sikhs failed to think beyond their mutual jealousies.

Back to London (1910): First Gurdwara in London

Upon return to London, Teja Singh had selected, with the help of a real estate agent, a beautiful big house (for free hold) for the Gurdwara. This was for twenty-five hundred pounds. However, the Sikhs of London, among whom most were students, thought it was too expensive. Accordingly a house, for sixty years' lease, was acquired for Gurdwara, and thus, the first ever Gurdwara was set up in London in 1910. Because Teja Singh had been working so hard for Sikh causes, at the time of Dewan in the Gurdwara, the Sangat requested that he go back to complete his studies.

Back to Academic Pursuits & Denial of Admission

Accepting Sangat's requests and remembering Sant Attar Singh's directive to acquire education, Teja Singh went to Cambridge University to complete the sixth and the last term. But they did not allow him to resume his studies and said that it was because of his political activities in Canada, a report of which had been received by the University. Teja Singh then approached Columbia University and a similar reply was received. Imagine the days when places of higher learning could be so narrow minded, simply because Indians were slaves—they were the subject of the British Empire whose cruel hands could extend far and wide.

At Harvard University (1911) and Financial Hardships

Then, Teja Singh thought of Harvard University, where he had gotten admission while he was still in India, and hoped that Harvard University might not have received information about his political activities in North America. And that was true. He was admitted at Harvard for an AM degree in English literature. He was to pay a $60 fee for the first term, but he was left with only $15 after paying his tickets from New York to Boston. He paid $4 for weekly rental of the house. These were days of great financial hardship for Teja Singh. But he faced these boldly. Together with his wife, they came up with a scheme. Teja Singh would buy plain cloth for pillow or sofa covers, and since his wife was skilled at sewing, she would make covers for Teja Singh to sell. This worked. The very first cover sold for nine dollars. Saving continued in order to reach the target of his school fee. Meanwhile, when the New York Sangat came to know of his presence at Harvard, they invited Teja Singh over for a lecture in New York for which they paid an honorarium of $25 besides the return ticket. Thus, Teja Singh had saved up $60 to pay the fee and was able to start his studies. Once the first term was finished, there were not enough funds to pay a fee of $60 for the second and the last term. The last day to pay the fee had passed, and the university sent a letter to Teja Singh prohibiting him from attending classes. Teja Singh wrote, "Me and my wife went to a park to think, and after praying for forgiveness for any selfish thoughts, we returned to the apartment. As soon as we sat down, there was a knock at the door." That was one of his professors named Bilso Perry who gave $60 to Teja Singh and told him to pay this forward to a needy student whenever he could. What a power of a prayer coming out from the depths of hearts with full faith. Here Teja Singh writes again that, contrary to what people think, one cannot carry on Gurbani Nitname when studying; it is actually a great support to ride over difficulties on the way to studies (2).

Teja Singh sent his wife and younger son to California where they were received by Baba Jawala Singh and Baba Vasakha Singh. Teja Singh's plan was to let his wife reach India via Shanghai, Hong Kong, and he would follow soon after completing his studies at Harvard. But Baba Jawala Singh and Baba Vasakha Singh would request his wife not to travel alone but to stay in Stockon until Teja Singh came.

The second term was over, and Teja Singh successfully completed his studies at Harvard and left for California with his elder son. Here it is interesting to note that Teja Singh started his journey to California with only fifty cents in his pocket. That was the amount left after he bought two train tickets to California. During the six days of journey they survived by eating pieces of bread with water. What an unflinching determination and faith.

Gurdwara in Stockton (1912) and Teja Singh's Contributions to Nationalistic Movements

Upon arrival at Holt Stockton, there was very warm reception by Baba Jawala Singh (36 years of age in 1912) and Baba Vasakha Singh (35 years of age in 1912). This gave renewed enthusiasm to Teja Singh who embarked upon his mission, given to him by Sant Attar Singh, to build Gurdwaras. Teja Singh had become a highly respected person in California due to his previous visits, and people could now easily rally around him. Here he played a pioneering role. At the next Sunday Dewan, about 20 Sikhs received Amrit, and a committee was formed to work towards setting up of a Gurdwara in California. The members of the committee were Teja Singh, Baba Vasakha Singh, Baba Jawala Singh, Tara Singh, and Bava Singh. Donations were collected at great speed, and a nice and open piece of land with a good house and a wind mill on it was purchased with $3400 in the city of Stockton, and thus, the first Gurdwara in the USA was established in 1912. Later, with an expenditure of $20,000, a brand new building, which still stands today, was built on the land. Construction of this Gurdwara proved to be truly eventful in the freedom struggle for India. This became a hub for the revolutionary activities of the Gadar movement. Students of India of all faiths would often visit and stay at the Gurdwara.

Analysis:
Professor Teja Singh's activities in British Columbia and on the western coast of America made him the uncrowned king not only of Sikhs but of all the East Indians. His humility, honesty, and dedication endeared him to everyone. In India, he was regarded as the champion of the nationalist movement trying to tell the British Government that their administrators were unjustly racial to Indians and that they should respect their feelings. It should be noted that this was in 1908–1912, well before the initiation of the Gaddar movement in 1913. In fact, Teja Singh's works in Canada and on the western coast of the USA provided the fertile breeding ground for the growth of the nationalistic feelings to help in the formation of the Gaddar movement. A

testimony to Teja Singh's leadership role in pioneering the struggle against British rule can be seen from the following statement of a British ruler:

> *Captain H.F.E. Freeland of the Punjab regiment, had been in India for 16 years, and had seen services in Burma and China, also. He was in Vancouver in December 1908, and at a party got up in his honor at Hotel Vancouver, he said that: The vast masses of the people in India are loyal to the British and there will be no general uprising... England's safety comes from the large number of races professing different creeds as well as the caste system... In dealing with Orientals you must act with a firm hand. If you show weakness they will not be slow to take advantage... I have read the seditious utterances of Professor Teja Singh who is said to be the leader of the local colony. The boldness of his utterances surprised me. If he returns to India and talks the same way, I think he would be speedily silenced... But John Bull has always been too lenient regarding the freedom of the press and free speech as safety valves. This may be good logic among whites but it does not apply among Orientals... I trust the people of British Columbia will treat the East Indians with justice and fairness. (10)*

It was during these times (1908–1912), the resentment against the demeaning and racial treatment of Indians, the majority of whom were Sikhs on the West Coast, was growing. Even some poor Americans would also come to have Langar at the Gurdwara. Baba Jawala Singh owned a big farm, and he established scholarships for students studying at UC Berkeley. How generous and forethoughtful was Jawala Singh who knew that higher education was the key to the doors of opportunities. How many more Gurdwaras and affluent Sikhs are there nowadays, yet the vision for promoting the pursuit of education among youths through scholarships is sadly absent among them. They worked in lumber mills in Oregon and on farms in California and had been gounded in faith by Teja Singh's visits. Later in April 1913 at Astoria, Oregon, they established the Hindi Association of the Pacific Coast which got converted into the Gaddar Movement named after the newspaper *Gaddar* of Hindi Association. Baba Sohan Singh Bakhana (43 years of age in 1913) was the founder president of the association. Although highly intellectual and prolific writers like Lala Hardyal and Ram Chandra have been given lots of credit because of their writings in the weekly newspaper *Gaddar*, the poems of Baba Vasakha Singh in Punjabi in the gaddar paper were no less forceful, and, in fact, were far more nationalistic. More will be covered by others on this, especially by Dr. Jasbir S. Mann as to how these shrewd intellectuals swayed away from their commitment and how the Gadderites, the majority of whom were Sikhs, never waived and laid down their lives. As such, the backbone of the Gaddar movement were the Sikhs and should have been acknowledged so.

Gurdwara in Victoria, BC

The Sangat of Victoria had collected enough funds by offering one to two months of their pay to build a Gurdwara on the land they purchased in 1909. Drawing of the blueprints, estimation, and contracts were all accomplished with speed. Teja Singh went to California for about two to three months to preach and organize the California Sikhs and then returned to Victoria. Meanwhile, the Gurdwara building was near completion. The opening ceremony was done with great pump and show with Nagar Keertan: After this, Teja Singh started his journey back to India.

Conclusion

1. Teja Singh's academic pursuits at London, Cambridge, and Columbia Universities are testimony to the value placed by Sant Attar Singh and through his inspiration by Teja Singh on higher education. Sikhs must not forget this.
2. Because of Teja Singh's deep spiritual strength born out of his grounding in Sikh faith, he was able to bring about profound changes in the minds and history of the English, Canadians, and Americans, and especially in the heart and soul of Indians for freedom.
3. Teja Singh's pioneering efforts to fight for justice for Sikhs and Indians and to initiate a national movement for the freedom of India are noteworthy and were historic. He essentially prepared the groundwork for the Gaddar movement to take root.
4. His fights against unjust and ill treatment of Indians in Canada and America were most remarkable and were even acknowledged by the governments of these countries. This was because of his thorough knowledge

of world history, his skills in the legislature, constitutional and organizational fields, and the way he articulated these in perfect English to Western audiences. We need spokesmen like him to further our progress in America.

Acknowledgements
Help extended by Avtar Singh Gill of Vancouver and Alison Wuerstle of Santa Clara University is gratefully acknowledged.

References
1. "Sant Teja Singh ji (Professor), (1877-1965)";by Dr. Gurbakhsh SinghGill, U.S.A.
2. "Life History of Sant AttarSingh ji" (in Punjabi) by Teja Singh, published by Director Language Dept., Punjab, Patiala, 1946 (First Edition), 1981 (4thEdition)
3. "Hindoos almost Caused Riots at Temple," "Hindus Refuse to Hear Report," The Vancouver and the World, Tuesday, December 8, 1908
4. "Hindoos Buy Valuable Tract," The Vancouver World, Thursday, December 10, 1908
5. "East Indian Labor is Needed": Governor Swayne says laboring men are difficult to get in Honduras and offers local Hindoos best of treatment; The Vancouver World, Friday, December 11, 1908
6. "Mystery and Power of TejaSingh," The Vancouver Daily Province, Vancouver, B.C., Saturday, December 12, 1908
7. "Governor Swayne's Mission Has Proven Fruitless; Swayne Mission Proves Failure," The Vancouver World, Monday, December 14, 1908
8. "Prof. Teja Singh and Light Housekeeper IrwinReach a Deadlock in Negotiations for North VancouverTract."TheVancouverDaily Province, December 18, 1908
9. "People of India in North America," I.M Muthanna, Bangalore, South India, 1975
10. "The Vancouver Daily Province," December 1908
11. Articles of Incorporation of Pacific Coast KhalsaDiwan Society, State of California, Chapter No.69371-dated the 27th May 1912

Reevaluating the Origin and Inspiration of "Sikh Gadar 1907-1918"

Jasbir Singh Mann MD, California

Many historians of the Gadar movement try to generalize the influence of communists, Arya Smaj, Abhinava Bharat, Western socialists, anarchists, and the 1857 Sepoy Mutinee mindset as a source of inspiration on the Ghadarites without any serious analysis of the actual content of historical evidence. I agree with Dr. Ganda Singh (1969 AD) based on the evidence by historians like Dr. Surendra Nath Sen, Dr. Romesh C. Majumdar, Maulana Abul Kalam Azad, and S. Acharya Kriplani. According to Dr. Ganda Singh, ". . . it would be a travesty of truth to describe the revolt of 1857 as a national war of independence." Without refuting this evidence, many historians still claim that Sikh Gadar (1907–1918) was the sequel of the Gadar (mutiny) of 1857. Dr. Harish K. Puri states, "The major source of Gadhar movement's Inspiration was V.D. Savarkar" (Introduction Page XII: 2011). Excerpts and chapters from *The Indian War of Independence* were published in various issues of Gadhar movement, overshadowing what really happened on the western coast of America. But evidence shows that the movement was launched from Sikh Gurudwaras and Guru Granth Sahib's teachings, and Guru Nanak's Salok 20 on page 1412 of *Guru Granth Sahib* was the motto of *Gadar* newspaper, ਜਉ ਤਉ ਪ੍ਰੇਮ ਖੇਲਣ ਕਾ ਚਾਉ (Jo Tau Prem Khaelan Kaa Chaao), published in the USA.

Historians do not try to explore the religious, social, cultural, and political beliefs and political activism of the new migrants to North America in the years 1904–14. More than 85% of these immigrants were male Sikhs, and this movement did not involve repudiation of their religious faith; instead, their faith strengthened their involvement in the Sikh Gadar revolution. That is why they went back to India to fight for the cause. Their religious conscience was their guiding force, and that's why the movement was non-sectarian and non-racial. The above facts are supported by the historical evidence from 1906–1914.

This paper argues that the movement started from India, but it began mainly by the Sikh Gadarites with an inspiration from Gurbani in the North America West Coast in 1907. Back in India, Sikh peasants and Sikh military personnel participated in extreme agitation against the new Colonization Act and the Doab Bari Act of 1907. In Vancouver, Canada, the Sikh lost voting rights in March 1907. September 4, 1907, was the day of the Bellingham Riots in the USA. Sikhs migrated to the West Coast of North America and worked as laborers but carried with them the dream of independent India. The consolidation of Sikh Gadarites is objectified by the Gurdwara Sahibs in Vancouver in 1908 and at Stockton, Abbotsford, and Victoria in 1912.

Many historians misrepresent the movement intentionally and ignore the evidence of all, including constitutional struggles of 1907–1913, and label the start of Gadar movement in North America from April 1913, ignoring what consolidated this movement. Based on evidence, this paper argues that this movement in fact was an International Anglo Sikh War that started in 1907. It was the first declared Indian freedom war fought by majority International Sikhs, also known as "Sikh Gadar 1907–1918."

From 1905 to 1913 in Europe, Shyamaji Krishna Varma's Arya Smaj mindset, Veer Savarkar's Abhinava Bharat mindset, and Bhikaiji Cama and Sardar Singh Rana's Social Democratic mindset were tried. But inspiration behind their thought process could not produce any international mass movement for the freedom of India in Europe, as compared to the West Coast of North America, where movement was finally produced and action taken through Sikh inspiration. Many Hindustani societies, armed rebellion, and explosive plans in North America's West Coast have been reported since 1907 as noted in significant year-wise events below.

In North America six newspapers were in circulation prior to November 1913, voicing the Gadar cause as noted below year wise. Their activities were noted by British viceroys in India from 1907 onwards, and they in turn planned Indian/Sikh exclusion from North America, and they were successful in Canada in 1908 and in 1914–1917 in the USA. Many Gadrites moved from Canada to America during those days and performed cheap labor, but did not give up the cause of free India. The secret British Gadar Directory list of revolutionaries in outside countries and India was first published in 1917 and then updated in 1934. It had total of 616 persons: 527 Sikhs, 54 Hindus, and 35 Muslims.

The Sikhs affirmed to fight back by consolidating with a vision of building Gurdwara Sahibs and fought for constitutional rights from 1907 to 1913, but got exhausted. Finally due to the vision of one leader, Lala Hardyal, in 1913, they fell into the trap of German imperialism and its money. The Germans were on the hunt to start a colonial/world dominance war against the British with an eye on India's industrial and mineral wealth, which made Sikhs vulnerable.

Harish K. Puri finds Lala Hardyal as a radical intellectual and "**inspirational genius**" (Introduction page XI, 2011). But author Emily Brown, who has done most extensive academic study on Lala Hardyal's life found him ". . . heroic, incisive, imaginative, exciting, and provocative; I have also found him **selfish, devious, petty, and pedestrian**" (Preface page XI, 1975). He was a god-gifted prolific writer but never wrote even a single line in remembering his compatriots when the armed revolutionary plan created by him failed on February 19, 1915. In December 1913, the German Consulate was with him in a Sacramento meeting, which shows that Hardyal has connection. This was an armed revolution, but why couldn't Lala Hardyal supply any arms to the revolutionaries in Panjab until February 19, 1915? Lala Hardyal himself surrendered to the British in February 1919 when he applied for amnesty. Gadar failed because Lala Hardyal had no vision as an armed revolutionary. He proved to be an armchair revolutionary only.

Gadrites reached India but failed because: There was no money nor any arms or explosives as promised to them. There was a lack of good and efficient leadership.

2. Lack of mass following and absence of national and political conscious.

3. Religious organization in India failed to support them. Only Bhai Randhir Singh Jatha supported them. The Arya Samaj and Chief Khalsa Diwan were against the Ghadrites and supported the British. Even from Sri Akal Takhat, the Hukanamas passed were against the Ghadrites.

4. British were smart and made Sikhs form local committees consisting of leading Sikhs in the districts, which could give information of the

Ghadrites among the rural population and assist the government in arresting them. . . .

5. There was efficiency of the British security system for communication between the foreign countries and India, and they passed new Security Acts before even Gadarites landed in India.

Harish K. Puri goes on to write, "Hardyal, who had aroused thousands of Indian immigrants in foreign lands against 'Willy British' shocked his comrades by his clean Volte Face. He was apparently upset by the alleged backwardness and lack of culture among the Turks and Germans" (Page 149, 2011). Writing in *New Statesman* (London) in March 1919, Lala Hardyal says, "Asia needs Britain's strong Arm for safety and progress." And this brought about the end of revolutionary Lala Hardyal.

Harish Puri hides from the readers what Hardyal wrote nine months earlier in June 1918 in *Der Neue Orient* in favor of German culture. His article, **"Orient and German culture,"** a lengthy piece which was published in June 1918, reads, "Germany has produced the intellectual figures of the 18th and 19th century and dramatist poets and magicians." Emily C. Brown also brings this out by saying, "He (Lala Hardyal) bowed only once to the fatherland of the 20th century in a perfunctory opening sentence. The oppressed people of the Orient now look up to Germany as their champion and their leader in the conflict against English and French imperialism" (Brown, p. 216, 1975).

Harish K. Puri goes on to say that Lala Hardyal was not aware that one of his mentors V.D. Savarkar, the main revolutionary, broke down under severe torture and was pleading from Andaman Jail for mercy and promising ". . . to serve the British government in any capacity" (pg.149, 2011). Here Puri hides the facts again as reported by A.G. Noorani in his book *Savarkar and Hindvata* (pp. 57–58). Savarkar won concession after his pleadings and was made foreman in Andaman jail. Majumdar says that Chakavarti also alleged in his memoirs *Jele Tirish Bochor* (Thirty years in jail), published in 1938, that Savarkar and his brother Ganpat, who was also there, secretly encouraged him and others to call a strike, but did not join it (R.C. Majumdar, Penal Settlements in Andaman's). A.G. Noorani also writes, "His (Savarkar) version of history is also determined to interpret Buddhism and Sikhism as integral branches of Hinduism though Buddhist and Sikhs see themselves as being distinct from Hindus" (p. 47).

In order to understand this important movement, knowledge of **Proclamation by the Queen** in 1858 is very important. After 1858, Sikhs were taken into military in large numbers and were promised protection under British Raj. Most of these men came to North America in the early twentieth century as British subjects. Their dreams for better living were shattered as the North American governments systematically discriminated against them by restricting their immigration, family reunions, and by disfranchising them. This was all done with support from the Indian/British Government (against the 1858 Proclamation by the Queen). They were successful for Indian/Sikh Exclusion from Canada in 1908 and United states in 1917 by passing various Exclusion Acts.

Proclamation by the Queen in Council, to the princes, chiefs, and people of India in 1858 reads:

"We hold ourselves bound to the natives of our Indian territories by the same obligations of duty which bind us to all our other subjects, and those obligations, by the blessings of Almighty God, we shall faithfully and conscientiously fulfill. Firmly relying ourselves on the truth of Christianity, and acknowledging with gratitude the solace of religion, we disclaim alike the right and desire to impose our convictions on any of our subjects. We declare it to be our royal will and pleasure that none be in anywise favored, none molested or disquieted, by reason of their religious faith or observances, but that all alike shall enjoy the equal and impartial protection of the law; and We do strictly charge and enjoin all those who may be in authority under us that they abstain from all interference with the religious belief or worship of any of our subjects on pain of our highest displeasure."

IN ORDER TO FULLY UNDERSTAND THE ORIGIN AND INSPIRATION, ONE HAS TO LOOK AT THE YEARLY ACCOUNTS OF MAJOR EVENTS.

1906 India

Doab Bari Act: In November 1906, the government increased the rates for water from the Bari Doab Canal, and this affected the Sikh landowners, many of them with military background in the districts of Amritsar, Gurdaspur, and Lahore. They greatly resented this increase.

Canal Colonization Act: The Chenab colony was **mostly inhabited by the peasants and military personnel of the central districts of Punjab.** They had secured the land either free or on very nominal rates. The new colonies were carefully planned and controlled by local officials. The Punjab Land Colonization Bill (1906) aimed at strengthening the "irksome system of regulations"; it was proposed to introduce inheritance by primogeniture in order to check the process of subdivision of land-holdings. It touched off widespread discontent in rural areas and affected the Sikhs in military, who got such land free, and other Jat Sikhs, who got it at cheaper rate. "Peasants in Punjab were on the boil against the new colonial laws—the new Colonization Act and the Doab Bari Act. The background to these acts was that the British Government had constructed canals to draw water from the Chenab river and take it to Lyallpur (now in Pakistan) to set up settlements in uninhabited areas. Promising to allot free land with several amenities, the government had persuaded peasants and ex-servicemen from Jalandhar, Amritsar, and Hoshiarpur to settle there. Peasants from these districts left behind land and property, settled in the new areas and toiled to make the barren land fit for cultivation. But as soon as they had done so, the government had enacted the new laws to declare itself master of this fertile land, denying the farmers the right to ownership! The new laws reduced the peasants to sharecroppers; they could neither sell trees on these lands, nor build houses or huts nor even sell or buy such land. If any farmer dared to defy the government diktat he could be punished with eviction from the land. Also the new laws decreed that only the eldest son of a sharecropper was allowed to have access to the land tilled by his father. If the eldest son died before reaching adulthood, the land would not pass to the younger son, rather it would become the property of the government. Not only this, through the taxes levied for more than one and half decades in lieu of canals on the Chenab river to irrigate these 20 lakh acres of land, the government had not only got back its initial investment, it was also able to extract more than 7 lakh rupees per annum on the *abpashi* tax. **Ajit Singh and his comrades put in all their efforts to channelize the widespread discontent and anxiety of the peasants (Sikhs) against the British policies** into a popular mass resistance."

1906 North America

In Canada and the USA, Sikhs started moving since 1897, but numbers in Canada increased suddenly (1904–1908 nearing a total of 5,079 in 1908; 98% of them were Sikhs and rest Muslims and Hindus) and the majority of them were military veterans. In the USA, they came via Vancouver or by land through Mexico (1904–1908 nearing 1746; the total number of Indian immigrants swelled to 20,000 by 1911 in the USA and Canada: 98% were Panjabi, 75% of whom were ex-soldiers).

In 1906, all Indians were British subjects, and their migrations threatened the local white labor, but employers wanted cheap labor. Devi Chand was the first person who brought the Sikhs in Canada from Punjab to British Columbia as the local saw millers assured him that they could give employment to 2000 of his countrymen in the lumber camps and saw mills.

In 1906, J.B. Hobson of Cariboo, an employer, said, *"These Hindus are all old soldiers. They know little outside of their regular drill . . . I would have White laborers of course if I can get them . . . But I would rather give employment to these old soldiers who have helped to fight for the British Empire than to entire aliens."*

The class of Hindu that have invaded British Columbia, are commonly known as Sikhs, entirely dependent upon their physical capabilities - those who have no set aim in life. They are the coolies of Calcutta. In stature the average Sikh is slender and his body gaunt. The complexion is dark-brown while his hair is long and black. In dress he copies the European with the exception of the head adornment which is substituted by the turban. (The Daily Province, October 1906)

Experience has shown that immigrants of this class, having been accustomed to the condition of a tropical climate, are wholly unsuited to this country and that their ability to readily adapt themselves to surroundings so entirely different inevitably brings upon them much suffering and privation, also that were such immigrants allowed to reach by considerable dimensions, it would result in a serious disturbance of the industrial and economic conditions in portion of the Dominion and especially in the province of British Columbia. (The Daily Province, October 1906)

In 1906, large numbers came. They had no place to live and *"with Pots and pans proceeded to Stanley park. Probably Devi Chand brought them by ship 'Athenian'"* (*Daily Province*, July 20, 21, 28 and Sept. 1, 1906).

The Mayor of Vancouver pitched and built a big tent: *"our duty is one of humanity . . ."* (*Daily Province* Nov. 19, 1906).

On November 19, 1906, *The Daily Province* also reported, "With prosperity, the blood of generations of fighting ancestors has made itself felt and to satisfy their ambitions of martial glory, the descendants of Aurangzeb are turning to the ranks of the militia regiments." It appears that the reporter was not familiar with Sikhs and probably that's why he called them descendants of Aurangzeb. <u>As jobs were less there were no other resources and Sikhs wanted to build a regiment of their own as they knew the profession very well</u>. Sikhs wanted to make a Sikh regiment of their own in Canada. In the city of Westminster, they stated their intention of applying the local militia regiment. As there were no jobs or no other resources and the Sikhs, who had been longer in the province, aspired to start a regiment of their own. The scheme for admitting the Sikhs to the militia came from those "tall, broad shouldered and bushy whiskered" men. <u>The Sikhs said that, if they were not admitted to the ranks with the white militia men, they would apply to Ottawa for permission to form a separate Company</u>.

1907

Paper "Circular-I-Azadi" in Urdu started by Ram Nath Puri from Oakland.

Initially the Viceroy of India, Minto, viewed Punjab unrest of 1907 as: (a) 50th anniversary of the Mutiny, (b) Punjab Colonization Bill, and (c) Plague. But later, Minto and as well as Ibbotson, the governor of Punjab, admitted, according to Syed Razi Wastil in *Lord Minto and Indian Nationalist Movement (1905–1910),* that the troubles started in the Punjab were largely agrarian in origin due to the Colonization Act and the Doab Bari Act.

But by 1907, Sikhs had good connections with their brethren outside India. The peasants/Sikhs, however, deeming their strength to be low, first approached the well-known Congress leader and lawyer, Lala Lajpat Rai, to lead the movement concerning the Doab Bari Act and Canal Colonization Act. **"However, Lala Lajpat Rai disappointed the peasants by arguing** that the Congress would be unable to do anything because the Bill had already been passed as a Law. It was then that the peasants (Sikhs) accepted the leadership of Ajit Singh." He fearlessly resisted the anti-peasant laws. He used pamphlets, meetings, and lectures and criticized the British rule in India—its repressive policies, destruction of Indian industries, and heavy taxation. "1907 being the 50th anniversary of 1857 revolt, the government got terrified. Maltreatment of Indians in army helped in bringing unrest and sudden signs of revolt in the army. The British Government itself helped in winning army support for me (Ajit Singh) by issuing circulars that they should not listen to Ajit Singh. This proved their contribution in alienating army trust and feelings for them. The sudden change in treatment of Indian soldiers, which were hitherto mistreated and also created doubts in the minds of India soldiers. The more the Indian soldiers were asked not to listen to me, the more the Indian soldiers drew towards me, if not for anything else only through curiosity."

As the Doab Bari Act and Canal Colonization Act touched off widespread discontent in rural areas with Sikhs who were a source of military recruitment, the Viceroy, Lord Minto, vetoed the bill in May 1907.

1907 – Natal Act passed in BC where (1) Asians must know English language, (2) cannot vote in local and federal elections, (3) are not allowed to buy land in certain parts of the city, (4) are not permitted to join any profession/serve on jury and unable to get any government contract, and (5) cannot bear arms. The penalty was a $500 fine or 12 months in jail.

1907 – Canada was a white country. British Columbia Interior Minister Browser said, "I regret that the federal government has taken a strong stance in regards to legislation of this character—but I ask the liberals of this house to break away from the party alliance and keep British Columbia a white man's country to the extent that is in power." The opposition leader W. McDonald also stated, "I would suggest that the government revise our election laws and while depriving those Hindus and naturalized foreigners of franchise, exclude also others who are unable to read even a ballot paper" (proceedings of the BC Legislature, March 26, 1907).

Sikhs started moving from Canada to adjacent cities in the USA, like Bellingham and Everett (Washington), as well as Oregon and California.

In 1907, the Asiatic Exclusion League was responsible for the Bellingham, Everett, and Vancouver Riots. The Asiatic Exclusion League was formed as the Japanese and Korean Exclusion League on May 14, 1905, in San

Francisco, California, by 67 labor unions. The group's stated aims were to spread anti-Asian propaganda and influence legislation restricting Asian immigration. Specifically targeted were Japanese, Chinese, Koreans, and Indians. The League was almost immediately successful in pressuring the San Francisco Board of Education to segregate Asian school children. By 1908, the Asiatic Exclusion League reported 231 organizations affiliated, 195 of them labor unions. A sister organization with the same name was formed in Vancouver, British Columbia, on August 12, 1907.

Then, September 4, 1907, was the dark day in the 20th century for the Sikhs, when they were beaten and had to leave town. But they struggled. Asian Exclusion League members damaged almost $250,000 worth of property, and the British counsel in the USA did not fight for the cause. Rather, they tried to make a policy for exclusion of the Sikh immigrants/Indians from Canada and the USA. The Bellingham riots, which were a planned atrocity by the Asian Exclusion society, took place on September 4, 1907, in Bellingham, Washington, USA. The *Bellingham Herald* writes that anti-Hindu riots started and 500 white workingmen attacked 250 of Bellingham's East Indian millworkers who were primarily Sikhs with military background. Many of them then moved to the nearby city of Everett. Their estimated damage was approximately $250,000, but the British Consulate did not help the Sikhs to recover such money from the US government. Therefore, on Nov 5, 1907, as reported by *The Daily Province*, Sikhs "supported their medals which they had earned while in military service of India." They reminded everybody about Queen Victoria's proclamation which was highlighted to them when they were in military service for the empire/John Bull. But nobody supported the British Citizens outside of India; No participants in the mob violence were prosecuted. In November 1907, again, a month and a half later, all Indians/Sikhs in Everett, Washington, were "rounded by 500 men." Indians "packed up and left." In January 1908, there was a riot in in Live Oak, California, and another at St. John, Oregon, in March 1910.

See news coverage by the *Bellingham Herald* September 5th 2007. For more news click http://www.wce.wwu.edu/resources/AACR/documents/bellingham/main/0.htm

Reevaluating the Origin and Inspiration of "Sikh Gadar 1907–1918"

SIKH GADAR LEHAR 1907–1918

BELLINGHAM MAN SLAYS TWO AND SELF

A. J. Murrey Shoots Jennie Jones, His Former Mistress, and Jack Rich, and Then Blows Brains Out.

COUPLE ACQUAINTED WHILE IN THIS CITY

Woman States That They Lived Together in Bellingham—Murderer Comes to Vallejo Direct From Puget Sound City.

[article text illegible]

NEW EVIDENCE IS DISCOVERED

District Attorney Having in Charge Standard Oil Case Develops Trial to Lay Important Facts Before Department.

[article text illegible]

TAFT MAY MISS THE OPENING SESSION

[article text illegible]

Crowd Numbering 500 Drags Dusky Orientals From Their Homes

While Police Strive in Vain to Restore Order, Men Escort Dusky Sons of India to City Limits and Easterners Scurry Panic-Stricken and Half-Clothed Through the Streets.

Labor Trouble and Insolence Are Causes

A MOB of between 400 and 500 white men and boys last night attacked the different colonies of Hindus employed in the mills. Many of the Hindus were hurried away from the mills, their quarters in their night clothes and sought refuge at the tide flats, where they were afterward found and escorted either to the city or to the police.

[remainder of article text illegible]

Hindus Fight Crowd and Policeman

[article text illegible]

Mob Attacks Hindu House

[article text illegible]

Reevaluating the Origin and Inspiration of "Sikh Gadar 1907–1918"

"*This is the type of man driven from the city as a result of last night's demonstration by a mob of 500 men.*"

REQUEST FOR RIGHT TO VOTE DENIED IN CANADA IN MARCH 1907

On March 27, 1907, Indians lost voting rights in Vancouver, Canada. Taraknath Das was a Bengali student at the University of Washington in Seattle who had worked as an interpreter in the Vancouver office of the US immigration service in 1907. Several members of the community petitioned for the right to vote, which the British Columbia legislation denied to all Asians.

In 1907, "Lord Kitchener commander-in-chief in India (1902-09) got terrified since peasantry was becoming rebellious, military and police were unreliable. John Morley, Secretary of State for India between 1905 and 1910 made a statement in the House of Commons that in all 33 meetings that took place in the Punjab, out of which 19 were addressed by S. Ajit Singh. That increase in land revenue was not the cause of this unrest. It was with a view to finishing British Rule in India that it was being used as a political stunt."

On March 5, 1907, Viceroy Minto wrote to Morley, "Heard today of the discovery of Mardan, the Headquarters of the guides of the circular addressed to native troops pointing out to them how easy it would be to overthrow British rule—the circular immented from some natives of India, now in united states" (from Minto and Morley, 1905–1910, London, Macmillan Press, 1934, p. 122).

According to the Home political proceedings (B) on July, 3–4, 1907, the prosecution of Athwal (Atwal) and Lala Pindi Das (editor "The India" of Rawal Pindi) was proposed due to the publication of a leaflet in which the troops were asked **Sipahi Na Bano (Do not become soldier). This pamphlet originated from North America. This pamphlet was taken from the custody of Sawan Singh.**

Aug 29, 1907 – While justifying the new act, it was reported as a "safeguard against the contamination of the Indian army." Minto reminded Morley of those mysterious stories of chapekars before the mutiny, which might have a warning but not evidence. The effects that stare us in the face are the circulation of the leaflets and seditious newspapers in the lines of native regiments (Minto and Morley, 1905–1910, Macmillan Press, pg 151.Sept 2, 1907). George Milton, the Secretary of State of India, wrote to Visqunt, "I think the real danger to our rule in India is not now but say fifty years hence in the gradual adoption and extension of Western ideas of education and organization."

1908

ETHINIC CLEANSING OF SIKHS FROM CANADA

1908 Free Hindustan newspaper in English started by Taraknath Dass in United States from Portland.

1908 – Because of the Natal Act, there was a deportation order against 200 Sikhs, but they were determined to fight for their liberty. During 1699, when Guru Gobind Singh created Khalsa, he preached that the khalsa for independence, liberty and equality, and the fight against oppression for the poor or any kind of injustice. The Sikhs saw that the penalty of the Natal Act, with its fine of $500 or 12 months in jail, was a disproportionate offense, and, on March 12, 1908, the Indian News Agency reported the Sikhs as saying, "In fact, we do not see any offense. We are loyal British subjects and some of us have fought the battles of the Empire under Lord Roberts and now this is our reward—12 months in prison at hard labor, because we cannot pass the education test as given in the Immigration Act." Ultimately, the Natal Act was repealed and withdrawn by the federal government but was replaced by the Continuous Journey Act.

March 1908 – Colonel John Smith was a political adviser to the Maharaja of Mysore, then a south Indian state of six million people. He was in Vancouver, and he spoke as reported by the Indian News Agency, March 18, 1908, "If the people of British Columbia are true British subjects and proud of the traditions of our common empire, they will not treat the Hindus harshly. Close your gates if you will against the Indians, but to not humiliate, prosecute or antagonize them, for the consequences in India may be horrible. The Hindus resident in this province will and possibly have already written home telling their relatives that the flag which they have served under in India does no protect them in Canada. It will create unrest and dissensions among the native troops and may precipitate an outbreak of far greater magnitude than the Indian mutiny. The danger is there." He also said, "Tolerate those unfortunate men who have been unable to get work. Respect the old soldiers for the memory of their velour in defense of our common empire. The toleration of British rule in regard to the freedom of the press and freedom of speech is remarkable. Probably repressive measures would aid the work of agitators who only now walk."

"As a British subject, I should treat the Hindu better than the Chinese or Japanese. Nearly all those I talked with are Sikhs. It distressed me to hear their tales of woe. The Sikhs are a brave, sensitive and proud people. I know all these from experience in many campaigns. Have sensitive feelings for them... In India it is a common sight in Hindus washing at the river banks. On the average I should say they are more cleanly than the white man and they are proudly sensitive to their ways of life and culture."

Deportation remained a threat through the winter of 1908–09. The 1907 recession, riot in September 1907, and pressure from organized labor moved the government to introduce another act to stop immigration from India. This was named the Continuous Journey Passage Act and gave immigration officers the power to refuse entry to immigrants who did not come to Canada on a single ticket directly booked from an Indian port. The regulation was ruled invalid in March 1908 when challenged in court but was amended again, and such act passed by the Canadian parliament in April which made a permanent seal for the entry of Indians in Canada. Its impact was reinforced by an additional regulation, issued in June 1908, requiring immigrants from India to be in possession of $200 when they landed. The requirement for Europeans was only $25.

The unjust Continuous Journey Law of 1908, combined with the $200 per person requirement, virtually eliminated Sikh immigration to Canada. It was a plan to undo the damage of having let 5,000 Sikhs into the country already. From 2,623 immigrants allowed into Canada in 1907, only 6 were allowed in 1908. Travel Company used to issue the following letters. One sample:

> Dear Sir:
>
> We are in receipt of your favor of the 12th instant and in reply beg to state that if the young man whose passage to British Columbia you wish us to arrange is an Indian we regret we cannot undertake same owing to the very strict immigration laws which have been passed recently. There is no direct steamer service to Canada from here and it is therefore impossible for us to issue a through ticket as required by the immigration law. If, however, the young man is European, we shall be pleased to arrange his passage, the second class fare from Calcutta to Vancouver by Apcar line to Hong Kong, thence per Nippon Yusen Kaisha to Victoria being Rs. 515/-or 34.68 Pounds. These services are fortnightly. ("Thomas Cook travel Company")

In May 1908, *The Daily Province* reported, "Sedition is rife amongst the Hindus in British Columbia town and that in their schools and meetings, Anti British sentiment is openly inoculated." Tarak Nat Das started his free Hindustan newspaper which preached the doctrine of political, social, and religious freedom. It raised a question of barring dominion immigration doors to the Hindus.

May 15, 1908: "A bomb was placed in the rail street car in Calcutta where four white persons were sitting. One of the suffering points was that one of those bomb outages in Calcutta had been fathered in the pacific cities like Vancouver, Seattle, Portland or San Francisco. From the investigations made, it was found that the Indians in Bellingham and Seattle furnished their 'brothers' at home with the recipe for the making of the bombs which were used at that time in India."

The Daily Province, May 21, 1908: "There is evidence that the traits of the East Indians are all of such a character that color is lent to the proposition that the information which led to the making of the bombs—all came from this side of the Pacific Ocean . . ."

1908 British Indian government plans Canada's exclusion of Indian/Sikh immigrants.

1908 – Hopkinson appeared in Canada in the spring of 1908 and published an article in the *London Times* against Indians making bombs on the West Coast. Hopkinson was an Indian/Canadian secret agent.

Hopkinson, the Indian British spy, was killed in October 14, 1914. Dr Johnston Writes, "The day following Hopkinson's murder, the Governor General asked what was being done to replace him. The reply from the Deputy Minister of the Interior, W.W. Cory, was that he assumed that the India Office would find an individual with similar qualifications and equal rank in the Indian service, although there had not yet been any correspondence on the subject: **Mr. Hopkinson was originally obtained by us from that service. Cory was the deputy minister who appointed Hopkinson in 1909; and his words might be construed to mean that the Indian government sent Hopkinson to India".** On November 4, India's secretary of state replied that there would be no replacement and that the Canadian immigration department should no longer be involved in surveillance of political activity among Indian emigrants, although he asked Canadian officials to pass on any information that came their way. **The employment of Mr. Hopkinson clearly showed that the "Indian government supported Canada's exclusion of Indian/Sikh immigrants."**

A delegation was sent to Honduras so that Sikhs could be removed to Honduras. Hopkinson was selected to be a translator with the delegate. While the deportation of the Sikhs to the Honduras was going on

On November 23, 1908, *The Daily Province* reported what Teja Singh spoke: "3000 dollars were offered to the Hindu delegates for making a favorable report on transporting their countrymen from British Columbia." "The delegates informed Teja Singh that the bribe was offered to them by Hopkinson at a town named Tancret. The money was filled in a small bag. They were told that they could keep it if they made a favorable report. They took the sack and found it contained the bills mostly in large denomination. As soon as they found it was money they returned it to them (to Harkin and Hopkinson)." Teja Singh also recalled the Queen's proclamation while speaking at O'Brien Hall in Vancouver: "If India's rights are not granted as prophesized by an English officer in India years ago, that will cause direct warfare."

On December 4, 1908, Capt. HFE Freeland of the Punjab regiment, who had been in India for 16 years, was in Vancouver at a hotel, and he said, "I have read the seditious utterances of Prof. Teja Singh who is said to be the leader of the local colony. The boldness of his utterances surprised me. If he returns to India and talks the same way I think he would be speedily silenced. But John Bull has always been too lenient regarding the freedom of the press and free speech as safety valves. This may be good logic among whites but it does not apply among Orientals. I trust the people of British Columbia will treat the East Indians with justice and fairness" (Dec. 4, 1908, *The Daily Province*).

While in India, the Britishers were recruiting Sikh soldiers and preferred that they be baptized, but they could not understand that the Sikh baptism teaches the basic principle of independence, equality, and liberty. While in North America, they were trying to insulate the Sikhs from the liberty and equality as practiced by the North Americans. In 1908, Sikhs bought 441 acres in Vancouver for their brethren to do farming at the cost of $41,000. The BC government was reporting that Sikhs had no work in BC, and that's why they wanted to transport them to Honduras.

On November 6, 1908, *The Daily Province* reported, "A conspiracy to manufacture bombs and supply them with arms to the political agitators in Calcutta, India was hatched." It was reported that East Indians at millside and British Columbia were busy operating a bomb factory at a secret place and the whole idea of such a project was imported through Hindu militants of Seattle. The entire affair seemed to have been a part of a bigger movement in India against the British Government. It also reported that this startling information was given by a Sikh worker who was in Bengal previously and who had known Bengali. "In a general way scores of Hindus of Millside are where of the manufacture of bombs and about securing money for the purpose by subscription from time to time, which is ultimately converted into firearms with which the yoke of Great Britain is to be thrown off by India's millions." The Sikh who is responsible for the exposure of the manufacturing of bombs and explosives resided in Millside and in a house where the chief plotters lived. The chief plotter was staying in Seattle, and he was there only for a year or two but had good influence on his countrymen. The newspaper also reported, "There was a room which was a mystery to all but the executive of this league of fanatical murderers. None others are permitted beyond the heavily barred and bolted portal."

Hugh Johnston was very right when he talked about Balwant Singh's seditious speeches in Japan, Britain, and California, and Harnam Singh Sahri's manufacturing of bombs, as well as items such as measuring glass and ten inches of fuse seized by Hopkinson during a search of Harnam Singh's store and house. **"Again what did not warrant prosecution in Canada, became a capital offense in the judgment of a tribunal in India."**

The Asiatic Exclusion League and its branches continued their work and from time to time promoted anti-Asian/Hindu rights in Seattle, Vancouver, Everett, Bellingham, and Portland. In northern California, around Stockton and Sacramento, the riots only happened one time in 1907 but after that, the Sikhs fought back, and no more riots happened thereafter.

Sikhs affirmed to fight back and stay back.

1908 Built first GURUDWARA in Vancouver

They collected money for the Sikh Gurdwara in Vancouver in 1907 and constructed the building in the first half of 1908, which became a focal center for all the Indians to fight back the anti-Oriental policy of the white Canadians. The leadership, however, concentrated its efforts on the immigration issue, beginning with resolutions, petitions, and deputations, and proceeding to direct challenges. They sought repeal of all discriminatory regulations blocking Indian immigration, but they emphasized the admission of women. A deputation of four met the Minister of the Interior in Ottawa.

VEDANTIC CENTERS in USA & their political activities in USA:
In 1893, Swami Vivekananda came to the Parliament of the World's Religions in Chicago (Yokohama to Vancouver to Chicago). The Rama Krishna Vedanta centers of New York and Chicago were founded in 1902. The San Francisco Rama Krishna Vedanta center (2963 Webster Street) was set up in 1905. No political activity against the British was noted in Vedanta centers. On the contrary, on January 6, 1913, Hopkinson landed in San Fransisco and met the British council Carnegie Ross and M.N. Guhai, an Indian, for details of anti-British activity. **Swami Trigunatita** reported the details of Hardyal's celebration on Christmas day (Harding Bombing case in Dec. 1912 in New Delhi). Henry Edward Pandion (student of history and philosophy at Berkley, a Guru Gobind Singh scholarship holder) became an informant for Hopkinson and the British council.

1909

1909 Pardesi Khalsa newspaper in Gurumukhi started by Hira Singh in Vancouver, Canada

Herbert Steven's speeches in 1909 and 1910 were full of empty Asian sentiment. He wrote, "The Hindu civilization is measurably older than ours: where as they as a race, were never known to open up a new territory, or extend civilization? Never! But they came creeping into the choicest parts of our empire, seeking to pluck some of the rich rewards resulting from the labors of a hardy race of pioneers who have opened up the country and made possible a comfortable life."

He was also of the opinion that the Hindus and Sikhs who lived in North America between CA and BC were all injected with a kind of Indian nationalism and anti-British feelings, but the Western people were quick to read the motives of these men who had indulged in seditious activities.

Unrest in India is well reported in various journals like *Yuguntar*, *Sandhya*, and *Bande Mataram* and gave a spirited call for Indian nationalism. Madan Lal Dhingra murdered Sir Curzon Wyllie. Such action shook most of the empire. Madan Lal was tried and hanged on August 17, 1909. At the court, he said, "I thank you, my Lord. I am proud to have the honor of laying down my humble life for my country. Your sentence of death is perfectly illegal. You are all powerful, and can do what you like but remember we will have the power some time. That is all I have to say."

In 1909, Harnam Singh Kahri Sahri and Guran Dutt Kumar (G.D. Kumar) reached Canada. They formed the **Hindustan Association** with Bhai Bhag Singh as President, G.D. Kumar as Secretary, and Bhai Balwant Singh as Treasurer, but, with G.D. Kumar's departure to Seattle (USA), the association came to an end. On December 15, 1911, however, a new organization was established known as the **United India League.**

October 1909 – "At Khalsa Diwan Society Vancouver, the Sikh soldiers in resentment burned their Uniforms and medals. Many of the immigrants were army veterans who had served in India and abroad. These men were in the vanguard of the immigration: the adventurers, who discovered North America and who encouraged others to follow. In Canada, they began to reassess their army service, and, although they did not all reach the same conclusions, those who emerged as community leaders all became militant opponents of British rule. Within three years of their arrival, these leaders were making a public display of their anti-British feelings. In October 1909, the executive committee of the Vancouver Gurudwara banned the wearing of military insignia, medals or uniforms by executive members. To dramatize this action, Bhag Singh, the secretary of the temple society, burned his honorable discharge, turning his back on five years in the Indian army cavalry, as well as several years in the police in Hong Kong and Shanghai. Service under the British, he declared, was the service of slavery. His position received mixed support from other veterans. In September 1912, when the Canadian Governor General visited Vancouver, officials invited Sikh veterans to take part in a military review. Bhag Singh and the executive rejected the invitation, but many Sikhs paraded in uniform."

1909 – Anti-Hindu riots continued by the Asiatic Exclusion League off and on, but no help was given by the British Consulates to Indians.

In 1909, Lord John Morley, who became the secretary of state in 1905, opposed Indian emigration to Canada by writing, "There is a socialist propaganda in Vancouver and the consequent danger of east Indians being imbued with socialist doctrines." Harish K. Puri, author of *The Ghadar Movement*, wrote, "Morley's fears were not unfounded as it was indeed Vancouver which became the first center of seditious propaganda among Indians in North America."

November 14, 1909 – "Two bombs were thrown at the carriage of Lord and Lady Minto, the Viceroy and Vicereigne of India while they drove along the streets of Ahmedabad, but they had a narrow escape." In Bengal cocoa shell bombs filled with poisoned needles were the weapons used by the revolutionaries. Various pamphlets were distributed which contained instructions to make bombs and incite people to kill white men. News reports from Calcutta in 1909 and on May 30, 1910, said, "We appear before you to preach our revolutionary doctrines to all for the redemption of our motherland from the atrocious hands of the white men. Your life is not worth the dust or straw if you do not soil your hand with the blood of our oppressor (white men). You must kill as many of these white sheep as you lay hands on whether men, women, or children."

1910

Beginning in January 1910, Guran Ditta Kumar and Harnam Singh Sahri produced a periodical in Gurumukhi called *Swadesh Sewak*, which he mailed to India for Sikhs in the Indian army. Its banner line was as follows:

> "Maran Bhala uska Jo apne leyay jeay, jita hai who jo mar chukka hai insan Key Leay."

This was followed, in second line, by **"ik-o^{N}kaar satgur sahai."**

Inspector Hopkinson obtained copies in Vancouver and forwarded them monthly to Ottawa. As a consequence, in March 1911, the Indian government prohibited the importation of this journal. In January 1910, Harnam Singh Sahri and G.D. Kumar started the Gurumukhi paper *Sudesh Sevak*, which continued till March 1911, and it, being anti-British, was stopped by the government with the efforts of Hopkinson.

1910 – *The Daily Province*, dated May 11 and June 1, reported that the Hindus in Vancouver, Seattle, and Portland "systemically milked for funds, for the purpose of assisting in the most militant manner the anti-British plots woven by seditious agitators." The India Office in London reported, "The most remarkable ramification of the anarchistic schemes of these turbaned plotters in India have been discovered in Vancouver which indicated little fear of detection or retribution."

This seemed like an international movement preparing for an insurrection against a government many thousand miles away by a stalwart race burning with a kind of spirit of nationalism. It was said, "As much as 2000 dollars have been raised in Vancouver on a single Sunday as a result of direct appeal to Hindus employed in about this city for funds with which to buy rifles, to aid the plots to overthrow the British rule in India." It is also said, "Some as high as 20,000 dollars was sent in one draft from Vancouver to London. And the government proceedings reported in June 1910." "A good amount was skillfully deflected for the individual enrichment of some—while the majority of the Hindus in British Columbia contributed to the seditious movement in India. Though the report was that everyone did not pay willingly. The secret service agents that operated in Vancouver had been in possession of information which enabled them to lay their hands on the leaders of the plotters at the moment's notice."

1910 – There was anti-British plotting in Vancouver, Seattle, and Portland, where money was collected for freedom of India. Hussein Rahim was charged of making bombs in Vancouver. It is reported, "Comprehensive notes respecting the handling and treatment of nitro glycerin with references to dynamites, acids, etc., well known to chemistry of high explosives." Rahim was noted to be a "walking textbook on explosives." Five hundred Hindus gathered in Vancouver and to claim equal rights.

17-9-10 "*KHALSA PAMPHLET*" POSTED AT HIGHGATE KHALSA PAMPHLET

Posted at High gate, London 17-9-1910 TO 21-10-1910.

Short excerpt from the khalsa pamphlet By Malwinderjit Singh Warriach (paper 2012 is as below. Original document is located at national archives of India, Complete document has been reproduced in appendices of Books by Nahar Singh [Struggle For free Hindustan] and Malwinderjit Warriach [War Against king Emperor; Gadar of 1914-1915]).

Bande Matram: Khalsa "He whose soul no slavery fills. He who rides the fiery steed. And to righteous battle speeds, Saves the weak, oppressor kills. He is of the Khalsa, He alone, and none "BY- Guru Gobind Singh.

He Said *"The insatiable Goddess of Duty demands a bloody sacrifice. Is there any one amongst you who will tear his heart and pour forth his blood instantaneously to propitiate this hungry Goddess?"* At this the surging multitude sank into dumb silence! It was in the year 1699 AD, that one of those historical movements which make or unmake an epoch dawned its eventful lights on the scenes of Anandpur. Great, was Plato, when he wrote his ideal *'Republic',* great was Geurgus when he translated his military ideal into gigantic fact of a *Spartan* State, but greater by far is the Republic 'of this great INDIAN THIS KHALSA OF GURU GOVIND SINGH'; so beautifully balanced in its philosophic and practical aspects that philanthropy ceases to be weak and becomes as sharp as a sword. "Such was the birth of the great Khalsa. The Guru himself tells us in his biography that he was sent to this earth to restore the 'Glory of God and for the liberation of man' by extirpating the wicked and the tyrannical. Before death he was asked who his successor was. He took up the Guru Granth Sahib and enthroned it and declared that no human being can succeed him as a leader of the Khalsa, but the Khalsa was to be led and commanded and ruled by Guru Granth Sahib and PRINCIPLES alone." "Wherever" said the dying Guru, "five of my disciples assemble, there know ME. TO BE PRESENT." "My disciples" O, Guru, where are those "MY Disciples"? To be your disciples, to be your true Sikhs is to be a lion, a Singh, to tolerate no oppression. It is to be a life-long warrior — not to prostitute the sword in the furtherance of the wrong, but to consecrate it by the propagation of virtue. "When, Oh, when shall we find "My Sikhs" to the number of five, for there our Guru will be present amongst us, and when Guru Govind Singh is present amongst us, Good. God! Then the woe and degradation and the downfall of our race and soil is gone forever! Indeed such five men as he breathed into life on that first day of Vaisakh are sufficient to ennoble the whole nation. Over the whole forest the jackals of famine and tyranny, and treachery are stalking, victorious — where is the Singh — the lion who at his thundering will assert the lordship of his native soil. This Khalsa — the Guru created as a sword in the hand of Mother Bharat — not far Punjab alone. The great Guru and his sons and followers poured forth their blood in unmeasured quantities, destroyed the tyrants and threw back the invaders. At present the whole body of the Motherland from Himalayas to Cape Camorin is dying. Her blood sucked off Punjab where every stone has a tale of some Sikh martyrdom to tell: Bengal where Guru Tegh Bahadur and Guru Nanak lived and preached; the

Deccan. Where the ashes of the mighty dead are treasured in the Godavari are groaning under the death disease. Patna, the very birth place. of the Guru is a weeping slave; and Anandpur, the city of Joy is buried under the heap of treachery and shame. The Guru told the Brahmins that to repeat the prayer is no Dharma but to act the prayer is real Dharma. Will he not hurl the same lance at us, when he sees us repeating the prayer like parrots unconcerned amidst the wailings and weeping's of the three hundred millions as if that was a music and keeping engaged ourselves in repeating our 'Japji and 'Shabads'. The sword which he gave to protect Dharm and Desh, has not that very sword traded on treachery. A Sikh was hailed as a patriot by the Motherland and as a hero by the world abroad. ` But Oh Shame! Now Sikh has become a nickname for tiller at home; a synonym for a laborer or *Kooli* in the coasts of both the Pacific and the Atlantic. But this cannot last long. The Guru will not leave us. Even as he said, the sparrows shall kill the hawks. The trumpet call of duty is sounded and it is never too late to mend. Therefore. Awake, Oh, Khalsa arise. Oh, Khalsa, and never again shall we be fallen.

Liberate BHARAT MATA from the clutches of MALECHCH FRANGIS. SAT SRI AKAL

(PS Note: Who could be the author of this Pamphlet? It was probably written by Harnam Singh Arora as Savarker left England in July 1910.)

Highgate is an area of North London on the north-eastern corner of Heath. Highgate is one of the most expensive London suburbs. India House: As many Indian students faced racist attitudes when seeking accommodations, Shyamaji Krishna Varma (ordained by Swami Dayanand Saraswati, the founder of Arya Samaj, Shyamji Krishan Verma arrived in London 1905) founded India House as a hostel for Indian students, based at 65, Cromwell Avenue, Highgate. This living accommodation for 25 students was formally inaugurated on July 1 by Henry Hyndman of the Social Democratic Federation. Shyamaji Krishna Varma left India House in 1907 for Paris until 1914, then finally Geneva died there in 1930. In 1907, Shyamaji Krishna Varma gave charge of India House to Vir Savarkar, who was sent to India in July 1910 (and surrendered to British in 1911). Others in India House were Madan Lal Dhingra, hanged to death August 2009, and Harnam Singh Arora, who was a good friend of Madan Lal Dhingra as they both were from Amritsar. Virendranath Chattopadhyaya moved to Germany then to the USSR (later shot dead by the Stalin regime in the USSR in 1937). Lala Hardayal moved to Paris in early 1909, to USA in 1911, on to Geneva Germany, and Turkey in

1914, and then to Sweden from 1918 to1927 (he surrendered to the British in 1918 onwards, moved to London in 1927, and died in the USA in 1939 when he came to give lecture). All of the above were associated with India House at Highgate. Others were Bhikaiji Cama and Sardarsinh Rana (France). **Only Harnam Singh Arora was left behind who probably wrote this Khalsa Pamphlet.**

1910 AD *RULES AND REGULATIONS OF HINDUSTANI ASSOCIATION OF VANCOUVER (CANADA)* (Issued under the signatures of SUNDER SINGH, the Secretary, on 23-10-1910).

"Some excerpts from these historic documents are reproduced from the original, which sounded an alarm at the highest echelons of the British Empire, i.e., India Office at London. of Pacific Coast in March 1913 at Portiand, U.S.A." Sundar Singh, G.D. Kumar, and Harnam Singh Lehri were important members. But G.D. Sharma and Harnam Singh Lehri were pushed out of Vancouver by Hopkinson in the beginning of 1911.

NAME: This association shall be called Hindustani Association. **OBJECT:** To establish LIBERTY, EQUALITY AND FRATERNITY of the Hindustani nation in their relations with the rest of the nations of the world. **MEMBERS:** Every Hindustani by his birth-right is eligible to become a member of this Association, and on the following conditions: (1) that he must sign an application that he will carry out the objects of the Association to the last of his ability, (2) that he will eliminate prejudice of caste, color and creed f or himself. **MANAGING COMMITTEE AND OFFICERS:** Managing Committee will be chosen by a ballot or vote in general meeting. The Committee will then choose other officers."

1910; "**Friends of Hindustan a society** of wealthy Californians, and a good number of white ladies, told the object of the society, firstly to secure unrestricted admission to Canada and secondly to advance the cause of freedom. Many whites and Indian students were the member of this society. One student told the security officer that his subject was chemistry and he was studying with the object of making use of the knowledge thus obtained in furthering the cause. Making of explosives was occupying the largest part of his attention. He also revealed that he was also a member of a secret military organization formed from the ranks of his fellow students of his country and their 'white friends of America'. He also produced his rifle, uniform, as a proof for all that he said."

Sikhs from 1910 to 1912 also made appeals to the Canadian government in Ottawa against Hindu discrimination. "Various petitions and memorandums which included (1) an appeal for fair play, (2) why not others also, (3) Hindus-good workers, (4) Hindus subjects of the same king, and (5) requested for removing of restrictions. The Hindus trying to stick on in these countries in North America for favorable opportunities and occupations and at the same time most of them indulging in the anti Government and anti British revolutionary activities with the help of the money they got from the Germans who were then the enemies of the British, made the position of the Hindus all the more worse. In fact, for some years things certainly seemed to have happened that way." The appeals to the Canadian government failed because of what happened toward the end of 1912 and even after that.

1911

1911 *KHALSA HERALD* newspaper in English started by Kartar Singh in Canada

1911 *ARYAN* newspaper in English started by Dr. Sundar Singh in Canada

1911 – Khan Koje finishes one-year degree from Mount Tamapias Military Academy at San Rafael, California, 1910, and his bachelors in Agriculture Sciences from Oregon State University in 1911. With the help of Kanshi Ram in Portland, he started a revolutionary society to obtain freedom for India through revolutionary means, and the society was named the **India Independence League.** Many students in Portland, Seattle, and Berkeley were among its members.

In 1911 in **Astoria** and **Winthrop**, another **HINDUSTANI ASSOCIATION** was formed in which Kesar Singh was president, Munshi Kareem Baksh was secretary, Shri Manshiram was treasurer.

1911 – Tarak nath das formed the **EAST INDIA ASSOCIATION.**

1911 – The proposal to form a Sikh militia is discussed again for a second time to establish a regiment of Hindus and Sikhs as reported in *The Daily Province* on Novemeber 14, 1911. Capt. Gordon Adjutant of the 72nd Highlanders, who had served in India, said that "It is a great pity to see excellent material being wasted, and it would give the old soldiers of the King, who are here in Canada an opportunity to take part in our national life to which they are naturally accustomed. This would do away with much of the discontent that now exists."

In November 1911, a delegation was sent to Ottawa which consisted of Dr. Sundar Singh of Victoria, Prof. Teja Singh, Raja Singh, and one Rev. C. W. Hall. A Presbyterian minister from Victoria prompted the Minster to send an immigration department official to Vancouver and Victoria to investigate.

> *There are today a number of women and children who are living lonely, wretched lives in Calcutta, whose husbands and fathers are waiting their arrival here. The steamship companies dare not bring them here, as the federal authorities will not allow them to land. In Hong Kong there are a number of relatives of men already here, and they are not allowed to come forward. (Victoria Daily Times, July 26, 1911)*

1912

1912 *SANSAAR* Punjabi newspaper started by Kartar Singh Hundal and Dr. Sundar Singh in Canada

Its title page cover had a slogan/motto by Salok from Asa Di Var 10 page 468 of Guru Granth Sahibs:

SACH SA<u>BH</u>NAA HO-AY <u>D</u>AAROO PAAP KA<u>DH</u>AI <u>DH</u>O-AY.
Truth is the medicine for all; it removes and washes away our sins.

Followed in line 2 by:

"IK-ONKAAR SATGUR PARSAAD".
One Universal Creator God. By The Grace Of The True Guru:

1912 – The **HINDUSTANI ASSOCIATION** was operating out of Portland (Oregon) with Sohan Singh Bhakna as president, G.D. Sharma as secretary, Kanshi Ram as treasurer. Others were Bhai Udham Singh Kasel, Bhai Harnam Singh, and Ram Rakha. Lala Hardayal, when contacted by

Sohan Singh Bhakna and others, promised to arrive on December 25, 1912, but he arrived at St. Joan in March 1913.

May–October 1912, a Gurdwara was established in Victoria and Abbotsford, and all three gurudwaras above were the focal points for Sikh revolutionaries and sites for social and political gatherings.

1912 – Sikhs in Stockton, CA, first started their Gurdwaras in their homes from 1904 onwards and at farms and finally opened the Sikh Stockton Gurdwara in 1912 under the Pacific Coast Khalsa Diwan Society. Teja Singh was president, and Tara Singh was Secretory. These were focal points for Sikh revolutionaries in the USA. The Sikh Temple in Stockton becomes a site for social and political gatherings in the USA.

Stevens speaks again, and two women arrive in Vancouver but were refused to land. The white man's illusions around 18 Asians were rebutted by Teja Singh. Those two women stayed on.

Sundar Singh and Teja Singh file an appeal for fair play. Why not others also? Hindus were good workmen, subjects of the same king, so they petitioned to remove restrictions.

A second deputation, named at a meeting in the Vancouver gurdwara in the summer of 1912, left the following spring to put the case to the British Colonial Secretary in London. This was a particularly fruitless mission because the British neither had jurisdiction over Canadian domestic policy (which included immigration matters) nor were they inclined to exert pressure on the Canadians.

In 1912, the delegates, led by Balwant Singh, went on to India where they secured an interview with the Governor of Punjab, Sir. Michael O'Dwyer, and the Viceroy of India. They found no friend in him either.

Many of the Indian revolutionaries joined together in India and other countries, and the situation was described as a great sleeping volcano. On May 10, 1912, J.M.G. Davis of a great banking house in Calcutta with branches in London, Paris, and Berlin, reports from Vancouver, "Canada made a mistake when it ever permitted Hindus and others to get in. It should lose no time to adopt a policy of exclusion like the Australian immigration policy. This country should be preserved as a white man's country. The east is waking up from a long sleep. One of these days the Oriental nations will be assuming rights."

1913

GHADAR (English, Gurumukhi, and Urdu) started by Hardial and Ram Chandra in November 1913.

In 1913, the Hindustani Association of Portland held various meetings on the following dates:
- March 31 in Bridalven, Oregon
- April 7 in Linton, Oregon
- April 14 in Wina, Oregon
- April 21 in Astoria, Oregon

On **April 21, 1913, the Hindi association of pacific coast was formed.** Then on December 31, 1913, a central body was made in California by Bhai Jawala Singh, Bhai Santokh Singh, Bhai Wasakha Singh, Bhai Nidhan Singh, Bhai Rur Singh, Bhai Chanan Singh, Pundit Jagat Ram Haryana, Bhai Karam Singh, Bhai Kartar Singh Latala, and Bhai Bhagat Singh.

Sohan Singh Bhakna was the president of this Hindi association, Lala Har Dyal was the secretary, and Kanshi Ram was the treasurer. It was decided to start the newspaper named *Gadar* to be published in Urdu, Hindi, Punjabi, and other Indian languages. The word *Gadar* was picked up as it is easier to use and was readily accepted by the members, most of whom were uneducated, and the movement became popularly known as the Gadar Movement. "Gradually the branches of the party were started in other countries especially in Gurdwaras. Shanghai where members were Santokh Singh, Kartar Singh Cheema, Nidhan Singh, Wasakha Singh, and Munshi ram. In Hong Kong members were Labh Singh, Bhagat Singh and Hardit Singh. In Philippines Hafiz Abdulla and Giani Bhagwan Singh. In Siam / Thailand the leading members were Jeevan Singh, Inder Singh, Chet Ram, Dharam Singh, Karam Chand and Babu Amar Singh. In panama, the members included Punjabis, Sindhis, and Bengalis and prominent among them were Rala Singh, Kabal Singh, Nidhan Singh, and Khuda Bax."

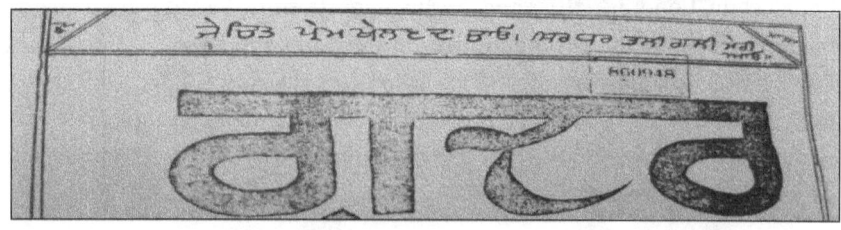

Started publishing in Novemeber 1913.

On November 15, 1913, the Gadar spokesman wrote, "The Germans have a great sympathy with our movement and liberty because they and ourselves have a common enemy. In future Germany can draw assistance from us and they can render a great assistance also."

On December 31, 1913, **in a meeting in Sacramento, while German Consulate Franz Bopp sat on stage, Lala Hardyal declared, "If I am turned out of this country, I can make preparation for the mutiny in another country ... I shall have to go to Germany to make arrangements for the approaching Gadhar."**

On December 31, 1913, during the Sacramento meeting: "Finally Lala Hardyal told the audience that Germany was preparing to go to war with England and that it was time to get ready to go to India for the coming revolution."

It is interesting to note the Gadhar report of these meetings made no mention of the presence of the German consulate nor does it account that Har Dyal had read a portion of General Frederic von Bernhardi's "Germany's next war" which had been written in 1911 and stated that Bengalis and Pan Islamics would produce disturbance in India in case the British went to fight with the Germans. On the screen in the background, they displayed the patriotic fervor of Mazzini, William Tell, Lenin, Sunyat Sen, Nanasaheb Peshwa, Rani Lakshmi, Tatya Tope, Chapekar, Kudiram Bose, Kanhaya Lal Dhutta, and other Indian martyrs. In between, the young Kartar Singh began to sing:

"Chalo, Chaliye deshu yudda karan,

E, ho akhirivachan, te farman hogiye"

(Come on! Join us, let us go fight the battle of our freedom, why waste time, the final order is given, let us go)

The suggestion that England would soon be involved in European war and that this would be the time to strike seemed to bring the movement to a head. After the Sacramento meeting, German support of the Gadhar movement became more evident, and money not only became available but German agents now helped to deliver published materials to places all over the world. Within six months, the British noted that Gadar literature was appearing at various places throughout the empire: Egypt, South Africa, Fiji, Canada, British East Africa, and British Guiana, Philippines, Hong Kong, Thailand, Burma, Dutch, East Indies, Mexico, Panama, and Brazil to mention a few. **Large numbers of sign boards were posted in Ashram in San Francisco and sent to other places in the world which read**, **"Do not oppose the Germans."**

1914

By January of 1914, a community of economic emigrants—men who had come to North America to make money—had become absorbed in militant nationalist politics. From 1906 to 1913, they tried all democratic methods of appeals and delegations but were without any success.

The Gadar Party began preparations to incite rebellion. The first meeting after Hardayal's exile took place on April 12, 1914, at Stockton Gurudwara under the auspices of the Khalsa Diwan Society. After that, a series of meetings were held at Fresno, Upland, Oxford, Claremont, and Los Angeles on May 10. On June 7, 1914, in the meeting at Astoria, Sohan Singh and Barkat-Ullah, who had come from Japan, roared that the time had come to expel British imperialists from India. Similar meetings took place in Wina, Washington, Aberdeen, Portlandm and Seattle on June 8, 11, 13, 14, and 15 respectively.

"First world war started on July 28, 1914. Some of the leaders like Sohan Singh Bhakna left U.S.A. on July 26. The party published 'Declaration of War' (Ailan-i-Jung) in 'Gadar' on 5 August 1914. The first batch of Ghadarites left for India on 19th August, 1914. Ram Chander said, your duty is clear. Go to India. Stir up rebellion in every corner of India."

Two developments during 1914 served to explode an already boiled atmosphere.

A. First was the attempt of 376 Punjabis on the converted Japanese freighter *Komagata Maru* to secure the right of entry into Canada. A spate of violence within Vancouver's Sikh community in the fall of 1914 became acute after *Komagata Maru* incident and the call to arms. This included few murders, a shooting in the Vancouver Gurdwara perpetrated by an immigration informant, Bela Singh, in which Bhag Singh and Battan Singh were killed and seven others were wounded. Finally, the shooting death of immigration inspector Hopkinson at the hands of Mewa Singh when Hopkinson was sent by the Indian/British Government for political policing and exclusion of Indians/Sikhs from Canada against the Queen's Proclamation of 1858 for all Indians of British raj.

B. Second was the declaration of war in Europe and the Gadar party's call for armed revolution against British in India. The Gadar party leaders fell into the trap of German imperialism and its money, where the Germans were looking to start a colonial/world dominance war against the British enemy with an eye on India's industrial and mineral wealth. This made the position of the Sikhs critical. From August 1914, Indians started moving back to fight the revolutionary war. About 8000 migrants left for India. Nearly everyone, and from anywhere, who had come from India rallied round the idea of freedom for the country. They left the shores of California by whatever ship they could and arrived in India to infiltrate in the army and incite rebellion. About 8000 who reached were nabbed by the government. About 5000 were let off, and out of the remaining 3000, about 400 were sent to jails to undergo various terms of imprisonment.

1915

On February 19, 1915, the Gadar Moment collapses in Punjab. Ram Chandra Bharadwaj, also known as Pandit Ram Chandra, was in charge of the Gadar Party from August 1914 onwards when all Gadarites left for India. He promised the Gadrites in August 1914 before their departure that they would receive arms and explosives upon their arrival in India. With German money, arms and explosives were finally planned to be sent on the schooner *Annie Larson* (**started April 15th 1915**). Then they were to be loaded onto the ship *Maverick*. Hari Singh Usman, who was the revolutionary in charge with the other four on the *Maverick*, which sailed on **April 23, 1915,** from Los Angles carrying arms to India, writes in his diary that Pandit Ram Chandra became a British agent and told all secret plans to the British Council about him (Hari Singh) being the leader on ship. The British council in turn notified the US council, and orders were given to blow up the *Maverick*. But, the German consulate notified Hari Singh Usman's party about it and *Maverick*'s route was detoured through New Guenia. Just three weeks later on May 15, 1915, the British Ambassador's correspondence to US State Sectary Larson shows that "British Ambassador Cecil Spring-Rice asked that a shipment of arms the Germans had purchased in New York for shipment to Mexico on the

Annie Larsen be investigated. British undercover agents knew the Germans planned to transfer the arms to the *Maverick* in Mexico and to ship them to Batavia for distribution to Indian revolutionaries." Read below statement of Hari Singh Usman directly from his diary edited by Malwinderjit Singh. In Punjab, the movement failed on February 19, 1915, whereas the arms shipment started from Los Angles on April 15, 1915, after the movement collapsed. It appears leaders were not serious about their revolutionary plan. Lala Lajpat Rai is noted to say that he had no role in this revolutionary movement. But on the contrary, evidence shows that he went with Hari Singh Usman and paid Rs.6 Lakhs by check to the German consulate through Shiv Ji Gupta. What does this incident tell us about the role of Lala Lajpat Rai?

Hari Singh Usman's diary states that Lala Lajpat Rai and Shiva Ji Gupta paid German Consulate Rs six lakhs in February 1915.

> ਅਮਰੀਕਾ ਜਾ ਪਹੁੰਚੇ । ਉਹਨਾਂ ਨੇ ਜਦ ਗਦਰ ਪਾਰਟੀ ਦਾ ਕੰਮ ਦੇਖਿਆ ਤਾਂ ਬੜੇ ਖੁਸ਼ ਹੋਏ । ਸ਼ਿਵਾ ਜੀ ਗੁਪਤਾ ਨੇ ਡੇਢ ਲੱਖ ਰੁਪਏ ਦਾ ਚੈੱਕ ਲਿਖ ਕੇ ਜਰਮਨ ਕੌਂਸਲ ਨੂੰ ਦਿੱਤਾ ਤੇ ਕਿਹਾ ਕਿ ਅਸੀਂ ਵੀ ਆਪਣੇ ਮੁਲਕ ਦੀ ਆਜ਼ਾਦੀ ਹਾਸਲ ਕਰਨ ਵਾਸਤੇ ਪੂਰੀ ਮਦਦ ਦੇਣ ਲਈ ਤਿਆਰ ਹਾਂ । ਜਰਮਨ ਕੌਂਸਲ ਨੂੰ ਯਕੀਨ ਹੋ ਗਿਆ ਕਿ ਹਿੰਦੁਸਤਾਨ ਦੇ ਅਮੀਰ ਲੋਕ ਵੀ ਅੰਗਰੇਜ਼ਾਂ ਨੂੰ ਦੇਸ਼ ਵਿਚੋਂ ਕੱਢ ਕੇ ਆਪਣੇ ਮੁਲਕ ਨੂੰ ਆਜ਼ਾਦ ਦੇਖਣਾ ਲੋਚਦੇ ਹਨ ।
>
> ਮੇਰੇ ਨਾਲ ਲਾਲਾ ਲਾਜਪਤ ਰਾਏ ਤੇ ਸ਼ਿਵਾ ਜੀ ਗੁਪਤਾ ਨੇ ਕਸਮ ਖਾ ਕੇ ਇਕਰਾਰ ਕੀਤਾ ਕਿ ਜੋ ਤੂੰ (ਹਰੀ ਸਿੰਘ) ਇਸ ਕੰਮ ਵਿਚ ਮਰ ਗਿਆ ਤਾਂ ਅਸੀਂ ਤੇਰੀ ਔਰਤ ਤੇ ਬੱਚਿਆਂ ਦੀ ਪੂਰੀ ਮਦਦ ਕਰਦੇ ਰਹਾਂਗੇ । ਜੇ ਉਹ ਡੇਢ ਲੱਖ ਰੁਪਏ ਨਾ ਵੀ ਦੇਂਦੇ ਤਾਂ ਹਥਿਆਰ ਵੈਸੇ ਵੀ ਮਿਲ ਹੀ ਜਾਂਦੇ ਪਰ ਪੈਸਾ ਮਿਲਣ ਨਾਲ ਜਰਮਨ ਕੌਂਸਲ ਨੂੰ ਯਕੀਨ ਹੋ ਗਿਆ ।
>
> ਤਦ ਜਰਮਨ ਕੌਂਸਲ ਨੇ ਅਮਰੀਕਾ ਦੀ ਸਟੈਂਡਰਡ ਆਇਲ ਕੰਪਨੀ ਤੋਂ ਮੈਵਰਿਕ ਨਾਂ ਦਾ ਜਹਾਜ਼ (650 ਟਨ ਬੋਝ ਉਠਾਉਣ ਵਾਲਾ) ਖਰੀਦ

1915-1918

Various conspiracy trials occurred about 10 miles from Ludhiana, the nearest to Gujjarwal - Narangwal. (Randhir Singh and many of his Jatha, later identified, were put on trial in the supplementary Lahore Conspiracy Case.) The wheels of government machinery swung into top gear after having "nipped the evil in the bud." Sir Michael O'Dwyer, the Punjab Governor (later notorious for having authorized the Jallianwala Massacre of 1919 and ultimately assassinated by Shahid Udham Singh in 1940), bared his fangs in manipulating a legislation by the British Parliament establishing a tribunal of one chief and two special commissioners (not judges) with untrammeled powers, both procedural and substantive.

"NA VAKIL. NA DALEEL NA APPEAL"

(SANS COUNSEL, SANS ARGUMENT, SANS APPEAL)

A. LAHORE CONSPIRACY CASE

This "blank cheque" put at the disposal of the tribunal, overshadowed by a rabid anti-Indian Punjab Governor, was exploited to hilt. Of the 61 accused before it in the Lahore Conspiracy Case, as many as 24 were sentenced to death, 27 to transportation for life with forfeiture of property, 6 to lesser sentences, and only 4 were acquitted. Most of the judgments passed on the accused were most casually worded, verging on the cryptic; they could not possibly have been able to bear the scrutiny of any appellate court. Be that as it may, death sentences were given to as many as 24 of those accused. All at once, this attracted the attention of the highest authorities in India i.e., the Governor General, as for the legal formalities. The Punjab Governor, being the final confirmatory authority, "duly confirmed" the sentenced. There was, of course, a provision petition of mercy which was availed by one or two of the 24. So for more practical rather than legal consideration, the matter went to the Governor General's Council. The judgment had been pronounced on September 13, 1915. These 24 prisoners were put in the "death cells." The date of their execution was fixed for October 5, 1915. Their "last night" was spent shouting greetings to each other from their individual cells and reciting poems expressing the vindication of their resolve to die at the altar of liberty. Early on the morning of October 5, they were waiting for the parting knock of the warden with a bucket full of water for their "last bath" when they were informed of the deferment of the executions. What actually prompted the Governor General to intervene is thus explained by Baba Sohan Singh Bhakna in his autobiography *JEEWAN-SANGRAM*, he himself being among these 24:

"We learnt that Sh. Raghunath Sahai and other well wishers of the national cause who had. on their own choosing been following the course of 'trial' constituted a Committee of Lawyers which went along the relevant documents to Pandit Moti Lal Nehru, father of Pandit Jawahar Lal Nehru at Allahabad. Pandit Nehru opined that of these 24 there were as many as 17 who had been arrested before they set their feet on the Indian soil. They then met the Indian Legal Members of Viceroy Council, like Sir Abi Imam who were persuaded to reason with the Governor General resulting in the said screening of the case." When the case evidence was reviewed from a legal angle, the lacunae were too glaring to be ignored. The Tribunal had proceeded on the simplistic presumption that the acts of all the conspirators (accused) done "up to July–August 1914 were acts of conspiracy to wage war acts thereafter when once the war started, acts in furtherance of war, and in abetment of such war."

Under the Indian Penal Code, the conspiracy charge attracts life sentence whereas waging war itself may be visited even by death sentence. "Prima facie" the Tribunal regarded the "Declaration of War" (Ailan-e-Jang) of August 4, 1915, as the clinching proof of "Waging of War" since all the subsequent criminal acts of conspirators would fall "ipso facto" in the category of acts of war per se by virtue of this unequivocal assertion, lending these acts the color of WAR. Be that as it may, there was no limit to the dismay of men like Sir Michael O'Dwyer to see persons like Baba Sohan Singh Bhakna, the arch conspirator and war monger, escaping the gallows whereas those unknown persons like three local collaborators from village Gilwali, Amritsar, namely Sardar Baksheesh Singh, Sardar Surain Singh s/o Sardar BurSingh, and Sardar Surain Singh s/o Sardar Ishar Singh, were sent to gallows (besides 4 leading revolutionists viz., Sardar Kartar Singh Sarabha, Sh. Vishnu Ganesh Pingle, Sardar Harnam Singh Siallkot, and Sardar Jagat Singh of Sursingh, Amritsar). The lessons of the post-judgement developments were duly learned by the Tribunal. This was visible even to the naked eye when they gave their verdict in the supplementary Lahore Conspiracy Case.

B. Supplementary Lahore Conspiracy Case

In sharp and glaring contrast, the overall trend of sentences awarded was towards moderation. Also because most of the luminaries of the movement had already been dealt with in the former case. Of the 74 tried, 5 (actually 4) were sentenced to death, 18 to transportation for life, and as many as 36 awarded lesser sentences, whereas the number of acquittals was 15. Later, there were subsequent trials in the series extending up to 4 Supplementary cases. These cases had a few odd accused that were arrested later (had been "absconding"). Besides, there were a chain of related cases, such as Mandi (H.P.) Conspiracy Case, Burma Conspiracy Cases (I and II), Ferozeshahr Murder Case, Anarkali Murder Case, Jagatpur Murder Case, Nangal Kalan Murder Case, Padri Murder Case, Walla Bridge Assault Case, Gurdaspur Arms Act and Dacoity Case.

Court Martials

However, as mentioned earlier, the extent and magnitude of sentences imposed on army men suspected of Gadrite activities may well run into hundreds of death sentences. Sardar Ram Singh "Majithia," in his memorable writing delineating the contribution of Punjab in the freedom struggle, had cited some data, admittedly sketchy in this regard. He has mentioned:

A 2-3-15 — 5TH NATIVE LIGHT INFANTRY posted at Singapore— Court-martial death sentence to 3.

B 13-3-15 — 2 more added.

C 23-3-15 — MALAYA STATE GUIDE (Singapore) — Court Martial, 5 shot dead.

D 105 LIGHT INFANTRY — Singapore — As many as 41 were ordered to be shot dead and 125 given prison sentences.

E 24-4-15 — 12TH CAVALRY — Court Martial at Meerut (UP.), 4 sentenced to death and hanged in Meerut Jail.

F 24-4-15 — 128 PIONEERS — (Meerut) Two hanged to death.

G 28-6-15 — SINGAPORE — a businessman hanged for inciting soldiers.

As the names mentioned in said text indicate, most of those executed at Singapore happen to be Muslim, and those in India were the Sikhs. It needs be mentioned that the Gadrities, while returning to India for Gadar, had been halting at the ports on the way and had openly approached the Indian troops stationed there for joining the movement. Even though the data cited above is scanty, it can be reasonably surmised that it exposes only a tip of the iceberg.

Hindu/San Francisco Conspiracy Case: "On March 6, 1914, Berliner Tageblatt published the article 'England's Indian trouble,' depicting a gloomy situation in India and suggesting that secret societies flourished and spread with help from outside. In California especially, it was said, there appeared to be an organized enterprise for the purpose of providing India with arms and explosives." A letter by M. Krug which was addressed to the German chancellor, Theobald von Bettman Hollweg, explained "that opportunities existed for undermining British authority on the Indian subcontinent." Because of the preponderance of the Royal Navy, Germany had been unable to strike at England with any real force. The alternative was to attack the enemy using artifice and intrigue. Krug followed the same reasoning in requesting the German army furnish him with a hundred well-equipped soldiers to incite a guerilla war in India, as the natives of Spain had done in 1809 to oust Napoleon. Krug conceded that there was a great probability such a venture would fail. On the other hand, even a small coup in India could create a healthy scare in England which would presumably be noticed by Indian troops fighting and dying for their British masters. An itemized bill detailing the cost of starting Gadar in India with 100 persons was drawn up by the Berlin Committee, which was established in September 1914, and was submitted to the foreign office:

- Amount for Gadar Party passage of 100 men @ 100 marks — 50,000
- Passage & Preliminary expenses for 25 students @ 1200 marks — 30,000
- Amount to be carried to India by 5 people @ 2000 marks — 10,000
- Transport, instruction & travel expenses — 10,000
- Expenses for 2 workers for 2 months @ 400 marks — 1,600
- Passage from Berlin to India — 800–52,000

Germans assisted Gadrites in funding the publishing of anti-British literature and its distribution worldwide, collection of arms and ammunition, and getting passports for free mobility through their consulates.

The Hindu–German conspiracy trial started in San Francisco on November 20, 1917, and finished on April 24, 1918. Conspiracy cases tried in India showed that San Francisco, USA, was the headquarters of the Gadhar Party. The British Government pressured the US government to take action against Gadarites. On April 7, 1917, the United States declared war on Germany. Its first act was to arrest those who had violated its neutrality in the preceding years. The German defendants were members of their country's consular corps who had passed money to the Indians. One hundred conspirators were named in the case, and, beginning in November 1917, 35 were arraigned before Mr. Justice Van Fleet at San Francisco and charged under Section 37 of the Federal Penal Code. Oren, the codename assigned to a Baltic-German double agent believed to be a man of Swedish descent, and Vincent Kraft, a German double agent who passed information to the British Consul, were instrumental in exposing parts of the Hindu–German Conspiracy. In particular, they revealed the plans to ship arms to India on board the SS *Maverick* in June 1915 and information on the operations of Jatindranath Mukherjee's agent Mohindra Nath Roy and of Jatin's plans for revolt in the Indian Army in Bengal in August 1915. Based on Oren and Kraft intelligence the *Maverick* was seized, and while in India, police shot Jatin Mukherjee on September 9, 1915. He died next day. The story of the chartering of the *Annie Larsen* and the *Maverick* and the purchase of arms was unfolded by one confessor after another. For the first time, many of the Indians accused heard of the extent of German participation in their fight for freedom, of Foreign Minister Zimmerman's instructions to the German Ambassador in Washington, of the contacts between German consulates in San Francisco and Japan with some of the Indian revolutionaries, and of the hundreds of thousands of dollars that the Germans had handed over to the Indians in the name of the Gadar Party. Where had all the money gone? The answer was partly provided by Dr. C. K. Chakravarty, who had become the chief liaison between the Germans and the Gadar Party some months before he was arrested. On one occasion, he had been given $60,000. The next day, he bought two apartments for himself in New York. He continued to feed his German paymasters with imaginary stories of the revolution around the corner. In the sixteen minutes he took to testify, he damned everyone he could. As he sat down, Bopp, the German Consul-General, asked him bitterly: "You say you were inspired by patriotism?"

Dr. Chakravarty: "Yes."

Bopp: "Patriotism and $60,000."

Dr. Chakravarty only accounted for a part of the money; bigger sums still remained to be accounted for. More than $15,000 in cash was reportedly deposited in banks in the name of Pundit's (Ram Chandra) wife, and properties were purchased in in name of Pundit's personal friends. Two plots on Wood Street were put in the name of Mr. Reed. Harish Chandra took $8,000 out of party funds and absconded. Ram Chandra was assassinated on April 24, 1918, on the last day of the Hindu–German Conspiracy Trial by fellow defendant Ram Singh, who was a big donor for Gadhar party.

The hearing lasted 155 days. Over 100 witnesses from around the world testified, with the British and US governments bearing a trial cost of over $3 million. The jury found Indians and Germans guilty under the Neutrality Act. Along with 15 Indian Gadarites, 16 German-American or Germans were also convicted. Franz Bopp, the German consul in San Francisco who was on stage with Lala Hardial on December 3, 1913, at the Sacramento meeting, was convicted and sentenced to 2 years imprisonment and a $10,000 fine.

German Sabotage of America (July 1914–April 1917)

This aspect has been entirely missed by scholars of this movement and needs to be highlighted. Before World War I, Germans thought they would make a short but decisive campaign through Belgium and North France, but they failed. On account of the miscalculation of a rapid victory, not much attention was given to the United States. Germans soon realized that America's resources might well be the key to the victory of the World War, because all the ammunition and arms were supplied from the US. Because the British navy was very strong, they were unable to destroy the ships on the way to Atlantic, and so they adopted the second option of sabotaging the American ammunition factories and Canadian Pacific railways to achieve their goals. Germany did not have many trained spies in United States prior to World War I. Therefore, Germany used diplomatic representatives to build the necessary organization. The German embassy was staffed by four executives: ambassador, commercial attaché, military attaché, naval attaché. Germany's Commercial Attaché was Privy Councilor Dr. Heinrich Albert. He paid out at least $30,000,000 for propaganda, sabotage, and secret service purposes.

Over 50 acts of sabotage were carried out on American targets from July 1914 to April 1917. Of those 50, nearly 30 occurred in the New York area alone. Not only did several factories and warehouses operate in the New York area, but ports in and around New York were the major staging point for shipping supplies to the western front in Europe. The outcome of only two cases (Black Tom and Kingsland cases) was at least $150,000,000 in damage done by the German agents. This does not include the huge loss in potential profits and potential contracts done to the factories. The weakness of the United States was that its counter-espionage service was not up to date.

Black Tom Island terminal was blown up on July 30, 1916, destroying 2,132,000 pounds of ammunition. The total estimated damage was $14,000,000. Three men and a child were killed. The Kingsland fire of January 11, 1917, damaged an ammunition plant which was used for assembling shells and was a subsidiary of Canadian Car and Foundry Company in Montreal. Their estimated damage was $17,000,000. In spring of 1915, the Canadian factory secured an $83,000,000 contract from the Russian government for 5,000,000 shells; the factory was turning out 3,000,000 shells per month. After the fire, there was damage to 275,000 loaded shells, 300,000 cartridge cases, 100,086 detonators, and 439,920 time fuses. Large stores of TNT and more than one million unloaded shells, which were waiting for shipment to Russia, were completely destroyed. Germans also committed passport fraud, tried to sabotage the shipping areas and ammunition factories, and planned to blow up Welland Canal. German military attaché

Van Papen wanted to sabotage Canadian Pacific in several places. A German agent named Schulenberg was in contact with Ram Chandra. Van Papen came to know about Hindu coolies in Vancouver and planned to employ coolies in the Canadian Northwest to dynamite railway bridges and tunnels. Von Papen personally paid $4000 to Schulenberg for buying one ton of dynamite and 50 rifles fitted with Maxim silencers to shoot any guards in the way. This plan was dropped because the *Annie Larson* schooner was caught at that time.

In summary, the United States wanted to stay neutral in World War I and probably wanted to go on selling arms to Britain and Russia. Germany soon realized that America's resources might well be the key to the victory of the World War I as all the ammunition and arms were supplied from the US. Therefore, they sabotaged the American ammunition factories and Canadian Pacific railways to achieve their goals. The British had two goals before them: How to reduce the German and German-American influence and how to induce the US to World War I. The British needed many collaborators who could bring inside information about the decisions of German leadership and who could provoke the US to jump into World War I. Hindu leaders of Arya Samaj, operating in the background, had larger goals of securing the Indian subcontinent for Hindus. Both Ram Chandra and Chakravarty, top Gadar officials in the USA, embezzled large amounts of German money meant for Indian freedom. Sikh Ghadrites were looking for secular/republican Indian nationalism by their fight for Indian independence. But as India became independent, Sikhs were legally assimilated into the Hindu fold in the constitution, which was against their dreams of gadarites who wanted a constitution like the US in which all religions are treated equal.

Later, German ambassador Bernstorff referred to the Hindu plot in his memoirs as "an absolute wild-goose chase." Years later, German military attaché Von Pappen wrote in his own memoirs that "he never really expected Germany to successfully export revolution to India, but rather create a diversion of British effort." In 1918, the Sedition committee headed by Rowlatt reported: "German arms scheme suggests that the revolutionaries concerned were far too sanguine and that the Germans with whom they got in touch, were very ignorant of the movement which they attempted to take advantage."

Sikh Ideology/Inspiration and Gadhar Lehar 1907-1918

As noted in the beginning of this paper, many historians of the Gadar movement tried to generalize the influence of communists, Arya Smaj, Abhinava Bharat, Western socialists, and anarchists on the Ghadarites without any serious analysis of the actual history. Many historians claim that this rebellion was the sequel of the Gadar (mutiny) of 1857 (Harish K. Puri. 2011 Page XII). "The major source of Gadhar movement's Inspiration was V.D. Savarkar exciting history of the rebellion *The Indian War of Independence 1857*. Excerpts and chapters from that book were published in various issues of Gadhar." But if one reads Savarkar's book, it clearly shows very strong anti-Sikh sentiment as it completely suppresses the glorious period of Sikh history in the 17th century. He (Savarkar) blames the Sikhs for supporting the British in the 1857 Mutiny which wanted to bring back the Mughal raj who massacred the Sikhs in the 17th century. But in his personal and political life, Sarvakar does it with preconceived motive to blame the Sikhs. On the contrary, evidence shows Sarvakar appealed for clemency, first in 1911 and then again in 1913, the latter during the visit of Sir Reginald Craddock. In a letter dated November 14, 1913, Savarkar (convict no. 32778) wrote to the Home Minister of the Government of India: "I hereby acknowledge that I had a fair trial and just sentence. I heartily abhor methods of violence resorted to in days gone by and I feel myself duty bound to *uphold law and constitution."* He started the Shhudi movement from Andaman jail from 1923 onwards. He served as president of Hindu Mahan Sabha from 1937 to 1942, and records show he supported the British against Quit India movement in 1942 and 2nd World War. He openly supported the British and criticized the Indian National Congress. It is well recorded that, in January 1913, Swami Trigunatita reported the details of Hardyal's celebration on Christmas day (Harding Bombing case in December 1912 in New Delhi) to Hopkinson.

It is necessary to explore the composition, cultural, social and political beliefs, and political activism of migrants to North America in general and Sikhs in North America on the West Coast in the years 1904–14. More than 90% of South Asian immigrants to North America at that time were male Sikhs who tended to come from the most populous states in the Punjab, from the Hoshiarpur, Jullundur, and Ferozepore districts in particular. It is crucial to understand that the revolutionary role of Sikh migrants did not involve a repudiation of their religious faith, and in some cases their faith was even further strengthened due to their involvement in the Sikh Gadhar revolution, and that is why they went back to India to fight for the cause. Their faith was founded in the teachings of Guru Nanak as enshrined in Sri Guru Granth Sahib and Khalsa principles as laid down by Guru Gobind Singh in 1699 when he created the Khalsa, the community of Sikhs who took the name Singh, kept unshorn hair, wore turbans, and carried kirpans along with other articles of faith. In North America the embracing of the socialistic ideology of equality and liberty by Sikh revolutionaries was already firmly grounded in the institution of the Khalsa Sikhs. Their religious consciousness was their guiding force, and that's why the movement was non-racial and non-sectarian.

Evidence shows that fighting stages in North American Gurughars in Stockton, Abbotsford, Victoria, and Vancouver played a significant role in this movement. It is worth noting that the work against British imperialism was started in North America primarily by the Granthis (Sikh religious preachers) who read the scripture in the Gurudwaras. Other spiritual personalities like Prof. Teja Singh, Wasakha Singh, Jwala Singh, Nidhan Singh Chugha, Gurdit Singh, Bhag Singh, Bhagwan Singh, Balwant Singh, and Hari Singh Malhi were Granthis who played significant role in the non-racial and non-sectarian Sikh Gadhar Movement. There is list of total 29 Granthis in Gadhar Movement as noted below. Balwant Singh was a Granthi as well as a Sikh religious revolutionary leader and was closely associated with the Socialist Party in Canada. He came to California in February 1909 to preach the Sikh religion and baptized a large number of Sikhs. No evidence exists anywhere that revolutionary Sikhs in Gadhar abandoned the Khalsa customs. Sohan Lal, for example, played an active role in the Vancouver Gurdwara and the Chief Khalsa Diwan (CKD), the central organizing body of the Khalsa Sikhs. It was part of the Khalsa tradition to respect the ideas of non-Khalsa Sikhs who understood the teachings of the Guru Granth Sahib. These Granthis understood the teachings of Guru Nanak as enshrined in Sri Guru Granth Sahib and Khalsa principles as laid down by Guru Gobind Singh in 1699, and they preached the socialist ideas and values of independence, equality, and liberty already enshrined in Guru Granth Sahib and as affirmed in the institution of the Khalsa.

"Marna Bhala Gulami di Zindagi Ton, nahin Sukhan ih manon Bhulavne da. Mulak Jagia chin ghook sutta dhol vajiya Hind Jagavane da. Saanun Lorr na Panditan Qazian di, nahin sauk hai berry dubavane da. **Jap Tap da wakt batit hoya, Vela aea gia Tegh Uthavane da.**"

The Stockton, Abbotsford, Victoria, and Vancouver Gurudwaras and others as noted in the section below played a significant role in this movement. "The Gurudwaras at Vancouver and Stockton played historic role in the freedom Movement and became central places for Indians to chalk out their program. The participants were mainly Sikhs in these organizations and they played historic role for the formation of Gadar organization and the movement. Perhaps due to these many claims, the Gadar movement was to a large extent, a Sikh movement."

All constitutional methods adapted from 1907 to 1914, which included appeals, protests, representations, and deputations were treated by the British as treason by many, including Sunder Singh, Bishen Singh, Taraknath, Sudhendra Bose, and Tishi Butia. However, Professor Teja Singh was the first Gadari who organized the community, established institutions, created Sikh awareness, and posed a real threat to the British in thwarting Honduras deportation and other constitutional appeals to Ottawa. The British used its resources to bring down his image in the Sikh community. Six newspapers prior to 1913 wrote for freedom but were shut down. When all constitutional methods failed, bearing tyranny patiently became worse in August 1914. The final resolve per Sikh tradition then was to revolt with arms as preached by Guru Gobind Singh. **"Kou Kise Ko Raj Na De Hai, jo Lai hai nij bal Se Lai Hai."**

Evidence shows that the teachings of Sikh Gurus strongly motivated the consciousness of Gadarites along with their response to racial discrimination in employment, finance, civic matters, sense of public humiliation, nagging immigration restrictions and ultimate exclusion, which compelled them to re-evaluate their status in light of the Queen's proclamation of 1958.

<u>Martyrdom in Sikhism is a fundamental concept and represents an important institution of the faith.</u> In Sikhism, the institution of martyrdom is a complete departure from the Indian tradition, and for that matter, it radically distinguishes the whole-life character of Sikhism from the earlier dichotomous or pacifist Indian religious traditions. It is significant that the concept was emphatically laid down by Guru Nanak, and the history of the Gurus (5th Guru and 9th Guru martyrdom) as well as the subsequent history of the Sikhs is an open express, in thought and deed, of this basic doctrine.

Sikh Gadar Movement is only a small part of the Stockton and Vancouver Gurudwara's history, whereas Sikhs played larger roles in India's freedom, which remains unrecognized till today. Our aim is to highlight the role of

Sikhs who have been accommodating other Indians for regaining and reorganizing lost national unity. Sikhs sacrificed and contributed, in all phases of the Indian independence movement, more than other Indian nationals though they comprise only about two percent of the total Indian population. According to the statistical record: (I) Out of 121 persons hanged to death, 93 were Sikhs; (ii) out of 2644 persons awarded the sentence for transportation of life, 2147 were Sikhs; (iii) out of 1300 persons killed at Jallianwala Bagh, Punjab, 799 were Sikhs; (iv) out of the 42,000 persons in the Indian National Army, 21000 were Sikhs; (v) on Kamagata Maru, out of a total of 376 passengers, 346 were Sikh. *Gadri* Sikhs had a vision of secular nationalism, perhaps a republican nationalism, similar to that of the United States.

But, what did Sikhs get for their selfless and patriotic role in Indian freedom movement? They received communal nationalism and lost their unique identity under article 25 (Section IIb) of the Constitution of India. Scholars may notice that none of the Sikh constituent members signed the ratification of the Indian constitution. Sikhism, Jainism, and Buddhism have been characterized as part and parcel of Hinduism. Analysts may disregard Gadar for failing to achieve its objectives, but they can't dismiss its role in awakening nationalistic fervor among Indians of all walks of life. In fact, Gadar is the only movement, which after 100 years of its journey, still shines as the true Ideal of Indian Nationalism and that has remained unfulfilled even after six decades of India's independence. Read the Report of the National Commission's Review of the Working of the Constitution set up, vide Government Resolution dated February 22, 2000, for change but no action taken. Santokh Singh, a senior member of institute of Sikh studies, wrote a detailed article on this issue in 2011 which reads "Article 25 Exterminates Sikhism."

In his biography, under "Amrit section," Ajit Singh writes, "As a kid I was taken along with my elder brother to Anandpur for the performance of the ceremony of Sikh Baptism which is called Pahoul or Amrit chhakna. It was the time of Holi festival which the Sikhs, after their masculine fashion, call Hola. I remember very well the sugar water given to us as a drink for making us Singh's and immortals, A part of it was sprinkled on the faces as a sign of sanctification. **This ceremony teaches the person who undergoes this, not to fear death, and to fight against the oppressors, tyrants and the unjust people and to protect the weak, the poor, the old, the children and womenfolk from all sorts of molestation. From that day onward one has to be** pure in body and heart. This is why the Sikhs are called Khalsa i.e. the pure. After the ceremony is performed, those having an out-wardly appearance of the Khalsa but having their hearts and sometime their bodies too full of impurities are a disgrace to the Panth and to the sacred cause. [This was] preached by the Guru." Under **"family section,"** Ajit Singh writes that his grandfather Fateh Singh was in Maharaja Ranjit Singh's army. "He joined the forces that were fighting against the British, and took valiant part in the famous battles at Mudki, Aliwal and Sabraon. As a result of fighting against the British, the Jagirs held by our family got reduced. But when some Chiefs and Rajas went to help the Britishers in 1857 against their own compatriots who were fighting a war of independence, sacrificing their lives for the liberation of their countrymen from the terrible yoke of the English imperialists. Sardar Fateh Singh, my dear grandfather was also invited by the Majithia Sardar Surat Singh, the father of late Sunder Singh. He bluntly refused to take up such an abject task."

Bhai Mewa Singh was like a Granthi who spent lot of time at Khalsa Diwan Society, Vancouver. On October 21, 1914, he shot William Hopkinson in the Agassiz court corridor with two revolvers. For, he believed him to be an unscrupulous and corrupt person who used informers to spy on Indian immigrants. At the trail in the court of Judge Morrison, Mr. Wood, the attorney of Mewa Singh, read the statement of his client, "My religion does not teach me to bear enmity with anybody, nor had I any enmity with Mr. Hopkinson. He was oppressing poor people very much. I, being a staunch Sikh, could no longer bear to see the wrong done, both to my countrymen and Dominion of Canada. This is what led me to take Hopkinson's life and sacrifice my own life. And I, performing the duty of a true Sikh and remembering the name of God, will proceed towards the scaffold with the same amount of pleasure as a hungry babe goes towards his mother. I am sure, God will take me into His blissful arms." In addition, Bhai Mewa Singh also paraphrased the words of the Tenth Sikh Guru, Guru Gobind Singh Ji: "He is truly a hero who fights on the side of the weak, gets questered and cuts limb by limb, but does not flee."

Read the exact quote from the inquiry committee report as follows;

> Muhammadans from the Shahpur district in the Punjab. These 17 Muhammadans managed to elude the efforts of their fellow passengers to detain them and entered the special train not only willingly but gladly, as they alleged that they had been subjected to great ill-treatment by Gurdit Singh on the voyage. The remainder of the passengers steadily refused to disembark, in spite of the efforts of the various officers to induce them to do. So finally, after a considerable delay, they were induced to take their luggage off the vessel, and disembarked. They then proceeded in a procession, headed by the Granth Sahib, the holy scripture of the Sikhs, which was carried by some of the passengers, up to a level-crossing close to the railway station. Here they again halted and refused to proceed to the station, alleging that they did not believe that the train provided for them was going to the Punjab, that they were being deceived and would be sent to Assam and that in any case they wished to go first to Howrah to deposit the...

Sikh passengers proceeded with Guru Granth Sahib on September 29, 1914, at Budge Budge Calcutta from "Report of Kamagata Maru Committee of Inquiry by Govt. of India 1915." Page 70, Introduction by Darshan Singh Tatla, Unistar Books 2007.

Santokh Singh, secretary of the Gadar party, carried with him "chhoti Bir of Guru Granth Sahib." His "Kirti Akhbar has main banner line from pauree 20, page 474 GGS" because it was part of HUKAMNAMA/VAK which he received when he did Akhand path sahib to start his *KIRTI* newspaper which reads, "aapay hee karnaa kee-o kal aapay hee tai Dhaaree-ai. (You Yourself created the creation; You Yourself infused Your power into) daykheh keetaa aapnaa Dhar kachee pakee saaree-ai. (You behold Your creation, like the losing and winning dice of the earth). jo aa-i-aa so chalsee sabh ko-ee aa-ee vaaree-ai. (Whoever has come, shall depart; all shall have their turn). jis kay jee-a paraan heh ki-o saahib manhu visaaree-ai. (He who owns our soul, and our very breath of life—why should we forget that Lord and Master from our minds?) **APNE HATHIN APNA AAPEY HI KAAJ SWARIEY** (We shall fulfill our task with our own hand)."

In 1926, Santokh Singh still had the Sikh religious inspiration he had in 1913.

> ਗੁਰੂ ਅਰਜਨ ਦੇਵ ਜੀ ਲੋਕਾਂ ਨੂੰ ਭਰੱਤੀ ਵਾਸਤੇ ਸੱਦ ਦੇ ਰਹੇ ਹਨ ਗੁਰੂ ਜੀ
> ਵੰਗਾਰ ਰਹੇ ਹਨ ਕਿ ਜਿਨ੍ਹਾਂ ਦੇ ਹਿਰਦੇ ਵਿੱਚ ਸਚਾਈ ਦੀ ਅੰਸ਼ ਹੈ, ਉਹ
> ਪਰਉਪਕਾਰੀਆਂ ਦੀ ਸੈਨਾ ਵਿੱਚ ਭਰਤੀ ਹੋਣ। ਸ੍ਰੀ ਗੁਰੂ ਜੀ ਭਰਤੀ ਵਾਸਤੇ ਸੱਦਾ ਦੇ
> ਰਹੇ ਹਨ ਅਤੇ ਨਾਲ ਹੀ ਦਿਖਾ ਰਹੇ ਹਨ ਕਿ ਭਰਤੀ ਕਿਸ ਕਿਸਮ ਦੀ ਕਾਰ ਵਾਸਤੇ
> ਖੋਲ੍ਹੀ ਗਈ ਹੈ। ਸ੍ਰੀ ਗੁਰੂ ਜੀ ਫਰਮਾ ਰਹੇ ਹਨ :-
> "ਜੇ ਤਉ ਪ੍ਰੇਮ ਖੇਲਣ ਕਾ ਚਾਉ ॥
> ਸਿਰ ਧਰਿ ਤਲੀ ਗਲੀ ਮੇਰੀ ਆਉ ॥"
> ਸ੍ਰੀ ਗੁਰੂ ਜੀ ਦਾ ਕੌਤਕ ਇਹ ਹੁਕਮ ਦੇ ਰਿਹਾ ਹੈ ਕਿ ਪਰਉਪਕਾਰ ਦੇ
> ਰਸਤੇ ਤੁਰਦਿਆਂ ਕਸ਼ਟ ਸਹਾਰਨ ਵਿੱਚ ਲਾਜ ਵਾਲੀ ਕੋਈ ਗੱਲ ਨਹੀਂ। ਲੋਕ-ਲਾਜ
> ਸਆਰਸ ਵਾਸਤੇ ਕਸ਼ਟ ਸਹਾਰਦਿਆਂ ਪਈ ਹੋਵੇ। ਪਰਉਪਕਾਰ ਵਾਸਤੇ ਦੁੱਖ ਉਠਾਉਣ

From Santokh Singh Kirti's June 1926 article "UBALDI DEG wich betha Ala da noor Piara Sri Guru Arjan." It shows that even in 1926 Santokh Singh still had Sikh religious inspiration from Shabad "Jau tau prem Khelan Ka Chao."

> ਇਹ ਕੋਈ ਨਵੇਂ ਨਹੀਂ ਹਨ। ਦੁਨੀਆਂ ਦੇ ਇਤਿਹਾਸ ਵਿੱਚ ਪਹਿਲਾਂ ਵੀ ਕਈ ਵਾਰੀ
> ਇਹ ਦੁਹਰਾਏ ਜਾ ਚੁੱਕੇ ਹਨ ਅਤੇ ਅੱਗੋਂ ਨੂੰ ਵੀ ਕਈ ਵਾਰੀ ਦੁਹਰਾਏ ਜਾਣਗੇ।
> ਭਗਤ ਫਰੀਦ ਜੀ ਨੇ ਵੀ ਇਹ ਕੁਝ ਕਿਹਾ ਸੀ ਜੋ ਕਿ ਸ੍ਰੀ ਗੁਰੂ ਗ੍ਰੰਥ ਸਾਹਿਬ ਵਿੱਚ ਵੀ
> ਦਰਜ ਹੈ :-
> "ਬਾਰ ਪਰਾਏ ਬੈਸਣਾ ਸਾਂਈ ਮੁਝੇ ਨ ਦੇਹਿ ॥
> ਜੇ ਤੂ ਏਵੈ ਰਖਸੀ ਜੀਉ ਸਰੀਰਹੁ ਲੇਹਿ ॥"

Santokh Singh article "Rang badaldi Rahegi sada Kudrat quotes Bhagat farid Hymn from Sri Guru Granth Sahib page 79-88 read detail article from book 'Gadri jodha bhai Santokh Singh.'"

Sohan Singh Bakna was the President of the Gadar party from 1913 to 1922. His biography *MERI RAM KAHANI* clearly shows that he became Namdhari before coming to the USA. He also quotes from Guru Granth nine times in his biography *Meri ram kahani* by Rajwinder. *Dn ipr... (page 7).AMimRq kOvw....(page 38).. suK duk ijh prsy...(page 40)..rihxI rhy soeI is`K myrw...(page 42)..Ab qo jry mry is`D pweIAY.....(page 67)..sIs vFy kir bYsn dIjY....(page 106)..duK dwrU suK rog BwieAw...(page10 7)..Din jIa iqh ko jg my...(page 110)..icMqw q kI kIjIey....(page 134).* Two detailed examples are as follows.

1. Movement failed because no leaders in India were ready to sacrifice. "sees va<u>dh</u>ay kar baisa<u>n</u> <u>d</u>eejai vi<u>n</u> sir sayv kareejai. (**Cutting off my head, I give it to Him to sit upon; without my head, I shall still**

serve Him [GGS 558])." This means that I will serve my Lord without questioning HIM.

2. Only those joined Gadar who considered death as life and to live as slaves is a life of death. "Dukh daaroo sukh rog bha-i-aa jaa sukh taam na ho-ee (**Suffering is the medicine, and pleasure the disease, because where there is pleasure, there is no desire for God** [GGS 469])."

The last poem by gadrites written before their hanging in 1915, "Gadri jodha Bhai santokh singh," from pages 89–91 taken from a *Kirti* issue published September 1926.

ਬੜੇ ਦਿਨਾਂ ਤਾਈਂ ਬੇੜਾ ਪਾਰ ਹੋਸੀ, ਸਰੂੰ ਹੱਥ ਤੇ ਅਸੀਂ ਜਾਮਾ ਦਿਆਂਗੇ !

ਸਾਡੇ ਵੀਰਨੋ ਤੁਸਾਂ ਨਾ ਫਿਕਰ ਕਰਨਾ, ਵਿਦਾ ਬਖਸ਼ਣੀ ਖੁਸ਼ੀ ਦੇ ਨਾਲ ਸਾਨੂੰ !
ਫਾਂਸੀ, ਤੋਪ, ਬੰਦੂਕ ਤੇ ਤੀਰ ਬਰਛੀ, ਕਟ ਸਕਦੀ ਨਹੀਂ ਤਲਵਾਰ ਸਾਨੂੰ !

ਸਾਡੀ ਆਤਮਾ ਸਦਾ ਅਡੋਲ ਵੀਰੋ, ਕਰੂ ਕੀ ਤੁਫੰਗ (ਗੋਨ) ਦਾ ਵਾਰ ਸਾਨੂੰ !
ਖਾਤਰ ਧਰਮ ਦੀ ਜਾਨਾਂ ਨੇ ਪਰਤ ਵਾਰੇ, ਦਿਸੇ ਚਮਕਦੀ ਨੋਕ ਮਿਸਾਲ ਸਾਨੂੰ !

Last common poem written by Gadrites in 1915 before they were hanged. It clearly reflects their Sikh religious inspiration.

Sikh Gurus compiled SGGS in 1604, and Khalsa revolution was created in 1699 by Guru Gobind Singh. Sikh Gadarites were aware of the teachings of Sikh Gurus, which included civil liberties, social reforms, universal equality and goodness, human freedom, independence, religious freedom (9th Guru), Trade (5th Guru), etc.

There is no evidence available of any influence of French philosophers on Sikh Gadar Lehar 1907–1918. Many of the French writers were not yet born or were only small children at the time of the Khalsa revolution of 1699: **Jean-Jacques Rousseau** (born 1712), Jacques Derrida (born 1930), **Paul Ricouer** (born 1913), or **Michel Foucault** (born 1926). **Montesquieu**, born 1689, was 10 years old at the time of the Sikh revolution of 1699. His literary work, first published in 1721, became popular only in 1748. **Francois Voltaire**, born in 1694, was only 5 years old at the time of Sikh revolution. Moreover, none of the French political thinkers showed any marked concern for the lower classes as compared to Sikh revolution of 1604–1699, which was not only egalitarian social revolution but was plebeian (for low class) also.

Similarly, there is no evidence which would support the influence of communist philosophies on Gadarites between 1907 and1918. Evidence shows that Santokh Singh and Rattan Singh went together to USSR first time in 1923. Rattan Singh admits during his speech on July 22, 1929, "Anti Imperialist League international Conference," which was published in the October 1929 *Gadar Hindustan* and reads, "Gadar means revolution." "In 1922, efforts were made to revive the failed Gadar Movement which was formed to destroy British Raj in India" (page 19, Gadar Lehr Vartik edited by Kirpal Singh Kasel 2008, Panjabi University). Gadar Party was reorganized again, and in 1927, the monthly *Hindustan Ghadar* paper was started again in the USA by Rattan Singh, Gurumukh Singh Lalton, Teja Singh Sutantar, and Achhar Singh Chhina. Bhai Santokh Singh, former secretary of Gadar Party USA, who was charged with conspiracy in 1918 and went to jail after the San Francisco conspiracy trial, was given a room in the Sikh missionary college Amritsar by SGPC to start his paper *Kirti* in 1926. He starts his paper with religious banner line on the top.

When Sohan Singh Josh took charge of *KIRTI* after the death of Santokh Singh on May 19, 1927, he removed the religious banner from the top—"**APNE HATHIN APNA AAPEY HI KARAJ SWARIEY**" (We shall fulfill our task with our own hand)—after one week of his death and replaces it in May 1927 with the words, "**Arise, Awake, ye works of the world, and unite.**" Read below about the death of Bhai Santokh Singh followed by a direct quote by Sohan Singh Josh from his book (pages 109 and 110).

ਘਰ 1926 ਅਤੇ 1927 ਵਿੱਚ ਉਪਰੋ, ਥਲੀ ਦੇ ਬੇਟਿਆਂ ਨੇ ਜਨਮ ਲਿਆ ਪਰ ਉਹ ਕੁਝ ਦਿਨਾਂ ਬਾਅਦ ਹੀ ਚੜ੍ਹਾਈ ਕਰਦੇ ਗਏ। ਭਾਈ ਸੰਤੋਖ ਸਿੰਘ ਇਹ ਸਦਮੇ ਵੀ ਸਹਿ ਗਏ ਪਰ ਤਪਦਿਕ ਦੀ ਨਾਮੁਰਾਦ ਅਤੇ ਉਸ ਵੇਲੇ ਦੀ ਲਾਇਲਾਜ ਬੀਮਾਰੀ ਨੇ ਉਨ੍ਹਾਂ ਦਾ ਪਿੱਛਾ ਨਾ ਛੱਡਿਆ। 19 ਮਈ, 1927 ਈ: ਨੂੰ ਸਵੇਰ ਦੇ 7 ਵੱਜ ਕੇ 40 ਮਿੰਟ ਉੱਤੇ ਉਨ੍ਹਾਂ ਨੇ ਆਖਰੀ ਸਵਾਸ ਲਿਆ ਅਤੇ 35 ਸਾਲ ਉਮਰ ਭੋਗ ਕੇ ਸਮਕਾਲੀ ਸਿਰਮੌਰ ਅਕਾਲੀ ਆਗੂ, ਮਾਸਟਰ ਤਾਰਾ ਸਿੰਘ ਜੀ, ਦੇ ਸ਼ਬਦਾਂ ਵਿੱਚ ਪਰਜਾ-ਪਰਜਾ ਕਰਕੇ ਸ਼ਹੀਦੀ ਪਾਯਤ ਕਰ ਗਏ।

Bhai Santokh Singh dies on May 19, 1927. The same month Sohan Singh Josh removes the religious banner from Kirti newspaper's May issue. Read below the statements by Sohan Singh Josh from his book, My Tryst with Secularism, pages 109–110.

shabad from Sikh scripture had appeared below the title of the issue, and on the top was a quotation from *Guru Granth Saheb* "We shall fulfil our task with our own hands". I felt that this was not only odd but also wrong. Why this bias in favour of the Sikh religion? *Kirti*

However, the other quotation: "We shall fulfil our tasks with our own hands" remained there in some more issues. There was nothing wrong in it politically, except the religious tinge of its origin. It was subsequently replaced in the May 1927 issue by the words, "Arise, awake, ye workers of the world, and unite!"

The above evidence by Rattan Singh and Sohan Singh Josh confirms communist influence on Gadar Lehar starts from 1927 onwards.

Reevaluating the Origin and Inspiration of "Sikh Gadar 1907–1918"

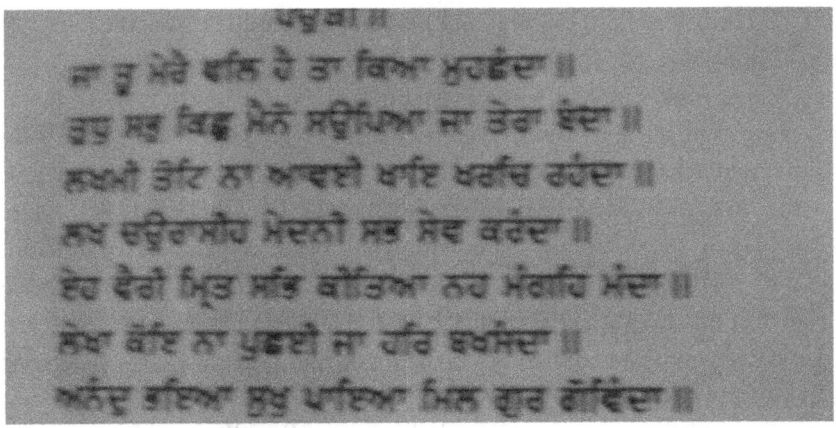

Fifth guru shabad from raag Gauri GGS page 201 used to be read in court during court proceedings. From R. Rahi "Gadar lehar Asli Gatha" part 2, page 201.

Fifth guru shabad from rag maru GGS page 1096, which Nidhan Singh Chugah used to recite. Rahi's "gadar lehar Asli."

The above substantial and preponderance evidence shows that Gadarites' source of inspiration was predominantly religious. Certainly there was existence of written evidence of teachings enshrined in Guru Granth Sahib since 1604, promoting the value of human freedom and equality, which were already ingrained in the minds of the Gadari Sikhs. After the establishment of Sikh Gurdwaras, teachings and sacrifices of Sikh Gurus and their followers were reminisced and relived in their consciousness. Records maintained at Pacific Coast Khalsa Diwan Society are a huge evidence of these factors.

Various Shabads in Gadar di Goonj

A. A.ਫਰੀਦਾ ਬਾਰਿ ਪਰਾਇਐ ਬੈਸਣਾ ਸਾਂਈ ਮੁਝੈ ਨ ਦੇਹਿ ॥ ਜੇ ਤੂ ਏਵੈ ਰਖਸੀ ਜੀਉ ਸਰੀਰਹੁ ਲੇਹਿ ॥੪੨॥ GGS page #1380 If this is the way you are going to keep me, then go ahead and take the life out of my body. ||42||

B. ਸਲੋਕ ਕਬੀਰ ਸੂਰਾ ਸੋ ਪਹਿਚਾਨੀਐ ਜੁ ਲਰੈ ਦੀਨ ਕੇ ਹੇਤ ॥ ਪੁਰਜਾ ਪੁਰਜਾ ਕਟਿ ਮਰੈ ਕਬਹੂ ਨ ਛਾਡੈ ਖੇਤੁ ॥੨॥੨॥ {GGS page #1105} He alone is known as a spiritual hero, who fights in defense of religion. He may be cut apart, piece by piece, but he never leaves the field of battle. ||2||2||

C. .ਮਃ ੧ ॥ ਸਚੁ ਸਭਨਾ ਹੋਇ ਦਾਰੂ ਪਾਪ ਕਢੈ ਧੋਇ ॥ ਨਾਨਕੁ ਵਖਾਣੈ ਬੇਨਤੀ ਜਿਨਿ ਸਚੁ ਪਲੈ ਹੋਇ ॥੨॥ {GGS page #468}Truth is the medicine for all; it removes and washes away our sins. Nanak speaks this prayer to those who have Truth in their laps.

D. D.Guru Nanak's teachings and his Salok 20 page 1412 was the motto of Gadar Newspaper.

Please note this Salok was written by Guru Nanak before 1539AD. It was in the psyche of Sikhs and in use since then. ਜਉ ਤਉ ਪ੍ਰੇਮ ਖੇਲਣ ਕਾ ਚਾਉ ॥Jo Tau Prem Khaelan Kaa Chaao ||If you desire to play this game of love with Me,ਸਿਰੁ ਧਰਿ ਤਲੀ ਗਲੀ ਮੇਰੀ ਆਉ ॥Sir Dhār Thales Gale Mare Ado ||Then step onto my Path with your head in palm of your hand. ਇਤੁ ਮਾਰਗਿ ਪੈਰੁ ਧਰੀਜੈ॥Edith Mara Pair Dhhareejai ||When you place your feet on this Path,ਸਿਰੁ ਦੀਜੈ ਕਾਣਿ ਨ ਕੀਜੈ ॥੨੦॥Sir Deejai Kaan N Keejai ||20||Give your head, and do not blame/fault/find imperfection with anyone /or pay any attention to public opinion. ||20|

"Nevertheless, they used 'Vande Mataram.' Sure 'Vande Mataram' was used. It was written in Bengali in 1882. Hindu MahaSabha was founded in 1915. Scholars supporting this contention must produce evidence what percentage of Gadari Babas knew Bengali at that time? But, What happened to the votaries of this 'Vande Mataram'? Tilk, Hardyal, Savarkar who believed in 'Vande Mataram' But surrendered to British very soon? As it was not in their psyche they could not follow Eith Maarag Pair Dhhareejai ||When you place your feet on this Path, Dheejai Kaan N Keejai ||20||Give your head, and do not blame/fault/find imperfection with anyone /or pay any attention to public opinion. **But brave Ghadrites who knew the significance of this Salok followed the path without any blame to anybody including Lala Hardial or Ram Chandra who promised them/ Gadarites going to India that they will get money and arms when they reach India.**

British efforts for insulation of freedom of Sikhs by getting ideas from free societies: Harold Gould in his excellent Book on the subject writes **about** it was the fear that Indians in open societies like Canada and united states were undergoing social and ideological changes which had revolutionary implications for the perpetuation of British rule in India, the British were eagerly searching for ways to prevent such Indians from getting Ideas." But **FREEDOM, liberty, Independence, and equality in Sikhs were already part in teachings of GGS and Khalsa institution created in 1699.**

Colonial Terrorism of Fear for respect versus Guru Granth Sahib on Fear (Kuka movement)

Blowing Sikhs by cannons, Budge Budge Ghat Firing, Jallianwallah Bagh firing, Gurudwara movement, Guru Ka Bagh and Jaiton Morchas, and the hanging of young Sikhs in Khalsa army (after 1849 annexation) were manifestations of colonial terrorism of fear for respect.

Lord Minto writes on the issue of deportation of Ajit Singh and Lala Lajpat Rai (page 100), "Minto was not very fond of policy of deportation and repressing, but could not see no alternative, as he wrote to Lord Roberts, who wrote, 'Morley was willing to support you in any repressive measures you may think necessary to take.' Lord Roberts further informed Minto that '<u>I told Morley that we govern India by respect based on Fear, remove the fear and the respect will soon disappear</u>'" (Reference Lord Roberts to Minto, May 17, 1907. M.C).

But, the final statements of Sikh Shaheeds Mewa Singh, Kartar Singh, Karam Singh, Bhagat Singh, and Udham Singh proved that Sikhs are a fearless nation as Guru Granth Sahib teaches against fear and hatred. Kartar Singh Sarabha's final statement reads, "You can only hang me, what more can you do? We are not afraid of that." "What sentence will I receive for my crime? Life-sentence or death? I would prefer death, so that I could be born again—as long as the India does not become free I would be born again and again—and would be hanged for my country. This is the only last wish I have."

Sachinder Nath Sanyal on Sikhs who participated in Sikh Ghadr Movement

The Bengali Revolutionary came to Punjab in 1914–1915 and met the Gadaris for the first time. He writes in his book, *Bandi Jiwan* (Incarcerated life), about his impression of the Sikhs having a simple way of life and talks about their openness, civility, honesty, daring, and courageous qualities. He uses the word "Sikh Dal" for the Gadaries and writes that, if someone had to meet the Sikh Dal members, one had to go to Gurdwaras, the only place they were seen. He writes that most of the members of the Sikh Dal were over 60 years of age, but they had courage and zeal like young men. These Sikh Dal members would start reciting Sikh scripture early in the morning after taking a bath. Baba Nidan Singh Chugha remembered Guru Granth Sahib by heart and always continued to do Paath orally. He also writes that 7000 to 8000 Gadaries came from different countries, and the majority of them were Sikhs and included only 20–25 the Hindus or Muslims.

M. Honoring of Sikh Gadrites By Central Sikh League and Association of Ghadries with SGPC and Sri akal Takhat.
Central Sikh League (1919–1933) was a political organization of the Sikhs, which guided their affairs until the Shiromani Akali Dal emerged as a mass force. The inaugural session of the Central Sikh League was held at Amritsar on December 29, 1919, coinciding with the annual sessions of the Indian National Congress and the Muslim League. It was dominated by the educated Sikhs from the middle strata, such as Sardul Singh Caveeshar, Harchand Singh Lyallpuri, and Master Sundar Singh Lyallpuri. The first president was Sardar Bahadur Gajjan Singh, representing moderate political opinion. But the leadership soon changed, and Baba Kharak Singh, an ardent nationalist, was elected president for its second **session** at Lahore in October 1920. The aims and objectives of the Central Sikh League, according to its new constitution adopted on July 22, 1921, were the attainment of swaraj, i.e., political autonomy for the country by legitimate, peaceful, and constitutional means and the promotion of Panthic unity, the fostering of patriotism and public spirit among the Sikhs and the development and organization of their political, moral, and economic resources.

Rajwinder Singh Rahi (Gadar Lahar Asli Gatha part III- In Press) writes as follows about the Gadris Honoring by Cetral Sikh League and other facts about Gadari involvement in newly formed SGPC and Sri Akal Takhat. These facts have been also supported by many other authors, and they can be summarized as follows:

Reevaluating the Origin and Inspiration of "Sikh Gadar 1907–1918"

1. Central Sikh League in October 1920 honored the Sikh Gadaris. In this program, Sant Visakha Singh, Bhai Piara Singh Langari, Bhai Bhakhtavar Singh, Bhai Bhag Singh Canadian, Master Mota Singh, and Bhai Kartar Singh Jhhabar, etc., participated. In this program, approximately 50 passengers of Kama Gata Maru were honored who were released from jail recently. All these 50 Kama Gata passengers were sitting on the stage on the right side. On the left side of the stage, there were seven empty chairs which were garlanded and were for Sant Visakha Singh, Bhai Randir Singh, Master Chatar Singh, Baba Nidan Singh, Baba Jawala Singh, Bhai Madan Singh Gaga, and Udam Singh Kasail, all of whom were in the jails at that time. In this program, Sikh Kaidi Prewar Sahaiak Committee was formed. From the stage, Harchand Singh Rahees Layl Puri openly appreciated the Panthic services by these courageous Gadari Sikhs and criticized all those who tried to label them anti-Sikh. Sangat labeled these Gadhri as "Kalgi Dhar De Sache Suptr" (October 20, 1920, report as published in Akali paper).
2. On January 10, 1931, Sant Wasaka Singh was selected one of the Panj Piara for the Kar Seva of Tarn Taran Gurdwara Sarvor.
3. On October 21, 1934, Sant Wasaka Singh was appointed as Jathedar Sri Akal Takhat unanimously by SGPC.
4. In 1932, for the opening ceremony of the building at Gurdwara Panja Sahib, three Ghadries were selected and participated as Panj Piaras, which included Sant Wasakha Singh, Baba Nidan Singh Chugha, and Bhai Randir Singh.
5. In 1936, the SGPC Committee first appointed Baba Wasakha Singh as a sole Salas/arbitrator/umpire for unanimous selection of SGPC President, but he went to Nilibar. Then in his place Gadri Baba Sohan Singh Bhakna was selected as sole arbitrator for such selection.
6. Nadan Singh Chugha became the president of Gurdwara Moga in 1936.
7. Bhai Piara Singh Langari was made member of SGPC and Central Sikh League in 1920.
8. In 1920, Canadian Bhai Bhag Singh became member of SGPC and in 1925 became a member of Gurdwara Central board.
9. Bhai Mit Singh Pandori became an SGPC member in 1926, and he was also a member of Gurdwara Parbhandak Committee Muktsar.

10. Jathedar Pratap Singh Kot Fatoohi became an SGPC member in 1920.
11. Baba Ishar Singh Marhana became member of SGPC in 1920, and in 1930, he was a member of the Darbar Sahib managing committee. On July 4, 1930, he became vice president of SGPC.
12. Bhai Santokh Singh was given a room in Sikh missionary college Amritsar by SGPC to start his paper *Kirti*.
13. 1920–1923, underground Baba Gurumukh Singh Lalto was provided a room near Sri Darbar Sahib by SGPC.
14. Bhai Hari Singh Chotia became a member of SGPC in 1920. He was Jathedar of the Guru Ka Bagh Morcha.
15. In July 1930, Baba Sohan Singh Bhakna was given Saropa at Sri Akal Takhat after he was released from jail.
16. In July 1930, Baba Sohan Singh Bhakna was also given Saropa at Gurdwara Dera Sahib Lahore, and after that, he became Sri Akal Takhat Jathedar.
17. With the help of SGPC, underground Udam Singh Kasail and underground Baba Gurmukh Singh Lalto were provided two months of residence in Sikh missionary college Amritsar by SGPC.
18. In 1926, Baba Gurdit Singh of Kama Gata Maru acted as president of Akali Dal party in absence of SARMUKH SINGH Jhabal. He took part in the Sarb Sampradai Conference (1934) on behalf of the Akalis.
19. **Sikh Preachers and gurudwaras who participated in Sikh Ghadr.**
    a. **Sikh Preachers (Granthis) who participated in Sikh Ghadr and were Indicted in various cases**
        1. Bhai Balwant Singh, Gurdwara Vancouver
        2. Bhai Hari Singh Chotin, Gurdwara Vancouver and Shanghai
        3. Bhai Piara Singh Langary, Gurdwara Vancouver
        4. Bhai Mit Singh Pandori, Gurdwara Abbotsford
        5. Bhai Munsha Singh Dhukhi, Gurdwara Victoria
        6. Bhai Bhagwant Singh Pritam, Gurdwara Pinang-Korea
        7. Bhai Waryam Singh-Sundar Singh, Gurdwara Vancouver
        8. Bhai Wasakha Singh Dadehar, Gurdwara Stockton
        9. Bhai Hazara Singh Dadehar, Gurdwara Stockton
        10. Bhai Inder Singh Malha, Gurdwara Stockton
        11. Bhai Budha Singh, Gurdwara Bangkok

12. Bhai Harnam Singh Kahuta, Gurdwara Hong Kong
13. Bhai Wasawa Singh, Gurdwara Ching Mei Thailand
14. Bhai Bhog Singh, Gurdwara Jharh Sahib Amritsar
15. Bhai Prem Singh, Gurdwara Pinang-Korea and Chomala Sahib-Lahore
16. Bhai Madan Singh Gaga, Gurdwara Lahore Cantonment (Chhauni)

b. **Sikh Preachers (Granthis) who participated in Sikh Ghadr but were not indicted in any case**
   1. Bhai Jagat Singh, Gurdwara Shanghai
   2. Bhai Kharak Singh, Gurdwara Hong Kong
   3. Bhai Bishan Singh, Gurdwara Hyan Shanghai
   4. Bhai Harnam Singh, Gurdwara Vancouver
   5. Bhai Naryan Singh Thhikriwal, Gurdwara Vancouver
   6. Bhai Bhagat Singh-Charanjit Singh, Gurdwara Stockton
   7. Bhai Sardara Singh, Gurdwara Burma
   8. Bhai Joga Singh, Gurdwara Singapore
   9. Bhai Uttar Singh, Gurdwara Dhikmanpur
   10. Bhai Chattar Singh, Gurdwara Baba Buddha Ji Ram Das and Khadoor Sahib
   11. 11.Bhai Ishar Singh Marhana, Gurdwara/SGPC Member
   12. Bhai Karam Singh Nathok Barki, Gurdwara Lahore
   13. Bhai Santa Singh/Sant Lakvir Singh, Gurdwara Chak Lyalpur / Faislabad

c. **List of 25 Gurudwara around the Globe who participated in Sikh Ghadr**
   1. Gurdwara Sahib Vancouver
   2. Gurdwara Sahib Victoria
   3. Gurdwara Sahib Abbotsford
   4. Gurdwara Sahib Stockton
   5. Gurdwara Sahib Hong Kong
   6. Gurdwara Sahib Shanghai
   7. Gurdwara Sahib Tianamen Shanghai
   8. Gurdwara Sahib Pinang, Korea
   9. Gurdwara Sahib Bangkok Thailand
   10. Gurdwara Sahib Chin Mei Siam-Bangkok Thailand
   11. Gurdwara Sahib Manila Philippines

12. Gurdwara Sahib Rangoon Burma
13. Gurdwara Sahib Singapore
14. Gurdwara Sahib Sant Gulab Singh Amritsar
15. Gurdwara Sahib Gharh Sahib Amritsar
16. Gurdwara Sahib Lohat Badi, near Rai Kot Ludhiana
17. Gurdwara Sahib Dera Sahib, near Lahore
18. Gurdwara Sahib Chomala Sahib Bhaigate Lahore
19. Gurdwara Sahib Cantonment Lahore
20. Gurdwara Sahib Singh Sabha Rawal Pindi
21. Gurdwara Sahib Singh Sabha Mardan - Peshawar
22. Gurdwara Sahib Kohat Peshawar
23. Gurdwara Sahib Peshmlak Afghanistan
24. Gurdwara Sahib Lal Para Afghanistan
25. Gurdwara Sahib Jalalabad Afghanistan

20. Only Randhir Singh Naragwal Jatha supported the Gadaries when they reached India. All members of this Jatha were baptized (Amritdhari). All of them were indicted in the Lahore 2nd supplementary case and were prisoned for life. Apart from Randhir Singh, other names were Bhai Arjan Singh, Bhai Atar Singh, Bhai Dalip Singh, Giani Harbhajan Singh, Bhai Dharam Singh, Bhai Harnam Singh, Bhai Harnam Singh, Bhaijagat Singh, Bhai Karam Singh, Bhai Lal Singh, Bhai Mohinder Singh, Bhai Mastan Singh, Bhainahar Singh, Bhai Ram Singh, Bhai Sajan Singh, Bhais Santa Singh, Bhai Surjan Singh, Bhai Kharak Singh, Bhai Kharak Singh, Bhai Pooran Singh, Bhai Kartar Singh.

Conclusion

In two world wars, a total of 169,700 Indians died, out of which 83,005 were turbaned Sikhs. The growing sense of their public humiliation, nagging immigration restrictions, and their ultimate exclusion compelled them to re-imagine their status in light of the Queen's proclamation of 1958. They realized that the British were taking advantage of their military and other services, and promising better treatment as a ploy to cheat them. They stood up for the same treatment which was given to other citizens. The feeling of being abandoned made them rebel against the unjust British Raj and initiation of constitutional efforts and planning for armed struggle. The revolution was started in India by Sikh peasants and Sikh military persons on extreme dissatisfaction against the new Colonization Act and the Doab Bari Act (1906–1907). In North America, Sikhs affirmed their fight by all means and avowed to stay back by building Gurudwaras in 1908 in Vancouver and 1912 in Stockton, Victoria, and Abbottsford as the center of their religious, social, and political activities. From 1907 to 1914, they made democratic appeals. Professor Teja Singh, Sunder Singh, and others in Canada, and Dr. Bishen Singh, Dr. Bose, and Tishi Butia in USA sent deputations to England and India. But all constitutional means failed.

Finally, in 1914, they recieved funding help from Germans, who were looking to start a colonial and world war against their British enemy with an eye on India's industrial and mineral wealth. The position of Indians and Sikhs became critical. Sikhs returned to India to start an armed fight but received no money or any arms or any institutional help as promised by leaders. Their leaders themselves later surrendered to the British and abandoned their compatriots who were hanged, sent to rigorous imprisonment for life, and lost their earned and ancestral property. Evidence shows Indian pioneers (majority Sikhs) fought with peaceful constitutional means, formed many Hindustani societies, and made armed rebellion and explosive plans from 1907 to 1914 on the West Coast. Six newspapers supporting Indian freedom were in circulation prior to November 1913. Twenty-nine Sikh religious preachers (also known as Granthis) and 25 Gurudwaras around the globe, including in India and Punjab, participated in this movement. No Vedanta center participated in this movement, although New York, Chicago, and San Francisco centers existed at that time. History being created by authors like H.K. Puri based on secondary sources is misleading. The evidence shows that Gadar Movement between 1907 and 1918 on the West Coast of North America was primarily inspired by Sikh thought. Scholars must take into consideration the concept of Sikh Martyrdom along with colonial and pre-colonial Sikh History. Based on above evidence, it is affirmed that this movement characterized by British as War against King/Sikh Ghadr, in fact was an International War against politically awakened Sikhs and their sympathizers 1907–1918. It was the first declared Indian freedom war fought by majority international Sikhs also known Sikh Gadarites (Gadri Babey). Please note my study is referring to Sikh Inspiration influence on this Indian freedom movement. It was not a religious movement. Communist influence in this movement is a late phenomenon, after 1922–1927 as is clearly supported by the writings of Sohan Singh Josh and Rattan Singh Ajnala. From 1905 to 1913 in Europe, Shyamaji Krishna Varma's Arya Smaj thought, Veer Savarkar's Abhinava Bharat thought, and Bhikaiji Cama and Sardar Singh Rana's Social Democratic thought could not produce any international mass movement in Europe. Evidence shows that the teachings of Sikh Gurus strongly motivated the consciousness of these Gadarites in the West Coast of North America along with racial discrimination in employment, finance, civic matters, a sense of public humiliation, nagging immigration restrictions, and their ultimate exclusion, which compelled them to re-imagine their status in light of the Queen's proclamation of 1858. The correct history of Ghadris/Sikh Pioneers must be recorded and saved for the coming generation of Sikhs in North America, who, if they read the right books, will know about the true contributions of Sikh pioneers from North America to the Indian war of independence.

APPENDIX.

Sikh Community Salutes and prays for many Hindus and Muslims who on being inspired by the archetype of martyrdom tradition , sacrificed their lives fearlessly and whose names include Kanshi Ram, Vishnu Ganesh Pingle, Khankhoje Pandurav, Sohan lal Pathak, Jatindranath Mukherjee, Mangu Ram, Taraknath Das , Maulvi Barktulla, Jagat Ram, Guran Ditta Kumar, Ram Rahim, Jatinder Lahiri, Munsi Ram, Babu Ram, Hafiz Abdulla, Chet Ram, Challia Ram, Kirparam, Ram Rakha, Ali ahmed Sidiqui, Lal Chand Falak Piyare Lal and others. All of them followed Gadhri Slogan Shabd (Jo Tau Praem Khaelan Kaa Chaao (If you desire to play this game of love with Me),Sir Dhhar Thalee Galee Maeree Aao |(Then step onto my Path with your head in palm of your hand)Eith Maarag Pair Dhhareejai|(When you place your feet on this Path),Sir Dheejai Kaan N Keejai (Give your head, and do not blame anyone).

Sikh Community also prays for Pandit Ram Chandra who played his role in this movement but was shot in April 1918 on suspicion of distrust. Sikh Community also prays for Lala Hardyal and Veer Damodar Savarkar. They were god-gifted prolific writers but never wrote even a single line in remembering their compatriots when the plan created by them failed on February 19th, 1915. Lala Hardyal died in 1939 and Veer Damodar Savarkar died in 1966.

1. Sikh Community also prays for many members of this movement including Dr C.K. Chakravarty who embezzled funds which were given By Germans for Indian Independence.

2. Sikh Community also prays for many Sikhs, including a Muslim, which can be noted from a list of 103 names in Professor Malwinderjit Singh Warriach's work " Sikhs and India's First War of Independence 1907-1918"who became Approvers in this war against King in the true sense.

Special thanks to Professor Malwinderjit Singh Warriach who provided from his research work posters for 2012 Sikh centennial conferences held on September 22nd and September 30th, 2012, at the University of Pacific Stockton California thru Col Perminder Singh Randhawa.

Babar Akali Lehar 1922-1923: Sikhs armed struggle for freedom from the British continued. A large number of Ex- Gadarites, became active Babars including Karam Singh Daulatpur, Karam Singh and Kartar Singh Jhingar, Baba Karam Singh Cheema, Bhag Singh Canadian, Assa Singh of Phukrudi, Kartar Singh Pindori Nijjaran, Hari Singh Sundh, Piara Singh Langheri, Battan Singh Kahri Sahri, Partap Singh Kot Fatuhi and many others.

Refrences and Bibliography

1,2: GANDA SINGH;THE INDIAN MUTINY OF 1857AND THE SIKHS,1969.GURDWARA PARBANDHAK COMMITTEE SISGANJ, CHANDNI CHOWK, DELHI

3. Kesar Singh Navalkar. Ghadr Lehar Di Kabita, Punjabi University, 1995., Giani Kesar Singh, Ghadr Lehar Di Wartak compiled by Kirpal Singh Kasail, Punjabi University, 2008.

4. Syed Razi Wasti, Lord Minto and the Indian Nationalist Movement 1905-1910, Clarendon Press, Oxford, 1964.

5. "People of India in North America," I.M Muthanna, Bangalore, South India, 1975

6. Paper read By DR. Paul Engles Berg at 2012 Sikh Centennial conference, University of Pacific Stockton California. Also See news coverage by Bellingham herald sept 5th 2007. click.http://www.wce.wwu.edu/resources/AACR/documents/bellingham/main/o.htm

7. Sedition Committee Report 1918 by Justice Rowlatt, O'Dwyer, Sir Michael Francis 1925. *India As I Know It – 1885-1925*, Constable & Co., London.,Isemonger, F. C.; Slattery, J (1919), *An Account of the Ghadr Conspiracy, 1913–1915*, Lahore: India Government Printing Office-Punjab and Lt.General Sir George MacMUNN, Turmoil and Tragedy in India; 1914 and after. Jarolds publishers, London

8. Hugh Johnston; Surveillance of Indian nationalist 1908 to 1918 prophet. library.ubc.ca/ojs/index.php/bcstudies/article/.

9. Prem Datta Varma. Indian Immigrants in USA: Struggle for Equality, Heritage publishers, 1995

10. The Ghadr Directory, 1934, Published by Punjabi University, Patiala, 1997

11. Karl Douglas Hoover, PhD unpublished thesis, The German-Hindu Conspiracy in California 1913-1918, June 1989

12. Harish K. Puri, Gadar Movement 'AShort History' National book Trust 2011. He is known as an academic Expert on this movement. Also read other books by Harish K. Puri, Ghadar Movement ideology Organisation and Strategy, GNDU, 1983, 1993

13,14. Brown, Emily C. 1975. *Har Dayal-Hindu Revolutionary and Rationalist,* University of Arizona Press, Tucson.

15, G.S. Deol, The Role of The Ghadar Party in the National Movement, Sterling Publishers, 1969

16. Harish K. Puri, Gadar Movement 'Short History' National book Trust 2011

17.18,19. Brown, Emily C. 1975. *Har Dayal-Hindu Revolutionary and Rationalist,* University of Arizona Press, Tucson. AND Forty Four Months in Germany and Turkey, P.S. King & Son. Ltd., 1920

20. Harish K. Puri, Gadar Movement 'AShort History' National book Trust 2011

21,22. A.G. Noorani, Savarkar and Hindutva, 2002, Leftward Books

23. Read Milestone documents. Click on http://www.milestonedocuments.com/documents/view/queen-victorias-proclamation-concerning-india

24. Ajit Singh Autobiography "BURIED ALIVE" http://www.shahidbhagatsingh.org/index.asp?link=about_ajit AND Syed Razi Wasti, Lord Minto and the Indian Nationalist Movement 1905-1910, Clarendon Press, Oxford, 1964.

25. Bhagat Singh, Canadian Society and Culture, Vikas Publishing, 1997

26. G.S. Deol, The Role of The Ghadar Party in the National Movement, Sterling Publishers, 1969

27. Syed Razi Wasti, Lord Minto and the Indian Nationalist Movement 1905-1910, Clarendon Press, Oxford, 1964

28, 29.34. Ajit Singh Autobiography "BURIED ALIVE" http://www.shahidbhagatsingh.org/index.asp?link=about_ajit

30,31,32. Paper read By DR. Paul Engles at 2012 Sikh Centennial conference University of Pacific Stockton California. Also see news coverage by Bellingham herald sept 5th 2007. Click.http://www.wce.wwu.edu/resources/AACR/documents/bellingham/main/o.htm

33. "People of India in North America," I.M Muthanna, Bangalore, South India, 1975

35. Gurcharan Singh Sainjsra 1961. *Gadar Party da Itihas*, Desh Bhagat Yadgar Committee, Jalandhar, India

36. B.N. Pande, from centenary of history of national congress, volume one, Vikas publishing house, 1985, pg 267

37, 38, 39.40, 41, 42, 43. 44,46   "People of India in North America," I.M Muthanna, Bangalore, South India, 1975.

45. Hugh Johnston; Surveillance of Indian nationalist 1908 to 1918 prophet. library.ubc.ca/ojs/index.php/bcstudies/article

47. Pritam Saini. Shaheed Madan Lal Ingra, Punjabi University, 1991

48. **Lives In The Pacific Northwest** *Sikh Community: Over 100 Years in the Pacific Northwest* http://www.wingluke.org/pages/sikhcommunity-website/lifeinthepnw.html And Sohan Singh Pooni "Paper read at 2012 Sikh Centennial conference Universty of Pacific Stockton California", Sohan Singh Pooni, Canada Dey Gadri Jodey, Singh Publishers, 2009

49. Harish K. Puri Gadar movement 1983, GNDU

50,51,52,53.   "People of India in North America," I.M Muthanna, Bangalore, South India, 1975

54,55   *"khalsa pamphlet"* Original document is located at national archives of India, Complete document has been reproduced in appendices of Books By Nahar singh[Struggle For free Hindustan] and Malwinderjit Warriach[War Against king Emperor; Dhadar of 1914-1915}.Short form the khalsa pamphlet read by Malwinderjit Singh Warriach "Paper read at 2012 Sikh Centennial conference Universty of Pacific Stockton California".

56. Malwinderjit Singh Warriach "Paper read at 2012 Sikh Centennial conference Universty of Pacific Stockton California".

57,58. "People of India in North America," I.M Muthanna, Bangalore, South India, 1975 AND G.S. Deol, The Role of The Gadar Party in the National Movement, Sterling Publishers, 1969

59. Savitry Sawhney, I Shall Never ask for Pardon: A memoir of Pandurang Khankoje, Penguin Books, 2008

60. Giani Kesar Singh, Ghadr Lehar Di Wartak compiled by Kirpal Singh Kasail, Punjabi University, 2008. Kesar Singh Navalkar. Ghadr Lehar Di Kabita, Punjabi University, 1995

61,62 "People of India in North America," I.M Muthanna, Bangalore, South India, 1975

63,64,65 Brown, Emily C. 1975. *Har Dayal-Hindu Revolutionary and Rationalist,* University of Arizona Press, Tucson.

66. G.S. Deol, The Role of The Gadar Party in the National Movement, Sterling Publishers, 1969

67. Malwinderjit Singh, Diary of Hari Singh Usman, SGPC. AND Joan M.Larsen, "The Hindu Conspiracy: A reassessment" Pacific historical review 1979 page 73Spring-Rice to Bryan May 12, 1915; Spring-Rice to Lansing June 14, 1915; Johann von Bernstorff to Lansing, July 2, 1915and Spring-Rice to Robert Lansing, Dec. 21, 1916; T. W. Gregory to Robert Lansing, Feb. 26, 1917, file 9-10-3, NA, RG 60.

68. Malwinder jit Singh, Harinder Singh. War against King Emperor Ghadr of 1914-1915, Nov 2001. Published by Bhai Sahib Randhir Singh Trust., Malwinderjit Singh Waraich, First Lahore Conspiracy Case Mercy Petition, Unistar Press, 2010.,

69. Karl Douglas Hoover, PhD unpublished thesis, The German-Hindu Conspiracy in California 1913-1918, June 1989, Jon M Jenson The Hindu conspiracy A Reassessment from PACIFIC HISTORICAL REVIEW 1979,Vol 48 (pages68to87) http://www.jstor.org/stable/3638938., Don K Digan The Hindu Conspiracy in Anglo-American Relations during World War

PACIFIC HISTORICAL REVIEW 1971,Vol 40 pages 57-76 http://www.jstor.org/stable/3637829?origin=JSTOR-pdf. Henry Landau, the Enemy Within; The Inside Story of German Sabotage in America, G.p. Putnam's Sons, 1937, Brown, Emily C. 1975. *Har Dayal-Hindu Revolutionary and Rationalist,* University of Arizona Press, Tucson., Harold A Gould. Sikhs, Swamis, Students and Spies, Sage Publications, 2006., Jagjit Singh. Ghadr Party Lehar, Navyog Publishers, New Delhi, 1979 AND Khushwant Singh; 'The Ghadr Rebellion' http://www.sikhpioneers.org/rebellion.html and 'Hindu german Cospiracy' Jesse Russell,Ronald Cohn, published by LENNEX Corp 2012

70. Veer Damodar Savarkar Book INDIAN WAR OF INDEPENDENCE 1857, London,1909

71. Peter Campbell South Asian militants and socialist party Canada,1904-1914 *International Journal of Canadian Studies / Revue internationald'études canadiennes* 20, Fall / Autumn 1999

72. Gadar Di Goonj No. 1 Couplet No. 5, Quoted by Dr. G.S. Aulakh, Veer Naik Kartar Singh Sarabha, Patiala, 1994 p.48.

73. Harbans Singh, The Heritage of the Sikhs, Delhi, 1983 pp. 263-64.

74. "SantTeja Singh ji (Professor), (1877-1965)";by Dr. Gurbakhsh Singh Gill, U.S.A. "Life History of Sant Attar Singh ji" (in Punjabi) by Teja Singh, published by DirectorLanguage Dept., Punjab, Patiala, 1946 (First Edition), 1981 (4thEdition) "Mystery and Power of TejaSingh," The Vancouver Daily Province, Vancouver, B.C., Saturday, December 12, 1908

75. Mewa Singh Justice(Retired), 2010"Religion and History of the Sikhs1469 – 2010"

76. Report of the National Commission Review to the Working of the Constitution set up vide Government Resolution dated 22 February, 2000. *http://www.lawmin.nic.in/ncrwc/finalreport.htm*

77. Santokh Singh **"Article 25 Exterminates Sikhism"** ABSTRACTS OF SIKH STUDIES, Published By institute of Sikh Studies, Chandigarh. Vol XIII, Issue 4.Oct-Dec 2011 / 543 NS click www.sikhinstitute.org

78. Last Statement of Bhai Mewa singh Shaheed

79. Sohan Singh Josh in his book ' My Tryst with Secularism pages 109 and 110" replaces religious banner from the top of 'Kirti newspaper started by Gadri Santokh Singh which Read" APNE HATHIN APNA AAPEY HI KARAJ SWARIEY(We shall fulfill our task with our own hand). There was nothing wrong in it politically, except religious tinge of its origin. It was subsequently replaced in the mat 1927 issue By words ' Arise,Awake,ye workers of the world, and unite'. Thanks to Rajwinder singh Rahi for providing me this evidence.

80. POEMS of GADAR DI GOONJ compiled by Kesar Singh Navalkar. 'Ghadr Lehar Di Kabita', Punjabi University, 1995.

81. Harold Gould "Sikhs, Swamis, Students and Spies: The India Lobby in the United States, 1900-1946 (2006)page 111 "

82. "Lord Minto and Indian nationalist movement 1905-1910" By SYED RAZI WASTI 1964 Clarendon Press Oxford page100"

83. SachiderNathSanyal"Bandi Jiwan/Incarcerated life"

84. 'Sikh Encyclopedia' edited by Harbans Singh Published by Panjabi university Patiala, 1998.

85. Rajwinder Singh Rahi forthcoming Book Gadar Lahar Asli Gatha part III- In Press

86. 'Bhai sahib Bhai Randhir Singh ji Simriti Granth' edited by Jaiteg Singh Anant, published by Hardarshan Memorial International Trust sector 40 Chandigarh. Excellent Didari Haraf By editor with collection of 99 articles on life and works of Bhai sahib including his contributions to Sikh Gadar

Lehr AND Rajwinder singh rahi ' Gadar Lehar Di Asli Gatha- Part 2.published by Sangam Publications, Samana. Punjab 2012

87. Bhupinder Singh Holland. How Europe is Indebted to the Sikhs, 2009, Sikh University Press

88. Gurcharan Singh Aulakh. 'Babbar Akali Movement: A Historical Survey', National Book Shop, 2001 and B.S. Nijjar. 'History of the Babar Akalis', ABS Publishing, 1987

Effect of the Sacrificial Traditions of Sikh Heritage on the Journalism of Ghadar Movement

Gurvinder Singh Dhaliwal

After the annexation of Punjab by the Britishers, a new form of revolution came in force in the shape of different movements. This began with Punjabis joining the British Army and going to reside in far-off colonies. Historically, this period can be taken as a reawakening of numerous movements. After defeat of the mutiny, many campaigns rose from the soil of Punjab and mobilized the people against British rule. Along with the economic aspect, even the religious awakening and political awareness also now became apparent as helpful elements in the uprise of these movements. In this context, the role of Namdhari Movement, known also as *kuka* movement, can be taken as most significant.[1] For the later-on birth of the revolutionary ghadar movement on the soil of North America, this kuka campaign can be taken as its base which re-enlivened the sacrificial traditions of Sikh heritage of medieval times and founded the revolutionary struggle in the most truthful and trustworthy ways. On getting an inkling of the mutinous mood of the Punjabis, the British masters undertook numerous ways and means to keep them under control. For this, Punjabis used to be sent to other colonies under British rule to maintain law and order there and, to suppress their mutinous intent, the foreign policy was put in use. On the other hand, the Punjabis, badly

---

1 Gurcharan Singh Sainsara, Gadar Party da Itihas, p.16

held in economic recession and other problems, had no other alternative. During the initial years of the twentieth century, the political and economic turmoils in Punjab compelled many Punjabi farmers to move out to alien lands in order to appeae their bellies, get rid of loans, and to make themselves prosperous. During these days, the lands in America and Canada were developing on the form of capitalism. Capitalists needed badly the cheap, strong, and skilled workers. When Punjabi farmers got wind of the need of workers in America and Canada at daily wages of five or six rupees, they set their caravans in that direction.[2] This was the time when the Punjabi soldiers in the British army were paid only nine rupees per month while fighting on the frontiers of east Africa, Egypt, Burma, China, Iran, or on the western borders of India. Meanwhile, the Sikh soldiers came to know about another English-ruled domain, Canada, where they could earn more while working and living in better conditions. Only after these revelations did the emigration of Punjabis to alien lands begin in a true sense. In America, Baba Visakha Singh Dadehar and Jawala Singh Thathian started organizing the Indians in these areas and, on October 24, 1912, established the Pacific Coast Khalsa Dewan Society Gurdwara. After formation of the National Organization like Vancouver, Baba Sohan Singh Bhakna mobilized other patriots to make the natives strung in one form and thus, on April 21, 1913, established the Hindi Association of Pacific Coast in Austria. Later, it became popular under the name of Ghadar Party. On November 1, 1913, a weekly paper in Urdu was started from San Francisco. In Gurmukhi, the weekly paper *Ghadar* in Punjabi began in December 1913. Afterwrds, the paper started getting published in other languages—Hindi, Gujarati, Bengali, Nepali, and Pushto. In initial editions of *Ghadar*, Gurbani hymns are found written in the center under somewhat alteration and "Bande" and "Matram" were written on end-corners separately. These are the editions of those times when Shahid Kartar Singh Sarabha was the editor of this Punjabi paper. After some time, the revolutionary veterans became active in the struggle for freedom in the country, and many of them sacrificed their lives or suffered long jail terms.

After these stalwarts, glaring changes were made on the title page of *Ghadar*. The Gurbani hymn was replaced with the words: "O valiant young Indians! Take up the weapons." Such changes on the title page of *Ghadar* did not come of their own, but were introduced in a planned way. Ram Chander started writing his name as Editor on the first page, and then, getting aside

---

2 Heera Singh Dard, Punjabi Dunia, February 1960,p14-15

of the party, he started a parallel paper, *Hindustan Ghadar*, at the party's expenses. Initially, S. Kartar Singh Sarabha remained Editor of the Punjabi version of this paper. Other revolutionary writers included S. Harnam Singh Tundilat, Bhai Santokh Singh Dhardeo, Bhagwan Singh Pritam, Munsha Singh Dukhi, Kartar Singh Latara, Basant Singh Chaunda, Mehbub ali, Inayat Khan, Ram Chander, Khem Chand Das, Mohan Lal, Pirthi Singh Azad, Bishan Singh Sada Singh Wala, and Nidhan Singh Maheshwari who remained associated with the paper. The writers used mostly their sub-names or the pen names. Under assumed names, such as Dukhia, Ghadar da Sipahi, Pritam, Faqir, Punjabi Singh, Sewak, Baghi, Jachak, Iqbal, Humdum, Azad, Yakdam, Nastik, Sach, Hind Sewak and Nidharak, the purpose was to highlight the real motive of the movement rather than individual popularity, and it was meant equally to keep secret the identity of *Ghadar* under state of political compulsions. The main purpose of the writers was to rouse political awakening among the migrants so as to prepare them for the struggle for freedom of India. These papers are so prominent in journalism that these proved milestones of awareness for the next generations. Under a missionary spirit, these journalists took cues from their past to make journalism a means of attaining independence. Through this paper, we come to know of cultural challenges, social sufferings, the horrors of the British rulers, and the sores of servility. Narrations of the *Ghadar* expose such issues to the readers that rise from coercions in foreign lands and slavery in the country. Enlightening the native slaves, *Ghadar* prompts them onto the path of struggle for freedom. He himself is proponent of the revolutionary zeal and stirs the reader also to take immediate step in this regard. For a journalist of *Ghadar*, his writing is not a mere writing only; it is struggle for freedom and he is committed to strengthen the movement by means of media. In these saffron robes, the *Ghadar* pronounces that we should bereave ourselves of fear and selfishness. Rubbishing aside the frivolous differences amongst ourselves, we should have neat and clean visions of our patriots of independence. What is this life? Numberless species go extinct while moving about on this earth. Millions of people die without doing anything worthwhile. Took meals, wore clothes, got married, bore children and brought them up, and then left forever. Worthwhile living is that wherein the individual does numerous deeds in this brief life. He should help in guiding others and fight against the tyrants.[3]

---

[3] Weekly magazine Gadar, 23 December 1913.

Ghadar appears in light of prompting the Punjabis to fight for human rights and motivate them to struggle for freedom of the country.

Ghadar—the proponent of ending British Empire through armed revolution—indulges in negotiations with the moderate leaders and presents those as mode of dual approach. While misleading the Indian youth, detracting them from the path of revolution and throwing their strugglesome effort in chilly bin, these leaders could not save themselves from the sharp tune of revolution. Whereas the pro-English Khans and Bahadurs and feudal lords remained stuck as pros of the critics of revolutionaries, even the anti-political national leaders also could not save themselves from this effect. It is found written in a Punjabi version of weekly *Ghadar* that sixty or seventy students had joined this influence of servility till then. That is this if all the pseudo leaders of India had bonded themselves to live in servitude. These proponents of slavery have been looting the honor and wealth of the country, and now they were depriving the Indian youth of education and wanted to sacrifice them for the English. At this time, it is clear to everyone that this is the right time to free ourselves of alien rule. But the ones who are engulfed with the tallow of slavery, they can see nothing but slavery only. The youth of the country are preaching for revolution. The ones doing hard labor for nine hours daily are sacrificing the Indians, and Gandhi has taken contract for the slavery of Indians. He is a bad example for the young Indians.[4] Severe criticism of the timely pro-British Indian political policies is found in *Ghadar* weekly.

Thus, to uplift the spirit of struggle for freedom and encourage the downtrodden, the valiants of *Ghadar* set aside, in total, self-interest, self-pride, and the bourgeois thought. The spirit reflects distinct in *Ghadar*. Notwithstanding literally with this profession, the journalists of *Ghadar* used this paper solely for the purpose of promoting the revolution. They shed away the psychic stain of illiteracy even from their mind. Rather, they could exhibit the leadership traits in themselves. Becoming aware of one's entity and contemplating over it, anguish arose against the British Empire after going through reasons behind it. Proding through our heritage under effect of anger and contemplation, the migrant Indians stood face to face before it to realize a creative and revolutionary vision of fearlessness. It was this revolutionary and creative consciousness out of the dynamism of which came into being a new future.[5]

---

4 Weekly magazine Gadar, 17 January 1915.
5 Amarjeet Singh, Gadar Lehar di Kavita de smaji ate syasi sarokar, p73

A prominent part of the *Ghadar* is that the editorials appear to give prominence towards exposing the coercions of the British Empire and thereby promulgation of initiating an armed revolution from foreign lands to finish these atrocities. In the first edition of *Ghadar* in Urdu and Punjabi, we find versions of the use of media force to organize a people's campaign as main issue against the British rule. "To-day, on 1st November 1913, a new era sets in the history of India when a struggle against the British rule begins from foreign lands in vernacular. It is an auspicious day when the word 'Ghadar'— the paper published in Urdu and Punjabi—forebodes the uprooting of British rule in India. Publication of this paper at a place ten thousand miles away from home is such an act that its glimpse makes our joy unlimited. What is our name? Ghadar. What is our aim? Ghadar. Where shall Ghadar be? In India. When shall it take place? In a few years. Why shall it be? Because the people have fed up from the atrocities of the British rule and they have become ready to sacrifice their lives for independence."[6]

Whereas *Ghadar* stimulated the people from foreign lands through the force of media and vernacular to take solid steps against slavery, it also included within it the silent role of media pertaining to these important issues in India in the form of *Ghadar*. Editorials in the form of argumentative and sarcastic tone in *Ghadar* hit the timely Indian newspapers hard. As is stated in *Ghadar*: "Punjab press is quite alert. On a minor lapse by a political leader, they drab him thrashingly. News come that Baba Gurbakhsh Singh Bedi arranged a show of dancing girls at the marriage of his son. As such, the Punjabi people are pushing him in a difficult plight." No doubt, we also express our dismay at this folly. But we question the Punjab newspapers who raise so many hue and cries on such matters but why do they entertain the English for months in Simla and offer gifts of millions of rupees to them when they leave for England with pension and loot of Indian treasures. Then why do these papers sorely? They don't utter a murmur even. These papers do express dismay on the social lapses of rich men, but we express sorrow on the timidity of these papers.[7] *Ghadar* was a movement rather than a mere paper. This newspaper ended up to be the first Punjabi paper at international level, and it used to reach the countries where even very few Punjabis lived. This

---

6 News Paper Gadar, December 1913.
7 Same July 1914

paper proffered honorable rank of status to the Punjabis living abroad for struggle for independence of the country.[8]

In line with the prose write-ups in this Punjabi *Ghadar* weekly, even the poetry also presents a specimen of meaningful literary journalism. These poems prepared the people to get rid of hardships by following the path of struggle. In this poetry of people's idiom, the victims took cue from their national legacy to forget their racial differences and fight against the tyranny of foreign rulers. In order to accomplish this ideal and revolutionary step, the contributors of *Ghadar* highlighted the particular elements of dynastic extinction, caste extinction, and class extinction and stressed upon the essence of equality, fraternity, cooperation, and unity. We quote a line as specimen of this ideal:

We think not of any caste or creed, we know not any low or fallen;

One brotherhood all the Indians have, and no crafty rite we follow.[9]

Writers of the contributions in *Ghadar* were absolute detractors of Manu's castes, and they were fully motivated under their glorious history towards uniting the people against atrocities. The message that *Ghadar* conveyed for getting rid of the clutches of slavery and making every sacrifice for independence is an invaluable contribution made by the literary journalism in Punjabi, and its effect is everlasting rather than timely. To quote an example, when Kartar Singh Sarabha was entrapped with his companions under some tip-off by informers, they, rather than running away, started reciting this verse written by Kesar Singh Thathgarh:

Nothing can save us from sacrificing our head.
Shall fight to the last though we be dead.
Shall ever we roar and never run away.
With sword in hand, we plunge in the fray.
Cut the enemy into pieces and suck their blood
We shall not run away though we be dead.
Kill the enemy or get ourselves killed.

---

8 Navneet Jauhal, Videshi Punjabi Pattarkaari de do daur: ik tulnatamik adhyain, Parvaasi Punjabi Sahit vishesh ank 40, Khoj Patrika, p.127
9 Desh Bhagatan di baani, Gadar di goonj, no.2, 1916, p.31

Effect of the Sacrificial Traditions of Sikh Heritage on the Journalism of Ghadar Movement

> *So shall we finish the malady of cowardice and poverty.*
> *As roaring lions, we shall sacrifice ourselves.*
> *And shall fight to the last though we be dead.*[10]

In the poetry of *Ghadar*, the Sikh revolutionary spirit reflects everywhere, and the revolutionary poets quote examples that give a jolt towards the struggle against tyranny and injustice in every way. This poetry hints towards those pages of history wherein we pass through various stages starting from the sacrifice of Sahibzadas of the tenth Master and then visualize the Sikh revolutionary spirit through the deeds of Banda Singh Bahadur, Akali Phoola Singh, Hari Singh Nalwa, and the Sher-e-Punjab Maharaja Ranjit Singh. In order to get freed of the colonial loot of the British Empire, the paper *Ghadar* idealizes the Sikh struggle against the Mughal Empire. Verily, this, like thought in *Ghadar*, prospered at such a time when the reins of this movement came in the hands of Panjabis wedded to revolutionary struggle. The daring bands who came forward for this armed revolution were none others but Punjabi migrants only. Not caring of their lives, they left the limits of America and Canada and set for India, especially Punjab, under a spirit of daredevilry. With arrest of Hardayal in April 1914, the movement came in the hands of Punjabis, and they, through exemplary sacrifices for a bright future, set such a path on which the revolutionary youth followed to consolidate it. A revolutionary legacy can be visualized among these valiant ones that was flowing in their veins as an inseparable part of Punjab's soil. That is why their revolutionary vigil against injustice made a quick rise and put them at such a struggle-some path as made death certain while pursuing the struggle. In the simple and straightforward politically awakening poetry of these veteran revolutionaries, the Sikh revolutionary spirit can be visualized everywhere.[11] The poem *"Panth Aggey Pukar"* published in *Ghadar* is an example of it, wherein the revolutionary poet quotes revolution from the national legacy.

> *He himself when prepared to leave for heaven,*
> *Sent Banda as our savior Singho!*
> *Banda did his best on coming here,*
> *The Panth did prosper all and well Singho!*
> *When Banda left for his heavenly abode,*

---

10 Gadar, Kesar Singh Thatthgarh, Kavita "Bni sir sheran"
11 Amarjeet Singh, Gadar Lehar di Kavita de smaji ate syasi sarokar, p.34-35.

The Panth took lead of all Singho!
Valiants were many there in Panth,
They became savior of the Panth Singho!
They suffered untold miseries,
But never left sword and shield Singho!
Then came Ranjit with might valorous,
Cruelly dealt with all rebels Singho!
Came warriors like Hari Singh Nalwa,
All liberal, pure and pious Singho!
Great warrior was Phoola Singh Akali,
Ever had his Faith in Akal Singho!
Did the sinners kill them splitting apart,
Ever they chanted Akal Akal Singho![12]

Such a politically awakening poetic composition is inspired from the proud legacy of Punjabis. Rather than making any entreaties, the writers preferred the path of sacrifice against the cruel tyrants. In order to put the people on this path, they used to cite the deeds of martyrs who, rather than submitting before the tyrants, sacrificed their lives and made firm the foundation of the Sikh nation. We find such reflection in a daring poem published in *Ghadar*:

Had there been like Deep Singh to-day,
Who could have scoffed the Singhs why!
Had there been like Mani Singh Bhai,
How could have Hindustan spoilt why!
People call the Singhs as bad tempered,
Sent back rebellion of Delhi why!
Country would have been free now,
Did they create the storm so why!
Sons of lions we die like lions,
In cages we lie dismayed why!
Roaringly we shout and kill the Whites,
Sitting so humiliated in shame why!
Thirty crore men has India,
These four crore do rule why!

---

12   News paper Gadar, Kavita 'panth di pukar', January 1914.

Effect of the Sacrificial Traditions of Sikh Heritage on the Journalism of Ghadar Movement

Look sharp to revolt for uprising,
You have abandoned the country's need why![13]

The literary writers and columnists of the *Ghadar* were not only pen-proficient but were equally true to the deeds. Whatever they wrote, they remained committed to. The poetry in *Ghadar* demands remembering the sacrifices of martyrs and following their foot marks. Historical references stand in support to the fact that Kartar Singh Sarabha, while in lock-up with his companions, always used to recite the lines of last message of martyrs that were published in *Ghadar* weekly.

Our death is life of the nation,
Shall do our duty before we go.
Our memory shall spur our sons ever,
To love the country after we go.
Ever shalt thou roar like sons of lions,
Never get called cowards erst you go!
Jails are colleges for the patriots of country,
Do engrave your name here before you go!
Gallows grant degree from the school here,
What misdeed you commit to pass before you go!
Many ones fail and pass a few,
Lose heart not countrymen before you go!
India is ours and Indians we are,
To children you teach this before you go!
O loving 'Pritama' wherever are we going,
You also come the same way to us.[14]

The literature published in *Ghadar* had such an effect on the Punjabis living abroad or in India that the paper became panacea for eradication of the caste-cult that was spreading in society as leprosy. References relating to death for freedom and living a life of self-respect were quoted from Sri Guru Granth Sahib. It was not only the Punjabis living in Canada and America who learned Punjabi to read the *Ghadar*; rather in India, many Indians in different parts of the country learned reading Punjabi enthusiastically to read

---

13 News paper Gadar, Kavita 'panth di pukar', January 1914
14 Gadar Kavita, qaumi shahidan da aakhari sandesh, 29 march 1915.

the *Ghadar*. After undergoing the revolutionary stirring made by this paper, the valiant living abroad developed such a spirit of unity that they fixed an aim to finish the slavery of the British Empire in India and establish home-rule in the country. In every edition of the paper, they talked of independence and advocated extermination of the ones opposing this move. Along with, the natives living abroad were asked to go back to the country and make the people united to begin the revolution. Giving detail of the hardships suffered under slavery on the alien land, the *Ghadar* pledged to uproot the rule of the British Empire. *Ghadar* can justifiably be called "Baba Bohar"—the grand root—of Punjabi journalism in foreign lands. The journalism of revolutionary movement, no doubt, was greatly influenced by the hereditary Sikh traditions of sacrifice; nevertheless, it also made an equally deep effect on Punjabi journalism in the country.

Central Role of Gurdwaras in Ghadri Movement

Rajwinder Singh Rahi

Born in Gurdwaras on the soil of America and Canada and concluded in Punjab, the Ghadar Movement is a glorious chapter in the struggle against British colonialism. The Gadarites living in Canada, America, Hongkong, Shanghai, Manila, Penang, and Bangkok came to Punjab like a storm, offered unlimited sacrifices, and mingled in the soil of their ancestors. No one can deny this historical fact that more than 85% of participants in this Movement were Sikhs who became the pivot of this campaign. Another fact that cannot be denied is that the majority in any campaign often get ignored of their natural influence on that Movement. And without comprehending the psyche of persons involved in this, the natural character and practice of this upsurge cannot be fully understood, because without observing the clear state of one's psycho-philosophy, it is difficult to visualize an individual's historical perspective in true light. So an insight for psycho-philosophy is an essential element for a historian; rather, it is a truly sensitive one.[1]

The saintly historian S. Jagjit Singh, the first one to write the history of Gadar Lehar, also lays stress on this element. He writes: "In order to comprehend any Movement, one has to know about the character and nature of its participants because these factors play a great role in affecting its effect. Nature and behavior of classes or castes do not get moulded of their own; the long time environing circumstances do help in moulding them."[2]

---

1 Harinder singh Mehboob, "sehjey rachyo Khalsa " p. XIV, Ashok book depot, Garhdiwala, 1988.
2 Jagjit singh 'Gadar party Lehar' p.25, Navyug publishers, New Delhi, September 2000.

In order to understand the reasons of the birth of Gadar Movement on the soil of America and Canada, the learned ones have, no doubt, enumerated numerous reasons and followed various political formulas for their analysis, but these formulas have remained a total failure to comprehend this Movement. These formulas, no doubt, do elucidate its thought, organization, struggle, strategy, and program, but they remain totally oblivious of the real environment which influenced its birth and how it affected the Sikh psyche only. Such Movements do not rise out of the blue; these need some soil to take birth. Though the outward condition is supported by the soil, much more depends on inner potency of the seed for its growth and development.

To date, the writers of the history of Gadar Movement have carried out its elucidation from the socio-economic point of view. They have followed this easy and convenient formula that the outward social and economic conditions make the people perceptive and conscious to take to the path of struggle. In similar manner, the outwardly suppressive social and economic conditions in America and Canada made the Punjabi migrants realize their state of slavery, and they set out in caravans to their country to free it. But this commentary gives rise to an important question: Why did the Sikhs only join this Movement in large numbers under effect of these suppressive conditions? In these foreign lands, there lived many Hindu students and Hindu migrants also; why did they remain unsoaked of this Movement? Sitting in Europe, the Hindu nationalists have been preaching for freedom since long ago; why did they not join the Gadar Movement? The suppressive conditions in South Africa were much more stringent than those in America or Canada. Then why was no effort made by Hindus living there for freedom of the country? Why did this impulse of freeing the country become so intense and irresistibly painful among the Sikhs only? The historians of Gadar Movement quite often ward off these questions. Suppressive conditions in any society or state are always alike for all the suffering people. But why do not all the suffering ones respond alike to such conditions? These conditions can evolve fear and indifference in someone and, among others, these can become the cause of fury to fight. The decisive fact is how much energy an individual or a group has to stand consciously against the suppressive forces. Verily, the strength and confidence of fighting erupts always from within. This inner might is not subservient to outer effects. That is why one has to go through to utmost depth to explore such delicate tissues while analyzing and explaining the Gadar Movement. Even the finding of sources is also essential as wherefrom the nations or groups find courage to fight against the suppressive forces. As we explore the source of their spiritual strength, it is found from the religion, history, and heritage of those people. When we investigate delicate layers to find the nucleus of their spiritual might, we again find their roots from their religion, history, and heritage. Historians of the Gadar Movement term these Sikhs as *"the wonderful human spice."* But wherefrom and how this *"wonderful human spice"* took birth is most essential to know.

Role of Gurdwaras in Ghadar Movement

When we probe into the already described birth procedure of Gadar Movement, we can say with firm belief that this *"wonderful human spice"*[3] so formed as the nucleus of Ghadar Movement was the outcome of Gurdwaras established in America and Canada and other islands. There were two dozen Gurdwaras in India and abroad that were active centers of the Movement, and these centers get full credit in performing their central role in this Movement. This truth can be firmly ascertained: If the Gurdwaras were not established in these lands, the Gadar Movement would not have come to the fore. Whether pushed by the circumstances or allured for better life, the Sikh farmers of Punjab, mostly Sikhs up to 70%, had already served in the British army. Beyond the islands, they had reached the limits of America and Canada. It was they, first of all, who had to be face to face with hurdles and hardships. Besides the necessities of sustenance and livelihood, those hardships were connected with their religion, identity, culture, religious symbols, self-respect, and lifestyle as only these issues collectively contribute towards building the cultural identity of an individual or of community.

Though the hatred cult against Asians was already prevalent in Canada and America, when the Sikhs started coming in hordes to these lands, their identity with turban and beard made them the butt of hatred of the racial Whites. When ship-loads of Sikhs reached Canada, the racial Whites termed it as a spate of turbans. Describing the Sikhs as dirty and disgusting, the Whites stirred winds of hatred and discrimination against them. As a result, the Sikhs were made the butt of attacks while they moved about in bazaars and streets. Restrictions were put on their work privilege also. However, one Mr. H. Gladstone, sympathizer of the Sikhs, put his words about Sikhs in a

---

3 Dr. Harish puri, 'Gadar party lehar: vichardhara, jathebandi, ranniti' Guru Nanak Dev university Amritsar 2006

newspaper, saying, "Sikhs are a nice community and they are very conscious of cleanliness."[4]

The apartheid newspapers of Canada used to ridicule the Sikhs daily. One paper printed a cartoon that had body of a sheep and the head of a Sikh.

Such humiliating overtures scalded the hearts of Sikhs. The biggest problem was their identity. Because of their distinct identity, they were detected from afar, and the English siblings took them as strange beings. The distinct, turban-and-beard identity was not letting them fit into their culture, but the Hindus had no such problem. With their outer appearance and dress, they could easily fit and merge into the culture of westerners. But the Sikhs' identity, with religious symbols and dress, was a big problem. This was an inseparable part of their "cultural entity." The religious symbols were a mark of their self-respect. The five religious symbols were the seal of their Guru.[5] Some weak-minded Sikhs, in line with Hindu people, did try to deceive the Whites by bidding adieu to their Sikh identity. But even those could not escape the attacks of racial Whites. And, with the abandonment of identity, they became spineless of their struggle for strength and could not stand against the assaults of Whites.

In Canada and America, as the crisis of "cultural entity" of Sikhs went on becoming more and more sharp and serious, so did their awareness for its safety go on to become intense and mighty.

Badly cornered in an alien land, surrounded by an alien language, subject to an alien government, emersed in an alien culture, and among alien people, when Sikhs found their cultural identity endangered from all sides, their first and foremost thought went towards building Gurdwaras as that way only they could safeguard their cultural entity.[6] Sitting in the foreign lands, every Sikh has maintained the urge to construct a Gurdwara, next only to filling their bellies. After going around in different lands, the veteran writer Giani Hira Singh Dard drew one conclusion, and that is the real truth about the natural instinct that stirs ever within a nation or community. He writes:

It is well-known about the English people—

---

4   Khushwant Singh & Satindra Singh, 'Ghadar 1915, India's First Armed Revolution', R&K Publishing House, New Delhi – 1966.
5   Baba Harnam singh Kotla Naudh Singh
6   'America vich Hindostani' (ed. Ganda Singh) bhai Kartar singh Nvan Chand da Byan

Central Role of Gurdwaras in Ghadri Movement

Solo English shall enjoy soda and whisky in full.
When two English meet, they make up a sport.
Should three English get together, there comes up a show.
Foundation of a new colony shall there at once be laid.

But here is what is popular about Sikhs:

One Sikh is Sikhs;
Two Sikhs make Sadh Sangat, the congregation;
Five represent the Almighty.

Wherever they go, the first project they undertake is building of Gurdwaras. It is a matter of immense pride and prestige for them because the people gone abroad can register their goodness or badness through their character and deeds only.[7]

When the migrant Sikhs assimilated this realization that only building Gurdwaras could safeguard their religious symbols and self-respect, they undertook the first project of building a Gurdwara in Canada. The majority of the Sikhs in this endeavor were ex-army men, and at the time of going from Punjab, they had gone under the influence of the Singh Sabha Movement. So they tried to establish a Singh Sabha–like society there also.[8] These Sikhs organized the Khalsa Diwan Society Vancouver in 1907. Before the formation of this society, the Sikhs formed some local committees in order to confirm their cultural status so the weak-minded Sikhs could be checked from running away from their religion, history, and heritage. Bhai Arjun Singh Malik was the first person to initiate in this matter. Under his initiative, a committee was formed that preached Gurmat Ideology. They asked the Sehjdhari Sikhs or Hindu to abstain from smoking and refrain from indulging in self-willed acts. They were brought on main line by offering them Amrit. Those who came ignorant of Sikhism from Punjab, they were also served Amrit by this committee. Likewise, thousands got adorned as Sikhs.[9]

Sikhs living in Canada completed the Gurdwara in Vancouver in 1908 and had its inauguration on January 19 with full Sikh-colored zeal and zest. The

---

7 Heera singh dard, Brij bhoomi te Malaya di Yaatra, p. 88-89, Dhanpat Rai & sons, Jalandhar & New Delhi, 1956
8 Jagjit singh 'Gadar party Lehar' p.18
9 America vich Hindostani' p.58

day was to introduce a glorious chapter in the history of Sikhs. Establishment of the Gurdwara did not mean it as a meeting place[10], as the leftists term it; the building of the gurdwaras on alien lands was meant to consolidate the firm hold of distinct identity and unique entity of the Sikhs. Along with, the Gurdwara was a source of spiritual inspiration for the Sikhs. With establishing of the Gurdwara in Vancouver, the Sikhs working away preferred to live in Vancouver. The Gurdwara became a center of their daily life.[11] For management of the Gurdwara and to deal with different problems of the Sikhs, the Khalsa Diwan Society Vancouver was registered in 1909. Since its establishment, the Gurdwara in Vancouver rose to be a symbol of confrontation against the British Empire and the racial Canadian government.

In the state of California in America, the country adjoining Canada, Sikhs in large numbers were working there. In nearby states like Oregon and Washington, a large number of Sikhs were working in factories. Though living in distant places, the Sikhs were in full coordination in every way. They frequently used to visit these places. After establishing the Gurdwara in Vancouver, the struggles undertaken by the Sikhs living there influenced the Sikhs living in America also. On this side, the Sikhs working on the construction of railway lines were confronting the racial assaults of Whites tooth and nail. In Holton, near Stockton city in California, Sant Baba Wasakha Singh Dadehar and Jawala Singh Thathian were farming a 500-acre parcel of land on contract. Afterwards, Bhai Santokh Singh Dhardeo also joined them. Since 1908, Prof. Teja Singh, who later on became popular as Sant Teja Singh Mastuana, had been preaching Sikhism in Canada and America. Under his inspiration, hundreds of Sikhs took Amrit to become committed Sikhs. Prof. Teja Singh had a cordial rapport with Sant Baba Wasakha Singh Dadehar and Baba Jawala Singh Thathian. In 1911, a Gurmat program was held at Holt Farm, and about twenty-five persons were served Amrit. In this program itself, a plan was built to erect a Gurdwara in Stockton and thus hoist the religious flag of Sikhism there.[12]

As per the writings of Sant Baba Wasakha Singh, it was in December of 1910 or the beginning of January 1911 that a large gathering was arranged

---

10   Gurcharan Singh Sainsara, Gadar Party da Itihas, p.73, desh Bhagat yadgar committee, 1969.
11   N. G. Barriers 'The Sikhs and their Literature', p. 100.
12   Jevan katha Gurmukh pyare sant atar singh Ji maharaj, p. 90-91, kalgidhar trust, baru sahib.

at Holt Farm to celebrate the birthday gurpurab of Guru Gobind Singh Ji. Akhand Path was arranged at the farm, and Dewan went on for the three days. At the concluding hour, a resolution was moved in the congregation to establish a Gurdwara at Stockton. The congregation granted approval in absolute gusto.[13] Money was collected here itself; a building worth $3400 was purchased; Guru Granth Sahib was installed in it, and the saffron flag was hoisted upon it.[14] With the unlimited enthusiasm of the Sikhs, the new Gurdwara was inaugurated in September 1912. As such, a firm hold of distinct identity and unique entity of Sikhs was established on the land of America, which has to remain firmly affirmed for centuries to come.

Creation of the Valiants

With the establishment of Gurdwaras in Canada in 1908 and in America in 1912, a strong wave of enthusiasm rose among the Sikhs. On every Sunday, the service meetings were held. Sikhs used to reach there from far and wide. But the leftist historians cunningly termed these religious congregations "Sunday Gatherings" on the tenor of Whites. But there is tremendous difference in "religious congregations" of the Sikhs and the "Sunday Gatherings"[15] of Whites. Among Sikhs, the tradition of congregational assemblies was started by Guru Ji themselves. The word "Diwan" was the word of Mughal culture, meaning "get-together." Meeting the people was termed "Diwan" by the Mughals.[16] Where the Emperor met common people was known as "Diwan-e-Aam"; it was "Diwan-e-Khas" where the Emperor met select people. Guru Sahib started organizing Diwans at equal level of the Mughals; it was a challenge to sovereignty of Mughals or being equal to them. So, in Sikh culture, the word "Diwan" has specific distinction. Assemblies in gurdwaras are specific unison of religious and political meets. To confront any Power, the confronting movements are the products of these Diwans. That is why the English CID Officer V. M. Smith took these Diwans as

---

13 'Atam katha sant baba vasakha singh dadehar' (ed. malwinderjit singh varhaich) p. 54-60, SGPC, Amritsar 2001.
14 Jevan katha Gurmukh pyare sant atar singh Ji maharaj, p. 90-91,
15 Gurcharan Singh Sainsara, Gadar Party da Itihas, p.73, desh Bhagat yadgar committee, 1969.
16 Bhai Kahan singh nabha, Mahan kosh, p639, bhasha vibhag Punjab.

very dangerous. He says: "When a single Sikh ploughs the fields, he is not dangerous. But when he reaches the 'Diwan,' he becomes a limitlessly dangerous fellow."[17]

The Sikh congregations assembling in gurdwaras of Canada and America did not have merely a single purpose to get together there, take parshad, have meals, and go on their ways. These Diwans were awakening those divine spirits within them by dint of which the Sikh Gurus had molded them into absolutely different molds. . . . The weapon-wielding fellow for human development and independence was built into a divine stalwart being absorbed in fighting for divine deeds and supreme human values. The symphony of religious hymns was used to transform the mind and the related essence of organization. With directions to sing the hymns in classic measures, the inner change was processed to form an organization. Thus, the hymn-singing and its reverberations connected with the nervous system were used as a forceful medium to bring about an ideological change.[18]

Prof. Puran Singh, in his carefree style, highlights the evident infusion of a neo-human spirit in the creation of Sikhs:

> *The tenth Master energized the latent power of the down-trodden ones in such a way that they were awakened with the spirit of social independence and ever blissfulness. . . . By virtue of the miraculous influence of Guru Gobind Singh Ji, they underwent change not only in their mental state, but the action proved pragmatic in materialistic form also. It brought about muscularity in their physical self.*[19]

What sort of environment that was in these Diwans organized in gurdwaras is distinctly reflected in the writing of Sant Baba Wasakha Singh Dadehar:

> *With improvement day by day, brothers got ready one after the other. As Khalsa got word of the tyrannies, many got ready in love abundant. Diwans were held daily, everyone got ready and alert.*

---

17 V. M. Smith, S.P,.C.I.D.Punjab, 22 February 1922, 'Punjab Past and Present' Oct 1967, p. 297

18 Gurbhagat singh, 'Punjab da qaumi msla khabbe pakkhi chintkan di nazar vich' (ed. malwinder singh maali) p.11, lok geet parkashan, Sarhind,1989.

19 Pro. Puran singh, 'Sikhi Di Atama' p.413, Lahaur book shop Ludhiana 2007.

Central Role of Gurdwaras in Ghadri Movement

Everyone exceeded the other in love, and all got alert together.
Having suffered cruelties unlimited, uttered loudly to kill or get killed.
As the cruel had oppressed their country, they twisted their moustaches and gave war cries.
Let's oust the foreigner from our country, thousands of cruelties have we undergone.[20]

What sort of issues were raised in these Diwans and how the people were connected with history can be clearly understood through writings of Baba Ji:

When the cruel committed cruelty, O Brothers, may be known to you!
They demolished the Gurdwara Rakab Ganj in Delhi and forcibly they destroyed the Masit in Kanpur.
They stopped the water flowing in pool of Amritsar.
To wipe out the College Khalsa, quite cunningly they raised their hand.
Following a novel way, they educated the children adversely.
Numberless cruelties they committed and resolved steps bad to worse.
Let India be free never, they resolved to keep it ever oppressed.
The Almighty felt gracious and stirred us to awaken and be alert.
Sitting on the hot plate, the fifth Master taught us to bear His Will.
Sacrificing his head in Delhi, the ninth Master did the holy deed.
We remember the sweet memory of Mati Dass who got his head sawed.
Limb by limb got Mani Singh cut himself and Taru Singh felt never disheartened.
Subeg sacrificed along with his son, Mehtab brought Massa's head cut.
We remember Baba Deep Singh Ji how he wielded his two-edged sword.
Wearing saffron robes somehow, we saw Gurakhsh Singh from somewhere.
Then from Punjab we visualized Hari Singh warrior and his threatening cry.
Off-springs we are of those valiant, why we waste our lives uselessly.

---

20 Atam katha sant baba Vasakha Singh Dadehar' p.61

Get up lions and hold high your head, why have you wasted your time aimlessly?[21]

These Diwans helped the Sikhs know the history of their religion. Twisting their whiskers, they felt proud of the religious symbols which they were thinking of doing away with in order to merge themselves in western culture, since their self-respect was connected with those religious symbols only.[22]

Remembering their religious heroes and the martyrs, the Sikhs realized the significance of their ancestors. Their inner self-pride became forceful. They also remembered their past when they ruled over Punjab as a sovereign independent nation. It is only the realization of self-respect that becomes a base of self-pride and spirit among the people. In same way, it is awareness of being a free nation that ignites the inner-self of national solidarity against slavery and servility. Howsoever strong is national awareness in a national community, so much stronger shall be the spirit of self-respect in that community and nation.[23]

The spirit of "Sikh Memory" had sprung up in the reminiscence of these Sikhs. "Sikh Memory" is the name of that pure and pious perception that can recognize clearly the true features of past events gone extinct.[24] Along with the Sikh Memory, there sprung up "Guru Conscience" in the minds of these Sikhs, and this gave birth to moral or ethical purity in them. Under this effect, they survived all the degradations and set themselves on the path of courage and bravery. The Guru Conscience refreshed Guru's vision in their memory. Because of this, they felt pinched at every step of insult and disgrace. The feeling of slavery disturbed their soul. Addressed hatefully as "coolie" by the racist Whites stirred their conscience. Sikhs felt it rather severely as they were the martial race. Their ancestors had brooked noses of the raiders and they had lived as rulers, indeed. Being addressed as "coolie," it reminded them of their slavish state.

---

21   Atam katha sant baba vasakha singh dadehar' p.81
22   Statement of Permanand Jhansi "The Maker of Modern Punjab' (Compiled by Dr. Kirpal Singh, Prithipal Singh Kapur) p. 133, Singh Brothers Amritsa - 2010
23   Ajmer singh, kis bidh rulli patshahi, p.35, singh brothers, Amritsar, 2007.
24   Harinder singh Mehboob, "sehjey rachyo Khalsa " p. XXi.

Central Role of Gurdwaras in Ghadri Movement

With severity and tyranny at every step, why don't the Sikhs retaliate?
Everyone calls us 'coolie'; why flutters nowhere our religious flag?
We were lions once, got changed to jackals, O Brothers; why change we not the course of time?
Being timid, the tyrant frowns at you; why hold not fist like men at them?[25]

Even before the forming of the Ghadar Party, the Sikhs living in Canada/America were already on the lookout to find some way to fight against slavery. When the Ghadar Party was formed in 1913, the iron was already hot to be struck. Only the lighting of the flame was awaited; ready for sacrifice, the moth ran at once towards it. Now the Sikhs had no problem in convincing others to join the Party. They had already become one with the historic conscience. Thus, the Sikhs, as per their nature, adopted the martial approach in politics. At this time, no human being was guiding them. History itself was leading them. It was such a stage where the people, having reached a decisive turn, accept no personal guidance, because, at this point, "they find unlimited hints from their ancestors in their dreams, conscience and ever blissful state. They find a close divine touch in their word and deeds. In such circumstances, the 'collective conscience' of nations becomes most fertile, miraculous, subtle and fine. Then the conscience accepts no principle of any adverse-development and stands free from every type of economic effect. Then its mobility becomes more powerful and vehement than common history because then history itself takes birth out of it."[26]

In Sikh religion and culture, peace and war-tactics get equal regard. But the Ghadari Sikhs had realized that the British colonials could not be thrown away now through peaceful means, as such weaponry means were essential. Taking cue from history, they took to martial path and not the violent polity as some learned ones say about this Movement.

When the Ghadar Party brought out its *Ghadar* newspaper, it used to be read out to the congregation in three gurdwaras—Vancouver, Victoria and Abtsford—in Canada. Evidently, the overall managing committee of Vancouver Gurdwara and the Khalsa Diwan Society literally became branches

---

25 Gadar lehar di Kavita (ed. kesar singh navalkaar) p. 93-116, punjabi university patiala, 1995.
26 Harinder singh Mehboob, "sehjey rachyo Khalsa " p. Viii.

of Ghadar Party. Similarly, the managing committee of Gurdwara Stockton also changed into a branch of Ghadar Movement. Sant Baba Wasakha Singh Dadehar, Baba Jawala Singh Thathian, Baba Nidhan Singh Chugha, Bhai Santokh Singh Dhardeo, Bhai Kartar Singh Latala, Bhai Hazara Singh Dadehar were the members here. As per secret reports of British colonies, "the most dangerous persons in Ghadar Party were the members of committees of Vancouver and Stockton gurdwaras."[27]

In August 1914, when the Ghadar Party gave a collective call to go to Punjab and start a strife against the British colonies, the Sikh-majority response given to it was par exemplary. The Sikhs quickly sold away their million-dollar properties, which they had built with their hard-earned money, on throw away prices. Not caring about consequences, they raised the *Khalsai* war cries—Bole So Nihal; Sat Sri Akal—and took seats in ships to reach their motherland—the Punjab. Seated in the ship, the Ghadarites felt as if enthused for the strife. They were going to do deeds on the footprints of their ancestors on the land of their birth. Boarding the *Masimamaru* ship, there was one approver Jawala Singh with the Ghadarite passengers. He tells about the daily speeches made by Ghadarites on the ship. Poems from *Ghadar di Goonj* were read out, and, standing before Guru Granth Sahib, they took oaths to sacrifice themselves in the rebellion.[28]

The historians analyzing this movement based on leftist formulas describe the open preaching by Ghadarites as a main reason of failure of this movement. According to them, the Ghadarites should have come to Punjab secretly in a changed disguise. They should have held secret meetings of the people, should have established party cells and then have grouped the people secretly. They should have practiced like this for twenty or thirty years and then have rebelled against the British Empire. But the Ghadar Movement cannot be understood through leftist formulas. Firstly, the leftists have no historic experience of Mass Upsurge; secondly, no one can comprehend the Sikh psychology. Ghadar Movement was a storm-like people's rise that has every action and activity open and expository. With free, open, and frank propaganda, people become part of this storm. They go on courting arrest in this storm and go on sacrificing their lives also. But the open and fearless propaganda of rebellion only is the soul and strength of this storm.

---

27 F. C. Icemonger & J. Slattery 'An Account of the Ghadar Conspiracy' p. 22.
28 'Lahore Conspiracy Case I and II (Editors, Malwinderjit Singh Waraich, Harinder singh) p. 150, Unistar Books, Chandigarh – 2008.

The second aspect to comprehend is the psycho-structure of Sikhs. After the martyrdom of fifth Master Guru Arjan Dev Ji, the peasantry passed through struggle and strife for about three centuries, and their nature has become struggle-some. They cannot submit before any injustice or accept it timidly through pleadings. A war-like upsurge erupts in their emotions, and their hand goes immediately to the sword or the gun. That is why he considers sacrifice an act of love and goes towards it happily. For Sikhs, the fervor to fight prepares them to forgo any sort of worldly attachments. "Spiritual structure of the Sikhs is such that without strife and struggle, he enjoys neither life in full and nor does he join it fully. If we remove struggle and strife from Khalsa perception, then the vehemence of his moral purity will go on the wane very soon. He shall be cut off from his spiritual sources and his skilful gaiety shall get no more grandeur. So much so, that his faith in non-violence shall also go weak."[29] It was not only the male Ghadarite Sikhs to feel excited against injustice; the female ones also were not left behind in this passion. When the ship carrying Ghadarites from Canada/America reached Manila, even there the Gurdwara was their main center.[30] They arranged congregational assemblies in the Gurdwara and planned to motivate the people on reaching Punjab for rebellion. Countless Sikhs living in Manila got ready to go to Punjab. Two Muslims—Hafiz Abdullah Jagraon and Rehmat Ali Wajidke (Barnala)—also joined them. One couple—Bibi Gulab Kaur—living in Manila also gave names to go to Punjab. But later on, her husband was frightened, and he refused to accompany the Jatha. Bibi Gulab Kaur was fully drenched in the colors of Khalsa strife. In full assembly of the Diwan, she cursed her coward husband and separated herself from him in this way:

O dirty pig! You have shown back to the religion.
You have brought slur on the name of Guru Gobind Singh.
It is OK if you are not going; I renounce you for the whole life.
I am nothing to you from to-day; my final adieu to you.
You have brought blot on the name of Sikh religion and your family.
But I shall not let this blot come to the Sikh religion.
In your place, I am going now. [31]

---

29 Harinder Singh Mehboob, "Sehjey Rachyo Khalsa " p.1054.
30 'Gadar lehar di kahani: Gadari babyan di zubani' (ed. Chain Singh Chain) Baba Harditt Singh lamme's statement p. 156, Desh Bhagat yadgar committee, Jalandhar.
31 Gurcharan Singh Sainsara 'Heroine of the Ghadar Party: Gulab Kaur' Journal of Sikh Studies, Vol IX

Gurdwara of Hongkong was the largest center of the Ghadar Party. In the decision given in Lahore Conspiracy case leveled against Ghadarites, there is mention of Hongkong gurdwara. Ships coming from abroad used to halt there for many days. Daily religious meetings were held here, and poems of *Ghadar di Goonj* were recited there. Speeches were made to undertake revolt on reaching Punjab. Since the day of beginning of *Ghadar* newspaper, the paper used to reach the Gurdwara. It used to be read out in the congregation. At first, Bhai Bhagwan Singh Pritam was Granthi in this Gurdwara. After he left, Bhai Harnam Singh Kahoota took over the position. In fact, the overall committee of Gurdwara Hongkong was converted into a branch of the Ghadar Party.[32] In this committee were members like Bhai Hira Singh Dard (who later suffered life-term jail in Hazari Bagh), Bhai Labh Singh, Bhai Jagat Singh, etc. In congregational assemblies held in this Gurdwara, Bibi Gulab Kaur, in her Khasai zest, used to throw bangles at males. Challenging them, she used to say if they were not to go for mutiny, let them wear the bangles.[33] Soldiers of the 26th Punjabi Platoon used to come to the religious assemblies held in this Gurdwara. They also were getting colored under the effect of Ghadar Movement. Bishan Singh, the Head Clerk of this Platoon, was whole-heartedly with the Ghadarites.[34] When the British authorities came to know about the change of Gurdwara into Ghadar Party, they dismissed the Gurdwara Committee and formed another one with their government people.[35] The 26th Punjabi Platoon was sent at Ferozepur. But this unit was fully drenched in the colors of Ghadar Party. When the Ghadarites were to give mutiny call at Ferozepur Cantt on February 19, 1915, then these soldiers of the Platoon were to give the call. The English Officers banned the visiting of sepoys in Gurdwara and deputed their spies all around the Gurdwara.[36]

The Gurdwara in Shanghai was also an active and strong center of Ghadar Movement. *Ghadar* newspaper used to come here, and it was read out to the congregation. The Gurdwara Committee was fully in support of Ghadar Party. When the Ghadarite Jathas from Canada and America came

---

32 Gadar lehar di kahani: Bhai Harnam Singh Gujjarwal's statement p.149.
33 Gurcharan Singh Sainsara 'Heroine of the Ghadar Party: Gulab Kaur' Journal of Sikh Studies, p.94
34 'Gadar lehar di kahani: Bhai Harnam singh koohta's statement p. 138-39.
35 Baba Bhagat singh bilga, 'Gadar lehar de anfoley verkey' p. 84, desh Bhagat yadgar committee, Jalandhar 1988.
36 'Lahore Conspiracy Case' I-II, p. 208.

Central Role of Gurdwaras in Ghadri Movement

for Punjab, the Gurdwara in Shanghai also became a center of activities. Rebellious speeches were made in the Gurdwara and the poems of *Ghadar di Goonj* were read out. According to the approver Jawala Singh, Bhai Harnam Singh and Bhai Veer Singh came to the Gurdwara to collect money and men. They made revolting speeches and showed the map of new republic in India.[37] Bhai Nidhan Singh Chugha, leader of this Ghadari Jatha, came in the Gurdwara, and the Committee gave him the help of five hundred rupees.[38] A big Jatha from Shanghai under leadership of Bhai Gujjar Singh Bhakna came to Punjab for revolt.

After Shanghai, the Gurdwara of Penang was most popular for Ghadar activities. When the ships of Ghadarites halted here, the Ghadarite leaders delivered revolting lectures. Prominent leaders were Baba Jawala Singh, Baba Kesar Singh, Bhai Jagat Ram, Bhai Roor Singh, Bhai Sher Singh, Baba Nidhan Singh Chugha, etc.[39] Bhai Prem Singh was Granthi of the Penang Gurdwara whom Baba Sohan Singh Bhakna called "an angel-faced Granthi."[40] He was leader of Ghada Party. He reached Punjab to cause mutiny, but he remained detained in his village.

In Siam, the gurdwara of Bangkok was the main center of Ghadar Movement. As per Granthi Mangal Singh, the *Ghadar* newspaper used to come there. Rebellious propaganda used to be done there.[41] Bhai Budha Singh, President of the Gurdwara, was the richest man who sacrificed his life during hunger strike in the jail of Andaman.

After Bangkok in Siam, another Gurdwara in Changmai was an active center of the Ghadar Movement. Bhai Wasawa Singh, Granthi of the Gurdwara, was hanged to death along with five other Ghadarites on November 16, 1916, in the Burma Conspiracy case.

In Burma, another gurdwara in Rangoon was a center of Ghadarite rebels. When the British Government dismissed these committees and formed committees of their own officials, spying agents were also spread all around. It became difficult for the Ghadarites to visit gurdwara. Bhai Santokh Singh, Bhai Sohan Lal Pathak, and Nhai Harnam Singh Sahri were to begin their activities after holding an Akhand Path on reaching Burma.

---

37 Ibid. p 125.
38 'Lahore Conspiracy Case' I-II , p 128.
39 Ibid p. 132
40 Baba Sohan Singh Bhakna, 'meri raam kahani', (ed. Rajwinder Singh Raahi) p.71, sangam publications Samana 2012
41 'Lahore Conspiracy Case' I-II p. 150.

But the gurdwaras had come under control of the British handymen. At last, Bhai Sohan Lal Pathak, with some other fellows, arranged Akhand Path secretly in some jungle area and took the pledge in presence of Sri Guru Granth Sahib to fight against the English. On this occasion, present were Hindus like Sohan Lal and Chalia Ram and Muslims like Mujtaba Hussain.[42]

In Singapore, there were two gurdwaras and both were centers of Ghadar activities. In these gurdwaras also, Baba Jawala Singh, Bhai Inder Singh, Nhai Kala Singh, Bhai Sher Singh, and Bhai Jagat Ram used to deliver mutinous speeches.[43] The Soldiers' mutiny that took place later on in Singapore was the outcome of inflammatory speeches delivered by Granthi Joga Singh and Bhai Santokh Singh Dhardeo. Since the *Ghadar* newspaper used to come in the Gurdwara and the Granthi helped it reach further to the soldiers.[44]

When the Ghadarites came to India, they chose Punjab to initiate their rebellion since it was motherland of the Sikh Ghadarites. They started their initial activity among Sikh soldiers. If there were any centers of activity of the Ghadarites, they were the gurdwaras only. When the revolutionary Sachinder Nath Sanyal from Bengal came to work with Ghadarites in Punjab, he was surprised to find gurdwaras as centers of stay for the Ghadarites.

"Religious places of Sikhs are called gurdwaras. . . . Gurdwaras were there in the revolutionary centres."[45]

According to Sanyal: "I asked if they had no centre of their own from where one could get each and every information. The answer was in 'negative'. It came to be known that these people would go for different jobs and shall come back at a fixed point after doing the job. If, under any reason, they are not able to meet in this way, there is no other way but the gurdwara to meet each other."[46]

Near Jhabal in district Amritsar, there is Gurdwara Jhar Sahib built in memory of the fifth Master Guru Arjan Dev Ji. It was the biggest center of the Ghadar Movement. Bogh Singh, the Granthi of this gurdwara, and

---

42   Sant Vasakha Singh ' malva sikh Itihas' jild dooji, p.362, Bhai Chatar Singh Jivan Singh, Amritsar.
43   'Lahore Conspiracy Case' I-II, p 150.
44   Bhagat Singh Bilga, nirbhai yodhe Gurmukh Singh lalton di jeevani, p.14, desh Bhagat yadgar committee, Jalandhar.
45   Sachinder nath sanyal, 'Bandi jeevan' p.9, lok geet parkashan Chandigarh
46   Sachinder nath sanyal, 'Bandi jeevan' p.24, lok geet parkashan Chandigarh

his mother and whole family were associated with the Ghadarites. In this gurdwara only, the important meetings of Ghadarites were held, and the high command of the Ghadar Party used to participate in it. In this gurdwara only, planning for capturing the Mian mir cantonment of Lahore was devised. On January 26, 1914, a momentous meeting of Ghadarites was held here, and the soldiers of the 23rd Cavalry were to participate in it. But they somehow went astray and could not reach this meeting.[47] The secret agencies got clue of this meeting, and the police cordoned around the Gurdwara Jhar Sahib. The Ghadari ones succeeded in escaping safely, but two or three soldiers of the 23rd Cavalry were arrested by the police. Afterwards, the Granthi Bhai Bogh Singh and his mother were also arrested. Bhai Bogh Singh was sentenced for life-imprisonment in the second Lahore Conspiracy Case. He underwent this punishment in company with the Jatha of Bhai Randhir Singh in Hazari Bagh jail. After the release, the jail authorities gave very thin clothes. With severe cold on the way, many ghadarites died on the way. Bhai Bogh Singh died after reaching home.

In Amritsar, the gurdwara of Sant Gulab Singh near Sri Darbar Sahib was a big halting place of Ghadarites. The Ghadarites used to make bombs in this gurdwara.[48] The gurdwara in the village of Lohatbaddi near Raikot town in Ludhiana district was also a halting place of the Ghadarites where they made bombs.[49] According to one approver, Bhai Nadhan Singh Chugha came in the gurdwara with a bag of explosive material for bombs.[50]

At last, it can be said that the Ghadar Movement took birth in gurdwaras and it prospered also in gurdwaras. It being a Sikh movement, they began every task after taking Order from Sri Guru Granth Sahib. When the Jatha of Bhai Randhir Singh was to march to Ferozepur for revolt on February 19, 1915, they at first organized an Akhand Path[51] at Dhandari Khurd. In reality, the Ghadar Movement did develop as per the nature of the Sikh Ghadarites. Though the Sikh Ghadarites were appealing to the Hindus and Muslims also to fight for freeing the country, these communities had no scope of cooperating with the Sikhs since their nature did not comply with that of the Sikhs

---

47 Gurcharan Singh Sainsara, Gadar Party da Itihas, p.106, Desh Bhagat yadgar committee
48 Parmanand Jhansi 'The Makers of Modern Punjab' p 138.
49 Same p 138
50 Lahore Conspiracy Case I-II, p 160.
51 'Gadar lehar di asli gatha'-2, (ed. Rajwinder Singh Raahi) p.122, sangam publications, Samana 2012.

as there is little difference in word and deed of Sikhs.[52] The political purpose may be pious and tempting to any extent, but every section of society does not bear the same response to it because big gaps exist in their natures. In Ghadar Movement, this fact cannot be ignored. No other community feels the same heat as the Sikhs, who swear against injustice with such anger and fury. Thus, the Ghadar Movement can be comprehended properly only by grasping the nature of Sikhs. About two dozen gurdwaras are there in foreign lands which remained prominent centers of the Ghadar Movement. Equal is the number of Granthies who suffered jail terms in this movement. So, in order to understand the Ghadar Movement, these facts have to be borne clearly in the mind.

Appendix

Gurdwaras as Centres of Activities of Ghadarites

1. Gurdwara Vancouver (Canada)
2. Gurdwara Victoria (Canada)
3. Gurdwara Abtsford (Canada)
4. Gurdwara Stockton (America)
5. Gurdwara Hongkong
6. Gurdwara Shanghai (China)
7. Gurdwara Penang (Korea)
8. Gurdwara Bangkok (Siam, now Thailand)
9. Gurdwara Chingmai (Siam)
10. Gurdwara Rangoon (Burma)
11. Gurdwara Manila (Philippine)
12. Gurdwara Singapore
13. Gurdwara Sant Gulab Singh Ji, Amritsar
14. Gurdwara Jharr Sahib near Jhabal, Amritsar
15. Gurdwara Dera Sahib, Lahore
16. Gurdwara Singh Sabha, Rawalpindi
17. Gurdwara Singh Sabha, Mardan (Peshawar)
18. Gurdwara Kohat
19. Gurdwara Pesh Palaak (Afghanistan)
20. Gurdwara Lohat Baddi, near Raikot, Ludhiana

---

52 Sachinder Nath Sanyal, 'Bandi jeevan' p.82.

21. Gurdwara Lalpura (Afghanistan). It was built by Master Udham singh Kasel.

Granthi Singhs who played central role in the Ghadar Movement
1. Bhai Sahib Bhai Balwant Singh Khurdpur (martyr) Gurdwara Vancouver.
2. Bhai Bhag Singh Bhikhiwnd (martyr) Gurdwara Vancouver
3. Bhai Batan Singh Dalel Singh Wala (martyr) Gurdwara Vancouver
4. Bhai Hari Singh Dhotian (suffered jail in Hazari Bagh) Gurdwara Shanghai-Vancouver
5. Bhai Piara Singh Langeri (suffered jail) Gurdwara Victoria-Vancouver
6. Bhai Mit Singh Pandori (suffered jail) Gurdwara Abtsford
7. Bhai Munsha Singh Dukhi (suffered jail) Gurdwara Victoria
8. Bhai Bhagwan Singh Pritam, Gurdwara Penang-Hongkong
9. Bhai Waryam Singh alias Sant Sunder Singh (exiled) Gurdwara Vancouver
10. Bhai Hazara Singh (jail) Gurdwara Stockton
11. Bhai Inder Singh Mallah (jail) Gurdwara Stockton
12. Bhai Budha Singh (martyr in Andaman) Gurdwara Bangkok
13. Bhai Harnam Singh Kahoota (jail) Gurdwara Hongkong
14. Bhai Wasawa Singh (martyr in Burma) Gurdwara Chinmai, Thailand
15. Bhai Bogh Singh (martyr in Hazari Bagh), Gurdwara Jharr Sahib, Sri Amritsar
16. Bhai Prem Singh (jail) Gurdwara Penang and Chomala Sahib, Lahore
17. Bhai Madan Singh Gaga (jail) Gurdwara Lahore Cantt
18. Bhai Attar Singh Dhikampur (suffered jail in Hazari Bagh) Gurdwara Bhai Satta Singh, Chakwal (Jhelum)
19. Bhai Chattar Singh (suffered jail), Gurdwara Baba Budha Ji Ramdas and Asst Manager of Gurdwara Khadur Sahib
20. Bhai Ishar Singh Marhana (suffered jail), Member SGPC
21. Bhai Santa Singh alias Sant Lakhmir Singh (suffered jail), Gurdwara Sudharke, Chak no. 67, Lyallpur.

Granthi Singhs and Preachers who kept safe their hair
1. Bhai Jagat Singh, Gurdwara Shanghai
2. Bhai Kharak Singh, Gurdwara Hankaoon
3. Bhai Bishan Singh, Gurdwara Tianzen (Shanghai)
4. Giani Harnam Singh, Gurdwara Vancouver

5. Giani Narayan Singh Theekriwala (Baranala), Bhai Balwant Singh Khurdpur and Bhai Nand Singh Seehra
6. Bhai Bhagat Singh alias Charanjit Singh Granthi Gurdwara Stockton follower of Sant Attar Singh Mastuana in Punjab
7. Bhai Sardara Singh Uthap, Gurdwara Burma
8. Bhai Joga Singh, Gurdwara Burma
9. Bhai Karam Singh Nathoke Barki, Lahore

Perspectives on the Ghadr Movement

Dr. Gurdarshan Singh Dhillon

Ghadr Movement, which played a pioneering role in the freedom struggle of India, has not found its due place in the contemporary historiography. Great injustice has been done to the sacred memory of the Ghadrites, who, as champions of the rights of their people, laid down their lives for the freedom and honor of their country. Popular history books have completely ignored the significance of the Ghadr movement in the country's struggle for freedom. Politically oriented and distorted versions of the movement have been propagated. Some historians, with their elitist approach, have ingeniously tried to deify and project Indian revolutionary intellectuals abroad as founders and guiding spirits of the movement, who galvanized the simple-minded, humble flock of people—the illiterate peasants and laborers—into revolutionary action. As a result of this misplaced emphasis, the heroic sacrifices of these simple, unknown and less sophisticated folks have been left unsaid and unsung by these historians.

Literature on India's freedom struggle is voluminous. New books are also being added to the list. These books are not objective in their approach and fail to provide a correct perspective on the Ghadr movement, which deserves to be called a forerunner of the country's freedom struggle. It is noteworthy that the Sikh Ghadrites conspicuously differed from the other freedom fighters, not only in their temperament and training but also in their principles and programs, their value system and world-view, their political convictions, agenda, and outlook. These issues are crucial to the understanding of the character and development of the movement. Harish K. Puri, in his Ph.D.

thesis on the Ghadr movement does not study the movement in the context of Sikh history and tradition. He takes no cognizance of the strong ideological moorings of the Ghadrites and calls it a peasant rebellion. He overlooks the social processes and the historical sequence of cause and effect in relation to this movement. Hence, his understanding of the movement is not very accurate.[1]

The Ghadr movement, which was founded on the Pacific coast of America in May 1913, was manned by immigrants from Punjab, the majority of whom were Sikhs from the Punjab countryside. There were several forces and factors that led to the emergence of this movement. Indian immigrants in America were the victims of racial discrimination. All sorts of insults, indignities, and humiliations were heaped upon them. They also faced racial attacks. Their efforts to secure justice in the courts of law failed. They looked up to the Indian government's intervention for remedial measures. They sent petitions and deputations to the Governor of Punjab and the Governor General of India appealing to their sense of justice and seeking help for their cause. These fervent prayers, petitions, and deputations evoked no response from the government. Immigrants came to realize that they could not be treated as equals in America until they were free. It was in these circumstances that Hindustan Association of the Pacific coast was formed. Sohan Singh Bhakna, a lumber mill worker, was elected its president, and Lala Hardayal was elected its general secretary. The headquarters of the association was established in San Francisco. The foremost objective of the Hindustan Association was to liberate India from the British rule, through an armed rebellion. "Rifles and blood would take the place of pen and ink," was their motto.[2] They believed that a revolutionary movement required a revolutionary response from the participants.

A historian must capture the passion, fervor, and ideological motivation of the creative and vibrant Sikh community which stood in the forefront of the Ghadr movement. He must take into account the spirit, ethos, world-view, and goal of these revolutionaries who were determined to root out discrimination and injustice and usher in an era of freedom and justice. Rallying centers of all Ghadrites, whether Sikh, Hindu, or Muslim, were the Gurdwaras. All communities pledged to fight under one banner, as the issue of communal identity was less important for them than efforts to combat British imperialism. They had the urge to stand united in the face of challenge. With a glorious heritage of chivalry, selfless service, and martyrdom, the Sikh character revealed itself at its best in deeds of kindly service to their fellow countrymen in foreign lands. Gurdwaras enabled them to seek inspiration from the Guru's word and relate to Sikh values and ideals. Institution of Langar emphasized the principle of equality and universal brotherhood. With their liberal social ethos and tradition of sacrifice embedded in their psyche, the Sikhs displayed enough moral strength to prove their patriotism for their motherland. Ghadr movement was almost wholly manned by the Sikhs, who listed the maximum volunteers and raised huge funds out of their hard earned money. Out of the 24 members of the working committees of the Hindustan Association, the majority were the Sikhs.

In Vancouver, the Khalsa Diwan Society and the United India League, with their headquarters in the same Gurdwara, mobilized their protest against the Alien Land Law (1913), which restricted the rights of Indians to own land in Canada.[3] They also directed their propaganda against British rule in India and coordinated their activities with the branch of Hindustan Association in Vancouver. Revolutionary activity in Canada was further intensified when the Canadian government passed stringent Immigration Law (1917) restricting the entry of Indians to Canada.

The Ghadrites launched a magazine called *Ghadr* in English, Urdu, and Punjabi for free distribution. Urdu and English editions of *Ghadr* were edited by Hardayal, whose powerful writings lent him an aura of romance as a revolutionary. Hardayal was inspired by his ideologue V.D. Savarkar. In *Ghadr* magazine, he extensively quoted from Savarkar's book, *The First War Of Indian Independence, 1857*. The book was published in London in 1909 and was instantly proscribed. The Punjabi edition of *Ghadr* was edited by Kartar Singh Sarabha, a stalwart of the revolutionaries. Every issue of the *Ghadr* exhorted the Indian people to unite and fight against the British rule. It launched a vigorous attack on the British imperialism. It highlighted the miserable plight of the Indians under the British rule and also the issues of racial discrimination and attacks against Indians in America and Canada. Written in such virile and compelling language, the *Ghadr* literature became quite popular in India, Europe, Canada, America, and several other countries. A few examples of this virile language are given below:

> Without blood O'patriots! will the country awake ?
> Rise, gird up your loins, Rise, Gird up your loins, Rise
> Rise, O, lions!, Rise, Pluck your courage, serve your country.

Why do you disgrace the name of Singhs? You have forgotten the majesty of lions.
O, Brave Khalsa, Wake up, country is in the throes of tyrnny.
Follow Guru's injunction: Play the game of love with your head on your palm[4]: This motto was written on the title page of every issue of *Ghadr*.

The British Government adopted various measures to stop the circulation of *Ghadr* and other such publications particularly in India. The outbreak of First World War in 1914 suited the object of the Ghadr party to spread an armed rebellion in India. The time was most suitable as the British were involved in war. British reverses involving large-scale casualties of Sikh soldiers from the rural areas seemed to the Ghadrites a right stage for their objective. They wanted army soldiers to join their revolt against the British. As Germany fought against England, the German Government and the Ghadrites had the British as their common enemies. The Ghadrites sought financial help from Germany to buy arms and ammunition in order to overthrow the British rule.[5] Berlin Committee was formed to help the Ghadrites. Overseas Indians were exhorted to reach India and launch a revolution. They formulated plans to infiltrate the Indian army and incite the soldiers to fight against the British. With financial support from Germany, several ships were chartered to carry arms and ammunitions to India. Filled with death-defying courage, hordes of immigrants rushed homewards to liberate their motherland. It was unfortunate that the plans of the revolutionaries were leaked out to the British. Ships, with arms and ammunition, commissioned to reach India were diverted elsewhere or taken captive on reaching India, by the British Government. Much harm was caused to the movement by the spies, informers, and loyalists of the British Government.[6]

The path, which the revolutionaries had chosen to tread for themselves, was beset with all kinds of obstacles and difficulties. They had envisaged that their countrymen would whole-heartedly join them in their revolutionary activities. But on reaching India, they soon realized that they had labored under an illusion. Gurdwaras in India were under the control of corrupt Hinduized Mahants and Pujaris, who enjoyed a patronage of the British Government. Whereas the overseas Indians prayed in the Gurdwaras for the success of the mission of the revolutionaries, these Mahats and Pujaris expressed no sympathy for their cause.[7] Lack of popular support was a big handicap for the revolutionaries. Yet, filled with an indomitable spirit and an unbounded optimism, starving, thirsting, and laboring hard, they toured the Punjab countryside in batches of 15 to 20, collected people with the beat of drums, inspired them with revolutionary speeches and poems, and exhorted them to overthrow the British. A young revolutionary Kartar Singh Sarabha used to cover a distance of 40 to 50 miles in the rural areas, each day, on his bicycle.[8]

Ghadrites achieved some success in organizing their revolutionary activities in central Punjab, but these activities were more in the nature of sporadic and impromptu guerilla operations. They could not rise to such dimensions as to assume the shape of a mass upsurge. Ghadrites were able to mobilize support of patriotic elements among the Indian soldiers of units, namely 23 Calvalry at Lahore and 26 Infantry at Ferozepur.[9] But their plans were intended to cover a far wider area, in a much wider network. Some of the Singh Sabhas were sympathetic to the Ghadrites; Bhai Takht Singh entertained the delegates of the Ghadr Party when they visited Ferozepur. Daljit Singh, Assistant Editor of the *Punjabi Bhain*, a monthly publication of the Sikh Kanya Maha Vidyala, Ferozepur, joined the Ghadrites and became a Secretary of Baba Gurdit Singh, a leader of the Ghadr party. According to a report, "the methods to be employed by the delegates of the Ghadr party in pushing the campaign in India appeared to have been discussed in the weekly meetings of the Singh Sabha at Lahore . . . A member of the Singh Sabha in advocating these measures spoke of creating a spirit of awakening among Hindus and Sikhs." Ghadrites also enjoyed the support of two popular Sikh mystics, Bhai Randhir Singh and Baba Vasakha Singh, who were sent to Andamans as life convicts.[10]

The unfortunate episode of *Koma Gata Maru* cast a gloom among the Ghadrites and intensified their anti-British fury. The barbarous manner in which the *Koma Gata Maru* tragedy was enacted at Budge Budge Ghat had no parallel. A group of Sikh immigrants returning from Canada became the victims of British high-handedness. Many innocent Sikhs were mercilessly killed, while others were wounded or imprisoned for no fault of theirs. This incident was universally condemned and the Sikh public opinion was greatly mobilized against the British. As a reaction, William Hopkinson, the hated Inspector in the Immigration Department at Vancouver, was killed by Mewa Singh, a Ghadrite who later made a confessional statement and was hanged.[11]

In a short span of 4 to 5 years, all the leading activists of the Ghadr movement were captured by the British. They were charged with criminal conspiracies. 291 accused were tried: 42 of them were sentenced to death, 114 transported for life, and 93 were awarded varying terms of imprisonment.[12] Annals of their courage, bravery, and martyrdom have few parallels in history.

A dispassionate historian has to analyze the factors and forces which caused a setback to the movement. It would be befitting to carry the torch of research into some of the hitherto overlooked aspects of the movement like the lack of centralized leadership, lack of unity and the cleavage that grew up between the communities. There were some who flaunted their rationalism, articulate speech, and intellectual gifts, but they lacked moral courage and would often shun to hold the gun. Lala Lajpat Rai observed that persons like Hardayal kept themselves in the background and avoided danger. They goaded the assassins but covered their own tracks skillfully. The ignominious story of their surrender to British imperialism is often concealed, although it constitutes a black chapter in the history of the Ghadr movement. Hailed as great freedom fighters and revolutionaries, they have to be tried and judged at the bar of history.

This was in sharp contrast to the revolutionaries, mostly Sikhs, who pledged that rifles and blood would take the place of pen and ink. They were simple-minded people, sincere and steadfast to their cause, who were never afraid to wield the gun, when needed. The image of a saint-soldier was imbedded in their psyche. The flame of liberty, lit in their hearts, could never be extinguished. They were subjected to innumerable oppressions and tortures, their houses were burnt, and their lands were confiscated. But they remained firm and unbending and fought for justice, freedom, and human dignity and laid down their lives for this cause. They truly deserve to be applauded, honored, and glorified. Here it is relevant to quote the confessional statement of Mewa Singh, in 1914, who had eliminated William Hopkinson. The statement reflects his socio-religious orientation and nobility of thought: "My religion does not teach me to bear enmity with anybody, no matter what class, creed or order he belongs to nor had I any enmity with Hopkinson. I heard that he was suppressing my poor people very much. I, being a staunch Sikh, could no longer bear to see the wrong done both to my innocent countrymen and the Dominion of Canada . . . and I, performing the duty of a Sikh and remembering the name of the God, will proceed towards the scaffold with the same amount of pleasure as the hungry babe does towards its mother. I shall have the rope around my neck, thinking it to be a rosary of

God's name."[13] Mewa Singh laid down his life upholding the glorious Sikh tradition of martyrdom for a righteous cause.

The two categories of revolutionaries had divergent views not only in terms of their revolutionary consciousness but also in their cultural orientation. Uneasy alliance between the two categories often resulted in friction between the two. Some Hindu activitists in the movement were proud of their intellectual attainments and looked down upon the immigrant Sikhs as an "unlettered people" and a "crowd of rustics." Hardyal's friend Daris Chenchiah described them as that "wonderful human material."[14]

The Sikhs, on the other hand, looked upon the Hindus as English-knowing Babus who were cowardly, crafty, and unscrupulous in the use of funds. A centralized leadership which could integrate the two elements was lacking. The British also played one community against the other. They openly manipulated and opened clear arenas for communal competition. Revolutionaries, who had rallied around Hardyal for leadership, found him lacking in the courage of his convictions. He could not cope with the mounting pressure of Ghadr enthusiasts for immediate sounding of the bugle and recourse to armed rebellion to synchronize with the out break of war. In such a situation only those leaders could prevail who were in tune with the overwhelming passion of the masses. Hardayal was at his wit's end. His arrest in April 1914 provided him an opportunity to quit the scene, escape, and conceal the inconsistencies in his attitude. He no longer remained an uncompromising revolutionary and turned a *volte face*. He declared that the cause of Indian nationalism could best be served by India's remaining in the British empire. He deplored terrorism as a "mixture of heroism and folly." He said that the majority of Hindu patriots now stood with the Indian Natonal Congress and followed Gandhi who preached and popularized passive resistance and who advised the nationalists to boycott the British schools, law courts, councils, and everything British in the country.[15]

After his stay in Germany for 44 months, where he had mustered support for Ghadrites, Hardyal moved to Sweden and turned his critical lens on Germany, describing it as the "hot bed of militarism and chauvinism"[16] which must be taught that her dream of emerging as a world-power cannot be realized. An issue of *India* (London) dated March 14, 1919, quoted Hardayal as saying, "I avow publicly my conversion to the principle of Imperial unity with progressive self-government for all civilized nations of Empire."[17] Hardayal disassociated himself from the revolutionary struggle against British imperialism in unequivocal terms: "The events and experiences of War have led me to modify my political opinion in some respects. I think that the British Empire in Asia and Africa is, after all, a necessary institution as those people cannot defend themselves against German, Turkish and Mohammedan invaders without the help of British officers and soldiers. In my opinion, the dissolution of the British Empire in Asia, would be a great calamity as it would not result in the establishment of independent nation-states, but only a change of masters. I have, therefore, come to the conclusion that the nations, which now form part of the British empire, should try to receive Home Rule within the Empire and should co-operate with England for the defense of their countries. English administrative genius has built up a fabric which should be improved and developed but not overthrown."[18] He voluntarily returned his German passport on February 2, 1919. The German Foreign Office reported with a touch of bitterness that, even after this date, Hardayal spoke of his plans to reorganize the Berlin Committee and to constantly ask for official German aid by letter and by telegraph.[19]

The man, who goaded the revolutionaries to gird up their loins against British imperialism, now wrote, "It is part of wisdom for us not to tempt fate but stay under the protection of the British fleet and arms in our quiet and sunny home of Hindustan, and to make the best of our position in our Empire."[20] Hardayal also waxed eloquent over the quality and blessings of English literature: "No Oriental nation would be loser if it forgot its own tongue and learned English instead . . . A primer of English history was worth more than all the histories of Asia."[21] At yet another place, he wrote, "The Empire cannot develop as an organic healthy state if the orientals prefer their barren literature and their uninspiring history to English literature and English history." The man who was a rebel against the British Government, taking part in anti-British propaganda during his stay in Germany (1914–1918), suddenly severed all connections with Germans after his departure from there. His book *Forty-Four Months in Germany and Turkey*, published in England, contains most vicious denunciation of Germany and an effusive praise of the British Empire. He lamented that "Indians have yet not learned to love and cherish the institution known as the British empire."[22] India Office London saw to it that the book was translated into Hindi and distributed free of charge in India.

While the revolutionaries clenched their fists, boiled with rage, and wrote threatening letters to the man who had blatantly ditched them and jeopardized their movement, it was no easy task for the British Government to judge the motives of a man who had undergone a sudden dramatic change of heart to come forward and shake hands with the British. According to a report of the Director of intelligence, Hardayal was still, at heart, a revolutionary, "who lacked courage to execute his convictions."[23] The report characterized him as "an opportunist who is apt to temper his conduct to the prevailing winds."[24] A judgement in the first Lahore Conspiracy Case described Hardayal as "a dangerous monomaniac, devoid of any trace of moral and physical courage, who while inducing his dupes to go to a certain fate, carefully kept himself out of trouble."[25] A man with such marked inconsistencies and profound contradictions in his character and career was certainly not fit to lead the way of revolutionaries.

As noted earlier, politically Hardayal had made a turn around and had safely aligned himself with the Gandhian ideal of Home Rule for India. Culturally, he toed the line of Damodar Das Savarkar, President of Hindu Maha Sabha, although he had leaned towards the Arya Samaj in his early days. In the *Ghadr* literature, frequent references were made to Savarkar's ideas and ideology. It is noteworthy that there are remarkable similarities between Hardyal and Savarkar. During his student days in England, Savarkar had started the Free India Society and had organized students for revolutionary activities. He was charged with murdering an Englishman and was tried and sent to the Andemans in 1910. During his detention in Andemans jail, under harsh conditions, Savarkar underwent a serious metamorphosis. He decided to renounce his struggle against British imperialism and focus on Hindutava which aimed at establishing Hindu Rashtra in India, through a process of Hindu identity building. One can find an echo of Savarkar's views in Hardayal's declaration, "Future of the Hindu race, of Hindustan and Punjab, rests on these four pillars: (i) Hindu Sangthan, (ii) Hindu Raj (iii) Shuddhi of Muslims and (iv) conquest and Shuddhi of Afghanistan and the frontiers. So long as the Hindu nation does not accomplish these four things, the safety of our children and great grand children will be ever in danger and the safety of the Hindu race will be impossible."[26] This was a declaration which Hardayal chose to call his "political testament." Both Hardayal and Savarkar passionately appealed to the communal instincts of the Hindus, both delinked themselves from mainstream nationalism and promoted Hindu nationalism instead. Both worked for the narrow sectarian ends of the Hindus, setting a very bad example for the revolutionaries who had pledged to work across communal lines. Secular character of the movement was undermined.

Both Hardayal and Sarvarkar appealed to the British Government for amnesty.[27] Both bartered the country's independence to secure their own personal freedom. They allowed their selfish interests to prevail over the wider interests of the movement. In a letter dated November 14, 1913, Savarkar wrote to the Home Minister of the Government of Inida, "If the government in its manifold beneficence and mercy releases me, I for one cannot but be the staunchest advocate of constitutional progress and loyalty to the English Government which is the foremost condition of that progress . . . Moreover, my conversion to the constitutional line would bring back all those misled youngmen in India and abroad who were once looking up to me as their guide . . . The mighty alone can afford to be merciful and therefore where else can the prodigal son return but to the parental doors of the government."[28] Hardayal toed the same line and bowed before the British Government for amnesty. When he received the letter from the India Office stating that he would be allowed to return to India without fear of arrest or subsequent prosecution, he replied, "I beg to thank the Secretary of State for India and the Punjab Government for their kindness and magnanimity in granting me a legal amnesty. I shall return to India in course of time in accordance with the stipulations which I beg to accept."[29] The two apostles of revolution threw off their mask and proved that they were singularly devoid of any sense of honor or grace. They came to serve their own interests, deceiving and leaving the lives and fortunes of their followers at stake. Factionalism and fights in the ranks of the revolutionaries were due to lack of sincere leadership which gave a fatal blow to the movement.

Gandhi's ideal of passive resistance to the British was not in tune with the revolutionary ideology of the Ghadrites. The story also brings into focus the parochial outlook and pseudo-nationalism of the Congress. Despite the ideological commitment of the Congress to a secular ideal, it failed to emerge as a champion of national unity. It faltered and failed to represent Indian nationalism in the true sense. It identified itself with the religion of the multitude and socio-political interests of the Hindus. Even Savarkar believed that his real "enemy" was not British imperialism but the minority religious groups and the secularists of India.[30] After many centuries of subjugation,

Hindus aspired to be arbiters and masters of their own destiny. They dreamt of a Hindu Raj and their emergence as a supreme power in the subcontinent. They tried to make a religious, cultural, and linguistic homogeneity as a sign of India's nationhood. Their notion of nationalism stemmed from the deeply felt insecurity of the urban Hindu middle class and was sustained, throughout, by their class interests as a counterweight to the imbalance of their position in Punjab. In its emphasis on Hindu interests, Punjab was far ahead of other states in the country. Resurgent Hinduism under the leadership of the Arya Samaj and the Hindu Maha Sabha, especially in Punjab, stood in the way of united political action against the British. The Ghadr Movement which originated in a foreign land, with the bold initiative of Punjabi immigrants, mostly Sikhs, could not rise to the desired dimensions due to lack of adequate support and cooperation from their own countrymen.

There were several forces at work which caused a setback to the Ghadr movement. In India, Congress leaders looked upon the Ghadrites with contempt. They were more sympathetic to the British than to the Ghadrites. Tilak, the so-called militant Congressite, had expressed his strong and open disapproval of the activities of the Ghadrites. Gokhle is said to have openly told the Viceroy that he would like the British to extend their stay in India. Gandhi chose to be loyal to the British during the war and the Zulu revolt against apartheid. Soon after the war, he was awarded the Kaisar-i-Hind Medal and the Zulu War Medal. In 1914, when he bade farewell to South Africa, his departing words were of praise for the British empire: "Rightly or wrongly, for good or for evil, Englishmen and Indians have been knit together, and it behoves both races so to mould themselves as to leave a splendid legacy to the generations yet to be born and to show that though the empires have gone and fallen, this Empire perhaps may be an exception and that this is an Empire not founded on material but on spiritual foundations."[31] Gandhi, the Father of non-violence, did not approve of the violent methods of the Ghadrites. By supporting the British empire, he did incalculable harm to the Ghadr Movement. The mendicant approach of Gandhi, along with his creed of non-violence and passive resistance, suited the British as compared to the radical tone and methods adopted by the revolutionaries for the overthrow of the British rule. British facilitated Gandhi's emergence as an iconic and central figure around whom the country's freedom struggle revolved. Moreover, Gandhi identified himself with the caste-oriented Hindu religious system. Even his call for Ram Rajya aimed at the revival of the Hindu cultural past, including the perpetuation of the caste system. Along with Jinnah, Gandhi too was responsible for the two-nation theory that divided India into two countries in 1947.

This was a period of political turmoil in the country. There was a split between the moderate and the extremist wings of the Congress but Gandhi, somehow, continued to be at the helm of affairs. During this period, Reform movements of the Hindus, Sikhs, and Muslims, which had religion as their prime motive force, were primarily concerned with the socio-religious reform of their respective communities. These movements, notably Singh Sabha Movement among the Sikhs and the Army Samaj of the Hindus, did not like to have open confrontation with the British. The British Government was also ready "to encourage freedom of thought, ideas of social reform on modern lines and even social revolt so long as these did not touch the dangerous ground of politics."[32] The policy of "divide and rule" also suited the British. Clashes between the communities stood in the way of united political action. Chief Khalsa Diwan, Amritsar, had, no doubt, undertaken "to protect the political rights of the Sikhs," but some of its leading members were patronized by the British Government. Therefore, Chief Khalsa Diwan could not help the Ghadrites. Government aimed at an erosion of the Sikh ideology and control of Sikh shrines through government nominated corrupt and Hinduized Mahants and Pujaris. Sikh tempers rose very high when the priests of Darbar Sahib condemned the *Koma Gata Maru* and Ghadrite Sikhs through a Hukamnama, issued at the Akal Takht. Two eminent religious personalities, Baba Wasakha Singh and Bhai Randhir Singh, who had supported the Ghadrites, were disowned and declared non-Sikhs by these priests. These events made it evident to the Sikhs that a political struggle with the British, with the dual objective of political freedom and the removal of government control over the Sikh Gurdwaras, was inevitable. A citadel of freedom was to be built on the ashes of martyrs of the Ghadr Movement. The grim tragedy of the Ghadr martyrs continued to cast its shadow on the future. Punjab remained in continuous ferment, while the situation in the rest of the country continued to be entirely different as a result of Gandhi's call for passive resistance. Time and again, the martial spirit of the Sikhs continued to assert itself against oppression and injustice. As a consequence of agitation against the Rowlatt Act, Punjab was thrown into the vortex of Martial Law.[33] Punjab bore the brunt of British high-handedness, as witnessed in the Jallianwala Bagh Massacre of 1919.

The Sikhs continued to be in the forefront of the country's struggle for freedom. The Babbar Akali Movement and the Gurdwara Reform Movement to release the Gurdwaras from government control were offshoots of the Ghadr movement which had created an atmosphere of popular discontent. All this paved the way for a new phase in India's struggle for freedom. This phase was marked by mutual distrust and rivalry among the communities. The battle for the country's freedom was not fought and won on a common political platform. The so-called national movement, led by the Congress in India, had nothing national about it. The idea of India being one nation could never take deep roots. Congress failed to prove its secular credentials.

A close study of India's freedom struggle reveals that leaders at the helm of affairs always pulled in different directions and played a double game to secure their own ends and interests. Gandhi, the greatest protagonist of truth and non-violence, failed in his experiments at the time of the country's partition. He displayed complete disregard for truth and fair play in very serious matters in which lives and fortunes of millions of his countrymen were at stake. Yet writing about Gandhi, historians have often mixed politics with history, by bestowing on him nobility, glory, and greatness which actually never belonged to him. No congnizance has been taken of the supreme sacrifices of the revolutionaries of the Ghadr Movement. It is time to put the record straight and accord a due place to these heroes in the history of the country's freedom struggle, even if it is a century after the events.

Conclusion

Ghadr Movement constitutes a very important landmark in India's struggle for freedom. Although it could not achieve its desired aim, it left a glorious legacy of chivalry, heroism, honesty, sincerity, and sacrifice. In their zeal for freedom, Ghadrites were far ahead of their countrymen. They were filled with amazing courage and death-defying fearlessness which emanates from a higher consciousness that impels men to suffer and sacrifice in order to uphold causes dear to their hearts. The saga of their colossal losses and sacrifices for the honor, glory, and freedom of their motherland deserves to be written in golden letters. The Movement, dominated by the Sikhs, has to be judged in the light of integrated Sikh world-view, revolutionary ideology of the Sikh Gurus, and Sikh historical experience, i.e., their tradition of martyrdom, which signifies the triumph of the human spirit against all odds.

Concealing or twisting of facts leads to erroneous and misleading interpretations of history.

Recent years have seen a great upsurge in empirical research, leading to a paradigm shift in the interpretation of Sikh history, especially in the West. These Western scholars, with their materialistic approach, take no cognizance of the spiritual dimension of human life. They are blind to the colossal spiritual energies generated by the revolutionary ideology of the Sikh Gurus and the phenomenal response they had over the centuries in shaping history. As a result, they provide materialistic interpretations of Sikh history, which are lopsided and misleading. In his book *Martyrdom In the Sikh Tradition: Playing the Game of Love*, Louis E. Fenech denies the role of ideas and ideology in Sikh history. He also undermines the Sikh tradition of martyrdom. He asserts that this tradition was trumped by the rhetoric of the Singh Sabha Movement. A correct evaluation of the Ghadr Movement cannot be made by applying materialistic yardsticks.

References

1. Puri, Harish K., *Ghadr Movement: Ideology, Organisation and Strategy*, (Guru Nanak Dev University, Amritsar, 1983), p. 176.
2. *Ghadr*, April, 4, 1915.
3. Khushwant Singh and Satinder Singh, *Ghadr 1915: India's First Armed Revolution*, (New Delhi, 1966), p. 17.
4. *Ghadr*, December 9, 1913.
5. *Ibid.*, January 6, 1914.
6. Pooni, Sohan Singh, *Canada de Ghadri Yodhe* (Amritsar, 2008), p. 90.
7. *Ibid.*, p. 85.
8. Puri, *op.cit.*, p. 158.
9. Pooni, *op.cit.*, p. 86.
10. Dhillon, G.S., *Insights Into Sikh Religion and History* (Chandigarh, 1991), p. 152.
11. Isemonger and Slattery, J.; *An Account of the Ghadr Conspiracy, 1913-15*, pp. 75-76.
12. *Ibid.*, Appendix.
13. Khushwant Singh, *A History of the Sikhs Vol. II* (New Delhi, 1977), p. 179.
14. Puri, *op. cit.*, p. 62.

15. Brown, Emily C., *Hardyal: Hindu Revolutinary and Rationalist* (Delhi, 1975), pp. 223-24.
16. *Ibid.*, p. 219.
17. *Ibid.*, p. 218.
18. *Ibid.*, p. 219.
19. *Ibid.*, p. 220.
20. Muthana, I.M. *People of India in North America* (Vancouver, 1982), p. 419.
21. *Ibid.*
22. Hardyal, *Forty Four Months in Germany and Turkey* (London, 1920), p. 71.
23. Brown, *op.cit.*, p. 265.
24. *Ibid.*
25. *Ibid.*, p. 264.
26. *Ibid.*, p. 233.
27. *Ibid.*, p 269.
28. *Mainstream*, September 25, 2004, pp. 14-15.
29. Brown, *op.cit.*, pp. 268-69.
30. Kuruvachira, J.; *Vinayak Damodar Sarvarkar: As a Narrow Visionary and A Hinduatva Hardliner*, p. 9, see on internet.
31. Singh, G.B. and Watron, Tom, *Gandhi: Under Cross-Examination* (Lathrop, C.A. 2009), p. 20.
32. Majumdar, R.C.: *History and Culture of the Indian People*, Vol X (Bombay, 1965), p. 103
33. Pooni, op. cit., p. 30

Bibliography

1. Brown, Emily C, *Hardyal: Hindu Revolutionary and Rationalist*, Manohar, Delhi, 1975.
2. Chain, Chain Singh (edited), *Ghadr Lehar Di Kahani; Ghadri Babian Di Jabani*, Jalandhar, 2002.
3. Dhillon, Gurdarshan Singh, *Insights Into Sikh Religion and History*, Chandigarh, 1991.
4. Fenech, Louis E., *Martyrdom In the Sikh Tradition: Playing the Game of Love*, Oxford, 2000.
5. Hardyal, *Forty-Four Months in Germany and Turkey – Feb 1915 to Oct 1918*, London 1920.

6. Kuruvachira, J., *Vinayak Damodar Savarkar, As a Narrow Visionary and A Hinduatava Hardliner* – Internet.
7. Majumdar, R.C., *History and Culture of the Indian People*, Bombay 1965.
8. Muthana, I. M., *People of India and North America*, Vancouver, 1982.
9. O, Dwyer, Michael, *India As I know It*, 3rd Edition, London, 1926.
10. Pooni, Sohan Singh, *Canada De Gadri Yodhe*, Amritsar, 2009.
11. Puri, Harish K., *Ghadr Movement, Ideology, Organisation and Strategy*, Guru Nanak Dev University, Amritsar, 1983.
12. Savarkar, Damodar Dass, *Revolt of 1857: The First Indian War of Independence*, London, 1909.
13. Singh, Jagjit, *Ghadr Party Di Lehar*, Tarn Taran, 1955.
14. Singh, Fauja, *Eminent Freedom Fighters of Punjab*, Punjabi. University, Patiala, 1972.
15. Singh, G.B., and Tim Watson, *Gandhi: Under Cross-Examination*, Lathrop, C.A., 2009.
16. Singh, Khushwant and Singh, Satindra, *Ghadr 1915 – India's First Armed Revolution*, New Delhi, 1966.
17. Singh, Khushwant, *A History of the Sikhs, 1839-1964*, Vol II, Princeton, 1966.

Relevance of Sikh Ideology for the Ghadar Movement

Dr. J.S. Grewal Former VC GNDU

(An Exploratory Note)

A large volume of literature has been produced on the Ghadar Movement since independence. It is well known that the Punjabis represented an overwhelming majority of the Ghadarites, and an overwhelming proportion of the Ghadarites were Sikhs. Therefore, the ideological moorings of the Sikh leaders of the Ghadar Movement become an important issue. Indeed, scholars have taken different views on this subject. We may take notice of a few to illustrate the point.

In his *Ghadar Party Lehar* (1955), Jagjit Singh underlined that the Singh Sabha movement served as a kind a renaissance among the peasants of the Central Punjab. For the first time under colonial rule, the tradition of sacrifice and martyrdom in Sikh history was made popular among the Sikh masses. It had created a social consciousness among the peasants who emigrated to North America and other countries and participated in the Ghadar movement. Though there was hardly any political consciousness among the Sikh peasantry in the early twentieth century, there was an awareness of new ideas with regard to social reform. This background had a great potentiality for inducing them to adopt a revolutionary path.[1]

Harish K. Puri completed his doctoral thesis on the Ghadar Movement in the 1970s. It was published as the *Ghadar Movement: Ideology, Organisation and Strategy* (1983). In his introduction, he talks of "the relevance or irrelevance of religion in political violence" as an important issue, and in his discussion of the "background," he notices that the Singh Sabha Movement had its followers in Canada. They were described in an intelligence report. As a section of "clannish Sikhs," their "jealously and bigotry" kept alive the ill feeling between the clean shaven and the other Sikhs. Teja Singh was referred to as "something of a religious fanatic," though he was concerned with "making life easier for the peasant" as well as with religious conversion.[2] This appears to suggest that the Singh Sabha ideology had no bearing on the Ghadar.

Indeed, an article published by Harish K. Puri in 1983 makes it clear that in his well-considered view the Singh Sabha and the Ghadar movements were two "divergent patterns of psychological orientations and structures of belief, values and attitudes towards political objects." The initiators of the Singh Sabha Movement were "landed aristocrats, mahants, pujaris and priests." Among them were also the Sehajdharis. The *mahants* and *pujaris* "condemned the Ghadarites as *patit* Sikhs and enemies of the panth." General Dyer was "honoured" and "initiated as a Sikh" at the initiative of the Chief Khalsa Diwan. The Nirankaris and the Namdharis had aimed at restoring "the pristine purity of Khalsa norms," with particular emphasis on "the observance of the five Ks" so that the Sikhs did not get "assimilated among the Hindus." Under the leadership of Baba Ram Singh, the Namdhari movement became "more radical and militant." The Singh Sabha Movement was "an alternative" to the Namdhari movement.[3] What Harish Puri had in mind was the militancy of the Namdharis and the loyalty of the Singh Sabhas. It may also be added that the Nirankaris did not assign any importance to the Khalsa initiation and the 5 Ks.

According to Harish Puri, the British wanted to strengthen "the loyalty of the Sikh soldier." They believed strongly that religious orthodoxy of the Sikh soldier in the army was "crucial for his loyalty to the empire." Therefore, they decided to enlist "only Keshadharis into regiments." Simultaneously, the control of Gurdwaras through government-appointed *sarbrahs* was sought to be strengthened through priests and *mahants* for promoting "the desired hegemonic influence." In this set of conditions, the Singh Sabha Movement was launched. Among its leaders were educated urban Sikhs and trading classes. Their conflict with the Arya Samaj strengthened the urge to assert that the Sikhs were a distinct community. "In the process, it developed among the community, largely in the urban areas, a distinct political orientation based

Relevance of Sikh Ideology for the Ghadar Movement

on separate community interests." The other two communities in the province were seen as "threats to the Sikh community."[4]

The Ghadar Movement, on the other hand, developed "just the contrary structure of political orientations." The Ghadarite interpretation of the community's heritage was "very different from, almost contrary" to the one argued by the Singh Sabhas and the Chief Khalsa Diwan and "what some near to that articulated by the Kukas." The Ghadarites sought inspiration from the teachings of Guru Gobind Singh for armed struggle in a righteous cause and from the brave Sikh crusaders like Banda Singh Bahadur, Dip Singh, Mahtab Singh, Hari Singh, and Phula Singh. For the Ghadarites, the Guru's "Singh" was distinguished not by "a ritualistic adherence to external forms, as the Singh Sabha advocated," but by "the bravery and self-sacrificing spirit to fight the enemy." The Ghadar poets referred to the Khalsa or the Panth as a force created for the defense of the country and for ending oppression of "Bharat Mata." "The Panth therefore was to be judged by its service in the cause of the country's freedom." The stress of the Ghadarites was on "the primacy of politics and rejection of preoccupation with matters of religion." At best, religion could be accepted as "a private affair." Casteism was completely rejected by the Ghadarites, and, in their social relations, they never cared much for keeping long hair and beards or eating *jhatka* or *halal*. "This orientation naturally aroused the wrath of the orthodox against the Ghadarites." In Harish Puri's view, the Gurdwara Reform Movement was a structure of orientations "somewhere midway between the two," the Singh Sabha and the Ghadar movements.[5]

We have outlined Harish K. Puri's well-considered view of the irrelevance of the Singh Sabha movement for the Ghadar partly because he has modified his view only slightly by now, but largely because his view does not appear to find support from the available evidence on the Singh Sabha Movement.

In *The Sikhs of the Punjab* (1990), my view of the relevance of the Singh Sabha Movement for the Ghadar was different from that of Harish Puri. I pointed out that some of the Sikh leaders of the Ghadar Movement recalled later that they had been inspired to live or die heroically by the novels of Bhai Vir Singh and the *Panth Prakash* of Giani Gian Singh. They acquired a genuinely "national" outlook, but their source of inspiration remained "almost exclusively Sikh." They evoked the memory of Sikh heroes and martyrs and referred to the Sikh past as a struggle for liberation. Not indifference to faith but a secular interpretation of the heritage distinguished them from the Singh Sabha reformers of the Punjab.⁶

In his *Ghadar Movement: A Short History* (2011), Harish K. Puri states at the outset that Lala Har Dyal was the "inspirational genius" of the Ghadar. However, it was mainly a movement of the Punjabi Sikh patriots of India. Their political ideas were shaped by their experience in Canada, USA, and other countries of the world. Harish Puri has outlined the historical, social, and political context of the Punjab at the time when Punjabis started migrating to North America. "The leading figures appeared to have carried with them some of the reformist ideas to the foreign lands." They kept the outward symbols of conduct associated with Guru Gobind Singh, which inspired respect for them among their brethren. "But they did not approve of orthodoxy in such matters."⁷ This assessment of the situation seems to suggest that even the leading figures among the Sikh emigrants were content with observing the outward symbols of the Khalsa, and they had no ideological moorings relevant for the Ghadar Movement.

The socio-religious reform movements mentioned by Harish Puri in this publication are the Brahmo Samaj and its offshoot the Dev Samaj, the Arya Samaj, and the Singh Sabha Movement. Baba Sohan Singh Bhakna was "a follower of the Namdhari Guru Baba Ram Singh." However, the influence of the Singh Sabha ideas or attitude is not visible in the case of any Sikh leader. The leader of the Amritsar Singh Saba were *Sanatan* Sikhs who looked upon Sikhism as an offshoot of Hinduism. The leaders of the Lahore Singh Sabha devoted their energy to the assertion of a distinct identity of the Sikhs and their boundary demarcation from the Hindus. "Sikhism in danger" was a major part of their rhetoric. The British military officials were keen to promote separate identity and religious orthodoxy among the Sikhs for their own reasons.⁸

It must be added, however, that in the *Ghadar Movement* Harish Puri noticed in the Sikh Ghadarites "a romance of *shaheedi* (shahadat; martyrdom) imbibed perhaps from the Sikh tradition."⁹ The qualifying "perhaps" indicates that the author is not exactly aware of the Singh Sabha emphasis on martyrdom as an essential feature of the Sikh tradition. Dedication of "*tan, man* and *dhan* (body, mind and money)" comes from the Sikh Scripture. The legendary bravery of the Sikh warriors in the Sikh wars against the British was invoked by Kartar Singh Sarabha and Harnam Singh. There are other such examples, but there is no need to list them. The essential point is that the empirical evidence used by Harish Puri himself bears witness to the relevance of Sikh ideology for the Sikh leaders even though this relevance is denied in the formulation by Harish Puri.

More recently, Baba Sohan Singh Bhakna's *Meri Ram Kahani* has been published in a book form. It was originally serialized in 1930–31 in the *Akali Te Pardesi*, started by Master Tara Singh in the 1920s. Master Tara Singh had earned the displeasure of the British officials for helping the deputation of Canadian Sikhs in 1913. He organized large meetings in Lyallpur and the Rawalpindi area, at which resolutions were passed in support of the Sikhs in Canada. In any case, *Meri Ram Kahani* presents fascinating evidence on the relevance of the Sikh faith and Sikh ideology for Baba Sohan Singh Bhakna. He was not indifferent to religion. For him, religion and politics were two ways of serving mankind. His observations on religion in general, and the Sikh Panth, and his understanding of Baba Ram Singh's position call for serious attention.[10]

Finally, there is the issue of "methodology." The quantum and the nature of evidence, and the question of its interpretation are of obvious importance. For a meaningful interpretation of evidence on the Ghadar Movement, it is absolutely essential to study the Sikh movements of the colonial period in some depth, and that too in the light of the pre-colonial Sikh Movement. Impressions formed on the basis of "secondary" works can be misleading and remain more or less inadequate.

NOTES

1. Jagjit Singh, *Ghadar Party Lehar*, New Delhi: Navyug, 2000 (3rd. edn.), p.56.
2. Harish K. Puri, *Ghadar Movement: Ideology, Organisation and Stratergy*, Amritsar: Guru Nanak Dev University, 1993 (2nd. edn.), pp.5,57-8.
3. Harish K.Puri, 'Singh Sabha and Ghadar Movements: Contending Political Orientations', in *Ghadar Movement to Bhagat Singh: A Collection of Essays*, Chandigarh: Unistar, 2012, pp. 44-7.
4. Ibid., pp. 47-50.
5. Ibid., pp. 50-9.
6. J.S. Grewal, *The Sikhs of the Punjab* (The New Cambridge History of India, II.3), Cambridge : Cambridge University press 1990, pp. 153-6.

7. Harish K.Puri, *Ghadar Movement : A Short History*, New Delhi : The National Book Trust, India, 2011, pp. xi-xiii, 14.
8. Ibid., pp. 11-13.
9. Ibid., p. xvi.
10. Baba Sohan Singh Bhakna, *Meri Ram Kahani*, ed., Rajwinder Singh Rahi, Samana : Sangam publications, 2012.

Sikh Pioneers in North America and the Crisis of Leadership

Dr. Amrik Singh

After Sikh pioneers settled in North America, they set up their social, religious, and political institutions. The role of Prof. Teja Singh, a Harvard alumnus, in organizing the community according to principles of Sikhism was noted among Punjabi settlers. He prepared them to face extreme discrimination of the racists with determination and urged them to live their lives as true Sikhs. As an authority on Sikhism, Teja Singh took no recourse to racial theories prevalent at that time. The very principle of race (Aryan) and caste becomes antithetical to the Sikh principle and the Ideal Indian Nationalism. But when Professor Teja Singh left the scene, Sikhs of North America fell into the in trap of "race diplomats," who used them for continuous financial support for a cause that was evidently pro-Aryan and anti-Sikh. In the subtle hands of the British, race diplomats became "reciprocal rebels, or freedom fighters." Without the tacit patronage of the British rulers, the Indian National Congress, Arya Samaj, and Singh Sabha movements could not have flourished. The British encouraged them to certain defined limits of conduct so that reciprocal rebels could create Alternative Indian Nationalism under the overall supervision of the British Empire.

The history of Pacific Coast Khalsa Diwan Society recorded campaigns of reciprocal "freedom fighters" who mostly used the rhetoric to deceive Sikhs both financially and ideologically. Sikhs' organizations on the Pacific coast appropriated the Khalsa legacy and made their mark in the agricultural economy of the US. As they were guided by Cambridge and Harvard educated Sant Teja Singh, they flourished socially and religiously. But as he left the scene, the race diplomats came in and impressed upon Sikhs to adopt race paradigm for their personal and social growth. It not only made them a living contradiction of their glorious legacy but also rendered them helpless victims in the hands of reciprocal freedom fighters.

In his book *Colored Cosmopolitanism: The Shared Struggle for Freedom in the United States and India,* Nico Slate records:

"The phrase 'pure-blood Hindus' was linked to caste by Akhay Kumar Mozumdar, the first Indian to gain naturalization on the West Coast. While obliquely referring to the same racial arguments that had bolstered the claims of Dolla and Balsara, Mozumdar relied more heavily on the racial purity of his ancestral caste-based lineage, implying that such purity made him 'more white' than most other Indians in the United States. Mozumdar stated, 'I am a high-caste, or ruling caste.' He distinguished himself from other Indians in America on the basis of caste, class, and religion. Mozumdar argued, 'The great bulk of the Hindus in this country are not high-caste Hindus, but are what are called sihks, [sic] and are of mixed blood.' Emphasizing the class, and religious differences between him and the 'mixed blood' Sikhs, Mozumdar stated, 'The laboring class, those who do the rough manual labor, are not high-caste Hindus at all, but are in an entirely separate class, having quite a different religion and a different ancestry.' He concluded, 'The high-caste Hindus always consider themselves to be members of the Aryan race.' Largely accepting his claim to racial purity and thus superiority, the court granted Mozumdar citizenship."[1]

When Punjabi pioneers started coming to the West, Punjab was a very active center not only for the Great Game of the British but also for Christian missionaries, Hindu sects, Sikh heretics, and secret lodges of freemasons and theosophical society. The object of all these societies was to create imaginary profiles of Sikhs for the consumption of the general Indian public and to a large extent of the western world. The purpose was to disable Sikhs' political leadership and strengthen imaginary religious identity for the obvious consumption of the Sikh soldier. Right at the time when migration started, Kooka movement and Dalip Singh's rebellion had occupied British leadership from top to bottom. The persecution of Kooka activists had again started the course of Sikh martyrdom. Dalip Singh's attempts to unify all fronts of Indian public against the British had wide-ranging effects on the

---

1 Nico Slate, Colored Cosmopolitanism: The Shared Struggle For Freedom in the United States and India (Cambridge, MA: Harvard University Press, 2012) 30

British to pioneer a political movement that could shock absorb the rising nationalistic energy. The British used the services and expertise of the secret societies to start an alternative freedom movement. Theosophical Society, with the active funding from Maharaja of Kashmir, took up an active role at the international level to start a series of actions, the purpose of which was to exhaust, isolate, and malign any movement that would follow the path of Ideal Indian Nationalism. Therefore, all reform movements and political campaigns in India started with the establishment of Theosophical Societies all over the world.

Madam Helene Blavatsky, a close confidante of Gulab Singh Dogra, the ruler of newly carved Kashmir State, and favorite friend of his son, Ranbir Singh, moved to India after being naturalized as American citizen in 1879. Colonel Henry Steel Olcott (1832–1907), the son of Presbyterian parents, accompanied her to Bombay. Maharaja of Kashmir, Ranbir Singh, had already set up contacts, programs, plans for launching secret missions at the global level. They set up Society's International Headquarters at Adyar, a suburb of Madras, where it has been still functioning. They visited Sri Lanka and defined Buddhism in their own way to Sri Lankans.

Theosophical Society got worldwide support from high-ranking officials of the British Empire, European establishments, and American political institutions. Along with secretive support of American and European leaders, the society also promoted its interests among journalists, intellectuals, artists, social scientists, spiritualists, anthropologists, rebels, anarchists, and harbingers of a universal government for the entire planet. Its specialization, in identifying the role of the Aryan race, in running the world, intrigued people across diverse interests. Theosophists' work among the Irish rebels, Russian lefts, and Indian activists ranged from high recognition to unending controversies. The society is credited with not only creating alternative political movements in different countries but also pioneering alternative religious movements mainly among South Asian religions. Its quick rise invited attention worldwide. When Punjabi pioneers came, theosophical societies had already created the imaginary profile of turban-wearing people among journalists and intellectuals. They regarded them only as Hindus, an Aryan outlook on all people of South Asia, the future subjects of the British-Hindu Empire.

"After, his two major co-founders departed for India in late 1878 to establish the international headquarters of the Society in Adyar, India, young attorney William Quan Judge diligently carried on the work of advancing interest in Theosophy within the United States. By 1886 he had established an American Section of the international Society comprised of branches in fourteen cities. Rapid growth took place under his guidance, so that by 1895 there were 102 American branches with nearly six thousand members."[2]

It is pertinent to mention here that, in 1885, the Theosophical Society played a crucial role in deflating Maharaja Dalip Singh's rebellion against the Raj on the one hand and creating a model of Alternative Indian Nationalism in the shape of Indian National Congress and the Arya Samaj. The use of occult, Mahatma, and the prophecy of the World Guru were all attempts to drain Punjab of Nankian dictum "brotherhood of mankind" and hoist all its universal principles on the British Empire. It was a new knowledge that the British obtained by promoting Anglo-Vedic Aryan sensibility, and over the course of time, it dismantled brick by brick what the Sikh soldier had achieved for Maharaja Ranjit Singh.

Annie Besant, president of Theosophical Society after Blavatsky, had a founding influence on M. K. Gandhi ever since she met him for the first time in England. Besant became the President of Indian National Congress in 1917. She quite often hinted at a world government and a World Guru in her addresses. "[. . .] We cannot in the Society permit any to be excluded, and the very moment that our General National Society excluded from its membership those who hold a particular belief, the belief in the near coming of a World Teacher, it was impossible that that National Society should continue to represent the Theosophical Society in Germany."[3]

Summing up views of Mrs. Annie Besant, Dr. H. N. Stokes demarcates how Christian ideals are coterminous with Vedic religions, and how the archetype of Great Teacher will establish lost authority for Hindus and will provide spiritual and temporal power to the British Empire. He states: "As Mrs. Besant says, we are confronted with the alternatives of self-sacrifice or revolution. The situation is wholly unique. We must either drift into intellectual and social anarchy or all of these forces must be whipped into line; they must be united into one harmonious movement for the realization of Theosophical—and that means Christian—ideals. And now a new idea

---

2 The official website of Theosophical Society in America. https//www.theosophical.org/about-us/1040 Retrieved on June 17, 2012. an
3 Annie Besant, *Super-Human Men in History and Religion* (Whitefish, MT: Kessinger Publishing ,1996) 131.

comes to the front—that of a Great Teacher or Leader who shall extract the kernel from all of these different schools; who shall point out, in language which cannot be misunderstood, the simple underlying principles of all and their practical application; who shall possess the force, the genius, the personal magnetism which will make him heard, respected and, if possible, obeyed."[4]

Stokes reiterates Besant's apprehension of a metaphysical threat to Christian ideals. The situation is, according to him, very grievous, requiring either radical action or acceptance of self-annihilation. He interprets it as a theosophical test in which the inaction is merely "intellectual and social anarchy," whereas declaring a war on antithetical forces is one of the choices. Physical force will bring these in line with a harmonious Theosophical worldview. A Great Teacher, according to Besant, was coming, who would have a magnetic personality possessing the force and genius to have power over the whole world. To achieve the power, Besant gives a theosophical interpretation to the Anglo-Vedic religions. The imaginary theorization results in an archetype of a World Teacher who is both "Christ in Christendom and Krshna in India." Besant writes: "They cannot understand how these strange likenesses to Christianity appear in a pre-Christian form of worship. They do not dream that the secret lies in the fact that it was the same World-Teacher who is the central Object of devotion in both, who is worshipped under the name of Krshna in India as He is worshipped under the name of Christ in Christendom. His great mission as the Christ was to the fifth sub-race of the Aryan people, those who spread over northern and Western Europe, and these fourth and fifth sub-races intermingle one with the other, and you find the great faith of Christianity dominating them both."[5]

The ruling principle of Besant's Indian Nation is Aryan hegemony. All other religions, nationalities, ethnicities, and races should conform to the Anglo-Vedic Empire. She asserts that she dreams of a time when India will help to build the Empire with that genius for statesmanship and clear insight which are found from time to time in great Indian ministers. These qualities will be utilized, according to her, for the good of the Empire, for the good of the mighty whole of which India is a part. "The times are gone by for

---

4   Dr. H.N.Stokes, "Moses and Prophets" in American Theosophist Magazine October 1913 to March 1914.(Kessinger publishing, 2003) 30-31
5   Annie Besant, *Theosophist Magazine*, July 1913-September 1913(Whitefish, MT: Kessinger Publishing, 2003)849.

small nations, for petty States, and for little peoples. The tendency now is towards raising a vast realm, united by common aims and common love. India should aid to build such an Empire, should help to bear its burdens and share its responsibilities. I dream of a time when India, England, Australasia and Canada will all join hands in the making of a common Empire, when India's children will bring their priceless treasures to the enriching of the Empire."[6]

Besant's Empire is a "mighty whole" in which India will seek its destiny not as an independent nation but a part of the British Empire. Writings of Gandhi and Nehru use theosophical rhetoric to express their views of Indian nation. While they talk about "Sawraj," glory of the Hindu past, and the birth of a new India, they strictly observe boundaries set by Western theosophists.

Alternative Indian Nationalism, promoted by Theosophical Society, had initially no place for Muslims. Indian National Congress, since its inception in the lap of Theosophy in 1885, enrolled for the first time any Muslim member in 1906. Their enrolment was more for striking a strategic alliance than for blending them in the mosaic of emerging nationalism. Punjab remained disturbed because it couldn't find outlines of the Ideal Indian Nationalism that could make Sikhs an integral part of national life. Memories of cultural integration of Muslims, Hindus, and Sikhs in Sovereign Punjab had not been completely erased from their memories. Sikhs could pose a threat by genuinely uniting Muslims, Hindus, Buddhists into a nation that would give them freedom to practice their faith without fear of conforming to the "mighty whole." In one of the reports from commissioners, inspectors, and other authority figures of the British Raj, the official identifies the regulation of the Sikh factor, an essential component of the British Empire:

> *The North Western Front Province and the Punjab divide India from Afghanistan and Central Asia. The Punjab has for year been ground for the Indian Army and to-day enjoys the same period of eminence. Of its population, 55 percent, is Muslim, 33 percent, Hindu, and 11 percent, is Sikh. But the most martial section is the Sikh, which during the present war, with less than one/100th of the population, has supplied about one-sixth of the fighting forces of the Indian Empire. The Punjab, however, has by no means escaped*

---

6 Annie W. Besant, The birth of new India (Adyar, India: Theosophical Publishing House) 106

> *revolutionary contagion, and our brief narrative must commence with the early months of year 1907 when as was noted at the time, by Sir Denzil Ibettson, the Lieutenant Governor, everywhere people were sensible of a change, of a "new air" which was blowing through men's minds and were waiting to what would come of it. It will be remembered that at this time the Jugantar and similar publications were pouring forth their poison among thousands in Bengal, while Alipore and Dacca conspirators were laying their plans, recruiting their ranks and collecting their weapons. It is not surprising that simultaneously new ideas should be fermenting elsewhere in India.*[7]

There was a great discontentment in Punjab, especially among the peasants who were deprived of their lands and means of subsistence. They looked for new pastures due to rising economic strain, stifling religious censuring, and disturbing stereotyping. As has been pointed out before, their overrepresentation in the Indian military compelled the British to design policies in which they could leave no aspect of Sikhs' life unregulated. Since Arya Samaj had generated a lot of heat in the past decades against them, there was no dearth of anti-Sikh volunteers to proliferate in their private and public life. There was always a voice that appealed to their religious, social, and political consciousness. The universal unity of all people always intrigued them, as the very principle is inalienably rooted in the Sikh scriptures. Calls to fight for rights of others can easily hook them even to stake their lives. The British benefited greatly from such a character of the Sikh soldier. The Battle of Saragarhi epitomizes the unfailing courage of Sikhs against all odds. The Hindu leaders of the newly born "freedom struggle" from 1885 to 1947, instead of benefiting from sacrifices of the militant Sikhs, only used it for raising their (Hindus') bargaining power at the doorsteps of the British Raj for a flawed and fractured nationalism. From the role of Dogras in Anglo-Sikh wars to Hindu nationalists of Gadhar and Gandhian movements, they flattered the Sikh militant only to an extent where the cause of Hindu nationalism is espoused, and the militant agent is destroyed within. The patterns that emerge from such a process are typical and trendy. The Hindu nationalist operates in two domains to achieve his illegitimate goals. He will either act as an *agent*

---

7 Reports from Commissioners, Inspectors, and Others, Great Britain, Parliament, House of Commons Session 12 Feb.1918- 21 Nov. 1918 (London: His Majesty's Stationery Office, 1918) viii, 60.

provocateur or a *reciprocal rebel*. The role of the first is to lend violent energy to the targeted movement. The objectives of the provocateur are to take the movement to a premature climax, and then get out of its direct and destructive trajectory. The moment the provocateur leaves, the reciprocal rebel gets in with all pretensions to statesmanship.

The age of reciprocal rebel starts with Ram Mohan Roy and Dwarkanath Tagore in the beginning of the nineteenth century. They visualized a royal role for themselves in manipulating secret desires of both the British and Muslim elites. Therefore, they offered their services to bring down the last hurdle in the British's way, the sovereign Panjab under Maharaja Ranjit Singh. They carve a role for themselves as reciprocal rebels.

"The most articulate advocate of European colonization was Rammohun Roy, who, with Dwarkanath in agreement, viewed the question in the broad context of India's history and future place in International society . . . Rammohun expected the most recent among the conquerors, the British, to follow the pattern and foresaw, in time, an India that was Christian (if not in the formal sense, at least in an ethical sense), modernized, prosperous, and, in some measure, associated with England. The Indian Empire of the future was to be a realm of British-Indian partnership in all spheres—political, economic, and cultural."[8]

At the beginning of their rule, the British had many ambitious plans. The foremost was to learn classical and vernacular languages, and then ameliorate the lot of millions of Untouchables who had suffered centuries of brutal treatment at the unjust hands of high-caste Brahmins and their collaborators (both foreign and domestic). The British brought the best vernacular teachers to teach Europeans Indian languages and cultures. But Ram Mohan Roy and Dwarkanath Tagore found it unsavory for their future alliance with Europeans. If the trend wasn't checked, India would have leadership from oppressed classes collaborating with Europeans. It was not only detrimental to hegemony of the upper-castes but was considered a threat to the Vedic language and culture. Roy and Tagore used the current circumstances to their advantage. They knew the British's secret desire to colonize Panjab was ruling their consciousness in the 1800s. They found a very welcoming entry into British rulers' minds. The second entry they made was lobbying for opening English schools in a big way. The Europeans who offered themselves

---

8   Blair B. Kling, *Partner in Empire: Dwarkanath Tagore and the Age of Enterprise in Eastern India*(Berkeley: University of California Press,1976) p.25

to be taught vernacular now were asked to teach Indians English and western cultures. The core of this alliance remained dominant ever since 1820 to the current times.

The British not only recognized Roy and Tagore as partners in the rising Empire but also allowed them freedom to publically criticize the Europeans so that they could become popular among unsuspecting masses. Tagore performed this role much better than Roy, and that is why succeeding generations of Tagores had been benefitting on both fronts (the white ruler and the masse leader). This reciprocity existed behind the scenes, and that is why India, in spite of experiencing great bouts of insurgencies, couldn't transform the radical energy into a new political system like Russia did in 1917 after World War One and China did after the Second World War in 1949.

The British developed multiple profiles of the "Reciprocal Rebel" and found it a very ingenious way to control mass consciousness. Reciprocal rebel replicates in all fields: anarchism, extremism, and communism, all varieties of nationalisms, sectarianism, and pacifism. The political scene may create the illusion of great uprising, but the ruler remains confident of his directorial role, both in creating the movement and suppressing the movement. The age of the Reciprocal Rebel starts with Roy and Tagore, and it is at its height of glory today.

Despite his leadership of the loyal opposition and his impassioned criticism of the administration, the Government of India encouraged Dwarkanath's civic activities and accorded him special honors. For one reason, British rule over the subcontinent was still incomplete. The Marathas had only recently been conquered, the Sikhs were strong and independent and the Russians were threatening the vulnerable northwestern frontier. Bengal, led by its loyal, reliable zamindars, was, in this period, the pillar of the Raj. Dwarkanath, the representative zamindar, might criticize the government, but he did so as an insider, a confidant of governors-general, a man whose social position and fortune depended on the British . . . In the age of evangelical humanitarianism it was necessary to clothe colonial activities with morality and to justify the East India Company as an agent of civilization. Dwarkanath was the symbol of the success of the company's government . . . He must be encourage in everyway, *held up for emulation as a man who would lead his people in the paths of westernization and loyalty.*⁹

A reciprocal rebel, also a theosophist overtly or covertly, is a trained revolutionary who is skilled in matters of civil rights, freedom, liberty, and fraternity. He theorizes on these issues and can easily pass for a genius. Lala Lajpat Rai's stay in America from the beginning of the Ghadr in 1914 to the times after Jallianwala massacre in 1919 makes a very interesting study of his activities. He was idolized by *The New York Times* twice. But after America's participation in World War I, he becomes controversial. Theosophical circles give him prominence which even talented Americans couldn't have had dreams of. On his return to India, Rai presides over the Calcutta session of the Congress and supports Gandhi's non-cooperation movement. The theater of his deportation changed to nationalism of Gandhi's dreams. His staunch revolutionary friend Ajit Singh could not adapt to the reciprocity and, therefore, was forgotten and thrown out of the memory.

In his book *The Wilsonian Moment: Self-Determination and the International Origins of Anticolonial Nationalism*, Erez Manela points out that Lajpat Rai set to work immediately upon arrival, traveling the country from Boston to New Orleans to Chicago to San Francisco. "Armed with letters of introduction from the British social reformer Sidney Webb, Lajpat Rai visited with progressive intellectuals at Columbia, Harvard, Stanford, and the University of California, Berkeley, as well as with Indian 'emigres in each locale.' Lajpat reported his impressions of the United States to readers in India in a book entitled *The United States of America: A Hindu's Impressions and a Study*, which was published in Calcutta in 1916."¹⁰

It is interesting to note how the rise of Woodrow Wilson in America in 1912 polarized major players of the Indian politics. Theosophists provided the central stage to deal with the Wilsonian impact in the international politics. Bal Gangadhar Tilk (1856–1920), Annie Besant, and Lala Lajpat Rai adopted the extremist line as a ploy to attract genuine freedom fighters into their circle of influence. On the other hand, Gandhi continued working on the pacifistic line of actions. Both groups controlled almost 85% of the popular opinion

---

9   Blair B. Kling, *Partner in Empire: Dwarkanath Tagore and the Age of Enterprise in Eastern India*(Berkeley: University of California Press,1976) p.167
10   Erez Manela, The Wilsonian Moment: Self-Determination and the International Origins of Anticolonial Nationalism (New York: Oxford University Press, 2007) 87.

of the masses. The effort of all groups was to save India for Anglo-Aryan trilogy against any empowerment of Shudra as it had taken place in the rise of Maharaja Ranjit Singh. The result of these efforts was the Lucknow Pact.

As Erez Manela has suggested, Tilk started organizing movement for Indian home rule in 1916 by incorporating Home Rule League with branches across the country. Annie Besant, who, though not a native Indian, served in 1917 as the INC president, also established a home rule league of her own, which sometimes collaborated and sometimes competed with Tilk's as it also set out to enlist grassroots support for self-government. But Besant stopped short of advocating Indian independence, asking only that India be a "Free Nation within the British Empire, under the Imperial Crown of His Majesty the King-Emperor George V and His successors."[11]

British's missive to the US authorities on Besant's support for Indian Home Rule was characterized as a mere ploy to trap the imagination of freedom-loving Indians. The same could be said about two groups: pacifists and extremists, in the National Congress and Hindu Mahasabha. Since Theosophical Society coordinated movements of all leaders, it made sure that no leader should cross the line by genuinely demanding complete freedom. Tilk's "Sawraj is my birthright" only meant some civil rights within the British Empire.

Clarifying it further, Manela underlines how the Indian nationalists tried to negotiate the emergence of the Wilsonian moment and launched what he called "concerted efforts to enlist support of "world opinion," and especially American opinion, on behalf of their cause. Besant's arrest for circulating copies of Wilson's war address helped their efforts, since it raised a furor among American theosophists, who launched a public campaign for her release and denounced Britain's "jailor's regime" in India. The pro-Besant campaign also caused some consternation at the British embassy in Washington, which attempted to neutralize it by telling the US authorities that Besant's support for Indian Home rule was not genuine but rather little more than a ploy calculated to attract Indians to the religion of which she was a "high priestess."[12]

The Wilsonian moment made Lala Lajpat Rai work with African American leader W.E.B Du Bois. Lala's deep-rooted faith in Aryan superiority

---

11 Erez Manela, The Wilsonian Moment: Self-Determination and the International Origins of Anticolonial Nationalism (New York: Oxford University Press, 2007)
12   ----ibid, 84.

was clearly contradictory to the interests of blacks to whom he equated with Dalits. Arya Samaj, as a reform movement, turned anti-Sikh; it maligned the founder of Sikhism, Nanak, and other saints as illiterate and unfit to question Aryan ideology. Swami became harsher towards Guru Nanak and other saints simply because some of them hailed from "Shudra" (Untouchable) backgrounds. Lajpat Rai's activism with black leaders in America was, therefore, merely "a ploy" to make an implied statement against Woodrow Wilson's liberalism, and thus to get accolade from their British masters via theosophical society. Lala Lajpat Rai's attitude towards Sikh pioneers in the United States was not different, as it was that of his mentor Swami Dayananda. Manela points out that, while traveling across the United States, Lajpat Rai also met numerous Indian revolutionaries but found most of them, with a few exceptions, uncouth, misguided, or simply corrupt. He was especially critical of their efforts to establish contacts with German agents, who they hoped would supply them with funds and arms to organize resistance against the British.[13]

The majority of Indian revolutionaries, at that time, were Sikhs. One of the leading Ghadrite Baba Jawala Singh, the founder of Stockton Sikh Temple and provider of the Guru Gobind Singh scholarship for students from India, belonged to Kumahar caste (one of the untouchable castes of Punjab). Lajpat Rai's dismissal of Indian revolutionaries as "uncouth, misguided, or simply corrupt" speaks of his hatred for "wretched of the earth."

In her book, *The Lives of Agnes Smedley*, Ruth Price comments on anti-Sikh prejudice that Agnes Smedley noticed while closely interacting with Lala Har Dayal, Lala Lajpat Rai, many Bengali intellectuals, and high-caste Punjabis. She writes:

> *In California, where the majority of America's two hundred thousand unskilled Asian immigrants lived, the nation's racist xenophobia was most extreme, and legislation was currently under consideration that would eliminate already tightly restricted Asian immigration entirely. Working-class laborers, middle-class progressive reformers, and even the Socialist Party looked down on California's Asian community as racially inferior, unassimilable, and a threat to wages. Of all the state's detested Asian populations, none was more reviled than the "ragheads"—the derisive*

---

13   -Manela,---ibid, 88-89.

term by which the Sikhs, who comprised the overwhelming majority of California's Indian immigrant population, were known. Stigmatized, ridiculed, and bullied for maintaining their customs in America, discriminated against in theaters, restaurants, and hotels, charged higher rents than Caucasians for substandard housing in undesirable sections of town they faced the most limited opportunities for work and the lowest wages of all Asian immigrant groups. Having made greater peace with her racial identity than with the working-class background she still battled to escape, Agnes found it easier to identify with California's beleaguered Asian community than with Bay Area Socialists who wore buttons urging workers of the world to unite while simultaneously advocating Asian exclusion.[14]

Lala Lajpat Rai in his role as a reciprocal rebel takes things too far where it becomes hard for him to maintain the façade of a secular nationalist. His seven-year stay in the US among scores of theosophists was part of the British Empire's international clout through diverse forms of art, literature, and emancipatory ideologies. The most important point is that all Indian nationalists sink their mutual differences when the route to Hindu nationalism started emerging. The Lucknow Pact of Bal Gangadhar Tilk in 1916 and Gandhi's support to Khilafat agitation prepared grounds for post-Jallianwala alliance to rather look for mutually exclusive nationalisms: Hindu India and Muslim Pakistan. The understanding might have reached with the British administration through offices of Theosophical Society. The British's identification of the trail left by the Ghadr movement as the model of Ideal Indian Nationalism might have prompted them to encourage sectarian interests. Otherwise, why would the British Raj allow Hindu and Muslim elites to own the Jallianwala site, for their mutually agreed flawed Indian Nationalism? Finding it impossible to suppress people of Punjab, the British paved the way for an Alternative Indian Freedom movement to take birth in the blood-soaked and haloed land of Jallianwala Bagh. In his book *The Butcher of Amritsar: General Reginald Dyer*, Nigel Collett reconstructs all background circumstances to analyze what actually led to the massacre of Jallianwala Bagh.

---

14 Ruth Price, The Lives of Agnes Smedley (New York: Oxford University Press, 2005) 44-45.

"On 14 February 1920 an appeal was launched for a Jallianwala Bagh Memorial Fund, and this was to play a part in Indian consciousness similar to that which the Dyer fund played in the British. 'We are glad to inform the public that the Jallianwala Bagh has now been acquired for the nation.' At a cost of 540,000 rupees, a committee including Gandhi, Madan Mohan Malaviya, Motilal Nehru, Swami Shraddhanand, Harkishan Lal, Kitchlew and Girdhari Lal purchased for the nascent Indian nation a focus of martyrology that would help to light and keep lit the flame of independent nationalism."[15]

One fails to understand that these very leaders had given a call of *hartal* and extended it to coincide with Sikhs' national festival of Vaisakhi, their arrest before the appointed date led to all disturbances, then under what circumstances the British make them custodians of the historical site? Where was the consent of 10 million Sikhs and 70 million Shudras?

Lala Lajpat Rai's time spent in the US was for building American opinion in favor of the British rule in comparison to that of the German on the one hand, and in favor of more rights under the overall control of the British administration on the other. Besant, Tilk, and Rai all concurred on getting partial rights for Indian citizens. This brings into focus questions about Rai's strident rhetoric against the British rule in his writings. It may be due to the Aryan trilogy of three seemingly unrelated elements, which actually work in perfect coordination underneath. The three elements, Theosophical Society, Indian National Congress, and the conglomerate of Hindu radicals, followed patterns that touched the imagination of the majority of the uneducated masses. Inassimilable Sikhs and Muslims were dangled as targets of the Aryan trilogy.

The British made sure the two (Sikhs and Muslims) should never identify with their common language, common belief (Sufism), and their common territory. Instead, hatred was encouraged in such a manner that Hindus might look like helpless victims of Muslim fundamentalism. This was to stimulate the historical memory of Sikhs as Hindus' savior during times of Aurangzeb, Nadar Shah, and Ahmad Shah Abdali. In the absence of strong political leadership, Sikhs again fell into the trap of hatred during partition in 1947. The natural consequence of their action was more embarrassment

---

15 Nigel Collett, The Butcher of Amritsar: General Reginald Dyer (New Delhi: Rupa & Co., 2005) 399.

to themselves, and the immorality of their acts could neither be sanctified culturally nor religiously.

Coming back to India, Rai presides over the specially convened Calcutta session of the Indian National Congress in 1920. His seven years in the US during World War I, Peace Conference in Paris, and Jallianwala Bagh massacre had great significance for starting a new course of action. With the death of Tilk in 1920, the Gandhian era started right with the ownership of the Jallianwala Bagh site in Amritsar where in December 1919 Congress annual session was held with great exhibition of Hindu-Muslim political relations. British recognized efforts of national leaders strictly for a limited Swaraj. Without this oblique understanding, the British could never have dared to strike at Jallianwala Bagh.

Jallianwala massacre was more to send symbolic message to the Sikhs of Ghadr movement and other villagers who were ready to join in any prospective and unregulated revolt. In Punjab, Rai continued to act as a patriot for complete freedom. Punjab was not aware of what he wrote to the US President Woodrow Wilson about granting freedom to India. Manela points out those colonial nationalists were looking for only extra concessions from their rulers. He writes, "Like other colonial nationalists, Indians also commonly held up US colonial rule in the Philippines at the time not as a blemish on the American record but as a model, which the British would do well to follow. Already in 1916, a review of Lajpat Rai's book on the United States published in Tilk's nationalist weekly, *Mahratta,* recommended that every patriotic Indian, as well as British colonial officials, study the chapter in the book that dealt with US rule in the Philippines as an example of colonial benevolence . . . And shortly after the armistice, Lajpat Rai wrote Wilson that India should be granted 'at least such progressive measures of Home Rule as the present administration has established in the Philippines.'"[16]

Philippines remained a colony of the US from 1898 to 1946. More than 100,000 Filipino nationalists died to free their islands from US control. The American War lasted until 1902, and an estimated 4,500 Americans died in the conflict. As the first colony of the US, the Philippines had invited a lot of criticism from both within and without. Rai's example of Philippines as the perfect model of freedom was not only a setback for Filipino nationalists but also for Ghadris who were fighting for total overthrow of the British from India.

---

16 Manela---92.

Indian National Congress, in its Delhi session in December 1918, adopted a resolution that appealed for the application of self-determination to India. "'In view of the pronouncements of President Wilson, Mr. Lloyd George, and other British statesmen, that to ensure the future peace of the world, the principle of Self-Determination should be applied to all progressive nations,' the INC demanded that India be recognized by the powers as 'one of the progressive nations to whom, the principle of self-determination should be applied.' The congress further urged that elected delegates represent India at the peace table, and it proceeded to nominate Tilak, Gandhi, and the Muslim leader Syed Hasan Imam as its delegates to the conference."[17]

Lala Lajpat Rai, an Arya Samaji, in his typical role of a Reciprocal Rebel, secured the position of a patriot in popular public parlance. But he remained in the United States from 1914–1919 on a very subtle and specific mission. Reciprocity of the British and the Indian National Congress was quite visible when a special session of the party was convened in his honor.

His two other devout followers, Lala Hardayal and Bhai Permanand, took up the opposite roles. In New York, Rai acted pro-British in the conflict between Great Britain and Germany. His India Home League of America was to show support of his community to the British. Lala Har Dayal, however, acted as a pro-German agent, an implacable enemy of the British. With all his posturing, Har Dayal won the trust of the German leaders. With scores of other bodies working simultaneously, their goal was to influence American public opinions against the Germans. By capitalizing on the popular discontent of Sikhs, they aroused Sikhs' sentiments against the British and thus provided evidence in shape of the German-Hindu Conspiracy for United States to jump in World War I.

But after the end of World War I, the British Empire never before felt as anxious and overwhelmed as when President Woodrow Wilson put forward his 14 points at the peace conference. The empire's wide-ranging influence within America also didn't bear desired fruits. It was primarily because President Wilson, being professor and then President of Princeton University, had tremendous capacity to influence others more than to be influenced by them. Later, as Governor of New Jersey, Wilson liked furrowing his own row. President Wilson may be the only president to have given perturbing time to the narcissistic British leaders. Manela states:

---

17   ----96.

> *British officials were gravely concerned about the effect that US influence at the peace table would be very difficult for the British, Montagu had noted even before the armistice, not to "fall in line" with the US program at the war's end given Wilson's preponderant power. "We have been so long accustomed to dictate to the world . . . our position," he wrote, that it was "rather galling now that we find ourselves playing second fiddle to the autocratic ruler of the United States . . .*
>
> *They hoped that Wilson's influence there, and his apparent determination to reconstruct the world according to the principles of self-determination and the equality of nations, would force the hand of the British and other imperialists and compel them to give their colonial possessions, if not complete independence, then at least a much greater measure of self-government. British officials, on the other hand, remained determined to prevent any discussion of issues related to their empire at the peace conference, where the United States and its president could meddle with them.[18]*

The very idea of sending a delegation to the peace conference was very annoying to the British. Therefore, the British instantly rejected it. Gandhi and his associates right away stopped to flirt with the idea of sending a delegation to the peace conference. Punjab disturbances originated in 1907 and decreased to some extent with the repealing of the Punjab Government's Land Colonies Act, but it created a lot of awareness in peasants and soldiers of Punjab. It was during these disturbances that Ajit Singh came to the notice of the police. He appealed to Sikh soldiers to openly revolt against the repressive policies of the British. Lala Lajpat Rai, being an associate of Ajit Singh, is said to have been deported to Burma. But on his explanation, the British became compliant to his reciprocal rebellious activities.

Arguing about revolutionary movement in the Punjab before World War I, Lajpat Rai writes in his book *The Political Future of India* that it was nothing until Ghadr activists came back to Punjab. Rai tries to wash his hands off any involvement with Ajit Singh. Commenting on a report about Ghadr party, he points out the Sikhs of Vancouver's revolutionary zeal had nothing to do with Hardayal and Barkat Ullah as they were separated from Sikhs by

---

18   --97.

their "religions, habits and associations." In his judgment, Rai tries to club Hindu-Muslim nationalism opposed to more aggressive nationalism of the Sikhs. "The revolutionary movement in the Punjab amounted to nothing until it was reinforced by the return of the Sikh members of the Ghadr party during the war. The committee has failed to answer the question: why did the Sikhs of Vancouver and California readily fall in with the schemes of Har Dayal and Barkat Ullah, the alleged founders of the revolutionary party of California. These latter had nothing in common with the Sikhs. In language, and religion, by habits and associations, they were poles apart from each other. Why did then Har Dayal's propaganda find such a ready soil among the Sikhs of Vancouver, BC?"[19]

Rai, in his compliant tone, tries to convince his interlocutors that "the Indian soil and the Indian atmosphere are not very congenial for revolutionary ideas and revolutionary methods. The people are too docile, gentle, law-abiding and spiritually incline to take to them readily. They are by nature and tradition neither vindictive nor revengeful. Their general spirit is opposed to all kind of violence. They have little faith in the virtues of force. Unless they are provoked, and that too terribly, and are face to face with serious danger they do not like the use of force, even when recourse to it may be legal and morally defensible."[20]

Lajpat Rai's conciliatory and reciprocal appeal to the British is quite evident when he suggests them to trust educated leaders working among young radicals. He demands a leeway for mixing with revolutionaries so that intelligence for interests of the British Empire could be gathered. That is exactly how a reciprocal rebel wins over amateur radicals to his side so that they could be used/annihilated to further Anglo-Vedic interests. Rai, in an effort to convince the governing classes about his reciprocal role, emphasizes, "As to the duty of the educated leaders in the matter of suppressing the growth of the revolutionary movement in future, we beg to point out that all depends on how much faith the governing classes place in the professions of the popular leaders . . . It is not likely that the educated leaders will in any way consciously and voluntarily digress from the limits of reasonable criticism of Government policy, nor have they very often done so in the past. What has so far prevented the educated leaders from exercising an effective check on

---

19 Rai, Lajpat (Lala), *The Political Future of India* (New York: B.W. Huebsch, Inc., 1919) p166
20 Ibid., 184

the growth of the revolutionary movement is their inability to associate on terms of friendship with the younger generation."[21]

Commenting on page 61 of the investigation committee report in which Lajpat Rai was charged for providing shelter to a certain "Chatarji," he defends himself by referring to the report, "'Chatarji's father too had ordered him home on discovering that he was staying with Hardayal in the house of Lajpat Rai.' The whole of this statement is absolutely false. I am prepared to swear and to prove that Chatarji did not stay in my house even for a single night. He came there a few time with Hardayal." Talking about Amir Chand, one of the accused in the Delhi Conspiracy Case, Lajpat Rai says, "I have no doubt that he was rightly convicted in this case but I have no doubt . . . up till 1910 the man had led an absolutely harmless life . . . His revolutionary career began in 1908. Before that he could not and would not have tolerated even the killing of an ant, much less that of human beings." [22]

Gopal K. Gokhale's intervention to get Rai released speaks more of his Arya Samaj's solidarity with the Raj than with the national movement of which Ajit Singh was a part. Gokhale's stress on "monstrous injustice" refers to ineptness of the British administration in "bracketing" the two on the same plane. Gokhale is using Rai's reciprocity as the valid ground for his release. His statement implies that Ajit Singh belongs to a different "cult" which Rai has nothing to do with. S.C. Mittal in *Freedom Movement in Punjab* describes that Gopal Krishan Gokhale personally intervened for the release of Lajpat Rai and wrote a letter to Mr. Dunlop Smith, the Private Secretary to Viceroy, pleading that Lajpat Rai's arrest was unjustified: "To bracket Ajit Singh with Lajpat Rai is monstrous injustice to the latter. When I was in Lahore in February last Ajit Singh had already begun to denounce Lajpat Rai as a coward, and a pro-government man because Lajpat Rai would have nothing to do with Ajit Singh's propaganda."[23]

Pacific Coast Khalsa Diwan Society 1912

The history of Pacific Coast Khalsa Diwan Society, Stockton, California, is a fascinating account of trials and toils of Punjabis on the western coast. It also reveals how the British Empire weaved an intricate web just to deal with

---

21 Ibid, 185
22 Ibid., 165
23 S.C. Mittal, Freedom Movement in Punjab (Concept Publishing Company, 1977) 55

an insignificant number of natives of India. The British not only used racial connections and the propaganda of the highest order to deprive Punjabi peasants of the Pacific coast of any decent life, but also treated them inhumanly for a highly complex international plot. They survived organized criminal conspiracies against them through sheer community wisdom that they had brought with them from India. The peasants started coming at a time when their exiled King had died in 1893 after suffering indignities at the hands of usurpers of his Kingdom. The Britain regulated his life in collaboration with shrewd Brahmins and by influencing political ambitions of Muslim elites.

The epic struggle that started from the Pacific coast laid the foundation of the freedom struggle of India and also had international implications in World War I. In order to keep the Empire through criminal conspiracies and impact the mind of world leaders, the British disguised their intentions in writings of poets, novelists, students, and swamis. It had well laid out plan to involve the United States in World War I and also had a very subtle posturing to get information of Germans through exploiting revolutionary activities. It had also preemptive design to push genuine freedom lovers to the gallows with or without trials. The design appears to have been laid to quarantine Sikh soldiers in the British army for deterring rebellious elements. After Anglo-Sikh Wars and the 1857 mutiny, the British were so shaken that they knew their survival was due to Sikh soldiers' relentless encounters with the mutineers. Sikh soldiers' aggressiveness was more due to their humiliation at the hands of the Raj's Sepoy and the treachery of Dogras in control of the Sikh Raj. The design of the British in Anglo-Sikh wars of 1845–1849 was to provoke the Sepoy against the Sikh Soldier of the Sovereign Punjab; and in the same way the leaderless Sikh soldier of the annexed Punjab was incited against the mutineer Sepoy in 1857.

The British collaboration hinged on promises of ushering Hindus and Muslims to have their respective nations at the cost of other minorities. The deft collaboration continued in deceptive forms until promises were fulfilled even by supporting one of worst carnages in the modern history of the world. The matter didn't end there. The newly born nations kept up their bloody politics to deny civil liberties to their citizens. The attempt to control public opinion of the world leaders is continuing uninterrupted. The politics of crime in the name of the civilized world is still occupying their mind. No lessons have been learned. Instead, the same impoverished minorities are continuously being targeted to deny them their fundamental rights in their home countries and abroad.

The documents that have been maintained at Stockton Gurdwara reveal valuable information not only from the point of view of the Sikhs but also of the history of colonialism, wars, and genocides. The documents reveal how pioneers' hard-earned dollar was marked for supporting liberty both in their home and adopted countries. The contours of Ideal Indian Nationalism already hovered in their consciousness; therefore, it didn't take much time to work their energies towards its goal. In America, they saw the prototype of Ideal Indian Nationalism in the American Revolution; they fantasized of making India just the "United States of India." Their twin purposes were getting civil rights through legitimate ways in the land they toiled day and night, and putting their sincerest efforts to liberate the country of their birth from parasites of humanity. They tried to be in the forefront of talks of unity of a nation that only remained divided in the known history of mankind. The dream they saw on the Pacific coast was strong, and it could have turned the table, had they been a little more careful of the intentions of their agent provocateurs.

Disguised in robes of patriotism and religious piety, agent provocateurs aimed at their imaginary nation that would follow the mythical route to Manu Samriti and Chankayan politics of unethical means. Aims of collaborators and agent provocateurs could be achieved only through the agency of the theatrical and covert event management. The stage and equipment was meant for a worldwide stage. The players too were of diverse backgrounds but united integrally in defining the world in their own way. They succeeded in having enormous sway but felt deprived of knowledge that was required to keep their gifts.

Gadaris, Gadar Party, and Anglo-Vedic Games of the British

Dr. Amrik Singh

Historians experience a dilemma when they take up their pen to write the history of the Ghadr movement. It is mainly because there are myriad aspects to the story, and it becomes tough to negotiate the transnational nature of the subject. Even the most realistic narration tends to end up in the dark alley of hegemonic interpretations. The writing of Ghadr history, according to these versions, has to conform to the imaginary view of Indian Nationalism. Historians, both in the East and West, attempt to pick only selective details, which may make the whole narrative either very simplistic or just an aberration of irrationally excited minds. They avoid engaging the core of the problem and fail to explain the contours of a wonderful dream that made thousands of countrymen, mostly Sikhs, die for their country. Before embarking on their journey, many of them were baptized in Gurdwara Stockton, California. According to the Sikh tradition, when one takes a vow to offer one's head, the fear of death disappears. Ghadris knew only one thing—that they would die for their country—and they didn't even look back to see if the so-called organizers had any actual plans for the great revolt. When the dream of one's own nation was born, it found its path to love, commitment, and sacrifice. For the ones who were initially in the forefront and who stayed back, the dream was just chimerical. They tried to run away from it but could not ward off the shame that haunted them even in their graves. For others, it was to carry their heads on their palms and bring the butchers of the British Empire to Indian people's justice. They honored all their heroes of the past and left a legacy for the future that will keep on ringing notes of love, liberty, equality, and fraternity.

The dream was so powerful that those who had it were transformed. The youngest Kartar Singh Sarabha's passionate energy to inspire others was undeniably irresistible. His friend Vishnu Ganesh Pingley demonstrated a rare courage in rejecting an appeal for mercy. The iron-will of many others horrified the judge who had to report to Viceroy Lord Hardinge about their nonchalance and fearlessness. He personally intervened and commuted death sentences of 17 to life imprisonment. Seven of them kissed the noose on November 17, 1915, about nine months after the scheduled date of the Ghadr. Vishnu Ganesh Pingley was fearless and resigned to his fate; he didn't least think of disappointing his beloved friend Kartar Singh Sarabha. They, along with many others, rejected the advice of filing an appeal, engaging a lawyer, and requesting any relief. They demonstrated their will to outright reject colonial occupation of their country. Baba Jawala Singh, known as the Potato King, objected to the pronouncement of lesser punishment awarded in his own case in comparison to his other fellow beings. Baba Jawala Singh challenged judges to send him also to gallows. Such was their spirit, brotherhood, and unity for a nation of their dreams.

The young Sarabha wrote a poem before going to the gallows that urged countrymen never to hesitate to walk on the path of freedom with their heads on their palms. He appealed to his countrymen to keep them in their memory and also pointed out that mere high-flown language wasn't enough for the love of their country. Before going on his journey, he had witnessed the empty enthusiasm of some leaders who he knew wouldn't take their first step in the path of service to their country. The following poem was written by Sarabha who was among the first seven to be hanged to death:

> O Indians, do remember us when we leave.
> Never throw us out of your mind.
> we are kissing the noose for our country
> Don't get scared to see us this way
> Our death will fill hearts of our countrymen
> with unbounded love for our nation
> O countrymen, shine like moon
> don't let dark clouds overpower your spirits
> O friends, never betray your country

That will mean slur on the name your land.
Like Moola Singh, Kirpal Singh and the Nowab
And Amar Singh who betrayed the nation
Jails are colleges for the patriots
take admission and get degrees there
Dear brothers, follow the same path
to reach the abode where we are going.

Har Dayal

> *The English are on the whole a truthful people; that are perhaps their characteristic virtue. Whatever policy the State may adopt, the individual Englishman is a reliable person. He keeps his word. And the English Government also keeps faith with its friends, partly from policy, and partly from the national habit of truthfulness. The Englishman has acquired a reputation for truthfulness in Asia. The Englishman has acquired a reputation for truthfulness in Asia. Several years ago a hotel proprietor in a small island in the West Indies said to me: "The English are different from other people. If an Englishman says he will do a thing, you may be sure that he will do it." The English also trusts others, as he wishes that he should be trusted. —Lala Har Dayal*[1]

Har Dayal makes the above statement in 1918 in his book *Forty-four Months in Germany and Turkey*, which, critics interpret, was his abject surrender to the British Empire. He begs for amnesty and seeks for permission to go back to India. His grand betrayal made many Ghadris introspect the whole genesis of Ghadr Party and what took place subsequently. Har Dayal's book came out when his closest friends in the Ghadr were executed and sent to life imprisonment. He could not write a word for them who went to gallows bravely. Most of them were called ideologically Ghadris until then but had committed no crime to be awarded the death sentence. So much blood had been shed, but Har Dayal, instead of taking any responsibility, doled out brazen advice to remain subservient to the British for long. Har Dayal asked Ghadris to betray their cause: "It is to be hoped that these young Indian

---
1 Lala Har Dayal *Forty Four Months in Germany* P. 86

enthusiasts will also give up the fruitless revolutionary methods which have made them the dupes of cunning German imperialists during this war."[2] Ghadris had only one cause, and that was total freedom for their country.

The idea of German help and connections was thrown by Lala Har Dayal at the behest of Virendranath Chattopadhyay and Chandrakant *Chakarvarty*. Whatever money came from the Germans was invested by Pandit Ram Chandra and C. Chakravarty in real estate. It is a known fact that Germans' help was never rendered to Ghadris who went to the battlefield.

The blood of freedom fighters only prompts Har Dayal to say, "Now they must be awaked to the sober reality, which teaches them that their destiny is linked with that of the English people for a very long time to come."[3]

Historians have never analyzed his statement in the context of what happened during the World War I and the Ghadr movement. What is the "sober reality" and who are "They"?

Sober Reality: Is it that so many have been shot dead at Budge Budge, and so many hanged, and hundreds of Sikh soldiers fatally shot by the firing squads for allegedly showing tendency to mutiny? For Dayal these sacrifices, instead of kindling the patriotic fire, must awake them, and teach them the hard lesson of the greatness of the British Empire. Har Dayal is often addressed as a Hindu intellectual and sometimes even called the "Chanakya" of Indian freedom movement. Was he following Chanakya when he played as an *agent provocateur* for sending so many to gallows? We know Chanakya's advice to Chandargupta: "Son, one should never be too upright. You have just returned from a hunt in the forest, haven't you? Didn't you notice that it is always the straight trees that are cut down where the crooked ones are left standing? asked Chanakya."[4] By the time Har Dayal wrote *Forty-four Months*, the First World War had ended with 80,482 deaths of Indian soldiers in which a large section of Sikh soldiers was represented.

THEY: We must interpret Dayal's "They" as Ghadris who were mostly Sikhs of California. Lala had two sets of opinions about his "They." We know nothing about what he told his American friends, who were among socialists, members of Asian Exclusion League, Theosophical Society, Presbyterians, Unitarians, and associates of Vedanta Society. Much has been written about what Har Dayal told Sikhs on the Pacific coast in 1913 when he extensively

---

2   Ibid., 95.
3   Ibid., 96.
4   Ashwin Sanghi, Chanakya's Chant (Chennai: Westland Ltd., 2010) 419

traveled to deliver lectures and raise funds for the newly constituted Ghadr Party. However, very little attention has been given to analyze his interaction with Americans.

Dayal won wide support among Sikhs for what he preached to them. Many historians elevate Dayal, on the basis of his lectures and a few essays, as the founder, architect, and the engine of the Ghadr Party. In such attempts, they delink Ghadr from the history of riots of Bellingham, Everett, and many other places in California. They hide the role of Asian Exclusion League and some Swamis' complicity with AEL. They refer to the Honduras episode sketchily but don't consider it a major incident. They tend to overlook the role of Professor Teja Singh in organizing the Sikh community in England, Canada, and USA. They only start with Lala Har Dayal, Vinay Sarvarkar, and Ras Bihari Boss. In order to get the complete picture, we need to reconstruct the whole story in the original context as it developed following the constitution of the Ghadr party.

Har Dayal's white audience quite often rallied around him for his Anglo-Vedic knowledge. Theosophical Society and Vedanta Society were attracting Americans for eastern mysticism that was interpreted as the fulfillment of western ideals. When Dayal's mentor Lala Lajpat Rai came to the US, he was armed with many letters of introduction to officers of Theosophical Societies. Similarly, Lala Har Dayal had many such connections through secret societies. His views in these circles were different from what he preached among Sikhs of California. We owe it to Agnes Smedley who left some traces of Har Dayal's opinions among whites.

When Lala Har Dayal was served warrants, he was ready to deliver his lecture to about 200 Americans from different walks of life. Some accounts say they were socialists. Smedley, a young American girl who socialized with Lala Har Dayal, Lala Lajpat Rai, Bhagwan Singh, M. N. Roy, and Chattopadhya at different times and places, and who had very intimate relations with most of them, has profiled them in her writings. As an American, she notes their overall personality and frankly states her impressions about them. To Smedley, Har Dayal is a high-caste Hindu, who had low opinion about the very people who he wanted to lead. Apparently, he considered Sikhs as low caste, uneducated, and savage in their thinking. According to laws of Manu and Chanakya maxims, Shudras' aspiration of liberty, equality, and fraternity are threats to Aryan nobility which should be preemptively dealt with. These codes also sanction a highly devious plot in which "awakened

Shudra" could be exterminated in a manner that their murders should glorify the Arya's hegemony on the one hand and teach a hard lesson of sobriety on the other.

Smedley noticed that the nation's racist xenophobia was most extreme in the case of California's Sikhs, who were vilified as racially inferior, unassimilable, "unclean," and "ragheads." The working-class laborers, middle-class progressive reformers, and even the Socialist Party expressed their hatred for "Hindus," a derisive term for Sikhs. "Stigmatized, ridiculed, and bullied for maintaining their customs in America, discriminated against in theaters, restaurants, and hotels, charged higher rents than Caucasians for substandard housing in undesirable sections of town they faced the most limited opportunities for work and the lowest wages of all Asian groups . . . Agnes found it easier to identify with California's beleaguered Asian community than with Bay Area Socialists who wore buttons urging workers of the world to unite while simultaneously advocating Asian exclusion."[5]

The biographer of Agnes Smedley, Ruth Price, illustrates how Har Dayal discouraged her (Smedley) from joining with Sikhs in their struggle to oppose the *Land Alienation Act* by which they couldn't own or lease land. "Many Indian immigrants as citizens under the British Crown considered appealing their right to own property in the United States through British constitutional channels. Har Dayal, for one, believed such efforts were futile."[6]

High-caste Hindus who identified with the Anglo-Aryan principles were naturalized as citizens. As mentioned earlier, the case of Akhay Kumar Mozumdar, the first Indian to gain naturalization on the West Coast refers to the phrase "pure-blood Hindus." Mozumdar distinguished himself from other Indians and argued, "The great bulk of the Hindus in this country are not high-caste Hindus, but are what are called sihks [sic], and are of mixed blood." Emphasizing the class and religious differences between him and the "mixed blood" Sikhs, Mozumdar stated, "The laboring class, those who do the rough manual labor, are not high-caste Hindus at all, but are in an entirely separate class, having quite a different religion and a different ancestry." He concluded, "The high-caste Hindus always consider themselves to be

---

[5] Ruth Price, *The Lives of Agnes Smedley* (New York: Oxford University Press, 2005) 44-45.
[6] Ibid., 46.

members of the Aryan race." Largely accepting his claim to racial purity and thus superiority, the court granted Mozumdar citizenship.[7]

It should also be seen in the background of the Congressional Hearing on February 14, 1914, in which Dr. Sudhindra Bose's "Aryan" card was basically used to exclude all Asians due to their non-Aryan backgrounds and low-caste status. But since "pure-blood" Hindus were few and educated, there was no bar for their naturalization, as the court granted Mozumdar citizenship on that basis. Testimony of Bose at the Congressional Hearing was a major damage to the immigration of all Asians. The irony of the case is that Pacific Coast Khalsa Diwan Society Stockton sponsored and funded the delegation mistakenly believing Har Dayal and Bose to be their loyal representatives. Later, the American immigration and justice department unabashedly followed the Aryan interpretation to deny citizenship rights to low-caste Asians. Bhagat Singh Thind, being a Sikh, is understood to have lost his high caste and, therefore, was denied citizenship on the basis of these arguments.

It is a fashion with many historians to download the official version of the Ghadr movement and make it the final truth of the struggle for freedom. Such a version starts with Lala Har Dayal and ends up with his scholarly accomplishments for freedom, the meaning of which he had no imagination, commitment, and will to achieve. His writings appear to be thought provoking and genuine expression of feelings, but Har Dayal couldn't sustain his argument when he was interrogated by the immigration officials at Angel Island on March 26, 1914. "But he stated that violence was not the answer." Besides giving an anti-British statement for the press, Hardayal backs out of his earlier stand on an armed revolt against Britain. 200 Sikhs attended his hearing and paid $1000 for his bail. The immigration official interrogated him about his illegal use of the country for spreading his propaganda; Har Dayal suggested to the immigration official that he could leave for some other country if he couldn't preach in the US. Commissioner General of Immigration Caminetti admitted there was no legal jurisdiction to deport him. One fails to understand why Har Dayal suggested himself that he would do his propaganda from some other country. Why was no lawyer engaged, or insisted?

But it is very important to review the activities of Canadian Immigration Inspector William C. Hopkinson and Lala Har Dayal from January, 1914, to

---

7   Nico Slate, *Colored Cosmopolitanism: The Shared Struggle For Freedom in the United States and India* (Cambridge, MA: Harvard University Press, 2012) 30

March 28, when Har Dayal jumps the bail to leave for Switzerland. After the meeting of December 31, 1913, in Sacramento, all Ghadris go to Stockton to celebrate Gurpurb of Guru Gobind Singh. On January 3, 1914, they participate in the First Sikh Parade organized with special permission of the city mayor. To accommodate the big gathering, a special hall was booked. All members and recruits of the Ghadr party planned the next phase of their activities. Two options were put before members: they should either join the bandwagon of the Ghadr to overthrow British in India, or they should suffer indignities living in America. As the information about Anti-Hindu immigration bills in the US Congress by two congressmen of California and the signing of the Land Alienation Act was provided, the second option appeared unattractive and unrewarding. Laws for restricting immigration of South Asians became more and more stringent and punitive. But the Pacific Coast Khalsa Diwan Society differed with Lala Har Dayal's contention that there was no use of wasting time on American citizenship, because he thought nothing would come out of it.

At this time, Har Dayal was looking for maximum funds for the Ghadr party. But when a large number of people suggested that they shouldn't give up on the legal battle, Har Dayal promised to recommend names for the delegation for the congressional hearing. Erika Lee and Judy Yung state that in February 1914 Har Dayal appeared as part of a delegation of South Asians who travel to Washington, DC, to protest against congressional bills. But before this, on January 19, 1914, Har Dayal appeared in a San Francisco court requesting an application for US citizenship.[8] Maybe Har Dayal wanted to get citizenship for himself on the basis of his education and high-caste Hindu status. It takes place 20 days after the Sacramento Ghadr conference, in which the decision is made to go back to India for waging an armed struggle. But three days before this, on January 16, 1914, Har Dayal throws a dinner party for Ram Chandra in which he announced that he (Ram Chandra) would take over the editorship.[9] It shows Har Dayal was already preparing for his sudden exit from the scene and, at the same time, was trying to get American citizenship so that he could return without any hassles. Har Dayal

---

8   Erika Lee, Judy Yung, Angel Island: Immigrant Gateway to America (Oxford University Press, 2010) 167

9   James Campbell Ker, Political Trouble in India: 1907-1917 (Calcutta: Superintendent Government Printing Press, 1917) p. 236

unilaterally took decision to appoint Ram Chandra without taking anybody of the Ghadr party executive member in confidence.

Next, his trip to Washinton, DC, is jointly monitored by the British Embassy and the US immigration department. The request to issue a warrant for Har Dayal's arrest is initiated by the British Embassy, and the subsequent theater of his interrogation was also followed with the express knowledge of the British officials. It was very common with the British administration to arrest some of its collaborators so that they could win an honorable place in people's minds. As the British Embassy had once convinced the US State Department that Annie Besant's arrest in India was merely a ploy. The US State Department was alarmed when she distributed copies of Woodrow Wilson's lecture in the public. The British were trying to establish Besant's credentials among educated Indians as a great freedom fighter. But when theosophists' propaganda against British India caught fire in international media, it made the British Embassy to write to the US authorities that "Besant's support for Indian home rule was not genuine, but rather little more than a ploy calculated to attract Indians to the religion of which she was a high priestess."[10] Likewise, did the British Embassy in the US tell American authorities that the arrest of Har Dayal was just a ploy to attract most "undesirable immigrants" to the Gadhr of which he was promoted as the architect, and whose plans were to discourage naturalization of "inassimilable Sikhs" and push them directly in the line of fire of British India?

What purpose did Har Dayal's arrest serve?

After Lala Har Dayal's departure, the British Embassy and the US immigration officials don't involve any other Ghadr activist in any case until the US enters the World War I. Har Dayal was removed on the plea that he was exciting South Asians against the British Empire. But there were many more in the Ghadr party who were recruiting Sikhs to go to India to wage an armed rebellion. Why didn't the British Embassy and the American immigration officials pay any heed to those activities? Wasn't the deportation of Har Dayal entirely a British ploy to advertise his case as the most important leader of the Indian freedom movement, and then to convince Germany of his great utility in World War I? Germany allowed him to be part of the

---

10   Erez Manela, *The Wilsonian Moment: Self-Determination and the International Origins of Anticolonial Nationalism* (New York: Oxford University Press, 2007) 84.

Berlin Committee. The forty-four months he spent there was the duration of World War I. On what basis did the British grant him amnesty if he had been the most dangerous among South Asians? How many less dangerous Ghadris had already been executed, imprisoned for life, and their properties confiscated? Was Har Dayal sent on a highly secret mission to Berlin? These questions need to be answered.

Free India destroys records of Ghadr history, but why?

Surviving leaders of the Gadhr movement tried to understand why they didn't receive any support from the public. Why was Ghadr's sphere confined only to Punjab? Why were only Sikh regiments asked to mutiny, not any other? Why didn't funds, weapons, and support follow Ghadris? On September 19, 1955, a committee consisting of seven members was constituted to write accurately the history of the Ghadr movement. Many surviving Ghadris were still alive. Baba Sohan Singh Bhakana, the founding president of the Ghadr Party, was again made the head of the committee for writing the history of Ghadr. Gurcharan Singh Sainsara became the secretary. Baba Gurmukh Singh Lalton, Dr. Bhag Singh, Ph.D., Professor Sant Singh Sekhon, Giani Hira Singh Dard, and Sohan Singh Josh were taken as members.

Gurcharan Singh Sainsara began his research in 1956. He interviewed former Ghadris, their families, went to many libraries and archives, and looked for letters and original manuscripts written by members of the Ghadr party. In March 1956, he got permission to research in National Archives New Delhi. The permission was granted to explore all British documents except military, intelligence, and covert action files. Sainsara and his colleagues spent six months' time in New Delhi's National Archives. After exhaustive search, Sainsara took 700 notes from various files. As per rules of the National Archives, all 700 notes were submitted to the concerned department for official permission to use them in writing the history of the Ghadr movement. To their utter shock and dismay, the Union Home Ministry revoked the permission to study related files, and all 700 handwritten notes were confiscated. The notes only covered the year 1914. They came back home and felt helpless to complete the true story behind Ghadr.

Baba Sohan Singh Bhakana decided to meet Prime Minister Jawahar Lal Nehru. He led a delegation of well-known nationalist leaders comprising of Dr. Saifudin Kitchlu, Raizada Hans Raj, Baba Gurmukh Singh, Baba Sher

Singh Beyeen Poyeen, and Dr. Bhag Singh. Nehru gave a very sympathetic hearing and promised to intervene in getting confiscated notes. But after two months, Nehru replied that the concerned files were secret and not meant to be shown to people. The files from which notes were taken were unclassified. The committee expressed its bewilderment in the following terms:

> *"We don't know why Indian Government wants to hide all cruelties and indignities that were inflicted on freedom fighters to suppress the movement? Why won't the Indian Government of Free India let the British policies toward Indian National freedom struggle come out in the public?"*[11]

The question of why the Indian Government would hide the British policies against India's freedom movement remains unanswered till today. The committee, expressing powerlessness, states, "The attitude of the Indian Government has rendered us helpless in throwing light on many aspects of this history. Ghadris who were hanged to death, and those who were thrown in prison in Third Lahore Conspiracy case couldn't be researched. The verification of Dr. Khankhoji's statement couldn't be completed. We could neither explain Burma and Siam expeditions nor the rebellion of Singapore and Mesopotamia. The atrocities suffered by Ghadris in Jails could not become part of the history."[12]

Great Britain destroys key documents related with Ghadr

It is a fact that records related with these struggles have been selectively destroyed both in India and Great Britain. Indian politicians who took over from the British were in active collaboration with them since the 1800s in times of Ram Mohan Roy and Dwarkanath Tagore. The Anglo-Vedic alliance jointly crafted policies to suppress genuine freedom fighters and promote the reciprocal rebels. Therefore, what is damaging for the British Empire, so is for the image of the Indian National Congress and Arya Samaj which were birthed by Theosophical Society of India. The destruction of records enabled

---

11 Gurcharan Singh Sainsara P. 8
12 Ibid., P. 8

Britain and India to write their official versions of history. In the absence of records, scholars appropriate whatever is available to them.

Sohan Singh Josh expressed similar doubts about British and Indian politicians. In an effort to correctly write the history of the Ghadr movement, he went to archives in England, Canada, and the USA. When he was in London in 1974, he researched India Office Library Records. He found that thousands of documents related with Ghadr in the indexes of subjects had been stamped "destroyed." He expressed his surprise that the same happened in India's National Archives in New Delhi. In India, Josh said he could not understand the meaning of "Not Available" or "Destroyed." Josh was also known as one of the Ghadris, who joined in the movement in 1920s. He had firsthand knowledge about how things shaped up, and how these are represented in modern histories of East and West. He comments:

> *Why have the former British rulers destroyed so many historical documents dealing with the fate of India? One must ask oneself this question. There is something fishy about it. The reason seems to be that the British rulers wanted to hide some of the most heinous and shameful crimes committed by them against the people of India in order to perpetuate their stranglehold over our motherland. The documents must be of a highly secret nature involving and implicating the British enslavers in political, social and moral crimes against our nation. They wanted to hide the criminal designs cooked up behind doors to kill lakhs of our innocent people . . . They wanted to hide the criminal plans hatched by them through which they set one community at the throat of another in order to create communal riots and mutual slaughter. They wanted to hide criminal schemes by which they now and then crushed our political movements and bribed traitors who stood by them in times of their need, and whose names they did not want to divulge. Some such must be the criminal motive in destroying these valuable documents.*[13]

Josh complains that Indian historians overlook these facts, perhaps, believing it a privilege of the British rulers to destroy historical documents. The history in school textbooks, according to Josh, only shows the British's

---

13 Sohn Singh Josh, *Hindustan Gadar Party: A Short History* (Jalandhar: Desh Bhagat Yadgar Committee, 1976) 17-18.

continued presence in India. The British contagion runs through theories like "academic neutrality" and "academic detachment."

Picturesque immigrants and threats to the white landscape

East Indian immigrants in the white landscape looked very picturesque due to their turbans. Their popular entry points on the Pacific ports were San Francisco, Seattle, Victoria, or Vancouver. A few also entered by way of New York, New Orleans, and Montreal. The presence of East Indians in the first decade of their arrival totally transformed the agenda of Exclusion Leagues meant for Japanese and Chinese. A few thousand East Indians posed so grave a threat to the white supremacists that they became hysterical in their response. The turbaned East Indians initially were identified as Sikhs, but as the Exclusion Leagues gathered their arsenals for driving East Indians out of Yankees lands, they were interpreted as Hindus. It became a convenient term to distinguish them from Red Indians but was also a vehicle for directing their derision to their low-caste status. It was also the time when hordes of Swamis had successfully set their spiritual centers in most of the US metropolises. They were high caste and highly educated. They freely interacted in circles of American professors, journalists, artists, and mystics. Average North Americans came to know about India from Swamis; they uniformly told that most Buddhists, Muslims, and Sikhs were converted originally from Hindu Untouchables. The majority of these immigrants were Sikhs and Muslims. Therefore, the term "Hindu" categorically got attached with uncleanliness, disease, and pestilence. The high-caste Hindus were known as Pundits, Brahmans, Swamis, and Eastern Mystics.

The clash of perspectives:

It is significant to reconstruct the site from where Ghadr developed and where mutually exclusive perspectives clashed. The three main actors were the Aryan Hindu, the Sikh, and the Exclusionist. What was the Aryan Hindu's standpoint? Where did he situate himself? How did he perceive the ongoing unrest among East Indians from 1906 to 1919? How did the Sikh consciousness react to the situation of extreme violence and humiliation? What premises did the Exclusionist provide for their violence and anti-immigration measures?

The Aryan Hindu Standpoint:
The place of Swamis, Brahmins, and Rajputs before and after the annexation of Sovereign Punjab makes an interesting study. In the beginning of nineteenth century, the grand alliance of Rammohan Roy and Dwarkanath Tagore with the East India Company consolidated British positions in India. Its brutal impact was witnessed when it permanently ended the Marattha power. In the following fifty years, the same alliance brought the fall of Punjab in 1849. The British didn't suitably reward Hindu-Muslim elites for the annexation of Punjab, and the trouble, therefore, kept brewing until it burst into the Mutiny of 1857. To reclaim the Hindu back to the heart of colonial policies, the British innovated entirely a new strategy. It also included isolating Muslims from the emerging breed of Hindu intellectuals until a suitable opportunity occurs.

The British policies after the Mutiny of 1857 mark a major turning point. The program to Christianize India was deferred for two decades. Missionaries got a new agenda which was more academic and attractive—a special curriculum for teaching them English through translations and reinterpretations of ancient manuscripts. They were given the task of educating upper-caste Hindus about their ancient systems of thought. The revival of Vedic periods and common Aryan ties achieved better results than the agenda of conversions. By the end of nineteenth century, a new breed of educated Aryan Hindus was ready to follow inscrutable directions. A spate of reform movements in the 1880s gave birth to numerous sects in major religions. Ahmadiya, Arya Samaj, Dev Samaj, Singh Sabha, Namdhari, Nirankari, Radha Swami, to name a few, created a lot of heat for mutual clashes. Surjit S. Gandhi, a Punjab historian, describes it in the following terms:

> *The Arya Attack on Sikhism attained a new fervor early in the twentieth century. It was the result of the increasing religious intensity of the militant Aryas as expressed in the public ritual of reconversion. These Aryas began in 1900 to convert low caste Sikhs en masse ... The attack on Sikhism on ideological level also harmed the Sikhs. The British scholars and Christian missionaries began to interpret Sikhism merely a social reform movement. The Arya scholars likewise treated Sikhism only part of Hinduism.*[14]

---

14 Surjit S. Gandhi, *Perspectives on Sikh Gurudwaras Legislation* (New Delhi: Atlantic Publishers & Distributors, 1993) p. 13

Swamis' English education and the British Empire's special interest in their career across continents promoted many organizations with a view to utilize their spiritual, intellectual, and strategic resources. Vedanta Society and Theosophical Society provided platforms for Eastern and Western perspectives to cohere together to form new parameters of peace in the world. Any other set of thought was considered disruptive, deviant, and derogatory. The Sikhs who came to settle on the Pacific coast were the unambiguous target of missionaries and Aryas. Therefore, they were vulnerable to misinterpretation, misrepresentations, and mistreatment of secret societies.

The Sikh Standpoint:

The majority of Sikhs, as mentioned before, came from the military backgrounds. Their overrepresentation in the British Army excelled in all fields. Sikhs had maximum number of deaths in the battlefields, maximum number of awards, and records of rare courage in key battles. The British encouraged the soldiers to be true Sikhs so long as they were fighting for them. The former soldiers in Canada and the US carried their war medals with them. They were given the impression that they would live respectable lives if they moved to British controlled territories outside India. First as citizens of British India and second as veterans of the British Army, they thought they would be welcome in foreign lands.

But when they faced the extremely hostile environment, they introspected on their loyalty to their British masters. The double-edged affliction wrought self-realization on the one hand and anguish of injustice on the other. Their experience with the British consulate office in Canada and America in the wake of atrocities, indignities, and violence, woke them to their statelessness and sterility. But Swamis, on the contrary, not only got a privileged status but also were at the center of ideological support to the colonial west. Their association, therefore, was more with the exclusion leagues than with the laborers. But the laborers, naïve as they were, couldn't understand these connections. They greatly relied on upper-caste Hindus, trusting their abilities and education to solve their problems.

The Exclusionist Standpoint:

On the other hand, some Americans perceived the situation from an entirely different angle. The tide of turbans was associated, in their minds, with territorial occupation by the most undesirable aliens. Sikhs' hunger for agriculture land, resolve to succeed in spite of all odds, and insistence to keep their picturesque lifestyle are nagging questions for the exclusionist Leagues.

In 1905, more than sixty anti-immigration groups jointly vowed to preserve the "Caucasian race upon American soil." Samuel Gompers, president of the American Federation of Labor in 1908, expressed the typical mood of the exclusionists at that time: "Sixty years' contact with the Chinese, and twenty five years' experience with the Japanese, and two or three years acquaintance with Hindus should be sufficient to convince any ordinarily intelligent person that they have no standards . . . by which a Caucasian may judge them."[15]

Gompers's Caucasian standards of judgment apparently apply only to India's Brahmins and their collaborators. Chinese, Japanese, and Hindus (Sikhs, Muslims, and Buddhists), according to these standards, don't fit anywhere in his design. Dr. Sudhindra Bose's argument before the congressional committee in 1914 compares with that of Gompers. Bose provided "ideological" basis to the lawmakers to fashion all their judgments according to the Caucasian standards. The contagion spreads to all branches of government and judiciary. Any contrary voices were either vetoed or just silenced in the name of European nationalism.

The constitution of the Asian Exclusion League advertised itself to be the true voice of American whites. Its business was run in a highly organized manner. Minutes of meeting, reasons for excluding undesirable aliens, and strategizing action plan were all recorded. Five hundred white militants represented the League's agenda when they attacked Sikh laborers in their deep sleep. The abrupt violence left them totally shattered. The weekly newspaper *The Outlook* analyzed data gathered from various newspapers in its issue of September 14, 1907, as such:

If the wrecking of a small Japanese restaurant in San Francisco by hoodlums, in the judgment of certain excitable people and newspapers, almost made war with Japan inevitable, how much greater,

---

15 Gordon Chang, ed., *Asian Americans and Politics: Perspectives, Experiences, Prospects* (Washington, D.C.: Woodrow Wilson Center Press, 2001) p. 261.

logically speaking, must be the danger of war between the United States and Great Britain if the story told last week in press dispatches from the State of Washington is a true one! According to this story, as a result of mob violence in the town of Bellingham, six badly beaten British subjects went to the hospital, four hundred fled to the jail for police protection, and seven hundred and fifty were driven away, beaten, hungry, and half clothed, to make their way to Canada and the protection of the British flag. The subjects of Great Britain who were thus maltreated were Hindus. Probably not one out of a hundred of our readers in the East, has been aware of the fact that a racial question with this class of Asiatic was brewing in the Northwest. It appears that many hundreds of Hindus have been employed in the mills in the neighborhood of Bellingham; that they were displacing white employees, and that the outbreak came from five hundred white men who raided the mills where the foreigners were employed, battered down the doors of lodging-houses, dragged the Hindus from their beds, and drove them with violence from the town. It is stated that most or all of the Hindus were Sikhs . . . As The Outlook has pointed out in other cases, the United States not only should have but does have authority to require from the State Government proper action in the way of redress and reparation. Meanwhile it is amusing to note, as a contrast to the Japanese flurry, that no human being predicts any serious disturbance of amicable relations between the United States and Great Britain.[16]

The reporter of *The Outlook* identifies accurately victims of violence as "the British subjects," Hindus, and Sikhs. He analyzes the truth by directing the attention of readers to the victims' powerlessness. The size of the British Empire was way bigger than that of the US. Normally, the humiliating treatment of "the British subjects" could strain bilateral relations of the two countries. But what the reporter emphasizes is that British India was only interested in using the Indian subject for the Empire, and could easily get away with moral obligations for their welfare in other countries. But Japan, in this regard, was entirely on the other end of the spectrum. The reporter tries to make clear by saying, "most or all of the Hindus were Sikhs."

---

16 Francis Rufus Bellamy, ed., "War With Great Britain ?" in *The Outlook*, Volume 87 (New York: The Outlook Company, 1907) 51-52

Their imaginary identity as "Hindus" or the "British Subjects" was a sign of their emasculation. To deal with their extreme alienation, they identify with the "Sikh culture" as the only recourse to put together their shattered selves. In their effort to reconstitute their response, they envision for themselves a larger role, the harbinger of freedom for their subjugated nation.

In a study, Nayan Shah comments on the Asian Exclusion League's activism in 1907 that propelled a spate of hate crimes against the "most undesirable aliens." The opening of League chapters in America and Canada prepared grounds for organized crimes. The collection of ten thousand three days after the Bellingham riot was seen as a mandate for exclusion of Sikhs. Arthur Fowler's advice of making the Bellingham riot exemplary only demonstrates how serious and complex the problems of Punjabi pioneers were in the first decade of the twentieth century. One month after the Bellingham riot, the murder of Darrah Singh, an educated and well-dressed Sikh, by Edward Bowen, a twenty-one-year-old English laborer, shocked the community to devise some plans for their defense. Bowen's version of portraying Darrah Singh as a sexual predator, and his killing as a defensive measure to save his honor, didn't go well with the jury. All evidence collected by the prosecutor established Darrah Singh's innocence and Bowen's inconsistent lifestyle. The decision of the jury to convict Bowen for murder restored some sense of justice in the beleaguered community. Shah provides details of circumstances that prevailed one month before Darrah Singh's murder:

"Three days after the Bellingham Riot, a crowd of 10,000 people gathered for an anti-Asian parade organized by Vancouver's newly established chapter of the Asiatic Exclusion League (AEL). The San Francisco-based white labor political organization had established chapters in Seattle, Bellingham, and Vancouver during the summer. Arthur Fowler of the AEL's Seattle chapter traveled to Bellingham on September 6, 1907, to assess the impact of the riots and traveled onward to Vancouver to participate in the parade. At the parade, he delivered a rousing speech and urged Vancouver residents to follow the example of the Bellingham driving-out campaign as a solution to Vancouver's Asian problem. He urged the crowd to march on Chinatown, and that night, a mob did so and destroyed the businesses and lodging houses of hundreds of Chinese and Japanese residents."[17]

---

17   Nayan Shah, *Stranger Intimacy: Contesting Race, Sexuality, and the Law in the North American West* (Berkeley and Los Angeles: University of California Press, 2001) p. 31

The conviction of Bowen did not dampen sprits of Asian Exclusion League. Its members made it their favorite sport to hunt "Hindus" and warn owners of sawmills against their employment. Exclusionists even pressured the city council to pass restrictions against business owners from employing East Indian labor. The Bellingham incursion against Sikhs provided whites to sink their ethnic differences and identify with white America. The valorization with their new persona had political implications as it could polarize the majority of votes to serious advocates of exclusionism. The election year was round the corner. The politics became more geared towards excluding Hindus first of all as they were more visible and inassimilable.

"From every standpoint it is most undesirable that these Asians should be permitted to remain in the United States. They are repulsive in appearance and disgusting in their manners. They are said to be without shame and, while no charges of immorality are brought against them, their actions and customs are so different from ours that there can never be tolerance of them. They contribute nothing to the growth and upbuilding of the city as the result of their labor. They work for small wages and do not put their money into circulation. They build no homes and while they numerically swell the population, it is of a class that we may well spare . . . There can no two sides to such a question. The Hindu is a detriment to the town, while the white man is a distinct advantage." [18]

An editorial in the *Bellingham Herald*, published September 5, 1907, condemns the senseless violence. He also upbraids the police's role in remaining mere spectators to the hoodlums. But the editor's conclusions are from the point of view American decency that was compromised. His views on Sikhs' assimilation are, however, the same as in most other editorials.

"The Hindu is not a good citizen. It would require centuries to assimilate him, and this country need not take the trouble. Our racial burdens are already heavy enough to bear . . . Our cloak of brotherly love is not large enough to include him as member of the body politic. His ways are not our ways; he is not adaptable, and will not in many generations make a good American citizen. Moreover he is not even a good workman . . . But such exhibition of man's inhumanity to man as that of last night should not be tolerated. Such lawlessness is an outrage upon American decency."[19]

---

18   "The Hindus Have Left Us" *Morning Reveille* September 6, 1907, P.4 (Editorial)
19   "A Public Disgrace" Bellingham Hearald, September 5, 1907, p. 4 (Editorial)

Seattle Morning Time's report analyzes the problem from a sociological standpoint. He interprets whites' preferences for meat and comfortable beds as being more urgent than Hindus' vegetarianism and alleged tendency to live in a filthy corner. A new definition of righteousness emerges from the reporter's standpoint, in which violence against the "undesirable aliens" can hardly be called "indignation."

"It is not a question of race, but of wages; not a question of men, but of modes of life; not a matter of nations, but of habits of life . . . When men who require meat to eat and real beds to sleep in are ousted from the employment to make room for vegetarians who can find the bliss of sleep in some filthy corner, it is rather difficult to say at what limit indignation ceases to be righteousness."[20]

Bellingham Herald's report of September 9, 1907, mentions white men indulging in stone throwing at "Hindus" who asked for police protection for all Sikhs living in other places. The report "Everett Hindus Ask For Police Protection" also points to the lackadaisical approach of the police.

On November 2, 1907, *Anaconda Standard* (Montana) reported "Assault On Hindus Thirty Shots Fired." The gun attack on Sikh laborers left one man, Bingwan [or Bhiningwan] Singh, dead. Six men were arrested though no reports of further action were recorded.

On November 6, 1907, *Bellingham Herald* (p. 2) reports "Rowdies are Arrested For Murdering Hindu." Five white men fired 30 rounds which killed Bhagwan Singh.

"Hindus living in a shack at 2607 Norton appealed to the police yesterday for protection. On Friday Night their shack was stoned by a number of white men, and the Hindus are in fear of a similar treatment to that given their countrymen in Bellingham." [21]

Mill owners resisted the pressure of the white laborers and retained East Indians at par with whites, but the labor leader started giving warnings of violence in case they failed to obey their dictates. The *Bellingham Herald* of October 2, 1907, gives the following title to the report, "HINDUS WARNED TO LEAVE EVERETT; Millmen Refuse to Discharge Dusky Workers and Replace Them at Same Wages by Whites – Claim is Made That It Is an

---

20 *Seattle Morning Times*, reprinted in *The American* September 7, 1907 (Halberg, pp.150-151)
21 "Everett Hindus Ask For Police Protection" *Bellingham Herald*, September 9, 1907.

Attempt to Force Down Wages. TRIED TO TROUBLE, Labor Leader Says Hindus Should Leave, as All Peaceful Means Have Been Exhausted."[22]

The *Everett Herald* reports on November 4, 1907, "HINDUS ARE LEAVING CITY ; ALIENS, ALARMED BY SATURDAY'S DEMONSTRATION, ARE TAKING DEPARTURE; MANY GOING TO PORTLAND; REPORTED THAT SHOTS WERE HEARD SATURDAY NIGHT – EMPTY SHELLS FOUND." The reporter's tone appears to be sympathetic, appreciative, and somber because Sikhs had finally decided to leave and try their luck somewhere else. Sikhs protest in a unique way. The majority of them were veterans of the British Army who fought and risked their lives for the British Raj. The treatment they received at white men's hands was worse than dogs. They organized a march wearing their military uniforms and medals to make a very significant statement. The message was undeniably strong and multidimensional. In spite of their military backgrounds, they chose to remain peaceful even when some of them had lost their lives in the unprovoked violence. Secondly, it was also a message to British India that instead of dying for their unjust Empire, they would prefer to die for their own free country.

"Every Hindu who owns a medal sported it today as the Asiatics walked the streets in the safety of daylight, making preparations to leave Everett for British Columbia and Portland, where they intend seeking new and friendlier pastures. Tall, erect, decorated with medals awarded for signal bravery while in the British military service in India, the Hindus went down with colors flying, bowing to the inevitable stoically, uncomplainingly, voicing no expressions of anger against their enemies, speaking nothing but regrets that the white man to whose free country they came, refused to permit them an opportunity to make a living . . ."[23]

In 1908, a White mob attacked Sikhs in Marysville, California. The help sought from the British Consul was denied. White mobs again struck in Oregon on March 22, 1910, in which many were seriously injured. The Mayor's intervention saved the situation from further escalation.

The British spread a very organized network of spies to monitor the behavior of veterans of the British Army. They found it to be a most important experiment because it didn't take too long for the contagion to spread in the

---

22   "Hindus Warned to Leave Everett" *Bellingham Herald* October 2, 1907, p 1
23   "Hindus Are Leaving City" *Everett Herald*, November 4, 1907.

army. The British didn't want to leave any segment unregulated. The height of resentment, especially among Sikhs, made headlines everywhere. During this time, the British spies spread their network, who successfully infiltrated in Punjabi gangs. They used the same old strategy of the Reciprocal Rebel. Many pamphlets, newspapers, and essays were written on the ruthlessness of the British rule.

The Honduras episode added fuel to the fire. During this time, Professor Teja Singh's role had already been mentioned. After he left, Theosophical Society, British intelligence, reciprocal rebels took over to create serious dissensions. Sikhs failed to understand the diplomatic game. *Komagata Maru* further fueled the anger. They formed the Ghadr party to express their nationalistic aspirations. When the world was in turmoil, Ghadris played their part with stunning devotion to the cause of freedom. But many others got lost in the maze of their own tricks. The trials, executions, prison sentences followed and many surrendered to the influence of the Empire.

The Birth of the Ghadr Party

The birth of the Ghadr Party after six years of organized violence of the Asian Exclusion League, white mobs, and network of British spies was not due to any single individual efforts as erroneously suggested by many Ghadr historians, but it was born out of the collective consciousness of Punjabi pioneers who sensed total absence of Indian Nationhood during their ordeals in Canada and the US. The Indian National Congress's failure to pass a resolution to condemn the racial violence of 1907, British Consulate Offices' apathy, and the White mobs' incursions made Sikhs explore their community resources to make up for the lack of nationhood. Most attacks were on Sikh identity and its inassimilable nature. Some gave in to pressures and changed their form, but others took cues from Sikh history and stuck to their stand. Professor Teja Singh's work and the incorporation of Sikh Gurdwaras brought change in the community's consciousness. Gurdwara became the site of Indian nationalism. They found some stability in their life which earlier was rocked by series of violent incidences against the Punjabi community.

Arya Samaj intellectuals' intense efforts from 1900 to 1907 were to arouse memories of the 1857 mutiny in which Sikhs' role was shown as a "missed opportunity" for Indian freedom. Arya Samaj and Hindu Mahasabha jointly used provocative idiom against the British and incited anger of young men.

But the extremist leadership took a U-turn after Madan Lal Dhingra killed Sir William Hutt Curzon-Wyllie at Imperial Institute, South Kensington, on July 1, 1909. Most of the Arya Samaj leaders, who earlier provoked young men, were now completely reconciled with the British.

The pioneering influence during the 50th anniversary of the 1857 mutiny was Ajit Singh, who had joined Arya Samajis for greater unity of Indian people. When Lala Lajpat Rai testified against Amir Chand, and endorsed his execution, Ajit felt totally isolated in his dreams and desires for independence of India. Close on the heels of the Delhi conspiracy, Ghadr movement arose with all its might. Ajit Singh experienced a sense of frustration when many Arya Samaji leaders reversed their position to save their skin. The Arya Samji leadership could not extricate itself from Theosophical influence, and that is why it could not understand clearly what it wanted.

Theosophy provoked Indians to seek limited freedom for India, while, for collaborators, it promised greater roles in the administration. As Gandhi's entry into the political system materialized, Ghadr looked like a violent and outdated movement. Gadhr changed into Babbar Akali Dal, Akali Dal, and communist movements. The original Ghadr transformed into myriad, tiny influences which were not big enough to dismantle the colonial administration. The two world wars had totally wrecked the Indian leadership, and people were left with no choice except Gandhi and Jawahar Lal Nehru. The greatest setback was the partition of the country.

The Surveillance of Indian Nationalists in North America, 1908-1918

Hugh Johnston

Immigrants from India, most of whom were Sikhs from Punjab, discovered North America in 1903 and 1904. The immigration of young men flourished briefly until shut off by Canadian authorities in 1908 and by American in 1910. By then a small community of Punjabi laborers had established itself in the Pacific coast states and in British Columbia. Associated with this community were a number of students and entrepreneurs from Bengal and elsewhere in India. The leaders of this community were under close surveillance, so that now, eighty years later, in the archives of four countries—Canada, India, Great Britain, and the United States—we can trace their movements with remarkable precision. Most of these men were political activists who were openly critical of the British regime in India and who called for Indian self-rule, either within or outside the British Empire. It is not surprising that these leaders were watched, given the paranoia of the British regime in India and the sentiments of the anti-Asiatic lobby in the Pacific coast states and in British Columbia. As time progressed, they warranted more watching. By the end of 1913, Indians in San Francisco had organized the Ghadar or Mutiny party with links in Vancouver, Victoria, and other points up and down the Pacific coast. In the first months of the First World War, the leaders of the Ghadar party tried to stage a rising in Punjab and encouraged emigrants to return to India to take part. Their efforts were ill organized and drew little support from the Sikh population in Punjab, but the Indian government met the threat with a severity that profoundly affected the outlooks of Sikhs and other Indians and contributed to the unrest that seized Punjab after the war ended.

Canadian immigration officials in Vancouver played a key role in the surveillance of Indian nationalists in North America. This role has been recognized in previous studies of the Punjabi community in British Columbia, but the nature of the surveillance and its consequences deserve closer examination.[1] The subject has a contemporary echo in the attention that the Canadian and Indian governments now pay to nationalist activity among Sikhs in Canada. The past provides a lesson for the present. Sikhs who came to Canada early in this century, like those who have come in the past twenty years, were economic immigrants, more interested in jobs than politics. The activist Har Dayal said that they were timid,[2] and a great many of these immigrants were uncomfortable with any community action that might be misconstrued by the government, whether Canadian or Indian.[3] Time and events, however, drove most of them into the hands of the activists. Surveillance was a contributing factor. A symbiotic relationship existed between the watchers and the watched: together they nurtured the ideal that political activity among Sikhs in North America was a threat to British rule in India. Each was a spur to the other. When they thought about it, Punjabi peasants had little affection for the British regime and much to resent. When they realized that they were under surveillance, even though they were far from home, they took a step towards political awareness. In this way, surveillance stimulated political activity among Indians, and political activity among Indians justified more surveillance. By tracing the ever increasing scope of Vancouver-based surveillance, one can see the process at work.

At the heart of the surveillance effort was one man, a former Calcutta police inspector, W. C. Hopkinson, who surfaced in Vancouver in 1908, and who was employed as a Canadian immigration inspector in Vancouver from 1909 until 1914, when he was shot and killed by a Sikh named Mewa Singh.

---

1   See Norman Buchignani and Doreen Indra with Ram Srivastiva, *Continuous Journey, A Social History of South Asians in Canada* (Toronto: McClelland and Stewart, 1985), 25-265 37, 51-53, 58-65, and Hugh Johnston, *The Voyage of the Komagata Maru, The Sikh Challenge to Canada's Colour Bar* (New Delhi: Oxford University Press, 1979), 1, 7-16, 124-29, 138.

2   Har Dayal, "India in America," *The Modern Review* (July 1911) : 1-11.

3   See the comments attributed to Husain Rahim at meeting of the Khalsa Diwan Society and United Indian League: Public Archives of Canada [PAC], RG 76, vol. 385, file 536999, Henry W. Gwyther to Malcolm R. J. Reid, 24 Feb. 1913.

As part of his job, Hopkinson did the routine work of an immigration inspector, but his main responsibility, and the reason he was hired, was for police work which, in all its implications, was of far greater interest to the India Office and the Government of India than to the Canadian government that employed him. A reading of the archival record indicates that the initiative in this work lay entirely with Hopkinson. He uncovered the presence of Indian nationalist agitators on the Pacific coast, convinced the authorities (without much difficulty) of its seriousness, and obtained a special commission and employment to investigate. His original mission in Vancouver is a mystery. He was probably sent by the Indian government to report on the situation among the Sikhs, but without much advance notion of what he might find. When he first arrived, he did not come in any official capacity or report his purpose to the Canadian government.

Hopkinson was a Eurasian born in Delhi in 1880, although he maintained the pretense that he was of English birth and English parentage.[4] For four years, from 1904 to 1907, he served as a sub-inspector of police in Calcutta. He started at the age of twenty-four at 80 rupees a month, and by 1907 his salary had risen to 125.[5] In the spring of 1908, he appeared unannounced in Vancouver without any clearly defined occupation but engaged in investigative work. His first overt act was to publicize Indian nationalist activity in Vancouver by planting a story with a *Times* of London correspondent.[6] The article, which appeared in the *Times* on May 22, alleged that Indians in Vancouver and Seattle were raising money, printing literature, and distributing instructions on the manufacture of bombs to support revolutionary agitation in India. In late May/early June, he was interviewed by the Deputy Minister of Labour, Mackenzie King, while the latter was conducting a Royal Commission of Inquiry into oriental immigration. King, impressed, wrote a nine-page confidential memorandum based on information that

---

4　When Hopkinson was first appointed as immigration inspector and Hindu interpreter, and required to complete a form for the Department of the Interior, he gave the correct birth date (16 June 1880) but the wrong birth place (Hull, Yorkshire, England). For nationality he wrote "English." See PAG, RG 76, vol. 561, file 808722, pt. 1. He must have claimed he was English consistently, because the obituaries that appeared in Vancouver newspapers after his death say that he came to India as a child. The baptismal records in the India Office Library show he was born in Delhi. He was taken for a Eurasian by people who worked with him: interview on 29 Oct. 1976 with former immigration inspector Fred "Cyclone" Taylor.
5　India Office Library, *Thacker's Indian Directory*, 1904-07.
6　PAG, RG 7, G 21, vol. 200, file 332, Report of Col. E. J. Swayne, "Information as to Hindu Agitators in Vancouver."

Hopkinson had supplied.⁷ This information, King concluded, provided all the more reason for controlling Indian immigration to Canada. In the next few months, Hopkinson was a fixture in and around the immigration office in Vancouver, although without regular employment. By his own account, he was on leave from the Calcutta police force,⁸ but his activities suggest that he was angling for better employment, and Canadian officials readily made use of him. "I had Hopkinson spend a day among the Hindus . . ." wrote J. B. Harkin, private secretary to the Minister of the Interior, in a letter of late July to W. D. Scott, Superintendent of Immigration in Ottawa; what is striking about the reference is that no further identification was needed: Superintendent Scott knew who Hopkinson was.⁹

In October and November 1908, Hopkinson was employed by Harkin as secretary and interpreter on a special delegation to investigate Indian labor conditions in British Honduras. The delegation included Harkin, Hopkinson, and two men selected by the Indian community in Vancouver, Nagar Singh, a Sikh, and Sham Singh, a Hindu. Expenses were paid by the Department of the Interior. The objective, sanctioned by the Colonial Office, was to disembarrass Vancouver of excess Indian laborers by shipping them to the West Indies or Honduras under indentured contracts.¹⁰ Nagar Singh and Sham Singh were taken to Belize to see the country at firsthand before any of their compatriots accepted transportation there, but they returned with negative reports and accusations of attempted bribery against Hopkinson.¹¹ The Honduras proposal was angrily rejected at a meeting in

---

7   PAG, RG 2/1, vol. 703, file 21, 21 July 1908.
8   Affidavit by Hopkinson, 7 Dec. 1908, copied in J. B. Harkin's report, *The East Indians in British Columbia* (Department of the Interior, 1909), 31-33.
9   Harkin, *The East Indians in British Columbia*, 8-9.
10 AC, RG 7, G 1, vol. 272, Crewe to Grey, 19 Sept. 1908, telegram.
11 Over the years, members of the Indian community repeatedly claimed that Hopkinson was corrupt. The case was not proved at the time and is unprovable now. In the office he held, and in the power he possessed over Indian immigrants, there was potential for abuse. On the other hand, department officials believed that charges against Hopkinson were manufactured to discredit him or to get him fired. The story that he tried to bribe the Honduras delegates seems implausible. (Nagar Singh said that Hopkinson wanted him to give a favourable report on conditions in Honduras and tempted him with a purse filled with $3,000 in cash, but Hopkinson did not have that kind of money, and it is difficult to believe that the Department of the Interior or anyone else gave it to him for such an unprofitable and unaccountable purpose.) In May 1911 a Mr. Von Guttenberg of the Department of the Interior was sent to Vancouver to investigate charges against Hopkinson. (Among the people he talked to was an Indian named Boga who said that Hopkinson had taken $50 from each of

the Vancouver Sikh Temple. None of this did any harm to Hopkinson's reputation in official quarters. Instead, the episode gave him prominence: it put him into correspondence with the Deputy Minister of the Interior and with the Prime Minister,[12] and, ultimately, it produced the recommendation that he be given permanent employment. Colonel E. J. Swayne, Governor of British Honduras, was in London when the idea of recruiting coolie labor in Vancouver was first raised; when he offered to return to Belize via Canada if the Canadian government paid his way, they said yes.[13] He arrived in Montreal and Ottawa in early December and discussed his mission, first of all with the Governor General, the 4th Earl Grey, and then with Prime Minister Sir Wilfrid Laurier and members of his cabinet. As an old India hand, Swayne was asked to look into the political as well as the labor situation among Indians in Vancouver, and, before he left the country at the end of the year, he submitted both written and personal reports to the government. In

---

eight people entering from the United States.) Hopkinson was not given warning or notice of the investigation, and found out about it indirectly. None the less, he was exonerated. In October 1913, when the Indian colony was in an uproar over Immigration Department efforts to deport the priest Bhagwan Singh, Hopkinson warned his superiors that there might be more allegations against him: he had received veiled threats from leaders of the Indian colony that they would say that he had landed Bhagwan Singh for money. (In fact, Bhagwan Singh had entered the country by using the name and documents of another man who had established residence in Canada.) Norman Buchignani and Doreen Indra cite the case of Mrs. Uday Ram, who was landed in Feb. 1910, as possible evidence that Hopkinson could be bought. Between April 1908 and March 1910 only thirteen Indian men and two Indian women (including Mrs. Ram) were permitted entry to Canada as new immigrants. The landing of an Indian woman was most exceptional and one can understand the suspicion among Indians that bribery was involved. Because it was exceptional, however, it would seem that even a most venal official would have been discouraged from taking a bribe. The decision to land Mrs. Ram was not made by Hopkinson alone, but in conjunction with the immigration agent, J. H. MacGill; and it was reported immediately to the Deputy Minister of the Interior, who watched Indian immigration cases like a hawk because the possible political repercussions were considerable. Hopkinson was loyal to British India and Anglo Canada and behaved accordingly. One does not need evidence of personal corruption to explain the part he played. On the Honduras bribe charge: affidavit by Sham Singh and diary by Sham Singh, copied in Harkin, 25-27, 29-31. On the Von Guttenberg investigation: RG 76, vol. 561, file 808722, G. D. Kumar to L. M. Fortier; and RG 7, G 21, vol. 201, file 332, Hopkinson to Gory, 6 April, 8 May & 25 May 1911. On the Bhagwan Singh case: RG 76, vol. 385, file 536999, Hopkinson to Gory, 20 Oct. 1913. On the Mrs. Uday Ram case: RG 7, G 21, vol. 200, file 332, Hopkinson to Gory, 19 Feb. 1910; and Buchignani and Indra, 49. See also RG 76, vol. 561, file 808722, MacGill to Scott, 15 July 1910. For more on the question of Hopkinson and bribes see Johnston, *The Voyage*, 143.
12   Harkin, 6-7.
13   PAG, RG 25, A 2, vol. 200, file 120/76.

his confidential report, Swayne recommended Hopkinson's appointment as a Dominion police inspector to keep a watch on Indian activists in Vancouver.

According to Swayne, Hopkinson was likely to return to India at any time. Before he did, he was hired as an immigration inspector stationed in Vancouver and charged with so-called Hindu work. The offer came from the Deputy Minister of the Interior, but the initiative, interest, and sense of urgency belonged to the Governor General, Earl Grey.[14] Grey was a popular governor general whose term, twice extended, lasted from 1904 to 1911. The office he held, although a largely formal one, still carried an aura that gave him personal influence with the Prime Minister and members of his government on some issues. He had to avoid the appearance of interference in domestic matters, but he could be sure that members of the government would listen to him when he represented imperial concerns. Oriental immigration was both a domestic and an international issue, and Grey kept a close watch because he saw imperial interests at stake.[15] By the end of 1907, following the anti-oriental riot in Vancouver that summer, he was convinced that Indian immigration to Vancouver would have to stop. But he wanted the government to act circumspectly. He was incensed when the Minister of the Interior, during the election campaign of 1908, announced that steps would be taken against Indian immigration. The publicity was potentially inflammatory in India. He accepted the policy but not the open advertisement. Similarly, although Grey was outraged by evidence that Indian nationalists were at work in Vancouver, he counseled restraint in dealing with them and their community. In his mind, the stakes were high. Quiet vigilance was wanted, and a man like Hopkinson could prove invaluable.

Hopkinson reported for duty in Vancouver on February 8, 1909, at a salary of $100 a month. At the prevailing rate of exchange, this was equivalent to 300 rupees or 2.4 times as much as he had earned on the Calcutta police force. His job was to keep a watch on the Indian community and to report regularly to the department. When this did not keep him busy, or when there was an overload in the immigration office, he could be assigned to ordinary immigration work. These were his instructions and those given

---

14   PAG, RG 7, G 21, vol. 200, file 332, Sir John Hanbury-Williams to W. W. Gory, 13 Jan. 1909, copy, and Gory to Hanbury-Williams, 18 Jan. 1909.

15   Mary E. Hallett, "A Governor General's Views on Oriental Immigration to British Columbia, 1904-1911," *BC Studies* 14 (Summer, 1972): 51-72.

the Immigration Agent, J. H. MacGill.[16] For the most part, Hopkinson worked independently. He concentrated his attention on the leaders of the Indian community in Vancouver. He collected their publications, recorded their public utterances, monitored and sometimes intercepted their mail, and assiduously kept track of their comings and goings. A matter as apparently inconsequential as a $20 money order sent to New York was grist for Hopkinson's mill. He collected what he could and sent weekly reports to the deputy minister, who forwarded a copy to the Governor General. Earl Grey had a great appetite for this material. When he stopped in Vancouver in August 1909, on his way to the Yukon, he spent an hour and a half with Hopkinson. On his return, five weeks later, he interviewed him again, and while he was in the north, he insisted that Hopkinson keep him up to date by sending reports via Skagway.[17] It was not long before Grey wanted three copies of Hopkinson's reports: one for himself, one for the Home Government, and one for the Director of Military Intelligence in Ottawa. This material found its way into the files of the Criminal Intelligence Office in India by one of two routes. Regularly, it went from the Governor General via London (the Colonial Office and the India Office) to the Viceroy; irregularly, it went from Military Intelligence Ottawa to Intelligence Branch, Simla.[18]

When he wanted information, Hopkinson had the resources of the Governor General's Office to draw on, and he could count on enthusiastic and expeditious action. Housain Rahim, who emerged as a leading figure in the Indian community in Vancouver, entered the country in 1910 via Honolulu and Japan. At Hopkinson's request the Governor General obtained reports through the British Ambassador in Japan on Rahim's activities in Kobe, where he was manager of the firm of Varma & Co.[19] When Hopkinson wanted information about Guran Ditta Kumar (whose business card read "Punjabi Buddhist" and "Worker in the cause of Temperance and Vegetarianism"), he suggested a trace by the Commissioner of Police in

---

16 PAG, RG 76, vol. 561, file 808722, W. W. Gory to J. H. MacGill, 3 Feb. 1909, copy; Gory to Hopkinson, 3 Feb. 1909, copy; MacGill to Cory, 8 Feb. 1909.
17 PAG, RG 7, G 21, vol. 200, file 332, Hopkinson to Gory, 5 Aug. and 9 Sept. 1909, copies.
18 Ibid., Captain Bruce Hay to Major the Earl of Lanesborough, 15 March 1910.
19 Ibid., vol. 201, file 332, Claude M. MacDonald to Grey, 2 Sept. 1911, enclosure. On the co-operation of the Japanese police in watching Indian nationalists, 1914-1918, see Grant K. Goodman, "Japanese Sources for the Study of the Indian Independence Movement," in Sisir K. Bose éd., *Netaji and India's Freedom* (Calcutta: Netaji Research Bureau, 1975), 76-108.

Calcutta. When he wanted to know what Teja Singh was doing in England, he recommended a watch by Scotland Yard.[20]

Teja Singh was a Khatri Sikh who had arrived in Vancouver in September 1908 by way of Montreal and New York. He had immediately assumed a leadership role in Vancouver's Sikh community, and, in 1909 and 1910, he absorbed much of Hopkinson's attention. The Punjab Government identified him as a former resident of Gujranwala city in Punjab, a graduate of Government College in Lahore and an M.A. from Punjab University.[21] He had also passed the intermediate law exam and had taught as headmaster of a school in the Shahpur District and at Khalsa College, Amritsar, where he had temporarily acted as principal. For a time, he had been a pleader or advocate in Rawalpindi. His father, who had been either an assistant surgeon or a hospital assistant, had died, and, with a large share of the estate at his disposal, Teja Singh had gone abroad to study natural science at Cambridge. In the summer of 1908, he had come to North America, and, although he had not yet taken his Cambridge exams, he had reportedly enrolled as a graduate student in education at Columbia. On his politics, the government of India relayed contrary assessments. By the first, his views were "not dangerous but fairly moderate." By the second, they were "bigoted."[22] He made no public statements that would brand him an extremist, and when he did undertake a series of lectures in Vancouver, his subject was theosophical: the principles of Buddhism. Hopkinson, however, had no doubt that he was subversive.[23] In March 1910, Teja Singh returned to Vancouver after a six-month absence. Hopkinson heard that he had had a meeting with Gandhi. "Gandhi," Hopkinson explained in his report, "is a prominent man in South Africa and is purported to be connected with some Hindu trouble in that country, and from what I can learn is at present in jail serving a sentence."[24]

Others watched by Hopkinson included Balwant Singh, millworker and priest in the Vancouver Sikh Temple; Bhag Singh, president of the temple management committee; Sundar Singh, self-styled doctor and editor of the *Aryan,* published monthly in Victoria; and a number of students—Behari Lai Varma, Harnam Singh, Surendra Mohan Bose, and others—who

---

20   PAC, RG 7, G 2i, vol. 200, file 332, Hopkinson to Cory, 12 Aug. and 6 Nov. 1909, copies.
21   Ibid., Crewe to Grey, 15 March 1909, enclosures.
22   Ibid.; and vol. 199, file 332, Lord Hardinge to Viscount Morley, telegram, 17 Dec. 1908, copy.
23   Ibid., vol. 200, file 332, Hopkinson to J. B. Harkin, 4 Jan. 1909, copy.
24   Ibid., Hopkinson to Gory, 7 March 1910, copy.

The Surveillance of Indian Nationalists in North America, 1908-1918

were enrolled in American colleges but who appeared from time to time in Vancouver. Most important, aside from Teja Singh, was Taraknath Das, a Bengali student enrolled at the University of Washington in Seattle. He was a graduate of Calcutta University who had arrived in North America in 1906. For a time, he was employed as an interpreter by the US immigration office in Vancouver. In 1908, he opened a school for Sikh immigrants, and it was this school that was exposed by Hopkinson and subsequently closed by the authorities. Part of the case against Das was guilt by association: he "was acquainted with" Arabindo Ghose, Professor of History and Political Science at National College, Calcutta, who was prosecuted for seditious journalism (and acquitted) in Calcutta in August 1907. He "knew" Surendranath Banerji, editor of *The Bengali* and a powerful voice in the 1905 agitation against the partition of Bengal.[25] Part of the case lay in the content of *Free Hindustan*, which Taraknath Das published between 1908 and 1910, attacking British rule in India on every page and drawing attention to unfair treatment of Indians in British colonies overseas.[26]

The men that Hopkinson watched were constantly on the move. For the first two and a half years of his employment, Hopkinson was comparatively immobile. In November-December 1909, he toured the lower Fraser Valley and the Kootenays. Subsequently, he made occasional quick trips into the interior, but, for the most part, he was confined to Vancouver and Victoria. With this, he was not satisfied. In February 1910, he identified Seattle as the headquarters of revolutionary activity. There Taraknath Das and his associates could operate without fear of arrest. "If enquiries should ever be directed and a strict watch be kept on their doings, there is no doubt whatever evidence would be forthcoming . . . "[27]

After June 1911, Hopkinson's field of inquiry expanded. He was told by informants that Taraknath Das was trying to speed up his application for American citizenship. The application had been pending for some time. Now rumours circulated about a meeting of Indians in Seattle who had resolved

---

25 Report of Col. E. J. Swayne.
26 Extracts from *Free Hindustan* can be found in James Campbell Ker, *Political Trouble in India*, confidential publication (Calcutta: Superintendent Government Printing, 1917), reprint (Delhi: Oriental Publishers, 1973), 119-22. Comments on *Free Hindustan* are given in Mackenzie King's *confidential memorandum of July 1908*, in Col. Swayne's report and in Hopkinson's report of 10 Feb. 1910. There is a copy of the first issue of *Free Hindustan* in PAC, RG 2/1, vol. 163.
27 PAC, RG 7, G 21, vol. 200, file 332, Hopkinson, "Report Re Hindus," 10 Feb. 191 0, copy.

to send Taraknath Das and Kumar back to India. There was a motive behind this, Hopkinson thought, and that was for Taraknath Das to return home with the protection of American citizenship to create a disturbance during the royal durbar, the visit of the new King, George V, and Queen Mary, to India that December.[28] Lord Grey was alarmed and promptly telegraphed the Colonial Office. In the doldrums of summer, it took several weeks for this message to work its way through the Colonial Office and India Office bureaucracies, and by September the matter had become one of urgency and high priority. Hopkinson was asked for more information for use in a diplomatic approach to the Americans to get Das's application stopped. He replied that he could produce what was wanted only if he were allowed to make an investigative foray across the border to Seattle, Portland, San Francisco, Berkeley, and Stockton, cities in which there were concentrations of Indians and which Das regularly visited. He had to do it himself, Hopkinson said, because there were practically no educated Indians on whom he could rely. Permission came immediately on the personal instructions of Lord Grey.[29] Go at once, Hopkinson was told, and he set off on a nineteen-day tour of the Pacific coast.

In Seattle, he went straight to the US immigration office and found the inspector who knew the most about the local Indian community. Similarly, in San Francisco, he started with the immigration office and with F. H. Ainsworth, the inspector who specialized in Indian immigrants. Ainsworth painted a dark picture of the activity of the Indian students on the Berkeley and Stanford campuses and expressed surprise that the British had paid no attention to it. From the immigration office, Hopkinson proceeded to the Asiatic Exclusion League and spent some time going through their clipping files. He also found an informant in Swami Trigu-natiti, teacher of the Vedanta Society of San Francisco, minister of the Hindu Temple on Webster St., a disciple of Swami Vivekananda and affiliated with Vivekananda's Ramakrishna Mission in Calcutta. Tarak-nath Das had joined the Vedanta Society and briefly lived with Trigu-natiti, but the Swami did not like his activism and accused him of using the society to recruit a political following, not just among Indian students but also among some of the white women attracted to the study of Indian philosophy. There had been a falling out, and

---

28   Ibid., vol. 201, file 332, Hopkinson to Cory, 29 June 1911, copy.
29   Ibid., Gory to D. O. Malcolm, 25 Sept. 1911 ; Malcolm to Gory, 26 Sept. 1911, copy.

the Swami happily gave Hopkinson copies of publications and letters he had received from Das and his associates.

Late in his stay in San Francisco, Hopkinson called at the office of the British Consul General. He found the staff there unaware of the menace (as he saw it) under their noses. His reports were to change that. He believed that he had uncovered enough to show that Das was the chief agent infecting Indian students and laborers with revolutionary propaganda and that this should be sufficient to deny Das his application for citizenship. Berkeley, San Francisco, and Seattle were the focal points of the agitation that Das was leading. The Berkeley campus in particular (which enrolled scarcely three dozen Indian students) was for Hopkinson a hotbed of intrigue: the situation there was far more serious than he had anticipated. What was needed, he recommended, was the appointment to the consular staff of a man knowledgeable about activity in the Indian community both in Canada and in the US.[30] It was a not-too-subtle case of writing up a job description to fit oneself, but, for the moment, nothing came of it.

In October 1911, while Hopkinson was in California, Lord Grey's term as Governor General ended, and that of His Royal Highness the Duke of Connaught began. Hopkinson's role was not affected, and the new Governor General acquired, in time, a high opinion of him and placed no small value on what he was doing. Nevertheless, in the months that followed, Hopkinson made noises about resigning from the Canadian immigration service. He was unhappy with his salary which, he argued, did not compensate him for the danger of his work. He had been paid $100 a month from February 1909 until March 1912, when he received a $25 increase. He wanted another $25.[31] During the summer of 1911, he had acted as Immigration Agent in the absence of J. H. MacGill, but when MacGill, a Liberal, was dismissed a few months after the Conservative election victory of 1911, the position went to another political appointee, Malcolm Reid. In November 1912, Reid tried to get Hopkinson a further increase, convinced he would resign without it. What happened in the next two months pushed that thought far from Hopkinson's mind.

---

30 Ibid., Hopkinson to Gory, 13, 16 and 23 Oct. 1911, copies.
31 Ibid., vol. 206, file 332, Joseph Pope to Governor General's Secretary, 5 Nov. 1914; RG 76, vol. 561, file 808722, Malcolm Reid to W. D. Scott, 5 Nov. 1912; Scott to Gory, 20 Feb. 1912. As of 5 Nov. 1912, in addition to his department salary of $125, Hopkinson received a retainer of $25 a month, for interpreting, from the U.S. Immigration in Vancouver; and he was paid $4.00 a day when required by the police or the Provincial Court.

A year after his first visit to California, Hopkinson asked for and received permission for another trip across the border,[32] and it was while he was in Seattle and San Francisco in November 1912 and January 1913 that he was alerted to the presence of Lala Har Dayal, a still greater danger, in his mind, than Taraknath Das. Hopkinson had not heard of Har Dayal before. He came across the name when he went to Seattle in November 1912 but attached no special significance to it and first described Har Dayal as "apparently a wealthy Hindu" who had offered a $500 scholarship for Indians studying at Berkeley.[33] (The information was inaccurate: the money for six scholarships had been pledged to Har Dayal by a Sikh farmer in the Stockton, California, area, Jawala Singh). When Hopkinson reached San Francisco in January 1913 and presented his credentials to Andrew Carnegie Ross, the new British Consul-General, he was told a story of great consequence: Har Dayal was connected with the bomb thrown at the Viceroy, Lord Hardinge, in New Delhi on December 23.[34] One source was a twenty-one-year-old student from Madras who had come to Berkeley five months previously with the promise of one of Har Dayal's scholarships. The money for the scholarship had not materialized, but he had stayed and was living in a house or hostel with Har Dayal and a number of Punjabi and Madrasi students. In that house, he inevitably overheard many conversations. He said that Har Dayal was the secretary of a Radical Club whose members included Russian and Polish socialists. On the 23rd of December, when news was received in Berkeley of the bomb thrown at Lord Hardinge in Delhi, Dayal called up many members of the club and in each instance said, "Have you heard the news? What one of my men have done in India to Lord Hardinge?" For Hopkinson, this was a statement of complicity. On the 25th of December, Har Dayal celebrated the attempted assassination by giving a party for fifteen or twenty Indian students from Berkeley. This news burned the wires to Ottawa within forty-eight hours of Hopkinson's arrival in San Francisco. With a little digging, he found out that Har Dayal was born in Delhi, had been a student at St. Stephen's College, Delhi, studied at Oxford, spent some time in France, and had arrived in the US about a year and a half before.

Har Dayal's biographer, Emily C. Brown, shows that, while he arrived in the US a fervent nationalist, he was unfocused in goals or activities: a student

32 PAG, RG 7, G 21, vol. 202, file 332, Hopkinson to Cory 17 Nov. 1912, copy.
33 Ibid., Hopkinson to Cory, 16 Nov. 1912, copy.
34 Ibid., vol. 203, file 332, Hopkinson to Cory, 11 Jan. 1913, copy.

of Buddhism at Harvard, a recluse in Hawaii, a lecturer in Indian Philosophy at Stanford — roles assumed and dropped in the brief time he had been in the country,[35] Once Hopkinson had discovered him, he came under close scrutiny. From Assistant Commissioner Edsall of the US immigration service at Angel Island, San Francisco, Hopkinson obtained a letter of introduction to Clayton Herrington, special agent of the US Department of Justice, and with Herrington's assistance he was able to place a watch on incoming and outgoing mail by paying $3 a day to a confidential clerk in the Berkeley Post Office and a little less to a letter carrier. After he had recruited agents to take notes at Har Dayal lectures and to try to infiltrate his circle of friends, Hopkinson insisted on coming back to Ottawa to report in person. "When you hear what I have to say," he told the deputy minister, "you won't consider it a waste of time and money."[36]

He was right. On February 28, he was dispatched by steamer from New York to London so that he could report personally to the India Office on Har Dayal's activities and more generally on the situation in the Indian colonies in North America. He had recommended that someone (himself) should be posted in San Francisco for six months of the year.[37] Ottawa was convinced and so was London. As a consequence, the India Office began paying him a stipend of £60 ($300) plus £60 expenses in addition to his $1,500 annual salary as an immigration inspector,[38] and he began reporting directly to an agent of the Indian government in London as well as to the Deputy Minister of the Interior in Ottawa. The Indian government agent was the Superintendent of Police in Bombay, J. A. Wallinger, who had been deputed to London for intelligence work; his correspondence with Hopkinson commenced in April 1913 when Hopkinson arrived back in Ottawa on his way home to Vancouver.[39]

So began a campaign to get Har Dayal deported from the United States. At the diplomatic level, the British Ambassador approached the State Department, and in June 1913, the US immigration officials on the Pacific

---
35 Emily G. Brown, *Har Dyal: Hindu Revolutionary and Rationalist* (Tucson, Arizona: The University of Arizona Press, 1975), 85-117.
36 PAC, RG 7, G 21, vol. 203, file 332, Hopkinson to Cory, 15 Jan. 1913.
37 Ibid.
38 Ibid., J. W. Hôlderness to Undersecretary of State, Colonial Office, 22 July 1913; Hopkinson to Gory, 11 Dec. 1914; vol. 204, file 332, Holderness to Undersecretary of State, Colonial Office, 21 Jan. 1914, copies.
39 Ibid., vol. 202, file 332, Cory to Governor General's Secretary, 23 April 1913.

coast were instructed to go to any lectures that Har Dayal gave and to take notes. At a subterranean level, Hopkinson sought evidence to make a case for the US immigration department. Diplomatic pressure secured the sanction of the US Department of Justice for the assistance of special agent Herrington.[40] Hopkinson knew that he had to build a case that would stand up in an American immigration inquiry—that is, a case with more to it than allegations of nationalist, anti-British, or anti-imperial activities—so he sought evidence of anarchist leanings, connections with the IWW (the Industrial Workers of the World) and with the anarchist lecturer Emma Goldman. He spent the winter of 1913–14 in the San Francisco area, bringing his wife and two children with him, and rented a furnished house in Oakland for $45 a month ($35 of which was paid by the Canadian government).[41] On March 25, 1914, US immigration officers arrested Har Dayal at the conclusion of a Socialist meeting at Bohemian Hall in San Francisco, charging that he was an anarchist and therefore an illegal immigrant. The event was well covered in San Francisco newspapers, and, to American journalists, Har Dayal appeared quite unruffled. "For many months," he was quoted as saying, "I have been spied upon by British secret service operatives, but have gone about my affairs openly and have not turned my statements or moderated my declarations because of their presence. My arrest was not a surprise; I had been expecting it for a long time."[42] He was not deported but released on bail, because the American immigration officials discovered, to their embarrassment, that he had been in the country for three years and was safely landed. He argued, moreover, that, if he could be called an anarchist now, he was not one when he arrived: his ideas had developed since then. They had confused his records with those of another Indian, a laborer named Hur Dial; as a consequence, they had kept his case pending for too long. One straw grasped at was the story given to Hopkinson by informants in Vancouver that Dayal had spent time in Honolulu and Suva (Fiji) since coming to the United States (and therefore did not have continuous residence), but it could not be authenticated.[43] In May, Hopkinson went to Washington and discussed the Dayal case with the US Commissioner-General of Immigration, Anthony

---

40   Ibid., vol. 203, file 332, Joseph Pope to Governor General's Secretary, 17 Nov. 1913.
41   Ibid., Hopkinson to Cory, 14 Nov. 1913, copy.
42   Ibid., vol. 205, file 332, clipping from *Los Angeles California Times*, 29 Mar. 1914.
43   Ibid., Hopkinson to Gory, 4 April 1914; Samuel W. Backus to Hopkinson, 1 April 1914; Hopkinson to Gory, 7 April 1914, copies.

Caminetti, who concluded that on the evidence available his department could not act.[44] Later that summer, Caminetti received a letter from Har Dayal mailed from Geneva. He had decided to leave on his own.[45]

In hindsight, the effort to have him deported appears counterproductive. If anything, it gave Indian revolutionaries in North America greater purpose and determination. In the year and a half beginning with Hopkinson's discovery of Har Dayal and ending with Dayal's departure for Switzerland, the revolutionary movement on the Pacific coast flowered. In May 1913, Har Dayal organized the Hindu Association of the Pacific Coast, of which the Ghadar party was an outgrowth, and in November 1913, the first issue of the *Ghadar* newspaper appeared. What distinguished the Ghadar movement from earlier organizations was its espousal of violence. No one in the India Office or in the Government of India was inclined to minimize what was going on. On May 11, 1914, C. R. Cleveland, the Director of Criminal Intelligence in Delhi, wrote: "I look on the rabid discontent of the Sikhs and other Punjabis on the Pacific coast as one of the worst features of the present political situation in India."[46] Yet, ironically, the Ghadar phenomenon occurred subsequent to Hopkinson's first report on Har Dayal. The alarm had been sounded before the fire. Without this kind of attention, the Ghadar party could not have made the mark it did.

Cleveland considered sending agents to California to counter Ghadar propaganda among the Sikhs, and he discussed the matter with army authorities, the Punjab government, and the Home and Commerce and Industry Departments of the Government of India.[47] Hopkinson saw a reference to this in a secret Criminal Intelligence Office circular he received from Wallinger. He thought it a bad idea, called it a missionary undertaking, and said that it would not work and would be dangerous for those involved. Instead, he promoted a Canadian-based secret intelligence organization in which, it went without saying, he would play a large part.[48] His sphere was increasing. He had suggested regular trips to New York to see US immigration authorities there and check arrivals from Europe, and he had been authorized to go. Now he had two coasts to cover, and he was spending more money—$ 1100

---

44   Ibid., vol. 204, file 332, Hopkinson to Gory, 3 May 1914, copy.
45   Brown, 166.
46   PAG, RG 7, G 21, vol. 205, file 332, Supplementary Note to Draft Circular, Criminal Intelligence Office, Simla, April 1914, copy.
47   Ibid.
48   RG 7, G 21, vol. 205, file 332, Hopkinson to Wallinger, 27 June 1914, copy.

for his winter in San Francisco and $350 on one trip to New York. On May 20, 1914, the Governor General, the Duke of Connaught, urged a new arrangement. In a secret dispatch to Lewis Harcourt, the Colonial Secretary, he described Hopkinson as a valuable officer doing work "of very considerable importance."[49] Connaught identified two problems. First, he thought that too much rested on the shoulders of one person, and if anything ever happened to Hopkinson, his intelligence system would collapse. Second, he observed that the government of Canada was paying most of the cost for investigations that were of imperial, rather than Canadian, concern. A lurking danger was the possibility that members of the House of Commons might discover Hopkinson's expenditures. If they made an issue of the matter, the publicity would jeopardize his work. The solution Connaught had in mind was to transfer Hopkinson permanently to the service of the Indian government and for that government to give him the means to set up a systematic intelligence organization.

Hopkinson spent a few days in Ottawa just before that dispatch was written, and one can presume that he had been putting his case to the Governor General.[50] For the next two months, he had little opportunity to renew the campaign, although he occupied center stage in a drama that commanded the attention of all concerned with the relations between India and Canada. From May 21 until July 23, 1914, he was occupied with the *Komagata Maru*, the shipload of Punjabi immigrants who unsuccessfully sought entry at the port of Vancouver, and he served the Canadian and imperial governments well in doing what he could to avert a violent encounter between officials and immigrants which would have given Indian nationalists the *cause célèbre* they sought. Less than two weeks after the *Komagata Maru* was ushered out of Canadian waters, Hopkinson's presence assumed a new importance. On August 4, Britain declared war on Germany. On August 11, Hopkinson reported that revolutionaries on the Pacific coast were promoting a general return of Indian immigrants to take up arms against the British while they were at war in Europe.[51] It was a campaign organized without much secrecy. Hopkinson was first alerted by a story in a Portland, Oregon, newspaper saying that half of the Indians employed at the Hammond Mills in Astoria had left by train or boat for San Francisco and that the other half were

---

49 Ibid., vol. 204, file 332, Connaught to Harcourt, 20 May 19.14, copy.
50 Ibid., Hopkinson to Wallinger, Ottawa, 14 May 1914, copy.
51 PAG, RG 76, vol. 388, file 536999, Hopkinson to Gory, 11 August 1914, copy.

preparing to go to take part in the expected revolution. Within days, the India Office, the British Foreign Office, and the Canadian Department of the Interior had set up a reporting system with Hopkinson at the hub. Lists of departures from San Francisco were sent by the British Consul General there, Carnegie Ross, to the Canadian Governor General, so they could be scrutinized by Hopkinson and then telegraphed to India.[52] He was now in direct correspondence with Sir Charles Cleveland, Director General of Criminal Intelligence, Delhi.[53] His letters and telegrams identified a good many of the most active members of the Ghadar party who were subsequently arrested on arrival in India.

On October 21, 1914, Hopkinson was shot and killed by a Sikh, Mewa Singh. This was no ordinary murder, but a political act. The shooting occurred in a public place, the Vancouver Court House; the assailant made no attempt to escape and pleaded guilty at his trial. A shot in a dark alley would have been as deadly, but Mewa Singh sought martyrdom, and he was granted it twelve weeks later when he was executed by hanging. The police charged several other men with complicity in Hopkinson's murder and then failed to obtain a conviction. If Mewa Singh did act on his own, he still understood the value of his deed for the community.[54] Hopkinson was his chosen target, not just for what he did, but for what he represented—the British regime in India. In the eyes of Sikhs and other Indians in Vancouver, he was the most appropriate target available. By shooting him, Mewa Singh sacrificed himself in a way calculated to affect the hearts and minds of his countrymen. His deed can be seen against the background of the Ghadar Party call to arms, as a moral lesson for Sikh emigrants who were being exhorted to return to India to fight the British. It was also one of a series of murders involving Hopkinson's informants and their enemies: an act of retribution following a shooting outrage in the Sikh Gurdwara seven weeks earlier when one of Hopkinson's informants went berserk, killing two men and wounding seven others. It may as well have been an act of expiation, a supreme attempt by Mewa Singh to rehabilitate his reputation, after he had given information against three leading members of his community to

---

52   PAG, RG 7, G 21, vol. 205, file 332, Pope to Governor General's Secretary, 15 Aug. 1914; telegram, British Ambassador, Washington, to Governor General) 31 Aug. 1914.
53   Ibid., vol. 206, file 332, Hopkinson to Cleveland, 16 Oct. 1914, copy.
54   See Mewa Singh's address to the Khalsa Diwan Society of Stockton, California, printed in "Khalsa Samachar" and translated for the immigration department by A. H. Burton: PAG, RG 7 G 21, vol. 206, file 332, copy.

avoid a long prison sentence for smuggling a revolver across the Canada-US border earlier that year.⁵⁵ The news that Hopkinson had been killed was relayed from the Canadian to the British and Indian governments. "Murder is the outcome of work done for India," the Secretary of State for India told the Viceroy by telegram on October 26.⁵⁶ Eventually, Hopkinson's widow received £500 ($2,500 Canadian) from the Indian government, paid out of the Secret Service Fund so that it would not have to be disclosed. Initially, the Viceroy expressed reservations about making such a payment, especially after he had read a parcel of newspaper clippings from Canada. He could see that Hopkinson's relationship with the Indian government had not been hinted at, either in press speculation or in the evidence brought forward at Mewa Singh's trial. Canadian newspapers connected the assassination with Hopkinson's immigration work, particularly with the immigrant ship, the *Komagata Maru*. The theory was plausible, the Viceroy suggested. Also, he thought that it might be unwise for the Indian government to compensate the family of a Canadian immigration officer and leave itself open to the charge that it supported Canada's exclusion of Indian immigrants. He was inclined to be cautious even though the payment would be made out of a secret fund and not disclosed. The reply from London did not equivocate: "India was . . . under obligation to Hopkinson."⁵⁷ With that the Viceroy quickly gave his assent: "We have already said that Hopkinson's family has every title to consideration."⁵⁸ The Canadian government, not as generous, offered Mrs. Hopkinson a stenographer's position in the Vancouver immigration office at $1,000 a year—but no lump-sum payment.⁵⁹

The day following Hopkinson's murder, the Governor General asked what was being done to replace him. The reply from the Deputy Minister of the Interior, W. W. Cory, was that he assumed that the India Office would find an individual with similar qualifications and equal rank in the Indian service, although there had not yet been any correspondence on the subject:

---

55   See Singh's statement at his trial: PAG, RG 13, vol. 1467, Rex vs. Mewa Singh, 30 Oct. 1914; and his statement of August 1914 concerning the purchase of revolvers: City Archives of Vancouver, H. H. Stevens Papers.
56   India Office Library, Home Dept. Proceedings (Political A), Jan. 1915, No. 3.
57   Ibid., Nos. 4 and 5, Viceroy to Secretary of State for India, telegram, 11 Dec. 1914, and Secretary of State to Viceroy, telegram, 26 Dec. 1914.
58   Ibid., no. 6.
59   PAG, RG 7, G 21, vol. 207, file 332, Joseph Pope to Governor General's Secretary, 27 April 1915.

"Mr. Hopkinson was originally obtained by us from that service."[60] Cory was the deputy minister who appointed Hopkinson in 1909, and his words might be construed to mean that the Indian government sent Hopkinson to Canada. On November 4, the Secretary of State for India replied that there would be no replacement and that the Canadian immigration department should no longer be involved in surveillance of political activity among Indian emigrants, although he asked Canadian officials to pass on any information that came their way. The India Office had decided that an immigration officer was too visible a target to do the work that Hopkinson had done, and there were no objections from the Canadian immigration branch. They had come to the same conclusion. Yet Canadian officials still assumed that he would be replaced in some way.[61] Further queries from Ottawa produced the following messages from the Colonial Secretary, Lord Harcourt, to the Governor General:

(21 January, 1915) ". . . The Government of India are not prepared at present to initiate any new system for watching seditious Indian movements on the Pacific Coast."[62]

(10 April, 1915) ". . . Lord Crewe [Secretary of State for India] has requested that it be made clear that the Government of India do not contemplate the appointment, during the war, of any official agent on the Pacific coast."[63]

These messages ought not to be taken at face value. In February 1915, there had been an abortive rising in Punjab led by emigrants returned from North America and inspired by revolutionary activists based in San Francisco, Vancouver, and Victoria.[64] In the words of the Colonial Secretary,

---

60 Ibid., vol. 206, file 332, Gory to A. F. Sladen, 23 Oct. 1914.
61 Ibid., Gory to Governor General's Secretary, 28 Dec. 1914, Gory to A. L. Jolliffe, 23 Feb. 1915, copy, and Gonnaught to Harcourt, 27 Feb. 1915, copy. PAG, RG 76, vol. 352, file 379496, Reid to Gory, 26 Nov. 1914.
62 PAG, RG 7, G 21, vol. 206, file 332, Harcourt to Gonnaught.
63 Ibid., vol. 207, file 332.
64 G. S. Deol, *The Role of the Ghadar Party in the National Movement* (Delhi: Sterling Publishers, 1969), 108-48.

this event "confirmed the value of Hopkinson's work."⁶⁵ And it was not finished. The trials of those apprehended began on April 26, 1915, and the government of India were amassing every scrap of evidence they could. They wanted to know how many more Indian emigrants in North America intended to return and which of these were dangerous.⁶⁶ They also wanted to know what the Germans were up to. Late in 1914, the German consulate in San Francisco made contact with the Ghadar party by locating Taraknath Das.⁶⁷ By the summer of 1915, Canadian officials were aware that Germans were spending money in North America to foment revolution in India.⁶⁸ The India Office and the government of India were far from indifferent about surveillance in North America.

Between 1916 and 1918, the archives yield traces of the undercover agent that the India Office did have in place. His name was Robert Nathan. He was a retired, top-level civil servant with twenty-six years of experience in India. His appointments had included those of private secretary to the Viceroy and chief secretary to the government of East Bengal and Assam.⁶⁹ His channel in London was the same J. A. Wallinger with whom Hopkinson had communicated.⁷⁰ He had a budget for paid informants, and his messages to and from his informants and Wallinger were regularly relayed in code through the Governor General's Office. To Canadian officials who cooperated with him, he was "our mutual friend." "I do not like to mention his name," Chief Press Censor Ernest J. Chambers explained to Malcolm Reid, Nathan's official contact in Vancouver.⁷¹ A year later, less cautiously, writing to the general manager of the North Western Telegraph Company, Chambers justified the interception of "Hindu" telegrams by citing the authority of

---

65   PAC, RG 25, series G 1, vol. 1156, file 40, Harcourt to Gonnaught, telegram, 19 April 1915.
66   Harcourt to Gonnaught, 10 April 1915.
67   Karl Hoover, "The Hindu Conspiracy Case in California, 1913-1918," *German Studies Review*, May 1985, 252.
68   For example: PAC, RG 6, E 1, vol. 571, file 251, Maj. R. O. Montgomery to Sir Richard McBride, 27 July 1915, copy.
69   *The India Office List for 1917*.
70   PAG, RG 7, G 21, vol. 207, file 332, paraphrases of cypher telegrams exchanged by Connaught and Harcourt containing messages between Nathan and Wallinger. The first in the file is dated 31 August 1916, but it mentions arrangements made in January. M. R. J. Reid's reference to "a mutual friend" in a letter to E. J. Chambers, 9 Jan. 1918, probably means Nathan. See PAC, RG 6, Series E, vol. 524, file 150-D.
71   RG 6, Series E, vol. 524, file 150-D, Chambers to Reid, 8 Aug. 1916, Copy; Reid to Chambers, 22 Aug. 1916.

"a very high official of the India Office who happens to be on the Coast at the present moment."[72] The assistance Nathan received in Canada was extensive. Beginning in 1916, telegraph companies were intercepting every telegraph message filed or received in Vancouver to or from any Indian in British Columbia or elsewhere. They were also intercepting Chinese telegrams.[73] Copies were passed on to Nathan as well as the Chief Press Censor and the Dominion Police Commissioner. Most of these messages appeared to be of no interest whatsoever. They chiefly concerned labor recruitment or job opportunities: "Let me know if you get job. What wages. I am alone," or, "Come to Wardner quick. Have job for you and Jagat Singh," or, "Yourself and Dhampol come quick. Mill starts Monday."[74] When the Dominion Police Commissioner suggested that these messages were not worth collecting, he was told that Nathan found them valuable, and the practice continued until December 1919—more than a year after the war ended.[75] It would have carried on longer if the wartime censorship system had remained in force.

Nathan was in close contact with Malcolm R. J. Reid, former Immigration Agent at Vancouver, who had been removed from that position in January 1915 and reappointed as Dominion Immigration Inspector for British Columbia.[76] The move had the appearance of a demotion, and Reid later complained that the man who recommended it, E. Blake Robertson, Assistant Superintendent of Immigration, was against him because "I had sat tight on the Oriental Question."[77] Still, Reid found a new function by picking up the bits and pieces of investigative work that Hopkinson's death left unattended. He had been involved in this work in the past when Hopkinson (his subordinate) had been absent from Vancouver, and he had

---

72 Ibid., Chambers to Geo. D. Perry, 6 Nov. 1917, copy.
73 Ibid., Chambers to Perry, 19 Jan. 1916, copy.
74 Ibid., Reid to A. P. Sherwood, 18 April 1916, copy.
75 Ibid., Chambers to Reid, 8 Aug. 1916, copy; Reid to Chambers, 22 Aug. 1916, copy; Chambers to John McMillan, 29 Dec. 1919, copy.
76 Reid was replaced by A. L. Jolliffe on 31 Dec. 1914, although he continued to sign correspondence as Immigration Agent until 17 January 1914. His removal was recommended 3 Dec. 1914. See W. D. Scott and E. B. Robertson to Dr. W. J. Roche: PAC, 76, vol. 561, file 808722. Reid's salary had been $2,400 since September 1912 and he was kept at the same salary after his reappointment as an inspector. His successor, A. L. Jolliffe, was raised to $2,000 from the $1,200 he had been earning as an inspector; in 1919-20, Jolliffe received $3,000 while Reid remained at $2,400 and by 1923-24 Jolliffe was earning $3,600 to Reid's $2,520: Auditor General's reports in *Sessional Papers, Canada*, 1915-25.
77 Vancouver City Archives, Stevens Papers, Reid to H. H. Stevens, 29 Feb. 1916.

pursued it with great relish. In 1911, Hopkinson had obtained, through the Deputy Minister of the Interior, a badge and a commission as a constable in the Dominion Police force (a small, unarmed federal force which depended heavily on other agencies in carrying out its intelligence gathering and other specialized responsibilities); Reid had angled for an appointment for himself as well because he found an allure in Hopkinson's secretive world.[78]

His role now developed despite instructions that, in light of what had happened, immigration officers should stick strictly to immigration work. The opportunity came because Vancouver immigration officers were also told to pass on any information that came their way. This they did, sending three copies of each item: one for the Department, one for the Governor General, and one for London. As a legacy from Hopkinson, they were receiving prohibited Indian newspapers that had been intercepted by the Post Office and reports from Andrew Carnegie Ross, the British Consul General in San Francisco. In August 1914, Ross had been instructed to send passenger lists to Vancouver for Hopkinson's scrutiny, and he continued to send Indian material through the Vancouver immigration office (rather than through the British Embassy in Washington).[79] Similarly, Hopkinson's Indian informants still turned up at the door of the immigration building.[80] In these ways, the surveillance activity continued, and Reid took it over. His position did not come under the supervision of the new Immigration Agent, A. F. Jolliffe, but he worked in the same building in a small second floor office at the head of the back stairs. The location suited him—although he complained it was cramped—because the back stairs allowed inconspicuous entry for his clientele.[81] By 1916, he was acting as Pacific coast agent for the Dominion Commissioner of Police and the press censorship service as well as liaison with Nathan,[82] and the watch he maintained on Indians and Chinese—which took him up and down the

---

78   PAG, RG 7, G 21, vol. 204, file 332, vol. 10 (B), Reid to Cory, 30 Dec. 1913.
79   PAG, RG 7, G 21, vol. 205, file 332, paraphrase of cypher telegram, Sir Cecil Spring Rice to Connaught, 31 Aug. 1914; see also correspondence in vol. 206 (1915)-
80   PAC, RG 76, vol. 385, file 536999, Reid to Scott, 10 Aug. 1915, with copy of letter from Baboo and Bela Singh to Reid, 20 July 1915; RG 7, G 21, vol. 207, file 332, Sir Joseph Pope to Governor General's Secretary, 27 May 1916, enclosures.
81   PAC, RG 76, vol. 352, file 379496, Reid to Scott, 6 June 1916.
82   PAG, RG 7, G 21, vol. 207, file 332, Chambers to Sir Joseph Pope, 20 Feb. 1916, copy. Between 1 May 1916 and 30 April 1918 Reid employed a Hindustani interpreter, A. H. Burton, apparently in connection with his work with Nathan. As Reid explained in a letter to the deputy minister, Burton was not employed by the Immigration department. His salary was paid out of a special appropriation by "those friends interested in Hindu work." Reid was

coast from British Columbia to the Mexican border—was extended to include radical labor unions. In this way, Reid became the key intelligence figure in British Columbia with a somewhat haphazard operation run out of his immigration office and his home. In 1918, the Royal Canadian North West Mounted Police took over security work in western Canada from the Dominion Police. The Mounties refused to employ Reid, despite the lobbying of his political patron, Vancouver MP H. H. Stevens. They wanted Reid's files, but they did not want him.[83] As an immigration officer, Reid seems to have continued his work with British Intelligence until his death in May 1936. His surveillance operation became formalized as the Vancouver Special Agency of the Immigration Department. In 1923–24, it had a budget of $7,927.28, which paid Reid's salary and expenses plus the salaries of two stenographers, a full-time Chinese interpreter, and a part time "Hindu."[84]

The main chapter in this story of surveillance ended in 1918. By August 1915, most of the Ghadar leaders were in jail in India or in Burma, and hundreds of emigrants who had returned from North America and the Far East were confined to their villages. German efforts to supply shiploads of arms and ammunition had been bungled. The Ghadar episode was over. What remained was a series of conspiracy trials in Lahore, Mandalay, San Francisco, and Chicago between 1915 and 1918. There had been little organization or coordination among the cells of the Ghadar party in North America and the Far East. The return of Ghadar sympathizers to India had been rash and ill concealed, and most of the Ghadar leaders had been arrested on arrival in India. In spite of this, Sir Michael O' Dwyer called the Ghadar conspiracy the most menacing threat to security he faced as Lieutenant Governor of Punjab.[85] He and his officials reacted accordingly. In the 1915 trial in Lahore, the tribunal sentenced 24 men to death although only six had been convicted of capital offenses. The Viceroy did not want "a holocaust of victims" and commuted the sentences of 18, but he was conscious that his clemency was unpopular among Anglo-Indians.[86] Altogether, 173 men were tried in Lahore

---

careful not to mention Nathan's name; and "those friends" looks like a reference to Nathan or to his superiors. See PAG, RG 76, vol. 388, file 536999, Reid to Cory, 4 Aug. 1919.
83   S. W. Horrall, "The Royal North-West Mounted Police and Labour Unrest in Western Canada, 1919," *Canadian Historical Review*, LXI, 2 (1980) : 177.
84   *Sessional Papers, Canada^* 1925, no. 2, H, 28.
85   Sir Michael O'Dwyer, *India as I Knew It, 1885-1925* (London: Constable and Co., 1925), 190-
86   Charles (Lord) Hardinge, *My Indian Years, 1910-1916* (London: John Murray, 1948), 130.

and Mandalay in connection with the Ghadar conspiracy: 23 were hanged and 88 received life sentences.

The cases of two of the hanged men, Balwant Singh, former priest in the Vancouver Sikh temple, and Harnam Singh, who owned a grocery store in Victoria, show how North American evidence was used in these trials. Harnam Singh was deported from San Francisco in September 1914 and subsequently arrested in Burma. The principal evidence against him had been uncovered by Hopkinson during the investigation of two Sikhs in Victoria who were caught with explosives. The evidence consisted of letters about the manufacture of bombs as well as items such as a measuring glass and ten inches of fuse seized by Hopkinson during a search of Harnam Singh's store and house.[87] The Indian government wanted a witness who could identify the letters in court. Hopkinson was dead, but his report mentioned Victoria detective Ezra Carlow. At the request of the Indian government, arrangements were made to send Carlow to Burma.[88] There had been no prosecution in Canada, but the evidence was enough to hang Harnam Singh in Rangoon. In the other case, Balwant Singh left Canada in December 1914. The Siamese police arrested him in Bangkok in August 1915 and deported him to Singapore. From Singapore, he was removed to Alipore jail in Calcutta and finally brought to Punjab in July 1916. He was charged with "waging war" or "abetting" or "attempting to wage war" in Moji, Yokohama, Victoria, Vancouver, Sumas, San Francisco, Honolulu, and Bangkok. The main witnesses against him were informants who had helped Hopkinson and Reid in Vancouver, and who had since returned to India, particularly Bela Singh and Dr. Ragunath Singh. What hanged Balwant Singh was their testimony that he had given seditious speeches to Sikh audiences in Japan, British Columbia, and California.[89] Again, what did not warrant prosecution in Canada became a capital offense in the judgment of a tribunal in India.

After the US entered the war in April 1917, the American government responded to British pressure by launching proceedings against those involved

---

87 PAG, RG 76, vol. 388, file 536999, Hopkinson to Gory, 17 Sept. 1914.
88 RG 7, G 21, vol. 207, file 332, Pope to Governor General's Secretary, 22 Feb. 1916; paraphrase of cypher telegram, Colonial Secretary (Andrew Bonar Law) to Governor General, 26 Feb. 1916; paraphrase of cypher telegram, Home Department, Delhi to Governor General, 12 March 1916; Reid to Scott, 6 March 1916, copy; Cory to E. A. Stanton, 14 March 1916.
89 National Archives of India, Lahore Conspiracy Case III (Second Supplementary Case, Judgment dated 4 Jan. 1917), accused no. 3, pp. 56-67.

in the German-Ghadar plot.[90] They included Franz Bopp, the German Consul General in San Francisco, a number of Germans and Americans, and seventeen Ghadar Party leaders. Nathan's sleuthing had contributed to the arrest in March 1917 of Chandra Kanta Chakravarty, the leader of the Ghadar party in the US since December 1915.[91] Chakravarty talked, and that led to further indictments. In June, the British Government brought seven prisoners from India to Canada as witnesses for trials in San Francisco and Chicago. These men came under Indian police escort. They were met by Malcolm Reid, placed in the custody of the immigration department, and escorted by rail from Vancouver to Regina, where they were held until the trials. In Regina, the prisoners could be isolated from other Indians but made available to American prosecutors. Thirty-five defendants stood trial in San Francisco for five months from November 1917. Four were tried in Chicago. At San Francisco, much of the evidence concerned activities from 1912–13 and earlier which Hopkinson's reports had brought to light. All seventeen Indians were convicted. One of the longest sentences—twenty-two months—went to one of Hopkinson's original discoveries, Taraknath Das, who had returned voluntarily from Japan to face charges.[92] A name that figured large in all the evidence was that of Har Dayal, who was relaxing at the expense of the German government at the best of German spas, far from the reach of American or British justice.[93]

The surveillance undertaken by Hopkinson and carried on by Reid was obtrusive, and it profoundly affected the expatriate Indian community on the Pacific coast. Early on, members of this community realized that, as a result of their activities here, police were making inquiries of their families.

---

90   Hoover, "The Hindu Conspiracy Case," 245-61; Kalyan Kumar Banerji, "The U.S.A. and Indian Revolutionary Activity: Early Phase of the Gadar Movement," *Modern Review* (Feb. 1965): 99-100. Giles T. Brown, "The Hindu Conspiracy, 1914-17," *Pacific Historical Quarterly* (Aug. 1948) : 307-08. Don K. Dignan, "The Hindu Conspiracy in Anglo-American Relations During World War I," *Pacific Historical Review* (Feb. 1971): 57-76.
91   PAC RG 7, G 21, vol. 207, file 332, vol. 15 (a).
92   Goodman, "Japanese Sources," 92-96.
93   Brown, 214.

The Komagata Maru Episode and the Ghadar Party

Dr. Hugh Johnston

After long and persistent lobbying, Canadian Sikhs have won recognition for the passengers of the *Komagata Maru*. Their victory has come nearly a century after fact and offers less compensation than some Sikhs expected, but it has included an apology by the prime minister of Canada and money for special *Komagata Maru* memorial projects, including publications, a museum, a website, and a monument. The monument—a joint project of the Vancouver Parks Board and the Vancouver Sikh Gurdwara—now stands beside the harbor where the passengers of the *Komagata Maru* rode at anchor during the long summer of 1914. At the unveiling on July 23 of this year—98 years after the passengers started their sad trip back to Asia—a long line of municipal, provincial and federal politicians spoke. Prominent among them were a number of well-known and influential Indo-Canadians. I was in the midst of writing this paper and found it striking, but not surprising, that not one speaker mentioned the Gadar (Rebellion) Party. Moreover, I was aware that for those who knew something about the subject, leaving out the Gadar Party was a conscious choice.

The platform party spoke appropriately against the wrongs committed by the Canadian government in 1914 when it stopped these immigrants from coming into the country, but they avoided the subject of the Gadar because they sensed a profitless controversy—an argument about the real purpose of the *Komagata Maru*. And they steered clear of the subject even though it is not that difficult to explain: it is fair and accurate to say that the passengers began their voyage as economic migrants—not as political agitators—and that the radicalization of some came afterwards. Despite this, it has become easier to tell a truncated story and not delve too deeply. That was evident in 2008, when the prime minister of Canada, Stephen Harper, apologized for the treatment of the passengers of the *Komagata Maru*, describing it as "a sad chapter in our [Canada's] history." He carefully kept his statement brief, mentioning only the "detention" and "turning away" of the passengers and the "hardship" they experienced and that the voyage ended for some in "terrible tragedy." Significantly, he too made no reference to the Gadar involvement, although it would have been familiar to many in his audience, given the settling in which he chose to speak.[1]

This was especially ironic because Harper delivered his apology at a Sikh festival in Surrey, BC, held in the honor of Gadar party patriots and martyrs, including several from Canada who were closely involved with the *Komagata Maru*. This was the annual Gadri Babian Da Mela, then in its thirteenth year, and while it was remarkable that he should appear and speak at the Mela and not mention the Gadar Party or Gadarites, it was also understandable—as at the later unveiling of the Vancouver Parks Board monument. The Gadar story would have complicated the inclusive and upbeat message tailored for all Canadians that encased his brief apology, so he kept his account simple and left the Gadar part out. He was walking a narrow path because he was simultaneously avoiding the wider attention of a formal apology on the floor of parliament in Ottawa—which Sikhs continue to demand—and seeking to deliver his apology to a targeted audience in a British Columbia constituency in which results turned on Sikh votes. He and his advisors were aiming at maximum political benefit and minimum loss—which proved hard to achieve—and in their miscalculation they provoked the immense and immediate ire of much of their Surrey Sikh audience, including members of the *Komagata Maru* Foundation and the Descendants of *Komagata Maru* Society. As a consequence, the apology issue has not been put to rest. Sikhs carry on campaigning for a statement in parliament, and the leftwing and centrist opposition parties in Canada are now lending them support. In this public discussion, however, the Gadar connection is still left out. No one of any national political stature has corrected or supplemented Harper on that.

---

1   *Globe and Mail*, 14 May, 2008; CBC News, 3 Aug., 2008 <http://www.cbc.ca/news>; Harsha Walia, "Komagata Maru and the Politics of Apology," *The Dominion*, 11 Sept. 2008; Rattan Mal, *Asian Journal*, 18 May, 2012; *Indo-Canadian Link*, 2 June, 2012; *World Sikh News*, 16 July, 2012;

The subject gets different emphasis in India, where the *Komagata Maru* is remembered as a chapter in the freedom movement. For nearly a decade, a Sikh scholar, Professor Malwinder Jit Singh Waraich of Chandigarh, has been determinedly petitioning the courts for official recognition of the passengers of the *Komagata Maru* as freedom fighters, seeking to make their families eligible for government pensions. The Government of India at first rejected the claim out of hand, but Professor Waraich has been staunchly persistent, and, by stages, he has nearly reached his goal. The Freedom Fighter Division of the Home Ministry now recognizes the place of the *Komagata Maru* in the freedom movement, and Waraich's remaining objective is to get the families onto the pension list. When he started his campaign, the Home Ministry told him flatly that the passengers were economic emigrants, not freedom fighters. But he has successfully insisted that they were transformed into revolutionaries by their treatment by Canada, and that reverberations from their experience shaped the independence struggle in Punjab. Moreover, what he says is a good interpretation of the extensive evidence that, while contradictory in its parts, does add up to a common picture. We can see this and generally agree with him by reviewing what is known. [2]

Professor Wairaich's explanation fits perfectly with the well-documented history of Gurmukh Singh Lalton, a passenger on the *Komagata Maru* who became active in the Gadar after his return to India and who was imprisoned for seven years by the British in India before escaping to the Soviet Union. With Moscow as his base, he traveled in and out of Afghanistan and the United States for the Gadar Party until 1934 when he was arrested in India during a surreptitious visit to Punjab, leading to his further imprisonment lasting until India's independence in 1947. As a young man, he had been a graduate of the English medium high school in the Punjab city of Ludhiana. He had failed to get into the army—for medical reasons—and had come to Hong Kong in 1913 before the *Komagata Maru* was organized. Following his six months on that ship, he was a confirmed revolutionary.[3] Admittedly, he

---

2   "Reinventing History: Komagata Maru's Role Denied," *People's Democracy*, XXVII, 11, 14 March , 2004; Vikas Kahol, Preserving the Past a Labour of Love for Him, *India Today*, 16 July, 2011; "Centre told to produce list of 267 eminent freedom fighters," *Times of India*, 16 Dec. 2011; "HC seeks Centre's reply on freedom fighters pension," *Daily, Post Chandigarh*, 22 February, 2012.

3   Harban Singh ed., *The Encyclopedia of Sikhism* (Patiala: Panjabi University, 4th edition 2002); *The Ghadr Directory, 1934*, Compiled by the Director, Intelligence Bureau, Home Department, Government of India (Published, Patiala: Punjabi University, 1997); *"Struggle*

took a more extreme path than all but a few of his fellow passengers, including his schoolmate from Ludhiana, Puran Singh Janetpura. Puran Singh was a leader on the *Komagata Maru*, acting as stores keeper throughout the voyage, and he was deeply affected by the bitter experience of the *Komagata Maru* but never aligned himself with the Gadar Party or the revolutionary approach.[4] He represented many of the passengers. Although they demonstrated great solidarity right up to the catastrophic end of their voyage, they made their own individual choices and followed their independent perspectives in the aftermath. That could mean becoming an active revolutionary like Gurmukh Singh, or seeking Indian independence by peaceful means, or even adopting a more passive role. We can assume, however, that once they had been turned back from Canada, their deeper sympathies were with the revolutionary cause.

Kartar Singh Mehli was one of the rank-and-file passengers on the *Komagata Maru* who never went to prison although, like most of his fellow passengers, he was confined to his village after he got back to Punjab. The author interviewed him twice thirty-six years ago in Vancouver, when Kartar Singh was ninety-two and in the home and the affectionate embrace of his Canadian Sikh relatives, speaking Punjabi during the interviews and communicating with the aid of a family member who translated. He remembered the events of 1914 with great clarity. He had been thirty years of age and retired from the army when he left his village in November 1913. After waiting in Calcutta until he found other Punjabi villagers to travel with, he passed through Hong Kong in January 1914 on his way to America without knowing anything about the *Komagata Maru*. His first attempt to land in North America, at Tacoma, Washington, failed when he got negative results on a medical exam, and he arrived back in Hong Kong in April 1914. It was then that he learned about the *Komagata Maru* and that it had already left. With a group of fourteen, he caught up at Yokohama, and he was with the *Komagata Maru* until the fateful ending of the voyage at Budge Budge. He was one of the ordinary passengers, never close to the leaders, never seeking attention for himself, but quietly of his own mind. He had wanted to farm in

---

for Free Hindustan: Ghadr Directory, Punjab Section, 1915 (published New Delhi: Gobind Sadan Institute for Advanced Studies in Comparative Religion, 1996).

4   Author's interviews with Puran Singh's grandsons, Raj Singh and Jas Singh Toor, November 2011; *Report of the Komagata Maru Committee of Inquiry*, (Calcutta, 1914); Kesar Singh, Canadian Sikhs and the Komagata Maru Massacre (Surrey: Kesar Singh, 1989).

America after reading in Urdu papers in Punjab of high wheat yields in the United States.⁵ That was the ambition that made him so determined to get to Canada or the United States, and it seems to have been the initial ambition of most of the men on the ship to eventually acquire land, even if it almost certainly meant starting as laborers.

For most of these men, it was incidental and unexpected that the ship became a classroom in religion and politics, but that is what happened. Gurdit Singh, the charterer and leader, was an actively religious man who had a gurdwara installed in the forecastle of the spar deck, with a finely carved platform with a canopy for the Sikh Holy Book, as attractively finished as in a major gurdwara. Having a granthi on board was as essential for him as having a doctor, and so he hired Sant Nabh Kanawal Singh from Nabha to lead worship. The chanting of kirtan was a continuing practice for the passengers, and it helped their mental and emotional stability and contributed to their cohesiveness throughout their long ordeal. And the gurdwara space was also place for political meetings and lectures. That was the speaking venue for Bhai Balwant Singh, and for Professor Moulana Barkatullah and Bhai Bhagwan Sing Jakh when they addressed the passengers in Japan on the ship's outward voyage. Balwant Singh—later a Gadar martyr—had arrived at Moji at the same time as the *Komagata Maru* and came on board then. He was on his way back to Canada after an absence over a year as a delegate for the Canadian Sikh community, during which he had met with the undersecretary for the colonial office in London, the governor of Punjab, and the viceroy of India to protest unsuccessfully Canada's immigration regulations. This he told the passengers when he addressed them in Moji, and when he was later interrogated by police in India, he told them that this was all he said. Barakatullah and Bhagwan Singh visited the ship after it reached Yokohama. Barkatullah—later a Gadar activist in San Francisco—was a Muslim from Bhopal, recently dismissed from Tokyo University and the former editor of an anti-British paper, *Islamic Fraternity*, that the Japanese government had shut down. Bhagwan Singh was his temporarily guest, staying with him from the moment he arrived in Japan after he had been thrown out of Canada for his anti-British political activity only months earlier. They were already corresponding with Gadar leaders in California, and when the

---

5 Interviews with author in Vancouver, 25 Sept., 1976 and 22 June, 1977.

Komagata Maru reached Yokohama, they brought on board copies of Gadar Party publications for distribution to the passengers.[6]

When they reconstructed these events, British officials in India had little doubt that that the Gadar Party was involved with the *Komagata Maru* and that its main objective was to engineer a confrontation in Canada that would inflame public opinion in India. When the police in India later questioned the passengers, they wanted to know what went on during shipboard meetings, and specifically what people like Balwant Singh had said, and also what the leaders among the passengers had said. Gurdit Singh had two principal secretaries, Daljit Singh and Bir Singh, young men in their early twenties from the same part of Punjab (villages near Muktsar). They were students, and they were traveling together on their way to study the United States when they stopped in Hong Kong and got involved with *Komagata Maru*. On board, they played leading roles, and Bir Singh in particular was prominent as a speaker and activist. They became confirmed Gadarites while on the *Komagata Maru*, and when it returned to Asia, Bir Singh disembarked in Japan and took another ship to Shanghai to collect Sikhs for the planned Gadar rising, while Daljit Singh escaped arrest at Budge Budge, found his way back to Punjab, and successfully evaded the police while working for the Gadar Party.[7]

British imperial authorities noted—with alarm—the distribution of Gadar publications on the *Komagata Maru*, the appearances on the ship in Japan of Balwant Singh, Bhagwan Singh and Barakatullah, and the reports by a few passengers of anti-British lectures during the passage to Vancouver. To imperial authorities, it had all the markings of an anti-government conspiracy. But it was not proof, and the Lahore tribunal that passed sentence on Balwant Singh and other Gadarites in 1917 stopped short of saying that it was. In Balwant Singh's case, the court admitted that he was within his rights when he spoke at public meetings in Punjab and also on the ship of the grievances of the Canadian Sikhs, or when he agitated to have Canadian immigration restrictions removed. The tribunal imagined that his language had

---

6 Jaswant Singh, Baba Gurdit Singh: Komagatamaru (Jalandhar: New Book Co., 1965), p. 61; National Archives of India, Lahore Conspiracy Case III (Second Supplementary Case, Judgment dated 4 Jan., 1917).

7 Struggle for Free Hindustan: Ghadr Directory, Punjab Section, 1915 (published Mehrauli, New Delhi: Gobind Sadan Institute for Advanced Studies in Comparative Religion, 1996); Jaswant Singh. Baba Gurdit Singh: Komagata Maru (Jallundhur: New Book Company, 1965), p. 58.

been inflammatory and that it had strained the limits of acceptable protest, but they could not say with certainty that what he had done up to the time he visited the *Komogata Maru* had been seditious. Instead, they judged him by what followed, and in this perspective, they saw him going from legitimate protest to intemperate language to seditious action, all within ten months in 1913–1914—the time frame of the *Komagata Maru*.

This time frame included the outbreak of war in Europe in late July 1914, and that world-shaking event dramatically advanced the Gadar Party timetable. To understand what the passengers and their friends and supporters planned and intended, we have to follow events as they unfolded. The founding of the Gadar party and the planning of the *Komagata Maru* were nearly simultaneous developments, and they took place against a background of dramatically changing circumstances. When the founding members of the Gadar party began organizing in the summer and fall of 1913, they were preparing for an armed struggle for India's freedom that they believed was some distance away. Their main propagandist in the beginning, Har Dyal, spoke at times of as much as a decade before the armed struggle would begin, although he also saw the moment that Britain and Germany went to war as the opportune time. Before that, whenever it might be, he believed there was a lot of work to do.

At the end of March 1914, when he was arrested and questioned under threat of deportation by American immigration officials, Har Dyal described himself as the organizer of a movement, a thinker, philosopher, and propagandist who understood very well that his work of preparing for a future revolution could be damaged by any immediate or associated act of terror whether in the United States or in India. The charge against him was that he was an anarchist who concealed that fact when came to the United States. Under questioning, he freely admitted he was an anarchist but denied that made him dangerous. Rather than incite his associates to acts of violence, he said, he had to control them. His immigration hearing took place on Angel Island in California at the end of March 1914—coincidentally about the time Gurdit Singh chartered the *Komagata Maru* in Hong Kong. The proceedings against Har Dyal stalled when the immigration department discovered that he had already been in the country for three years and had legal residence, but he took no chances and left for Switzerland in May and that took him out of the Gadar circle. Although he was protecting himself from deportation during his Angel Island hearing, his answers have the ring of truth. His work and that of his closest associates in the Gadar at that point was education and propaganda, not action, and their main effort was the *Gadar* paper from its first appearance at the beginning of November 1913. Up to the time that Har Dyal left California, the Gadar party had no direct connection with the *Komagata Maru*.[8]

Moreover, the *Komagata Maru* enterprise grew out of a campaign by legal means that had been going on for more than five years before Gadar party was organized. From this perspective, we can see the *Komagata Maru*'s challenge to Canada's immigration regulations as a major chapter in a struggle that had begun in 1908 when Canada first barred immigration from India. Canada's South Asian immigrant community had been contesting this policy from the start: in the courts, through delegations to Ottawa, London, and Delhi, and by seeking publicity in Canada and abroad. We can demonstrate the story with one immigrant, Behari Lal Verma, who arrived in Vancouver on early in 1908 and who returned to Hong Kong in December 1913, seeking to charter a ship to bring Punjabi immigrants to Canada. He was an activist whose efforts led directly to Gurdit Singh's decision to hire the *Komagata Maru*.

Behari Lal Verma was a Punjabi Hindu educated in the reformed Hindu (Arya Samajist) Anglo-Vernacular High School in Hoshiarpur. He had spent four years in the police in Suva, Fiji, and was in still in his mid-twenties when he came to Canada on the SS *Monteagle* from Hong Kong with another 182 Punjabi immigrants. These were the first immigrants from India that Canada tried to reject with a newly instituted continuous journey regulation—a regulation aimed at Japanese coming via Hawaii and then used against Punjabis coming via Hong Kong. Their case went to court—with Behari Lal Verma heading the list of appellants—and they won, and he and the others were landed. That did not open the way for other South Asian immigrants to follow because the government passed new legislation to close the loophole that the court had identified. But it established Behari Lal on the West Coast of North America, and over the next few year, he moved many times to study in Seattle, Oakland, and Vancouver and briefly to work in a sawmill in Portland before settling in Vancouver as a real estate broker

---

8   Struggle for Free Hindustan: Ghadr Directory, Punjab Section, 1915 (published Mehrauli, New Delhi: Gobind Sadan Institute for Advanced Studies in Comparative Religion, 1996); Jaswant Singh. Baba Gurdit Singh: Komagata Maru (Jallundhur: New Book Company, 1965), p. 58.

and court interpreter. In this time, he got to know personally the leading activists in the South Asian community in California and British Columbia.⁹

Behari Lal was living in Vancouver and was active in local South Asian community in October 1913 when the SS *Panama Maru* arrived in Victoria, BC, with 56 South Asian passengers. This became a court case after the immigration department rejected all but 17 (who already had Canadian domicile), and the local South Asian community came to their defense by hiring a warmly sympathetic and politically committed Canadian lawyer. And it became a victory that seemed to open Canada to further immigration from India when the judge in this case found the regulations that the Canada was using to be invalid. This included the latest version of the continuous journey regulation. The judge made his ruling on very technical grounds, and it was a short-lived victory for the South Asian community because the Canadian government immediately prepared to reissue its regulations with revisions to meet the judge's objects. But the community saw a window of opportunity, and shortly after the ruling came down, Behari Lal left Vancouver on behalf of his countrymen to hire a ship to bring more immigrants to Canada. His arrival in Hong Kong in December 1914 generated excitement among Punjabis there, and that was how the *Komagata Maru* challenge began.

From Hong Kong, Behari Lal continued to report to the community leadership in Vancouver, but he was not able to obtain a ship, and very quickly the initiative passed into Gurdit Singh's hands—that is, into the hands of a man who had never been to Canada but who had the experience and personality to put this enterprise together. Gurdit Singh was a successful businessman whose maturity, knowledge, bearing, and manner commanded respect. He had spent years in Malaysia and Singapore, with regular returns to his village in the Amritsar District of Punjab, and for the previous several years, he had been living in his village of Sirhali. But he had come to Hong Kong on business in January 1914 and immediately became aware of the talk of Canada among Punjabis there, and the issue of finding a ship.¹⁰

Gurdit Singh, like Behari Lal Verma, soon discovered that hiring a ship was difficult—British shipping agents in Hong Kong and elsewhere were

---

9   Transcript of US Immigration Hearing in Har Dyal Case, 26 March, 1914, copy, Library and Archives Canada, RG 7, G21, Vol. 205, File 332, Vol. 11(b).
10 Struggle for Free Hindustan: Ghadr Directory, 1915; Hopkinson to Cory, 27 May, 1914, Library and Archives Canada, Governor General's Files, RG 7 G21, Vol. 200, File 332, Vol. 2 (b); L.W. Crippen to the Times of London, 30 March 1908; Jaswant Singh, Baba Gurdit Singh: Komagata Maru, p. 40.

unwilling to have anything to do with a venture that was so obviously loaded with political problems, given the hostility of the Canadian and Indian governments. It took Gurdit Singh over two months to secure a ship, and he had success only when he turned to a German shipping agent in Hong Kong who provided him with a ship owned by a Japanese firm. Even then, the Japanese owners were unhappy when they realized fully what their shipping agent had done. With that, the *Komagata Maru* venture was launched. The planning had taken place in Hong Kong with information and encouragement from Vancouver—the Vancouver Sikhs were ready for the *Komagata Maru* with a supportive Shore Committee appointed several days before it arrived.[11] Gurdit Singh, who said the *Komagata Maru* began as a business undertaking, can be taken at his word. He had no connections with the Gadar Party and no record with Central Intelligence Department in India, although they kept files on all known activists. Gurdit Singh was a nationalist and had no qualms about meeting with revolutionaries like Bhagwan Singh Jakh. But when the two of them talked on board the *Komagata Maru* in Yokohama, their conversation was about the practicality of the enterprise rather than its political value. Bhagwan Singh, who knew what he was talking about, said that the Canadian government would not let the passengers in, and Gurdit Singh refused to believe him. He thought that the law was on his side.

During the months that the *Komagata Maru* was in Vancouver, Canadian officials became convinced that a core group of the passengers were dangerously revolutionary. This opinion they passed on to the British and ultimately to the Indian governments. Their main source of information was the ship's doctor, Dr. Raghunath Singh, who early in the *Komagata Maru* saga became estranged from Gurdit Singh and most of the passengers. Dr. Raghunath Singh was a junior medical officer attached to the 8th Rajput Regiment stationed in Hong Kong. He had taken his position on the *Komagata Maru* during a two-month leave from his regiment, and he brought his wife and small son with him. When the ship and its passengers were detained offshore in Vancouver, he thought that he and his family should be given special

---

11   Jaswant Singh. Baba Gurdit Singh: Komagata Maru, pp. 40-51; Harban Singh ed., The Encyclopedia of Sikhism (Patiala: Panjabi University, 4th edition 2002), pp.142-43; Ramsharan Vidyarthi, Komagata Maru ki Sumudri Yatra (Mirajpur: Kramtikara Publications, 1970), pp. 9-15; Gurdit Singh, Voyage of Komgta Maru or India's Slavery Abroad (Calcutta, n.d.), pp. 16-44; Darshan S.Tatla with Mandeep K. Tatla, Gurdit Singh 'Komagata Maru': A Short Biography (Chandigarh: Unistar & Punjab Centre for Migration Studies, 2007); Report of the Komagata Maru Committee of Inquiry, (Calcutta, 1914).

treatment and be allowed to return to Asia on another ship. As the ship's doctor, he was permitted by the immigration department to go ashore in Vancouver to purchase medical supplies—while the rest of the passengers were kept on the ship—and he had a number of conversations with immigration officials and the Vancouver Member of Parliament, H. H. Stevens. It was then that he pressed his own case while describing seditious lectures on the ship and political divisions among the passengers. Eventually he and his family did disembark, and after some time, he did get back to Hong Kong on a regular steamer to rejoin his regiment. His testimony, given while on the ship and afterwards, was taken very seriously by Canadian and Indian officials who already suspected a seditious purpose behind the *Komagata Maru*.[12]

Suspicion worked both ways, because in their time in Vancouver, the passengers of the *Komagata Maru* acquired a powerful mistrust of Canadian immigration officials, especially a mistrust of their promises of food and water for a return journey. On the other side, with the officials, deep mistrust began with a conviction that the passengers had no regard for Canadian law and would do whatever they could to get into the country, legally or illegally. That was a starting point, and every hint that the leadership on the ship was militantly anti-Empire and fundamentally anti-British added another vigilant level of antagonism and paranoia with the officials. Gurdit Singh's public statement after the ship reached Vancouver fed this paranoia in a way that he probably did not intend. When he said that what happened to the passengers on the *Komagata Maru* would determine whether or not there was peace in the Empire, Canadian officials heard it as a threat, while he intended it as a warning. His words encouraged them to think that the *Komagata Maru* was a deliberate provocation with incendiary trouble as its chief purpose, while he wanted to emphasize the importance for the Empire of conciliating public opinion in India.

In the background, the newly formed Gadar party was operating from its headquarters in San Francisco and publishing its emotionally worded, patriotic, and revolutionary paper, and Canadian and British officials were becoming aware of it and were unquestionably upset by its tone and potential influence. They believed—and thought they had evidence—that Gadar sympathizers were foremost among the leaders both on the ship and on the Shore Committee, the committee organized in Vancouver by the local

---

12 Bhai Arjan Singh 'Chand' di Itihasak Dairy (1908-1947), Sunpadak, Dr. Puran Singh (Vancouver), 2008, p. 66.

gurdwara society to help the passengers. Immigration officials and the influential anti-Asianist MP H. H. Stevens were quick to assume the worst, and that prevented them from seeing the Shore Committee for what it was—a broad-based South Asian community effort, drawing together moderates and militants, Hindus, Sikhs, and Muslims, and the various regional sectors in the Vancouver Punjabi community—Majhail, Malwai, Doabi. The officials were more interested in discovering plots and divisions in the community, which did indeed exist, than in recognizing its common cause which was to support the efforts of the passengers to land in Canada and find work there.

An over-blown story linking the Gadar Party and the *Komagata Maru* was about the purchase of pistols by members of the Shore Committee while they were on a brief visit to the United States. Canadian officials were sure that these men intended to slip the weapons onto the *Komagata Maru*, and they may well have, but the incident caused more excitement and alarm than it needed to. It happened only a few days before the Canadian cruiser *Rainbow* escorted the *Komagata Maru* out of Vancouver's harbor to send it back to Asia. The passengers had lost their case in court and had agreed to leave Canada, but they were refusing to let the Japanese crew raise the anchor until the Canadian government had loaded provisions for the return Pacific crossing. The ship was still in the harbor when nine or ten South Asian community leaders from Canada and the United States gathered in the American border town of Sumas. Among them were prominent activists like Bhagwan Singh and Taraknath Das from California and Bhag Singh, Balwant Singh, and Harnam Singh, all members of the Shore Committee, from Canada. While in Sumas, three of these men went into a hardware store and bought two semi-automatic pocket pistols and two cheap revolvers and ammunition. Soon after that, one of them crossed the border ahead of the others, going through the woods to evade the regular check point only to run into a provincial constable who found the pistol this man was carrying in the crotch of his trousers and the ammunition he had in his pockets. That was how this attempt to secure pistols became known.[13]

Buying pistols and ammunition in a hardware store in the US was not a crime, and no American charges resulted. The only person liable to be

---

13 Stenographic notes from conversation between HH Stevens and Dr. Rughunath Singh, 4 July 1914, Vancouver City Archives, Stevens Papers; Lahore Conspiracy Case III (Second Supplementary Case, Judgment dated 4 Jan., 1917) accused no 3), National Archives of India; Indian Army Quarterly List for 1 Jan., 1912 (Calcutta, 1912), online database.

criminally charged and convicted was the one who smuggled a pistol and rounds of ammunition over the border into Canada. This was Mewa Singh—later remembered and honored in the Sikh community as the martyr who was hanged for shooting and killing immigration inspector W. C. Hopkinson. But Mewa Singh was not given a heavy sentence for the act of smuggling a pistol over the border, and that was because Canadian immigration officials did not consider him a major player. Still, they passed on information about this weapons shopping expedition to the British and Indian intelligence services, building a case for Gadar Party involvement with the *Komagata Maru*. In 1917, the Lahore tribunal that tried Balwant Singh saw the Sumas incident as incriminating for him. In his defense, Balwant Singh said that he had crossed the border to see about a plot of land for a gurdwara in Seattle, and it does seem more plausible that a large group—including the Bengali activist Taraknath Das—should get together to arrange a property transfer rather than to buy pistols, which could more easily and inconspicuously be purchased by one or two. Moreover, with the *Komagata Maru* still in Vancouver, they had much else to discuss, and pistol shopping looks like something done on impulse—the three involved had gone into the hardware store after breakfast on their second day in Sumas and after seeing pistols displayed in the window.

From the day the *Komagata Maru* arrived in Vancouver, some members of the South Asian community had repeatedly tried to buy handguns from local hardware stores only to be refused because they did not have the necessary permits from the city police magistrate. Their desire to get weapons was inspired by the Gadar leadership, which advocated the collection of rifles and revolvers "to rain a sweet shower of guns on Punjab" to arm and train fighters for the coming revolutionary struggle. But this was looking to the future. Even in late July 1914, one could not have predicted that the moment for action was coming so soon Har Dyal, for one, still imagined it five or ten years away. And arming the passengers of the *Komagata Maru* was not anyone's objective. In fact, up to the first week of July, the community hoped and expected that the passengers would win their case and come ashore in Canada, freeing the ship to take on cargo and homeward bound, fare-paying passengers for its return to Asia. The immediate opportunity of the ship, from the Gadarite perspective, was the possibility of getting weapons back to India. With this objective, Gadarites in San Francisco sent their president, Baba Sohan Singh Bhakna, to Japan with 100 or 200 American revolvers, and these weapons were taken onto the *Komagata Maru* at night shortly after it reached Yokohama on its return journey. It was between Sohan Singh's departure from San Francisco and his arrival in Japan that war broke out in Europe. The revolvers that he carried to Japan were secreted on the *Komagata Maru* only days after the Gadar Party's call to arms. This timing tells us that these revolvers were intended for a rising in a more distant future, and it was coincidence that put them on the ship at the dramatic moment when all calculations and considerations changed.[14]

All of the passengers, apparently, knew about the revolvers, and it is likely that very few saw anything wrong with having them on board (other than potential trouble with the police in India). But only a handful knew where they were hidden or had anything to do with them directly. What the passengers knew, the police in India—especially at the headquarters of the CID (Criminal Intelligence Department)—also suspected. The police were more vigilant than ever and had more arbitrary power over civilians now that war had begun and now that the Gadar Party had urged its supporters to return for the expected uprising. David Petrie, the CID officer who came came from Simla to Kolkata to meet the *Komagata Maru*, was in the police party that boarded the *Komagata Maru* before the passengers landed, and— searching a crowded ship with no easy way to separate the passengers from their kits and hesitating to do anything so offensive as remove turbans or examine loin clothes—found virtually nothing, no firearms and just a single copy of the *Gadar* newspaper that an absent-minded or disorganized passenger still had in his kit. (Most of the handguns and literature had been either hidden or jettisoned beforehand.)[15]

Significantly—and Petrie had been briefed beforehand by his police colleagues in Simla—he was not expecting the majority of the passengers to be hostile, and at the end of the searches, he thought that they were reasonably friendly. Nonetheless, he was surprised by the unity they showed and their strong attachment to Gurdit Singh, even after their months of trial and privation. He had expected a sharp division between a majority and a small

---

14   Hopkinson to Cory, 16 July, 1914, Public Record Office, London, Colonial Office 42/290; Reid to Scott, 25 July, 1914, Vancouver City Archives, Stevens Papers.

15   Harish K. Puri, Ghadar Movement: Ideology, Organization, Strategy, 2nd ed. (Amritsar: Guru Nanak Deve University, 1993), pp. 91-96, 167, 175, 189; The Ghadr Directory, 1934; Sohan Singh Josh, Tragedy of Komagata Maru (New Delhi: People's Publishing House, 1975), p. 65; Jaswant Singh. Baba Gurdit Singh: Komagata Maru, pp. 68-69; Report of the Komagata Maru Committee of Inquiry, p. 23.

group of radicals (or "mischief-makers" as he called them). He thought that the police could separate the majority from this small group of eight men—as he counted them—but he was wrong, and that miscalculation was a major factor in the tragedy at Budge Budge where the passengers disembarked and where twenty were fatally shot in an encounter with police and troops at the end of a long contentious day.

Even after it had happened, an official Committee of Inquiry into the Budge Budge tragedy agreed with what Petrie said of the passengers. The Inquiry Committee had a good chance to form an opinion because it questioned most of the men, those who were held as prisoners in Kolkata as well as those who had been escorted back to Punjab. While predictably putting the blame for Budge Budge solely on the passengers, the Committee described the majority as "harmless" and focused on just thirteen leaders close to Gurdit Singh whom the Committee judged to be "violent and dangerous characters."[16] Although the Committee saw no threat with the majority, they were still subject to harsh treatment—first of all at Budge Budge and then detention in the Kalighat Central Jail of Kolkata and finally transportation back to Punjab and confinement to their villages for the next several years.

The passengers received this treatment mainly because British India officials were afraid that—if free to do so—they would instigate an agitation in Punjab.[17] That is what lay behind government actions from the moment the *Komagata Maru* arrived off the coast of India on its approach to Kolkata. And it lay behind the automatic control—in a country long under press censorship—of news about Budge Budge. The government shut down two Urdu papers in Punjab after they made strong statements about the *Komagata Maru*. To make matters worse for the passengers, moderate politicians in India were supporting the British against their German enemies in the belief that India would be rewarded with independence when the war was over. The Indian-owned English language press struck a careful balance between mild criticism of the government and censure of the passengers for their "folly" (as one paper put it). And the leaders of the Indian National Congress and even government-friendly Sikh and Punjabi leaders in Punjab and Calcutta criticized the passengers. In the beginning, there was little open support in India for the passengers of the *Komagata Maru*, and that did not change until the

---

16   D. Petrie, "Note on Budge Budge Riot," Exhibit 116, File 5028, Public and Judicial Department Records, Indian Office Library, London.
17   Report of the Komagata Maru Committee of Inquiry, p. 26.

Indian public's attitude to the British soured after the war ended. Only then did Gurdit Singh, having escaped arrest at Budge Budge, come out of hiding and begin publicizing his account of the *Komagata Maru*.[18]

Up to that time, only the Gadar Party had publicly taken the passengers' side—praising, condoling with, and eulogizing them. It did so in publications that were banned in India but circulated through expatriate Punjabi colonies and kept and read in Punjabi emigrant homes for years to come. Bhagwan Singh, who had boarded the ship in Yokohama, then briefly assumed the presidency of the Gadar party in San Francisco, and who had met with Shore Committee members in Sumas, was the author of a Gadar booklet on the *Komagata Maru* circulated in Punjabi in 1915. He wrote in emotive and heroic language, invoking the voices of the passengers in calling for patriotic action: "We have sounded the bugle call and the scattered forces are gathering. Death awaits us all, but when we know not; if it should come in heroic deeds, don't fear it. Arise. Arise." Throughout 1914, he had been a primary link between the *Komagata Maru* and the Gadar Party. He had met and talked with Gurdit Singh, and he knew the leaders on the Shore Committee, and then he had become an early narrator of the *Komagata Maru* story. Understandably, given his revolutionary aims, he merged his perspective with that of the passenger to create a powerful image that emphasized the political meaning of the *Komagata Maru* without saying much about it as a business venture. It is his version of the story that Canadian politicians today choose to avoid.[19]

The formation of the Gadar Party and the episode of the *Komagata Maru* were a foreshadowing of the future for the British Empire—which appeared to be at its greatest when its days were actually numbered. The Sikh community leaders who encouraged the *Komagata Maru* and its passengers to test Canada's immigration laws, and those who spoke and organized against British rule in India have been vindicated by what has happened since. The freedoms and equality that they sought have come to be respected. At the time, however, neither the demand for the right to live in a British country (Canada) nor the demand that British rule should end in India, was accepted, understood, or even considered by a majority of Canadians. And the suggestion by Canadian officials that the Gadar Party was behind the *Komagata*

---

18 Petrie, "Note on Budge Budge Riot."
19 *The Bengalee*, 4, 6, 7, 14 October, 1914. Translation of Gadar di Goonj No. 2, 1915, pp 10-19, attached to Reid to Stevens, 20 March 1915, Stevens Papers, Vancouver City Archives.

Maru strengthened the negative feelings of most Canadians towards the passengers and their ambitions. But the evidence we have seen suggests that the Gadar party was only incidentally involved. A close look shows that, while the passengers and their leaders had pride of nationality and sympathized with the independence movement, the great majority were first and foremost economic emigrants seeking opportunity in North America.

Social and Political Lives of Early Sikh Settlers in California: 1897-1946

Dr. Bruce La Brack[1]

Although this early period can be generally and correctly characterized as one of almost continuous population decline and socio-economic

---

[1] Dr. Bruce La Brack, Professor Emeritus, School of International Studies, University of the Pacific Stockton, California

marginalization, it was also simultaneously a time of rising political consciousness, activism, and resistance to discriminatory government laws in the United States and to the rule of the British Raj in India. The story of this relatively small community's difficult transformation from struggling economic sojourners to acquiring full US citizenship shortly after India herself achieved independence remains one of the most remarkable, but under appreciated, in American immigration history.

It is also a story about how the founding of the Stockton *gurdwara* in 1912 created both a physical place and a symbolic center for Sikh life that played a crucial role in community life over the next forty years. It created the sole Sikh worship center in the US until 1947. The Stockton *gurdwara* remains a revered historic structure and is an icon known to Sikhs around the world. It is an important cultural touchstone and holds a major place in the history of the Sikh Diaspora, particularly in California.

However, the second act in the American Sikh story, the period from 1946 to the present, is more remarkable still, resulting in an even more spectacular half-century of growth involving Sikh/Punjabi communities across the United States, beginning in the mid-20th century and continuing to today. The last 60 years are all the more remarkable when contrasted with chronic uncertainty that characterized the first five decades of their immigration history. If someone objectively examined the status and conditions of the original Pioneer Sikhs in California in the late 1940s, they would logically conclude that it was not at all clear that Sikhs could even survive, let alone ever prosper, in America.

Nevertheless, it was during those initial long decades of general economic and demographic decline, social discrimination, and facing a continual and increasingly hostile, anti-Asian set of legal decisions, that Sikhs found ways to resist and circumvent these disadvantages. The community, especially in rural California, became galvanized by both domestic and international injustices. Sikhs responded to colonialism, institutionalized racism, and local discriminatory practices by seeking legal redress and supporting Sikh causes in America and India. The locus of much of this activity, secular and sacred, was, then as now, centered in the Stockton *gurdwara*.

I expect that this audience knows the basic outlines of Sikh early history in the US, but a brief review of how precarious the Sikh position was from the beginning can be summarized thus:

Social and Political Lives of Early Sikh Settlers in California: 1897–1946

- The first immigrants to North America were largely Punjabi male peasant farmers from the northwest of British-controlled India.
- Eighty-five to ninety percent of whom identified themselves as Sikhs; ten to twelve percent were Punjabi Muslims, with the remainder Punjabi Hindus.
- There were almost no South Asian women on the West Coast in the first decade of immigration, and perhaps no more than one hundred ever entered the US prior to 1945. It was all but impossible to find a Sikh mate.
- Concentrated on the West Coast, there were never more than six or seven thousand legal South Asians in residence, the majority (6,100) arriving between 1904 and 1911. They came largely from agrarian and/or military backgrounds. Moreover, in 1912, an Immigration Commission estimated that between one-half and three-fifths of the South Asian immigrants of that time could neither read nor write.
- Between 1915 and 1929, some 1650 additional Sikhs arrived, but during the Depression years and throughout World War II, only 183 additional South Asian legal immigrants were recorded.
- However, in the first two decades of the 20th century, some 6,750 South Asians were either deported or "voluntarily" left, many to support *Gadar* and other anti-British political activities in India or abroad, or for personal reasons.
- By 1930, the so-called "Hindu" population in California had declined to 3,130; by 1940, to 2,405; and by the end of the Second World War, to less than 1,600 individuals.
- Even factoring in a further possible 3000 illegals who sporadically filtered in via Mexico in the 1920s to 1930s, <u>fewer than a total of ten thousand Sikhs ever came to the United States in the first half of the 20th century, and only fifteen percent of those remained by mid-century.</u>
- The slow but inexorable decline of the original populations was somewhat offset by the formation in California of "Hindu-Mexican" (a.k.a. "Mexidu") family units whose story has been most fully documented and detailed by Karen Leonard. This unusual social component was composed of some 400 bi-cultural families headed by South Asian Punjabi Sikh or Muslim males, their Spanish-heritage wives, and their offspring, eventually forming networks statewide.

For practical terms, these mixed marriages formed a loose social network that provided Pioneer men with the only domestic stability they could create at the time.

To say that the initial conditions of Sikh immigration to America were not auspicious would be a Himalayan understatement.

The *Gurdwara* and *Gadar*: Religion and Politics

Throughout all this time, in spite of difficult economic circumstances, a series of prejudicial, restrictive legislative acts (e.g., Alien Land Laws, 1913; Barred Zone Provision, 1917; Thind Supreme Court decision, 1923) and sporadic US government surveillance, Sikhs in America continued to organize and lobby for their rights. The locus of much of this activity was the Stockton *gurdwara*. Although severely restricted for fifty years in their choices of occupation, marriage partners, freedom to travel abroad, own land, and participate in mainstream political activities, they continued to gather at the Stockton *gurdwara* to debate and organize.

From the beginning, the *gurdwara* served as an important nexus of Sikh social, religious, and political life. It simultaneously functioned as the combination of church, dining hall, rest home, guest house, employment information center, meeting place, and sanctuary where Punjabi culture and language were understood and appreciated.

The role of the Sikh temple as a political actor has been well-documented as part of the *Gadar*-era, so well in fact that the political machinations and in-fighting among the various *partis* (political factions) tends to sometimes overshadow the more mundane and central functions of the *gurdwara* as a social institution and welfare society. Nevertheless, it is difficult to discuss the *gurdwara* during the early years of Punjabi presence in America *without* referring to *Gadar* activities, because the Pacific Coast Khalsa Diwan Society (PCKDS) and the *Gadar* Party were largely composed of the same membership and financially supported by the same people. It is somewhat paradoxical that although the two organizations differed dramatically in their specific institutional goals and activities, the PCKDS and the *gurdwara* were the only two constants in terms of formal organizations available to Sikhs for many decades.

The PCKDS in that era was a socio-religious collective which was interested primarily in managing the *gurdwara* and providing support to its members, most of whom were, of course, Sikhs. It was, strictly speaking, the governing body for the Sikh worship site.

On the other hand, the *Gadar* Party was clearly a militant political association dedicated to violent overthrow of British rule in India. It originated in California as an indigenous response to external circumstances, although it certainly was a modern revolutionary movement, one which eventually achieved international dimensions. Beginning as a home-grown organization, within a few years it forged extensive global networks, including links to Hong Kong, Thailand, Russia, and Ireland. It became a force that eventually directly affected international relations among many European countries, including Germany and England, as well as influencing both Canadian and American foreign relations.

This caused political problems for the entire California Sikh community, because it regularly attracted the unwanted attentions of the immigration service, FBI, British Secret Service, and state and local authorities in California and elsewhere. The *Gadar* Party was a spectacular and exciting element in the lives of California Sikhs, but its international heyday lasted roughly seven years, from 1913 until the end of World War I. Thereafter, *Gadar* became almost wholly a Sikh enterprise, and, as it was from the beginning, Punjabi farmers throughout the American West were its main financial backers from 1913 until as late as 1947.

Never particularly effective in implementing its primary goal, *Gadar* nevertheless survived British, British-Indian, and American government surveillance and counter-intelligence, the deportation of some leaders, and the spectacular "Hindu Conspiracy Trial" of 1917–1918 in San Francisco, California. Sikhs also continued to publish *Gadar* materials throughout the early period and only ceased upon Indian Independence.

For all its political activity, the *Gadar* was also an important social institution that facilitated all manner of communication among its members. Although sometimes debates over policy and tactics could cause divisiveness, it also provided a feeling of cultural solidarity, and provided a rationale and impetus for action. In the face of continuous economic discrimination and social exclusion, it gave the Sikhs and other South Asians a "party" and cause of their own, one with a clear purpose and high ideals. Both the *gurdwara* and *Gadar* organizations provided a reason to band together. For many men these activities were the only "social functions" they had besides group drinking and religious services.

While *Gadar* meetings took place across California, the Stockton *gurdwara* frequently provided a forum for *Gadar* discussions and planning. Men and their Mexican wives remembered traveling to Stockton from around the state five or six times a year, and how these occasions combined attendance at religious services with *Gadar* fundraising, strategy sessions, and political discussions. As one old timer characterized it, "One day was for praying and the other for plotting."

Following World War One, *Gadar* ideals and goals continued to impact the political thinking and ambitions of many California Sikhs, but its importance gradually diminished over the decades. In retrospect, it seems that the social and religious aspects of the *gurdwara* as a social institution became dominant over time. The longer the community resided in California, the more they realized that Sikhs had serious domestic obstacles to overcome. While they never abandoned the *Gadar* goal, they increasingly turned their political attention to issues of social and legal rights within America during the later inter-war years. They also continued to work hard and take advantage of any economic opportunities that arose. Similarly, once they realized that, for whatever reasons, they were unlikely to be able to return home, they shifted mentally from being sojourners and temporary economic migrants, and began to realize that their future and their fortunes were going to be forged primarily within an American context.

In spite of severe social and legal barriers, many South Asians did well on the West Coast. Within less than a decade of their arrival, many had established themselves in farming ventures, often in partnership with other Punjabis. They quickly and expertly assessed the local markets and crops. And while they worked at almost anything that came to hand in the early period, including building railroads and bridges, logging, mining, and road construction in Canada and the American Northwest, it was in California agriculture that they found their most promising and lasting niche.

California land records show an initial Sikh pattern of leasing, followed, if possible, by purchase. Sikhs were already in the Central California valley by 1906. A few became successfully involved in establishing rice culture in the Northern Sacramento Valley, as well as undertaking orchard and vineyard cultivation in Yuba and Sutter Counties. By 1908, they were in the Imperial Valley of southern California where they helped initiate cotton growing, and, later, vegetable row crops. A 1920 state report listed 85,000 acres in the

Sacramento and San Joaquin valleys as under the control of "Hindus" and an additional 30,000 in the Imperial Valley, most of which was leased.

Ninety miles north of us in Yuba and Sutter counties of the northern Sacramento Valley, the Sikhs began to coalesce very early and eventually settled down, forming a northern nucleus that served as a small, but relatively stable, California Sikh community throughout their early history. Much of their success can be traced to cultivating 10–30 acre peach, prune, almond, or walnut farms in the Yuba City-Marysville area. This pattern endured through the difficult 1920–1940 period, when the local Sikh population eventually dwindled to around 350–400 persons owning less than 1,000 acres by 1946. Not surprisingly, in spite of the limited opportunities and legal restrictions the early Sikhs endured, this same location currently contains the largest agricultural concentration of Sikhs outside of India (10,000+) and now boasts third- and, even, forth-generation Sikh farm families.

In the difficult interwar period, just as Sikhs shifted their attitudes towards making a life in America, American attitudes towards empire and other peoples was beginning to change. Colonial attitudes towards India that had been so common in the society up to that time were giving way to growing support for Indian self-determination and self-governance in South Asia and elsewhere.

Simultaneously, the widespread reflexive racism at home was diminishing somewhat. By the end of the 1930s, in addition to *Gadar*, a second wave of South Asian organizations arose to promote both Indian Independence abroad and the right of citizenship for South Asians who already resided in the US or might wish immigrate. This time, new political centers arose outside of California in New York, Chicago, and even Arizona, and they became ever more effective in lobbying, public relations, and garnering support from mainstream media and federal governmental figures and agencies.

After decades of generally unsuccessful political activity, Sikhs saw the tide of public opinion regarding South Asians, domestic and foreign, turn more positive during the late 1930s and early 1940s. Many individuals, American and South Asian, were involved in achieving the rights of citizenship that were finally confirmed on July 2, 1946, when the US Congress passed the Luce–Celler bill. However, Sardar Jigit (J.J.) Singh, a successful New York businessman, was a key figure whose political savvy and contacts in mainstream journalism were crucial factors that led to passage of this historic legislation.

Incidentally, this legal victory was the first and, to that time, <u>only</u> successful outcome achieved by Sikhs at the national level since they arrived nearly a half-century earlier. It is also symbolic that the legislation in America was passed over a year before India herself became independent on August 15, 1947.

Although this law eliminated the ban on Indian immigration and allowed Indians to become naturalized citizens, it was far from a total success. The impact of obtaining citizenship remained greatly restricted as the total number of East Indians allowed to immigrate was set at a mere 100 per year, a quota which can only be considered simultaneously symbolic and ludicrous given that India had a population of 400 million. More important, of course, than the actual numbers, was the legal precedent. After nearly thirty years of systematic exclusion and another quarter century of being denied citizenship, the Luce–Celler bill restored to East Indians the option of United States' residence and naturalization, and the freedom to travel freely to India and return.

However, in a final perverse twist of fate, Indian Independence did not result in a whole nation-state, but a bifurcated, "Partitioned" India. Thus, as the first half of the 20th century wound down, events occurred which paradoxically brought both vindication and redress for Sikhs in America, but also contained the devastating reality that, shortly following their American victory, the gaining of independence was achieved at a tragically high cost in lives and loss of territory. It literally left the Punjabi homeland shattered, and large swaths of it ceded to the new nation of Pakistan.

Of course, over the subsequent sixty years, the growth of the Sikh community in America has surpassed all expectations and resulted in transformation beyond any the Pioneer Sikhs could have imagined. But the foundations of this renaissance were built on the financial and legal struggles of those early Sikhs in California, which was inextricably intertwined with history of the Stockton *gurdwara*. All South Asians in America owe a great debt to those Pioneer ancestors. It is fitting that we should be here today recognizing the Stockton *gurdwara* as the foundational Sikh religious institution in the United States.

As we celebrate the Centenary of the founding of this key North American religious center, it is appropriate to take a minute or two to discuss some links between the Stockton *gurdwara* and the institution that is

Social and Political Lives of Early Sikh Settlers in California: 1897–1946

our host today, the University of the Pacific. There are some interesting but little-known connections between this university and the California Sikhs.

The University of the Pacific is a private university originally chartered in 1851 in Santa Clara. It moved to San Jose in 1871 and remained in the Bay area until 1925, when it relocated to Stockton. Although the University was established in California long before the Sikhs arrived, the *gurdwara* was constructed thirteen years *before* Pacific arrived in the central valley. This put both organizations in the geographic center of California Sikh culture and community, because within a 500-mile radius of Stockton lived the majority of American Sikhs in the US from 1900 to 1965 (95% of Sikhs in the US resided therein until the 1960s). In other words, Stockton and greater Central Valley generally constituted the historic core of Pioneer Sikh communities.

However, very few historians or social scientists of that time took much note of early Sikh presence. One notable exception was Harold S. "Jake" Jacoby (1907–2000). He graduated from Pacific in 1928 and returned for a long career here as a beloved teacher and administrator, serving for 37 years as a faculty member. I mention him only because Jake was one of the very earliest US scholars who took any interest in the Sikh communities in their own backyards.

In fact, in 1956, he published one of the first, detailed, and still-useful pamphlets on Sikhs in America titled, "A Half-Century Appraisal of East Indians in the United States." The material was based on fifteen years of interviews with Pioneer Sikhs. The report was originally written as an invited research lecture he gave to the faculty on this campus. He maintained a life-long interest in and friendships with Sikhs from throughout California. It is therefore appropriate that a half-century later we should acknowledge his early scholarly interest at this time and in this place.

I sincerely hope that further academic research focusing on the earlier periods of Sikh history continues, because I am convinced that although there has been an explosion of literature on Diasporic Sikhs around the world, I do not believe that the present picture of the first half-century is anywhere near as complete as it could be.

For example, in the past six months, I have become aware of some very interesting historical research being done in the Pacific Northwest, primarily in Oregon and Washington, using a combination of newspaper archives and public records that seems to have the potential to expand our understanding of what the "facts on the ground" were in certain Pacific Northwest locales where Sikhs had settled in the first few decades on immigration to North America. The first is an article by Johanna Ogden titled, "*Gadar*, Historical Silences, and Notions of Belonging: Early 1900s Punjabis of the Columbia River," published in July in the *Oregon Historical Quarterly*, Vol. 113 (Summer 2012), No. 2, pp. 164–197, Portland, Oregon. As part of her analysis, she begins by discussing a keynote address by Har Dayal in Astoria, Oregon, on May 30, 1913.

She considers this meeting and speech as the opening salvo in the founding of *Gadar*. She then reviews both the responses of local Sikhs and Hindus to this call-to-arms and the social, political, and economic backlash that the presence of Punjabis in the Columbia River basin provoked from the general public. Her larger question is why this chapter of Oregon history has been essentially erased from the prevailing dominant narrative. She notes:

> "... while they were not physically driven from the state, the Punjabis have been run out of Oregon historically. There are no identifiable vestiges of them in Oregon's landscape, little recognition of their lives or accomplishments exists in our collective memory, and the watershed founding of Gadar is largely forgotten. If remembered at all, Gadar's Oregon story is eclipsed by that of San Francisco, the later home of its office and press."
>
> Ogden, 2012, p.166

In fact, the press she refers to, which was located in Oakland and produced much of the *Gadar* literature of the inter-war period, was recently acquired by the Stockton *gurdwara* where it will be on public display.

A second article on Sikh activities in the Pacific Northwest, which has not been published yet, is titled "(In)visible Minority: The Indian Community in the Pacific Northwest after the 'Anti-Hindoo' Riots of 1907-8." The author effectively argues that, in the aftermath of various violent encounters between Sikhs and local communities in Washington and Oregon, rather than leaving those locations as some previous researchers have suggested, they remained for decades in those Pacific Northwest regions. However, isolated and discriminated against, many of these micro-communities persisted for decades but kept such a low profile that they seemed to almost disappear from the historical record.

Both authors have gleaned new, and often surprising, information about the lives of early Sikh sojourners who lived far from the California nexus and endured significant hardship to do so. Much more of this kind of finely detailed and documented research would be welcome by anyone interested in constructing the whole story of immigration on the West Coast, and who wishes to include fully and accurately all the myriad groups who participated in the building of America, including the Sikhs.

So let me conclude by offering two quotes I think are *apropos* to our subject today. The first is the well-known Shakespearean line: "The Past is Prologue," from his play *The Tempest*, because it seems a particularly apt metaphor to describe the arc of Sikh history from the first half of the 20th century until today.

The second is from William Faulkner, who so wisely noted, "The past is never dead. It's not even past."

It seems fitting that we periodically express our collective appreciation for the sacrifices and hard work of the Sikh Pioneers. It was those early efforts that set the foundation, which, eventually, created the successes that all Sikhs in America benefit from. The role of the Stockton *gurdwara* lies at the core of this achievement. It continues to play a key role in California Sikh religious life. This heritage is therefore, in every sense, a living legacy . . . one which we honor and celebrate today.

Paper Presented at the *Sikhs beyond Boundaries: Imagined Profiles and the Real People* Conference, sponsored by the Sikh American Research Center of the Pacific Coast Khalsa Diwan Society as part of the Centenary celebration of the founding of the Stockton Gurdwara, University of the Pacific, Stockton, California, September 22, 2012

Social and Political Lives of Punjabi Settlers of the Columbia River, Oregon 1910-1920

Johana Ogden

Thank you to all the capable organizers of this conference and for including me.

I also thank the many participants for enriching our understanding of the political and cultural events of the Punjab and of the white colonial regimes like South Africa and Australia that combined to propel people towards North America and, once here, the faith, politics and simple ingenuity drawn upon by migrants to navigate the obstacles that the Canadian and US settler regimes threw at them. I can't and won't attempt to cover that ground that others are doing so capably.

Instead, I am going to focus on an under-told story regarding Punjabi settlers, largely Sikh, in Oregon, a community that was concentrated along about 175 miles of the Columbia River at the north end of the state. I am not an Indian, Ghadar, Sikh, or Canadian scholar. I've had to learn aspects of these as a part of my research. But I am an historian of Oregon, which is my home. And if this history proves nothing else, it drives home the fact that local history cannot be a narrow recounting of place and that seeming backwaters are thoroughly entwined in the world's currents and processes, often in surprising ways.

I find the story of Ghadar's ties to Oregon fascinating, and, for the most part, Oregonians have no idea there were Sikh pioneers in the state, let alone know they were a part of a groundbreaking international movement. I was no different when I stumbled upon this story.

But it's not just the public who has not known this story. Ghadar's roots in Oregon have been lost to historians of the American West. By contrast, Indian historians of Ghadar have provided details about the Punjabi presence and activity along the Columbia River and are the source of many of the particulars used in my work. Reading these Indian accounts, I was both elated but perplexed by the fact that historians on the other side of the world knew more about happenings in Oregon seemingly than those close by.

For example, in her seminal work on Asian Indians in North America, which I have relied on heavily, American Joan Jensen argues that the violence typified in Bellingham and amplified in its wake "eventually pushed Indians out of many areas and jobs in Washington, Oregon, and much of northern California, forcing their retreat into agricultural regions of central California where other Indians had already settled, Euro-American workers had not yet organized, and growers were expanding their operations."[1] This centrality of California is picked up and argued by others, such as Ronald Takaki.[2] The erasure of the Oregon leg of Punjabi experience continues in the excellent catalogue produced at UC Berkeley about Punjabis in California.[3] The catalogue's cover is a photo taken of the Dhillon family while in Astoria, Oregon. A Sikh family was a distinct rarity. Yet, other than one partial phrase, Oregon is not otherwise mentioned in the catalogue. The issue is not one of an improper credit. More, it is a subtle, and certainly unintentional, erasure of what I argue is a critical component to understanding the broader historical experience of Punjabis in North America, especially their ingenuity and flexibility in responding to shifting and often constricting political and economic possibilities, including their formation and pursuit of Ghadar.

There are several intersecting issues that might explain these omissions, including language capabilities of Western authors (like myself) and the demographics of California which, unlike Oregon, boasts a significant and continuous Punjabi community that can foster a tendency to view California as the singular locus in South Asian migration in the US. But there are also

---

1   Joan Jensen, *Passage to India*, (New Haven and London: Yale Uni Press, 1988), 42.
2   Ronald Takaki, *Strangers From A Different Shore, A History of Asian Americans*, (New York: Penguin Books, 1989), 301.
3   Suzanne McMahon, *Echoes of Freedom: South Asian Pioneers in California, 1899-1965* (Berkeley:Uni. Of California, 2001), front cover. This catalogue also depicts Ghadar as wholly centered in San Francisco.

the simple workings of our business as historians. Within each historical work there inheres the possibility of learning from and building upon it—and I am deeply indebted to these authors—along with the pitfall of being blinded by its received wisdom. Appreciating the historicity of our trade is critical.

This story of Punjabis in Oregon has also made me think differently about "legacy," because the men in Oregon left nothing in the built environment, no ongoing community, and mere shreds in the stories of our region. Yet they were a critical part of an earthshaking history. And that has become really the most important component of this research for me: trying to understand and unravel on a deeper level how this became a silenced history. From that I have come to believe this story is a window into the construal of belonging that continues to haunt and shape our domestic politics, especially in post-9/11 America, politics which propelled me into this research in the first place.

My claim is that Ghadar's initial formation occurred in Astoria, Oregon. I stand in good company with my claim, notably with Professor Harish Puri whose work I relied upon, and whose help I've been lucky enough to receive, in tracking down the details of Ghadar and the people behind it in the Oregon landscape.[4] The British Colonial government, judging from their court cases in Lahore and San Francisco, seem to have agreed as well.[5] On that note, I'm extremely pleased to announce that the Mayor and City Council of Astoria have recently agreed to commemorate the 100 year anniversary of Ghadar's founding. I invite everyone here to attend and contribute to the celebration in whatever way they can.

So while I am not alone in this claim about Oregon's role in Ghadar, it has without doubt been overshadowed especially by San Francisco, the later home of the Ghadarite press and its public office on Wood Street. That such a public manifestation of Ghadar has overwhelmed Oregon's landscape that bears no temple, no business, no farm, and no office, is not surprising. I would also argue that the tendency to make SF ground zero for Ghadar is linked with a tendency to focus on the role of students and intellectuals in Ghadar and underplay the laborers at its core.[6] Clearly, it was the joining

---

4   Harish K. Puri, *Ghadar Movement: Ideology, Organisation and Strategy*, (Amritsar: Guru Nanak Dev University, 1983), *passim*.
5   UC Berkeley Bancroft Library, Judgements of the Lahore Conspiracy Case In *re:* King Emperor *versus* Anand Kishore and Others, 112-114, etc.
6   For example, Bose; Arun Coomer Bose, *Indian Revolutionarires Abroad, 1905-1922: In the Background of International Developments* (Allahabad: Indian Press Private, Ltd., 1971), 48.

SIKH GADAR LEHAR 1907–1918

together of both groups that made Ghadar. Oregon was home to few students, intellectuals, or religious leaders, but hundreds of laborers were there actively organizing for Ghadar. In fact, I believe that the main reason there is no ongoing presence of Punjabis and Sikhs in Oregon is because these men left in droves in 1914 to overthrow the British.

Here's where I know there were communities.[7] One of my working theories is that the value of hiring Punjabis in the lumber mills of the Columbia River was passed along the river, likely by mill managers. For example, the Bridal Veil manager used to be at Hammond Mill, the major employer of Punjabis in Astoria, and there was a similar connection at Linnton.

It is interesting that in many of the towns along the river the existence of the Punjabi communities take no public expression, such as in the newspapers or court records, despite their clear presence. Further, the *Oregonian*, the major press of the state and region, made no mention of the Sikh community as a whole in the state, wrote little on the community in Portland, where the paper is based, but instead ran articles on the so-called "Hindu menace," and reports on the riots in Bellingham and Vancouver.

Most of these names on the map you see here are gleaned from the 1910 census. In towns like Goble, Rainier, Cathlamet, Hood River, Winans, and Bridal Veil, the census is about the only mention I have found of them despite, in all of those towns, scanning years of newspapers, legal and court documents, birth and death records. It's as if they were never there, and this is, I think, an important point to consider and one I will return to.

---

7   Map of Oregon, 1906, American Geographical Society Library, Uni. Of Wisconsin-Milwaukee Libraries. Digital image: am0063337. The names of the men appearing on the map have been gleaned from a number of sources: U.S. Census Bureau, 1910 Census, Records of Oregon, Soundex records K500 ("Khan") and S520 ("Singh"); OHS microfilm; the *Portland City Directory* (Portland: R.L. Polk & Co., 1910), unknown pages but searched under "Singh" and "Khan", OHS library; *Astoria City and Clatsop County Directory*, (Portland:R.L. Polk & Co., 1910), 101, 163-165, CCHS library; Multnomah County Circuit Court archives, Multnomah County Circuit Court, *The State of Oregon vs. Dickey,*" "Indictment (4/26/1910), "Order for Clerk to Issue Subpoenas" (6/4/1910), "Affidavit of DA Garland for Witnesses" (6/1/1910); Mult. Co. Justice Court, *State of Oregon vs. John Does,* "Information of Felony" (3/22/1910); *Oregonian* 3/24/1910:4; 3/25/1910:4; 3/25/1910:6; *St. Johns Review* 3/25/1910:1&5. The numbers of Punjabis along the Columbia River are roughly corroborated by R.K. Das who reported that according to the 1910 US Census, there were 208 "Hindustanis" living in Oregon. R.K. Das, *Hindustani Workers on the Pacific Coast,* (Berlin: Walter de Guyer, 1923), 17. The photo of Hammond Mill is CCHS Photo 3957.625. The GIS map was prepared by Gregory A. Greene, M.Sc. Candidate (Geography), UBC.

This next map is a sharp contrast to the *lack* of coverage this community received as it details where Ghadar organized. Some of these same towns had absolutely no record of the Punjabi communities, yet you can see by this map they organized for Ghadar. Look at, for example, Winans, which is basically a whistle stop south of Hood River, a bend in the tracks really, and consistently brought together 100 men for Ghadar meetings, as did Bridal Veil downriver, another bump in the road that was mainly just a mill and a bunkhouse at the time.

Oregon was not an initial point of entry for these migrants. More common was Vancouver, San Francisco, and sometimes Blaine, Washington, right on the Canadian border. They traveled to Oregon *after* they had been elsewhere, and I believe, largely in response to the 1907 riots and their aftermath in Bellingham and Vancouver, BC.

These Declarations of Intention help to illustrate my point. Declarations of Intention were the first papers filed when a person applied for US citizenship. These papers were filed in The Dalles—the easternmost community on the River I've located—between June and August of 1908. Often several men filed on the same day after having arrived in North America in the same port at the same time, assumedly on the same ship. Oregon was not their first destination. Of the 17 Declarations I located, 15 of them indicate that the men emigrated from Vancouver, BC, and traveled by train to settle in The Dalles.[8] It's not hard to imagine why in 1908 they might feel inclined to do so given the continuous journey provisions and other restrictions that were pushed through in those years. Interestingly, The Dalles, though a small Sikh community, was a place I saw the most signs of intended permanence of anywhere along the river based on the filings to become citizens (a high percentage for the few men there) and the purchasing of land. The climate of The Dalles is the driest of any Punjabi community along the Columbia River and was known for its wheat farming and orchards. The Dalles is the only place where I've found records of people buying land, and I am guessing that, like California, it is because of its greater resemblance to farming conditions back home. It seems, however, these land purchase plans met with some complications as Bishn Singh, the seeming driver behind them, was charged and convicted of "obtaining money by false pretenses" and sentenced to the

---

8 Wasco County Courthouse, Oregon, Circuit Court, Wasco County, Declarations of Intention: Bishn, Uttam, Hookam, Vir, Visawa, Bhola, Eson, Son, Sham, Talok, Jay, Sunder and Tebe Singh, along with Shib Diyal, "Ker," and "Kehru, " 1908.

Oregon State Penitentiary for two years. Inexplicably, he was pardoned and released after six months.[9]

I have located a few more Declarations of Intention in Portland. But the bulk of citizenship filings I've found are from Astoria, Oregon, at the mouth of the Columbia River, and which also seem to indicate arrival in Oregon after the Bellingham and BC riots. While I've found no record of land purchases there, the Dhillon family, the only Punjabi Sikh family in Oregon, did build their own home in town, renting the land from the mill.[10] There are also other signs of seeking roots: an interracial marriage occurred. It didn't seem to go well, but it happened, however briefly. But more than anything, what is notable about Astoria is the presence of these men in the town's newspapers, which carried many articles about them over the years, including about deaths and cremation, mill strikes, and often front-page sports coverage on wrestler Dodan Singh, well known in the town, and who remained when most others left for India.[11] Significantly, that press coverage included Ghadar itself. In no other town in Oregon did this happen, and I think it is reflective of the degree of the Punjabi migrants' acceptance in Astoria, though not without complication.

Astoria's records are worth examining in some detail.

The Astoria City Directory of 1906, essentially the telephone book of its day, shows two people with the last name Singh: Dahna and Sunder, both laborers at the Tongue Point Lumber Company The 1908–1909 Directory notes the same two men. But by 1910, almost 50 men with the last name of Singh were in that same Directory.[12] I think this is indicative, taken with the naturalization declarations that the population of Punjabi Sikhs came to Oregon largely after the riots in 1907 in Bellingham and Vancouver, BC, and the increasingly constricting atmosphere in Vancouver in their wake, including the passage of the continuous journey provisions. And there would

---

9   Oregon State Archives (OSA), Inmate Case Files, Box 5930-6072, File # 5965; OSA Justice Court Criminal, Wasco Co., File Folder #20 (Sickler through Singh), Criminal Complaint: State of Oregon v. Bisin Singh, 1909.
10 Dhillon, Kartar. "Astoria Revisited: A Search for the East Indian Presence in Astoria." Cumtux, Vol 15, No. 2 (Spring 1995):2-9
11 *ADB* 4/14/1914:5; *ADB* 4/22/194:1; The Morning Astorian (MA), 1/11/1920:2; CCHS, Hindu File: *Astoria Evening Budget (AEB)* 9/12/18; 10/18/1918
12 CCHS, Astoria City Directories, 1906, 1908-09, 1910. This is not conclusive, merely indicative. For example, the 1913 Directory lists only Dodan Singh, the wrestler, at the height of the Ghadarite organizing in Astoria and when it is known many Punjabis were in Astoria.

Social and Political Lives of Punjabi Settlers of the Columbia River, Oregon 1910-1920

have been a good reason to do so. Unlike most of the West Coast, Oregon saw no communal violence against Punjabis in 1907–08. That changed in 1910. But in 1907, when the floodgates of hate were unleashed, Oregon was safe. I agree with historian Chris Friday that in a multitude of ways "people consistently negotiated to empower themselves and make their lives more tolerable within large and rather harsh structural constraints."[13] Part of that involved moving to a safer place. A closer examination of the Astoria press highlights the wisdom of the migrants' choice and their active role in developing its potential.

This is the first article I located about any Sikh in Astoria, or in the state for that matter. On Halloween 1906, a small notice appeared on page 6 of the *Astoria Daily Budget*. It told of the death of a "Hindoo" by consumption after an illness of several weeks. "Sunday Sing [sic]" died in the local hospital after having been found ill on the city streets two weeks earlier. The story, a paragraph in length and sandwiched between notices concerning the price of eggs and a boat sale, ends with "[v]ery little if anything is known of him altho [sic] there are some Hindoos working at the Hume mill who visited him when he was first taken to the hospital." In the days that follow, the press writes of the plans for, and struggle over, the burial of "Sing." Interestingly, the spelling of "Sing" seemingly comes from the writer's experience with a significant community in Astoria, that being the Chinese who comprised nearly a third of the town. Throughout the next few days the press coverage changed in small ways, such as the spelling of Singh was corrected. More, the papers report that the men went to British Vice Consul Cherry in Astoria, who assisted them in petitioning the coroner and later the court, to allow them to claim the body and cremate it. On November 2, 1906, a procession comprised of the Deputy Coroner, the city physician, and the sheet-wrapped body of Rauma Singh in a horse-drawn carriage, accompanied by many of Astoria's prominent citizens arrived at the cremation site and formally turned the body over to the Hindu workers.[14]

From this beginning with Rauma "Sing" I want to fast forward to this article from 1913.

---

13   Chris Friday, *Organizing Asian American Labor: The Pacific Coast Canned-Salmon Industry, 1870-1942* (Philadelphia: Temple Uni Press, 1994), 1. Friday unfortunately confines his argument to the economic sphere and not the broader historical stage. That said, his point still has wider implications and truth.

14   *Astoria Daily Budget (ADB)* 10/31/06:6; 11/1/06:1; *The Daily Astorian*, 8/21/1981:6.

Under the title "Hindu Scholar Coming," the *Budget* reprinted an invitation from "Munsii Ram, Secretary of the Hindu Association, Astoria, Oregon" to the Astoria community to attend a lecture by Mr. Har Dyal, a "noted philosopher and revolutionist in India," including a specific "lecture on India for the American residents of Astoria." This oddly familiar, community announcement-type article was actually a notice for the foundational meeting of the revolutionary Ghadar Party.[15]

The more I consider this article, the more astounding I think it is. Munsii Ram's notice reflects a trust in their relationship with Astoria broadly. It was written in impeccable English, highlighting both a skill and a desire to reach out to the wider Astoria community. It was addressed to the editor of the paper, itself a confident move. Ram speaks as both the "Secretary of the Hindu Association of Astoria" and "on behalf of the Hindu residents of Astoria," revealing an assumption about Astoria's knowledge of the "Hindu residents" and their organization, and reflecting a change from "the Hindoo Sunday Sing's" death seven years prior when, "[v]ery little if anything is known of him . . ."[16] Munsii Ram describes the keynote speaker, Mr. Har Dyal, as a "noted philosopher and revolutionist in India" who is to be "accompanied by Mr. R. Chandra, a well known Hindu journalist and author, who is at present a political refugee in this country." There is no concealing the politics of the event or those involved but instead highlighted a "revolutionist" and a "political refugee." Ram also promoted the time, place, and plans for the arrival of the speakers, promising a "splendid reception" by the Hindu community, revealing no fear of their arrival being known, if not an overt invitation to join in that reception. Finally, Mr. Ram noted the specific "lecture on India for the American residents of Astoria," a clear attempt to speak to a wide audience. All of this bespeaks a comfort in and openness with the community in which these men lived. At a time of openly violent attacks throughout the West against Punjabis and others, most of which were endorsed by the powers within those communities, this level of comfort is significant, even more so given the openness about the politics being promoted.

Further, that Ram attempted publication in the local paper *and* that the notice was published are both notable. Both are suggestive of the important

---

15   *Astoria Budget,* 5/30/1913, page unknown, Clatsop County Historical Society ("CCHS") "Hindu" archive file.
16   *ADB*, 10/31/1906:6.

Social and Political Lives of Punjabi Settlers of the Columbia River, Oregon 1910–1920

openings allowed by life in Oregon generally, and Astoria more particularly, that I believe the Punjabi laborers recognized, cultivated, and utilized in their creation of Ghadar in 1913.

But while there was an opening that I believe attracted migrants here especially after 1907, and this took particularly favorable form in Astoria, I want to be clear: This did not mean that Oregon was a racial mecca. If I were to characterize the state's racial policy, it would be that the leader's, especially of Western Oregon, had catcher's mitts on, hoping to make a million dollars and build "paradise" utilizing the labor of peoples, whether Chinese, Japanese, or Punjabi, burned and run out of the rest of the West Coast by racial violence—and then make sure that they didn't stay.

Oregon was the first state admitted to the union with an explicitly anti-Chinese constitution. Barred from citizenship, Chinese were also explicitly excluded from both the right to vote (as were Negroes, Mulattos, and women) and from property ownership. Yet, in the midst of virulent anti-Chinese violence in the American West in the late 1800s, Oregon's Chinese population increased with Portland's Chinatown second only to San Francisco. This seeming contradiction was due, historian Rose Wong argues, to two critical factors. First, Matthew Deady, a key framer of the Oregon constitution, including its anti-Asian stance, was also a law-and-order judge concerned about vigilante violence and, with Portland's mayor, took strong stands against it. Second, was Harvey Scott, the *Oregonian's* leading journalist and editor for fifty years. Although Scott openly supported Oregon's Chinese Exclusion Act and opposed Chinese citizenship, he used his editorship to lobby against Oregonians imitating the vigilante violence of Washington and California. Deady and Scott promoted the "good sense" of Oregon growing rich by utilizing Asian laborers driven out elsewhere, while also assuring the public the Chinese would depart once the work was done. It was a use 'em and lose 'em standpoint, and gained considerable currency in Western Oregon. Thus, Oregon, judged by the times, was relatively safe for Punjabis and very much wanted their labor. This, I would argue, is a big reason Punjabis came to Oregon.[17]

---

17   I am indebted to the argument put forward by Marie Rose Wong, *Sweet Cakes, Long Journey: The Chinatowns of Portland, Oregon* (Seattle and London, Uni. Of Washington Press, 2004), 29-74. It is worth noting that Wong argues Washington was largely emptied of Chinese in the 1880s through a similar process as used against Punjabis in that state in 1907/08. But like the later Punjabi example, the 1880s campaign in Washington against Chinese had an opposite result on the Chinese population in Oregon (Wong 43-47). Thus,

In addition to this general view of Editor Scott's influencing the state, there were particular social and political features of Astoria that I think factored into it being the site of Ghadar's public launch. While not the only Oregon town without anti-Asian riots, Astoria was home to the largest Punjabi settlement in the state, numbering at least a 100. Their staying power and development of political resistance is entwined with the histories of the Chinese and Finnish communities of Astoria, communities I believe shaped Astoria's relative racial tolerance and its strong radical currents.

The Punjabi community in Astoria was initially largely the outcome of their recruitment for work at the Hammond Lumber Mill, which built boxes for the Columbia River's salmon canning industry, an industry that trailed only lumber and wheat in economic importance for the region. Astoria was at the heart of salmon-canning, reliant on Finnish fishermen, Chinese cannery crews, and international millworkers.[18]

Besides expanding local industry, the Hume/Hammond mill diversified Astoria's labor force as noted in the following local historical account:

> It is estimated that in the early 1900s the Hammond Mill in Astoria employed about six hundred people of different nationalities. Besides Italian, Greek, Japanese and Middle Eastern workers, there were nearly one hundred East Indians living in bunkhouses along the waterfront near the mill in Alderbrook [a district of Astoria]. Beginning in about 1906, until the mill burned on September 11, 1922, Birch Street between Fifty-first and Fifty-second streets was Astoria's so-called "Hindu Alley."[19]

The men of this "Hindu Alley," and the communities in and around it, were overwhelmingly single, laboring men ranging in age from 19 to 50. There was also the Dhillon family, Bakhshish Singh Dhillon, his wife Rattan Kaur and their four children (Kartar, Budh, Kapur, and Karm) who attended the Alderbrook public school.[20]

---

there does seem to be some historical precedence for people migrating to Oregon in the wake of racial violence.
18 Friday, citing Johansen, Gates Craig and Hacker, 2; 8-9.
19 Karen L. Leedom, *Astoria An Oregon History*, (Pittsburg:The Local History Company, 2008), 119.
20 CCHS, Photo 10,506-00D.

The "Hindus" of Astoria were primarily Sikhs but also included Hindus and Muslims. A college student, Bhagat Singh Thind, worked summers in the Astoria lumber mill to pay for his fees at the University of Berkeley and later challenged US federal citizenship criteria in a landmark court case.[21] Leading intellectuals occasionally spent time amongst the laborers. For example, on the invitation of the Hammond workers, Rama Chandra, a principal propagandist for the soon-to-be-formed Ghadar press, visited, talked politics, and briefly convalesced in Astoria.[22]

During their years in Astoria, the Punjabis were an active and diverse community. They were involved in wage strikes,[23] taught wrestling and fielded competitive wrestlers, like Dodam Singh[24] and Basanta Singh,[25] sued one another in court,[26] got in fights with fellow employees, got arrested for drinking and fighting,[27] filed for citizenship,[28] played with the Punjabi children,[29] cared for one another, talked, and otherwise entertained themselves in the times they were not working.

That in Astoria a picture of a Punjabi community emerges, especially in contrast to places such as Bellingham, I believe is related to the history of the Chinese in the town, especially in shaping Astoria's racial tolerance. By the time the Punjabis arrived in Astoria, Chinese settlers were already integral to the town, particularly to the running and profitability of the salmon canneries and thus to Astoria's and the entire region's wealth. By 1880, more than

---

21   CCHS, 3/06/2006 Email correspondence from David Bhagat Thind to Liisa Penner, archivist CCHS. Bhagat Singh Thind is known for his spiritual leadership and his legal case challenging citizenship standards for non-Europeans. For more on the Thind case see: http://www.pbs.org/rootsinthesand/i_bhagat1.html and United States vs. Bhagat Singh Thind (261 US 204).
22   UC Berkeley, Bancroft Special Collection, BANC MSS, 2002/78 CZ Box 4, Transcript of Interview of Padma Chandra, 11/18/1972, 34, 41.
23   *ADB*, 5/3/1909:6.
24   *The Daily* Astorian, 3/16/1988. Interestingly, Puri argues that wrestling was one of the means of training Ghadarites (Puri, 129).
25   *The Morning Astorian*, 1/11/1920:2.
26   CCHS "Hindu file" records, *Singh v. Lall*, Clatsop County Circuit Court Complaint dated 2/28/1920.
27   CCHS, City of Astoria Police Ledger, July 1910 – July 1916, unpaginated.
28   CCHS, "Hindu File," "Declaration of Intent" of Amin Chand Sherma, 3/02/1911; Behari Lall Verma, 8/31/1910; ____ [illegible] Singh, 7/26/1910; Behari Lal, 7/13/1910; S. Chhajju, 6/15/1921
29   Kartar Dhillon, "Astoria Revisited: A Search for the East Indian Presence in Astoria," *Cumtux*, 15, no. 2 (Spring 1995), 7.

a third of Astoria was Chinese, overwhelmingly men employed in the canneries.[30] They certainly experienced exclusion and racism, but there seemed to be acknowledged limits. For example, in 1886, the *Weekly Astorian* commented, "'they [the Chinese] congregate here [Astoria] in the same fashion [as San Francisco] because they are driven off elsewhere and have no place else to go,'" and reasoned that "[m]any Astorians refrained from anti-Chinese activities because they believed the laborers might abandon the canneries, thereby causing the collapse of the local economy."[31] Seemingly Astorians understood that their prosperity was based on tolerance. This shaped the town's relative racial peace and influenced and eased the entry of Punjabis into Astoria.

Life was not idyllic for Asian Indians in Astoria. Racist and anti-immigrant justifications were used to argue for their expulsion from the mill, cut their wages, or justify individual acts of physical violence.[32] But Punjabis were in no way driven out of Astoria. The first major exodus of Punjabis occurred in 1914, a direct outgrowth of Ghadar's influence, as captured in another amazing local article: "The Hindus employed at the Hammond Lumber company's mill are planning to return to India in the immediate future for the purpose of joining in the revolution that is expected to ensue, while England is involved in the war with Germany."[33] Finally, it was the destruction of Hammond Mill by fire in 1922, not a pogrom, which marked the end of the Punjabi community in Astoria.

But beyond simply developing as a community, Punjabis developed Astoria as a center of open radicalism. Again, think about that front page article in the town's mainstream press about Munshi Ram in 1913, or the report of men leaving to join the revolution in 1914. Their ability to do this, I believe, is directly related to the broad community influence of and camaraderie with another group in Astoria, the Finns.

By 1905, Finns were almost twenty percent of the town, many of them fishermen and many radicals.[34] In 1904, they formed the Astoria Finnish

---

30   CCHS, County Archives of Oregon, No. 4, Clatsop County Oregon, prepared by Oregon Historical records Survey Division, WPA, Portland, OR 9/1940; Friday, 56, 57. The Chinese wives of laborers were barred from entering the U.S.
31   Friday, quoting the *Weekly Astorian*, 58.
32   Denise Alborn, "The Hindus of Uppertown," *Cumtux*, 10, no. 1 (Winter 1989), 15.
33   ADB, 8/6/1914:4.
34   While outside the bounds of this paper, I do think it important to note that there were other factors than radicalism that undercut anti-Asian sentiments amongst the Finnish

Socialist Club, the most active Finnish group in Astoria, and one of the most influential in the US. In 1905, they built a five-story hall, the second largest hall in Astoria and a hub of the town's, and the socialists' social life.[35] This is the hall Punjabis used for the foundational meeting of Ghadar.

At the core of that Finnish socialist influence was their belief in a nation's right to self-rule and in the unity of laborers regardless of national origin. That radical message resonated across many of Astoria's communities. Chinese nationalist Sun Yat-Sen's fundraising visit to Astoria suggests one quarter.[36] Descendants of the Bakhshish Singh Dhillon family recount tales of Finns and IWW representatives meeting in their grandfather's house.[37] British surveillance files describe then-student Bhagat Singh Thind as "ke[eping] company with a bunch of socialistic I.W.W. anarchistic Finns."[38] Both stories evidence the explicit affiliations for which both the Finnish socialists and Punjabi nationalists were known.

Astoria, then, can be imagined as a place with strong currents of explicit radical sympathies and of relative social ease for its international community of workers. For Punjabis, it became a place with political allies, away from the hotbed of political spies and surveillance of especially Vancouver, BC, which, as a British colony, had high stakes in dealing with the increasingly radicalized community whose experiences and shifting aspirations are so well captured in this poem:

---

community. First, as fisherman, they were largely dependent on the Chinese cannery workers and international millworkers. Secondly, their hatred for Russia's occupation of their country, and their elation at the Japanese defeat of Russia in 1905 is significant. There were many laudatory articles about the Japanese in the Astoria press during this time period. My analysis of the effect of the Russian-Japanese war on the Finns of Astoria is derived from reading the *Astoria Daily Budget* from roughly December 1904 through March of 1905 which had almost daily front page coverage of the conflict. For some examples, see ADB 1/4/1905:1 and 1/23/1905:1.
35 Paul George Hummasti, Finnish Radicals in Astoria, Oregon 1904-1940: A Study in Immigrant Socialism, (New York:Arno Press, 1979), especially 3-74. Further on the centrality of internationalism to the Finnish socialist movement, see The Tyomies Society (Photographs) Records, Finnish American Collection, Immigration History Research Center, University of Minnesota.
36 Friday, 60-67.
37 Author's discussion with family members, May 2010.
38 Nayan Shah, *Stranger Intimacy: Contesting Race, Sexuality, and the Law in the North American West* (Berkeley: University of California Press, 2011), 242.

Some push us around, some curse us.
Where is your splendor and prestige today?
The whole world calls us black thieves,
The whole world calls us "coolie."
Why doesn't our flag fly anywhere?
Why do we feel low and humiliated?
Why is there no respect for us in the whole world?[39]

Ghadar represented a political shift from people working to build a better life back home, or a home in North America, to working to free their homeland. This political change was the product of the entire West Coast Punjabi community and its response to the restrictions, riots, and police spies marshaled against them. Confronting colonial and exclusionary policies the world over underscored that simply leaving India was not enough to escape their colonized status. Further, people mixed with radicals and nationalists tied with uprisings the world over. Finally, and seemingly contradictorily, Ghadar was also the result of the experience of living in the US which, though targeted, Punjabis witnessed life without an imperium extracting everything, as Britain was doing in Hindustan. This poem captures these varied sentiments and experiences.

Analyzing exactly how, why, and where a movement begins resists a firm grip and is not within the bounds of this talk. But with the briefest of strokes, the case of Ghadar included students and nationalists from India and Europe, like Bengali student activists Taraknath Das and Surendra Mohan Bose, and nationalist orator Gyani Bhagwan Singh, congregating in Vancouver.[40] These and other individuals and groups cajoled, threatened, and otherwise attempted to convince the authorities of British Columbia, Canada, India, and England of the injustice of their policies towards Punjabis. Such efforts became well known and sympathized with throughout not only North America but in India and the migrant Punjabi communities of the world, due to their newspapers, Gurdwaras, and other such networks.[41]

Organizations that were important hubs in the spiritual, social, and eventually political life of émigrés in Vancouver influenced the entire West,

---

39   Takaki, 301
40   Puri, 50.
41   Puri, 38-53.

many of them becoming binational.⁴² Of particular note was the Khalsa Diwan Society in Pt. Moody. Filmmaker Ali Kazimi argues Ghadar was foreshadowed in 1909 when Bhai Bhag Singh, a former Bengali Lancer and Secretary of the Khalsa Diwan Society, "made a bonfire with his certificate of 'honorable discharge'" outside the Gurdwara, and the Executive Committee of the Sikh Temple condemned the further wearing of British military medals.⁴³ By 1911, the Khalsa Diwan Society worked closely with the Hindustani Association and United India League, explicitly nationalist political organizations in Vancouver, sharing both building space and organizational positions.⁴⁴

The Canadian, British, and US response was increased border monitoring and cross-border spying, including in the form of one William C. Hopkinson who worked what were thought to be the key points in the radical network: Vancouver, Seattle, and San Francisco (all areas from which Punjabis in Oregon had migrated).⁴⁵ Oregon, to my knowledge but continued investigation, was not a focus of these political-policing efforts but became identified by the government(s) as a hub only after the fact as documented in the interrelated conspiracy trials in Lahore and San Francisco.

To this admittedly thumbnail sketch of the roots of Ghadar that I will leave to others to elaborate, I would add the March 1910 riot in St. Johns, Oregon, as an important moment in the lead up to Ghadar. The riot, I believe, achieved two important things. First, it made clear that Oregon, formerly a haven and perhaps even a pressure release valve, was not immune to the worst racial politics of the time. Secondly, it put radical workers living in the area on the radar of and in direct touch with radical intellectuals, such as Taraknath Das of Seattle.

The riot occurred on March 21, 1910, and began when a group of men gathered outside a St. Johns' saloon. Gordon Dickey, the foreman of the St. Johns Pulp Mill was the ringleader. "Speeches," read rabble rousing, took place. Soon the crowd, which had grown to nearly 300 men, moved towards the Punjabi laborers' homes, ransacked them, beat and robbed the men (it was right after payday), and pushed or caused men to jump from their second

---

42 Seema Sohi, unpublished paper "Race, Surveillance, and Indian Anticolonialism in the Western U.S.-Canadian Borderlands, .5
43 Kazimi, informal discussion 4/2009; Puri, 46.
44 Puri, 46.
45 Sohi, 5-6.

floor boarding rooms. The mob also went to the mill and forced the Asian Indians to leave work. According to the *Oregonian*, all of the Punjabi men left St. Johns that night, many after having been forced onto the streetcar bound for Portland proper.[46]

But the next day, a number of the Punjabis were back in St. Johns, the county District Attorney in tow, identifying those who had participated in the riot against them. They bravely named the mayor, police chief, a newspaper reporter, two volunteer firefighters, some shop owners, and numerous laborers from the local mills. 190 warrants were issued for beating and robbing 38 "Hindu workmen" and a grand jury was convened to investigate the riot.[47] Moreover, the mayor, city attorney, and police chief were charged with dereliction of duty.[48] Ultimately, only one conviction was sustained against Gordon Dickey, a mill foreman. The British Consulate acted in concert with the local prosecutor, and the US Federal prosecutors were also brought in to investigate the case. Such staunch involvement by Oregon authorities through the District Attorney, and the wide prosecution of participants, is indicative of Oregon's policy of intolerance of racial violence so as to better attract Punjabi, Chinese, and other laborers to the State's gain while enacting and maintaining constitutional bars to their permanence.[49]

The mill, the main employer of the Punjabis in St. Johns, continued to employ the men, its owners asserting that "(t)he Hindus employed by us do work that other men will not touch."[50] Moreover, the mill manager, N. E. Mayer, sat in on the trial and took an active role on behalf of the Punjabis.[51]

---

46   An interesting possible preamble to the riot appeared one month prior in the *Oregonian* on 2/15/1910:14. The article reported on a factory fire in St. Johns, suspected of being arson. The article states, "A Hindu has been arrested on suspicion of having set the fire, but the evidence against him is said to be slight." The St. Johns Lumber Company, a mill that employed many "Hindus," was immediately next door to the burned factory. This arson certainly could have been a coincidence, but it is not hard to imagine an arson being planned with the intention of stoking more anti-Hindu sentiment in the small town.
47   This riot sketch is drawn from numerous press articles other than those directly quoted. See *Oregonian* 3/24/1910:4; 3/25/1910:4; 3/26/1910:6; *St. Johns Review* 3/25/1910:1&5.
48   *Oregonian*, 4/19/1910:4.
49   It is different to note the difference in the tone of coverage between the *St. Johns Review* and the *Oregonian*, the seat of Harvey Scott's power. The differing coverage of the St. Johns riot, including the response to the legal battle could be read as a microcosm of the larger battle over the state's racial policy.
50   *St. Johns Review* 3/25/1910:1&5.
51   *Oregonian*, 3/29/1910: 12.

Most of the Punjabis returned to work immediately, but several were arrested for carrying revolvers and stating, "We have no protection."[52]

Besides arming, the Punjabis stayed active throughout the long course of the St. Johns riot legal battle, testifying in many court cases. As a part of this fight for justice, Taraknath Das penned this commentary which ran in the *Oregonian*. Besides finding it somewhat amazing the paper ran it, it also reflects close contact with the developments in the rioters' trial.[53] That Punjabis so insistently fought for justice in the face of violence is notable due both to its occurrence a few short years before Ghadar's formation and to the involvement of two men, Sohan Singh Bhakna and Kanshi Ram, pivotal in Ghadar's later formation.

Bhakna, from the Amritsar area, had arrived in Portland in 1909 aiming to pay off his mortgage debt back home with the earnings from his job at the Monarch lumber mill.[54] But instead, within a year of the riot, he was reportedly in contact with the United India League in Vancouver, and by 1912, he became a leader in Ghadar—its first president, the overseer of the San Francisco office with the departure of Ghadar's chief propagandist Har Dyal, and, finally, its trusted frontrunner to India at the outbreak of WWI.[55] Kanshi Ram, a successful labor contractor with a rented home in St. Johns, was a Ghadar founder and its first treasurer, and was executed upon his return to India after the Feroze Sharar Murder Case against Ghadarites in 1915.[56] Both men were involved in the opposition to the St. Johns riot. In the context of the rising tide of radicalism developing amongst the migrants, the armed and legal opposition shown in St. Johns could be considered indicative of a growing resolve to no longer be treated, as the Ghadar poem put it, like "black thieves" everywhere.[57]

Ghadar's genesis, like the men who made it, flowed through borders. From BC to Baja, the community was restive. But the critical bridging of

---

52   *Oregonian*, 3/25/1910:4.
53   *Oregonian*, 4/1/1910:14
54   This mill employed an array of workers from around the globe: China, Japan, Turkey, India and Russia, S.S. Josh, *Baba Sohan Singh Bhakna* (New Delhi, Ahmedabad, Bomby, People's Publishing House, 1970), 13.
55   Josh, ix, xii, 35.
56   Harold Gould, *Sikhs, Swamis, Students and Spies*, (Sage Publications, New Delhi 2006); also letter to this author from Harish Puri, Spring 2012.
57   This is my opinion. However, Puri seems to argue similarly regarding the importance of the resistance to the St. Johns riot (Puri, 52).

Vancouver's political ferment to the broader laboring migrants of the West and its gelling into an organization took place in Oregon.

In 1912, Ram and Bhakna met with G. D. Kumar, who left BC due to the political heat his publications garnered, and joined Taraknath Das who was then publishing *Free Hindustan,* a nationalist paper, in Seattle. Together, the two ran the press and established United India House in Seattle, which attracted a small group of laborers and students to its weekly lectures. Kumar visited laborers around the Pacific Northwest, and in early 1912, he went to Portland.

This 1912 meeting was held in the rented house of Kanshi Ram in St. Johns, Oregon, and resulted in the formation of the Hindustani Association. Sohan Singh Bhakna was elected president, Kanshi Ram treasurer, and Kumar the general secretary. Later that year, a second chapter was formed after Bhakna and Udham Singh Kasel, laid off from the Monarch Mill, approached Kesar Singh in Astoria to form a like organization. That branch was headed by Kesar Singh, Munshi Karim Bakhsh, and Munshi Ram (later penning the call for Ghadar published in the *Astoria Budget*), respectively President, Secretary, and Treasurer. The groups held weekly Sunday meetings to discuss politics and produced a short-lived press in Urdu, the latter ending when Kumar was hospitalized.[58]

With Kumar ill, Ram, Das, and Bhakna sent for Dyal of Stanford. On the evening of March 25, 1913, workers gathered in Ram's St. Johns house to meet with Dyal. In that historic meeting, they decided on immediate, direct, and radical political propaganda directed to the thousands of men of the West Coast, to "gird their loins to liberate India and work on revolutionary lines."[59]

From this gathering in St. Johns, Bhakna, Ram, and others organized meetings in the mill towns scattered along the Columbia River, working to establish chapters united by the March 25 resolutions of the Hindustani Association of America, commonly known as Ghadar. From March 31 through April 1—two weeks—they organized meetings in Bridal Veil (twenty

---

58   G.S. Deol, *The Role of The Ghadar Party in the National Movement* (Delhi and Jullundur:Sterling Publishers, 1969), 56-57. **Please note: I have learned of the controversy surrounding Deol's work, but have not yet had the opportunity to find an alternative cites that I know exists. Before any possible publication, I would wish to have that opportunity.**
59   Deol, 56-57.

men), Linnton (one hundred men), and Winans (one hundred men).[60] By late spring, they were ready for the culminating meeting in Astoria.

The founding meeting of Ghadar on May 30, 1913, was announced in Astoria's newspaper and keynoted by Har Dyal. It was attended by the Punjabis of Astoria and by delegates from along the river and beyond. Ghadar's official program was proposed and passed. Looking to England's engagement in World War I, its strategy was convincing the armed forces in India to turn their guns against the British colonizers, which they believed would be followed by a general uprising.

From Oregon, the movement established a weekly press published out of San Francisco in numerous languages—Urdu, Punjabi, and occasionally Gujerati. Har Dyal oversaw the office and publications in San Francisco. The first issue of *Ghadr*, carrying news of the organization's formation, garnered great interest among Punjabi farmers in California, and a second organizational conference was held in Sacramento in December 1913. Chapters spread throughout North America and on to India and the far-flung communities of Punjabis in Shanghai, Hong Kong, Manila, Siam, and Panama, weaving thousands of men across the globe into a movement for power.[61]

In sum, the Punjabi community gained strength in Oregon and Astoria; they were not driven out as historians have argued and I assumed when beginning this study. Instead, they left Oregon largely because they chose to go home and fight. Few visible traces of their presence endure as these men built Ghadar and not farms and Gurdwaras. The legacy, then, of Punjabis in Oregon is not one of ethnic cleansing but one of people empowering themselves and finding community and aid in their environs.

But while they were not physically run out of Oregon, they have been run out of Oregon historically and narratively.[62] How and why does that happen? How does such an important story get forgotten and lost when these were NOT unknown men in their times? In India, they were heroes. In Oregon, they worked in mills side by side with other men. Storekeeps sold them produce, and bank tellers took their money. They were listed in city directories and state censuses. People sold them land, and title clerks recorded

---

60   Deol, 59-60.
61   Deol, 60-61.
62   One notable exception is Clatsop County Historical Society, which has attempted a retroactive fix of sorts to its archive, largely due to the herculean efforts of Liisa Penner to make the local story of Punjabis in Astoria known.

their deeds and sometimes their marriages. Wardens had them as prisoners. Newspapers reported on riots against them and their desire to overthrow the British. Wobblies and socialists wrote of their collusions.

Accounting for this loss requires taking a step back to consider what history itself is. Historian Michel Trouillot argues that history is composed of two overlapping but distinct elements. On one hand, there's a real world out there and things happen in it. But on the other hand, we are humans, and the only way we can relay or remember events is through a story, and not lists of undigested "facts." Such narratives are where history lives, believes Trouillot, who argues that "history reveals itself only through the production of specific narratives," which have real stakes. His approach is to examine our narratives as an insight into our beliefs and relations of power.[63] Applying that perspective here, what is the narrative that has supplanted the Punjabis and Ghadar from our collective memory?

I would argue it is the conception of America as a white, Christian nation that has stripped our known history and our archives of the many people that have shaped it. The North American West the Punjabis landed in in the early 1900s had been promised to those whites left out of the American dream. But the reality of Westward expansion was not stoked simply by internal domestic migration but by infusions of men from every corner of the globe. That mix created any number of political and social tensions like accepted domestic arrangements given the dearth of women and about the relative rights and privileges of whites versus other laborers. Historian Nayan Shah writes that in these times the United States and Canada responded with "a system of democratic government in which large swaths of their residents were proscribed from full participation," with race a crucial divide.[64] This meant international workers were used to build the west but not included within its political covenant, barred both from citizenship and from the national stories. The US and Canadian governments had essential agreement that they were to be white, Christian nations, an attitude well captured in Canada's most popular bar song of the day entitled, what else, "White Canada Forever."[65]

---

63 See Michel-Rolph Trouillot, *Silencing The Past: Power and the Production of History*, (Boston:Beacon Press, 1995), *passim*, for an extended discussion of these matters.
64 Shah, 2-3.
65 Jensen, 62.

Social and Political Lives of Punjabi Settlers of the Columbia River, Oregon 1910–1920

But that conception of a White Canada or America is far different from the reality of the West and speaks to the power of narrative. Our narratives omit whole peoples who, despite their critical roles, were not considered real participants or principals in the project of building the US or the West in particular. It has concretely affected the stories we tell about ourselves. It has also affected the archives from which we can continue to tell those stories. So African slaves, indigenous peoples, or the many peoples from China and the Punjab have been late to be included in US and Oregon history, and often when done are done so as a sideline story and not as formative or central.

I'd like to give some concrete examples of how this affected finding this story in Oregon. As I've said, books from India led me to look for the story in Winans, Bridal Veil, Linnton, and St. Johns, because the received wisdom from US historians was that Punjabis had been driven out of Oregon.

More particularly, what I found when combing county and state records to find the traces of these men is, as you might guess, the records in our archives are very, very thin. But as I looked, and thought about it, you could almost see the filter that had kept them out of our narrative, our stories. Here are some examples: It's common for local libraries or museums to have big, leather-bound ledgers listing things like their area's pioneer names or local deaths. But they never listed the name Singh despite their presence. The local sheriff also had big, bound arrest ledgers listing the date, name, and what the person was arrested for. But under the heading of "nativity" these contrasted "American" with Jew, Negro, or Indian. Marriages were recorded, but not the many other domestic associations and liaisons among laboring men, whether they be cross-racial heterosexual unions or anything else. And those Finnish Socialists who should have had a lot to say about this story? Their radical newspapers and other records got left to mold in barns, not brought in to tell us of the multi-ethnic efforts and alternate hopes discussed in mills and camps everywhere.

A thousand seemingly benign acts of overlooking and erasure undergird and feed the persistent foundational myth of Oregon as a land of white, pioneer families. The records from the myriad who do not fit that storyline often never find their way into our archives or our stories due not to conspiracy but to social assumptions about who counts or belongs. Ultimately, I think that is how one immigrant in our stories and mythology becomes the pioneer and citizen, a historical sidebar or simply forgotten altogether. In short, our narrative is revelatory of deeply held cultural beliefs and assumptions.

But why does this matter? Why should we care? We lose some stories; someone resurrects them; so what? The real "so what" for me is that that attitude is still at work and, ultimately, I think is implicated in the suspicion of Muslims and Sikhs in the wake of 9/11, very much including the shootings in the Wisconsin Gurdwara last August.

It is true that many formerly denied citizenship in this country—the Chinese, Japanese, or Punjabis—have since been granted access to citizenship in both Canada and the US. But such changes in status have also proven to be socially and legally tenuous if not revocable. During World War II, Japanese-American citizenship was stunningly negated based on ethnicity.[66]

Now fast forward to post-9/11 America with the Quran burnings, opposition to mosques, not only in NYC's ground zero, but in towns across the country, or the NYPD and CIA's wholesale spying on New Jersey's Muslim community simply because they *are* Muslim and, seemingly by definition, then suspect. Further, remember that the first fatal hate crime post-9/11 was the murder of Balbir Sodhi Singh outside of his gas station in AZ, his only crime having been facial hair and a turban.[67] Since 9/11, the Sikh Coalition has reported more than 700 hate crimes against Sikhs in the US. Arguably, there remains a menacing, stubborn undercurrent in America that "immigrants are aliens, not citizens," as historian Mae Ngai so aptly puts it.[68]

This, I believe, also underlies the tragic shootings in Wisconsin last summer. You can argue it is mental illness that allows someone to walk into a Sikh temple and open fire—and it certainly is. But what do you argue when NYPD and CIA are spying on Muslims simply because they are Muslims?

---

66 Mae M. Ngai, *Impossible Subjects: Illegal Aliens and the Making of Modern America*, (Princeton and Oxford: Princeton Uni. Press, 2004), 175. I am indebted heavily to Dr. Ngai's overall argument of this book.
67 Amy Goodman, Democracy Now, April 17, 2012, available at http://www.democracynow.org/2012/4/17 /ap_wins_pulitzer_for_exposing_growth#transcript (accessed May 2, 2012). The U.S. government detained and interrogated over a thousand Arabs, Muslims, and South Asians in the wake of 9/11, irrespective of their citizenship status or activities. See Ngai, Impossible Subjects, 269. On the murder of Balbir Singh Sodhi, see "US 9/11 Revenge Killer Convicted," http://news.bbc.co.uk/2/hi/americas/315417 0.stm (accessed May 16, 2012). See also "Stories Put Spotlight on NYPD Surveillance Program," Fresh Air, WHYY, available at http://www.npr.org/2012/04/18/150805767 / stories-put-spotlight-on-nypd-surveillanceprogram (accessed May 2, 2012); Is America Islamophobic?", Time Magazine, August 30, 2010; "Across Nation, Mosque Projects Meet Opposition," New York Times, August 7, 2010; and Oregonian, February 15, 2012, C1, C3; Oregonian April 13, 2012, A1, A5.
68 Ngai, 229.

Ultimately, I think both are rooted in the fact that citizenship in America has always involved conferring legal rights on a select, worthy few, defined by gender and race. Citizenship has not trumped our cultural assumptions but instead sprang from and codified them. The bestowal of citizenship on the "right people" imaginatively and practically established Americans as white, Christian, family men in contradistinction to the non-white and non-Christian peoples, with varied interpersonal relations, who have been in and built up North America from day one. That, I think, is the shared narrative between those who are spying on whole communities and the lone, whacked-out gunman in Wisconsin.

But as angry and worried as I am about such things, I don't believe that's the only take-away from this story. For me, this story of the radical Punjabis in Oregon is also the story of the unexpected experience of so-called common people—Chinese, Punjabi, Finns, Socialists, Sikhs, or whoever—stepping outside traditions of rigid nationalism. Re-remembering Ghadar's ties to Oregon means remembering a time and a place where people managed to do better than what their times and their so-called place might suggest. It is likewise a story we can't afford to ignore about the importance of radicalism in subverting social norms and creating camaraderie. Our task is not so easy as to simply resurrect those earlier radical dreams. But their kernels and hopes need to be known and mined. Hopefully, knowing such alternatives exist not just in theory but in our lived past will provide perspective and mettle for our very difficult present.

BIBLIOGRAPHY

Newspapers:
Astoria Budget
The Astoria Daily Budget
The Daily Astorian
The Morning Astorian
Oregonian
St. Johns Review

Books, Articles and Films

Bose, Arun Coomer. *Indian Revolutionaries Abroad, 1905-1922: In the Background of International Developments.* Allahabad:Bharati Ghawan, Patna-1, 1971.

Deol, G.S. *The Role of The Ghadar Party in the National Movement.* Delhi and Jullundur:Sterling Publishers, 1969.

Dhillon, Kartar. "Astoria Revisited: A Search for the East Indian Presence in Astoria." *Cumtux*, Vol 15, No. 2 (Spring 1995):2-9

Friday, Chris. *Organizing Asian American Labor: The Pacific Coast Canned-Salmon Industry, 1870-1942.* Philadelphia:Temple Uni Press, 1994.

Gould, Harold, *Sikhs, Swamis, Students and Spies,* (Sage Publications, New Delhi 2006)

Hummasti, Paul George. *Finnish Radicals in Astoria, Oregon 1904-1940: A Study in Immigrant Socialism.* New York:Arno Press, 1979.

Jensen, Joan. *Passage to India.* New Haven and London:Yale Uni Press, 1988.

Josh, S.S. *Baba Sohan Singh Bhakna.* New Delhi, Ahmedabad, Bombay:People's Publishing House, 1970.

Kazimi, Ali. Continuous Journey. Dir./Ed., DVD, Peripheral Visions Film & Video Inc., 2004

Leedom, Karen L. *Astoria An Oregon History.* Pittsburg:The Local History Company, 2008.

McMahon, Suzanne. *Echoes of Freedom: South Asian Pioneers in California, 1899-1965.* Berkeley:Uni. Of California, 2001.

Ngai, Mae M. *Impossible Subjects: Illegal Aliens and the Making of Modern America*. Princeton and Oxford:Princeton Uni. Press, 2004.

Puri, Harish K. *Ghadar Movement: Ideology, Organisation and Strategy*, (Amritsar: Guru Nanak Dev University, 1983).

Sareen, Dr. T.R. *Select Documents on the Ghadr Party*. New Delhi: Munto Publishing House: 1994.

Seema Sohi, unpublished paper "Race, Surveillance, and Indian Anticolonialism in the Western U.S.-Canadian Borderlands, (2007?)

Shah, Nayan, *Stranger Intimacy: Contesting Race, Sexuality, and the Law in the North American West* (Berkeley: University of California Press, 2011)

Takaki, Ronald. *Strangers from A Different Shore*. New York:Penguin, 1989.

Trouillot, Michel-Rolph. *Silencing The Past: Power and the Production of History*. Boston:Beacon Press, 1995.

Wong, Marie Rose. *Sweet Cakes, Long Journey: The Chinatowns of Portland, Oregon*. Seattle and London:Uni. Of Washington Press, 2004.

Websites

Amy Goodman, Democracy Now, April 17, 2012, available at http://www.democracynow.org/2012/4/17 /ap_wins_pulitzer_for_exposing_ growth#transcript (accessed May 2, 2012).

"US 9/11 Revenge Killer Convicted," http://news.bbc.co.uk/2/hi/americas/315417 0.stm (accessed May 16, 2012).

"Stories Put Spotlight on NYPD Surveillance Program," Fresh Air, WHYY, available at http://www.npr.org/2012/04/18/150805767 / stories-put-spotlight-on-nypd-surveillanceprogram (accessed May 2, 2012).

Archival Materials

Clatsop County Historical Society ("CCHS"), Astoria City Directories, 1906, 1908-09, 1910.

CCHS, City of Astoria Police Ledger, July 1910 – July 1916.

CCHS, County Archives of Oregon, No. 4, Clatsop County Oregon, prepared by Oregon Historical records Survey Division, WPA, Portland, OR 9/1940.

CCHS, "Hindu File."
CCHS Photo 10,506-00D, 3957.625, 21041.540.
Map of Oregon, 1906, American Geographical Society Library, University of Wisconsin-Milwaukee Libraries. Digital image: am006337.
Multnomah County Circuit Court archives, *The State of Oregon vs. Dickey*, 1910.
Oregon State Archives (OSA), Inmate Case Files, Box 5930-6072, File # 5965; OSA Justice Court Criminal, Wasco Co., File Folder #20 (Sickler through Singh), Criminal Complaint: *State of Oregon v. Bisin Singh*, 1909.
UC Berkeley, Bancroft Special Collection, BANC MSS, 2002/78 CZ Box 4, Transcript of Interview of Padma Chandra, 11/18/1972.
UC Berkeley Bancroft Library, Judgements of the Lahore Conspiracy Case In *re:* King Emperor *versus* Anand Kishore and Others, 112-114.
United States Government Census Bureau, 1910, Records of Oregon, Soundex records K500 ("Khan") and S520 ("Singh"); OHS microfilm.
Wasco County Courthouse, Oregon, Circuit Court, Wasco County, Declarations of Intention, 1906-09.

The 1907 Bellingham Riot and Anti-Asian Hostilities in the Pacific Northwest

Paul Englesberg

Introduction:

The forced mass expulsions of Punjabi immigrants by mobs in Bellingham and Everett, Washington, in 1907 stand out as some of the earliest challenges that Sikhs faced in North America. Although these events have received far less attention than the more violent and more politically charged *Komagata Maru* struggle and Gadar activism, the 1907 riots were significant in influencing the immigration debates and policies in Canada and the US, and in serving as a prelude to an extended period of struggle by Sikhs and other South Asians in North America, from farmworkers to Gadar militants. Historians have emphasized various factors and aspects of the 1907 attacks, including labor strife, racial supremacist ideology, fears due to socio-cultural differences, and reaction to nationalism and radicalism. More recently, historians have paid particular attention to the legal and political implications and results on a national level on both sides of the US–Canadian border.[1] Through my study of Asian immigration in the Northwest region and Bellingham in particular, I have concluded that there was a concerted effort to harass the Punjabi Sikhs and arouse popular animosity that began a full year before the 1907 riot. Considering the focus of this conference on Gadar

---

1 Sohi, S., *Echoes of Mutiny, 2008*; Chang, K. *Pacific Connections*, 2012; Lee, E. "Hemispheric Orientalism and the 1907 Pacific Coast Race Riot" 2007.

history, I should make it clear from the outset that racial, xenophobic, and labor (economic) factors fueled this animosity, rather than any pro-colonial or anti-Gadar sympathies or motives.

In this paper, I focus first on the local and historical context going back to the first arrivals and reactions in the community; second, how the Bellingham riot and other attacks were portrayed in the press and how various individuals and groups responded at the local level; and conclude with a brief account of the second wave of immigration and the establishment of the Sikh community more recently in Whatcom County. The basic events of the Bellingham riot of 1907 may be familiar because they have been recounted in many histories of Asian Americans, and especially in accounts of South Asian and Sikh migration. I want to go behind these events and to show how the Bellingham riot was part of a pattern of hostilities against Sikhs and other Punjabi immigrants in the Pacific Northwest of the US and British Columbia. I also want to place the riots in the context of the politics of Asian exclusion and the deprivation of rights of Asian immigrants.

Historical Background

The northernmost port on the Pacific Coast of the lower 48 states, surrounded by salmon-rich waters to the west and massive old-growth timber on the slopes of the Cascade range, Bellingham's location and resources made it ripe for rapid growth at the beginning of the twentieth century. Located just 20 miles south of the Canadian border and approximately 45 miles south of Vancouver and 90 miles north of Seattle, Bellingham was connected to both by both rail and shipping lines. The white settlements that later became the towns of Whatcom, Sehome, Fairhaven, and Bellingham were built on land traditionally inhabited by Coast Salish natives who fished the Puget Sound and tidal waters around the Nooksack estuary and nearby islands. The Lummi Indian and several other tribes were relegated to 15,000 acres of land adjacent to Bellingham and Ferndale by treaty in 1855, and by the early 1900s, the Lummi Nation members had decreased to only around 450 individuals.

By 1907, the booming population of the city had reached 35,000, steadily increasing due to immigration due to expanding employment opportunities. Most of this immigration was from other states, and to a lesser extent from Canada and other countries. By the summer of 1907, the Asian population included approximately 300 Japanese, over 200 Punjabis, a number of Filipinos, and on a seasonal basis some large crews of Chinese workers brought in to work at the salmon canneries and housed in segregated Chinese bunkhouses.

On the evening of September 4, 1907, in Bellingham, Washington, a mob attacked and drove out over two hundred immigrant laborers from India, referred to commonly as "Hindus." The goal of the rioters was to force these South Asian workers from the mills and the city, using beatings and the threat of force to round up the men from their beds and mills. By the end of the evening, over a hundred had been herded into the city jail in the basement of the City Hall upon an agreement worked out with the police chief. Within a few days, the goals of the mob were fulfilled; all of the South Asian millworkers had either left by train or steamship for points further south along the Pacific coast or on foot to cross back into Canada. Several of the South Asian workers were beaten, and according to spokesmen for the group, many took the threats seriously and were afraid for their lives. Although the local papers downplayed the injuries and mentioned only one of the Sikh men being taken to a hospital briefly, according to a wire dispatch, six were badly beaten and hospitalized.[2]

The action was the first in a series of attacks on "Hindus" in Washington State and British Columbia, but it was not the first anti-Asian action in the Bellingham area. In October 1885, an anti-Chinese movement incited by the local newspaper and the Knights of Labor drove out over 25 Chinese residents from the towns that would later combine to form Bellingham.

There was a series of warnings and attacks in the days before the riot. After a massive Labor Day parade and gatherings of workers, unnamed speakers issued threats, and several violent incidents against Punjabis broke out.[3] On the day preceding the riot, workers at one mill had made a plan to attack the South Asians, claiming that white workers had been fired and replaced by Punjabi workers.

Although there have been speculations of the involvement of the Japanese and Korean Exclusion League based in San Francisco and with an office in Seattle, the evidence suggests that the Bellingham action probably caught Seattle Exclusion League Secretary A. E. Fowler by surprise. In fact, Fowler's organization and the president of the Vancouver, Canada, branch had been

---

2 *New York Times*, Sept. 5, 1907.
3 *Bellingham Reveille* [abbrev. BR.] Sept. 6, 1907, p. 1

jointly planning a mass demonstration for September 7 in Vancouver, BC, with delegates "from all points on the Pacific Coast."[4]

On the very morning of the riot, an editorial suggested that citizens had been unwelcoming toward the "Hindu" workers. Over the previous months, several editorials and local news articles included warnings that conflict and antagonism were escalating. Judging from press accounts, fights and taunts of Sikhs in the mills and on the streets were frequent, and the city records suggest a pattern of police harassment and discriminatory treatment.

The rioters were said to number at least five hundred, but accounts describe a mob that grew and separated into groups through the night, some attacking living quarters and others marching to lumber mills. Their composition was sometimes referred to as "white," but according to newspapers, some Filipino and black workers also participated. Some descriptions in the press emphasized participation of boys, but others described the rioters as persons of all ages, with millworkers in the majority. The five persons arrested and jailed were described as working men; police had also handcuffed two others described as boys who were released when an angry mob surrounded the police.

After the riot, press reports identified both immediate and long-standing grievances that were attributed as causes. The most commonly voiced reasons were the economic threats to mill jobs and wages, as the South Asian laborers were believed to be willing to work for lower wages than the prevailing rate for European Americans, therefore taking jobs from others. A further complaint was that the immigrant workers spent little, lived very frugally, and saved much of their pay to send to family in India. Immediate grievances mentioned as triggering the violence were several South Asian men refusing to yield the sidewalk to women, boisterous fighting outside of taverns, and a white female tenant being displaced by "Hindu" men. "Home-made wooden sandals" found in the quarters of the displaced Punjabis were later seen by some as evidence that "the cobbler and the merchant cannot afford to have the foreigners in the country," justifying calls for exclusionist policies.[5] Not everyone placed the blame on the immigrant workers themselves. The Bellingham City Council, in a controversial resolution, singled out the lumber mill owners as culprits for employing the South Asian workers.[6]

---

4 *Vancouver World*, Aug. 26, 1907, cited in Chang, 2012, p. 106.
5 *Bellingham Herald* [abbrev. BH] Sept. 13, 1907
6 BH Sept. 10, 1907

The reactions of the two local newspapers and most of the western US press were similar. They disapproved of the lawlessness of the method but celebrated the outcome of the eviction of these "undesirable" immigrants. Widespread public antagonism toward the South Asian population was suggested by the reports of jeering, harassment, and in private correspondence. Following the riot, several ministers spoke out to criticize the lawlessness and lack of tolerance, and one newspaper published sermon excerpts.[7] The Mayor publicly denounced the riot, called for additional police deputy assistance, and pledged to protect the workers.

The response of organized labor was mixed. Most labor voices were supportive of the aims and outcome of the anti-Asian movement but not necessarily of the tactics. The following week, the Central Labor Council of the city issued a resolution condemning the riots. Strong opposition to the riot also came from the IWW (Industrial Workers of the World), which had a very small presence in the Bellingham area. The IWW issued a statement denouncing the riot as injurious to the welfare of workers.

Most of the South Asian immigrants were young male Sikh farmers from the Punjab region of India who arrived by steamship in British Columbia beginning in 1906. Finding that employment opportunities were limited in the Vancouver and Victoria area, and hearing of employment opportunities and higher wages in Washington State, hundreds crossed the border in 1906 and 1907. Bellingham, located only twenty miles south of the border and having some of the largest lumber mills in the world, was the closest destination, and several lumber mills offered jobs to willing immigrants during periods of boom in a very volatile economy. The appearance of these men varied, with some wearing the traditional turban over uncut hair and bearded, and others clean shaven or with trimmed mustache and wearing Western hats covering their short hair. Although there were reports that a few South Asian women were living in Bellingham, these rumors were probably mistaken.

Canadian Entry

In February 1906, the Athenian, a CPR steamer from Hong Kong arrived in Victoria carrying large numbers of steerage passengers from Japan and India. The major news that Canadian passengers brought was of the growing anti-foreign feeling and riots in China. The immigration of "Hindus"

---

7   BH Sept. 9, 1907, p. 1

was barely noted.⁸ Perhaps it was some of these newly arrived passengers who were described the following month as the "turbaned Hindus who have been haunting the city hall for weeks past hunting for work." The *Colonist* reported the total of these Indian immigrants in BC was over 160, and that 40 were being hired by a sawmill in Revelstoke for $1.35 per day.⁹

By August 1906, the *Colonist* was referring to the "Hindoo invasion" and discussing the possibility of barring them from entry with the planned investigation by an immigration inspector from Ottawa. The paper focused on several economic and social complaints:

> these dark-skinned natives of India threaten to turn the labor market upside down, at least such is the opinion of labor men . . . More than Japanese or Chinese they enter into competition with whites in the labor market and they are equally unassimilative . . . they have, according to police records, cause proportionately more trouble for the police than any other race represented here. Judging from the number of them who have appeared [in various courts], they are by nature quarrelsome and litigious.10

The fears of thousands of additional immigrants from India arriving were reinforced by the regular landing of ships from Asia, such as the *Empress* from China which carried 219 and arrived in Victoria in August, most of whom sailed on to disembark in Vancouver.¹¹ Newspaper accounts tended to refer to the immigration in similar terms to those that had been used with other Asian immigrant groups that invoked fear and anxiety. "Sikh invasion,"¹² "hordes of Hindus" and "brown men,"¹³ "Hindu invasion."¹⁴

At least one BC newspaper, the *Armstrong Advertiser*, began to call for driving the East Asian works out of their cities in late 1906 which provoked a strong critical editorial in the *Victoria Colonist*.¹⁵ The *Colonist* was by no

---

8   *Victoria Daily Colonist* [abbrev. VDC] Feb. 20, 1906 p. 8
9   VDC March 16, 1906 p. 2
10 VDC Aug. 11, 1906, p. 6
11 VDC Aug. 22, 1906, p. 7
12 VDC Oct. 11, 1906, p. 2
13 VDC Nov. 14, 1906, p. 9
14 VDC Nov. 15, 1907, p. 4.
15 VDC Nov. 27, 1906, p. 4.

means welcoming, however, and summed up the official assessment and attitude in the province in quite negative terms. "They are, according to the reports of the Dominion authorities, a very undesirable lass of immigration. The feeling in British Columbia is strong against them on account of their habits and unsanitary methods of living."[16]

A shortage of labor in Washington State and a boom in the lumber industry in the summer of 1907, partly due to rebuilding of San Francisco following the great earthquake and fire, led to an increase in the migration of South Asian workers crossing the border from British Columbia. Attracted by offers of higher wages ($2.50 to $2.75 a day) and by hopes of warmer weather, hundred left jobs in mills in the Vancouver area where they had been earning $2 a day. A report in the *Victoria Colonist* included a rare voice one of the sojourners, a nameless "Hindu," heading for Tacoma, just south of Seattle, rendered in dialectical spelling reminiscent of American caricatures of "darkeys."

> One of the Hindus was spoken to as he was leaving the city [New Westminster?] last night on the Great Northern train and asked where he was going. "T'come. Mebbe lan of prom. This is not. Too cole ere. Say warmer in T'come." . . . Although they made lots of money in this country they are finding that it is not the promised land and are now taking further steps to find that place.[17]

The conditions of work were often dangerous, and risks to health could be quite severe. Workers at a cement plant near Victoria at Tod Inlet became infected with tuberculosis which caused the death of a Sikh immigrant, Tar Gool Singh, on April 11, 1907. His public cremation on a pyre was the first such ceremonies in the region and drew some attention in the news.[18]

South Asian immigrants first entered Bellingham the previous year, when two men without immigration documents arrived on foot from Vancouver, BC, and were arrested and turned over to immigration officials. Their appearance was described in detail as strange and curious, and one paper included an artist's drawings of the two men. Their vegetarian customs

---

16   VDC Dec. 30, 1906, p. 1
17   VDC July 6, 1907, p. 15.
18   VDC April 12, 1907 p. 10

were also seen as a curiosity when they refused the Bellingham jail food despite having gone for two days without eating.[19]

By September 1906, at least seventeen "Hindu" workers were reported to be living in Bellingham, and the expected arrival of many more South Asian immigrants became a frequent theme in the local press. One local paper devoted an entire page to the situation with a large banner headline about the "dusky peril" and several artistic depictions of the "Hindu." At the same time, the first organized effort to expel the Asian immigrant workers occurred at one of the lumber mills.[20]

A year before the riot, an editorial proclaimed "the dusky peril of the Hindus" as "the latest to threaten American labor," commenting on the report of Anglo mill workers protesting the hiring of South Asian workers.[21] The editorial was followed two days later by an astonishing full page newspaper article that warned Bellingham readers of the "Hindu hordes invading the state" and "floods of Hindus coming." The large banner heading asked, "Have we a dusky peril?" with a 6-inch question mark, invoking racial fears, as "dusky" was also sometimes used to describe African Americans. The article surrounded several illustrations of Sanda Singh, one of the 17 East Indian workers in Bellingham, who apparently had posed for Carroll Dibble, a local commercial artist and sign painter known for his caricatures. Dibble's drawing of Sanda Singh in turban and full beard must have seemed quite exotic and likely threatening to the Bellingham readers, and in the middle of the portraits, Dibble added an even more exotic image of a bearded man with turban and flowing robe charming a cobra with a woodwind instrument.[22]

Having rapidly expanded during this boom period, the population of Bellingham in 1906 had grown to over 35,000. Why were 17 lumber mill workers from India and the expected influx of dozens more seen as a threat deserving of an entire page and a hired illustrator? After all, several positive qualities were mentioned and attributed to immigration officials—they were "tall, well-formed, and stand erect" and in general were "intelligent, polite, neat, and clean." The article offers some explanations of the foreseen peril. Racial antagonism suggested by the term "dusky" was further intoned with a heading proclaiming, "Whites oppose Hindus." But labor and economic

---

19   BR Jan. 13, 1906, p.6
20   *Puget Sound American* [abbrev. PSA] (Sept. 16, 1906)
21   PSA Sept. 14, 1906 pp. 1; 4
22   PSA Sept. 16, 1906 p. 16.

fears were the most prominent—"wages will be reduced if repressive measures are not taken in the beginning," and they "will act as a brake on the city's progress" because these men "live cheaply and save their little earnings to return to India to spend them." Mill workers, the article warned, were making efforts "to oust them, and thus discourage further immigration to Bellingham." The fear of these turbaned strangers was linked to the legacy of the anti-Chinese movement of the late 1800s when mobs drove out many hundreds of Chinese residents from Bellingham, Olympia, Seattle, Tacoma, and many other Northwest cities, and in some cases vigilantes massacred Chinese miners or field laborers. Somehow, although the Punjabis appeared handsome and polite, the editor expressed the "fear that the dusky Asiatics with their turbans will prove a worse menace to the working classes than the 'Yellow Peril.'"[23] Just as the local papers had played a major role in inciting the anti-Chinese fervor in 1885, it is possible that this struggling paper was attempting to churn up sentiments to fuel a campaign that would increase readership and enhance its appeal. It was also championing an anti-vice campaign, pushing the mayor police to crack down on the thriving brothel business. As it was, the *Puget Sound American* went out of business two months later, bought out by the publisher of the *Bellingham Herald*.

In the same issue, it was also reported that workers at one of the lumber mills were circulating a petition demanding the firing of the Sikh workers, and that three representatives of the Sikh workers met with the local immigration inspector to complain of threats and harassment over their wearing of turbans.[24]

In contrast to the fear-mongering tone of the *Puget Sound American*, the *Bellingham Reveille* (Sept. 11, 1906) adopted a more balanced tone, several days earlier, reporting that the alarm was "all too premature" and that the fear was "judged as being without proper cause" from by employers and "other kindred observers." The major fear was identified as that a future "Asiatic invasion" could bring down wages of "the average American laborer." The *Reveille*, however, had also stirred up fears of the Sikhs with a story about a struggle in the brothel district which was described as "an attempt on the part of a dozen Hindus to capture the quarters by storm."[25] In reprinting an editorial from the *Anacortes Citizen* titled "Hindus, Chinks, and Dagos,"

---

23 PSA Sept. 16, 1906 p. 16
24 PSA, Sept. 16, 1906 p. 2
25 BR Aug. 28, 1906. p.2

the *Reveille* also appeared to endorse a strong antagonistic stance toward the immigrant workers.[26]

The following month, a third daily newspaper in town carried a Canadian report about the hundreds of South Asians arriving in British Columbia and the alarm voice by the Canadian government, with a fear-arousing headline "Hindoo Invasion is Menacing Northwest – Two Thousand Orientals Already Enroute for America."[27] In November, a Saturday night fight between Sikhs and others who were reportedly taunting them over their turbans resulted in "the Hindus being knocked senseless" with some 200 spectators encircling the fighters. Despite the provocation and the beating they received, it was the Sikhs whom the police arrested.[28]

Police arrests were part of the harassment that Sikhs encountered in Bellingham. For several months before the riot, police arrested Sikhs for drunkenness, and after being held overnight, instead of the typical treatment for whites arrested, release "per order of the police chief," the Sikhs were fined from $12 to $29. (As further evidence of racial profiling, when blacks were arrested to drunkenness or disorderly behavior, they were "fired out of town" the next day, a practice that continued in Bellingham at least into the 1960s.)[29]

In May 1907, another kind of opposition to the South Asians in Bellingham developed. The newspaper appeared to be the instigator, proclaiming that the "Hindus of Bellingham" were a "public nuisance," a "menace," a "pestilence," and that residents were in "mortal fear for their lives." By this time, their numbers had increased to fifty or sixty, and the press repeated diatribes about them being dirty, offensive, and belligerent. Charges against the "brown intruders" and "dark skinned sons of India" included indecent exposure, stealing neighbors' chickens, and dumping refuse around their housing, resulting in some calling for the deportation of the immigrants as "undesirable citizens," a view repeated in subsequent editorials. The strident tone of the article warned the "indignant citizens" would "rise up and deal with the brown intruders in their own way."[30]

---

26   BR Sept. 28, 1906, p. 4.
27   BH, Oct. 11, 1906
28   BH, Nov. 5, 1906
29   Bellingham Arrest Log; Tut Asmundson, 2004 Interview, Bellingham Centennial Oral History Project, Center for Pacific Northwest Studies)
30   BR May 21, 1907, p. 4

Press and Public Opinion

The most extensive sources on the riot and the surrounding issues, events, and opinions, of course, are the newspapers of the day. Readership was quite high, and in 1906, Bellingham supported three daily newspapers (consolidated into two in 1907) and also a Norwegian language weekly. I have searched and collected approximately 40 articles from the Bellingham press published between January 1906 and Sept 4, 1907, pertaining to the Punjabi immigrations and workers, and over 90 published from Sept 4, 1907, through the end of the year. The press likely exerted a strong influence on public opinion. At the same time, clearly the opinions in the papers also reflected the views of segments of the public. Analysis of the tone, language, and content of the press coverage would require a separate study. Overall, Wolf's characterization of the press coverage seems quite accurate:

> [Both newspapers] used their articles to further dehumanize the riot victims . . . [T]he newspapers both mixed and matched imagery seemingly at whim . . . The local newspapers provide a key element in discussing the racial attributes assigned to Hindus. These newspapers manipulated racial images of unassimilable Orientals held by the people of Bellingham and in turn helped to modify these images to justify the violence of the riot.[31]

The influence of the media is always a challenge to evaluate, and after 100 years, it is impossible to assess the impact which the press may have had in shaping public opinion about the Punjabi immigrants and in inciting the mob actions. However, the congruence between the press accounts of the Punjabi immigrants and the views of the public can be examined with the example of the private correspondence of A. W. Mangum (1876–1924), a 31-year-old soil scientist who was living and working in the area in 1907. In writing to his mother in North Carolina, Mangum tried to explain the riot and the antipathy felt toward the South Asian workers. His explanation and description was strikingly similar to the views in the press.

> We had a riot here about a week ago, the people ran out the Hindos [sic], who have come here in great numbers and have

---

[31] Wolf, Christopher. *Casting the "Hindu" in the Crucible of Nationhood.* University of Oregon, Masters thesis, 2001, pp. 22-23)

been working in the lumber mills. These Hindos came here from India and are British subjects so the English gov. may investigate the riots and make the people here pay for what they did. These Hindos are very undesirable citizens. They are dirty and mean and will work for wages that a white man can't live on. I am not in sympathy with the laboring men who started this riot, because they ought to mob the mill men who hire these laborers rather than mob the Hindos themselves. If the mill owners did not hire them, they would not come here in such crowds. They are worse than the Japs and China men and have caused trouble ever since they began to be numerous. The Japans and China-men have flooded this county and it begins to look like they intend to take possession of everything out here. There is going to be a race war out here pretty soon if this government don't [sic] keep them out, and when it comes, they are going to clean out the Japs and China-men, and we will have war with Japan. The people in the east cant realize what these people are up against with these Orientals. They will live in crowds, in one house and as nobody can live near them, people begin to move out of the neighborhood, and soon they will practically own a whole section of a town, and the value of property in that section will take a drop, to about ½ of what it was before they came. They can live on "nothing per day" and it looks like they will eventually crowd out the American workman. I believe if you could see and become personally acquainted with this out-fit, you would get the Keely-Cure, on the missionary question for you would see what kind of an out-fit you were working for, and would be ready to say you "had enough."[32]

Although, following the riot, the press and the city leaders denied that race was a motive and focused on the perceived threats to workers' jobs and wages as well as charges of immoral behavior, the language and tone in many of the newspaper accounts and editorials suggests that race and xenophobia were indeed major factors.

---

32   Adolphus W. Mangum Jr., letter. September 8, 1907. From Mangum Family Papers #483, folder #11, Southern Historical Collection, Wilson Library, University of North Carolina at Chapel Hill

Business Community

The *Bellingham Herald* editorial on the first day following the riot supported the mills in hiring the immigrant workers in order meet the demands of the market: "In doing so they are contributing to the prosperity of the community." The editorial then went further in pointing out the positive role that the Punjabi workers played, though couched in a negative hypothetical construction: "If no Hindus had been set to work the community would have been poorer by the amount of wealth their labor has created."[33]

However, the overall sentiments of the *Bellingham Herald* editor were to strongly deplore the lawlessness, rather than to fault the outcome of the removal of the Punjabi workers. "But such exhibition of man's inhumanity to man as that of last night should not be tolerated. Such lawlessness is an outrage upon American decency."[34]

Evidence of the outlook of the business community suggests that business leaders were more concerned with the lawlessness than with the plight of the Sikhs and other immigrant workers. G. C. Hyatt, the land agent for the Bellingham Bay Improvement Co., in a letter to the company president in San Francisco, saw the militancy of workers in driving out the Punjabi workers as a sign of the strength of organized labor:

> I do not think that this would have been classified as a riot in San Francisco. There was not bloodshed and the crowd was composed to a large extent of boys, although most every branch of organized labor was represented and the movement has doubtless their full approval. This is in all probability the first step toward Unionizing the mills and is the end which I feared last summer and is the reason that prompted me to refuse to Unionize my small force of builders. This condition will soon effect business in all lines and is a diversion to be regretted.[35]

The sympathies of the city council majority, at least one of whom was an avowed socialist, were with the workers rather than management, and they passed a resolution condemning the mill owners for employing the

---

33   BH Sept. 5, 1907, p.4
34   BH Sept. 5, 1907, p.4
35   Hyatt, Sept. 5, 1907, Bellingham Bay Improvement Company collection, Center for Pacific Northwest Studies.

immigrants from India. Due to the controversy surrounding this issue, the press published the responses of several mill owners. Most were highly critical of the city council's resolution and all denied hiring any contract laborers. One mill owner claimed that the Punjabi workers had received the same pay as the white workers.[36]

The business community in Bellingham seems to have responded to vigilante-ism, the city council's censure, and labor's hue and cry, despite the apparent shortage of labor with the departure not only of the entire Punjabi work force but also a portion of the 300 Japanese residents. Later that month when four Punjabis arrived in the city looking for employment, they were unable to find any work, and the Herald proclaimed on page one that they "are now notifying their compatriots to 'pass up' this city" and were heading across the border to New Westminster.[37]

Race and Ethnic Divides

Skin color featured prominently in nearly most news stories and editorials of the period in the West Coast press. Sikhs and other Punjabi immigrants were described as "dusky," "brown," "dark-skinned" and occasionally as "black" [note African Americans were described in the NW press in this period as "negro," "colored," and sometimes as "black" or "dusky"[38]]. Stories also commonly described them as aliens and emphasized otherness especially referring to the turban worn by many of the Sikhs with terms such as "turbaned," "foreign," "Asiatic," "Orientals," "sons of India," and "from India's coral strands."

Racial prejudice was acknowledged at times in the press. For example, an editorial about Italian immigrants commented, "As there are no race prejudices against the Italians a few thousand of them might be imported, with advantage to Whatcom county to develop the industry of market gardening on logged-off lands."[39] Another editorial on the failure of police in arresting an alleged attacker commented that with "too many Orientals on this coast" who "look pretty much alike" and are "clannish and inclined to protect each other," it was becoming difficult to pursue criminals among them.[40] A sports

---

36   BR Sept. 11, 1907
37   BR Sept. 26, 1907 p.1
38   BH Dec. 26, 1906 p.1
39   BH April 25, 1907 p.4
40   BH April 2, 1907 p. 4

article entitled "White Athletes Must Wake Up" deplored that "Negroes, Indians, Japs and Chinese are winning athletic honors and palefaces are not given even a look-in," and after citing several examples, concluded, "It's up to the white athletes to get busy, for the reds, yellows, browns, and blacks are copping all the honors."[41]

Although racial terms and general racial stereotypes were frequently used, more nuanced and complex perceptions and responses of ethnic difference were also demonstrated. There had been fears that mob actions would target Japanese and Filipino residents of Bellingham following the movement against the Punjabis and the attacks on Chinese and Japanese in Vancouver, Canada, that ensued, and the Japanese community demanded protection from the city and began to arm in preparation. The *Reveille* explained, however, that Filipinos were considered to be "good citizens," and "nothing but praise of the Filipinos is now heard in the city." It was reported that some Filipinos had actually taken part in the riot "along with the Americans." Although the Japanese were not similarly praised, the paper explained that due to their employment in areas not competing with white workers, they were "not disliked strongly enough by any class in the city to make it possible to stir up rabid sentiment against them."[42] In fact, the following day the *Reveille* published what it called "A Word of Solemn Warning" against a similar attack on Japanese residents of Bellingham. It speculated that a riot against Japanese could precipitate a war with Japan and rioters would be severely prosecuted. The editors concluded, "we warn the mob to keep its hands off the Japanese" and instead join with the Exclusion League in pushing for restrictive immigration legislation.[43] Several days later, the editors worried, along with the manager of the Pacific American Fisheries Company, that if Chinese and Japanese workers were also driven away in fear of anti-Asian mobs, the canneries that depended so heavily on their seasonal labor might have to close because few white workers could replace them.[44]

Commentators in national publications also discussed the racial element quite openly. Agnes Buchanan contrasted the immigrants from India with those from China and Japan, and reminded readers that "this last is a brother of our own race – a full-blooded Aryan, men of like progenitors with us."

41 BR May 2, 1907 p.2
42 BR Sept 7, 1907 p.1
43 BR Sept 8, 1907
44 BR Sept. 2, 1907 p.4

However, despite that recognition, Buchanan joined the prevailing racial discourse: "The Hindus and the Hindu Invasion is the latest racial problem with which we of the West have to deal with."[45] Buchanan revealed the complexities of ethnic and religious acceptance in the US with the story of Bingha Singh, a Sikh working in the boiler room of an iron factory, who described himself to her as a Brahmin who had lived for years in Hong Kong. Bingha Singh told her that he had applied for US citizenship but was unable to take the oath because the judge demanded that he remove his turban, which he refused to do.[46]

Similarly, poet and translator Herman Scheffauer (1878–1927), writing in 1910, also acknowledged common "ancient Aryan stock" but explained that Americans "find it difficult to accept the Hindoo as a brother of the blood. Between him and this dark, mystic race lies a pit almost as profound as that which he has dug between himself and the negro."[47]

During this time, some South Asians without turbans were also first making applications for citizenship. A Muslim from Punjab, Mohammed Akbar, applied for citizenship in Butte County, California, in 1908.[48] By 1913, A. K. Mozumdar, a resident of Spokane, Washington, became the first South Asian to obtain American citizenship, convincing a federal judge that by virtue of his "high-caste Hindu" status as a Brahmin he met the criterion of being "white." Ironically, Mozumdar, a Hindu mystic, had polished his English during a term of study in 1905 at the State Normal School in Bellingham on the hill overlooking the same mills where 200 or more Punjabis were to be forcibly evicted two years later.[49] Taraknath Das, who had studied at the University of Washington, also took out citizenship papers in Seattle in 1911 and was finally granted citizenship in San Francisco in 1914.[50] [Following the US Supreme Court's 1923 decision in the Thind case, Mozumdar, Das, and over sixty others of Indian origin has their US citizenship revoked.]

---

45   Buchanan, 1908, p. 309
46   Buchanan, p. 312; Scheffauer, 1910, p. 618
47   Scheffauer, 1910, p. 616
48   *Daily Appeal*, Jan. 30, 1908, p. 6
49   U.S. District Court, Eastern District of Washington, Jan. 6, 1913, no. 992 Order; *The Messenger, State Normal School*, 1905).
50   Shah, p. 241

Gender

Rumors of "Hindu women disguised as men," allegedly from Canadian sources, caused the immigration inspector in Bellingham to investigate, but apparently none were found. The report that "fully one third of the immigrants coming to Canada are women disguised as men," seems likely to have been fabricated.[51] In Bellingham, similar rumors of females living among the Sikh workers appeared in the press and were presented as fact but without substantiation. "The Hindu colony contains a few women, who, as they dress like the men in trousers and coats, are not to be distinguished from them on the streets. These women sleep in the same crowded apartments with the men."[52] Shah interprets such reports as white gender anxieties about the turban and the hidden long black hair of the Sikh men.[53] Earlier historians, such as Hallberg, Melendy, and Wynne, tended to treat newspaper accounts as fact and thus rumors or questionable reports have been accepted uncritically and repeated in other sources. Hallberg stated, "The Hindu colony contained a few women . . ." and repeated almost verbatim the Reveille's claim.[54] According to Saint Nihal Singh, in 1909 there was only one "Hindu woman" in North America, married to an Indian doctor in Vancouver. Singh believed himself to be the only man from India with an American wife.[55] In 1910, a few Sikh leaders in British Columbia made plans to bring their wives from India, but the report indicated that this would be unprecedented.[56]

[Note: Melendy and Wynne also accepted the questionable *New York Times* reports, stating that, "six East Indians were hospitalized, 410 gained protective custody, in the Bellingham jail, and 750 fled northward . . . to the Canadian border."[57]]

---

51 BH Dec. 14, 1906
52 BR Sept. 6, 1907, p. 3
53 Shah, p. 39
54 Hallberg, "Bellingham, Washington's Anti-Hindu Riot." *Journal of the West*, vol. 12, 1973, p. 169
55 Singh, S.N. "The Picturesque Immigrant from India's Coral Strand." *Outwest*, 1909, p. 45
56 BH Jan. 1, 1910, p. 7
57 Melendy, 1977, p. 192; similar in Wynne, *Pacific Northwest Quarterly* vol. 57 n.4., Oct. 1966, p. 174

Social Class and Caste: Two "High Caste Hindus" in Bellingham

How was it that during the period when "Hindu" was a term of revulsion and extreme prejudice in Bellingham and elsewhere in the Pacific Northwest, a young man from India lived as a family member with a prominent Bellingham family and was treated with much kindness by them? Was it a matter of social class, as the *Bellingham Herald* suggested on its editorial page the morning before the riot broke out? The pithy editorial is worth quoting in full:

> There will probably not be the same race prejudice against the prominent Hindu who is to attend the normal as against his fellow countrymen who are working in the mills. And yet there is no such thing as caste in this democratic country of our! [sic]58

Was this young man considered a "Prince of India," as the *Reveille* referred to him? Or were school principal Dr. Edward Mathes and his family unusual in their warmth, hospitality, and open-mindedness?59 Mathes was certainly unique in Bellingham in his support and generosity toward students from India. In 1905, the first international student at the Normal School, A. K. Mozumdar, was enrolled as a special student, and two years later the much younger Nabhi Ram Joshi became the second. The first issue of the nationalist *Free Hindustan* newspaper, published in Vancouver, BC, by Taraknath Das, proclaimed Dr. Mathes as "a good friend of India" who had "expressed his desire to and capacity to help a few more Hindu students in different institutions."60

Nabhi Ram Joshi was 19 when he enrolled at the State Normal School in Bellingham in the fall of 1907, one of the few male students there. He spoke English and several other languages and had first attended a university in India. He had worked at a mill across the border in New Westminster, British Columbia, where his older brother worked as foreman, and apparently his enrollment was arranged by the mill superintendent, W. P. Fowle, who had previously been superintendent of the Bellingham Bay Lumber Co. mill in Bellingham.61

---

58   BH Sept 4, 1907 p. 4
59   BH 9/5/1907 p. 4; AR 9/4/1907 p. 2
60   *Free Hindustan* VI no1 April 2908, p.3
61   BH 9/3/1907, p. 5; AR 9/4/1907 p. 2

Nabhi Ram's arrival as a student in Bellingham was unusual enough to warrant the attention of the city's two newspapers. Both news stories made special note of his status in India as "representing the highest caste" and "a member of the Brahmin class." He was described in glowing language, in stark contrast to the way that "Hindu" immigrants were commonly described in these papers. He was "good looking," "well educated," "able to converse in several languages," and "well supplied with money."[62] Mathes grew concerned when the riot broke out and spoke with some labor leaders who gave him assurances that they would not harm the student from India. He later spoke about the issue of racial conflict and the Bellingham events during lectures to other educators, but no records of the contents have been found.

Over many years of correspondence with the Mathes family, Nabhi Ram continued to express his affection for the family and fond memories of his year in Bellingham. Because of the strong relationship, Edward Mathes' daughter-in-law Miriam Snow Mathes created a scholarship for Indian students at Western Washington University in Nabhi Ram's name, one of the few such privately funded scholarships in the US expressly for students from India. As the *Bellingham Herald* editor had predicted, the hospitable reception of both A. K. Mozumdar and Nabhi Ram Joshi stood in sharp contrast to Bellingham's harsh attack on the working class Punjabis, "in this democratic country."

Certainly there were those who opposed the mob action and like the Mathes family may have been sympathetic to those from other lands and of other ethnicities and religions. The press accounts described the general public as generally supporting the mob, and street-corner agitators urged others to "help drive out the cheap labor." However, one woman witness was reported as walking "boldly through the thickest of the mob" declaring that is was "a shame."[63] However, the major voices that were recorded as opposing of the expulsion and in some sympathy with the Punjabis were from the clergy.

---

62 BH 9/3/1907, p. 5; AR 9/4/1907 p. 2
63 BR. Sept 5, 1907, p.3

SIKH GADAR LEHAR 1907-1918

Religion [Much of the following section was contributed by Adam Raas]

In terms of religion, Bellingham in 1907 had a strong Protestant dominance, typical in the Pacific Northwest region. The listing of Sunday services in 1907 included some 25 churches. A door-to-door census of approximately 4,500 families and households conducted by the YMCA and 200 church volunteers counted 3,430 Protestants of various denominations, 447 Catholics, 26 Jews. 562 declared "no preference," and 5 marked "unbelievers."[64] Otherness in terms of religion was mostly identified in terms of the wearing of the turban and by jailed Punjabis refusing to eat meat. The term "Hindu" or "Hindoo" was most commonly used, "East Indian" was less common, and only occasionally were they referred to as Sikhs. The term "heathen" appeared, but it was much less frequently applied to the Sikhs than it had been used in describing the Chinese during the anti-Chinese hysteria of 1885–1886.[65]

In the account of one criminal court case in 1907, the claim was made that the Sikh defendants were unfamiliar with the term "God," and when the oath was translated for them, so the interpreter "made them swear by the god of the jungle." The judge allowed Sikh witnesses to wear their turbans in the courtroom after an interpreter explained that it was required by their religion.[66]

Four days after the riots occurred, residents of Bellingham woke up on Sunday morning, September 8, 1907, and went to church. The local religious leaders had not forgotten the riot, and several of them sermonized on the actions of the rioters and the reaction of the police. Initially, the clergy responded vehemently to the rioters and the officials that allowed the riots to happen. One minister in particular, Reverend William Orr Wark, responded most passionately to the riots. He was a Congregationalist minister of the same denomination that supported the Chinese immigrants in 1885. The Monday following the riots, the *Bellingham Herald* printed excerpts of several sermons obtained from several local churches.[67] These sermons touched upon the general themes of workers' greed, immigration in general, and criticism of the police. The four religious leaders whose sermons were published

---

64   BR June 12, 1907
65   BR Sept. 6, 1907 p.4
66   BH Feb 28, 1907 p.3; BH May 2, 1907 p.10
67   BH Sept 8, 1907, 1, 5. "Denunciations Hurled From Pulpits" [(This section relies heavily on this article,)]

were Reverend Wark, Reverend Cheatham of St. Paul's Episcopal Church, Reverend Thomas Cornish of the First Baptist Church, and Reverend John W. Flesher of the First Methodist. Of the four sermons excerpted by the *Herald*, Reverend Wark's stands out as the most scathing.

All four religious leaders were critical of the greed and material motives of the rioting workers. Reverend Flesher argued that those who rioted did not represent the majority of the workers.[68] In continued agreement, Reverend Wark asked his congregation rhetorically, "Must we . . . refuse these outsiders because they . . . do not ask the same wages?"[69] All four sermons expressed shame for the mob actions taken in the name of greed and intolerance.

The sermons also touched upon the problem of immigration in general. In discussing immigration from Punjab, Reverend Cornish told of the many advances made in India in terms of education, communication, and infrastructure, noting the number of universities, the amount of trade, and the miles of railroad built in India. He argued that rather than spurn their entrance into the country and assault those who have come to work in the United States, they should be accepted and taught to become Christian: "The Hindu people, as well as showing a capacity for western learning and western enterprise, are very susceptible to the teachings of Christianity."[70] Reverend Wark again asked, "Must we admit to the world that we do not know how to deal with the Hindu and are simply keeping them out by brute force until we solve the problem? This is no way to solve it. We face the problem, and it must be settled sooner or later. The world must not believe we settle our differences in cowboy style."[71]

Both ministers Cheatham and Wark publicly criticized the police for allowing the lawlessness. Reverend Wark's solution was simple, that "Instead of organizing exclusion leagues, let us inaugurate an era of education."[72] Specifically, the minister looked to religious teachings to help "fortify our race and our nation while affording less favored peoples our aid in their struggle."[73] In fact, Wark himself turned to education and international work when he left the ministry in 1909, guiding Europe tours and, during World War I, working in France for the YWCA.

68 Ibid., "Local Pastor Gets Flattering Offers," *Bellingham Herald*, Aug. 31, 1907, p.12
69 "Denunciations Hurled From Pulpits."
70 Ibid.
71 Ibid.
72 Ibid.
73 Ibid.

However, Reverend Wark was not the last religious leader in Bellingham in 1907 to be heard on the topic of immigration. From late October through November, the *Bellingham Herald* published a series of four full-length sermons by Reverend J. R. Macartney of the First Presbyterian Church titled "The Alien Invasion," which raised fears of immigrants from Asia as well as from European countries. Macartney advocated strict controls on the numbers of immigrants allowed to enter the country, as well as the radical step of moving port of entry sites to Europe so that the potential immigrants could be screened before crossing the ocean. Macartney also addressed the issue of immigrants already in the US, calling for an evangelical crusade to convert immigrants already in America to Protestant Americans.[74] "God has set Protestant Christianity a gigantic task, nothing less than the assimilation of all these foreign people . . . into one common Americanism, so that they shall form a united free Christian people."[75] For Reverend Macartney, the problem was not just immigration but also assimilation and conversion.

Thus, the Bellingham press provided a platform from which religious leaders initially reacted to the lawless riots by condemning the participants and those who aided them, but also lent even more public space for a series of sermons that flamed anti-immigrant sentiment.

Threats, Harassment, and Planning

The day before the riot, a plan had been made "to drive out the cheap labor," according to one press account after the riot. The previous Sunday night, some of the immigrant workers were "congregating on the sidewalk" and a struggle with police ensued. The paper also reported that with the crowd of union members parading through the city on Labor Day, some of the Punjabis were attacked, and there had been at least five incidents of violence Tuesday night, though none of this had been reported in the paper until after the riot occurred. Several explanations were given of the immediate trigger of the riot. One trigger was the angry reaction of millworkers at the Whatcom Falls Mill Company when allegedly some white workers were discharged and replaced by Sikhs.[76] Other accounts attributed the start of the riot to taunting by "a gang of young rowdies" or a dispute over several Punjabis renting

---

74   Macartney, "Alien Invasion, pt. 4," *Bellingham Herald*, Nov. 16, 1907, p. 12
75   Ibid.
76   BR Sept. 5, 1907 p.1

of a shack and displacing a woman who had been living there.[77] The police chief reported that the riot was not spontaneous, but had been planned in advance.[78] However, following criticisms about how the police handled the riot and accusations that they had received warnings, Chief Thomas denied that he had any advance notice.[79]

Bellingham's weekly Norwegian paper, *Nya Varlden*, issued a strong criticism of the mob and the city for not taking stronger action to quell the lawlessness, comparing Bellingham to "the darkest of Russia." However, the editor made it clear that he was not a "friend of the Hindus" and blamed the mill owners for employing them.[80]

The only critical analysis of the racial character of the riot was provided by the editor and publisher of the *Seattle Republican*, Horace Cayton, under a column titled "Always ready to riot." Cayton (1859–1940), an African American and former slave who was born in Mississippi, lived in Seattle for most of his life.

> Whether it be North, South, East, or West in the United States, it is always a safe bet that the white man is ever ready to do violence to some class of human beings if they happen to have a darker skin than their own. But a few days ago the white folk of Shelbyville, Ind. were driving a number of Negroes out of the town . . . so common to the Southern states that comment is unnecessary. Another day the report comes that the citizens of Bellingham are mobbing a lot of Hindu people because they not only wanted to work, but were actually working and the Lord only knows what would have been the result if the British flag had not been displayed, the Hindus being British subjects, which alarmed the whites.[81]

Describing the rioters as "white," however, was problematic, because, as Wolf has discussed, both local newspapers identified Filipinos and at least one African American among the rioters.[82]

---

77 BR Sept 5, 1907 p.1
78 Ibid.
79 BR Sept. 10, 1907 p. 3
80 NV Sept. 13, 1907
81 SR Sept. 13, 1907
82 Wolf, pp. 25-27

The liberal *Nation* offered only passing ridicule in its comment on the riots. "On the Pacific Coast no form of Saturday night and Sunday afternoon diversion can compare in popularity with the baiting of Asiatic Laborers."[83] Referring to the agitation by American exclusion league leaders in Vancouver, the *Nation* noted that "White supremacy, like love and justice, knows no boundaries."[84]

Colliers magazine had dispatched writer Will Irwin to investigate the Japanese labor situation on the Pacific coast, and shortly after the Bellingham riot occurred, Irwin arranged a visit to interview city officials and others. In the second part of his series of four articles on "The Japanese and the Pacific Coast," Irwin reviewed several anti-Japanese incidents in the region, including threats against a Japanese owned shingle mill in Bellingham, which led to closure, and then Irwin described the Bellingham "anti-Hindu riot" as "a screaming farce."[85] Irwin's almost comical telling of the story portrayed the police and, in particular, Police Chief Thomas as being in sympathy with the mob and not up to the task of maintaining the law. If Irwin's account is at all accurate, then Chief Thomas offered to aid and abet the rioters.

> "But say, if you fellows keep 'em in them shacks, some bad man may start a riot. Why don't you take 'em down to the police station? They'll be safer there, and in the morning we'll all chuck 'em out together." The mob shouted approval of Chief Thomas, swept into the shacks and herded the Hindus forthwith to the station. So the chief made two thousand volunteer deputies out of a mob. But there were one hundred more Hindus still at large. How should he protect them? The chief was equal to producing the idea: "Now boys, let's make a clean sweep of it. You done a good job with these fellows, go out and get the rest."[86]

The *Bellingham Herald* editor also faulted the police chief and some of the officers.

---

83 *Nation*, Sept. 12, 1907, p. 220
84 *Nation*, Sept. 19, 1907
85 Irwin, Will. "The Japanese and the Pacific Coast" *Colliers*, Oct. 12, 1907
86 Ibid.

"... probably ... several of the officers on duty were strongly in sympathy with the anti-Hindu movement and did not object to the clamorous method pursued by the crown, since it was not violent."[87]

We have *Collier's* magazine to thank for the printing of the best quality photographs of the riot that have been preserved, as Irwin must have obtained negatives from the *Bellingham Herald* or its photographer. In a previous issue of *Colliers* (Sept. 28), two photographs of the Bellingham incident to accompany the first part of Irwin's series were printed on glossy paper in a montage along with photographs of Japanese on the coast. The photographs show the Punjabis in the city hall basement jail area and another outside the city hall the next day. Similar photographs from the Bellingham riot were also reprinted with a magazine article by *Bellingham Herald* editor Werter Dodd, along with photographs of Sikhs at the Bellingham rail station, posing on the sidewalk in front of a restaurant, and at a lumber mill.[88]

Police and Justice [portions of this section were contributed by Adam Raas]

On one hand, the Bellingham Police, led by Chief of Police Thomas, were hailed as heroes for their role in the anti-Hindu riots in facilitating the bloodless expulsion. On the other hand, others viewed the police as failing to act even though they were informed of the riot ahead of time and standing by while lawless mobs ruled the night in the city in which the police had been tasked to uphold the law. These two different versions of the actions of the police during the riots provide insight into the riots themselves and serve as a useful lens through which the race relations in Whatcom County in the early 20th century can be viewed. Also, it may be possible to speculate about the intentions of the police and Chief Thomas by examining the actions that they took when trying to protect the Japanese community in Bellingham during a potentially violent situation that took place shortly after the riots.

On the night of September 4, 1907, the police were alerted when neighbors of the immigrant community heard "the crashing of window panes and

---

87   BH Sept. 6, 1907, p.4
88   Dodd, Werter, "The Hindu in the Northwest." *World Today* v13 Oct. 1907, pp. 1157-1160.

... loud yells."⁸⁹ There were a total of five incidents of violence reported to the police that night, yet only a handful of officers responded to the disturbances. First to arrive at the homes where the immigrant laborers were being dragged out of their beds into the street were Chief Thomas and a patrolman. Initially, according to some reports, the patrolman arrested two youths throwing rocks at one of the Indian men. However, after the mob heard of these arrests, they forced the police to let the offenders rejoin the mob as it forced more of its targets out of their homes. Although the police tried to stop the mob, they were only able to protect themselves and prevent further violence. After another immigrant lodging home had been raided by the crowd, and the arrival of two more officers, the police were able to get control over the situation. The five members of the Bellingham police who were now on the scene guided the immigrants to the basement of city hall under their protection. This protection was that the crowd was only allowed to follow and jeer the immigrants as they were escorted by the police. Over the course of the night, smaller groups brought more immigrants from other parts of town to the city hall where they were kept under guard of the police until the morning when they were forced out of town.⁹⁰ The police were seen by some as heroes. They had reestablished order without serious injury or loss of life in a volatile situation.

Alternatively, the police may have allowed the riot to occur and acted only when it became necessary to prevent serious violence. Blame for the riot immediately fell on Chief Thomas' shoulders. The criticism that stands out the strongest was that the police knew the riots were going to occur and did nothing to stop them. The *Bellingham Herald* printed a commonly held belief that "the officers were secretly in sympathy with the rioters and . . . they knew the trouble was to occur."⁹¹

Yet, whether the police had foreknowledge will never be known. Chief Thomas argued that the response of his men was prudent and prevented further violence. Thomas "considered it folly for only four or five men to endeavor to stay the will of a howling mob."⁹² In looking back, it is hard to determine whether he took the correct actions: he prevented violence, but at

---

89   BR Sept. 5, 1907 pp. 1, 3
90   Ibid.
91   *BH* Sept. 5, 1907, pp. 1-2
92   Ibid.

the cost of driving an immigrant community and an entire cultural group out of town.

Chief Thomas left the meeting of the City Council the morning after the riots and began deputizing citizens. Of those fifty that Chief Thomas was ordered to deputize, only twenty-eight were actually sworn in to prevent further violence. In their day of duty, these extra officers conducted patrols of the areas where rioting had occurred the previous night and escorted the Punjabi immigrants to receive payment for their work in the mills before leaving town on trains bound for Canada, to the south, and on foot.[93] The Punjabi immigrants that remained relied on these officers for protection the day after the riots, especially the next night. Officers also guarded a group of Punjabis living in south Bellingham throughout the day and into the night after the riots.

On the day after the evening riots, Chief Thomas issued arrest warrants for five men involved in the riots: Fred Knowlton, E. H. Anderson, William Wankworth, Fred Nolan, and J. Brickbealer. These men were arrested by the County Sheriff that night and booked into the county jail.[94] According to the jail registry, the men arrested for rioting were released either on September 6th or 7th after they were able to post bail. As with scores of lawless actions against Chinese immigrants in the 1880s, which in some cases included cold-blooded murder, no one was prosecuted in the end because "no witnesses could be found to swear against the defendants." The prosecutor claimed that "the officers were unable to find a single person in the city who would swear that he could identify the defendants as participants in the outbreak against the Orientals," and the defendants were released.[95]

Once the case was dismissed and the last of the Sikhs had left Bellingham, there was little reference to the matter, and there seemed to be a deliberate attempt to forget the embarrassing lawlessness. One of the few official acknowledgements of the riot in subsequent years was in the *Souvenir Album* printed in 1916 as a form of publicity for the Bellingham police force. According to this retelling of "The Hindu Riots," as a great accomplishment, the police, led by Chief Thomas, enabled "some two thousand Hindus" to be "expelled from the city" following three days of "the so-called 'riots'" during which "no single man was hurt." The police chief "recognized the universal

---

93 BH Sept. 6, 1907, p. 1
94 Ibid.
95 BH Sept. 21, 1907 p.8

demand of the whites that the brown men be expelled, and while not aiding in rounding up the Hindus, the police were simply watchful to see that no violence was offered the aliens." The pamphlet concluded in a congratulatory tone that "like the Chinamen, who have never returned to Tacoma, the Hindu has given Bellingham a wide berth since."[96] In just a few years, some of the basic facts of the event were distorted, but pride and approval remained for both the expulsion and for the admitted complicity of the police.

Aftermath Exodus to Canada, Oregon, and California

Little is known about the Punjabi men who were driven out of Bellingham. The names of approximately 35 have been gleaned from various records, and many were believed to have returned to Canada or traveled south to Oregon and California in pursuit of work. The only documented story of the Bellingham exodus from the Punjabi perspective is that of Thakar (Tuly) Singh Johl, who was interviewed in Yuba City by Joan Jensen in 1975 for her book *Passage from India*. Tuly, the youngest of four sons, was born in 1878. He married, and after their first baby was born in 1903, he left his wife and baby son to find work in Canada in 1904 or 1905. According to Tuly's two sons, Gulzar and Kartar, whom I interviewed in 2008, Tuly traveled to Canada with six other men from his village of Jundiala and then crossed the border to the US with five of them. Tuly and five of the group were Sikh farmers. The sixth, Gurditta Mal, who was a Hindu, stayed in Victoria where he worked in labor and trucking jobs and had close ties to the Sikh community. The Bellingham lumber mill where Tuly and his friends worked was at some distance from the mills and residences attacked by the mob. But all the Sikh workers left town within days out of fear. According to his sons, Tuly said little about the experience in Bellingham except to marvel at the gigantic size of the logs that were milled.

They worked together on the railroad grading in Marysville and then became a crew on a fruit orchard. According to Verma, this pattern of several men from the same village forming a crew or team was typical of Punjabis who emigrated to Canada at that time.[97] Often they would live and work together with men learning to cook for the team as the women would do for the family in India. Tuly's family and the local Punjabi Heritage Association

---

96 Bellingham Police, Souvenir Album, 1916
97 Verma, 2002

introduced me to descendants of some of the other members of his crew who had worked with him in Canada and Bellingham, and then settled in the Yuba City, California, area. I also later met and interviewed two of Gurditta Mal's sons in Victoria, BC.

Tuly never attended school, and like most of the Punjabis, he was illiterate when he arrived in Canada; however, he was quite intelligent and somehow he taught himself English and kept written records for his crew. One report estimated that between 50% to three-fifth of the East Indian immigrants were illiterate.[98] Tuly returned home to India where he was placed under house arrest for many years for his sympathies with and support of the nationalist Gadar movement. He returned to Yuba City in 1924 with some difficulty via Mexico. Two of Tuly's sons, Kartar and Gulzar, who grew up in India, eventually were brought to California by their father, who encouraged them to study and supported them. Gulzar, his second son, studied agriculture and earned a masters degree and farmed like his father. Gulzar joined his father in Yuba City in 1948, studied medicine, and became an ophthamologist. He was the first Sikh in the region to earn an MD. He expressed some regret at not learning more about his father's experiences as one of the early immigrants and supporters of the nationalist movement:

> Things were simple at that time. I wish I had known that some day I would want my children and grandchildren to know everything about my father and the others. And it would have been so easy if I just, all the stories that I heard I wrote down. But I thought they were just like you know, just like we talk about I played this game or played that game and didn't pay any attention. And now all of a sudden—it would have been very important. At first I wasn't interested in those things. All I was interested in was working and first going to school and then being a doctor. I had nothing else that I wanted to do.[99]

Tuly lived to nearly 100, and as of 2003, his son wrote that Tuly had 19 grandchildren, 53 great-grandchildren, and 36 great-great-grandchildren. Tuly's descendants mostly stayed in the Sacramento Valley area and

---

98   Immigration Commission report, "Japanese and Other Immigrant Races in the Pacific Coast and Rocky Mountain States, 1911, p. 67.
99   Gulzar S. Johl, author's interview, Feb. 2008

contributed to the community in farming, profession occupations, education, business, and law enforcement. Through the single lens of Tuly's life and his descendants, one can imagine the collective contributions that the 200–300 Sikhs might have made to Bellingham and the Puget Sound region. Seen from this vantage, the 1907 vigilante action fueled by ethnic fears and wage competition most likely resulted in a tremendous sustained human and material loss to the local community.

Unlike the neighboring communities across the border of Abbotsford, Vancouver, Victoria, and various smaller communities in the Fraser Valley of British Columbia, Whatcom County had no Punjabi presence until the mid 1980s—a hiatus of about 75 years. Now there are approximately 2,000 Sikh and other South Asians in the County, double the number from the 2000 census. A Gurdwara was established in 2000, as the center of a Sikh community of over 450 families. Before the commemoration of the riot that was organized for the centennial in 2007, few in the community were aware of the history of these early pioneers and how they were driven out.

Spreading Actions and Responses

Several days following the riot in Bellingham, a larger race riot broke out in Vancouver, BC, in which a mob attacked Chinese, Japanese, and East Indian residents that seemed to have been triggered by the Bellingham events and agitation by the Asiatic Exclusion League in Vancouver and in the US. Exclusion League secretary A. E. Fowler visited Bellingham from Seattle only after the Bellingham riot had occurred and publically expressed disapproval of the action, favoring pushing for national exclusion policies to bar Asian laborers from entering. Immediately following the riot in Bellingham, the Exclusion League in Seattle issued a letter to President Roosevelt calling for halting Asian immigration to the Northwest, ominously warning that "if something were not done soon the agitation started in Bellingham would spread all over the Sound country and massacres of the Eastern aliens was likely to result."[100] Fowler was one of the speakers in Vancouver and some blamed him and League organizers from the US for setting off the riot in Canada.

In months following the riots in Bellingham and Vancouver, anti-Punjabi hostilities occurred in other locations in the Puget Sound region of Washington

---

100   BR Sept, 6, 1907, p.1

State, including Everett and Aberdeen, causing many more South Asian immigrants to flee the region. Fathe Mohammed, a Punjabi Muslim working at a mill in Aberdeen, left in fear following threats of violence. After relocating to Marysville, California, he became a successful rice farmer along with a group of other Punjabi Muslims in the Sacramento Valley.[101]

Several days after the Bellingham riot, the dwelling of several Punjabis in Everett was stoned, and they appealed for police protection. On October 2, an Everett labor leader issued a veiled threat to Punjabi workers advising them to leave, and on November 2, 1907, an armed mob of 500 rounded up all of the South Asian residents, who feared they might be shot. The police, having been warned in advance, used the Bellingham method of sheltering the immigrants in the jail to prevent bloodshed, releasing them the next day for a swift departure.[102] As in Bellingham, the local editor expressed disapproval of the means, but applauded the outcome:

> While everyone who believes in fairplay condemns Saturday night's anti-Hindu demonstration, there cannot but be a feeling of general satisfaction over the departure of the Hindus from the city as a result. One dislikes to see them driven out in that manner, but once it is done, perhaps we should be thankful that nothing worse occurred.[103]

In August 1908, a riot occurred between striking Italian workers and Punjabis at a railroad yard, and although shots were fired and rocks were hurled, no serious injuries were reported. This was the first incident in which Punjabis were reported to be armed for self-protection.

No one was prosecuted in any of these mob actions in Washington State, but when a similar outbreak occurred in St. John, Oregon, in 1908, several rioters were indicted and brought to trial. Apparently, however, like the anti-Chinese terror and the case of the massacre of 34 Chinese miners in Hells Canyon, Oregon, in the 1880s, no one arrested was ever convicted and sentenced.[104]

---

101 Robert Mohammed, author's interview, Feb. 2008
102 EDH, Nov. 4, 1907 p 1.
103 EDH, Nov. 5, 1907 p.5
104 Nokes, Greg *Massacred for Gold*, 2009

Conclusion: Sikhs Return to Whatcom County
[Satpal Sidhu contributed to this section]

After the 1907 riots, it took almost 75 years before Sikhs would again call Whatcom County their home. The first Sikh temple in the northwest was built in Abbotsford, BC, by the Khalsa Diwan society in 1908. In the early 1980s, a few Sikh families started to arrive in Whatcom County, and these newcomers found an uneasy silence or amnesia about the past. These newcomers were mainly farmers migrating from California, attracted by opportunities of inexpensive agricultural land and prime conditions for berry cultivation. By the early 1990s, a community had developed of 30–35 Sikh families in Whatcom County, and in 1994, the community decided to purchase land to build a Gurdwara. The first gathering in the new temple building was celebrated on January 1, 2000. Today there are more than 450 Sikh families living in Whatcom and Skagit County, and the 2010 Census found 1,922 Asian Indians in Whatcom County compared with 980 in 2000. Sikh farmers and their many employees produce 50 million pounds of raspberries and blueberries annually. Production accounts for over half of the total of 95 million pounds of the berry crop grown in Whatcom County, the largest in the US. In addition to agriculture, Sikh families own or are engaged in a variety of businesses and professional services and provide jobs for hundreds of employees.

In 2007, upon the hundredth anniversary of the events, the Human Rights Commemorative Project was organized in the Bellingham area, led by John McGarrity, Satpal Sidhu, myself (Paul Englesberg), and several other members of the local Sikh community, with the intent of raising public awareness of the events of the past. The group worked with local government officials, media, and non-profit organizations to organize a series of events, including a Day of Healing and Remembrance with a public gathering at the County Courthouse and educational displays at the public library and Western Washington University (WWU) Library. The Sikh Gurdwara in nearby Lynden also held an open house and a commemorative event. Mary Anne Gallagher, a *Bellingham Herald* reporter, wrote a series of in-depth articles about the history of the intolerance against the Punjabi residents and the development of the Sikh community in Whatcom County since the 1980s.[105] *Bellingham Herald* published an apology for the paper's role in the hostilities

---

105   BH Sept. 2, 2007; Sept. 3, 1907

against the South Asian immigrants, and the Mayor of Bellingham and the Whatcom County Executive declared a day of remembrance and healing.[106]

A panel discussion was also held at Fairhaven College, WWU, with several scholarly presentations related to the 1907 riot and immigration issues, including the showing of the trailer of a documentary video made by two WWU students, Ian Morgan and Andrew Hedden. The complete documentary, *Present in All that We Do*, can now be viewed online through the South Asian Digital Archive [SAADA] project at http://www.saadigitalarchive.org/item/20111122-470.

Following the tragic attack on the Sikh temple in Wisconsin, the Whatcom County Sikh community organized a prayer meeting and open house at the Lynden Gurdwara on August 12, 2012. Many civic leaders spoke at the event and expressed their condolences and support for the Sikh community. The legacy in Bellingham and Whatcom County of intolerance and hostility toward native people, Chinese, Japanese, African Americans, Sikhs, and other South Asians is slowly being replaced with such actions large and small that demonstrate respect, cooperation, and solidarity.

---

106   BH Sept. 2, 2007

References:

Buchanan, Agnes F. "The West and the Hindu Invasion" *Overland Monthly,* April 1908.

Chang, Kornel. *Pacific Connections: The Making of the US-Canadian Borderlands.* Berkeley: University of California Press, 2012.

Dodd, Werter. "The Hindu in the Northwest." *World Today* v13 Oct. 1907. pp. 1157-1160.

Hallberg, Gerald. N. "Bellingham, Washington's Anti-Hindu Riot." *Journal of the West, 12* (1973): 163-175.

Jensen, Joan. *Passage From India: Asian Indian Immigrants in North America.* New Haven: Yale Press, 1988.

Lee, Erika. "Hemispheric Orientalism and the 1907 Pacific Coast Race Riot." Amerasia Journal, 33(2) (2007): 19-48.

Melendy, Brett Asians in America: Filipinos, Koreans, and Asian Indians. Boston: Twayne Publishers 1977.

Nokes, Greg. Massacred for Gold. Corvallis, OR: Oregon State University Press, 2009

Shah, Nayan. *Stranger Intimacy:* Contesting Race, Sexuality and the Law in the North American West. Berkeley: University of California Press, 2011.

Sheffauer, Herman, "The Tide of Turbans." The Forum, 1910.

Singh, Saint Nihal. "The Picturesque Immigrant from India's Coral Strand." *Outwest,* 1909

Sohi, Seema. *Echoes of Mutiny: Race, Empire, and Indian Anticolonialism in North America.* PhD Dissertation, University of Washington, 2008.

Verma, Archana B. *The Making of Little Punjab in Canada.* New Delhi: Sage, 2002.

Wolf, Christopher, *Casting the "Hindu" in the Crucible of Nationhood.* University of Oregon, Masters thesis, 2001

Wunder, John R. "South Asians, Civil Rights, and the Pacific Northwest: The 1907 Bellingham Anti-Indian Riot and Subsequent Citizenship Deportation Struggles." *Western Legal History 4,* (1991): 59-68.

Wynne Robert, "American Labor Leaders and the Vancouver Anti-Oriental Riot." *Pacific Northwest Quarterly* vol. 57 n.4., Oct. 1966/

Newspapers and magazines:

Bellingham Reveille [BR]; Bellingham Herald [BH]; Colliers Magazine, Sept. 28, 1907; Oct. 12, 1907; *Nation; Nya Varlden* [NV]; *Puget Sound American [PSA]; Seattle Republican* [SR]; *Victoria Daily Colonist [VDC]; Everett Daily Herald [EDH]; Free Hindustan; Whatcom Reveille [WR]*

The Ghadar Movement: Its Aims and Objectives and the Effect of this Movement on the Tragedy of Komagata Maru.

Dr. Puran Singh

The Ghadar Movement is an inseparable part and important historical struggle of India's movement for independence. The movement infused courage among the Indian people in foreign lands for national campaign and prepared them to free their country from the British Empire through armed rebellion. There are no two opinions about it that farming was the main vocation of the people in Punjab, but this vocation was not sufficient for them to make both ends meet. They were little aware of the main reasons of this economic misery, but a few knew well that they were suffering economically because of the policies of British Empire. They got a clue somehow that by working in Canada and America they could improve their economic plight. All the same, laborers were needed there. With the hope of better wages there, they dreamt of bettering the plight of their families, so many Punjabis migrated to Canada and America.

Even before this, many Punjabis had gone to countries like Malaya, Sumatra, and Shangai in China where they served in police or army and very soon preferred to reach Canada and America. When these Punjabi farmers or ex-army men reached America, they had to face the wrath of racial discrimination.

Punjabis started coming to America and Canada in the beginning of 20th century. Ninety percent out of them were Sikhs. In Canada, these migrants started living in British Columbia, especially around Vancouver. Of the others who went to America, most started living in cities in California and Oregon. There they could find work at farms or in saw mills. During the autumn days of 1906, about 1500 Punjabi laborers worked around Vancouver.[1]

In his life story, Baba Sohan Singh Bhakna, the great veteran of Ghadar Movement, has described such episodes. After reading these, we become clear that the reason of humiliation of Punjabis everywhere was their slavery only. As he describes, many times Americans used to jolt them asking, how could the Britishers enslave the thirty crore Indians?[2]

As is already told, prior to going to North America, Punjabi Sikhs went to Malaya, Shanghai, and Hong Kong to serve in British army or police. They also established gurdwaras there as in Penang in 1901 and then in Hong Kong. Gurdwara was also established in Shanghai in China. By virtue of the establishment of these gurdwaras, Punjabis or non-Punjabis had the privilege of staying or dining there during the journey. It cannot be denied that, after establishment of Ghadar movement, these gurdwaras played a great role in motivating the people to join the Ghadar movement. Granthis of these gurdwaras made a fearless contribution in this movement by preaching firmly the lessons of sacrifice through Gurbani. The "Ghadar Lehar" used to be available there, and its topics were discussed openly.

In 1906, the Khalsa Dewan Society was established in Vancouver, Canada. Construction of Gurdwara started in October of 1907, and it was inaugurated on January 19, 1908.[3] Thus, the Indians around Vancouver had found a central place to assemble and discuss their problems.

First of all, the state government of British Columbia tried to pass a special law in 1900 to restrict the Asian people from entering Canada, but, in 1901, Governor General Minto rejected it. Thereafter in 1902, 1903, and 1904, the BC government tried to make new laws to check the entry of Asian people, but the central government did not give approval to these.[4]

---

1   Khushwant Singh & Satindra Singh, Ghadar 1915: India;s First Armed Revolution; New Delhi, R. K. Publishing 1966. P.1
2   Baba Sohan Singh Bhakna, 'meri raam kahani', (ed. Rajwinder Singh Raahi) p.67, sangam publications Samana 2012.
3   Report Khalsa Diwan Society, Vancouver, July 22, 1905 to Oct 20 1909.
4   Lower, R.M. "Case Against Immigration, Queen Quarterly, Vol. 37; p. 571

Being British subjects, the Indians had the right of voting in BC. But the Provincial Act of 1907 withdrew the right of voting from all the people of Asian origin. On August 12, 1907, a new organization came into being, and its aim was to restrict the entry of Asian people in Canada. The body was named the Asiatic Exclusion League.[5]

The law for continuous voyage by sea for Asians and especially for Indian people was passed on January 8, 1908, which was also known as PC 27. Under Section 26 and 27 of the Act, any emigrant could be restricted from entering Canada if he did not reach Canada direct from the country of his birth or by means of uninterrupted sea route.[6]

The Canadian government also devised a secret conspiracy to oust the Indians from here. Hopkinson was used to implement this scheme as he motivated the Sikhs by telling them that good jobs were only possible in Honduras. In a special meeting, the Sikhs passed a resolution to go to the place to verify the suitability of the place as per climate and area. The community deputed Bhai Sham Singh and Nagar Singh for the purpose, and they reached Honduras on October 25, 1908.[7]

On November 22, 1908, Khalsa Diwan Society passed a resolution stating that no Indian shall go to Honduras since its climate was not good and the general state of living was very bad.[8] When the Canadian government failed totally in its conspiracy to convince the Sikhs or Indians to go to Honduras, they tried to ban the entry of Indian people in Canada. For this purpose, a Privy Council order no. 920 was presented in the parliament on May 9, 1910. Similarly, another order, no. 926, was introduced to constitute another law.[9]

In Canada, the Indians and Punjabis organized themselves to oppose the racial discrimination laws based on the racial discriminatory policies of the Canadian government. Khalsa Diwan Society and United India League passed a resolution collectively to send a deputation to Ottawa. Dr. Sunder

---

5   Hallet, M. E. Governor Generals Views on Oriental Immigration to B. C. Studies No. 14, 50; 1972; p. 58.
6   Mehta, Sampat R. "International Barriers, Ottawa", Canada Research Bureau, 1973. Pp 133-134.
7   Jass, jaswant Singh, ' Baba Gurditt Singh' p.28-29, Jalandhar; new book company, 1983.
8   Harkin, J.B. The Indians in British Columbis; pp 27-28.
9   Parliament of the United Kingdom of Great Britain and Ireland, Ninth Edwars VII, 1909, Chapter 27 pp14-15.

Singh, Professor Teja Singh, Raja Singh, and L. W. Hall joined. This deputation reached Ottawa on December 15, 1911. There they disclosed their problems to the minister, Mr. Rozers.[10] But nobody bothered about these problems put before the minister. After this, a deputation of three members—Bhai Balwant Singh (Granthi), S. Narain Singh Theekriwala, and Nand Singh Seehra—was sent to the British and Indian governments. They set for England on March 14, 1913. Their meetings with high officials bore no useful outcome, and they all returned dismayed.[11]

Founding of the Gadar Party

Racial discrimination came up against the Indians in Canada, and the apartheid laws were formed and followed. On the other hand, the Punjabis continued their struggle against racial discrimination and the laws. They foiled the wicked plots of the Canada government. Giani Bhagwan Singh, Granthi of the Gurdwara, stimulated the people through his lectures to keep the struggle continued against British Empire. People got excited to sacrifice their lives for independence of the country. It is clear that the seeds of Gadar Movement were sown in Vancouver, and the gurdwara of Khalsa Diwan Society was its chief center. At last, San Francisco became its main center of establishment.[12]

The spirit of revolution was strengthened among the Indian people in America. First of all, at the end of 1912 or in the beginning of 1913, the Indian Association was established. This organization came into being in Astoria, Oregon. In one of its meetings, Munshi Ram, Karim Bakhsh Nawab Khan, Kesar Singh, Balwant Singh, and Kartar Singh delivered their lectures.[13]

According to one statement made by S. Bhag Singh, Canadian, a meeting was held in Astoria in May or June 1913. Many people came there from the nearby mills. It was a grand gathering and Lala Hardyal delivered his lecture. He gave inspiration to establish the party and start a paper. Thus, Baba Sohan Singh became President; Lala Hardyal, General Secretary; Munshi Ram, Assistant Secretary; Kanshi Ram, Treasurer; and Kesar Singh

---

10 Jass, Jaswant Singh, ' Baba Gurditt Singh' Jalandhar; new book company, 1983.
11 Gurdit Singh "The Voyage of Kamagata Maru", Calcuttan.d. pp13-14
12 Jagjit Singh, Gadar party lehar, Delhi, navyug publishers, 1979,p.37
13 Same page 38

Thathgarh as Vice President. I gave one hundred dollars and in all ten thousand dollars were collected.[14]

In many writings, there are indications of the forming of the "Hindustani Association" at first and then the "Hindi Association." Actually, the full name of the organization was Hindi Association of Pacific Coast. But under the name of the *Gadar* publication, this body too came to be known as Gadar Party.

Objectives

"The main objective of this organization is to free the country from British Empire by means of armed rebellion and establish self-rule in the country based on the concept of liberty, equality and fraternity; there should be clean administration for maximum benefit of the people."[15]

In the first edition of *Gadar*, published in November 1913, the objectives of Gadar party were in a way that "on this first of November 1913, there begins a new era since on the alien land but in our own language, the struggle has started against the British rule."

Our name: Ghadar

Place of Ghadar: India

When shall it begin? Very soon in India because the people cannot bear now the tyranny and torture of British rule and are ready to fight and die for freedom of the country.

General rules and duties of the Gadar Party and its members are found written in detail in the biography of Baba Sohan Singh Bhakna.

1. Irrespective of any caste, creed, or country, every lover of freedom can join this Hindi Association.
2. Every member of the Party shall have mutual national relation. No discussion based on religion shall be allowed in the Party.
3. Everyone shall be free in food habits. One may be vegetarian or non-vegetarian in any manner or kind.
4. No one shall be considered self-styled leader. Positions shall be held as per Party decisions.

---

14 Statement Bhag Singh Canadian, Gadar lehar di kahani (ed. chain singh chain) p.120-21.
15 The Seventh Report of the Senate Fact Finding Committee on Un-American Activities in California (1953) p. 216

5. This organization shall have two wings: one apparent and the other as secret with three members.
6. If any organizer or member of the secret committee commits forgery or leaks out secrets of the Society to enemies, he shall be sentenced to death on realization of the crime.
7. No member of the Gadar Party shall use any type of drug.
8. Every member shall be committed to obey every order of the Society. In case of any laxity, the individual can be given punishment.

Duties

1. A committed soldier of the Gadar Party shall be ever ready to help the supporters of liberty and equality in any part of the world where the struggle takes place.
2. For the sake of freedom of India, no revolutionary shall back out from sacrifice in body, mind, and money.
3. Every member is committed towards setting democratic rule in India after finishing the one-man dictatorship.
4. Even after failure of the revolution, no one shall get back from the mission. This struggle has to continue till even a single member of the Party is alive.16

The Ghadar Newspaper

The Gadar Party decided to start a newspaper. The Party entrusted Lala Hardyal with total responsibility of the paper, but he showed some laxity in performing this duty. At last, Kartar Singh Sarabha and Gupta carried out the responsibility of editing the paper in true spirit and might. Because of the *Gadar* newspaper, the Hindi Association of Pacific Coast became popularly known as Gadar Party. The paper started to be sent to other countries like Canada, Japan, China, Malaya, Burma, Manila, and India.

The first edition of the paper came out in November 1913. In addition, other literature was also published in which "Gadar di Goonj" became very popular.17

---

16   Baba Sohan Singh Bhakna, 'meri raam kahani', (ed. Rajwinder Singh Raahi) p.83-84, sangam publications Samana 2012. Same page
17   Same page 84-87

So far as the thinking of Gadarites is concerned, they were workers in true spirit and zeal, and 90% of them were Sikhs. As we observe the stipulated aims and objectives of Gadar Party, we find that the source of inspiration for the high ideals among them was Sri Guru Granth Sahib—the scripture of Sikh Faith. There is total negation of any caste or creed in it; the message is for human welfare; there is inspiration to stand fearlessly against tyranny or the tyrant; there are sermons against any race or gender discrimination; and there is appreciation of sacrifice for humanity and human rights. As expressed by Bhai Harnam Singh Tundilat, the main objective of Gadar Party was to oust the English from India and then establish the democratic and secular state in India. After eliminating the economic gaps among farmers, landlords, and capitalists, they were to give priority to works of public welfare. On observing prosperity in America, Indians had a firm view that the main cause of their poverty and misery was British rule only. No member of Gadar Party had any knowledge about Marxism, capitalism, communism, Bolsheviks, or any such "ism."[18]

When the Gadar Party did not succeed in its mission, some of them thought about the Russian revolution since they had succeeded in achieving their objective. The Gadar Party sent some of its members to Moscow to learn about Marxism. S. Santokh Singh, General Secretary of the Party, himself went to Moscow. After returning, he started the *Kirti* paper in Punjab.

Reasons of the Failure of Ghadar Party

Under process of self-assessment, S. Sohan Singh Bhakna, President of Gadar Party, enumerates the reasons as follows which caused failure to the Party:

1. Gadar Party was not yet one year old when the war started in Europe, and no solid preparation could be made.
2. It was new experience for members of the Party. They thought that the leadership and public in India would cooperate with them, but this did not become possible.

---

18   Gadar lehar di kahani, Chain Singh Chain, Jalandhar: Itihas sub committee 2002, p.68-69 (statements of Harnam Singh tundi laat, Kotla Naudh Singh at 22/6/1955) p.30-31(statement of baba Sohan Singh Bhakna in 1949)

3. There was no well-known leader in Gadar Party around whom the people could assemble. There were only poor farmers and laborers in Gadar Party.
4. It being their first venture in revolution, they were short of experience. Most of the rebels were caught while getting down the ship.

In addition, it was the miscalculation of Indian leadership which could not identify the opportunity. Secondly, there was absence of awareness among the people. Whatever assessment the Gadar Party leaders had made about the situation in India, it was wrong; however, the army men had extended full hope.[19]

Though the Gadarites were of firm mind, they could not consolidate their central command. Besides this, the British Government had become quite alert, and the Gadarites returning to foreign lands were arrested and put behind the bars. Secondly, the role of informers and traitors did not let the Gadarites succeed in their mission.[20]

As expressed by Baba Sohan Singh Bhakna, the Muslims did not have good opinion about Lala Hardyal, because when students from different states of India were called for higher education in America, Gobind Bihari Lal was preferred in place of the Muslim boy Mehmud from Madras. Lala Hardyal was incapable of doing the real job; secondly, he went away very soon after leaving the Society. Further, when the firm-minded ones, like Bhai Santokh Singh, Bhai Bhagwan Singh, Maulana Baratulla, Bhai Kesar Singh, Bhai Nidhan Singh, Bhai Jawala Singh, Bhai Wasakha Singh, Arur Singh, and Pandit Kanshi Ram, also left America, then Ram Chandar started exercising his self-will. At last, he was murdered by some patriot, since he had embezzled funds of the Society.[21]

Gadar Party was the first secular Movement that began with the notion of liberating the country through armed rebellion. The Sikhs were always in majority in the Movement and the Gadar literature was also published in Punjabi. Their meetings, secret or open, were usually held in Gurdwaras. But this Movement had no relation with Sikh religion in any way. Even Hindus

---

19 Gadar lehar di kahani, Chain Singh Chain, Jalandhar: Itihas sub committee 2002, p.30-31(statement of Baba Sohan Singh Bhakna in 1949)
20 Khushwant Singh, Ghadar 1915, Delhi, R&K Publishing House, 1966, p. 54-55
21 Baba Sohan Singh Bhakna, 'meri raam kahani', (ed. Rajwinder Singh Raahi) p.88, 90,93, sangam publications Samana 2012.

and Muslims also joined this Movement, and it influenced the rebellious campaigns in India also to work in secular spirit.[22]

Tragedy of the Komagata Maru

The racial policies of the Canadian government have already been conveyed in detail, particularly that a regular law for the voyage of Indian people was formed by the Canadian government. This law was passed in 1908. Before this, even the voting right of Indian people was withdrawn in 1907. In 1908, Honduras made up a conspiracy by means of which the Indian people were to be coaxed to go to Honduras. This time, the Indian people, under direction of Professor Teja Singh, refused to go to Honduras. Thereafter, the Canada government passed orders no. 920 and 926 which restricted Indians' entry in Canada.

On December 17, 1913, 56 new Sikh migrants reached the Victoria (BC) harbor. They all had come by the ship *Empress of Panama Maru*. The Sikhs of Vancouver had hired services of lawyer Mr. Bird for legal help.[23] Judge Hunter found some legal flaw in the Order in Council and allowed 35 voyagers to enter Canada.[24]

When Narain Singh and other migrants won the right of entry in Canada, it was natural for the news to spread far and wide. But the problem was that no ship company was prepared to sell tickets to Indian people. The biggest hurdle was the law to reach Canada through non-stop journey. But it could be possible if some ship was be hired. Up to 1914, there were rumours of buying a ship even; the dream became reality in 1914 when Baba Gurdit Singh Sarhali hired the *Komagata Maru*. In the words of Baba Gurdit Singh himself: "I was in Malaya when some persons came to me and related to me the sad tale of their woes."[25]

In Punjab, the Indian delegates—Bhai Balwant Singh (Granthi), Bhai Nand Singh Sehra, and Bhai Harnam Singh—met Bhai Takht Singh at Ferozepur. They gave him total information about Canada and asked him to contact Baba Gurdit Singh and convince him to hire a ship.[26]

---

22   Khushwant Singh & Satindra Singh, Ghadar 1915, Delhi, R&K Publishing House, 1966, p. 57
23   Johnston Hugh, "The Voyage of the Kamagata Maru, Delhi: Oxford UP, 1979 pp 17-18.
24   British Columbia Reports, Vol. 18, 1913, pp. 506-509
25   Gurjit Singh, opp cit, p. 14.
26   Kesar singh ' meri svai jeevani'

Baba Gurdit Singh started his efforts to hire a ship, but the British spies put hurdles in the way and he could not succeed in hiring a ship at Calcutta. Even the Khalsa Diwan Society at Vancouver also pressed Baba Gurdit Singh to hire a ship at the earliest. When the ship was to begin its sail from Hongkong on March 30, 1914, Baba Ji was arrested but very soon he was released.

Crossing over all the hurdles, the ship left Hongkong on April 4, 1914. The Governor of Hongkong informed the Governor General of Canada about this.[27] With 376 passengers, the *Komagata Maru* reached Vancouver on May 23, 1914, but the immigration authorities asked the ship to stop a good distance away from the harbor in deep water. Even the local Sikhs of Vancouver were not allowed to go near the ship. Baba Gurdit Singh expressed resentment against these restrictions, but it made no effect on the authorities. They were not allowed to meet the media and nor could the media people meet the passengers.[28]

All rules and protocols regarding *Komagata Maru* were thrown to the wind. Baba Gurdit Singh and the passengers were forcibly detained within the ship. The Secretary of Khalsa Diwan Society asked Mr. Bird, the lawyer, to prepare the case. Mr. Bird then asked permission to meet Baba Gurdit Singh, but Malcolm Reid did not permit it.[29]

It was really astonishing that even the lawyer was not allowed to meet Baba Gurdit Singh. It becomes evident that the people had no privilege to enjoy their rights. The lawyer Mr. Bird wrote about this injustice to Prime Minister Borden.[30] The Sikhs of Vancouver changed the charter of the ship at the names of Bhai Bhag Singh and Hassan Rahim. It was an effort that might have helped the passengers alight from the ship. Dr. Raghunath Singh, who boarded the ship from Hongkong, proved to be a man of immigration. He gave total information to the immigration department. In brief, it can be said that no appeals could affect the central government. Based on the policies of racial discrimination, the Canadian government was firm on sending back the *Komagata Maru*. The government requisitioned services of the Navy's ship *Rainbow* to forcibly compel the ship to move away. As

---

27 Telegram from Governor of Hong Kong to the Governor General of Canada, Borden papers. Letter 17490.
28 Malcolm Reid to W. D. Scott (June 9, 1914) Steven File, p. 158.
29 Ferguson, Ted 'White Man's Country". Pp 24-25
30 Telegram from F. J. Edward Bird to R. L. Borden (Prime Minister), June 23, 1914 Borden papers.

such, the passengers of *Komagata Maru* remained detained in the sea for two months, suffered numberless miseries, tried hard for legal help, and appealed for amnesty also. But the Canadian government showed no sense of mercy. And on July 23, 1914, the ship was forcibly sent back.

The captain of the ship was given special instruction by the Colonial Secretary of Hongkong to not come to Hongkong. Thereafter, the ship was not allowed to embark even at Singapore harbor. On September 29, 1914, the ship was intercepted at Budge Budge, which was 17 miles away from Calcutta. The passengers were asked to leave for Punjab by a special train; however, they refused to comply with this enforced order. The police fired at the passengers whereat many were wounded and many got killed. A few succeeded in running away safely, and 60 of them boarded the train to Punjab silently.

The Indian government announced a special "immigration proclamation" on September 5, 1914, so that restrictions could be imposed upon the rebels and their activities could be kept under control. In a way, their entry also may be checked.[31]

Effect on the Ghadar Movement

When the *Komagata Maru* was heaving to sail, the Gadar Party was being established in America at that time. Though the Sikhs did struggle in Canada against racial discrimination a good time before and also organized themselves, the efforts came up quite late, no doubt, in America. But the Sikhs of Canada were the real incumbents in establishing the Gadar Party in America and also became its members. In reality, there was no patronage for the *Komagata Maru* plan on behalf of the Gadar Party.

It was the Khalsa Diwan Society of Vancouver that emboldened the hiring of the *Komagata Maru* and gave consent for support also. On the way, Bhai Balwant Singh met Baba Gurdit Singh and traveled on the ship for some time. Then, he took a fast steamer to reach Vancouver before the reaching of this ship there.

Khalsa Diwan Society Vancouver did fight the legal battle for disembarking of passengers of the ship and did collect money also for payment of installments of the ship. But despite the severe struggle, the ship was sent back.

---

31   MacMunn, George, Sir "Turmoil and Tragedyin India" London, Jarrolds Publishers, 1935. Pp 94-95.

The Gadar Party brought out a special edition of *Gadar* wherein a detailed version was given about the excesses made by the Canadian government on the patrons and passengers of the *Komagata Maru*. The Party did contribute financially towards the Shore Committee of Vancouver. Through the Shore Committee, some copies of the *Gadar* were made to reach the passengers. When the Gadar Party came to know of the withdrawal of the *Komagata Maru*, they called an emergency meeting. It was decided that any member who met the passengers must tell them about the aims and policies of the Ghadar Party.[32]

The decision was to equip the passengers with 200 pistols and cartridges. Sohan Singh Bhakna took personal responsibility for this task. The responsibility of delivering the weapon boxes was assigned to Kartar Singh Sarabha and Giani Bhagwan Singh.[33] Baba Sohan Singh Bhakna developed a rapport of revolutionary views with the passengers and prepared them to take part in the revolution against British Empire. When a meeting in connection with *Komagata Maru* was held in the Dominion Hall of Vancouver, the speakers declared openly that since the ship had been sent back forcibly, all the Indians should go back to India and rebel against British rule.[34]

The treatment meted out to passengers at Vancouver and Budge Budge on return expedited the revolution in foreign lands. In the words of Michael O'Dyer: "It has energized the already prevailing proclamations in this rebellious move."[35]

Regarding its effect on the Gadar Movement, the Indian Sedition Committee writes in its report: "This notion has instigated some of the Sikhs in Punjab to this extent that the government is all out weighed against them. This further strengthened the hands of revolutionaries who were insisting the Sikhs living abroad to return home and take part in the revolution. They expected it to happen very soon. Many migrants heard this call and started returning to India from Canada, USA, Philippines, Hongkong and China."[36]

After this episode of *Komagata Maru*, many passengers became staunch revolutionaries. Prime among them were Baba Gurmukh Singh Lalton

---

32 Puran singh, 'Kamagata Maru da dukhant' Vancouver, Canadian Sikh studies & teaching society, 2008,p.137
33 Same page 137
34 Gurcharan Singh Sainsara, Gadar Party da Itihas, desh Bhagat yadgar committee 1969, p.151.
35 O'Dwyer, Michael Francis, Sir, "India As I Knew It", London: Constables, 1926, p. 194.
36 The Indian Sedition Committee Report, 1918, Calcutta, p. 148-149.

and Baba Harnam Singh Gujjarwal. Bhai Parmanand writes: "If there had been no *Komagata Maru* episode, no awareness would have risen among the Indians living in Canada and America."[37]

The *Komagata Maru* tragedy added fuel to the fire. The inhuman treatment meted to the passengers, making laws for putting a permanent ban on entry of Indians in Canada, and designing Honduras-like conspiracies excited all the Indians living abroad to struggle for absolute independence of the country.[38] They realized that living in slavery was nothing short of living in hell. But in addition to North America, branches of Gadar Party were everywhere, in Philippines, China, Siam, Burma, and Singapore. They all used to get information through *Gadar*—the newspaper. Even from there also, the Gadarites got ready for sacrifice and started returning to their country.

---

37 Perma Nand, "The Story of My Life", Lahore; The Indian Sedition Committee Report, Hindu Sabha, 1934; p. 75.
38 Jagjit singh, Gadar party lehar, Delhi, navyug publishers, 1979,p.71.

Bhai Mewa Singh Lopoke - The Immortal Martyr of Canada

Sohan Singh Pooni

In this paper, we will talk about Bhai Mewa Singh Lopoke—the immortal martyr of Canada.

Bhai Mewa Singh had shot dead a White Officer named William Hopkinson working in the immigration office. After the resulting suit against Bhai Mewa Singh, he was executed. Who was this William Hopkinson and who was Bhai Mewa Singh? What enmity did Bhai Mewa Singh have with Hopkinson? Why did Bhai Mewa Singh shoot at Hopkinson? Many writers have presented Bhai Mewa Singh as the murderer. No doubt, it is a bad act to kill someone by shooting. But the Canadian community has ever been taking Bhai Mewa Singh as martyr, and his day of martyrdom is celebrated every year. Was Bhai Mewa Singh a murderer or a martyr? We probe the questions in this paper, though in brief.

Bhai Mewa Singh was born in the village of Lopoke in Tehsil Ajnala of the Amritsar district in 1880. The village is about fourteen or fifteen miles away on north-west side of Amritsar. His father's name was Bhai Nand Singh Aulakh. Bhai Mewa Singh also had one brother named Dewa Singh. Like other migrants, Bhai Mewa Singh also had come to Canada in 1906 for better prospects of livelihood. Here he worked at the Green Chain of Frazer Mill in Westminster near Vancouver.

While living there, Bhai Mewa Singh came in close contact with Sikh community leaders like Bhai Bhag Singh Bhikhiwind and Bhai Balwant Singh Khurdpur. In company with them, he visited the numerous Indian dwellings to collect funds for building the first Gurdwara of North America in Vancouver. Inaugurated on January 19, 1908, Bhai Mewa Singh took Amrit in this gurdwara of Vancouver on June 28, 1908. He was a gentleman of religious nature. After his job hours, he spent most of his time in meditation and serving the visitors in the gurdwara. Bhai Mewa Singh was not married.

By 1908, about 5200 Indians had entered Canada. The majority of them, about 90%, were Sikhs from Punjab. Among these Sikhs, a good number had served in the British Indian Army. The Sikhs were very proud of their services rendered in honor and favor of the British battles. They considered themselves as loving sons of the British Empire. Since Canada was a colony of the British Empire, the Sikhs considered it their right to come to the land of their Emperor to live and work. But they were disillusioned upon coming to Canada. They had to undergo disgrace and humiliation on the roads of Vancouver. They fell prey to racial discrimination. While walking along the roads, their hearts felt knife-cut when they were called "Hindu slaves." These racial differences bruised the soul of Bhai Mewa Singh.

Even the Canadian government was discriminating against the Indian migrants in an organizational way. In 1907, the voting right was withdrawn from the Indian migrants. No doubt, the Indian migrants coming to Whites' colonies got political awareness which was dangerous for British Empire. So to restrict the entry of Indians in Canada, the Canadian Government in consultation with the British government devised racial rules in 1908 for "direct voyage" with at least 200 hundred dollars in pocket as a necessary condition. With the promulgation of these racial rules, the entry of Indians in Canada was totally stopped. Because of the "direct voyage" condition, the Indian migrants already living in Canada could not afford to call their families from India. In October–November of 1908, the Canadian government concocted a conspiracy to send all the Indians living in Canada to British Honduras, but the Canadian Sikhs did not let it succeed. Under effect of such a bad treatment, the Indians living in Canada started realizing that the main reason of such maltreatment to them was the slavery of India. They also started realizing that the only way to get rid of this slavery was through armed struggle.

The Indians living in Canada and America joined together to form Ghadar Party in April 1913. Its aim was to undertake an armed struggle to free India and then establish an American-like Secular Democratic Republic there. All members of the Ghadar Party considered themselves Indians. No religious matter was discussed in the Party. Religion was the individual issue of everyone. It was the obligation of every member of the Party to support the freedom struggle; it may be in any part of the world.[1] Bhai Mewa Singh too started working for the Party in company with workers like Bhai Bhag Singh and Bhai Balwant Singh.

Doing dire injustice with the passengers of the *Komagata Maru* ship on reaching Vancouver on May 23, 1914, the Appeal Court of British Columbia announced a verdict against the passengers on July 6, 1914. Orders were issued for the return of the ship. The Ghadari leaders of Vancouver wanted that, so, upon reaching India, the passengers of the *Komagata Maru* would take part in the rebellion to be undertaken for the freedom of the country. For this purpose, they kept supplying Ghadar literature to passengers in the ship, and later they also tried to send them weapons.

The Ghadri leaders in Vancouver tried to purchase weapons in Canada. Not succeeding in the purpose of getting the weapons here, Bhai Mewa Singh, Bhai Bhag Singh, Bhai Balwant Singh, and Babu Harnam Singh Sahree reached the city of Sumas on July 16, 1914, across the American border from Abbottsford to purchase weapons. Babu Tarknath Dass, the Bangali revolutionary leader, had already reached Sumas from Seattle in America. They spent the night in hotel "Sumel" there. After breakfast on the next day, they purchased revolvers from the Ridge Thomas store. After some time, Bhai Mewa Singh was arrested while crossing the border through bushes to reach Canada. On searching, the police found two revolvers hidden in the possessions of Bhai Mewa Singh. Packets containing 500 rounds were also found from the left and right stockings and his inner wear.[2] Bhai Mewa Singh was imprisoned in New Westminster Jail.

Malcolm Reid, Head of Vancouver Immigration Department, and the interlocutor William Hopkinson had a meeting with Bhai Mewa Singh in the New Westminster Jail. Police Inspector William Hopkinson had come from Calcutta to Vancouver in 1908. He worked as an interlocutor in the Canadian Immigration Department in Vancouver Centre, but his actual job was to spy for the governments of India, England, Canada, and America. He kept vigilance on the activities of Indians residing on the western coast of Canada and America. His main job was to encourage a rift in the Indian community and

---

[1] .Baba Sohan Singh Bhakna naal mulakaat" 1967; Prem Singh Bjaj, Do pairhan Itihas dian (Ludhiana, Punjabi Sahit academy 2004) p.55

[2] W. C. Hopkinson to Samuel Backus, Commissioner of US Immigration, San Francisco, July 20, 1914, PRO. C.O 42/980

harm the patriotic group of Indians. He had built up a pro-government lobby by "purchasing" Bela Singh Jian, Babu Singh Litran, and Ganga Ram Barian (Sahota Jatt) from the Indian community in Vancouver. With help of these people, he spied on the Indian community and informed the government about activities of the Ghadarites.

Malcolm Reid and William Hopkinson made an offer to Bhai Mewa Singh in jail to give a statement that the weapons found on him belonged to Bhai Balwant Singh, Bhai Bhag Singh, and Babu Harnam Singh Sahri, and that they had sent these weapons for the Gujarati revolutionary Hussain Rahim living in Vancouver. As such, he would be released after minor punishment. He threatened him also that in case of non-compliance, he would be sentenced for five or ten years. But Bhai Mewa Singh refused to give such an anti-Ghadarite statement. He said clearly: "You may cut me into pieces but I shall not tell a lie for your sake."[3]

Malcolm Reid and William Hopkinson were very much disappointed with Bhai Mewa Singh. But still, with the hope that he might give the anti-Ghadarite statement in time to come, he was released on August 7, 1914, after a fine of fifty dollars. But Bhai Mewa Singh could see through all their tricks.

On August 4, 1914, the First World War began. Hardly seventeen months had passed after formation of the Ghadar Party. The Party had not prepared well for creating rebellion upon reaching India. But finding the enemy entangled in war, the Ghadar Party gave a call to the Ghadarites to create rebellion when they reached India. Under compliance of the order, the Ghadarites of Canada also started boarding the ships for rebellion on reaching the country. Hopkinson, who till date had been trying not to let any Indian reach Canada, was now trying his utmost to not let any Indian go from Canada to India for rebellion. It was foremost for him to stop Bhai Bhag Singh from going, and for this, he was ready to take any step. In order to torpedo the Ghadarite activities, Bela Singh Jian, under abetment of Hopkinson, shot dead Bhai Bhag Singh Bhikhiwind, President of the Khalsa Diwan Society and prominent leader of Ghada Party, and his companion Bhai Badan Singh in the gurdwara of Vancouver on September 5, 1914. Bibi Harnam Kaur, wife of Bhai Bhag Singh, had already died in January 1914. With the death of Bhai Bhag Singh, his three-year-old son Joginder Singh and nine-month-old

---

3   Statement read for Mewa Singh by his lawyer at his trial of October 30, 1914; Trial Transcript.

daughter Karm Kaur became orphans. Bhai Mewa Singh could not tolerate all this. Bhai Mewa Singh made up his mind to murder the Hopkinson, the force in fact behind the traitor Bela Singh.

In reality, there were many reasons behind the decision of Mewa Singh to murder Hopkinson. There was a long list of wicked deeds with Hopkinson behind it. Hopkinson had caused great harm to the group of patriots of the country. Immediately after reaching Vancouver, he had written articles in newspapers about the revolutionary activities of Tarknath Dass. As a result, Tarknath Dass had to go to America after leaving Vancouver. Hopkinson had sent reports to the governments of Canada, England, and India that the migrants of Vancouver were getting influenced by socialist views, which were dangerous for the British Empire in India. Consequently, the Canadian government framed such laws of immigration that made the migration of Indians to Canada impossible. In the conspiracy concocted in October–November 1908 to send all the Indians in Canada to Honduras, Hopkinson was at the forefront. He made repeated efforts to expatriate Hussain Rahim, a popular leader of the Indian community, from Canada. Likewise, he influenced the expulsion of Giani Bhagwan Singh, another popular and revolutionary leader, from Canada in 1913. In the strife of the *Komagata Maru*, Hopkinson had played a villainous role.

The secret activities of Hopkinson were not confined to the limits of Canada only. He used to keep a watch on the activities of the Ghadarites living on the West Coast of America. He used to get secret reports of the Ghadarites living in Seattle, Portland, Astoria, San Francisco, and Stockton. He had collected proofs against Lala Hardyal and had him declared anarchist and then expelled from America. In August 1914, thousands of Ghadarites were boarding ships after leaving Canada and America to go to India and create mutiny in the country. Hopkinson was trying his level best to stop the Ghadarites boarding the ships and was sending lists of these people to the British Government in India. And now he had orchestrated the murder of Bhai Bhag Singh, the most loving and popular leader of the Indian community.

The case was going on in Vancouver in the Provincial Court of British Columbia against Bela Singh Jian, the murderer of Bhai Bhag Singh. A few days before, Hopkinson had "one" fellow of Bela Singh released from the murder case, who was connected with a "pro-government" group,[4] and now the same person was coming to the jury to give evidence in favor of Bela Singh. It was the 21st day of October 1914, twelve minutes past ten in the morning. Hopkinson was standing reclined against the wall in the veranda quite close to the entry room of the court. Walking in the veranda, Bhai Mewa Singh reached quite near Hopkinson. He had both of his hands in the pockets of his trousers. Reaching close to Hopkinson, he took out his pistol, and, moving a step forward, he shot at Hopkinson with his right hand. Hopkinson tried to catch hold of Bhai Mewa Singh, but Mewa Singh, in haste, fired more shots at him. Struck by the bullets, Hopkinson fell on his knees and caught the thighs of Mewa Singh. Bhai Mewa Singh hit Hopkinson on his head many times with the butt of the pistol held in his right hand. Then he threw the revolver down, took another revolver from his left hand in his right hand, and shot at him more.[5] Many people present in the court saw the murder committed. But they were threatened with fear. They could dare not come out and quietly closed the door of the court room.[6]

Hopkinson had received four shots. One shot pierced through the lower part of his left thigh and went out. A second shot hit him at the left side of his back. With these two shots, no vital organs of his body were damaged. But two more shots proved fatal for Hopkinson. One of these had hit him on the sixth rib of the lower part of his chest. This shot passed through his right lung, tore open the heart, and then got stuck near the third rib on the left side of chest.[7] Hopkinson died on the spot. Mewa Singh had committed the murder of Hopkinson at a "public place." After committing murder, he did not try to run away. Quietly, he gave the revolver to a sweeper and said: "I shoot. I go station."[8] Upon arrival of police, Mewa Singh offered himself over to the police without any resistance.

Regarding Hopkinson's death, telegrams were rung from Vancouver to Ottawa, Ottawa to London, and then to Delhi in India. Immediate

---

4   Mr. Justice Aulay Morrison to Secretary of State, Ottawa, November 9, 1914. Archives Canada, RG 13, Vol. 1467.
5   Evidence of witness W. A. Campbell, REX VS MEWA Singh, Vancouver, October 30, 1914, Trial Transcript.
6   Ibid
7   Evidence of Dr. George F. Curtis who performed post mortem examination of Hopkinson's body, REX VS MEWA SINFG, Vancouver, October 30, 1914, Trial Transcript.
8   Evidence of James McCann, REX VS MEWA sINGH, Vancouver, October 30, 1914, Trial Transcript.

information was sent to the Governor General of Canada, the Secretary for State sitting in London, and Lord Harding, the Viceroy of India. H. H. Stevens, MP of the Conservative Party in Vancouver and enemy of India, at once asked Prime Minister Borden in writing to forcefully deport all the Indians from Canada.[9]

The Canadian government arranged a big funeral procession for Hopkinson in Vancouver. Hundreds of police officials, firemen, immigration-custom officers, and employees of American Immigration Department and CPR were in the funeral procession. More than two thousand people were there in the procession. On the way, there was one policeman in civil clothes after every Indian. Police were scared that the Indian migrants might try to shoot at Malcolm Reid, Head of Immigration Department, and the Chief of Police.[10] Malcolm was to be shot dead alongside Hopkinson. On October 21, he was to accompany Hopkinson from the Immigration Office to the Court. But he had reached his office late. Hopkinson, after a long wait, went himself all alone.[11] Thus, luck had saved Malcolm Reid.

Nine days after Hopkinson's murder, on October 30, 1914, hearing of the case against Mewa Singh started. The government had delayed the process of the case of Bela Singh Jian, murderer of Bhag Singh, so that Mewa Singh could be sentenced at the earliest. Hearing of the case was going on with Mister Oile Morrison, Chief Justice of the BC Supreme Court. He was to decide the case with the help of a 12-member jury. Mr. Taylor was Crown prosecutor and. Mr Wood was the defense pleader. The courtroom was full at its capacity with hearers of proceedings of the case, but all those were Whites except four Indians. Officials of the Court had mischievously not allowed Indians to enter the court. Bhai Balwant Singh, Granthi of the Vancouver Gurdwara, and other Indians were standing outside the court. They hoped to look at Bhai Mewa Singh from outside, but this hope was not fulfilled. Doors of the court were closed, and a sign reading, "court is full," was put out.

Proceedings of the case started. Bhai Mewa Singh was told that he was accused of murdering Hopkinson. W. A. Cambel, James Macain, and Paul Caldwell were put as eyewitness. Detective Samstrum and MacDonald gave their statements. The "Report of Coroner" was presented. In this report,

---

9   H. H. Stevens to Borden, October 21, 1914. Archives Canada, File 536999, pt 9.
10 The Sun, Vancouver, October 26, 1914.
11 Melcolm R. J. Reid to W. D. Scott, October 22, 1914, Archives Canada, RO 76, Vol 561, File 808722, pt 2

detail was given of the shots fired and the damage they caused. The two revolvers used by Bhai Mewa Singh during the murder and the bullets taken out of Hopkinson's body were put before the court.[12] During this time, Bhai Mewa Singh kept standing calm and quiet and all carefree of the proceedings of the court.

During the proceedings, Mewa Singh stood in the witness box, took oath, and answered the questions asked by the defense counsel Mr. Wood. Mewa Singh confessed to the allegation of murdering Hopkinson. Thereafter, the defense counsel Mr. Wood read the written statement of Mewa Singh to the court. Mr. Wood had prepared that statement on the same morning with the help of the court interpreter, Mrs. Dalton. Bhai Mewa Singh had given this statement not in his defense but had done so with the purpose to make his plea public through the court. In this statement, Bhai Mewa Singh had tried to disclose all those atrocities committed upon Indians in Canada and why he had committed the murder of Hopkinson. Bhai Mewa Singh had said in the statement:

> "My name is Mewa Singh. I am a God-fearing man and offer prayer daily. I have no words on my tongue to tell what various difficulties, hardships and harassments I had to pass through in Vancouver. . . . We Sikhs go in gurdwaras to offer prayer but these wicked ones opened fire in the Gurdwara, killed Bhai Bhag Singh and thus desecrated the sanctity of Gurdwara. These sinners have orphaned two innocent children. The treacheries committed by these wicked ones in the Gurdwara have put my heart on fire. Mr Reed and Mr Hopkinson are responsible for all this. For the honour and prestige of my religion and community, I have killed Hopkinson. It was beyond me to tolerate all this."[13]

It was further said in the statement:

> ". . . Had all this taken place in your church, you Christians even could not have tolerated this because, by doing so, you would have

---

12   REX VS MEWA SINGH, Vancouver, October 30, 1914, Trial Transcript.
13   Statement read for Mewa Singh by his lawyer at his trial of October 30, 1914, Trial Transcript.

taken yourself as a dead nation. For a Sikh also, it is better to die than bearing with such acts in gurdwaras. . . ."[14]

"*. . . I have all the time been insisting that I need no Vakil. I hope for no justice. I know that I have shot at Hopkinson and I have to die for this. I am giving this statement for this purpose that the public may know what suffering we have been going through. We have never got any justice from judges, police or from any other source. I am giving my life for this purpose that the people may know all this. . . .*"[15]

"*. . . Our worthy judges and lawyers must realize as why Hopkinson has been fired at. The ones who always do misdeeds and commit crimes after drinking are considered correct by the Immigration Officers and we, the God-fearing true people, are trampled under feet. Abiding by God's Order, I can bear this no more. . . .*"[16]

Bhai Mewa Singh also mentioned in his statement how Hopkinson was compelling them to give evidence in favor of Bela Singh, the killer of Bhai Bhag Singh:

"*. . . When we going to post office, Hopkinson spoke to me on the way: 'Now you are to stand witness in the case of Bela Singh. You change sides to stand in favour of Bela Singh; otherwise, it shall be very bad for you. You also shall have to go on the same way on which Bhag Singh and Badan Singh have gone.' He threatened me. I asked him: Mr Hopkinson! You have taken bribery from me and now you are threatening me. Who are you telling to that I shall be killed like Bhag Singh and Badan Singh? What is all this going on? After taking dollars from me, now you are asking me to stand witness in favour of Bela Singh, and you are threatening to kill me.*"[17]

Further it was said in the statement:

---

14 Same
15 Statement read for Mewa Singh by his lawyer at his trial of October 30, 1914, Trial Transcript.
16 Ibid
17 Statement read for Mewa Singh by his lawyer at his trial of October 30, 1914, Trial Transcript.

"... For the whole night, the thing has been gnawing me that it is me on one side who does meditation and these people are coaxing me for false statements. They are trying to humiliate me and entangle me in problems. The wicked thing has been pricking me throughout night and, thinking so, I could not sleep that I shall suffer bad name for this. ... It is a matter of about three days after this that I was passing through Hastings street where I met Babu Singh. He said: 'Which side are going to witness? To our side or to the other one?' I said I shall speak the truth. I shall tell the same thing what I saw in the Gurdwara. Then Babu Singh started abusing Bhag Singh, who had been killed, and said: 'We have killed him.' Again he called him severe names. ... Then Babu Singh threatened me; 'If you did not give evidence in our favour, we shall have to do something with you.' Babu Singh kept calling me severe abuses but I said nothing. Babu Singh said again: 'It is our rule in Vancouver. We can do whatever we like. Immigration is at my back. I can set you right. You can do nothing. My writ runs here. I shall set right all of you.' After coming back from Babu Singh, I started thinking about it seriously that all that shall have to be stopped. Then I gave true evidence in the Court. After that, I fearfully moved about in Vancouver. Once again Babu Singh met when I was going alone. He said: 'If ever again you are seen walking in Vancouver, we shall not spare you.' I thought seriously about it again that I must do something about it. I thought it better to die rather than suffer such humiliation. I shall die a brave man's death ..."[18]

"... These people have defamed us. They think that Sikhs are nothing. We have been humiliated. There is no judge to listen to us. These four persons are everything. Bela Singh, Babu Singh, Mr Reed and Hopkinson consider themselves God. ... The government listens to Hopkinson only. We are never bothered about. For the government, we are two-pice valued starving coolies and Hopkinson's every word is law. Because of this, I have murdered Hopkinson and am sacrificing my life ..."[19]

---

18 Statement read for Mewa Singh by his lawyer at his trial of October 30, 1914, Trial Transcript.
19

The crime having been admitted to by Mewa Singh, the hearing of the case only took one hour and forty minutes. On the basis of the decision of the jury, the Judge Morrison indicted Mewa Singh as criminal and ordered him to be hanged on January 11, 1915.[20] On hearing the punishment, there was no sign of any remorse or regret on the face of Bhai Mewa Singh. He wanted to see the nine-month-old orphan child of Bhai Bhag Singh. When he could not see the child from the crowd outside, he started reciting these Gurbani hymns loudly:

Sura so pehchaniye jo larey din ke heit ||
Purja purja kat marey kabhun na chhadey khet ||

While reciting these hymns, he started walking calmly to the prison cell.[21]
The defense counsel Mr. Wood wanted to enter "mercy appeal" to save the life of Bhai Mewa Singh, but Bhai Mewa Singh did not allow him to do so. Not finding any way out, Mr. Wood pleaded before Justice Minister in December that Bhai Mewa Singh was not in the right mental balance, so he should be sent for a medical checkup. On January 3, 1915, Justice Minister C. G. Doerty ordered the superintendent of New Westminster Mental Health Institute to examine Mewa Singh and send the report as soon as possible.

J. G. Mackem, the Superintendent of the Mental Health Institute, examined Bhai Mewa Singh on the 5th of January. Mewa Singh did not do any untoward action which may show that he was not mentally sound and his life could be saved. Bhai Mewa Singh declared that he had killed Hopkinson in quite safe and alert mind, and he was ready to undergo any punishment for this. Mr. Mackem sent the report on the same day to Justice Minister that Bhai Mewa Singh was absolutely well mentally.[22]

Waiting for his D-day in the Provincial Jail of New Westminster, Bhai Mewa Singh was living in high spirits.[23] At 7:30 a.m. on January 11, 1915, Bhai Mewa Singh went to the gallows while reciting, "*Har jas re mana gae lae jo sangi hae tere.*" At the time of hanging, Bhai Mit Singh Pandori, as Granthi, performed the final religious rites. At quarter to eight, Bhai Mewa Singh was hanged till death. Despite rain and severe cold, four hundred Indians had

---

20 19 Ibid
21
22 J. G. Mackay, Acting Superintendent, Insane Asylum, New Westminster, January 3, 1915
23 Malcolm R. J. Reid to W. D. Scott, October 22, 1914.

collected outside the New Westminster Jail. As soon as the dead body was brought out, they shouted slogans, *"Long live the immortal martyr Bhai Mewa Singh!"* Marching in rows of five each and reciting hymns from Sri Guru Granth Sahib, they reached the Frazer Mill, four miles away, with dead body of Bhai Mewa Singh and performed the cremation with full solemn rites.[24]

Bhai Mewa Singh had nowhere given any hint of the like that may show any connection of the Ghadar Party with this murder. Neither was it expected of Bhai Mewa Singh that he would give some statement that might have entangled the Ghadri leaders in this murder. But the Canadian officials were fully sure that the act of killing Hopkinson was not the sole job of Mewa Singh only. They knew that firing at Hopkinson was carried out under consultation of Ghadri leaders, and it was carried out as per their plans. Even the newspapers of Vancouver had written this.[25] So the police charged the Ghadri leaders Hussain Rahim, Bhai Balwant Singh, Sohan Lal, Kartar Singh Nawanchand, and Bhai Mit Singh Pandori under allegation of inciting Bhai Mewa Singh to murder Hopkinson. Natha Singh, Naina Singh, Ganga Ram, Partap Singh, Bhagat Singh, Thakar Singh, Bela Singh, and Dr. Raghunath, the pet touts of Hopkinson, appeared as witnesses in the case against the Ghadarites. But their statements did not tally with each other, and since Bhai Mewa Singh had taken sole responsibility of the murder, the judge had to free all the Ghadri leaders.[26]

Actually, the Ghadar Party should have gone through this case of Hopkinson's murder by Bhai Mewa Singh in reference with the call given for rebellion on reaching the country. Like the British Empire targets they were going to hit in India, a similar one was here in Vancouver. Hopkinson was a symbol of the British Empire ruling in India. He was doing an important job for the British Empire in Canada and America. The caretakers of the British Empire knew the importance of the "work" being carried out by Hopkinson, and they were very worrisome of his safety. The Duke of Cannaught, the Governor-General of Canada, had written to Colonial Secretary Beus Harcourt on May 20, 1914, that ". . . Hopkinson is an invaluable officer. He is doing a very important job. If something wrong happens to him, the total

---

24   " Written statement of Mitt Singh Canadian " , America vich Hindostani, p.144
25   The Sun, Vancouver, October 22, 1914; The World, Vancouver, October 21, 1914; The Province, Vancouver, October 22, 1914; The News-Advertiser, October 22, 1914.
26   Hugh Johnston, The Voyage of Kamagata maru, p. 132.

structure of secret network set by him shall be demolished."[27] Ghadri leaders of Vancouver understood well the job of spying being carried out for British Empire by Hopkinson. That is why Hopkinson was an appropriate target in their eyes. By killing Hopkinson, they were trying to demolish this network of spying and wanted to devastate the caucus of Hopkinson that eroded the activities of Ghadar Party. With the murder of Hopkinson, a horrid fear spread all around in the traitorous clique, and the heads and hearts of revolutionaries were fully excited.

On the day of the martyrdom of Bhai Mewa Singh, the Sikh congregation performed the conclusion of the "sehj path" in gurdwara of Stockton in California. The martyrdom of Bhai Mewa Singh was highly praised in the revolutionary literature of Ghadar Party. The Indians of Canada celebrated the first anniversary of the martyrdom in the gurdwara of Frazer Mill in January 1916. In 1917, about 500 Indians gathered in the Frazer Mill to celebrate the martyrdom day of Bhai Mewa Singh. At that time, only 1000 Indians resided in Canada.

For the Canadian government, Bhai Mewa Singh was a murderer. But the Indian community in Canada has always regarded him a martyr. Bhai Mewa Singh was a soldier of the Ghadar Party that was fighting a war against the British Empire for freedom of the country. Bhai Mewa Singh was martyr of this freedom struggle of India. Therefore, the Indian community of Canada acclaims Bhai Mewa Singh "the immortal martyr of Canada."

In memory of Bhai Mewa Singh, the Khalsa Diwan Society of Vancouver has named the Langar Hall of gurdwara in Ross Street "Shaheed Bhai Mewa Singh Hall." The Akali Sikh Society in Vancouver has established "Shaheed Bhai Mewa Singh Library" in his memory. East India Defense Committee organizes a tournament every year in memory of Bhai Mewa Singh. On January 11, many gurdwaras in Vancouver hold Akhand Paths in his memory; the speakers throw light on his unique life, and respectful tributes are offered to him. In this way, Bhai Mewa Singh, the ever-living martyr of Canada, is a symbol of struggle against tyranny for the Canadian Indians.

---

27 H. R. H. Arthur, Duke of Connaught, Governor General, to Lewis Hardourt, Colonial Secretary, May 20, 1914. Archives Canada

Pen-profiles of the Renowned Ghadarites of Canada and America

Sohan Singh Pooni

The first Punjabi person to come to reside in America was perhaps Bakhshish Singh Dhillon from Sursingh village in Lahore District, now Amritsar. He disembarked from a San Francisco port along with his three companions in 1899. Indians started coming to Canada in 1903–04. By 1908, about 5200 Indians had migrated to Canada.[1] About half of them very soon left Canada and went to America. That way, by 1912, 2500–3000 Indians were residing in Canada,[2] and in America, the number of Indians had gone up to 7–8 thousand.

These migrants living in Canada and America formed the Ghadar Party in 1913. Its purpose was to free India under force of arms. On the beginning of First World War in 1914, the Ghadarites living in Canada, America, and other countries tried for the revolution on reaching India, but they could not succeed. The British Government in India hanged to death dozens of Ghadarites and imprisoned hundreds with life-term sentences or a little less. Who were these Ghadarites? What was their background? What for had they come to Canada and America? How did they become Ghadarites? What did they do for freedom of the country? Why could they not succeed? What is their contribution towards freedom of the country? To discuss over all these

---

1 Private Memorandum by F. C Blair, Immigration Branch, Department of the Interior, 26 January, 1912, VCA
2 Sansar, Victoria, July 1913.

questions, this paper aims at describing the lives of four Ghadarites who carried out important role in the Ghadar Movement. In addition to undertaking struggle for freedom of the country, the Ghadarites of Canada did strive for their rights in Canada also. So this role of the Ghadarites for their rights in Canada has also been discussed in this Paper.

Though the Ghadar Party was established in the city Astoria of America in middle of 1913 and its headquarter was in San Francisco, its beginning had already come up a few years before in Canada. Giving verdict of the Lahore Conspiracy Case against Ghadarites in September 1915, the Tribunal Commissioner wrote: "The beginning of this conspiracy has begun from the western coast of America. Its two big centres are Vancouver and San Francisco. The centre, at first, was Vancouver and this continued till San Francisco took its place."[3]

The spirit and soul of the Ghadar Movement in Canada was Bhai Balwant Singh Khurdpur, the Granthi of Vancouver gurdwara. He was born in 1882 in Khurdpur village near Adampur in Jalandhar district. After passing Middle, he joined the army service. He resigned after serving in the army for some time and then reached the city of Vancouver in Canada in 1906. The majority of the Indian migrants here were 90% Punjabi Sikhs. Many of them had already served in the British Indian Army. Like other Indians in Canada, Bhai Balwant Singh thought that Canada was also a colony of the British Empire. Being subject of the British Empire, Bahi Balwant Singh considered it his right to enter Canada and live and work there. Queen Victoria had also declared this after the mutiny of 1857 that she shall hold all subjects of British Empire equally, wherein Indians are also included. But on coming in Canada, Bhai Balwant Singh had to face severe hardships. He, along with others, became the victim of racial discrimination. The government of Canada also discriminated against the Indians in an organizational way. On March 27, 1907, voting rights were also withdrawn from Indians. In September 1907, in the city Bellingham near Vancouver in America, the racial Whites threw Indian workers out of the city after thrashing them bitterly. A few days after this, the racial Whites attacked Asians in Vancouver. All these events bruised bitterly the heart of Bhai Balwant Singh.

In July 1906, the Sikhs of Vancouver had formed one organization named "Khalsa Diwan Society Vancouver." With the cooperation of this

---

3   Lahore Conspiracy Case Judgement, September 13, 1915, Part 3, The History of the conspiracy and war, p. 1

organization, Bhai Balwant Singh carried out an important role in building the first Gurdwara of North America in Vancouver. Inaugurated on January 19, 1908, Bhai Balwant Singh was designated the first Granthi of this Gurdwara. This Gurdwara was not a religious center of Sikhs only but was a center of social and political activities of all the Indians. On the weekends, meetings concerning immigration, racialism, and political issues were held there, and Muslims and Hindus also joined in it.

Living in the free environment of Canada, the Indian migrants felt enlightened and, no doubt, realized their slavish status. It was dangerous for the British Government in India. So, in order to restrict entry of Indians in Canada, the Canada government consulted with British and Indian governments and, in 1908, formed rules of immigration on racial basis for "direct voyage with two hundred dollars in pocket." During that time, no ship company had any ship for direct voyage from India to Canada. It was clear that the only basic purpose of this law was to ban the entry of Indians in Canada. With formation of these laws, the entry of Indians in Canada was almost stopped.

Every effort was being made to restrict entry of Indians in White colonies of British Empire. With the Australian government's passing of the Immigration Restriction Act and the Labour Recruitment Act of 1901, the entry of Indians in Australia had already stopped. Similar discriminatory rules were already formed in New Zealand, and now the entry of Indians in Canada was banned. Bhai Balwant Singh was much disturbed under this step-motherly treatment of Indians in the British Empire.

In October–November of 1908, the Canadian government built up a conspiracy to send all the Indians in Canada to Honduras, the British Colony in Central America. The Canadian government put utmost pressure on Indian migrants to leave Canada and go to Honduras. But Bhai Balwant Singh, in support with Sant Teja Singh and Bhai Bhag Singh, refused to submit before this proposal of the Canadian government. In this way, Bhai Balwant Singh, in support with his companions, saved the Indian community from ruination.

While living in Vancouver, Bhai Balwant Singh came in close with a Bengali revolutionary Babu Tarknath Dass. Living in the free environment of Canada and getting in contact with revolutionaries like Babu Tarknath Dass, Bhai Balwant Singh became politically awake. He started realizing that the real reason for all the miseries of the Indians was their slavery, and they could not live an honorable life till India was freed. He realized also that freedom could not be achieved on the basis of "truth" only. It rather requires an armed struggle. He realized also that only a sword's sharp edge could cut the shackles of slavery. He also came to know that the English people only understood the language of a striking sword, nothing else. Living in North America, Bhai Balwant Singh also knew that America had snatched freedom from England with the force of weapons only. Gurbani also sermonized this only: "bal hoa bandhan chhutai—*with might all shackles get shattered.*" With the support of his companions, Bhai Balwant Singh started giving political awakening to the Sikh emigrants in Canada. He started preparing them to shun proship of the English and take to the path of armed struggle for freedom of the country.

Among the Indians living in Canada, there was good number of former Sikh army men who had done service in the British Indian Army. They were very proud of their army favors and valiant roles played in Imperial battles. They were in possession of army uniforms, medals, and honorable discharge certificates from English Officers. They moved out on Vancouver roads fully decked in army uniforms, medals on their chests, and recommendatory letters from English Officers in their pockets to tell the Whites that they were the most favorable and faithful men of the British Empire. Bhai Balwant Singh in company with his companions tried to clarify the fact to them that their role in the British Indian Army was not that of the Sikhs in the army of Guru Gobind Singh who not only caught hold of the reins of the horses of Pathan tyrants trampling the honor of Indian women under hoofs of their horses, but they rather turned back their faces from east to west and pushed them beyond the Khyber Pass. By dint of such preaching by Bhai Balwant Singh, these ex-army men felt ashamed that their role in the British Indian Army was nothing short of hired fighters who not only helped the English in keeping India in slavery, but rather carried that slavery to other countries also. With this newly imparted awareness, they started feeling ashamed of their uniforms, medals, and certificates. Under these effects, a very important happening took place in the gurdwara of Vancouver.

Bhai Natha Singh Bilga, a wonderful Sikh and friend of Bhai Balwant Singh, stood before the congregation. He delivered a lecture describing the miserable condition of Indians in India as well in other parts of the world and especially in British Columbia. He held forth the plea: "The medals they are wearing show that they are hired army men who fought for the English against their own countrymen and the free men of other lands. Medals won by fighting for the English are not signs of bravery; these can be called medals of slavery."[4] After this, he put a resolution: "No member of the gurdwara executive committee shall wear such medal, button, uniform or insignia that may show that the wearer is nothing more than a slave."[5] The resolution got full acclamation with resonant *Jaikaras*. In the evening, the Sikh army men set ablaze, in the gurdwara yard, all their medals, uniforms, and certificates of their honorable discharge.[6]

Burning the uniforms, medals, and certificates in the yard of gurdwara Vancouver was not an ordinary incident. On behalf of Sikhs, it was a beginning of doing away with the pro-English approach and plunging into the struggle for freedom of the country. This happening did not take place on its own. Such a change in thinking of the Sikhs in Vancouver did not come just like that. This change was the result of political preaching carried out by Bhai Balwant Singh and his companions. For Bhai Balwant Singh and his companions, it was easy to politically enlighten the Sikhs in Canada, in contrast with those in Punjab, and mobilize them for struggle against the British Empire, because there was no pro-English Sikh leadership there to frighten, terrorize, instigate, or mislead them.

Bhai Balwant Singh was a very wonderful and truthful Sikh of the Gurus. He was a proponent from Bhai Lalo's camp. He was an ideal Sikh, following the tenets of Sikh religion, such as: "Welfare of All; Doing labor and Sharing with others; Equality and Cooperation." Socialist Ideology also talks about "equality and cooperation" and condemns the loot of man by man. Thus, Bhai Balwant Singh saw no difference in Sikh Ideology and the Socialist philosophy. Therefore, he became member of the Socialist Party of Canada. In reality, Bhai Balwant Singh and other executives of Khalsa Diwan Society joined with Hussain Rahim to constitute a special branch of the Socialist Party of Canada in Vancouver.[7]

Bhai Balwant Singh took the lead in fighting for the right of Indians in Canada to bring their families to Canada. Because of the law of "direct voyage" enacted by the Canadian government in 1908, the Indian migrants

---

4   Free Hindustan, September-October,1909
5   Ibid
6   Ibid
7   Hugh Johnston, The Voyage of the Komagata Maru: The Sikh Challenge to Canada's Colour Bar(Delhi: Oxford University Press, 1979), p.11.

in Canada could not bring their families to Canada. The Canadian government feared that, if Indians brought their families, they would settle there by establishing a "permanent Hindu Colony" there. It was a well-thought-out plan of the Canadian government to check permanent settlement of Indian migrants by not allowing their wives and children to come to Canada. The Canadian government had the idea that, when faced with the refusal of entry for their families, the Indian migrants in Canada would go back permanently after working and earning money. But Bhai Balwant Singh and his Ghadri companions wanted to sharpen the wrath of Indians by unmasking the real faces of the Canadian government and British Empire and then put them on the path of armed aggression for freedom of the country. To unmask the face of the British Empire and challenge the Racial Immigration Law of Canada, Bhai Balwant Singh and Bhai Bhag Singh, President of Khalsa Diwan Society in Vancouver, decided to go to India to bring back their families.

Bhai Balwant Singh and Bhai Bhag Singh went to India to bring their families. After a distress of about one year, when they reached the Vancouver port, Bhai Balwant Singh and Bhai Bhag Singh were allowed to disembark, but their wives and children were put under detention. Both the families were released on bail. Only a year prior in 1911, 11932 Chinese and 2986 Japanese immigrants came to Canada, and there were 1037 women with them. Indian migrants were enraged that the Chinese and Japanese, who were not subjects of the British Empire, were being allowed to come to Canada, but Indian families, who were residents of the British Empire, were not being allowed to enter Canada. Indian migrants were going away from the weak-minded groups and were joining the militants with revolutionary minds. The revolutionary group was getting stronger. With a view to mollify the wrath of Indians and thus weaken the revolutionary movement, Hopkinson advised the Canadian government to allow both the families to live in Canada on mercy ground.[8] Even before the decision of the court, on June 3, 1912, the Immigration Authorities permitted both families to live in Canada on mercy ground. Since the decision was from the court, it did not open the way for other families to come to Canada.

Not getting any justice from the Canadian government in the case of families, the Indians of Canada sent one deputation to India in March 1913 under the leadership of Bhai Balwant Singh. This deputation pleaded with

---

8   Sansar, Victoria, July 1912 P.4.
9   W. C. Hopkinson to W. W. Cory, May16, 1912

the Indian government to stress upon the Canadian government to give rights to the Indian migrants to bring their families in Canada. The second motive of the deputation was to acquaint the Indian people with the racial discrimination meted out to them, awaken them politically, and prepare them for struggle for freedom of the country.

On reaching Punjab and before making any appeal to the government, Bhai Balwant Singh tried to awaken the people by going from village to village. During his lectures in these meetings, Bhai Balwant Singh held the British and Indian governments responsible for the miseries of Indians in Canada. In one of his lectures in Lahore, Bhai Balwant Singh, while addressing the people, said: "The British Empire has encircled you like a snake. To get rid of it, it is necessary to rub its hood on thorns."[9]

Michael O'Dwyer, Lt. Governor of Punjab, feared that, with lectures of Bhai Balwant Singh, the Sikhs of Punjab would become politically aware. It was dangerous for the British Empire, because this awareness among Sikhs could influence the Sikh armies. Sikhs of Punjab were considered the backbone of the English army. Punjab was the most important state for recruitment in the army. Sensing these dangers, O'Dwyer gave strict warning to Bhai Balwant Singh. O'Dwyer writes about this in his book: ". . . He held meetings in all states. In these meetings, many people were such whose loyalty was doubtful. After some time, the tone of these meetings changed. Rather than criticizing the Laws of Immigration, they started giving inciting lectures full of threats. At this, I warned the delegates that if all that remained continued, I shall be compelled to take strict action."[10]

O'Dwyer wished that Bhai Balwant Singh would keep himself confined to criticizing only the Immigration Laws of Canada and say nothing about the British and Indian governments. But Bhai Balwant Singh was not ready to accept this, because the real motive of bringing their deputation to India was to denude the Indian and British governments and make the people in India politically aware, incite their wrath, and then put them on the path of armed struggle. O'Dwyer wrote about this later: ". . . After a year when the storm of revolution rose in the state, then we realized that these three persons

---

9   Second Supplementary Lahore Conspiracy Case, Judgement, January 4, 1917, Individual Case of Balwant Singh, accused no. 3.

10   Sir Michael O'Dwyer, India As I know It 1885-1925, 3rd ed. (London: Constable and Company Ltd. 1926) p. 191

have been most ferociously but secretively spreading rebellion in Punjab."[11] O'Dwyer wrote further: ". . . Though we did not know at that time, but they were in reality the advance agents of Ghadar Party."[12]

Bhai Balwant Singh and his companions reached Shimla on September 18, 1913, and held a public meeting there. There they met Michael O'Dwyer, the Lt. Governor of Punjab.[13] With absolute firmness and fearlessness, Bhai Balwant Singh put before O'Dwyer the case of Indian migrants and asked him to do something. During this meeting with O'Dwyer, Bhai Balwant Singh talked with him while holding his head high and keeping eye contact. Michael perhaps was seeing such a person for the first time. Bhai Balwant Singh had no inferiority complex, and he had no reason to feel small before O'Dwyer. He rather felt fearful before Bhai Balwant Singh. O'Dwyer writes about Bhai Balwant Singh in his book: ". . . the way and style of this third man appeared like that of an inimitable revolutionary. They wanted to meet the Viceroy. Sending them to the Viceroy, I asked the Viceroy to be specially cautious of the third man."[14] In Shimla, Bhai Balwant Singh met Viceroy Lord Hardinge also. But for showing his sympathy, he expressed helplessness in taking some concrete step.

Gone to India under leadership of Bhai Balwant Singh, this deputation got no help from the Indian and British governments in taking their families to Canada. But they got profuse response from media and the people. They could see closely and understand the social, religious, and political conditions. But Bhai Balwant Singh also felt disappointed of some leaders and organizations. Lala Lajpat Rai, the prominent leader of Congress in Punjab, refused to help by saying these words: ". . . This issue is purely of Sikhs only."[15]

Bhai Balwant Singh felt sorely dismayed of Chief Khalsa Diwan, the impotent, pro-English organization of Sikhs. He aspired to see such an organization of Sikhs in Punjab that could shed away the pro-English stance and excite the people for an armed struggle against the British Empire to achieve freedom for the country. On getting back in Canada, Bhai Balwant Singh wrote a letter to Harchand Singh Lyallpuri asking him for a daring dissent against the English government and to shatter away the influence of Chief

---

11   Ibid.
12   Ibid.
13   Isemonger and Slattery, An Account of the Ghadr Conspiracy 1913-15, p. 7
14   Sir Michael O'Dwyer, India As I Know It, p. 191
15   Kirti, Amritsar, October 1926,p.5

Khalsa Diwan. In this letter, Bhai Balwant Singh had suggested to Harchand Singh Lyalluri that the Sikhs living in India and abroad should form a joint body, the headquarters of which shall be at Lahore. This body should bring out a newspaper that may put the Sikhs on an armed war-path for freedom of the country.[16]

The *Komagata Maru* ship reached Vancouver on May 23, 1914, with 376 Indian passengers. Bhai Balwant Singh, along with his Indian companions living in Canada, formed a 15-member "shore committee." This committee helped the passengers a lot and struggled for their disembarking. It was obligatory to pay the next installment of the ship by June 11. If the same was not paid in time, the owners of the ship would take the ship back along with its passengers. With the cooperation of his companions, Bhai Balwant Singh collected money from the community and paid the installment of the ship.

Bhai Balwant Singh and his companions strove hard for the disembarkment of the passengers. But the Canadian government, throwing its own laws to the wind, gave its decision to send back the *Komagata Maru* ship. The Ghadri leaders wanted the returning passengers to go to India and take part in the rebellion to liberate their country. For this purpose, Bhai Balwant Singh, in company with Bhai Bhag Singh and Babu Harnam Singh Sahri, members of the "shore committee," went to the town of Sumas in America to purchase weapons. The American police arrested them there on July 17. At the time the *Komagata Maru* returned from Canada, with the help of warrior ship *Rainbow* on July 23, 1914, the three most militant Ghadri members out of the four "shore committee" members were in prison in America. Only Hussain Rahim was there in Vancouver. Under pressure of the Canadian government, he agreed for the return of the *Komagata Maru*. Had Bhai Balwant Singh been present, along with Bhai Bhag Singh and Babu Harnam Singh Sahree, the history of *Komagata Maru* and the British regime in India would have been something different.

Because the purchase and keeping of weapons in America is not a crime, Bhai Balwant Singh and the companions were released on July 30, 1914, a week after the sailing away of *Komagata Maru* from Vancouver, and they returned to Vancouver. The First World War started on August 4, 1914. The Ghadar Party gave a call to the Ghadarites to go to the country and declare mutiny. Bhai Balwant Singh was as yet preparing to leave when, on September 5, 1914, Bela Singh Jian opened fire in the Vancouver gurdwara

---

16 Isomonger and Slattery, An Account of the Ghadr Conspiracy 1913-15, p. 7-8

and killed Bhai Bhag Singh and Bhai Badan Singh. Since Bhai Balwant Singh had to appear as witness, he had to stay back for some time. In the meantime on October 21, 1914, Bhai Mewa Singh murdered Hopkinson. The police accused Balwant Singh of inciting Mewa Singh to commit the murder of Hopkinson and thus implicated him in the case. But for want of proofs and the confession of Bhai Mewa Singh as solely responsible for the murder, Bhai Balwant Singh was freed of the case on December 4, 1914.

A few weeks after this relief, Bhai Balwant Singh set out for India. With him was his family and two Ghadri companions—Bhai Batan Singh Kahri and Kartar Singh Nawanchand. They stayed for some days in Yugantar Ashram in San Francisco. Boarding the ship from there, they reached Shanghai on January 23, 1915. From Shanghai, Bhai Balwant Singh sent his family to India with Batan Singh Kahri, and he himself stayed in Shanghai. His mind was to work on the eastern front of the Ghadar Party. For five months, he worked among Indians of China. On June 26, 1915, Bhai Balwant Singh took a ship to reach Savato on July 2 and then Bangkok on July 13. The purpose of his coming to Siam was to work in the company of those Ghadarites who had come from America and Canada and wanted to cause mutiny in Burma.

Very soon after reaching Bangkok, Bhai Balwant Singh fell ill. He was admitted in the hospital. There the doctor, out of ignorance, did a painful operation without serving chloroform, because of which Bhai Sahib had to undergo severe suffering for some days. He had not recovered fully and the doctors discharged him from the hospital. Such haste was made because the police waited for him outside.[17] On first of August 1915, the Siam police arrested Bhai Sahib outside the hospital of Bangkok. Not caring about the international law, the Siam government handed him over to the English.

The English had established one interrogation center at Singapore for interrogating the Ghadarites arrested from far-off eastern countries. In this interrogation center, the senior officers were all English but, for the purpose of torturing and physical thrashing, all the lower ones were the butchers of Punjab Police. Here a severe torture was perpetrated upon Bhai Balwant Singh. He was given brutal tortures of different kinds. In this butcher-house, Bhai Balwant Singh was interrogated for six months, but no one could shatter the revolutionary determination of this committed valiant. After terrorizing him for six months in Singapore, Bhai Balwant Singh was taken to India and

---

17 Kirti, Amritsar, October 1926, p.45

was put in Alipur jail of Calcutta. After six months in jail, he was brought to Punjab in July 1916, where he was dragged into the Second Supplementary Lahore Conspiracy Case.

This case started in Lahore Central Jail on November 8, 1916. Its hearing was going on before three commissioners of a special tribunal. The case of Bhai Balwant Singh was being pursued by the lawyers Lala Devraj and Dhanraj Shah. In this suit, total 18 Ghadarites were entrapped, and 9 of them were from Canada. From Vancouver, there were Bhai Batan Singh Kahri, Kartar Singh Nawanchand, Munsha Singh Dukhi, and Hari Singh Chotian, who joined Bhai Balwant Singh here. Bhai Balwant Singh was accused of being one of the Ghadar Party and sending many Ghadarites to India to topple over the throne of British Empire.

The Tribunal gave verdict of the case on January 5, 1917. Commissioners of the Tribunal had said in the verdict: "We have no doubt that the culprit is man of Ghadar Party and he incites the people most forcefully to actuate mutiny after reaching India. As a result, good many people have come to India cause mutiny in India." It was further written in the verdict that "the accused is one of the ring-leader of Ghadar Party. Taking benefit of his position, he has used others to commit crimes and murders. He is one of the prominent leaders inciting others and he deserves the punishment in full justice that his allies undergo under his orders."[18] Commissioners of the Tribunal indicted Bhai Balwant Singh under IPC Codes 121 and 121 A. The Commissioners pronounced capital punishment for him and ordered the confiscation of all his properties that were worthy.

These were the War days, and the government was very much fearful. Therefore, the officials while submitting to government orders remained on the lookout to award death penalties to political prisoners, and when they found that proper, they did not give the dead bodies to their heirs. Even the date of hanging Bhai Balwant Singh was not told to his family. On 18 Chaitra, when Bibi Kartar Kaur, wife of Bhai Balwant Singh, went to meet him, the jail officials placed before her the mini-form of Guru Granth Sahib and his other belongings and told her that her husband was hanged the other day on 17 Chaitra, i.e., March 29, 1917.[19]

---

18   Second Supplementary Lahore Conspiracy Case, Judgement, January 4, 1917, Individual Case of Balwant Singh, accused no. 3.
19   Kirti, Amritsar, October 1926, p.45-46.

Babu Harnam Singh Sahri was another prominent revolutionary in Canada to carry out an important role in Ghadar Movement. He was born in 1884 in the village of Sahri in Hoshiarpur district. He had passed Middle. After serving some time in the army, he went to Hongkong in 1904 and further reached Canada in 1907. He lived in Victoria near Vancouver for 9 months and then went to Seattle in May 1908. During 1908–09 in Seattle, he studied first in Lincoln High School and then in University College of Seattle. After spending one and half years in Seattle, he came back to Vancouver in November 1909. Here he joined with G. D. Kumar and formed an organization named "Hindustani Association." Its motive was to secure a status for the Indian community equal to that of other nations in the world. In December 1909, Babu Harnam Singh formed "Swadesh Sewak Home" in Vancouver on the line of "India House" of Shiamji Krishan Verma in London. Here the Indian emigrants were given political education. Again in association with G. D. Kumar in January 1910, Babu Harnam Singh brought out a monthly Punjabi newspaper *Sudesh Sewak* from Vancouver. Anywhere in the world away from India, it was the first newspaper published in Punjabi. In this paper, articles were published about the racial discriminatory laws constituted by the Canadian government with the purpose of keeping the Indians away from Canada, withdrawing the voting rights from Indians, and many other issues and problems faced by them.[20] Through these writings, the Indian emigrants were told that the reason for their suffering was the slavery of India. This paper was sent to India in large numbers. Senior English Officers in CID, later on, quipped about *Sudesh Sewak* thus: "By and by, its tone went on becoming objectionable. Since this Paper was addressed to the Sikh Sepoys of British Indian Army in their own language and was sent to India in large number, so its entry in India was banned in 1911." [21]

Canadian Officials felt very irritated upon reading the write-ups of Babu Harnam Singh in *Sudesh Sewak* and likewise from other political activities. They wanted to get rid of him. Very soon, an opportunity came in their hands. In the summer of 1910, Babu Harnam Singh crossed the border to America to meet the Indians living there and collect donations from them for *Sudesh Sewak*. On July 4, 1910, when he was returning from Seattle to Vancouver, a Canadian immigration official disallowed his entry into Canada. Babu Harnam Singh was stuck in Seattle. During 1910–12, he

---

20 Sudesh Sevak, Vancouver, May 1910.
21 J.C. Kerr, Political Trouble in India, 1907-17, pp 230-31.

studied at the University of Washington in Seattle. Babu Harnam Singh and G. D. Kumar kept on preaching political awareness among workers in the saw mills set on the bank of the Columbia River on the border of Washington and Oregon states and also kept preaching political awareness among workers working there.

In the beginning of 1913, Babu Harnam Singh succeeded in coming to Canada from America. In mid-1913, Ghadar Party was established in America, and he started working actively for it. He brought together many Indians living in Canada with the Party. On the advent of *Komagata Maru* at Vancouver in 1914, he was member of the 15-member shore committee to help the passengers. On sending back of the ship in July 1914, the Ghadar Party deputed Babu Harnam Singh the duty of supplying weapons to passengers in the ship. He tried to purchase weapons from the areas of Vancouver, Victoria, and the city of Port Angels on the America side, but he did not succeed. Then Babu Harnam Singh, in company with Bhai Balwant Singh, Bhai Bhag Singh, and Bhai Mewa Singh, tried to purchase weapons on July 17, 1914, from the town of Sumas near the border of America. In Sumas, the American officials arrested them all. The Canada immigration officials did take back Bhai Balwant Singh and Bhai Bhag Singh, but the immigration officials said that Babu Harnam Singh was not a citizen of Canada and they could deport him.[22]

In the second week of September, when Babu Harnam Singh was in jail in America, the police raided his house in Victoria. Police recovered from there the letters which were written to him by Babu Tarknath Dass and Surinder Mohan Bose, and important information was found implying that Babu Harnam Singh was an expert among the Indians in Canada in bomb making and he was collecting necessary material for the purpose. Upon searching the store of Babu Harnam Singh, the police found a huge quantity of such material that was to be used in bomb making.[23]

Babu Harnam Singh was in jail when the First World War started on August 4, 1914. On September 26, 1914, the American government deported Babu Harnam Singh. When his ship reached the port Yokohama in Japan, he gave away a slip. He made contact with Ghadar activists there. Here, in company with Sohan Lal Pathak and Santokh Singh Dhardeo, he took over the command of the Siam-Burma plan of Ghadar Party. Under this

---

22   Melcolm R. J. Reid to W. D. Scott, July 25, 1914. VCA, Add. Ass, No. 69, Vol. 1.
23   J. C. Kerr, Political Trouble in India, 1907-17, pp 249-50

plan, the Indians living in Siam and other eastern countries having sympathy with Ghadar Party were to be gathered in Siam. German officers were to train them for fighting, and they were to be equipped with weapons supplied from Germany. After getting training in Siam, these Ghadarites were to attack Burma.

Burma was state of India at that time. The White forces had gone from there to Europe to take part in War. In Burma, there was strong police force of 15 thousand Punjabi Sikhs and Muslims. In order to maintain their forceful effect, this police force was converted to military police after giving them army weapons. The Ghadar leaders were to preach to the Indian Military Police of Burma and then knot with them. It was to be made sure that it would help the revolutionary forces from Siam to attack Burma. In this way, the Ghadar forces in Siam, with help from the Military Police in Burma, were to capture Burma. Making Burma their foothold, they were to attack further at India.

Going from Siam to Burma, Babu Harnam Singh worked among the Indian soldiers. After activating and strengthening the Ghadar Party branch in Rangoon, Babu Harnam Singh set for North Burma. There he went in cantonments and distributed revolutionary literature. Among the Muslim soldiers, he distributed the decree issued by the *khalifa* of Turkey in which Muslims all over the world were directed to fight against the British Empire. By that time, reports of the failure of Ghadar in Punjab came over. In April 1915, the government came to know of the Siam-Burma Plan. Arrests of revolutionaries began in Burma. Trying to get out of Burma to reach Siam, Babu Harnam Singh was arrested at the border on the Burma side. Brought from there, he was imprisoned in Molmeen jail of Burma.

Babu Harnam Singh and some of his companions ran away from jail on September 1, 1915, after cutting the bars of the jail. But they were caught again on September 9, 1915. Babu Harnam Singh and his other revolutionary leaders were entangled in the First Burma Conspiracy Case in Mandalay jail of Burma. The allegation upon them was that they had planned a conspiracy to topple the British Government in India. Seventeen revolutionaries were entangled in this case. As per the decision of this case, on July 27, 1916, Babu Harnam Singh was awarded capital punishment, and on November 14, 1916, this grand revolutionary was hanged till death in Mandalay Jail.

Baba Sohan Singh Bhakna was President of Ghadar Party in America. He was born in January 1870 in his maternal village of Khutrai Khurd near

Guru ka Bagh in Amritsar district. His ancestral village was Bhakna. His father, S. Karm Singh Shergill, was a rich farmer who owned 65 acres. He studied up to primary level but knew Urdu and Punjabi very well. In the early days, he used to be a *shrabi-kbabi*, but in 1897, at the age of 27, he joined with Namdhari Movement. Tired of economic problems, he reached America in April 1909. Here he spent his first night in the house of Babu Harnam Singh Sahri who, after coming from Vancouver, was living in Seattle. With Babu Harnam Singh, he talked about the *"Pagri Sambhal Jatta"* movement of 1907.[24] Here he worked in a saw mill near Portland, Oregon. While living in America, he also had to face racial discrimination like other Indian emigrants. In his own words: "Going on the way, even children used to mock at us calling 'hello Hindu slave'. We were taunted as – 'you thirty crore are men or sheep who can't get rid of two lakh Englishmen. We were pricked 'you Hindus are not humans. You rats to spread plague'."[25]

Indian imigrants in Canada were already getting mobilized against this racialism. They had taught the Indian emigrants and Sohan Singh Bhakna living in America that ". . . an organizational struggle is essential to safeguard mutual rights." Bhakna and his people were influenced by Americans for fighting against the British for their independence. So they knew that taking to arms was very essential for independence. In his own words of Sohan Singh Bhakna: "After a long thought and discussion, we have reached the conclusion that till we become independent, we don't have value of two *kaudis* even. And nobody gives independence, it is snatched. Without armed revolution, neither independence can be achieved, nor can democracy be and nor can the national pride be saved."[26]

In order to enlighten politically and mobilize the Indian laborers living in Oregon and Washington States, the revolutionaries like Sohan Singh Bhakna and G. D. Kumar joined together to form Hindustan Association of Pacific Coast in Portland in 1912. Sohan Singh Bhakna was made its President and G. D. Kumar its Secretary. It was decided to bring out a newspaper named *Hindustan*. But hardly four or five meetings were held before G. D. Kumar

---

24 "Baba Sohan Singh Bhakna naal mulakaat" Prem Singh Bjaj, Do pairhan Itihas dian (Ludhiana, Punjabi Sahit academy 2004) p.50.
25 Baba Sohan Singh Bhakna naal mulakaat" Prem Singh Bjaj, Do pairhan Itihas dian (Ludhiana, punjabi Sahit academy 2004) p.52.
26 auhI, pMnw 53

fell ill. The launch of the newspaper got delayed and, by and by, work of the organization fizzled out.[27]

In these days, Thakur Das Dhuri suggested that Sohan Singh Bhakna call Lala Hardyal from California and entrust him this work of the organization. Bhakna wrote a letter to Lala Hardyal. On March 25, 1913, Lala Hardyal reached Oregon. Lala Hardyal and Sohan Singh Bhakna moved around Portland and held three or four meetings with the Indian laborers working in saw mills. Then a large meeting was called in Astoria at the end of third week of April. Here all those decisions taken in the St. John's meeting were re-approved, and the organization named "Hindi Association of Pacific Coast" was established. Sohan Singh Bhakna was made its President, Lala Hardyal its Secretary, and Pandit Kanshi Ram the Treasurer.[28] A three-member commission was formed for secret works. Sohan Singh Bhakna, Lala Hardyal, and Pandit Kanshi Ram became members of this secret commission. The main motive of the organization was to achieve freedom for India through armed revolution and then establish a Secular Democratic Republic as in America. The headquarters of the organization was to be at San Francisco, wherefrom the newspaper *Ghadar* was to be brought out. Later, it was due to the name of the newspaper, *Ghadar*, that this organization became famously known as "Ghadar Party."

The headquarters of the Party, named "Yugantar Ashram," was established in a rented house in San Francisco. On November 1, 1913, the weekly newspaper *Ghadar* started publishing from here. Through this paper, the Indians living in Canada, America, and other countries started joining Ghadar Party. Observing the increasing influence of Ghadar Party, the British Government felt baffled. They pressured the American government. Under this pressure, the American government arrested Lala Hardyal on March 25, 1914, but he was released on a surety of one thousand dollars. Later on, fearing the American government would hand over Lala Hardyal to the British Government, Lala Hardyal left America and went to Europe, as advised by the Party. In place of Lala Hardyal, Bhai Santokh Singh Dhardeo was designated General Secretary of the Party.

After Lala Hardyal left America, the responsibility of Sohan Singh Bhakna, being President of the Ghadar Party, increased much more. He left his job in the saw mill and started living in Ghadar Ashram in San Francisco.

---

27   Sohan Singh Josh, ik inklab: ik jeevani(Chandigarh :Punjab book centre, 1969) p. 26-27.
28   Sohan Singh Josh, ik inklab: ik jeevani(Chandigarh :Punjab book centre, 1969) p. 26-27.

He became full-time worker of the Party. He himself supervised all the activities in the Ashram. To make the Party strong and united, he worked day and night. Going out at the staying sites of Indian workers, he told them the programs of Ghadar Party, recruited new members, opened new branches of the Party, and collected funds for the Party.

Keeping the *Komagata Maru* held up at Vancouver harbor for two months, the Canadian government sent it back on July 23, 1914. In the *Komagata Maru* struggle, the Ghadarites of America helped the Ghadarites of Canada in every way. Because of the inhuman treatment meted out to them and after reading the literature sent by Ghadar Party, the passengers of the ship started hating the British rule and became sympathetic towards the Ghadar Party and its programs. In consonance with the duty assigned by the Party, Baba Sohan Singh Bhakna boarded the ship from San Francisco on July 21, 1914, with boxes of pistols and ammunition. On reaching the Yokohama port in Japan, Baba Bhakna reloaded these boxes onto the *Komagata Maru*.

At this time, the First World War had already begun. On October 14, 1914, Baba Bhakna reached Calcutta by a ship named *Namsang*. Police arrested Baba Bhajna from the ship itself. He was taken to Punjab and then imprisoned in Multan jail. To obtain secrets from him, the police offered him many temptations and, no doubt, threats also. But the police could not succeed in drawing any secret from him. Despite the fact that he was arrested from the ship at Calcutta, even then he was indicted in the Lahore Conspiracy Case and then was announced capital punishment which, later on, was changed, out of the fear of defamation, into life imprisonment by the Viceroy Lord Harding.

On December 10, 1915, Baba Bhakna was taken out of Punjab to Andaman and was put in the Cellular Jail. In Cellular Jail, numerous inhuman atrocities were thrust upon inmates. They were made to do severe labor, extracting 30 lbs. of oil daily in expellers. In case of non-completion of the hard labor, the prisoners were given very stringent punishments. In company with his Ghadar companions, Baba Bhakna undertook the struggle against this oppression. They took to hunger strikes many a time. In this turmoil, Bhakna's seven companions died in Cellular Jail. In August 1921, Baba Bhakna was brought to India from Andaman, and he was kept in various jails. There also, Baba Bhakna took to hunger strikes against bad conditions of jails. In Yadwada jail of Bombay, Baba Bhakna was made to remove his kachhehra, underwear, and turban, and he was made to wear knickers and cap. Baba Bhakna went on hunger strike for his religious rights. Parmanand Jhansi and Hirderam, though with Hindu background, joined Baba Bhakna in his hunger strike. In those days, Mahatma Gandhi also was in Yadwada Jail. Gandhi Ji showed no sympathy with Baba Bhakna and others in this case. Rather on asking, he said: "It is their religious matter."[29]

After spending sixteen years in different jails, Baba Bhakna got releasd in 1930. Even after coming out, Baba Bhakna kept struggling for freedom of the country and in favor of the rights of workers and peasants. The English government sent him to jail many times. After the English went away, the Indian government also sent Baba Bhakna to jail many times. Baba Bhakna got his hunchback in the jail of free India.

In alliance with progressive partners, Baba Bhakna kept striving to establish rule of the dreams of Ghadarites. His health had become very weak. On November 16, 1968, he reached Sarabha to celebrate martyrdom day of Kartar Singh Sarabha. On coming back, he was struck by pneumonia. Suffering under this illness, this veteran valiant of Ghadar Movement passed away on December 20, 1968.

Shaheed Kartar Singh Sarabha was another great Ghadarite who went to the gallowas at a very young age. Kartar Singh Sarabha was born in 1896 in the village of Sarabha in Ludhiana district. After passing matriculation at young age of 16, Karatar Singh came to study in America in 1912. Here he studied in Berkley University near San Francisco. Under the influence of the free American atmosphere and in observance of bad treatment meted out towards Indians, the slavery of India started tormenting Kartar Singh. In April 1913, Ghadar Party was established, and Kartar Singh Sarabha became its member. The Ghadar Party started bringing out the *Ghadar* newspaper in Urdu on the first of November 1913. Then Kartar Singh went to San Francisco and started living in Ghadar Ashram. He used to help with the printing press. In December 1913, the Party started publishing the newspaper in Punjabi. Kartar Singh used to translate and publish in Punjabi the articles of Lala Hardyal and other writers published in the Urdu version of *Ghadar*.

On beginning of the First World War on August 4, 1914, the Ghadar Party gave a call to reach India and declare mutiny there. But Kartar Singh Sarabha left for India even before this call by the ship *Nipon Maru*. Going via Colombo, he succeeded in reaching India by the third week of September. But other prominent leaders like Sohan Singh Bhakna, who were to reach

---

29   Prem Singh Bjaj, Do pairhan Itihas dian, p.69.

later, were arrested from the ship itself and, as such, the already formed organization was broken. Out of the Ghadarites outside, Kartar Singh Sarabha was the only competent leader to lead the Ghadar Party. With the cooperation of his companions, Kartar Singh reconstituted the Party afresh.

Ghadarites going to India were assured that they would be provided arms on reaching India. But the arms did not come. Money was required to purchase arms. To meet the shortage of money, Kartar Singh, under compulsion, suggested the Party to go for political robberies. Under lead of Sarabha, the Party committed robberies at many places. But these robberies brought a bad name to the Ghadarites.

Members of the Ghadar Party were very short of experience. To make up this deficiency, Kartar Singh Sarabha made contacts with Bengali revolutionaries. Sachinder Nath Sanyal, the Bengali revolutionary, came to Punjab at the end of November 1914 and took cognizance of the situation. The Ghadar Party had no headquarters of its own so far. As suggested by Sanyal, the headquarters of the Party was set up at Lahore. Rass Bihari Bose, the popular Bangali revolutionary, reached Punjab in the last of January 1915 and took command of the Ghadar Party. Kartar Singh Sarabha took the company of Vishnu Ganesh Pingley (having come from America) and visited the cantonments at Meerut, Agra, Lucknow, Kanpur, Allahbad, and Benaras and brought them round to join the mutiny. [30]

With reports received from different places, Sarabha and his companions decided to declare mutiny on February 21, 1915. As per Sarabha's plan, an attack was to be made at the cantonments of Lahore and Feroxpur, and the Whites standing guard at the magazines were to be overpowered and then, with help of "mixed" Indian soldiers, a national ghadari force was to come up. After this, it would have become easy for the other Indian forces "mixed" with Ghadarites to raise mutiny and join the Ghadarites. Then, with the force of this revolutionary army and the revolutionaries, all the Whites could be thrown out of India. Because of the leakage of information by the informer Kirpal Singh, the Ghadarites changed the date of the mutiny from February 21 to February 19. The government came to know this date also. On February 19, Kartar Singh Sarabha reached the Ferozpur cantonment with his companions to declare mutiny. But the pro-Ghadar soldiers were either sent home or they were put under strict surveillance, and the White soldiers

---

30 Lahore Conspiracy Case, Judgement, September 13, 1915, Individual Case of Kartar Singh, accused no. 39.

were standing at guard of the magazines. In the cantonment at Lahore also, the Indian soldiers were disarmed.

Because of leakage of secrecy, the mutiny could not be successful. Arrests of Ghadarites started. Kartar Singh Sarabha succeeded in escaping safely out of Lahore, but, on March 2, 1915, he was arrested along with his companions Harnam Singh Tundilat and Jagat Singh Sursingh from a house in Chak no. 5 near Sargodha. At that time, Kartar Singh Sarabha was reading out poems from *Ghadar ki Goonj* to the people gathered there. According to the police Sub-Inspector Sadardin, Sarabha, at the time of arrest, started giving lecture to the people that they should take to arms against the English.[31]

It being war time, the government could not afford to displease the Sikhs in Punjab, the nursery of recruitment in army. So while demolishing the Ghadar Movement and maintaining the trust of Sikhs for the English, Lt. Governor Michael O'Dwyer called a meeting of Sikh Sardars in "Govt House Lahore" on February 27, 1915. In this meeting, O'Dwyer asked for help of Sikh Sardars to suppress the Ghadar Movement forcefully. Sikh Sardars, one above the other, assured O'Dwyer that they considered themselves fortunate while serving the British Government. They assured O'Dwyer of their full cooperation and would use their good influence in getting the Ghadaries arrested. Sikh Sardars were rather strict in dealing with the Ghadarites. Out of the 3200 persons who came from abroad, 200 had been already put in jails and 700 were confined to village limits. But the Sikh Sardars suggested to O'Dwyer that all the 3200 persons who came from abroad should be thrown in the jails.[32]

Sardar Bahadur Gajjan Singh, who was a member of Provincial Legislative Council and was himself a lawyer, proposed to O'Dwyer that any form of leniency in dealing with the Ghadarites shall affect the people badly. Therefore, rather than filing suits against Ghadarites in general courts, they should be put under "Summary Trials."[33] Other Sikh Sardars confirmed the proposal of Gajjan Singh.

Getting assured of the loyalty of Sikhs through Sikh Sardars, O'Dwyer adopted a still more stringent policy. Acting upon the proposal of Gajjan Singh, O'Dwyer got the Defence of India Act passed from Viceroy Lord

---

31   Lahore Conspiracy Case, Judgement, September 13, 1915, Part 3, The History of the Conspiracy and War, p. 107.
32   Sir Michael O'Dwyer, India As I knew It, 1885-1925, p. 204.
33   Isemonger and Slattery, An Account of the Ghadr Conspiracy 1913-15, pp 75-76.

Harding. O'Dwyer had dictatorial powers to crush the Ghadarites. Kartar Singh Sarabha and all other Ghadarites caught so far were put together in Lahore Central Jail.[82] Ghadarites were sued vide Defence of India Act. This most infamous Lahore Conspiracy Case went on from April 26, 1915, to September 13, 1915, in Lahore Central Jail.

Special arrangements were made for this suit. Special police guards were standing at the jail's gate, inside on the jail's yard, and on the roofs also. CID men were roaming about on all sides. No one could go inside to witness proceedings of the case, not even the relatives of those involved in the case. Press people could not write reports of the case. Whatever reports appeared in newspapers were government reports.

Hearing of the case was going on under a special tribunal of three judges nominated by the government. Under the Defense of India Act, this special tribunal had been given unbridled powers. The decision of the tribunal was the last and final decision. No appeal in any court could be entered against this decision. No "authority" had any legal right to reopen the inquiry of decision given in this case, neither about its legal aspect, nor about the facts and proper or improper award of punishment. Only the Viceroy Lord Harding had the right to interfere or listen to appeals regarding the decision of the tribunal.

The accusation against Kartar Singh Sarabha and his comrades was that they had made up a conspiracy to topple the throne of British Government in India, and, to make this plot successful, they had instigated the Indian soldiers of the army and incited them for mutiny. They were also accused of committing robberies to collect money to purchase armaments, ultimately in order to make this conspiracy successful. Also, they had printed and distributed literature for mutiny. And they committed murders of the officials and police officers who tried to restrict their path. They had tried to blow off railway lines and the bridges.

While giving verdict of the case, the commissioners wrote about Sarabha: ". . . Despite his young age, he is the most dreadful culprit out of these 61 accused ones and his file of crimes is the largest one. In actual, whether in America or on the ship on way to his country or in India, there is no part of the conspiracy where this culprit would not have taken part. . . . He has admitted that he was there in the robbery committed at Sahnewal. He has accepted that he had relations with Lala Hardyal in America and he used to work in the Ghadar Press in San Francisco." The commissioners wrote further that "He is young man of tender age but he is one the most dreadful conspirators and no pity can be shown to him."[34]

Commissioners of the tribunal pronounced capital punishment to Kartar Singh Sarabha and his 23 cohorts. 27 were given life imprisonment and six were punished for less than six years. Later on, Lord Harding converted capital punishment of 17 Ghadarites into life imprisonment. But the capital punishment of Kartar Singh Sarabha was kept *status quo*. On November 16, 1915, Kartar Singh Sarabha was executed in Lahore Central Jail along with his six fellows. Among those who were hanged were Vishnu Ganesh Pingley, who came from America, and Jagat Singh Sursingh, the famous revolutionary of Vancouver.

Many of the historians, especially the western ones, have given more than due importance to Lala Hardyal. In their view, Lala Hardyal alone was the soul-self of Ghadar Party. But I do not agree with these views. Ghadar Party was not the creation of some single person. The Indian laborers working in saw mills around Portland were already wakeful by virtue of the preaching of Ghadarites like G. D. Kumar, Babu Harnam Singh Sahree, and Babu Tarknath of Vancouver. These workers had only called Lala Hardyal from San Francisco to form the Ghadar Party. Lala Hardyal reached the area of Portland in the last of March 1913. After holding meetings for about three weeks with the workers working in saw mills around the Columbia River, Lala Hardyal constituted the Ghadar Party in Astoria on April 21, 1913. This could become possible only because the workers were already awake politically. Otherwise, what other wild-horn did Lala Hardyal have to form the Ghadar Party in three weeks? (No doubt, much credit goes to Lala Hardyal by starting the *Ghadar* newspaper and then in projecting the Ghadar Movement to such acme heights among other revolutionary parties in other countries as to make the movement worthy of international fame). The British Government had the thinking that, with Lala Hardyal leaving America, the Ghadar Party would come to its close, but it did not happen so. In the words of Baba Sohan Singh Bhakna: "Hardyal worked with us for five months only. Had he been spirit and soul of the Party, this Movement would definitely have died after his going; but it did not happen so. Rather, the Movement grew stronger. Preparation for the mutiny was done after his

---

34 Lahore Conspiracy Case Judgement, September 13, 1915, Individual Case of Kartar singh, accused no. 39.

going."[35] So I would like to say that for the formation and for the running of Ghadar Party, it was not single-self Hardyal only. It was the result of collective efforts of many Ghadarites.

As such, we realize that in reality the true spirit and soul of Ghadar Movement were the Sikhs having come from central districts of Punjab. They were not much awake politically while living in India, and they did not consider the British rule there to be bad. They had come to Canada and America in search of better work and living means. Racialism, the free atmosphere of Canada and America, association with revolutionaries from different countries of the world, and the non-existence of pro-English Sikh leadership were prominent reasons of their becoming politically awake and then establishing the Ghadar Party. If they had not come to Canada, America, or other foreign countries, they would perhaps have lived their lives as most faithful servants of the English government. Being the best Sikhs, they adopted a secular approach and, in togetherness with Hindus, Muslims, and non-believers in religion, struggled for freedom of the country. Insufficient experience in revolutionary undertakings and non-cooperation from the native people were prominent reasons of non-success of the Ghadar Movement. No doubt, they had direct involvement in Akali Lehar, Babbar Akali Lehar, Kirti Lehar, and Communist Lehar—all for freedom of the country. Bhagat Singh and his likes of the Hindustan Socialist Republican Association were much under the influence of the Ghadarites. As such, these revolutionary giants of Canada and America had made a momentous contribution for freedom of the country.

Along with their struggle for freedom of the country, these Ghadarites of Canada had fought battles for their rights in Canada also. Ghadarites of Canada made that conspiracy of the Canadian Government unsuccessful in November 1908 by means of which all the Indians in Canada were to be thrown out to live in British Honduras. These Ghadarites had also won the right of bringing their families into Canada. After a long strife of forty years, they had also won the voting right in Canada on April 2, 1947.

Whatever the honorable living the Indian community is enjoying in Canada these days, absolute credit for all this goes as a tribute to the sacrifices made by those Ghadarites.

---

35 Prem Singh Bjaj, Do pairhan Itihas dian, p.57.

Bhai Randhir Singh: An Uncommon Personality

Dr. Balwant Singh Dhillon

Director Centre on Studies in Sri Guru Granth Sahib
G. N. D. University, Amritsar-143005

During the second half of nineteenth century, the Sikh Panth was passing through a very serious internal as well as external crisis. With the annexation of Punjab by the British in 1849, the Sikhs had lost political authority over the Punjab. The doctrinal originality of Sikhism and social unity of the Sikhs which were the hallmark of eighteenth-century Sikhism were now at their lowest ebb. All the social and religious evils which the Sikh Gurus had eradicated had again crept into Sikhism. Instead of tasting excelsior of the perennial spring of spirituality, the Sikhs had fallen prey to personality cult, blind faith, and ritualism. Aboard the bandwagon of British Raj, the Christian missionaries had penetrated deep into the Punjab, subsequently to embarkon an aggressive agenda to proselytize the Punjabis. The Hindu revivalist movements, such as Brahmo Samaj and Arya Samaj, were also testing the waters of Punjab in order to assimilate the Sikhs into their fold. The evidence at hand suggests that the Sikhs were really a vulnerable lot. Though the Sikh reform movements, namely the Nirankaris and the Namdharis, had come on the scene with a motive to stem the rot within, erosion of Sikhism at doctrinal level had not yet receded. It was the Singh Sabha Movement which set the ball rolling for the renaissance of Sikhism. Born on July 8, 1878, at Narangwal (District Ludhiana), Bhai Randhir Singh attained his adulthood when the socio- religious movements of different denominations were competing with each other in such a manner that their polemics had made the atmosphere of Punjab really very surcharged.

Bhai Randhir Singh's father, S. Natha Singh, was a magistrate in the state of Nabha. We can well imagine that Bhai Randhir Singh belonged to an elite family which brought him up in the best tradition of Sikhi. After his schooling in Nabha, in 1900 he graduated from F.C. College, Lahore, which was a very rare distinction in those times. Subsequently, he joined the civil services as Tehsildar and served the people with dedication when Punjab was experiencing a serious epidemic of bubonic plague. After a short stint in the civil services, in 1902 Bhai Sahib resigned from the job. Actually, his mind and soul was yearning for the service of Sikh Panth. With the creation of Khalsa by Guru Gobind Singh in 1699, the caste system had been uprooted from the social life of the Sikhs, but with the passage of time, it had again raised its ugly head. Resultantly, the so-called Dalit Sikhs were discriminated against at social and religious levels. Even their *Parsad* was not accepted by the priests of Darbar Sahib, Amritsar, and they were not baptized along with the upper-caste Sikhs. It was a variety of social injustice which was utterly in violation of the principles of Sikhism. Bhai Sahib took upon himself to remove this social evil and, in order to set an example, decided to partake *Khande di Pahul* along with the Sikhs who belonged to the Dalits and Muslims as well. It happened on June 14, 1903, in a huge public gathering (*Diwan*) held at Bakapur near Phillour. Thereafter, he took upon himself the mantle of a Sikh missionary which he remained till his death in 1961. In 1905–1906, he served as the Superintendent of the boarding house of Khalsa Collegiate School, Amritsar, where he inspired many of his colleagues and students by his unflinching faith in Sri Guru Granth Sahib.

Bhai Randhir Singh was a great organizer who knew well how to motivate the people for a common cause. In fact, he possessed the quality of a mass leader who, alike the traditional Akalis of Misl Shahidan, was always in the vanguard. His deep knowledge of Gurbani coupled with his rendering of Gurbani Kirtan in an absorbing and enchanting manner proved to be a crowd puller. It helped him to establish an instant rapport with his audience. In order to preach the message of Sikhism in the Malwa region of Punjab as well as to eradicate the social evils, in 1908 he established Khalsa Diwan at Talwandi Sabo. With his dedicated band of companions, he roamed from one place to another, held numerous congregations, and motivated the Sikh masses to reconnect with the Sabad Guru. In 1914, he followed vigorously an agenda that was to get rid of the un-Sikh like practices that had gotten currency at the historical Sikh Gurdwaras, namely Anandpur Sahib, Chamkour Sahib, and Fatehgarh Sahib. Significantly, it was done when the Gurdwara Reform Movement had not yet got full momentum. Credit goes to his leadership that it was done purely in a peaceful manner and with the least use of force.

Bhai Randhir Singh was a person whose allegiance was only to Akal Purakh and his Guru, i.e., Sri Guru Granth Sahib. In public life, he personified the quality of a saint-soldier for whom not personal but community matters were of utmost priority. In 1912, when the Colonial government of India was building a new capital in New Delhi, it acquired land of the Gurdwara from the Mahant and demolished the boundary wall of Gurdwara Riqab Ganj Sahib in New Delhi. The Sikh masses were highly perturbed over this act of sacrilege. However, the Sikh leadership of those times, namely the Chief Khalsa Diwan, were loyalists of the British and were not ready to confront the government over this issue. Bhai Randhir Singh, in association with S. Harchand Singh Layalpuri, took the matter in his own hands. In 1914, they shot of a telegram to Viceroy in which they strongly protested against the demolition of Gurdwara property. Resultantly, the government understood the gravity of the issue and subsequently the demolished wall was rebuilt. Now the Sikh masses had realized that the Chief Khalsa Diwan people could not protect their rights in an effective manner. A new Sikh leadership was the need of the hour at that time. This vacuum was filled by the Ghadarites and the Akalis who instantly took the imagination of the Sikh masses.

Bhai Randhir Singh's role in the Ghadar Movement was very significant, but unfortunately with the exception of S. Malwinderjit Singh, an advocate and historian on the Ghadarites, no known Sikh or non-Sikh historian has commented upon it. In other words, his contribution in the freedom movement of India has been totally overlooked by the modern Indian historians for the reasons best known to them. It is now well known that towards the beginning of twentieth century, though on a very small scale, the Sikhs had started migrating to North America. The Sikh immigrants in Canada were highly upset over its immigration policy which was not only racial in nature but also deprived them of their fundamental rights. Because the Indian immigrants were the British subjects thus the Canadian government had implemented this policy in close consultation with the British Government.

Therefore, unrest was simmering on against both the Colonial as well as the Canadian government. In this situation, many of the Sikh immigrants in Canada crossed over to the United States. Besides the Khalsa Diwan Society Vancouver, mainly representing the Sikhs, other outfits, such as the United India League and Hindustani Association of the Pacific Coast, had been set up in order to safeguard the interests of Indian immigrants. Out of these organizations, another party flourished which was known as the Hindustani Workers of the Pacific Coast. Since many of its members were Sikhs, usually its meetings were held in the Sikh Gurdwaras in North America. Subsequently, this organization came to be known as the Ghadar Party, and its chief objective was war against the British Raj. Significantly, most of the Sikh members of the Ghadar Party were the Khalsa Sikhs. The plight of passengers of *Komagata Maru* in Canadian waters near Vancouver and subsequently on returning to India firing on them at Budge Budge harbor in Hoogly in Sep. 1914, had convinced the Sikh Ghadarites that for their travails British Government is responsible. Meanwhile, the World War had broken out. The Ghadarites, who were active in North America, thought that now they had the chance to liberate India from the yoke of British Raj. Many of them returned to India with an aim to raise an armed struggle against the colonial government of India.

Bhai Randhir Singh had already shown his disenchantment with the British over the demolition of wall of Gurdwara Riqab Ganj in Delhi. The Ghadarite leaders realized that Bhai Randhir Singh carried a great clout among the Sikh masses and, to succeed in their mission, his support was of crucial importance. Consequently, S. Kartar Singh Sarabha, a noted Ghadarite leader, developed an immediate rapport with Bhai Randhir Singh and was successful in enlisting his support for war against the British Raj. However, the Ghadarites' plan of general uprising in Feb. 1915 was foiled because the British had got its information in advance. Bhai Randhir Singh, who had boarded a train for Ferozpur with a motive to join the revolutionaries there, had to return to his village. Meanwhile, the British Government had gotten information regarding his association with the revolutionaries. Consequently, on May 9, 1915, Bhai Randhir Singh was arrested and put on trial in Lahore. The case is known as Lahore Conspiracy Case (Supplementary), and judgement was pronounced on June 30, 1916, whereby Bhai Randhir Singh (Accused No. 69) was imprisoned for life and his property was confiscated. The rest is history: how Bhai Randhir Singh went through the ordeals of jail life in Lahore, Multan, Hazari Bagh, Rajamundari, and Nagpur. For his insistence on the Khalsa code of conduct in jail life, he had to undergo hunger strikes. For that matter, British officials had to amend the jail manuals. Ultimately, he was released from jail on Oct. 4, 1930. After that, till his death on April 16, 1961, he devoted his whole time to the organization of Akhand Kirtani Jatha, which even today stands as a living testimony to his rich legacy.

Bhai Randhir Singh belonged to a rare breed of the Sikhs which is very difficult to find in these days. His was a personality which always stood on a very high moral pedestal among his companions. He was a very strong-willed person who did not hesitate to take up the cudgels for the welfare of society. For his strict adherence to the Khalsa code, he had to face the might of British officials. For that matter, he had to bear tremendous physical and mental pressure. The source of his physical and moral courage was his unparalleled faith in the truthfulness of Gurbani. His writings prove that he was a creative genius. It establishes him not only as a man of letters but a mystic as well who cherished writings on Sikh spirituality. He combined in himself the qualities of a reformer and a revolutionary. In that way, he was a trailblazer for the freedom fighters and the Gurdwara reformists as well.

Life and Times of Pakher Singh Gill: A Panjabi Californian in the Early Twentieth Century

Nirmal S. Mann, MD

Introduction

Today the California Society is considered diverse, tolerant, and relatively liberal. At this time the American Society is one of the best in the world; it is basically a meritocracy. In present-day California, the minority groups like the Chinese, Japanese, Blacks, Hispanics, East Indians, Filipinos, etc., constitute a significant percentage of the population. They have political power and many are economically well off. However, it was not always like this. American-Indians in California were first brutalized by the Spaniards and Franciscan missionaries. After 1850, when California became a state, the Mexican-Californians suffered the full fury of white injustice, bigotry, prejudice, and cruelty (1). The blacks and American-Indians did not have the right to vote. Between 1850 and 1880, the Chinese population grew rapidly. During this time, Japanese also started arriving to California. Like other minority groups, they were subjected to harsh and brutal discrimination. They were not eligible for citizenship and had no voting rights. Anti-miscegenation laws were on the books in California till 1949. The immigration acts of 1924 revoked the American citizenship of Chinese, Japanese, and East Indians. In general, California was the most racist, bigoted, and cruel state at that time.

We study the past to understand the present and plan for the future. The present is evanescent, the future is unknown, but the past is etched in stone.

Even God cannot change our past. The present is already becoming the past as we speak. Remember the present is the past of the future (2).

By presenting the biography of Parkher Singh Gill (P.S. Gill), we intend to shed light on the socio-politico-economic conditions in California in the late 19th and early 20th century. His story will also highlight the struggles carried on by Panjabi Jutt Sikhs in California (2). P.S. Gill was first an Indian, then he was a Panjabi, then he was a Sikh, then he was a Jutt Sikh. Later on, he became a Californian and an American. But always remember, to begin with he was a Scythian. To understand his actions and thoughts, it will be necessary to trace his Scythian and Jutt Sikh roots.

Historical and Cultural Background

The Jutts of Panjab are descendants of Asian Scythians whose original home was Asian Steppe which is a large landmass extending from Southern Siberia in the east to an area around the Black Sea in the west. It is mainly a grassland suitable for a nomadic way of life. In 700 BC, the Scythians occupied Southern Russia. The average Scythian was a superb horseman, tall and sturdy. The Russian Cossacks like the Jutts of Panjab are of Scythian descent. "What men! They are real Scythians!" Napoleon is said to have exclaimed at the sight of a thundering charge by Cossack cavalry, as his tattered forces fought endless rear guard actions on the wintry retreat from Moscow. Although the Scythians formed confederacies, they remained ruggedly individualistic. Their original religion was Shamanism. They did not generally admit authority or superiority and tried to maintain equality of status among them; that is one reason, their Indian descendants, i.e., the Jutts of Panjab, were not easily influenced by the Brahamanic Caste System of the Hindu Society. They ate a wholesome diet of grain, meat, and milk. The Scythian considered owning a horse a status symbol. The horse enabled them to launch swift and effective raids on the enemy. They practically lived in the horse-saddle. In 650 BC, they intended their influence up to Egypt. In 514 BC, they humiliated a large Persian force of 700,000 men under Darius the Great. They loved music and left behind beautifully carved gold ornaments. In 310 BC, they were defeated by the Sasmartarians. Their main migration to India occurred between 50 BC and AD 50. After their arrival in India, first they became Buddhist but later became Hindus, Muslims, and Sikhs. Migration of Scythians also occurred westward up to Scandinavia and Baltic countries. In Panjab, they gave up their nomadic ways and settled into communities of land cultivators and farmers. It is interesting to note that some of the traits and characteristics of Scythians are found among the modern Jutts of Panjab, namely rugged individualism, bravery, frankness, and contempt for authority.

P.S. Gill was a Jutt Sikh, a descendant of Scythians. He was not an ordinary criminal motivated by greed or money but was a self-respecting honorable patriot with a great sense of honor and pride. Moreover, like Cesar Chavez (3), but at a much earlier time in the history of California, he was a supporter of the rights of farm workers and was very popular among them. To understand his character fully, we will need to briefly review the history of the Sikhs (4–6). His Scythian descent (7, 8) was responsible for his actions and thoughts.

P.S. Gill was born in the village of Choorchuck, now in Moga District, on May 7, 1889; Baba Ruhr Singh, one of the Gadarite, early 20th century California Sikh revolutionaries, was also from the same village as was Lacchman S. Gill, one of the Chief Ministries of post-partition Panjab. P.S. Gill studied at Govt High School and had an 8th grade education. The story of P.S. Gill, his struggles, and trials will illustrate the hardships suffered and eventual triumph of East Indians in California (2, 9–34).

Panjab is the land of the Sikhs. Of their 10 Gurus, 9 were born in Panjab. Initially the emphasis was on spiritualism. The first Guru Nanak traveled far and wide in a peaceful teaching style. He had learnt Hindi, Sanskrit, Persian, and Arabic. He developed a large following by the time he settled at Kartarpur. With each martyrdom, the Sikhs became more militant. After the execution of the 5th Guru Arjan Dev, his son wore two swords and maintained a cavalry force. After the martyrdom of the 9th Guru Tegh Bahadur, the 10th Guru Gobind Singh completely militarized the sect and fought many successful battles against the Mughals and their Hindu supporter Hill Rajahs. After the assassination of Guru Gobind Singh, his appointee Banda Singh Bahadur successfully challenged the Mughal Empire almost at its zenith and established territorial Sikh presence in Panjab and Western Oudh. In the 18th century, Sikhs were controlling vast territories in Panjab through the 12 Missals. Bhagel Singh occupied Delhi in 1783 and proceeded to build Sikh Gurudwaras in and around Delhi. The Sikh kingdom was established at Lahore in 1799 under Ranjit Singh. Some battles during the two Anglo-Sikh wars are memorable. For the first time during their long successful military campaigns in India, the British were soundly and decisively beaten by the Sikhs in two battles, one at Ferozeshahr and the other at Chellianwalla.

Panjab was annexed by the British in 1849. After 1849, most of the Jutt Sikhs went to their ancestral occupation of farming; some joined the British army; the religious matters were largely left in the hands of Khatris and Sahjdhari Sikhs. A splinter group known as Nirankaris came in conflict with the British and started the kooka movement. Their leader Baba Ram Singh was deported to Burma. Many organizations, such as Chief Khalsa Dewan and Singh Sabhas, were started; they had branches in California and British Columbia. During the period of 1900 onwards, Sikhs migrated to countries such as Burma, Thailand, Hong Kong, Philippines, Fiji, Malaya, Singapore, East Africa, Australia, New Zealand, Canada, and California. In Panjab, a canal system converted the barren lands of Lyallpur and Montgomery into fertile agricultural lands. The government increased the water and land tax in 1907. The Sikh farmers of those two districts led a successful campaign against the tax increase. Incidentally, this was the first successful non-violent campaign against the British in India. The Sikhs joined the British army and won many Victoria Crosses in WWI and WWII. The Sikhs who settled outside India realized that they were not getting the respect they deserved because India was being ruled by the British.

The Ghadar (Revolutionary) party was formed at Astoria, Oregon, on April 21, 1913, and later was head-quartered at San Francisco. As we will note later, P.S. Gill was very active in the affairs of the Ghadar Party. The incidence of the *Komagata Maru* occurred in 1914. In its aftermath, 12 people were hanged in India including a 17-year-old lad, Kartar Singh Saraba. During the *Komagata Maru* episode, a Canadian Anglo-Indian policeman, who treated Indians brutally was, in the typical Sikh trait for revenge, killed by Mewa Singh Lopoke who was hanged in Vancouver on Jan 11, 1915. In India, Pandit Kanshi Ram from the village Marauli Kalan (author's village) near Morinda was hanged. On April 13, 1919, the massacre at Jallianwalla occurred on the orders of M. O'Dwyer, British Governor of Panjab; hundreds of innocents were killed. Again in the Sikh tradition of revenge, M. O'Dwyer was shot dead by Udham Singh in London in 1940. In 1920, the Gurdwara Reform movement also known as the Akali movement successfully wrested the control of Sikh Gurudwaras from corrupt Hindu Mahants who were supported by the British. This was the first major successful non-violent Movement against the British; this was achieved by the Sikhs and not by M.K. Gandhi's

Life and Times of Pakher Singh Gill: A Panjabi Californian in the Early Twentieth Century

Congress party. In a non-violent movement, the British police clubbed to death Lajpat Rai. To avenge this death, Bhagat Singh Sandhu killed a British police officer, and he was hanged on March 23, 1931, at the age of 23.

During WWII, the British forces were defeated by the Japanese in South-East Asia and Burma. Indian National Army was formed first under the command of Capt. Mohan Singh and Col. Niranjan Singh Gill and later led by S.C. Bose. In 1947, India was partitioned into Pakistan and India; this was accompanied by lot of violence and mass migration of populations. Again Sikhs paid a heavy price; thousands were killed and displaced. However, they, by dint of hard work and persistence, re-established themselves. They have made significant contribution to India's progress in all spheres of activity, including, military, economics, education, agriculture, and science. The Sikh leaders at this time were Master Tara Singh and S. Baldev Singh, the latter from the village of Dumna (author's mother's village). Thanks to the hard work of Panjabis, Panjab had the highest per capita income in India.

The Sikh soldiers and generals played important roles in 1947 in the first India-Pakistan war over Kashmir. In 1965, Sikhs again played a significant role in India's military victory. In 1966, Panjab was divided into three states Viz Haryana, Panjab, and Himachal. All these three states subsequently have made impressive economic gains. Almost two million Sikhs are settled abroad, and they have made a name for themselves in their chosen professions; many among them are Sahjadhari Sikhs. Their remittances to Panjab, in no small measure, are contributing to Panjab's prosperity and wealth. This short history of the Sikhs will help explain the actions and thoughts of P.S. Gill. When P.S. Gill left India in 1908, the British Empire was at its zenith; Panjab and India were firmly in their grip.

After a three days' train journey from Ludhiana, P.S. Gill arrived in Calcutta in 1908. Calcutta at that time already had a sizeable Sikh community with well-established Gurdwaras and social life. P.S. Gill was popular with the local Sikhs and was considered a quiet, likeable lad. But like all Sikh youth at that time he was restless and looking for adventure. He stayed in Calcutta for a short two years. Sikhs have been serving in the British army and as policemen in Hong Kong since the 1880s. They were able to remit money back home to hang on to their lands. P.S. Gill, being outgoing and gregarious, made many Bengali friends and also learned to speak the Bengali language. After working hard, he saved money and sailed for Hong Kong in 1910. In Hong Kong, an elderly Chinese lady became a godmother to him and helped him in every way she could. He learned Mandarin and became quite fluent in it. He already could speak, read, and write Panjabi, Urdu, and also had a smattering of English. He spent about two years in Hong Kong and one year in Shanghai. From Shanghai, he sent home about 120 pound sterling. He reached Seattle in 1913 when he was 24 years old. At this time, he became a Sahjdhari Sikh. He had an impressive physique, 6 feet tall, and had a handsome face. In Seattle, he worked in the lumber mills. He took active part in the affairs of the small Sikh community and had developed political savvy. Being a Jutt, he was looking for farm land. That search brought him to Imperial Valley, California, in 1917.

People from India (generally derisively called "Hindoos," although a large majority were Jutt Sikhs) started arriving in British Columbia, Washington, Oregon, and California in 1890s and suffered prejudice and discrimination, particularly as a result of California's Alien Land Law, similar to what happened to the Chinese and Japanese. The Japanese and Chinese could expect some help from their governments; the East Indians had no such recourse as India was ruled by the British at that time.

In the period from 1890 to 1923, immigrants from India were generally illiterate with agricultural/military backgrounds; however, a small number were educated professors and students. The East Indians came long after the Chinese and Japanese presence had already caused resentment and hostility in the white population of Canada and America. The Sikhs in California faced many legal sanctions and restrictions, because the prejudice and fear of "yellow peril" was transferred to the Sikhs, who were perceived as the next "invasion" and got characterized as the "Turbaned Tide." They were stereotyped as being filthy, illiterate, and clannish. They lived in segregated areas along with Chinese, Japanese, and other Asiatics. Sporadic violence occurred against them and some were murdered. Panjabi men mostly settled in Sacramento Valley, Central California, and the Imperial Valley. Being expert farmers, very soon they started leasing land and began farming on their own. This alarmed the Anglo farmers who felt threatened by their progress upwards on the agricultural ladder. In 1913, the California Alien Land Law was passed whereby Asians could not own land. The relatively more humiliating treatment meted out to the Panjabis relative to the Japanese convinced some of the Panjabi intellectuals in Berkeley and San Francisco to form the Ghadar Party, whose aim was to fight for India's freedom from the British with arms. P.S. Gill took active part in the affairs of the Ghadar Party, lectured to the

Sikh farmers, and contributed money to the movement. Sikh Gurdwaras were established in many towns; the earliest was at Vancouver, BC. The Gurudwara at Stockton served as a meeting place for Sikhs, Hindus, and Muslims. P.S. Gill, as already mentioned, was fluent in Mandarin, Panjabi, Hindi, and Urdu and was politically erudite. He regularly read newspapers to keep himself informed about current events. Many Anglo landlords, bankers, and lawyers fronted for the Sikhs; they had high praise for the Sikh farmer. Because of the Alien Land Law, all agreements were verbal. A few dishonest Anglo landlords cheated their Sikh farmers and reneged on the verbal agreements. Many Sikhs married Mexican women and put the land in the name of their spouses and children; they continued to farm as their childrens' trustees and guardians. The Panjabis mainly grew cotton in the Imperial Valley, but some got into growing lettuce and fruit in the orchards.

Before Imperial Canal was built, the Imperial Valley was a hot, barren, arid, and inhospitable desert. In 1901, water arrived in the valley. During the next 30 years, many towns were established; farms and ranches were brought under cultivation. In 1907, the first electric lights were installed and auto cars appeared on the dusty streets. P.S. Gill arrived in the Imperial Valley in 1917. The town of Calipatria was established in 1914; one of the founders of Calipatria was Victor R. Stereling. After water came to Calipatria, rapid and effective development occurred. Hard-working Anglo pioneers met their match in the equally hard-working and persistent Jutt Sikhs working in Imperial Valley at that time. P.S. Gill, through friends and newspapers, kept himself informed about the Akali movement in Panjab and made liberal contributions to the cause. The Sikh farmers, depending entirely on the honesty and goodwill of Anglo friends, lawyers, and bankers in the matter of verbal leases, successfully cultivated cotton, lettuce, and alfalfa on hundreds of acres in the Imperial Valley. P.S. Gill, being relatively better educated than other Panjabis, assumed a leadership role. He conducted negotiations on their behalf. He was a supporter of the farm laborer. Some old timers describe him as tall, handsome, pleasant, kind, and considerate. He had a high sense of pride in his ethnic identity and was politically active. He spoke out against the British occupation of India; when people from Ghadar party approached, he gave them full support. P.S. Gill entered into a verbal lease with Victor R. Sterling, John B. Hager, and William Thornburg, and cultivated lettuce on 320 acres near Calipatria. The contract stated that P.S. Gill would be paid within three days after the crop was shipped out. John B. Hager and Victor

R. Sterling were extremely bigoted and prejudiced against the Panjabis; they missed no opportunity to humiliate and insult Panjabi farm workers. P.S. Gill was assigned to chastise them as he had to deal with them on a daily basis and bore the brunt of their humiliating racial comments.

April 1, 1925, in Calipatria in the north end of the Imperial Valley was a typical spring day. P.S. Gill got up early, and after a bath, he did his morning Sikh prayer using a Gutka (Religious Hand Book). After breakfast, he drove to Bradford Ranch south east of Calipatria. Sterliong and Hager were shipping lettuce out from P.S. Gill's leased land; the whole crop was worth $50,000; he politely requested Sterling for his share of the money. They refused to give him any money. Because of the Alien Land Law, he could not get any legal help. At 5:00 p.m., he again confronted Sterling and Hager about his share of the crop money. As usual, Victor R. Sterling rudely informed him that he owned nothing there and said, "Go away, you Goddamn Hindoo." At that moment, P.S. Gill decided that the time had come to settle the score: the time for pleadings and entreaties was abruptly terminated by that comment, "Goddamn Hindoo." At 5:30 p.m., Sterling was shot dead. Hager tried to run away and pleaded with Gill not to shoot him that he would give Gill a cheque for $25,000. P.S. Gill told him it was not a matter of money anymore and shot him dead. After this, P.S. Gill drove to the office of William R. Thornburg in Calipatria. When he reached there, Mrs. Thornburg who was 8 months pregnant came in front of her husband and pleaded with P.S. Gill not to shoot her husband. Seeing her, P.S Gill said, "I am Guru Ka Sikh, I do not raise my hand on women and children." Saying this, he threw away his gun and waited for the sheriff.

The trial of P.S. Gill galvanized the Sikh community behind him. Hundreds of Sikh men, women, and children were present in the court. Lots of money was raised for his defense. The Mexican farm workers were sympathetic towards him. He was convicted of second degree murder and sentenced to 14 years prison time at San Quentin.

P.S. Gill was in prison from 1925 to 1940. He is described as a model prisoner, who followed all the rules and got along well with prison officials and other inmates. In prison, he kept himself informed about political activities in India, Canada, England, and the USA. P.S. Gill was paroled on November 20, 1940, and on July 1, 1946, he became a completely free person.

He tried to do farming in Phoenix, Arizona, and again in the Imperial Valley but was not successful. At the age of 62, in 1951 he married Juliana,

Life and Times of Pakher Singh Gill: A Panjabi Californian in the Early Twentieth Century

the widow of his former partner Mota Singh Sandhu. It was not a marriage of convenience as by now Panjabis were no longer alien ineligible for citizenship. However, the marriage did not last long. He followed the fate of Indian National Army in Burma and raised funds for the three INA officers on trial in 1946. In the mid-1950s, he was elected president of El Centro Sikh Temple and continued community work there. Also in the mid-1950s, P S. Gill. became a naturalized US citizen. In 1955, at the age of 66, he married an 18-year-old Mexican girl named Alicia. Between 1955 and 1962, he fathered four sons; when his youngest son was born, he was 73 years old. His sons have done well; one is a lawyer.

Armed with an American passport, P.S. Gill visited India in 1970. He met his relatives and visited his old school. When a native son returns after 62 years, there are bound to be emotional reunions. He praised the modern California Society as being fair, just, and basically a meritocracy. He advised his grandnephews and grandnieces to migrate to California. He commented that in 1925, if he had killed two white men in India, England, or Canada, he would surely be hanged, whereas a reasonable US jury found him guilty of 2nd degree murder because they felt there was enough provocation and his action to some extent was justified. After about one month, he returned to California, on January 10, 1971. He then visited his nephews and grandnephews in England in August 1971. He visited the grave of Maharaja Dalip Singh. He stayed in England for two weeks.

In 1971, he was 82 years old. In 1973, his health began to deteriorate. He was diagnosed with lymphoma and died at Scripps Clinic La Jolla at 9:00 a.m. on September 9, 1973; he was 84 years old. At that time, there were no crematoria in Southern California; his body was taken to Yuma, Arizona. The caravan passed through the Imperial Valley towns, including Calipatria. The journey, which had started with a train ride from Ludhiana in 1908, ended 65 years later, half-way around the world in the Arizona desert.

Analysis

As is evident from the biography of P.S. Gill, the pioneer Jutt Sikhs of California had to struggle hard to gain respect and acceptance in the society. Many legal and social sanctions and restrictions were placed on them. Hard-working pioneer Anglo farmers met their match in equally hard-working and persistent Jutt Sikhs. In spite of all the hurdles, they were successful in raising profitable crops, such as cotton, lettuce, and alfalfa on hundreds of acres. Even though many were illiterate, they had the wisdom to organize and support movements such as the Gadar, Chief Khalsa Diwan, and Singh Sabhas. Sikh Gurudawaras played an important role providing a venue for social political interaction. Since there were not many East Indian women and they could not go to India to get married, many married Mexican women who played an important role in helping them get established. After 1946 (Lucy-Cuellar Law), the California Society was changing albeit slowly. As in the rest of the country, multiethinicism and multiculturalism was taking root. The passage of the Civil Rights Act of 1964 and desegregation in the south under J.F. Kennedy and Robert Kennedy's encouragement heralded a new era in America. The previously persecuted, disadvantaged, and disenfranchised minorities, such as the Chinese, the Japanese, African-Americans, and East-Indians, as if released after years of bondage, started to realize the American dream like the Europeans had done before. After the 1965 immigration amendment act, people from Asia stated migrating to the US in relatively large numbers. East Indians mainly came as much sought-after professionals, e.g., doctors, engineers, and scientists. But the Panjabi farmers who settled in the Imperial Valley and elsewhere in rural California also sponsored their relatives and provided for them to start anew like in California. This new wave of Panjabi immigrants had a significant impact on the Mexican-Panjabi couples and their children.

Discussion

The California Society has come a long way in the matter of diversity, equality, and tolerance. Today it represents the model for the rest of the country. Gone are the days of Alien Land Law and other restrictive laws both at the personal and institutional level. Today the minority groups are prominently represented in all academic, professional, and business entities and are enjoying the fruits of free and just society. It is really a meritocracy. California really has become a melting pot where various ethnic groups freely intermingle socially and professionally. No wonder California is the most populous state in the union. It is a tribute to the change which has occurred in the American and particularly the Californian Society that the progeny of P.S. Gill, a convicted felon, have done as well or better than the progeny of William R. Thornburg, the third intended victim of P.S. Gill. One of P.S.

Gill's sons is a lawyer; the other three sons are also successful in real estate and have management positions. They seem to have been completely assimilated in the American "melting pot."

Conclusions

At this time, the American Society is probably the best in the world; it is basically a meritocracy which gives a fighting chance for success to a prepared and disciplined mind, and it is still a land of opportunity. However, the present situation should not lull us into complacence; there is need to stay vigilant lest the latent prejudice may surface again (1).

The newly arrived immigrants from India, whether farmers, businessmen, or professionals, should always remember the sacrifices made and political struggles carried out by Panjabi farmers in the Imperial Valley and rest of rural California. Above all, they should never forget the contributions made by courageous and stout-hearted Mexican women who, defying the law, married aliens ineligible for US citizenship and enabled them to gain a foothold in the Imperial Valley and rural California. By the same token, the present generations of Panjabi-Mexicans are our people; we should always extend a hand of love and friendship towards them.

Bibliography

1. Heizer RF, Almquist AJ. The Other Californians. Univ of Calif Press Berkeley 1971.
2. Mann NS: The Life and Times of Pakher Singh Gill; A Panjabi Californian in the Early Twentieth Century. Dorrance Publications, Pittsburgh, 2005.
3. Hammerbach JC, Jensen RJ. The Rhetorical Career of Cesar Chavcz. TX A&M Univ Press, College Station TX, 1998.
4. Read A, Fisher D. The Proudest Day, India's Long Road to Independence. W.W. Norton & Co N.Y. 1997.
5. Singh Gopal. A History of the Sikh People (1469 to 1988). Allied Publishers Ltd N. Delhi 1988.
6. Singh Khushwant. A History of the Sikhs. Oxford Univ Pess, Delhi 1966.
7. Mahal B.S.: Panjab; The Nomads and the Mavericks. Sunbun Publishers N. Delhi 2000.

8. Ainsworth M. The Scythians, Fierce Horsemen of the Steppes. The World's Last Mysteries. Readers' Digest, 1978.
9. Leonard K.I. The Pakhar Singh Murders: A Panjabi Response to California's Alien Land Law. Amerasia Journal 11: 75-87, 1984.
10. Leonard KI. Making Ethnic Choices: California's Panjabi-Mexican Americans. Temple University Press, Philadelphia PA 1992.
11. Meeting with Balbir Singh Gill, nephew of P.S. Gill and Village headman of village Choorchuck, Distt Moga, Panjab, India Nov- 2001.
12. Meeting with eldest son of P.S. Gill at a San Jose Restaurant Dinner 4/24/2002 6:30 p.m. to 8:30 p.m.
13. Numerous telephone conversations with Mrs. Anna Sanhu of Oklahoma, who is related to P.S. Gill 2001-2003.
14. Telephone Interview with Vir Singh Gill, nephew of P.S. Gill of East Hounslow, England 3/26/2002 8:15 a.m. (PST).
15. Telephone Interview with Harinder Singh Gill (son of Vir Singh Gill) of England 3/16/2002 at 8:30 a.m. (PST).
16. Telephone discussion with William J. Thornburg, son of Wilham R. Thornburg 2002.
17. Meeting with Wilham J. Thornburg, Holtville 3/20/2002.
18. Letter of Vir Singh Gill to the author. Letter is dated Jan 12, 2004.
19. Telephone Interview with Vir Singh Gill of England 1/7/2004 10:00 to 10:30 p.m. (PST).
20. Leonard KI. Punjabi Farmers and Californian's Alien Land Law. Agricultural History 59:549-562, 1985.
21. Interview with Rose Singh, Calipatria 4/13/2002.
22. The People, Respondent vs Parker Singh Appellant. Crim No. 1286. 78 Cal App U76 248 p981 June 22, 1926.
23. The People Respondent Vs Parker Singh Appellant 78 Cal App 488 June 22, 1926.
24. Telephone Interview with Vir Singh Gill of England 1/24/2004 8:00 a.m. (PST).
25. Telephone Interview with Chamkaur S. Gill son of Vir S. Gill of Fremont Calif. 3/16/2003 7:00 p.m. (PST).
26. Imperial Valley Press April 2, 1925.
27. Holtville Tribune April 3, 1925.
28. Holtville Tribune April 10, 1925.
29. Holtville Tribune April 17, 1925.

30. Criminal Case #1U575, Court Transcript Riverside County
31. Imperial Valley Press June 4, 1925.
32. Holtville Tribune June 5, 1925.
33. Holtville Tribune May 1, 1925.
34. San Quentin Prison Record of P.S. Gill 3/12/1927.

Role of Gadrites in Babbar Akali Movement and India's Freedom Struggle

Dr. Baljeet Singh Sahi and
Dr. Gurcharan Singh Aulkh

Gadarite's (Ghadarite's) dreams had great significance and made their impact in the history of India in general and particulary in the history of the Punjab. Gadarite's were the first to raise a standard of rebellion against the British Imperialism to throw away the yoke of slavery from the United States of America and Canada.

The Punjab Province (after 1947, it has been divided into two parts—western Panjab lies in Pakistan, whereas the eastern part is in India) was a great source of immigration to the United States and Canada.

The first immigrants arrived in Vancouver (British Columbia) to celebrate Queen Victoria's Diamond Jubilee on June 20, 1897. The Punjabis were fascinated at the sight of vast fields and rich forests, affluence and prosperity of the new world. It is estimated that between 1899 and 1920 about 7348 Asians migrated to Canada. The number of Indians in Canada in 1901 was 2312, and in the USA it was 6313, which subsequently increased to 30,000.[1]

The flow of migrants was not always steady. In 1905, only 45 Indians reached Canada, while the number rose to 2623 in 1908. In British Columbia alone, the number of Indians was 258 in 1904 whereas their strength in 1908 was 5175.[2] The number rose to 10,000 in 1910. The emigrants mainly went

---

1 Sahensasha, 6.S., *Gadar Party Da Ithihas*, Vol. I, Jallandhar, 1961, P.20
2 K.M. Pannikar, *The Problem of Greater India*, p.248

either to British Columbia (Canada) or to California (USA). About 90% of migrants to Canada settled in San Francisco. The reasons are not far off to seek. The climate of these two places was very akin to that of Punjab. This fact cannot be precluded as one of the reasons. Another was that of economic hardship. The economic downturn in India during the early 1900s witnessed a high level of emigration. In Panjab, the government introduced a bill which affected the newly colonized lands opened by the canals in the Western Punjab. This circumvented the rights of the peasants as well as provided for higher rates on Bari Doab. This led to a grave discontent among the Jat Sikhs and made the Punjab a fertile soil for revolutionary seed.[3] The nationalist leaders like Lala Lajpat Rai and Ajit Singh made the peasantry politically conscious.

The soul stirring song "Pagri sambal oe' Jatta Pagri sambal" (Take Care of your turban) written by Banke Dyal added to their zeal.[4]

The agrarian agitation had brought the economic issue to the fore. It was a warning to the Punjab government, but it took no steps to ameliorate the lot of the Punjabis. Some of the hard-pressed and enterprising Punjabis, mostly the Sikhs, decided to emigrate in search of better opportunities, leaving others behind to keep the flame of revolution burning.[5]

The influx of the Punjabis to Canada and the USA led to the increased number of emigrants. This increase in number whipped up the anti-Indian feelings, and the Indians became victim of discrimination.[6]

It is estimated that in 1908 about 5000 Indians had entered Canada, out of which 99% were Punjabis, and out of them 90% were Sikhs. Many were studying at various universities all over America. Those Punjabi Hindu and Sikhs went to Canada, as it was under British rule. They worked there as laborers. Some of them crossed the border and settled on the West Coast of the Pacific in cities like Portland, San Francisco, San Jose, and Los Angeles.

The Canadian government decided to curtail this influx with a series of laws which were aimed at limiting the entry of South Asians into the country and restricting the political rights of those already in the country. The Punjabi community had hitherto been an important loyal force of the

---

3 Khuswant Singh, *A History of the Sikhs*, Vol.II p.159
4 Barrier, N.G. *The Punjab Disturbances of 1907* vide the Modern Asian Studies No. 1, Vol 1967, pp-353-83
5 Satya M. Ray, *Punjabi Heroic Tradition*, Patiala, 1970, p.28
6 Aulakh, G.S. (Dr.), *Babbar Akali Movement, A Historical Survey*, 2001, Delhi, p.37

British Empire, and the community had expected equal welcome and rights from the British and commonwealth governments as extended to British and white immigrants. This led to growing discontent, protests, and anti-colonial demonstrations. Faced with an increasingly difficult situation the community began organizing itself into political groups. A large number of Punjabis who moved into the United States also encountered similar political and social problems.

The anger and wrath against Punjabi emigrants, and especially against Sikhs, was acute as they were hardworking and were always ready to work for less wages as compared to the migrant laborers from China and Japan.[7]

The white laborers compelled their government to restrict entry of immigrant laborers. All sorts of excuses were made to debar the entry of ships which carried Indians. Many examples can be cited.

In 1906, a ship was granted permission to enter Vancouver harbor, and it had to seek permission at Victoria Harbour in October 1906. The Canadian Coasts were closed for Indians vide order-in-council in 1908, though many orders were annulled by the courts. In 1908, the Canadian government tried to lure Indian immigrants to settle in the Island of Honduras. This proposal was vetoed by Indians, and they passed a resolution against the scheme in the Gurudwara of Vancouver. The Secretary of Home, Govt. of Canada, tried to entrap some of Indian representatives, but he did not succeed.[8]

The Indians were debarred to work in factories. Victoria Municipal Committee decided not to give employment to any Indian.

In 1910, Canadian Privy Council order No. 920 was passed which envisaged that the immigrants must come by continuous journey and on through ticket from the country of their birth or citizenship and they must have 200 dollars in cash as well. These restrictions made entry of Indians in Canada impossible as in these days no direct ship sailed to Canada. Even those who had migrated to Canada were not allowed to call their families.[9]

This compelled the immigrants to start simultaneous struggles against the Immigration Act as well as against colonial rule. Since most of the immigrants were Sikhs, the earliest organizations were established to build Gurudwaras which soon came up in the cities like Vancouver, Victoria,

---

7 Khuswant Singh, A History of the Sikhs, 1966, p.169
8 Waiz, S.A., *Indians abroad*, Bombay, 1927, p.650
9 Ibid, p.661

etc.¹⁰ It is not surprising, therefore, that work against British Imperialism was started in those countries mainly by the granthis, i.e., the scripture readers in the Sikh Guruduaras.¹¹ The Punjabis had to fight hard against the government. From 1911 to 1913, seventeen thousand Chinese and Japanese along with families were allowed to settle in Canada, and, contrary to this, not a single Indian was allowed to bring his family.¹²

A deputation of immigrants consisting of Nand Singh Sihra (a Ramgarhia Sikh of Phillaur), Bhai Balwant Singh Khuradpur, ex-soldier and granthi of Vancouver Gurudwara, and Bhai Narain Singh first reached London and after that they met viceroy of India in Delhi on December 20, 1913, but got no relief.¹³ When the deputation went to the Punjab, the then Governor of Punjab Sir Michael O'Dwyer compelled them to go back empty-handed.¹⁴ Then the episode of the *Komgata Maru* broke the bone of the camel. It was a ship chartered by Baba Gudit Singh of Sarhali on March 20, 1914, to satisfy the condition of the Canadian Privy Council order No. 920. There were 376 passengers, out of whom 346 were Sikhs. The ship was not allowed entry and was compelled to leave Canadian waters on July 23, 1914.¹⁵ The police insisted that passengers should board the train bound for the Punjab. Only 50 men and 2 children boarded the train. About 203 were arrested, 32 absconded, and 19 were killed. Baba Gurdit escaped the police net.¹⁶

The conditions of the Sikhs in USA were not different. The Indian Immigrants were attacked by the white laborers on September 5, 1907. Indians were attacked in Belligham Saw Mills in the state of Washington. Then again on January 25, 1908, the Indian workers were forcibly loaded into street cars, driven to the wilderness of the forest, and left there. The victims approached the English Counsellor for the redressal of the grievances but to no avail. One such attack was organized by the American workers against the Japanese workers.¹⁷

The latter complained to their government which took such a serious cognizance of the situation that the American government had to pay

---

10   Satya M. Rai, *Punjabi Heroic Tradition*, Patiala, 1978, p.34
11   Nahar Singh, Documents Relating to Bhai Maharaj Singh p(⊠)
12   Partap Singh, Giani, *Akali Lehar Da Itihas*, Amritsar, 1975
13   Sehansara, G.S. *Gadar Party da Itihas*, P.69
14   Sir Michael O Dwyer, *India as I knew it*, P.191
15   Sehansara, G.S., *Gadar Party Da Itihas*, p.130
16   Josh, Sohan Singh, *Hindustan Gadar Party*, New Delhi, 1976, p.156
17   Sehansara, G.S., *Gadar Party Da Itihas*, p.90

compensation and assured that Japanese would be protected in future. It dawned upon Indians that nobody cared for them because they were slaves.

There were other incidents of discrimination as well. Once, Sant Teja Singh of the Mastuana and Sohan Singh Bhakna went for lunch in an American restaurant in the city of Portland. The owner of restaurant refused entry and told them that the Indians and dogs were not allowed. They took their food in a Japanese restaurant.

Again Sohan Singh Bhakna went along with his friend to find work in a mill. The superintendent of the mill said, "There is a lot of work but not for you. Instead, I feel like shooting you." When they asked the reason, he said, "You are 30 crores. Are you sheep or human beings? If you are human beings why are you leading the life of slaves? Go back to your country and get it free. After achieving freedom, when you come to America, I will be the first to welcome you."

Whenever the Indian workers took a stand, they compelled the white mob to run. Some white workers attacked the Sikhs in a factory in Washington. Ghaniya Singh Maur aimed his pistol at the attackers and performed his job fearlessly.[18] Another Punjabi, Vir Singh also faced the mob valiantly. Pakhar Singh became a terror for the whites when he attacked a white farm-owner because of his abusive behavior, thrashed him mercilessly, and cut his horse to pieces by his sword.[19]

The maltreatment and discrimination brought the stark reality to their faces that a slave has no life worth living. They were insulted even in the homeland and in foreign countries as well. They were not considered human beings. The state of their mind had been captured in the following words:

> In our mother land, from pillar to post we are thrown,
> In the foreign lands we get no refuge, none is our own,
> We aliens have no hearth and home
> We cannot say this is the country by which we are known.[20]

---

18   Jaswant Singh Jas, *Baba Sohan Singh Bakna*, 1968, Jullundher, P.69
19   Gagan Pakistani, *Samdarshi*, July Sept 1989 p .48. (Parvasi Punjabian Da Adikh Muhandra P.48)
20   Bhagat Singh Bilga, Unsearched pages of Gadar Lehar p.32
Gadar Lehar De unfole Varke
Desh pain Dhakke, Bahar Miley Dhoi Na
Sada Pardesian da desh koi na

The people had come all the way from Punjab and elsewhere leaving their home and hearth for a dignified livelihood. Now their demeaning status, arbitrary racist immigration laws turned them into an incendiary human stuff ready to change this state of affairs.

The latent discontent surging against the British and the will to change their condition in the racist milieu, got focused in one idea to get freedom for the country whatever the price. Only people from a free country, it was felt, could live in dignity and fight for their rights in alien land. This became a credo with the Indian immigrants who toiled hard in lumber mills in the states of Washington and Oregon and on the farms in California. The situation was so desperate for immigrants that their inner furry against the British came to the fore, and the idea of their mobilization was mooted. Nearly everywhere, everyone who had come from India rallied round the idea of freedom of the country. The idea of justice, freedom, and equality smote their consciousness. This led to the formation of a society, the Hindustan Association of Pacific Coast, more popularly called "Gadar Movement." Thus, die was cast and history was made.

Formation of Gadar Party and aftermath

The story of the formation of Ghadar Movement is long and winding. From the very beginning, those Indian emigrants who reached England, Canada (Vancouver, etc.), New York, and Seattle who came in search of livelihood were also imbued with patriotic fervor and were forefront in the struggle against slavery.

In 1905, Gopal Singh and Amar Singh reached America. In 1906, Tarak Nath Dass and Ramnath Puri of Khem Karan reached there. Ramnath Puri was a government employee in India. He published a pamphlet against the government. To avoid arrest, he escaped to the USA. He issued a circular of freedom upon reaching there.

At this juncture of time, the Indo-American Society and the New York Bar Association gave support to Indians through papers and lectures. They also established "India House" to extend help to Indian patriots and students who arrived there. The students who reached the USA on the invitation and with the help of these societies included Sri Surendra Mohan Bose, Sant Teja Singh Mastuana, and Hari Singh Cheema.

The rebels of the British Government, like Tarak Nath Das, Ram Nath Puri, Thakur Dass Dhuri, Malauvi Barkat-Ullah of Bhopal, became members of this society after their arrival in New York.[21]

In 1909, when the Indo-American Society was disbanded and India House was closed, the students, who earned money doing some work in Industrial east, shifted to the western coast. Hari Singh Cheema went to Chicago, Teja Singh to Vancouver, Surendra Mohan Dass and Tarak Nath Dass to Seattle, Thakur Dass Dhuri to St. Joan (Oregon), Ram Nath Puri to California, and Maulavi Barkat-Ullah left for Japan after getting appointment as Lecturer in Arabic in Tokyo University.

During this period, the Indian emigrants started a "pamphlet war." In 1907, the pamphlet *Khalsa* urged the Sikhs to lead the struggle for freedom against the British. In 1909 *Maro Farangi* was brought out, and *Bhaibandh* in Panjabi was published to throw light on racial discrimination. Tarak Nath Dass brought out *Desh Sewak*. As a result of these pamphlets, the Indian immigrants began to discuss their problems in groups.

It was in Canada where organizations were set up. The pioneer of this organizational set up was Sant Teja Singh. The Khalsa Diwan Society was founded in Vancouver, and Sant Teja Singh built a Gurudwara there at the cost of $25,000 in 1909. The branches of this society were established in Victoria, Abbotsford, New West Minster, Frazer Mills, Coombs, Ocean Falls, etc., and more Gurudwaras were built in Victoria and other cities.[22]

The Gurudwara at Vancouver played a historic role in the freedom Movement and became a central place for Indians to chalk out their program. The participants were mainly Sikhs in these organizations, and they played a historic role in the formation of Ghadar organizations and the movement. Perhaps due to this, many claim, the Ghadar movement was to a large extent "a sikh movement."[23]

Despite this, it can be safely asserted that these religious organizations and Ghadar Movement were nationalistic and secular in outlook. The ideology of the party was strongly secular. Sohan Singh Bhakna rightly said, "We were not Sikhs or Punjabis. Our religion was patriotism." The mouthpiece of the party the *Ghadar* newspaper also brought into limelight the party's secular character. The ideological aims and dreams of Gadarites have been

---

21 Sohanasara, G.S., *Ghadar Party Da Itihas* p.28
22 Khuswant Singh, *A History of the Sikhs*, Vol.II p.174
23 Harbans Singh, *The Heritage of the Sikhs*, Delhi, 1983 pp. 263-64

amplified in their literature. A poem written by Harnam Singh Tundilat is enough to quote as an example. He writes: "Death is better than the life of slavery and this is never to be forgotten. Even a country like China, which was once in deep slumber has awakened. Now it is time to awaken India with a beat of drum. We do not need Pundits or Qazis as we are not eager to see our boats sunk. The time of meditation is also over. It is time to wield sword now. After reading Gadar Paper we believe that time for rebellion is ripe." ("Marna Bhala Gulami di Zindagi Ton, nahin Sukhan ih manon Bhulavne da. Mulak Jagia chin ghook sutta dhol vajiya Hind Jagavane da. Saanun Lorr na Panditan Qazian di, nahin sauk hai berry dubavane da. Jap Tap da wakt batit hoya, Vela aea gia Tegh Uthavane da.")[24]

The formation of Gadar Party was neither sudden nor spontaneous. Its origin can be traced in associations formed in Canada, and later on, its transformation into a movement took place in the United States.

In 1909, Harnam Singh Kahri Sahri and Guru Dutt Kumar (G. D. Kumar) reached Canada. They formed the Hindustan Association with Bhai Bhag Singh as President, G. D. Kumar as Secretary, and Bhai Balwant Singh as its treasurer. With G. D. Kumar's departure to Seattle (USA), the association came to an end, and on December 15, 1911, a new organization was established which was known as United India League. In April 1913, this organization was strengthened with the arrival of Giani Bhagwan Singh. He gave the same slogan to the Indian emigrants in Canada which later on was given by Lala Hardayal in the USA. But the oppression of the Canadian Government compelled them to cross over to the USA.

When the Canadian Sikhs were, thus, active in their struggle, the Sikhs in the USA, like Baba Jawala Singh Thathian, Santa Wasakha Singh Dadher, and others, established the Pacific Coast Khalsa Diwan Society and built a Gurudwara at Stockton (California) in September 1912. Besides, they built a boarding housing and started Langar (Common Kitchen) for Indians who had no place to live and no job to earn food. They gave shelter to many a student who later on worked in Gadar Movement along with their compatriots who worked as laborers in the fields and factories.[25] They used to take farms

---

24 *Gadar Di Goonj* No. 1 Couplet No. 5, Quoted by Dr. G.S. Aulakh, *Veer Naik Kartar Singh Sarabha*, Patiala, 1994 p.48.
25 Jagjit Singh, *Ghadar Party Lehar* pp.18, 22.

on lease and thus provided a common bond to students and workers. This society thus became a nucleus and nursery of Gadar Movement.[26]

In the beginning of 1912, Babu Harnam Singh Kahri Sahri and G. D. Kumar, who had their center of activities in Seattle, visited Portland. Their activities centered round the idea of social reform and publishing some leaflets, but they could not build any movement. Many other seasoned patriots, such as Kishanji Verma, Madam Cama, Lala Hardayal, Tarak Nath Dass, and Sardar Ajit Singh, were also unable to turn their ideas into any mass movement. Harnam Singh and G. D. Kumar interacted with Indian workers in mills around Portland. They discovered that they were not in favor of mere reformist program. It was discussed and decided to form a revolutionary association. Thus, the Hindustan Association of Pacific Coast was set up at Portland in 1912 where Bhai Harnam Singh Tundilat reached from Bridelveil, Pandit Kanshi Ram Marholi Ram Rakha Saroa from St. Joan, and Baba Sohan Singh Bhakna and Udham Singh Kasel arrived from Monarch Hill.

Baba Sohan Singh Bhakna, G. D. Kumar, and Pandit Kanshi Ram were elected President, General Secretary, and Treasurer respectively.

Those days, Kartar Singh Sarabha too had arrived and was staying with his co-villager Rulia Singh and worked in Astoria Mill. They set up office in a rented building.[27] Hardly after half a dozen meetings G. D. Kumar fell ill. Thakur Dass Dhuri, who arrived in Portland, advised Sohan Singh Bhakna to send for Lala Hardayal from California. Lala Hardayal reached San Francisco in 1911. He was a polymath who turned down a career in the Indian Civil Service. He started writing harsh articles in newspapers, and the British Government decided to impose a ban upon his writings. Lala Lajpat Rai advised him to go abroad. He went to Paris in 1909, moved to Algeria, then to Martinique, and then reached the USA. First, he reached Boston and then went to California. He taught Indian Philosophy and Sanskrit at Leyland Stanford University and then shifted to the University of Berkeley.

He had developed contacts with Indian-American farmers in Stockton, California. He encouraged young Indians to gain scientific education. With the help of Teja Singh, Tarak Nath Dass, Arthur Pope, and funding from Jawala Singh, a rich farmer from Stockton, he set up the Guru Gobind Singh scholarship for Indian students. He also established his house

---

26 Dr. G.S. Aulakh, *Veer Naik Kartar Singh Srabha*, 1994, Panjabi University, Patiala pp.28-29.
27 Statement of Harnam Singh Tundilat

as a home for these students on the model of Shamji Krishna Verma's India House in London. Amongst the six students who responded to the offer were Nand Singh Sihra, Darisi Chenchiah, and Gobind Bahari Lal, his wife's cousin. They lived together in a rented apartment close to the University of California, Berkeley.

Lala Hardayal, when contacted by Sohan Singh Bhakna and others, promised to reach on December 25, 1912, but he arrived at St. Joan in March 1913. After some spade work, and a number of meetings in Bridleville, (March 31, 1913) Linton (7 April), and Wina (April 14), it was decided to give a final shape. The most important meeting took place in a saw mill of Astoria on April 21, 1913.

The representatives from Portland, Wina, St. Joan, Linton, and other places participated. Lala Hardayal spoke to the gathering and exhorted them to sacrifice everything for the freedom of the motherland. Sohan Singh Bhakna offered himself for the cause. The members gave generous donations for running the office of the party and the newspapers. Pandit Kanshi Ram donated ten thousand dollars in cash and a piece of land to the party. Now, it was decided to give a concrete program to the emigrants to liberate the country. The office bearers of the Hindustan Association of Pacific Coast were mostly same except G. D. Kumar.

The following were elected:

President: Bhai Sohan Singh, Bhakna
Vice President: Bhai Kesar Singh, Thathgarh
Generel Secretary: Lala Hardayal
Joint Secretary: Lala Thakur Dass Dhuri
Treasurer: Pandit Kanshi Ram Marholi

It was also decided that *Ghadar* Akhbar be brought out. But Lala Hardayal, who was entrusted with the task, could not keep his promise due to health reasons. Then the work of *Ghadar* was entrusted to Kartar Singh Sarabha, who gave 200 dollars received from home. He, along with Harnam Singh Tundilat and Pandit Kanshi Ram, took steps to bring out the first issue of *Ghadar* on November 1, 1913.

Now there occurred only one change in the name of the association: "Hidustan" was replaced by "Hindi" and thus nomenclature became "Hindi Association of the Pacific Coast," which ultimately came to be known as

"Ghadar Movemnt." The alternative Indian organizations were Hindustan Association of the USA, composed mainly of students and educated men, and the other was the Sikh Khalsa Diwan with its headquarters at Stockton, California. Both got ideologically merged with Ghadar Party.

The Ghadar Party had its headquarters at 5 Wood Street, San Francisco, where it had a printing press. Apart from Lala Hardayal and Kartar Singh Sarabha, who worked actively at the headquarters, i.e., Yugantar Ashram, others who worked actively were Munshi Ram and Hari Singh Tundilat, the poet.

Yugantar Ashram became a center of revolutionary activities. In the beginning, Lala Hardayal and Lala Raghubir Dyal Gupta lived there. Baba Sohan Singh Bhakna remained busy in organizing the party. He toured farms and factories along with Bhagat Singh of Kachar Bhan, Kanshi Ram, Kartar Singh Dukki, and Kartar Singh Sarabha.[28]

The backbone of the movement were the peasants who had trickled into the USA and Canada from their distant land where they had been facing economic misery due to the inhuman policy of plunder. They had a reputation of being determined fighters. They were always proud of their heritage and the sacrifices their forefathers had made in their fight against the Mughal oppressors. They were imbued with the tales of Kukas who were blown to pieces by the British rulers.

Hardayal, in his capacity as secretary of the Hindu Association of the Pacific Coast, along with the idea of armed revolution, addressed a gathering of Indian workers in Astoria on June 2, 1913. He said, "You have come to America and seen with your own eyes the prosperity of this country. What is the cause of this prosperity? Why nothing more than this, that America is ruled by its own people." On June 4, 1913, he said, "The Roman Empire was not worse than the British Government in India. It could not be reformed and it must be abolished."

Lala Hardayal was, though, not founder of the Movement, but he was the brain of the movement and gave it a revolutionary direction during his stay in the USA. His message given in the first issue of *Gadar* had an electrifying effect on the immigrants who were ready to do everything for the freedom of their country.

---

28   Sohann Singh Bhakna, *Jiwan Sangram*, p.45

The message was:

What is our name?	Ghadar
What is our work?	Ghadar
Where will it take place?	India

The party was built around a weekly paper, *Ghadar*, which carried the caption on the masthead, "Angreezi Raj ka Dushman" (an enemy of the British Rule). The *Ghadar* declared they "wanted brave soldiers to start up rebellion in India. Pay – Death; Price – Martyrdom; Pension – Liberty; Field of Battle – India."

The foundation of the party and the publication of *Ghadar* was a big blow to the imperialists. As a result, restrictions were imposed on *Ghadar*, and CID reports confirmed that Lala Hardyal was the brain behind the movement. On March 25, 1914, Hardyal delivered a speech in San Francisco, and his arrest warrants were issued. He was released on a surety of 1000 dollars given by an American lady. Bhai Jawala Singh and Bhai Santokh Singh took steps to send Hardayal to Europe. In the first week of April 1914, he was sent to Italy by airplane from where he went to Switzerland. The work of Ghadar Party fell on the shoulders of Bhai Sohan Singh Bhakna, Bhai Santokh Singh, Ram Chander, and others. After Hardayal's exile, the party took the revolutionary line with vengeance. Kartar Singh Sarabha was sent to Europe to get training in aviation.[29] Harnam Singh Tundilat, Pirthi Singh Lalru, and Master Udham Singh began to prepare bombs. It was during these activities that Harnam Singh lost one of his arms when a bomb exploded on July 5, 1914, in the Jawala Singh Farm.[30]

Gadar Party began preparations to incite rebellion. The first meeting after Hardayal's exile took place on April 12, 1914, at Stockton Gurudwara under the auspices of Khalsa Diwan Society. After that, a series of meetings were held at Presno, Upland, Oxford, Clairmont, and Los Angeles on May 10. On June 7, 1914, in a meeting at Astoria, Sohan Singh and Barkat-Ullah, who had come from Japan, roared that the time had come to expel British Imperialists from India. Similar meetings took place in Wina, Washington, Aberdeen, Portland, and Seattle on June 8, 11, 13, 14, and 15 respectively.

---

29   Bhagat Singh Bilga, *Gadar Lehar De Unfroley Varkey*, p.31
30   Dr. G.S.Aulakh, *Veer Naik Kartar Singh Sarabha*, p.39

Role of Gadrites in Babbar Akali Movement and India's Freedom Struggle

The First World War started on July 28, 1914. Some of the leaders, like Sohan Singh Bhakna, left the USA on July 26. The party published "Declaration of War" (Ailan-i-Jung) in *Ghadar* on August 5, 1914. The first batch of Ghadarites left for India on August 19, 1914. Ram Chander[31] said, "Your duty is clear. Go to India. Stir up rebellion in every corner of India."[32]

The exodus started with alacrity. Kartar Singh Sarabha, accompanied by Vishnu Ganesh Pingle, Satya Sen, and a large number of Gadarites, reached Colombo on board SS *Salamin* on November 16, 1914.

Several thousand left the shores of California by whatever ship they could get and arrived in India to infiltrate in the army and incite them to rebel against the British Government.

The exodus began and *Portland Telegram* reported that "If exodus takes place no Indian will be left in Astoria."[33] The first group of Gadarites left the USA in a ship named *Korea* on August 19 with Kesar Singh Thathgarh, Jawala Singh Thathian, Pandit Jagat Ram, Nidhan Singh Chugha, and others. On August 22, 1914, Bhai Sher Singh Vein Bhoein left with 26 Indians. Then the number of Ghadarites who left USA and Canada after the *Komagata Maru* episode began to reach India. 2,312 Indians returned from October 12, 1914, to February 25, 1915. They went on pouring in, and their strength rose upto 8,000.[34] According to Department of Justice Records Roll No. 6 (N.A.I.) from September 5, 1914, to March 9, 1915, 1,125 reached India.[35]

About 3,125 who came via Calcutta were nabbed by Panjab Police on February 16, 1915, and out of them 2,211 were let off. According to Rowlatt Report from October 19, 1914, till December, 331 were sent to jails and 2,576 were confined to their villages.[36]

Out of 295 passengers who came through Colombo, many escaped. Those who escaped were Kartar Singh Sarabha, Harnam Singh Tindilat, Jagat Singh, Nidham Singh, Gandha Singh nee Bhagat Singh, Bibi Gulab Kaur, Kanshi Ram, and some others.

---

31 Ramchandra, Bhagwan Singh & Maulavi Barkat-Ullah were key figures in mobilizing Ghadarites for exodus to India. Later on Ram Chandra was assassinated by Ram Singh on the suspicion of being a British agent.
32 Satya M.Ray, *Punjabi Heroic Tradition* P.53
33 The Statement of Harnam Singh Tundilat.
34 Sir Michael O Dwyer, *India as I knew it*, p. 106.
35 Quoted in T.R.Sareen, *Indian Revolutionary abroad*, p.97
36 Rowlatt Report, pp. 156-160.

Lord Harding[37] gives the strength of Gadarites who came to India as 7,000, but Punjab Governor Sir Michael O'Dwyer estimated 8,000.[38] Out of them, 2,500 were arrested, 400 were sent to prisons, and about 5,000 were let off.

On reaching India, the Gadarites found that the situation was not ripe for any revolutionary activity. Many sections of the society were agog to act as stooges of the government. The Mahants of the Sikh Gurudwaras and some other Sikh organizations passed resolutions against the Gadarites.[39] They had no money nor weapons. To get these, they resorted to dacoities and robberies. The might of the government was so much that a few hundred Gadarites could not do much.

After the arrival of Rash Behari Bose at Amritsar on January 25, 1915, it was decided that after capturing the cantonments of Mian Mir and Ferozepur, mutiny was to be engineered in Ambala and Delhi. The betrayal of Kirpal Singh, who was insider and who became a mole (a police informer), led to the collapse of the movement. A large number of members were arrested on February 19, the changed date of revolt. The government also disarmed the native soldiers in the cantonments of Mian Mir, Ferozepur, etc.

After the failure of the movement, the members who had escaped arrest decided to leave India. Kartar Singh, Harnam Singh, and Jagat Singh were asked to go to Afghanistan. They did cross the Indian border, but then Kartar Singh Sarabha's conscience did not permit him to run away when all his comrades had been arrested. On March 2, 1915, he came back with two friends and reached Chak No. 5 in Sargodha and stayed with ex-soldier Risaldar Ganda Singh. He became a traitor and got arrested. The Gadarites were tried. The judgement in respect of 63 Ghadarites was pronounced on September 13, 1915, at the Central Jail Lahore, in the first conspiracy case of 1914–15. Twenty-four Gadarites were sentenced to death; Kartar Singh Sarabha was one of them. He was hanged in the Central Jail of Lahore on November 16, 1915, at the age of 19. He became the symbol of martyrdom, and many heroes of freedom were influenced from his bravery and sacrifice. The lesson of his sacrifice and the other heroes was not lost upon the succeeding events. The movements, like that of Akalis, Babbar Akalis, and Hindustan Socialist Republic Association (revolutionary party of Bhagat

---

37 Lord Harding was Viceroy of India from 1910 to 1915.
38 Sir Michael O Dwyer, *India as I knew it*, p.200.
39 Teja Singh, Gurudwara Reform Movement and the Sikh awakening, p.v. (Foreword)

Singh and others), were deeply influenced by the Ghadar Movement. Of all movements, the Ghadarites strove hard to realize their dreams by participating in Babbar Akali Lehar. The Ghadarites who returned to Punjab and were not nabbed by the authorities were mostly Sikhs and belonged to the Central Punjab. Their source of inspiration was exclusively Sikh Lore and History to fight against tyranny of this kind, which was the duty of a true Sikh.

The Sikh heritage of struggle was presented in terms of a struggle for liberation substituting the Khalsa Panth by the country.[40] A veteran journalist, the late Patwant Singh, also echoed this view when he wrote that the clash of the Sikhs against the British Government during the Ghadar Movement remains etched in the collective memory of the Sikhs.[41]

If we look the events of Panjab History with acute accuracy, then we will find a great similarity in Gadar and Babbar Akali Movement. Babbar Akali Movement was outcome of Akali Movement in its conception and origin, yet it was an extension of the Gadar Movement in its objectives and modus operandi. Ironically and surprisingly, both failed in their immediate objectives due to lack of secrecy, hasty actions, treachery of insiders, and the paucity of resources.

Such revolutionary movements need long preparedness to succeed, but in these cases, both movements ran into wilderness. Of course, they made their impact and ultimately were helpful in bringing the country closer to the reality of Independence.

Gadarite Dreams, Babbar Akali Lehar, and reality of Independence are different segments of the same structure. One gave strength to the other. Briefly, each movement stirred the people and spurred them to achieve the goal of independence.

After the failure of the Ghadar Movement, the Sikhs came into conflict with the government over the issue of the Gurudwaras. The Gurudwaras belonged to the Sikh Community and the Mahants were simply the custodians, but they had begun to grab proprietary rights. They began to exercise personal rights in the endowments, and the resultant accumulation of wealth led to the deterioration of their character. These men were becoming unacceptable to the community. Their baptism and five symbols became a mere anomaly.[42]

---

40 Dr. J.S.Grewal, *The Sikhs of the Punjab*, P.156
41 Patwant Singh, *The Sikhs*, P.189
42 Teja Singh, *Gurudwara Reform Movement and the Sikh awakening*, p.34

The British sided with the Mahants because they never wanted the Sikhs to be the masters of their gurudwaras. A letter of Lietunant R. E. Eagerton, written to the Viceroy of India.

Lord of Ripon on August 8, 1881, showed them in their true colors. He wrote, "I think it would be politically dangerous to allow the management of the Sikh temples to fall into the hands of the committee emancipated from government control."[43]

The British Government went on honeymooning with the moderate Sikhs and also lured jat Sikhs by offering liberal recruitments in the army, but it all came to an end when the government committed blunders by interfering in Sikh Gurudwara affairs by crushing Gadarites and getting them excommunicated from the fold of Sikhism.[44] The Mahants also gave Siropa to Sir Michael O'Dwyer, Lieutenant Governor of the Punjab, and offered Kirpan (Sword of Honor) to General Dyer, the butcher of Jallianwala Bag Tragedy leading to 379 deaths.

The Mahants had degenerated and disgraced themselves in the eyes of the Sikhs by their role as sychophants of the British.[45]

The Sikhs wanted to wrest control from the Mahants by conciliation and compromise, peacefully and non-violently. To them, the liberation of Gurudwaras was as important as the Khilafat Movement was to Mohammedans. Swaraj, to them, included in its concept the liberation of the Gurudwaras. The Mahants on the instigation and overt and covert support of the government defied the Sikhs. Such a situation could not be tolerated indefinitely.[46]

It was on December 14, 1920, that the Shiromani Akali Dal was formed to assist the Shiromani Gurudawara Parbandhak Committee formed earlier on November 15, 1920. It was a prelude of the coming struggle for the control of Gurudwaras. The Akali Dal sent Jathas to different Gurudwaras, captured, and handed them over to the SGPC. The Gurudwaras like Babe Di Ber (Sialkot) Gurudwaras Bhai Joga Singh (Peshawar), Panja Sahib, and CHOLA Sahib passed into the hands of the Sikhs. All this happened peacefully, but the Akali zealots had their baptism of fire at Tarantaran on January

---

43 Quoted by H.S.Dilgir; Shiromani Akali Dal
44 Teja Singh, *Gurudwara Reform Movement and the Sikh Awakening*, p.V
45 Gulati, K.C., *The Akalis Past and Present*
46 Akali Te Pardesi, Amritsar, Oct. 22, 1922

25, 1921, when the two Akalis fell victim to the priestly aggression.[47] It was only a prelude to what happened at Nankana Sahib, in which 130 persons were killed.[48]

The Sikhs now realized that they would be able to oust the Mahants only if the government was compelled to withdraw its support of the latter. The Nankana tragedy had drawn the line. The Punjab government sided with the Mahants, and the Akalis drew sustenance from national forces. Indian National Congress and Mahatma Gandhi supported Gurudwara Reform Movement. The struggle continued leading to the Key-Morcha and Guru Ka Bagh Morcha in which the Sikhs came out victorious. When the government was compelled to hand over the keys of the Tosakhana of Darbar Sahib to the President of SGPC, (Baba) Kharak Singh Gandhiji congratulated him and called it the first victory of the freedom movement.

Thus, the Sikhs won, "First Decisive Battle for India's freedom."[49] In the key affair, the Punjab government had to eat a humble pie before the Shiromani Parbandhak Committee.

To retrieve its prestige lost in the key affair, the government committed another folly by taking the side of Mahant Sunder Dass of Guru Ka Bagh. The Sikhs launched a non-violent struggle. They offered themselves for arrest on August 9, 1922, and the arrests continued up to November 17, bringing the total number of arrests up to 5,605. The government failed to cowdown the non-violent Akalis. The police beat the Akalis with iron-tipped rods and batons till blood began to flow and the brave Sikhs fell unconscious. M. R. Jayakar wrote that it was a new heroism steeled by suffering, a war of spirit.[50] The Akalis had undergone their baptism of fire but won in the end, leading to the passage of Sikh Gurudwara Bill.

But there were a number of Akalis who lost faith in non-violence. They were in favor of punishing those who were responsible for the Nankana tragedy. They cherished the memories of the courage and bravery of the Ghadarites. They ridiculed the Gandhian policy of passive resistance.[51] Kishen Singh Gargaj asked SGPC Secretary Bhagat Jaswant Singh and sent a

---

47 Giani Pratap Singh, *Gurudwar Sudhar Arthat Akalai Lehar*, p. 96
48 Gurbax Singh Jhabalia, *Sahidi Jiwan*, p.573 gives a list of 86 Sikhs, but government report conceded 130 killed, vide Punjab Legislature Council debated, p. 304.
49 Ganda Singh, *Some confidential Papers of the Akali Movement*, p.11
50 Jayakar, M.R., *The story of my Life*, Vol. II 1922-25, New York, 1959, pp.34-35.
51 Partap Singh, *Gurudwara Sudhar Arthat Akali Lehar*, p.135.

letter asking him to make recourse to the sword. No doubt, the Babbar Akali morcha took its final shape during the Guru ka Bagh Morcha.

A large number of ex-Gadarites became active Babars, including Karam Singh Daulatpur, Karam Singh and Kartar Singh Jhingar, Baba Karam Singh Cheema, Bhag Singh Canadian, Assa Singh of Bhugrudi, Kartar Singh Pindori Nijjaran, Hari Singh Sundh, Piara Singh Langheri, Battan Singh Kahri Sahri, Partap Singh Kot Fatuhi, and many others. Some were active as members of the Jathas, while others were symphathisers and well-wishers. The ex-Ghadrites were powder keg, and they turned out to be the leaders of the Babbar Akali Jatha.[52] Even Sir Michael O'Dwyer considered these Ghadrites the nucleus of the new revolutionary movement of the Akali Sikhs.[53]

Thus, it is clear that a large number of emigrants from North America, whose enthusiasm had not yet languished, living in Doaba Bist, Jalandhar, gave new color to the peaceful Akali Movement. Thus, the Babbar Akali Movement came into existence when the Gurudwara Reform Movement was passing through a crucial stage.

The movement took place during the years 1921 to 1925. The Babbar Akalis made their first appearance during the Sikh Educational Conference held at Hoshiarpur from March 15 to 27, 1921, after Nankana holocaust.[54] Some radicals led by Master Mota Singh and Kishen Singh Gargaj, a retired Havildar of the Indian Army, held a secret meeting and made up a plan to avenge themselves upon those who were responsible for the killings at Nankana Sahib. It was generally felt that Mr. C. M. King, Commissioner of Police, Mahantas Devi Dass, Basant Dass Sunder Singh Majithia, and Baba Kartar Singh Bedi, who were responsible for the massacre, be taught a lesson. For this purpose, Bela Singh and Ganda Singh were sent to Lahore to eliminate Mr. J. W. Bowring. They were suspected by the police at Lahore Railway Station and arrested on May 23, 1921. During interrogation, the two let out the secrets, leading to the arrests of Amar Singh, Narain Singh, Tota Singh, Chattar Singh, Chanchal Singh, and many others. Warrants were issued for the arrest of Master Mota Singh, Bijla Singh, and Kishan Singh. They had managed to dodge the police. They became fugitive. Kishan Singh Gargaj formed a secret organization called the Chakarwati Jatha and started

---

52 Labh Singh Jassowal, *Sankhep Itihas Babbar Akali*, Hoshiarpur, 1962, p.1
53 O'Dwyer, *India as I knew it*, p.209
54 Charan Singh, The work of the Sikh Education Conference, 1944, p.26, Akali Lahore, March 31, 1921 p.4. the date of 19-21 March are not correct.

working among the peasantry and soldiers inciting them against the government. While Master Mota Singh was arrested from his village on June 16, 1922, Kishan Singh and his band carried on the campaign in Jalandhar district and neighboring areas of Hoshiarpur with the frequent incursions in the district of Ambala, Sangrur, and state of Kapurthala.

In his itinerary and campaign of awakening the people, he delivered 327 speeches against the British Government. His poems and articles in the various newspapers brought an awakening in the people of Doaba. At the same time, Karam Singh, an ex-ghadrite, orgnized a band of extremists in Hoshiarpur district around Nawanshahar on similar lines. Towards the end of August 1922, the two jathas were merged and the organization came to be called Babbar Akali Jatha. Kishen Singh was chosen President, Dalip Singh Gossal, Karam Singh Jhingar, and Babu Santa Singh were appointed Secretary, Joint Secretary, and Treasurer respectively.

Another top most leader, S. Karam Singh Daulatpur, was authorized to bring out the Akhbar Babbar Akali Doaba. The formation of this Jatha took place at Rajowal (district Hoshiarpur) in the hermitage of Sant Thakur Singh.[55]

It is pertinent to note that the main centers of Babbar activities were Gurudwaras or Kutiyas such as Kutiya (Hermitage) of Kartar Singh at Pragpur near Birring (Village of Kishen Singh Gargaj) Gurudwara Kishanpura where Sant Mitsingh lived, Kutiya of Sant Thakur Singh at Rajowal, where Jassowal lived, and Kutiya of Sant Charan Singh in Jassowal. The main centers of Babbar activity were Pindori Nijjaran, Rajowal, Jaswal, and Patara (Village of Master Mota Singh). As the Gadarites started their work by forming the Pacific Coast Khalsa Diwan Society Stockton and Stockton Gurudwara became a nucleus of the Gadar program, so were the Gurudwaras in the Babbar Akali Movement.

The whole of the Doaba was practically humming with the Diwans held by them. The participants in the different cases belonged to no fewer than 110 villages, whereas the people of more than 60 villages harbored the Babbar Akali on various occasions.[56]

Under the leadership of Kishen Singh, Babbar Akalis became a force to reckon with till his arrest on February 26, 1923, due to the perfidy of a confidant. The Babbars were very active during 1921–25 and were at the

---

55 Dr. G.S.Aulakh, *A concise History of the Sikhs*, (Men and Movements) p.189
56 Maksuspuri, .S.S, *Ithihas Babbar Akali Lehar*, pp. 295-97

height of their glory in 1922 and 23. They challenged the leaders of Akali Movement to follow a policy of violence and give up the kneed policy for the liberation of the Gurudwaras. They were out to paralyze the supporters of the British Government, such as Zaildars, Sufed Poshes Lambardars, Patwaris and police-informers, and other toadies. Accordingly an attempt was made to take care of Arjan Singh Patwari of Haripur who had alledgedly helped the arrest of Master Mota Singh. Zaildar Bishan Singh of Rani Thus, a retired official of the Canal Department, was shot dead on February 23, 1923.

The activities of the Babbars alarmed the government. It announced rewards for the arrest of the Babbars. The toadies became very active, and due to the information supplied by them, Babbars like Sunder Singh, Master Mota Singh and Jathedar Kishen Singh were caught in their snare. The arrest of these leaders actuated the rest of the Babbars to chalkout a program of eliminating the supporters of the government. The government published rewards for the arrest of the Babbars, and the Babbars offered their names taking responsibility of the murders. A game of hide and seek was on.

Consequently, a series of continuous eliminations took place. Buta Singh Lambaradar and his grandson were killed in his village, Nangal Shamman, on March 11, 1923. On March 19, Labh Singh, an employee of the Police Training School Phillaur, was killed on March 27, 1923. On April 17, ex-subedar Genda Singh was shot dead in his village Ghurial. They killed Diwan of Hayatpur on May 20, 1923, and Atta Mohammad Patwari on June 6, 1923.

At that time, the British Government considered every Akali a Babbar Akali. The number of committed Babbars was only about 500 or so, yet their activities sent a shiver in the supina of the British Government.[57] Even the members in the British Parliament like Sir Charles Yates, Lt. Colonel Howard, and Hope Simpson gave the Government many anxious moments. On June 4, 1923, Sir Charles Yates urged the British Government in Parliament to merge Doaba with some native state if the Government was unable to put down the Babbar terrorists.[58] Again on June 14, 1923, the seriousness of the Babbar Akali Movement was felt and the motion was tabled. Upon pressure of the British Parliament, the Babbar hideouts were raided. The raids were carried out in Pandori Nijjaran, Kishanpura, Jassowal, Paragpur, Kot Fatuhi, and Daulatpur. As a result, 186 arrests were made. During this period, the

---

57 Labh Singh Jassowal, *Tawarikh Babbar Akali*, p.12 gives the number as 55 thousands where as Teja Singh, *Arsi*, published in 1958, gives their number as 40000.
58 Dr. G.S.Aulakh, *A concise History of the Sikhs*, (Men & Movements) p.191

Babbars performed some rare feats of daring and self-sacrifice. Among these daring encounters, one took place on August 31, 1923, in which Karam Singh, Editor of *Babbar Akali*, Udey Singh, Bishen Singh, and Mohinder Singh were killed due to the betrayal of Anup Singh Manko. On October 25, 1923, Dhanna Singh Behabalpur exploded a bomb, leading to the death of nine policemen, wounding A. F. Harton S.P. and A.S.P. W. H. P. Jenkins, who died subsequently on November 3, 1923, at Hoshiarpur and at Calcutta respectively.[59] On December 12, 1923, Banta Singh Dhamian and Jawala Singh were killed at Munder in an encounter with the police.

Waryam Singh Dhugga, who escaped from Munder, was killed at Chak No. 54, Lyallpur, in an encounter with the police headed by S.P. Degale. It was a befitting finale of the Babbar heroism.

The Babbar Movement lingered on till 1944, but by 1925, it was a spent force. The Congress leaders did not approve their methods, and Shiromani Gurudwara Parbandhak Committee issued Communiques appealing to the Sikhs to dissociate with the activities of the Babbars. Despite this, the Babbar Movement, like the Gaddar Movement, played historic role in bringing the goal of freedom nearer. It inspired Bhagat Singh and Udham Singh to perform glorious deeds and make supreme sacrifices. The Babbars also increased the bargaining power of the Akalis, and this compelled the government to come to terms with them.

The sacrifice of Babbar Akalis, like that of Gadarites, has become a part of History. In the main Babbar case, there were 133 alleged criminals, of whom six (Kishan Singh Gargaj, Nand Singh Ghurial, Dalipa Dhamian, Karam Singh Haripur, Dharam Singh Hayatpur, and BABU Santa Singh Chhoti Harion were hanged on February 27, 1926). In Babbar Supplementary Case, 37 persons were brought to the trial, of whom six (Banta Singh Gurusar Satlani, Gujjar Singh Dhapai, Mukand Singh Jassowal, Nikka Singh Gill, Sunder Sing Lokhe, and Alowal) were sent to gallows on February 27, 1927.

The role of the Sikhs in the struggle of India's freedom must be written in the words of gold. They were in front in every struggle, whether it was Agrarian agitation of 1907, Gadar Movement, Babbar Akali Movement, Hindustan Socialist Republican Organisation, National Congress Movement, or Indian National Army led by Subash.

Out of 2,175 Indian martyrs for freedom, 1,557 were Sikhs. Out of 2,646 sent to Andaman Islands for life imprisonment, 2,147 were Sikhs. Out of

---

59 Maksuspuri, S.S., *Babbar Akali Lehar*, p.192

127 Indians who were hanged, 92 were Sikhs. Out of 20,000 who joined INA, 12,000 were Sikhs. And the Sikhs constitute only 2% of India's total population.[60]

Gadarites dreams were realized to some extent in Babbar Akali Lehar as the latter provided continuity to the struggle. The armed struggle against the foreigners emboldened the masses, and they shook off their lassitude. Their sacrifices brought the goal of freedom nearer.

There are many who study history not merely as a warning reminder of man's follies and crimes but also as an encouraging remembrance of generative souls, thereby the past ceases to be a depressing chamber of horrors.[61]

The impact of the Gadar Movement and the realization of their dream in Babbar Akali Movement can be gauged only keeping in view the freedom struggle. The impact of these on national leaders, on national politics, as well as on Punjab History cannot be underestimated.

It has brought home to us that to realize the dream of freedom, the country should be free from want, misery, and squalor.

The Gadarites went abroad in search of employment to seek better living. But they were disappointed as they could not get equal treatment. They fought against discrimination. When they returned home and entered into the ranks of Babbar Akalis, they did perform daring deeds and cowed down the government and its stooges. They made selfless sacrifices for the liberation of the country.

When they failed to realize their dreams, their brethren Gadarites in America, though disappointed, appreciated their role. They truly regarded Babbar Movement as an extension and continuation of the Gadar Movement. Giani Harnam Singh of Khalsa Diwan Society Vancouver eulogized the exploits of Babbar Akalis and collected subscription for their relief in May 1926. Sammund Singh of Khalsa Diwan Society condemned the British Government for the repression of Babbars in a letter written on April 5, 1926.

The Secretary of the Pacific Coast Khalsa Diwan, Stockton, Ajmer Singh, delivered a warning to the toadies. The Sikhs in America sent Rs. 37000/- for the relief of Babbar Akalis and their families.

It gave many sleepless nights as the Babbar Movement had transcended national frontiers. The letters written by Giani Harnam Singh to Gurdit Singh of *Komagata Maru* fame, "Desh Sewak," and "Babbar Sher" were

---

60 Rajinder Puri, *Recovery of India*, p.100
61 Will Durant, *The Lesson of History*

intercepted by the CID in August 1926. The activities of the Khalsa Diwan Society Victoria, Doaba Press Society were considered the beginning of the new "Babbar Akali cult."[62]

This assumption of the CID leaves no doubt that the Gadar Movement played a significant role in the rise of the Babbar Akali Movement. Perhaps Gadarites were making bid to realize their dreams. When the Babbars, like Gadarites, too failed, their dreams could not be realized.

But it is naive to say that they failed. On the contrary, they lit a torch for many courageous souls, like Bhagat Singh and Subhash Chander Bose, who put new life into a listless nation. Their activities brought the goal of freedom nearer, and it enabled the Indian Congress to wear the crown of glory. But for them, the reality of the Independence Movement could have been elusive.

Now Free India cannot claim to have fulfilled the dreams of the Babbars and Gadarites. When India becomes a land of plenty, every able-bodied person gets employment and does not hanker after passports, then and only then, the dream of Gadarites would be realized and reality of Independence visualized and achieved.

These dreams become true only when the home government makes India fascinating for her sons and daughters living in foreign lands. Only then, the dream of the Gadarites would become a reality.

---

62 Home – Political Tele No. 200/1926 p.12

Bibliography

Aulakh, G.S. (Dr.) 1988, Babbar Kav Sangrah (Pbi) Panjabi University, Patiala,2001: Babbar Akali Movement, National Book, Delhi.1994; Veer Naik Kartar Singh Sarabha, Panjabi University, Patiala.2010A concise History of the Sikhs (Men and Movements, 1469-2009) B.Chittar Singh, Jiwan Singh, Amritsar'

Barrier, N.G. 1970, The Sikhs and their sacred Literature, Manohar Book Service, New Delhi The Punjab Disturbances of 1907 Jiwan Sangram. Bhakna Sohan Singh, Jiwan Sangram

Bilga, Bhagat Singh, 1989, Gadar Lehar De Unfrole Varkey, D.B.Y.C. Jallandhar

Charan Singh 1944, The work of Sikh Education and Darbara Singh, Conference, Amritsar.

Grewal, J.S.(Dr.) 1994, The Sikhs of the Panjab Cambridge University Press

Gulati, K.C.(Dr.) 1974, The Akalis, Past and Present, Asha Janak Publications, Delhi

Harbans Singh, 1983, The Heritage of the Sikhs, Delhi.

Jayakar, M.R., 1959, The Story of my Life, New York.

Jagjit Singh, 1979, Gadar Party Lehar, Delhi.

Jass, Jaswant Singh, 1969, Baba Sohan Singh Bhakna, Jallandhar

Jhabalia Gurubux Singh, 1938, Sahidi Jiwan, Nankana.

Josh, Sohan Singh, 1976, Hindustan Gadar Party, New Delhi.

Khushwant Singh, 2005, A History of the Sikhs, Oxford University Press.

Makhsuspuri, .S.S, 1970, Ithihas Babbar Akali Lehar, Amritsar.

Nahar Singh, 1969, Documents relating to Bhai Maharaj Singh, Karamsar.

O'Dwyer, Sir Charles, Michael, 1925, India as I knew it.

Pannikar K.M., The Problem Of Greater India.

Partap Singh Giani, 1976, Gurudwara Sudhar Arthat Akali Lehar, Amritsar.

Patwant Singh, 1999, The Sikhs, Delhi.

Rajinder Puri, Recovery of India.

Ray, S.M., 1970, Panjabi Heroic Tradition, Patiala.

Sahensana, G.S., 1961, Gadar Party Da Ithihas, Jallandhar.

Teja Singh, 1922, The Gurudwara Reform Movement and Sikh Awakening, Jallandhar.

Waiz, S.A., 1958, Arri, Amritsar.

Will Durant, The Lessons of History.

Miscellaneous

Akali Lehar, March 31, 1921.
Akali Te Pardesi, Oct. 22, 1922, Amritsar.
Gadar De Goonj.
Modern Asian Studies, Vol. I, 1967.
Rowlatt Act.
Statements of Baba Sihan Singh Bhakna, D. Chanchiah and Harnam Singh Tundilat.

Ghadar Movement: Its Origin and Impact on Jallianwala Bagh Massacre and Indian Freedom Struggle

Dr. Tarlochan Singh Nahal

The purpose of this paper is to shed light on the Ghadar Movement, the Jallianawala Bagh massacre, and their impact on the Indian freedom movement. These events played a significant role in shaping various political and religious movements in Punjab which led to the freedom of India. The Ghadar movement originated in 1912 out of discontent, injustice, and discrimination against the Sikh/Indian immigrants in the USA who came to North America to seek better life.

The Jallianawala Bagh massacre occurred because people opposed the oppressive and draconian Rowlatt Bills which gave almost unlimited power to the British police and authorities to arrest anyone and send them to jail for any reason or no reason, without following proper legal procedures. It was an oppressive act which was passed primarily to suppress the demand for freedom of India. A martial law was declared and announcements were made by banging a tin in different parts of Amritsar on that doomed day which warned people not to gather. Most people who gathered at the Jallianwala Bagh had come from many neighboring villages to participate in the Vaisakhi celebrations. Jallianawala Bagh was a 6–7 acre open area, which was walled from all sides except for five entrances. Four of them were quite narrow, admitting only a few people at one time. Jallianwala Bagh is only few hundred yards from the Golden Temple, which is the most sacred Sikh shrine in India. Khalsa was established on the Vaisakhi day by the tenth Guru of the Sikhs—Guru Gobind Singh. It is also a major festival in Punjab celebrated by all communities. Most people were not even aware of any such announcements. Many of them had gathered over there because of a call from the Indian National Congress party in order to protest the Rowlatt Bills commonly known as Rowlatt Act. People gathered peacefully at a place called Jallianwala Bagh at Amritsar and were listening to speeches by various leaders. They were massacred by the British Indian army led by General Reginald Dyer by blocking all the entry and exit gates and opening fire. This took place on April 13, 1919, at Amritsar.

Regardless of how these events unfolded, the fundamental reason behind them was the India's slavery of the British.

Sikh Emigration to Canada and US

In order to understand the Ghadar movement, it is important to understand its underlying reasons. The Sikhs and other Indians came to Canada and the US for better life and opportunities for themselves and their families. The agricultural land was being subdivided into smaller landholdings, and it was becoming more and more difficult to survive on smaller pieces of land. In order to fund their own lavish lifestyle in India and Great Britain and to fund WWI, the British Indian government levied heavy taxes which were getting heavier for a common person. Emigration to other countries was a good way of improving one's financial status, because the pay was much higher in other countries. They did not have any political agenda at that time. Most of them were Sikhs who were marginal farmers and artisans in Punjab. There was a series of droughts in Punjab after the British took over Punjab. Many Sikh farmers had lost quite a bit of their ancestral lands to Hindu moneylenders and were in financial trouble. Drought and failed crops had sapped the energies of the general population and of farmers.

Punjabis had heard about better opportunities abroad and, by their very enterprising nature, were not afraid to take risks. Most immigrants from India who came to Canada and the US were Sikhs. They started to come to Canada as laborers and semi-skilled workers towards the end of the 19th century and in the beginning of the 20th century. Many of them were former soldiers in the British army in India, Singapore, and Hong Kong. However, they had never even imagined that, being part of the British colonial Empire, they would face discrimination, inequity, and injustice on foreign lands, because Great Britain had announced that all subjects would be treated on equal basis in all its colonies. They experienced discrimination firsthand in Canada and the US. The US was the former British colony over which the British held a significant sway. Thus, the Sikh discontent and the Ghadar movement grew out of discrimination and humiliation in foreign lands. Their "King Emperor" did precious little to alleviate their misery.

The first Sikhs ever to enter Canada were on an official trip as part of the Hong Kong army regiments which were traveling through Canada in commemoration of Queen Victoria of England's Diamond Jubilee in 1897. They liked the land and vastness of the country, and some of them stayed there and invited their relatives and friends.

Things went unnoticed until about 1906. However, when the Sikhs started to emigrate to Canada in more noticeable numbers, the Canadian government wanted to stop their emigration to Canada. In fact, it wanted to get rid of the Indians who were already there and tried to force them to move to British Honduras (now an independent and almost a tiny, third-world country known as Belize).

A religious function was held at the second floor of Gurdwara Sahib Vancouver to discuss this situation. An Indian delegation of two Sikhs named Bhai Nagar Singh and Bhai Sham Singh Rajput were selected to go to British Honduras for a fact-finding mission. They were instructed to write a signed letter daily from that country describing full details, circumstances, climate, and labor situation at every stay of their journey to the Chief Khalsa Diwan. These two individuals were most reliable and honest people who knew English well.

This delegation went to British Honduras and found out that the climatic conditions were very poor, wages were too low, and some Indian families over there were living in miserable conditions and in abject poverty. There was a great danger of malaria and yellow fever. The Indian delegation did not agree to move to Honduras in spite of great pressure and financial lure by the Canadian government.

The seed of discontent that manifested itself as the Ghadar movement in the US was actually sown in Canada as early as 1907 with the establishment of Khalsa Diwan Society in Vancouver. It provided a place of worship, communal consciousness, rallying point, and even practical help by providing food, housing, and legal assistance. This was the place where the Sikhs discussed their issues and took important community decisions. Most of them worked in the lumber mills, at construction, and on farms where they often encountered jealousy, racial slurs, and even physical attacks from the white people. In 1907, racial riots broke out in Bellingham, about 20 miles south of the Canadian border in Washington state. All the Sikhs and Indians were driven from their homes by the white mobs. All of these factors solidified the unity of the Indians regardless of their faith. A similar episode happened in Marysville near Yuba City in California in 1908.

"Twenty citizens of Live Oak Saturday night attacked two housed occupied by seventy Hindus who had been discharged from Southern Pacific Company and ordered the Hindus to leave town.

"The Hindus were driven to the edge of the town and told to travel. One went to Yuba City and swore to complaints charging the members of the mob with stealing $1950. He also took the case to the British Consul at San Francisco."

The Indians were not allowed to bring their wives and children to Canada. To make things even more difficult, the Canadian government came up with another plan to keep the Indians out. They used a three-prong approach:

1. Put a condition on all immigrants that their sea voyage should be direct and continuous from India and they must not change the ship at any port between India and Canada.
2. Made it mandatory for each passenger coming from India to show $200 cash.
3. Worked up the Canadian public against the Indians and spread hatred against them. That put a great stress on them and their families and created hatred towards them in the minds of the majority white community.

A Canadian immigration law was specially designed to keep the Indians out because there was no direct ship voyage from India to Canada. Most people could not afford to show $200 for each family member, which was a very large sum over 100 years ago. The *Komagata Maru* ship incident of 1914 is a textbook example of such extremely biased and unfair treatment of the Indians. The *Komagata Maru* was a Japanese ship which was hired and renamed "*Guru Nanak Jahaj*" by Gurdit Singh in 1914 to bring the Indian passengers to Canada.

According to Baba Sohan Singh Bhakna, "Bhai Sahib [Gudit Singh] hired the Komagata Maru (Guru Nanak Jahaj), a Japanese ship for six or more months and directly reached from the port of Calcutta to Vancounver." According to some other accounts, the *Komagata Maru* sailed from Hong Kong to Shanghai, Yokohama, and then to Vancouver, British Columbia, as per plan. 376 travelers on the ship were Indians, out of which 340 were the Sikhs, 24 Muslims, and 12 Hindus. The *Komagata Maru* ship was not allowed to dock at the Canadian shore and was forcibly returned to India from Vancouver. When the ship reached at Calcutta, India, at the Baj Baj *ghat*, about 17 km from the Calcutta port, a train was waiting for the passengers to take them directly to Punjab. The Sikh insisted upon depositing their holy book *Sri Guru Granth Sahib* to a local Gurdwara and many of them did not want to go back to Punjab. They were fired upon by the police. As a result many people were injured and killed. This incident gave boost the Ghadar party and its cause.

Sikh Emigration to the US

The Sikhs started to emigrate to the United States of America well over 100 years ago. *San Francisco Chronicle* writes, "The four Sikhs who arrived on the Nippon Maru the other day were permitted yesterday to land by the immigration officials. The quartet formed the most picturesque group that has been seen on the Pacific Mall dock for many a day. One of them, Bakkshlled [sic] Singh, speaks English with fluency, the others just a little. They are all fine-looking men, Bakkshlled Singh in particular being a marvel of physical beauty. He stands 6 feet 2 inches and is built in proportion. His companions-Bood [sic] Singh, Variam [sic] Singh and Sohava Singh-are not quite so big. All of them have been soldiers and policemen in China. They were in the Royal Artillery, and the tall one with the unpronounceable name was a police sergeant in Hong Kong prior to coming to this country. They hope to make their fortunes here and return to their homes in the Lahore district, which they left some twenty years ago."

World War I had just ended in 1918, and India, especially Punjab, paid a hefty price both in terms of human lives lost and money spent on the war. At least 400,000 Punjabis were forced to go to war in various parts of the world. A large number of them died in different theatres of war. Even though the original Ghadar movement started and ended before the Jallianwala Bagh massacre, it continued to shape various political events in Punjab. The Ghadar movement had a major impact on various Sikh Morchas (agitations) in Punjab in the 1920s and gave rise to the Babbar Akali movement which had a significant impact in the Doaba region (Jalandhar, Kapurthala, and Hoshiarpur districts) of Punjab. The Sikh lost hundreds of people in those *morchas*. The Ghadar movement peaked with the murder of Michael O'Dwyer at Caxton Hall in London on March 13, 1940, who was the former Lt. Governor of Punjab. (It was he who had ordered the massacre of the Punjabis at Jallianwala Bagh). Both these events created political turbulence that had worldwide consequences. Both these events shook the very foundation of the British Empire in India.

Figure 1. Michael Francis O'Dwyer (Lt. Governor of Punjab 1912–1919)

Babbar Akali movement was a great threat to the British Indian government after the Ghadar movement. The government was acutely aware of the hostilities of the Canadian Sikhs towards the government for executing many Babbar Akalis. This is evident from a letter written to His Magesty's Under Secretary of State for India by H. G. Haig, Officiating Secretary to the Government of India:

"In May last a letter written by one Giani Harnam Singh of the Khalsa Diwan Society, Vancouver, to a Sikh newspaper in Amritsar, Punjab was intercepted. This letter described the proceeding of the Diwan of the Society held at Vancouver in the preceding March. At that meeting Resolutions were passed expressing sympathy with the families of the executed Babbar Akalis, condemning the actions of the Punjab Government and calling upon Sikhs to help the families. . . . 5. In the opinion of the Government of India the interest in the Babbar Akali spirit displayed by Sikhs in Canada and America points to a general revival of the seditious activity among the Sikhs in those countries which was originally associated what is known as Ghadr movement."

Figure 2. Brigadier General Reginald Dyer

"Hindu" Discrimination in California

According to the official report to Gov. W. D. Stephens, called "California and the Oriental," published by State Board of Control of California in 1922, makes these comments about the Hindus, (as all Indians were called black then):

"The Hindu, in the opinion of the Commissioner of the State Bureau of Labor Statistics, is the most undesirable immigrant in the state. His lack of personal cleanliness, his low morals and his blind adherence to theories and teachings, so entirely repugnant to American principles, make him unfit for association with American people. These references apply to the low caste Hindu or Sikhs. Reports from official authorities concerning these people on file in the office in the State Board of Control are unfit for publication."

This statement smacks of pure racism and bias against Sikhs and other persons of India.

The State Board of Control of California report paints a dismal picture of the "Hindus" in California. A letter written by Shaughnessy and Atherton Attorneys at Law of Stockton, California (counsel for the Hindus in California), dated February 16, 1920, to State Board of Control in Sacramento says,

"The number of Hindus in California is fast decreasing. About five hundred of them have left for India the last year. A rough estimation of their distribution over this state is given below:

Sikhs	2000	Imperial Valley	300
Mohammadens	500	Sacramento County	500
Hindus	100	Around Willows	600
Total	2,600	San Joaquin County	300
		Fresno County	300
		Scattered	600
		Total	2,600

You are familiar, of course, with the fact that none of them are now permitted to enter the United States; and none of them have been permitted to bring wives and children here and a very few of them have married here."

According to this report, there were about 77% Sikhs, 19.2% Muslims, and only 3.8% Hindus in California in 1922. Even though this report is prepared primarily against the growing influence and presence of the Oriental immigrants, especially the Japanese, it was the Sikhs who were the primary victims.

The report makes extremely derogatory comments about the Hindus and Sikhs and says, "The Hindu has no morals . . . The low caste Hindus and Sikhs not eligible to citizenship in the United States, but in a very few cases natives of India of high caste have proven to the satisfaction of the courts their Caucasian blood and have been admitted to citizenship . . . One investigator for the State Board of Control state that Hindus, although ineligible to citizenship and therefore not entitled to legal ownership of land under the California alien land act, nevertheless own many parcels of land in California and are purchasing more land."

This document shows how the racial bias and caste system propagated by the Brahmanism in India found its way to the US government and how it was used to determine the eligibility for granting citizenship.

While the Indians were prohibited from bringing their wives and children from India, a wave of "picture brides" were arriving from Japan in large numbers. Many Japanese marriages were initiated by the exchange of photographs between the parties. Usually, a young man from the US would send a picture to his parents and they would take it to the parents of a prospective bride and negotiate a marriage. When both parties agreed, immigration papers were initiated and visa was issued to the "picture bride" to come to the United States. The marriage was often consummated at the arriving dock with a marriage ceremony. This practice was approved both by the Japanese and American governments. The following table shows the number of picture brides from Japan to the US.

The figures given for the periods from July 1, 1911, to February 29, 1920, have been added by State Board of Control of California gathered at the United States Immigration Station at Angel Island, just outside San Francisco.

Picture Brides Arriving at the San Francisco Port	
July 1, 1911 to June 30, 1912	879
July 1, 1912 to June 30, 1913	625
July 1, 1913 to June 30, 1914	768
July 1, 1914 to June 30, 1915	823
July 1, 1915 to June 30, 1916	486
July 1, 1916 to June 30, 1917	504
July 1, 1917 to June 30, 1918	522
July 1, 1918 to June 30, 1919	668
July 1, 1919 to December 30, 1919	379
January 1, 1920 to February 29, 1920	95
Total 8 years, 8 months	5,749

On the other hand, there was a virtual ban on bringing wives from India. Only a handful of women from India arrived during this period, and the population of the Indian immigrants decreased rapidly and almost came near extinction by 1946.

The "Hindus" (which implies Sikhs here) came to the US and farm laborers, but due to their hard work and frugal habits, they were slowly turning from laborers to landlords. Before they were able to buy land, they started to lease it, employed other Indians and Americans, and eventually started to become landlords. They were employed in Fresno, Kings, Madera, and Tulare counties in orchards and vineyards. They were employed in Yolo County and Salinas Valley in the sugar beet farms. The *California and the Oriental* reports highlights this fact, "The number is rapidly growing less, for the change from employed to employer or lessee is rapidly placing the Hindu in the position of 'little land lord.' The Hindu will not farm poor land. He wants the best and will pay for it. Consequently the American owner who can get a big rental for his land desired the Hindu. He will pay."

Congressional Hearing Related to Indian Immigration to the US at Washington

The Indians fought hard against the repressive immigration policy of the US and used whichever avenues were open to them. A hearing took place before the Committee on Immigration in the House of Representatives (Sixty-Third Congress) on February 13, 19 and 26, 1914, and on April 16 and 30, 1914, in which the "Hindu Immigration" case was heard and decided.

Two Indians, Sudhindra Bose and Bishen Singh, submitted a letter and pleaded the case of the Indians in front of this committee on behalf of the Pacific Khalsa Dewan Society and the Hindustan Association of America on February 12, 1914. In this letter, they tried to present the Indian population in the US as the subjects of the British Government and claimed some privileges and protection under international law. They also argued that in the event such protection is not provided to them, this would create a diplomatic stalemate between those two nations. The fact is the British Government did not want to protect them because they were simply considered troublemakers. It further argued,

"At present the Hindus are the citizens of the British Empire, and have the same international civil status as the Canadians or Australasians. In international law a Hindu is protected by the British flag. Any attempts to place an important portion of the British Empire in a position of irritation with the United States would be unfortunate at this moment, as it might create another cause of diplomatic friction between the United States and Great Britain."

The fact is that there were no treaties between the US and Great Britain that would prohibit the United States from excluding Indians when it came to immigration to the US. Sudhindra Bose did try his best in answering a battery of questions in front of this powerful committee, but gauging the mood of the Committee, no answer could have ever satisfied them. This letter was perhaps written with all the good intentions, but it did not produce the desired results. Since there was a racial tension and opposition to the "Orientals" at the time who are considered to be of the Mongolian origin, the Indians wanted to differentiate themselves and argued that the Hindus are not "Mongolians." They said that the Hindus are of the Caucasian race and that their classic language, Sanskrit, points to their unmistakable kinship to all Aryan races of modern Europe.

Even though this may be technically correct in the case of the Northern Indians, it is not entirely true. Indians from the South are of Dravidian origin. This argument does not make sense from the Sikh perspective, because Sikhism believes in equality of human race. This argument was probably made due to two reasons: 1) The Indians did not want to be bracketed with Chinese and Japanese and they thought proving themselves as Caucasian race might give them some break; and 2) there might have been the influence of Brahmanism working behind such statements, because the spokesman of the Indians was Sudhindra Bose, a Hindu.

This committee had 15 members. Almost the entire committee was extremely biased against the Indians from the very beginning. Here is an excerpt from the hearing and a statement from Mr. Denver S. Church, a member of Congress (7th District) from the State of California:

"That brings me this proposition: While we can get along, yet there are 350,000,000 of them over there, and they are coming and they going to continue to come, because conditions are so bad over in their own country. It is a self-evident fact that sooner or later we will have to exclude them. Why not do it now when we are masters of the situation?

The Chairman: Have you heard of any of the leaders teaching any anarchistic ideas

Mr. Church: Of course, the Hindus down in my country, in the interior of California, are there for the purpose of getting jobs so as to earn money to send back to India. I have heard that occurs in the sections around the bay. I cannot give you any definite information as to whether they teach revolution and anarchy. There is no doubt from what I have heard that they do and that these people are acquiring all the knowledge they can do as to be in a position in the future to rebel against the form of government under which they are at the time living."

This indicates how biased the Immigration Committee in the US Congress was and how they were worried about "revolution" in India against the British, against whom the United States itself had rebelled and freed itself from the British slavery. It also indicates that the California Indian immigrants, who were predominantly Sikhs, were active in throwing the British out of India.

Ghadar Movement, Its Origin and Development

Sohan Singh Josh writes about the birth of Pacific Coast Hindustani Association,

"On some day in July 1912, the Indian mill workers gathered at Portland. Harnam Singh Kotlanaudh Singh, and some others from Bridal Veil, Pandit Kashi Ram and others from Saint John, and Bhai Sohan Singh Bhakna and others companions participated in this meeting. A decision was taken to establish Pacific Coast Hindustan Association and to open its office by renting a house. All those who were present, became its members. Bhai Sohan Singh Bhakna was appointed its president, Babu Guru Dutt was appointed its general secretary and Pandit Kashi Ram was appointed its treasurer. . . Lala Thakur Das, who was working with Pandit Kashi Ram in Saint John, suggested to President Sohan Singh Bhakna and others to invite Lala Har Dayal who lived in San Francisco, to lead this effort. This suggestion was accepted in the Portland meeting and Lala Thakur Das was given the responsibility of persuading Lala Har Dayal to accept this role."

Thus, the ground work for the solidarity of the Indians had begun in the US. One Thakur Das wrote a letter to Lala Har Dayal in 1912 to come to Oregon. "In a reply Har Dayal notified him about his visit to Saint John on December 25, during the Christmas holiday. All the friends were happy about this news that the work will now begin. However, only 3-4 days before the appointed date, they were disappointed to know that Har Dayal would not be able to make it to Saint John then, but during the last week of March 1913."

According to Baba Sohan Singh Bhakna, one of the founders of this association, "In 1912 our factory 'Lifton' was closed for one month due to Christmas holidays. So I went to a factory in Astoria where approximately 250 Indians worked. Among them Bhai Kesar Singh was highly regarded by all and they all particularly trusted him and I also stayed with him. When we discussed the pros and cons of the national independence, then we reached a conclusion that without action and sacrifice and the ability to show the results, one cannot achieve freedom. So it is important to start a national war and to prepare an army of the Indians patriots in the US which should be above communal lines, and being an Indian each of its soldier should enroll himself in it to achieve freedom for his motherland. . . . At the end, both of us decided that we should call a meeting on the coming Sunday in order to establish a society for that purpose. . . . At the end, the society was established which was called "Hindi Maha Sabha. Its president was Bhai Kesar Singh, Vice President a Muslim and I was elected the Secretary. The primary goal of this association was set "to free India after uniting all Indians into a national chain."

Thus, the "Hindi Maha Sabha," also known as "Pacific Coast Hindustan Association," was established in the city of Astoria, in the state of Oregon of the United States of America. This was later known as Ghadar Party.

According to a statement published in the *Stockton Daily Evening Record* of December 6, 1913, "International (foreign) money order to the amount of $26,282.82 were sold by the Stockton post office during the month of October. The Indians had transmitted $18,489.27 in October. Of this amount, $18,469.27 was sent to British Indian offices." This amount was sent in a single month which amounted to 70.30% of the total foreign money orders sent by the residents of 16 other countries living in the Stockton area, most of which were Europeans. The next second highest was Japan, where $3908.00 were sent. This became a cause of alarm in the US, and this issue was raised in the US Congress.

Role of Lala Har Dayal

Lala Har Dayal was born in Delhi in a Hindu "Kaisth" family in 1884. He was a brilliant student. He received his M.A. in English from Government

College Lahore and an M.A. in History the next year. Then he went to Oxford University for further studies. He came back to India in 1908 and returned to England again where he published the *Bande Matram* newspaper. According to British Intelligence documents,

"He was the cleverest of the young Indian extremists in Paris, but he was quite unbalanced in his views and much handicapped by ill health. In April 1911, he was in California and contributed to the *Modern Review* (July 1911) an excellent article on 'India in America,' giving his address as Berkeley, the suburbs of San Francisco where the University of California is situated. In 1912 he was appointed lecturer on Philosophy and Sanskrit at Stanford University."

In February 1912, he was appointed the General Secretary of the Ghadar Party and the Chief Editor of the *Ghadar* (*Ghadar Di Goonj*) newspaper. He wrote revolutionary articles in *Ghadar* which originally started in Urdu. Later, it was published in Gurmukhi and other India languages. He had lectured on anarchism at Stanford University before he joined the Pacific Coast Hindustani Association. According to Giani Wadhawa Singh, the former Granthi of Stockton Gurdwara, "After this, Lala Har Dayal did not have any correspondence or connection with the Ghadar Party. He died in Philadelphia in 1939. There is no doubt that the foundation of the Ghadar Party was laid down before he joined the party, the work of the party went on with full force after he left, but the office work that he did for the party and the work he did for the newspaper for five-and-a-half months will stay alive in the history of the Ghadar Party."

Har Dayal also addressed meetings in various towns in America in support of the Indian revolutionary movement until March 1914. Then he was arrested by the authorities of the United States Government, with a view to his deportation as an undesirable alien. Released on bail, he escaped to Switzerland possibly with the help of the Ghadar party. After the war broke out, he joined the Indian National Party, which worked in Berlin under the directions of the German Foreign Office. It seems like his love affair with Germany did not last long. In his book, he described his experiences and the reasons that have led him to change his attitude towards British rule in India. Har Dayal writes, "The history of Germany during the last fifty years may be described as the tragedy of a whole society. This nation is utterly sick in head and heart. It has lost its wits, and it has killed its conscience. 'Whom the gods destroy, they first make mad.' It will take a very long time to restore this demented and demoralised people to health and sanity."

Har Dayal almost became a mouthpiece of the British Government in his later years. He expressed that England had been in the field of creating colonies and France was not far behind. Thus, it was a good idea to support them in their endeavor and cooperate with them. He writes, "Among European nations, England has been already in the field for a century, and France has also acquired vast dependencies in Asia and Africa. It is; therefore, wise to co-operate with these nations for the establishment and continuance of good government in Asiatic countries, whatever colour the flag may have."

In short, he propagated perpetual slavery of India and all the other nations colonized by Great Britain and France. After reading this statement, one wonders what kind of mindset he possessed and why he flip-flopped on independence of India and other slave nations. His book leaves little doubt that he was in league with the British intelligence.

Here are the views of Michael O'Dwyer about Lala Har Dayal:

"He arrived in the United States early in 1911, and established himself at Berkeley, California, where seditious movement had been at work for some years to corrupt the Indian immigrants, chiefly Sikhs, of whom several thousand had settled since 1907 along the Pacific coast from Vancouver to San Francisco.

Har Dayal found the ground prepared and at once set to work to sow the seed. . . . The infamous Ghadar newspaper, which openly incited to murder and mutiny and urged all Indians to return to India with express object of murdering the British and causing revolution by any and every means, was started by Har Dayal in 1913."

Ghadar Party published the first issue of *Ghadar di Gunj* (Echo of Mutiny) in November 1913. Kartar Singh Sarabha wrote in the first issue: "Today there begins 'Ghadar' in foreign lands, but in our country's tongue, a war against the British Raj. What is our name? Ghadar. What is our work? Ghadar. Where will be the Revolution? In India. The time will soon come when rifles and blood will take the place of pens and ink."

Modern Hindu historians, especially those under the influence of the Hindu nationalist BJP (Bhartiya Janata Party) give much credit to people like Har Dyal to push their Hindutiva agenda. He worked with the Gadharites for less than six months. He seemed to have revolutionary ideas and played an important role in the formation of the Ghadar movement in its initial phase. However, he did not stick with the Ghadar ideology very long and made an about turn soon after he left the United States. His views and deeds are at variance. On the other hand, the Sikh Ghadarites fought fearlessly, and their commitment to the Ghadar movement was unflinching. There were some Hindu and Muslim Ghadarites like Rash Bihari Bose, V. G. Pingle, Sachindranath Sanyal, and Maulana Barkatulla who fought with great passion and paid a heavy price.

Khushwant Singh, while paying a tribute to Har Dyal writes,

"What made his reputation impregnable was the fact that he was also a revolutionary who spurned government patronage, directed the Ghadar Movement in its early years in the US and Canada, became the principal adviser of the German Government's attempt to foment a revolt against the British Raj during World War I. Then like his equally distinguished contemporary Veer Savarkar, he took a complete somersault, apologised for his past errors and pledged loyalty to them. . . . He became an ardent admirer of the British as a 'truthful people . . . who had a moral and historical mission in India.' The British government had his pronouncements translated into Hindi and distributed free in India." This pretty much sums up his commitment to the Ghadar movement and the cause that he so dearly espoused.

Ghadar Movement Operations and Plans

Even though the Ghadar movement originated in the North America, its operational field and primary target was India. Its primary purpose was to cause a rebellion against the British Government in India and set India free from the British yoke with the help of arms. Its initial goal was to inculcate the Ghadar thinking in the minds of the people of India and the British Indian army and attack British establishments using all means, including violence.

It is often said that the Sikhs have been making history, but they have been careless in preserving it. This is also true of the Ghadar movement. The Ghadar movement was conceived and organized by the Sikhs in North America, but various communist parties in India, who were not even on the scene for many more years, have tried to misappropriate it and claim its ownership. The Ghadar movement was not a communist-inspired movement at all. It is true that some communists did join it, but they did so at a much later stage when the original Ghadar movement was gone for the most part. They were allowed to join it because of the secular nature of the fight against the

British. The fault lies primarily with the Sikhs who abdicated their responsibility in preserving the Sikh legacy. It is encouraging that the Sikhs have finally become aware of this issue in the last few years.

The British Indian army was not only settled in India, but also got involved in various war theatres throughout the world where they were ordered to go as British mercenaries. The British in India had hit a sweet spot when it came to getting army recruits from Punjab. They exploited the young men of Punjab and used them as fodder in both World Wars. In order to accomplish their goal, they pitted one community against another in getting maximum number of recruits. Both Muslims and Sikhs were the backbone of the British Indian army. Interestingly, Sikhs, who made only 2% of the total Indian population, provided at least 25% of the military recruits.

While the goal of the Ghadarites was to throw the British out of India as quickly as possible, the princely states tried to outdo each other in sycophancy of the British. They spent enormous amounts of money on WWI and WWII and sent a large number of soldiers to international war theatres. The Maharaja of Kapurthala during the visit of Viceroy of India Montagu Chelmsford spared no words for the praise of the Viceroy and told him how his state had contributed more than 4000 recruits towards the war efforts and how he had extended war loans totaling 1.2 million rupees and over 300,000 rupees toward war efforts. The Viceroy, in turn, praises him for subverting the Ghadarites in this state: "Your Highness has recently given one more proof, though none was needed, of the loyalty of the Kapurthala State to the British Government. During the recent troublous times through which the Punjab passed as a result of the influx of seditious agitators and returned emigrants the State co-operated whole-heartedly with the Punjab Government in its efforts to expatriate crime and to bring the guilty to justice. The movements of such of these persons as entered the States were kept under careful surveillance, and the efficiency of State Police was demonstrated by the success which was achieved."

During WWI, the Germans were fishing in the troubled waters of India through Persia and Afghanistan through the tribal areas of the border. This is documented by none other than the infamous General Reginald Dyer (also known as butcher of Amritsar) who writes, "They were pouring their agents, with their lying propaganda, into India via Persia and Afghanistan. Afghanistan, like Persia, was nominally neutral, but she was breaking her neutrality by many open acts of aggression, and was offering every facility in her power to the German agents in their passage through her territories, and thence into the Punjab." On the other hand, Germany's ally Turkey was Mahommedan, and the Muslims in India were asked by the British to fight against their co-religionists by the British.

According to General Dyer, "These tribes were generally friendly with the British, but Germans had bribed them heavily and had moreover assured them that Germany had turned Islam [sic] and that the Kaiser William himself was a convert to their religion. As the Sarhad tribes were always out for a good thing for themselves, and as they believed the lie about the German conversion, they had allowed themselves to be tricked into helping the Germans."

General Dyer was a ruthless man who did not hesitate to bend the law or bluff people in order to achieve his goals. When dealing with the lawless rebels near the border of Iran and Baluchistan in 1916, he acted as a general when he was not. He writes,

"Meanwhile, though I was not yet a General I determined to act the part. The 28th Light Cavalry made crossed swords for my shoulders and the necessary red tabs. The former were considerably bigger than the regulation pattern, but were otherwise well made. Then Landon and I went off by car to Nasaratabad."

Plan to Infiltrate and Attack Military Cantonments

The Ghadarites had infiltrated at least 20 military cantonments in Punjab, UP, and other parts of India in order to create a rebellion. However, their first targets were the Lahore and Ferozepur cantonments in Punjab. The soldiers of 23rd Regiment had asked for an earlier date. The soldiers had another reason to be piqued at the British Government. They were being sent to other countries as fodder for WWI for the British. The expectation was that once the revolt is launched at these two military bases, it was going to spread in other military bases in India as well. The date for the army revolt was set for the night of February 21, 1915. Contacts were made with the army men in these bases. Due to the treachery of one Kirpal Singh, the plans of revolt were leaked to the police. As a result, most of the Ghadar leaders were arrested and the plan died.

Various groups of revolutionaries had gathered at Ferozepur in large numbers. Bhai Randhir Singh (founder of Akhand Kirtani Jatha) arrived at

Ferozepur railway station with a party of about 60 men with him to participate in the revolt. They sang hymns with harmonium as they passed. The white policemen thought they were a singing party and let them pass without any problem. Bhai Randhir Singh was arrested and sent to jail by a special tribunal in the Second Lahore Conspiracy case. He was sentenced to death along with 23 other people by this tribunal. However, due to the intervention of the Viceroy of India Lord Hardinge, only six people were hanged including Kartar Singh Sarabha. Bhai Randhir Singh, along with 17 other people were sent to prison for life. This account is provided by Lord Hardinge (Viceroy of India) himself in his biography, *My Indian Years 1910-1916*.

"The Lahore Conspiracy gave me much trouble at this time. No less than twenty-four men were condemned to death by a Special Tribunal. I went to Lahore to see the Lieutenant Governor, Sir M. O'Dwyer, and told him categorically that I absolutely declined to allow a holocaust of victims in a case where only six men had been proved to be actually guilty of murder and dacoity. He recommended that only six [sic] of the twenty-four should have their sentences commuted. I agreed to commutation in these cases but submitted the remaining eighteen cases to the judgment of the Law Member. He proved to me conclusively that in the case of all except six actually guilty of murder and dacoity, they had been convicted under a clause of the penal code which could not entail a death sentence."

Jallianwala Bagh Massacre

On December 10, 1917, the Viceroy of India Lord Chelmsford appointed a Sedition Committee, popularly known as Rowlatt Committee named after its chairman. Its charter was to investigate and report on the nature and extent of the criminal conspiracies connected with the revolutionary movement in India, and to advise as to the legislation necessary to deal with them. Harbans Singh writes, ". . . Based on the recommendations of this committee, two bills, popularly called Rowlatt Bills, were published in the Government of India Gazette on 18 January 1919. Mahatma Gandhi decided to organize a satyagrah (non-violent civil disobedience campaign) against the bills. One of the bills became an Act, nevertheless, on 21 March 1919. Call for a countrywide hartal or general strike on 30 March, later postponed to 6 April 1919, was given by Mahatma Gandhi."

There were riots in Amritsar and Lahore in April 1919 along with "passive resistance" against the Rowlatt Bills that the government had passed. Dr. Saif-ud-Din Kitchlu and Mr. Satya Pal, the two main agitators, were called to the Deputy Commissioner's office, arrested, and sent off to Dharamshala (now in Himachal Pradesh) by car. This led to a general strike in Amritsar and mobs attacked some government buildings and banks. They injured and killed a European guard named Robinson. The Town Hall, the telegraph office, and the National Bank buildings were wrecked. Two European officials of the bank, Mr. Stewart and Mr. Scott, were murdered. The crowd was stopped and fired upon near the railway foot-bridge.

On April 13, 1919, several thousand unarmed Indians peacefully assembled in Jallianwala Bagh, Amritsar, to listen to several prominent local leaders speak out against British colonial rule in India and against the arrest and deportation of Dr. Satya Pal, Dr. Saif-ud-Din Kitchlew, and few others under the unpopular Rowlatt Act. Michael O'Dwyer had declared a martial law which had not been announced. He probably made some announcements about it in some localities in the city beforehand, but the general population was not aware of it. The political instability made it very difficult for him to stay in Punjab much longer after the Amritsar massacre. He says, "I arrived in India in November, 1885, and was posted to Lahore, the capital of the Punjab. I left Lahore and the Punjab for good in May, 1919."

General Reginald Dyer brought in fifty riflemen; forty Gurkhas, armed with their traditional weapon, the kukris, and two armored cars, marched towards the Jallianwala Bagh with a clear intention of killing a large number of people and thus teaching the Punjabis a lesson.

Ghadar Movement

Figure 3. Entrance Gate of Jallianwala Bagh

Figure 4. Martyrs' Well At Jallianwala Bagh

Figure 5. Ashes of Sardar Udham Singh Brought to India from England on July 19, 1974, kept at the Jallianwala Bagh Museum, Amritsar

Sardar Udham Singh's ashes were brought back from England to India in July 1974. They were paraded throughout Punjab and other parts of India in a specially decorated bus. That bus also visited my college, Guru Gobind Singh Republic College, Jandiala, Jalandhar in Punjab. All the students and college staff received the float with great enthusiasm. Various leaders of Punjab accompanied Sardar Udham Singh's ashes and briefly spoke on that occasion. Among them was S. Amar Singh Dosanjh, the editor of *Akali Patrika*.

Figure 6. Reception of Holy Ashes of Shahid Udham Singh at Guru Gobind Singh Republic College, Jandiala, Jalandar (this picture is taken from the college Magazine The Baaz, 1975–76.)

"Dyer had a minute glimpse of the assembly of the people in the Bagh where the seventh speaker, Durga Das was speaking from the platform. The earlier six speakers were Rai Ram Singh, Dar Singh, Abdul Majid, Brij Gopi Nath, Hans Raj and Gurbakash Rai. Dyer, who was in independent commands of the force under him, was not to consul anybody at this point of time. He had already made up his mind to act in a way which might be a lesson-giving to the people of Punjab. Not losing even a minute, he at once ordered his sepoys to adopt kneeling position, a usual posture for a soldier to fire. The firing order was given and the numerous volleys of shots began to pierce into the bodies of the people in the Bagh."

Firing continued for about ten minutes until the ammunition was exhausted. It panicked the crowd and they ran in all directions. Many jumped into the well in the hope that it might save their lives. They were soon drowned. Those who held on for some time drowned under the weight of others. There was no one to pull them out. That well is still present. All the exits and escape routes were blocked by the army. General Dyer personally directed the fire where the crowd was the thickest or in the direction people were rushing in order to save themselves.

Figure 7. Jallianwala Bagh Memorial

General Dyer knew well in advance that people were gathering at the Jallianwala Bagh, but he did nothing to disperse them nor did he give them the chance to escape. The Martial Law was in place, but most people came from villages far away from the city and they were not aware of it.

Ironically many people in England supported General Dyer. Joseph Rudyard Kipling, an India-born British writer who won a Nobel Prize in

Literature in 1907, supported the actions of General Dyer. He claimed Dyer was "the man who saved India." He started a benefit fund which raised over 26,000 pounds sterling, including 50 pounds contributed by Kipling himself. The money was presented to Dyer when he settled in England on his retirement. On the other hand, Rabindra Nath Tagore, who later won the Indian Nobel Prize in poetry, condemned this barbarous act and renounced his "Knighthood" that the British Crown had granted him in 1915 by writing this letter:

"Your Excellency,

The enormity of the measures taken by the Government in the Punjab for quelling some local disturbances has, with a rude shock, revealed to our minds the helplessness of our position as British subjects in India. The disproportionate severity of the punishments inflicted upon the unfortunate people and the methods of carrying them out, we are convinced, are without parallel in the history of civilised governments, barring some conspicuous exceptions, recent and remote."

B. G. Horniman writes,

"Floggings were a common feature of the administration of Martial Law in Amritsar as in other areas. The sentences were inflicted by summary courts for trivial offences on trumpery evidence. The public flogging of some men who were alleged to have been concerned in the assault on Miss Sherwood, was an exceptional incident, akin to the crawling order. These men had not been tried or convicted for the crime. They were awaiting trial. But to create an example, they were brought to the scene of the assault, and publicly flogged in the street."

Murder of Michael O'Dwyer by Udham Singh

Udham Singh was an eyewitness to this horrible event and it had a major impact on him. On August 30, 1927, Udham Singh was arrested at Amritsar for possession of unlicensed arms. Some revolvers, a quantity of ammunition, and copies of a prohibited Ghadar Party paper called *Ghadr-di-Gunj* ("Voice or Echo of Revolt") were confiscated from him. He was prosecuted under section 20 of the Arms Act. It took him another 21 years to take revenge, after he reached England and shot Michael O'Dwyer dead at Caxton Hall in London on March 13, 1940. Udham Singh did not try to flee the scene and took full responsibility of his act of bravery. In fact, he defiantly said,

"I did it because I had a grudge against him. He deserved it. He was the real culprit. He wanted to crush the spirit of my people, so I have crushed him. For full 21 years, I have been trying to wreak vengeance. I am happy that I have done the job. I am not scared of death. I am dying for my country. I have seen my people starving in India under the British rule. I have protested against this, it was my duty. What a greater honour could be bestowed on me than death for the sake of my motherland?"

On June 4, 1940, he was committed to trial, at the Central Criminal Court, Old Bailey, before Justice Atkinson. When the court asked about his name, he replied, "Ram Mohammad Singh Azad," (Ram as a Hindu name, Mohammad as a Muslim name, and Singh as a Sikh name). Azad means to be free. On April 1, 1940, Udham Singh was formally charged with the murder of Michael O'Dwyer. He was hanged at Pentonville Prison on July 31, 1940.

Role of Michael O'Dwyer and General Reginald Dyer

Michael O'Dwyer, the Lt. Governor of Punjab, was the lynchpin of the Jallianwala Bagh massacre. There is quite a bit of controversy about Michael O'Dwyer, who approved the actions of General Dyer. Michael O'Dwyer writes, "General Beynon told me he was conveying approval of his action to Dyer and asked if he might add mine. I had at first some hesitation, as Dyer's action was a military one, but on fuller consideration I thought it advisable to endorse General Beynon's approval. He then sent the message (by aeroplane, I think) to Dyer." The fact is this massacre could not have happened without the express approval of Michael O'Dwyer. It was Michael O'Dwyer who had endorsed General Dyer and called the massacre a "correct" action.

There was a curfew order in place in the city. People were afraid to go about their business and kept their businesses and shops closed. General Dyer issued another warning to Punjabis by issuing a notice in Urdu which is translated here:

"You people know well that I am a Sepoy and soldier. Do you want war or peace? If you wish for a war, the Government is prepared for it, and if you want peace, then obey my orders and open all your shops; else I will shoot. For me the battlefield of France or Amritsar is the same. I am a military man and I will go straight. Neither shall I move to the right nor to the left. Speak up, if you want war? In case there is to be peace, my order is to open all shops at once. You people talk against the Government and persons educated in Germany and Bengal talk sedition. I shall report all these. Obey my orders. I do not wish to have anything else. I have served in the military for over 30 years. I understand the Indian Sepoy and Sikh people very well. You will have to obey my orders and observe peace. Otherwise the shops will be opened by force and rifles. You will have to report to me of the Badmash [scoundrel]. I will shoot them. Obey my orders and open shops. Speak up if you want war? You have committed a bad act in killing the English. The revenge will be taken upon you and upon your children."

General Dyer was a military man who looked at even a normal social discord and protest as a "military problem" and tried to deal with it accordingly as if fighting a foreign invading army. One person who fully exposed the Amritsar atrocities was a fearless British editor of *Bombay Chronicle*, B. G. Horniman. He writes,

"General Dyer said he fired, and fired well, because he did not want anyone to have to shoot again in the Punjab. What followed on the Amritsar *battue*—and it is not unreasonable to argue that it was a result—was wholesale shooting and bombing of unarmed people in other parts of the Punjab, and six weeks' agony under Martial Law."

A British woman, Miss Sherwood, lived in Amritsar and was attacked by the mob a few days before the April 13, 1919, incident. She was saved by the local residents who lived on the same street. General Dyer issued a "crawling order" and made all the people to crawl on all fours who happened to pass through that street. This was a humiliating act for the honorable people who lived on that street or had to go through that street.

Bombing of Gujranwala on April 14, 1919

The Amritsar massacre is a well-known fact. However, the Gujranwala bombing, which is equally serious, is often overlooked by the historians. This occurred during the martial law which was declared by Michael O'Dwyer with the approval of the Indian government (Montagu Chelmsford, Viceroy of India).

On April 14, 1919, well over 100 people perished in Gujranwala when three airplanes of the Royal Air Force dropped bombs on civilians and fired machine gun rounds from the air. The bombing operation was carried out by two RAF officers, Major Carberry and Lieutenant Dodkins. A bomb fell near the Khalsa School hostel and injured one student. There were serious protests in Amritsar, Lahore, Gujranwala, and Kasur after the Rowlatt Bills were passed. On April 14, 1919, the telegraph office, post office, and railway station and collector's office, a church, a school, and a railway shed were set on fire. There were also some minor incidents at some other places. A Commission called "Hunter Commission" was appointed by the British Indian government to investigate the incidents of Punjab. An independent committee was appointed by the Indian National Congress which had collected mass evidence by talking to a large number of people, but it was not heard by the Hunter Commission. B. G. Horniman adds,

"If Dyerarchy in Amritsar had begun and ended with this incident, the disgrace to Britain would have been sufficiently deep. But it was brought to still further depths by the iniquities which followed during the six weeks of administration of Martial Law under Dyer, with the continued approval, knowledge, and co-operation of Sir Michael O'Dwyer, and also the Government of India, who had given the Lieutenant Governor a blank cheque and provided him, by a series of proclamations and ordinances, with unlimited power to override the ordinary law and destroy liberty."

Qutubuddin Aziz writes,

> "With Martial Law clamped on the Punjab by its sadist Lieutenant-Governor, Sir Michael O'Dwyer, who hated all educated Indians and relished inflicting the vilest humiliation and atrocities on the locals, the bloody year 1919 also witnessed the ruthless bombing of the small town of Gujranwala, barely 60 miles from Lahore, by three war-planes of the nascent British Royal Air Force the next day after British guns had mowed down unarmed Indians in the killing field of Jalianwala Bagh in Amritsar."

The Civil and Military Gazette provided an "official report" in which the government provided its own version and downplayed the incident. According to the report, only nine people were killed due to airplane bombing, twenty-seven were wounded by police and aeroplanes. The report was obviously dishonest which tried to convince people that dropping of at least three 20-lbs bombs and 255 rounds of machine-gun fired at close quarters into crowds of people killed only nine people.

Akali Morchas Joined by Former Ghadarites

There is enough evidence available that even those Sikhs, who had served in the British army in India, Singapore, Hong Kong, etc., were quite dismayed by the treatment meted out to them by the Canadian government and citizens. So much so that they had burned their military discharge certificates and war medals that they had won in the British Indian army in different war theatres. Someone named J.A.W. (who seems to be an influential person) writes,

"After a study of the files – which unfortunately are somewhat meager – referring to the Indian agitation in Canada looking to the general movement in Europe that the situation in Canada and specially on the West Pacific Coast is such that it behooves us, to at least keep well in touch with the Anti-British agitation there. In a recent conversation with a well-educated Indian gentleman – who had visited the locality – he told me that the agitation has worked up the Sikh labourers there to such an extent that those of them who had been soldiers in the Indian army, and had War Medals, and Army Discharge Certificates, in their possession, burnt them on a bonfire at a public meeting, at the same time denouncing the British in violent terms."

There are some intelligence documents that shed light on the former Ghadarites joining various Akali morchas or agitations. Many Gadharite Sikhs, who returned to India during the peak of the Ghadar movement, joined the Akalis against the British Government after the Ghadar movement had faded. There were several Akali *morchas* or agitations in the 1920s, which included Nanakana Sahib Morcha (1921), Chabian Da Morcha (1921–22, agitation related to the keys of most important Sikh shrines), Guru Ka Bagh Morcha (1922), and Jaito Da Morcha (1923).

> "6. Mit Singh. – Mit Singh, a prominent member of the Ghadr Party, who recently returned to India from America (vide paragraphs 5, Weekly Report, dated 29th August) has been appointed a Jathedar at Muketsar."

The CID (Criminal Investigation Department) was keeping tabs on them. "5. Arrival of four Akalis in Shanghai for secret work. – Four Akalis, two of whom named Harnam Singh and Gurdit Singh alias Gopha Singh, were associated with the notorious Gurdit Singh of the Komagata Maru fame, are reported to have been in Shanghai since May last, 'with the object of working secretly with the Sikhs'. Harnam Singh is still there, but Gurdit Singh has gone to Mexico. Further inquiries are being made."

Murder of Michael O'Dwyer and Ghadar Party Connection

There seems to be a direct connection between the murder of Michael O'Dwyer and the Ghadar Party of California. The fact is FBI was tipped off by an Indian about a possible attempt on the life of Michael O'Dwyer which, in turn, had warned Michael O'Dwyer in writing about the pending danger to his life from the Sikh Ghadarites in California. In fact, FBI had advised Michael O'Dwyer to stay home if at all possible and he must go out, he should do so under a police guard. The murder of Michael O'Dwyer seems to be planned by the Ghadar party, but it was Udham Singh who actually executed that plan very carefully and without divulging any details to any person.

The British India Office Library released some documents in 1997 which included many documents related to the Ghadar movements and Udham Singh. One of the secret reports from the British Consulate says,

> "Local police state that they have received report from an Indian informant that Indian extremists in California may be contemplating attempt on the life of Mr. O'Dwyer. In view of the

criminal record of many Indians in California police consider this report should not be disregarded.

I have requested the police to take protective measures but they maintain that it is impossible to guarantee that attack by some fanatic may not take place. I am also consulting F.B.I. In the meantime all reasonable precautions will be taken.

Repeated to Washington telegram No. 62."

There is another similar coded message:

"IMMEDIATE.

Your telegram No. 22 [of the 22nd March] concerning threats to Mr. Dwyer's life]

If you think advisable arrange for Mr. O'Dwyer to stay in his house or other safe place with police guard until position is clarified. If after consultation with police and or F. B. I. you think Mr. O'Dwyer should take leave local or otherwise you may instruct him accordingly. As we see it no question of prestige is involved. It would be deplorable if any incident were to occur.

Repeated to Washington No. 462."

Unfortunately, the historical facts are so twisted and beaten out of shape by some vested interests that the whole Ghadar movement is presented as if it were the brainchild of the Communists or inspired by its principles. The Ghadar movement was started and dominated by the Sikhs, but they welcomed any other Indian communities into its fold regardless of religious beliefs or practices. This was a joint effort by the Sikhs, Muslims, and Hindus, and its primary purpose was to drive the British out of India by force.

In conclusion, the Ghadar movement lasted only 6–7 years, but it had a lasting effect on the Indian freedom struggle. In almost all Akali morchas, there were ex-Ghadarites who had returned from USA or Canada. Sikhs, the real heroes of the India's freedom, are being ignored by the modern historians who are either brainwashed by the Hindu nationalism or by the communists who have a tacit collusion with the Congress party and have lived off doles thrown at them by China and former USSR. By the time the Babbar Akali movement was suppressed in the Doaba region of Punjab, it had spread in other countries like Afghanistan, the US, and Canada. It continued with great strength until at least 1926.

In summary, all the sacrifices made by the Ghadarites played a key role towards the freedom of India. It is sad that the history is being sliced, diced, and corrupted by some modern historians in India to please one political party or another or to push one's own political agenda. One needs to look at this issue in a more objective manner and investigate the truth. During any sincere and diligent research, one would find that the roles played by the Ghadarites acted as a trigger point which unleashed many political events, and each one of them brought India closer to its freedom. It was a joint effort by the Sikhs, Hindus, and Muslims, but the Ghadar movement was spearheaded by the Sikhs, and its thrust and trajectory were also provided by the Sikhs, in which the Khalsa Pacific Diwan Society (Gurdwara Sahib Stockton) played a key role as it provided the necessary refuge, infrastructure, and support. There are hundreds, perhaps thousands, of unsung Ghadarite heroes whose names are never seen in the newspapers or history books, but they too played a key role in the freedom of India.

It is quite disturbing that there are too many so-called "melas" (festivals) that are being organized in name of the Ghadri Babas throughout the US and Canada. Unfortunately, these have nothing to do with the Ghadri Babas, because these festivals are all about business, dance, merry-making, and self-promotion. In fact, they do great injustice to our forefathers. Sikhs should shun and totally discard such fake memorials which not only belittle the sacrifices of the Ghadri Babas, but also twist our history. Sikhs need to wake up and reclaim their rich heritage.

There has also been a positive development lately. Two Sikh centennial scholarly conferences are being organized by Pacific Coast Khalsa Diwan Society (Stockton Gurdwara Sahib in California). It is a step in the right direction in which almost 30 historians and top-notch scholars from the East and West are presenting their papers related to the Ghadar movement. Similar efforts are also taking place in other parts of the US and Canada. These efforts leave no doubt in anyone's mind that the real heroes of the Ghadar movements were the Sikhs who suffered the most for the freedom of India.

[This paper was presented at the Eastern Scholars Conference as part of the Sikh Centennial Celebrations, organized by the Pacific Khalsa Diwan Society, Stockton (Sikh Temple, Stockton), California in September 2012 at the University of the Pacific, Stockton.]

Gadar Lehar and Lala Har Dayal: Life, Activities, & Ideology

Jatinder Singh Hundal

1. Gadar: A Sikh-centric Movement

A Sikh-led revolutionary movement, more popularly known and recognized by its vernacular name, Ghadr Lehar, rather than English translation, Gadar Movement, has left its mark on the history of Sikhs in North America, especially on the West Coast of the United States and Canada. It was based on core Sikh values that all people should have the freedom to live their lives as they wish. Freedom of thought by an individual, society, and nation is a principle that Sikhs throughout their short history have fought for and made sacrifices of unparalleled magnitude to defend. It is indeed a matter of pride for the young faith that it has made significant contributions to development of human civilization to further the cause of freedom of all people to profess and follow a faith of their own choice and practice it free from fear of oppression.

Gadar Lehar was originally a brain child of Sikhs living on the West Coast, mostly those concentrated in the California Central Valley and British Columbia. It was and still is completely natural and justified to claim this movement to be described as a Sikh-centric movement, and the use of Sikh Gurduaras in Stockton, Abbotsford, and Vancouver as its bases for gathering of its members as well as collect donations on its behalf also lends strong support to this argument.

Even though generally its beginning is contributed to the idea of freedom of India, there was an underlying frustration and disappointment with injustice system in American society against men of color that fueled the resentment among immigrants. This movement was a combination and result of these two factors that led to its acceptance not only by Sikhs but also non-Sikhs from South Asian region, mostly of Punjab origin, but also many non-Punjabis as well.

This movement was seen as a common ground for unity to fight for rights of individuals in their adopted land and at the same time provide a stage to raise voice against British imperialism in India. Many of the members who joined its rank and file were fighting the battle on two fronts, the front to free India and the struggle for justice and equal rights in America. Ghadr Lehar was seen as supportive organization for both of these ideas, and thus it was an easily acceptable movement in its message to all South Asian immigrants.

There were immigrants from all segments of the society of Punjab, but Sikhs, who were generally from the rural communities of Punjab, were better suited and equipped to establish themselves in the harsh and physically demanding agricultural and forest product based production environment of California Central Valley and British Columbia. This was somewhat less true for the urban immigrants who preferred to work in traditional white collar environments. Due to prevalent racial discrimination, many of these urban raised and educated young men found it difficult to fully utilize their white collar skills to the fullest. This lent itself to further anger and resentment against the system, and ultimately the British were blamed for the unfriendly and unfair system in India which forced these educated elites to seek employment overseas.

Sikhs adapted well to hard and demanding but growing agricultural and lumber based economy and were financially at stronger footing then other Punjabis. This contributed to the fact that this community collectively became the base of a freedom movement under the banner of Ghadr Lehar.

Funds collected for its operations were mostly from Sikhs working in the farms of California, and donations given to Stockton Gurduara were also utilized for this purpose. Leading members and office bearers were mostly from Sikh families of Punjab, which provides sufficient weight to the argument that Ghadr Lehar was a Sikh institution devoted to freedom of all people of India. This agenda of "freedom for all," and not just Sikhs, made it acceptable to non-Sikhs as well, and they also made contributions to help sustain this Lehar, at least in the beginning.

From the very beginning of this Lehar, its leadership was influenced by non-Sikhs who infiltrated its upper echelons. Its membership consisted of mostly Sikhs, but other Punjabis, both Hindus and Muslims, also joined it for the fact that there was no other institution dedicated to the freedom of India and non-Sikhs were not organized in the manner that Sikhs had organized themselves under the Khalsa Diwan Society and the Ghadr Lehar. Even though its members came from all sections of Indian society, its major financial contributors remained Sikh farm workers, laborers, and contractors of California Central Valley that stretched from Chico/Yuba City up in the north to as far as Fresno/Bakersfield in the south.

It was during its time of inception that some of the less than dedicated and opportunist individuals entered the ranks of the leadership of the Lehar. Many of these were accepted into its ranks of leadership by Sikhs either unknowingly, innocently, or at the recommendations of other non-Sikhs. If not most, at least many Sikhs in the area were not well versed in language or the laws of the adopted land. It was the need of the Sikh community that allowed many unknown and unproven personalities to be trusted with highly responsible positions within the Lehar.

2. Guardians of the Gadar: Sikh Pioneers

Sikh leadership of the Gadar from the beginning of this movement was not either fully prepared to accept a leadership from outside or trusted the non-Sikhs with leadership roles without fully investigating the backgrounds of individuals. Since the majority of the upper leadership was drawn from the Punjab region, these individuals either were known to each other or were familiar with the backgrounds of the families and villages of each other. They found their personalities to be at par and compatible with each other during times of struggle. They understood the mental state of others who came from similar family, social, and financial backgrounds and found a common bond of unity to fight not only for the freedom of India but also to continue the struggle for equality and justice in their newly acquired homeland. They were united at both fronts and were equally affected by the injustice served to them by American society and its unjust, unfair, and discriminatory system.

It was their common struggle that created a strong bond among them and served to unify their approach and behavior in the face of difficulties and hardships. It was also this reason of unity that outsiders, especially non-Sikhs, found it difficult to infiltrate and take control of the Ghadr Lehar and this remained a solely Sikh movement, especially Sikhs belonging to Punjab region who shared a common background and bond of clanship.

Sikhs were also the guardians of the Ghadr Lehar as the tradition of opposing oppression in any and all forms was a core value of Sikhism. They viewed British imperialism in India and white racial discrimination in US as discriminatory and aggressive segregation against downtrodden. They viewed racial discrimination in American society as a form of oppression that must be resisted. It was this core value of opposing social aggression which played a major role in shaping the thought process of Sikhs who actively sought to implement this philosophy of Sikhism through Ghadr Lehar.

Trust in fellow members is of utmost importance and pre-request to success of any organization, and Ghadr Lehar was no exception. Many Sikhs settled on the West Coast had served in the British army at one time or another and trusted fellow Sikh soldiers with their lives. This trust was transferred to the new land, where many ex-soldiers were united in the new war of independence. Many were either probably known to each other or had known about others who were now "soldiers of struggle" under the banner of Gadar.

It was easy and natural for these ex-soldiers and comrades in arms to form a bond that was not possible with non-Sikhs. This accounted for another fact that these foot soldiers of the Gadar worked closely and confidentially with each other for the success of the Lehar. This further strengthen our argument that Ghadr Lehar was a purely Sikh organization that was led and financed by Sikhs, while non-Sikh participated in its activities only to a very limited degree.

Traveling to faraway places usually widens not only the sphere of one's knowledge but also helps develop a broader approach to life in general. Sikhs were by far the most traveled men in India at the time of the Ghadr Lehar formation. There has been a long history of Sikhs traveling to all parts of the commonwealth to either protect English rule or to work in the new developed frontiers in Africa and other parts of Asia. Returning soldiers would infuse a spirit of freedom in young males who grew up to expect this freedom for their own society. Many of the earlier immigrants to the West Coast had been themselves in the British army and had served overseas in various capacities.

This exposure to world stage had instilled a sense of freedom in Sikhs but was not found to the same degree in non-Sikhs from India who had come to the USA. For example, centuries of belief of Hinduism that it is a sin to cross an ocean had kept the Hindus from exploring other parts of the globe and learning about the equality and freedom enjoyed by inhabitants of other societies. This created a pacifist approach to life and hindered the acceptance of freedom struggle by many Hindus. Status Quo of subjugation was not acceptable to Sikhs, and they were far ahead in their demand for a free and just society, not only in India but also in their newly adopted homelands.

The role played by non-Sikhs in the organization and its success has been greatly exaggerated by the fact that some internationally active non-Sikhs used Ghadr as a stepping stone to achieve their own narrow-minded and lop-sided goals. They appeared to have tried to gain control of the organization to further their own personal agenda rather than benefit the movement for liberation of India.

Either misinformed or ill-intentioned historians have attempted to re-write a fact-less history of Ghadr to promote personalities that associated themselves with this Lehar either to gain acceptance by Sikh freedom fighters or to use this stage to move forward with their own plans. These were opportunists who used the Ghadr financial and public base to develop their own agenda for themselves.

One such personality usually associated with Ghadr is Har Dayal even though his contribution was negligible at best. His weak and immaterial relationship with Ghadr Lehar from 1912 to 1914 was eventless and unproductive. He was mostly based in the urban areas of San Francisco while the Ghadr had its roots and support in the rural area of Central Valley, especially Sacramento/Stockton area.

Har Dayal took Sikhs into confidence to fight on behalf of the Indians for freedom from British rule. After his brief stopover on the East Coast, and meeting with Teja Singh, a young student at Harvard, he arrived in California in 1911. He was made aware of the existence of several "colonies" of Sikhs in California, especially around the towns of Stockton and Sacramento.

Upon his arrival in Northern California, he immediately established contacts with leading personalities of the Sikh community. He worked with Sikhs who had already designed the infrastructure of contacts and supporters who would carry out the responsibilities of the movement. Har Dayal offered little in the form of encouragement or knowledge to an organization that had already been set up by Sikhs. As an experienced writer, his offer to work with the *Ghadr*, the official publication of the Ghadr Lehar, was accepted by its founders and office holders of Khalsa Diwan Society.

Even while associated with Ghadr Lehar in California, he managed to visit Oregon and set up another organization under the name of "Hindi Association of Pacific Coast." The funds collected by Ghadr Lehar were mostly likely put to use to develop this organization, thus splitting up the movement for the freedom of India. This does not speak very highly of his contribution to or dedication for Ghadr Lehar. It clearly shows that he was looking for an opportunity to develop his own agenda with his own organization fully in his control. This throws a monkey wrench into the argument that he was a dedicated soldier of the Ghadr. His dedication to the cause of Ghadr as argued by some historians is questionable given the fact that he was busy collecting and using funds for establishing another organization in Oregon while claiming to work with Sikhs in California under the banner of Ghadr Lehar and Khalsa Diwan Society.

Real guardians of the movement were Sikhs of California and British Columbia who had dedicated themselves to the cause of India's freedom, contributed financially for its success, suffered untold economic hardships for its success, and paid far greater a price for this cause than any other community. A price they paid in lost lives and devastated families was far greater in proportion to their numbers in India and even more so for a small Sikh community on the West Coast of North America.

"Har Dayal's Hindi Association of the Pacific Coast was an uneasy coalition between Hindu intellectuals and Sikh farmers, peasants, and lumber mill workers. This does mean that there were not both Muslims and Hindus of the lower classes who were members, but the Sikhs were in the majority and provided most of the financial support to the organization and its proposed program" (Brown, 1975, 140).

3. Har Dayal: Time Line and Childhood Influences

Har Dayal was born in the township of Cheera Khana in Chandni Chowk, which are of Old Delhi, and now this township has been renamed as Har Dayal Katra. He belonged to an aristocratic Punjabi family of Mathur background. He was born on October 14, 1884, exactly 46 days before Bhai Ram Singh Kooka passed away in Prison in Rangoon, Myanmar, after spending 12 years in Jail as a freedom fighter.

His father, Gauri Dayal, was a Reader in the District Court at Delhi. It was his father's status that helped Har Dayal establish contact with institutes of higher learning and with educated/affluent families of Delhi. These families must have established trust of the British authorities in order to maintain their upper class status. This influenced Har Dayal's loyalty and acceptance of British as masters. His childhood was spent with pro-British neighbors and family friends and helped him establish a thought pattern that was based, not only on accepting the English as masters, but also on considering Indians as the subject of British Masters.

It was the pro-British thinking pattern that he grew up with as a child of the privileged and affluent family that had established itself by serving the British. It could not have been possible for the family to keep its status without loyalty to English rule, and Har Dayal had watched and learned from his surroundings and developed a pro-English attitude at an early age. This influenced him as a child and left a permanent mark on his thinking, and he continued to hold pro-establishment and pro-British feelings for the rest of his life as this is apparent from his writings published later in life.

In 1901, at the age of 17 he was married Sunder Rani, daughter of Lala Gopal Chand, a Sessions Judge (Nazim) in Patiala State. Sunder's Grandfather was Chief Minister (Divaan) in Patiala State, and this aristocrat family belonged originally to Barnala (30.378602, 75.546506). They had one daughter from this marriage, Shanti Devi, who was born in 1908. Even after his marriage, he continued his studies, and in 1904, he graduated from Government College Lahore with a Master degree. Har Dayal left India on August 2, 1908, and Shanti was born on August 8, only 6 days after his escape, and he never saw his daughter and only learned about her birth after he left India and was in Colombo. He never had a chance to see his daughter during his life.

In 1905, Har Dayal joined Oxford University in England, but in 1907, he resigned his state scholarship at Oxford. It was possible for him to be accepted to a British university only because of family's tested and trusted pro-British attitude. He traveled to Switzerland and took over as editor of a new publication called *Bande Mataram* in 1909.

Originally, *Bande Mataram* was published from Calcutta but had ceased publication in 1908. The first edition of the new *Bande Mataram* appeared from Paris, France, on September 10, 1909, and Har Dayal praised Madan Lal Dhingra in its editorial for killing Sir William Curzon Wyllie on July 1,

1909. Dhingra was hanged on August 17, 1909, in London, and Har Dayal's statement read, "Dhingra has behaved at each stage of his trial like a hero of ancient times, he has reminded us of the history of medieval Rajputs and Sikhs who loved death like a bride. England thinks she killed Dhingra, in reality he lives forever, and has given the deathblow to English sovereignty in India."

In 1911, he arrived in Cambridge, Massachusetts. While in Cambridge, he came in contact with (Sant) Teja Singh at Harvard University, who gave him details of Sikh pioneers in Northern and Central California.

In 1911, after getting details about Sikhs living in California, he arrived in San Francisco. On April 28, 1911, he published an article which provides clues to his mental state during his arrival in California. In this write up, he explains that he is currently trying to find a suitable place for meditation that would be similar to the Hindu holy city of Hardwar in its peaceful and worry-free environment. This clearly indicates that he may have been an intellectual in his thoughts but was certainly not a revolutionary fighting to end colonialism in India.

In February 1912, he was appointed a Lecturer on Indian Philosophy at Stanford University. He was forced to resign his position in September 1912 due to his views expressed in several articles published in San Francisco. In order to be accepted by the leaders and members, he took an oath at Yugantar Ashram in San Francisco in 1913 with a vow to fight for freedom of India as part of the Ghadr Lehar.

On October 13, 1912, he set up a communist ideology based organization in San Francisco. He named it "The Fraternity of the Red Flag" and invited all and anyone who was willing to "renounce all wealth, promises not to earn money or be a parent at any time, repudiates all other social ties and obligations, and lives a life of simplicity and hardships." This clearly indicates that Har Dayal did not believe in family life. He asked others not to "be a parent at any time," while he was himself a father of one daughter.

In December 1912 issue of *Modern Review*, he stressed his earlier ideology that "study of Hindu philosophy, or any philosophy, for that matter, was a waste of time." He continued with a similar theme of his ideas while writing in 1913 in *Modern Review*, and he recommends that "Pilgrimages should be made to European capitals rather than to time-honored religious sites in India, such as Hardwar and Puri." This indicates that while he is claimed to be working with Sikhs of California in setting up of Ghadr Party, he is also advocating that Indians are in some ways inferior and must lean on the Europeans for survival of the Indian society.

In May 1913, he visited Saint Johns, Astoria, and other cities in Oregon to meet with other Indians working in the lumber industry. He not only explained his ideology but also solicited financial contributions to fund his plans.

However, he was arrested on March 16, 1914, and released on bail. He was arrested for speaking against the King Czar of Russia as at it was allied with the US against German. Another reason for his arrest appears to be his setting up of the communist ideology based organization called "The Fraternity of the Red Flag." His arrest did not seem to be based on his opposition to British Rule in India as he wrote very little against it and never appeared to be stressing in his lectures he delivered to gatherings outside of the Indian community.

As documented in the Deportation files of Har Dayal dated May 26, 1914, the Bureau of Immigration filed charges against Har Dayal and he was ordered to be arrested "on charges of being a member of excluded classes, and anarchist or advocating the overthrow of the United States government by force." There was no mention of his activity against the British rule in India or the freedom movement working for its overthrow. In fact, it directly accuses him of belonging to an "excluded class," indicating his involvement with the communist ideological based organization that seeks anarchy as its goal. He was taken into custody while actually attending a meeting which was described by local media as a "Socialist" gathering.

After his arrest, he was interrogated by the immigration authorities, and he was asked about his speech delivered on October 31, 1913. This speech was described and discussed the Russian revolution in which he had made comments that Indians should learn from the revolution. He commented that all revolutionaries should take the Russian revolution seriously "because of many lessons we can derive from it and because of its tremendous importance for the future of the race."

He escaped to Europe but only after a long and revealing interrogation by the Immigration Authorities of the United States. During this interrogation, he strongly criticized freedom fighters like Madan Lal Dhingra and others as social terrorists. The true personality of Har Dayal was exposed during this interrogation. He made derogatory remarks not only against individuals involved in the freedom struggle, but also distanced himself from the movement entirely.

For about a decade from 1915 to 1925, he wandered around Europe either establishing contacts with nationalist Indians or the German sympathizers of free India. Either he did not receive a positive response or was mistrusted by both nationalists and the Germans. He decided to settle in a more peaceful environment of Sweden, far removed from active Indian communities of Europe. He lived a life of reclusion and remained focused on his study of Buddhism which he pursued further after going to England.

In 1931, he married Agda Erikson in Sweden (both wives never knew about existence of each other during his life time). He died on March 4, 1939, in Philadelphia during his visit to the US, and a rumor was circulated by no other than Gobind Bihari Lal, his brother-in-law, that Har Dayal was poisoned to death by Sikhs.

4. Activities for Self-Promotion

Har Dayal's early life during his education was basically an un-eventful life that was devoid of involvement in any nationalist or freedom movement. There is no documentation of his serious involvement in politics or nationalist movement during those days. This fact, along with his father being in the service of the English, contributed to his being accepted at Oxford which would not have been possible if he had shown a nationalistic ideology in his behavior or writings. Even while a student at Oxford in the UK, he showed absolutely no inclination towards Indian community or the country's freedom struggle. He did not join any student or community based organization that worked for the Indian community or raised voice for a free India. He lived a life of isolation and absorbed in his education.

His stay in the UK was a quiet period as he focused on his studies and kept himself isolated from the community and its activities. This was either due to the fact that he was busy with finishing his studies or most likely due to his upbringing as a loyal British subject not to question its ways and authority. This loyalty, ingrained from childhood, finally showed up in his writings at the final stage of his life when he published his works praising the British Empire and denounced nationalists fighting for India's freedom.

He neither arrived in the US directly from the UK nor did he go there with any plan to work for the freedom of India. He left the UK and arrived in Paris, France, looking for a peaceful environment away from the struggles of a hectic life in England. Disillusioned with life in Paris, he left for Algeria at the end of September 1910. He was equally dissatisfied with life in Algeria and decided to live on an island, surrounded by water and away from metropolitan centers. He was still trying to locate a hideout that would provide him with suitable environment for meditation. Unable to find the inner peace he was looking for, he returned to France and then arrived in Martinique Island in the West Indies. He met another active Indian, Bhai Parma Nand, and told him that, like the Mahatama Buddh, he wanted to bring into light another peaceful religion like the Buddhism.

While in Martinique, he earned his living by teaching English to the mostly French speaking population. He continued to meditate in the hills during his free time and proclaimed that his ideal man was Buddha, whom he held in great esteem. He tried to follow Buddha's teaching by living as an ascetic by renouncing the world and living in isolation. This behavior clearly indicates that he did not hold any revolutionary ideology in his heart and would be a misfit in any revolutionary movement.

While in Martinique, Har Dayal held long discourses with Parmanand about religious beliefs and Har Dayal's plan to lay foundation of a new religion. He also disclosed to Parmanand that his religion was to be based on atheism and moral law. Even though he did not go into details about his "moral laws," his writings later in life, especially during his brief stay at Stanford University, provide clue to his "moral laws." He believed in "moral freedom" rather than "moral restrains" to ensure peace and tranquility in life. The fact that he had a change of mind from living a life of reclusion and isolation to a life at Harvard in an intellectually challenging environment indicates that he had not yet settled himself emotionally and was still looking for a purpose in life.

At the insistence of Parmanand, from Martinique he arrived in Harvard University to study Buddhism. Even though he had come to the US to study, he did not enroll at Harvard but simply used its library to continue his study. At Harvard, he met Sant Teja Singh and decided to move to California where there was a large Sikh community. Even after arriving in California, he had no plans to initiate any political action or launch any freedom movement. In fact, after staying for a short while in California, he went to Honolulu, again looking for a peaceful place for meditation. He arrived back in San Francisco from Honolulu, completely disappointed and unable to find the inner peace he sought. His friend Parmanand, who had been keeping touch with him throughout Har Dayal's journeys, described him at this stage as "moody, needy and unfriendly."

Har Dayal lived in a cave-like environment near Waikiki beach. He continued his study of Buddhism but also concentrated on the works of Karl Marx. But he found his life full of disillusionment and decided to return to California. His focusing on both Buddha on one extreme and Marx on the other end of the spectrum shows his inability to focus on a set of values that he could pursue for a lifetime of study and make his goal in life.

In the magazine *Modern Review* dated April 28, 1911, he published a lengthy article from Berkeley that outlined his search for a peaceful heavenly place on earth where he could find space for what he called "Self Development." He also wrote and felt that southern California might offer such tranquility where he could meditate.

He accepted a teaching position with Stanford University in 1912. He wrote several papers during his stay at Stanford that were mostly philosophical in their contents. In one such article published from San Francisco in a local paper, he advocated the theory of "free love." He wrote that he supported those who defy customs and normal conventional ways and enter into a contract of "free love." He wrote that he was "a consistent and convinced opponent of the entire fabric of slavery and hypocrisy that is called the marriage system." This was a cause of his termination of contract with Stanford University. It is evident that he did not support the civilized society where marriage and family life was the backbone of the society.

His relationship with one of his students, Ms. Frieda Hauswirth of Switzerland, also became public following publication of the "free love" theory. She had spent many long days and nights with him while working on her papers. Their letters written to each other shed light to a relationship that was more than just a teacher–pupil communication.

It is evident that Har Dayal was never politically active or had any militant ideology prior to coming into contact with politically active Sikhs in California, and only then, he appears to have taken, hesitatingly, any interest in freedom struggle. His minor political involvements were limited to Europe and North America. His activities can be divided into roughly four phases of his politically active life that had a beginning in Stockton, California.

Phase 1:

His association with Sikhs in California was a short lived and virtually uneventful association with Pacific Coast Khalsa Diwan Society and the Ghadr Lehar. This included his contribution to the official publication *Ghadr*. Few of his writings, mostly mild in tone, appeared in this publication.

In April 1911, he published an article titled "India in America" in the magazine *Modern Review*, in which he describes Sikhs as "timid, shabby, and ignorant" who are being "transformed" by America. This article appeared while he was actively pursuing his contacts with Sikhs to further his idea of war of independence for India and needed Sikhs' help to achieve it. With this kind of mindset of opinions about Sikhs, he set out to work with Sikhs in Stockton to set up the Guru Gobind Singh Scholarship with himself as one of the selection committee members. The only Sikh on this committee was Sant Teja Singh. This was also the year when Pacific Coast Khalsa Diwan Society (Khalsa Diwan) was formed.

Under Guru Gobind Singh Scholarship, one of the 6 selected from over 600 candidates was Har Dayal's brother-in-law, Gobind Bihari Lal, a cousin of his wife in India, Sundar. Was this a coincidence, or did Har Dayal influence the decision making—we will never know. Also as a reminder, it was the same Gobind Bihari Lal who spread the false rumors that Har Dayal had been poisoned to death by Sikhs in 1939.

One year after Khalsa Diwan was formed, in May 1913, he visited Portland, Oregon, set up another organization and named it "Hindi Association of Pacific Coast." This is despite the fact that he was based in and working with Sikhs in California under the banner of Khalsa Diwan. Also important to note is that there were hardly any Hindus in Oregon and most Indians were in fact Sikhs. Sikhs were made officers of this organization, including Sohan Singh Bhakna as President.

Funds collected by Sikhs to launch a newspaper by Pacific Coast Khalsa Diwan Society might have been used to start Hindi association in Oregon as the first issue of *Ghadr* did not come out until November 1913. If he was seriously involved in the affairs of the Ghadr Lehar, he would not have worked to initiate the formation of yet another organization that he claimed was fighting for the cause of India's freedom. This conflicting interest clearly indicates that his involvement with Ghadr Lehar and its mother organization, Pacific Coast Khalsa Diwan Society, was only superficial at best and non-involvement at worst.

On March 25, 1914, he was arrested in San Francisco and released on bail the same day. During his interview with immigration authorities, he made very derogatory and damaging comments on the activities of those involved in the freedom movement of India. As documented in his interrogation report no. 12016 dated 3/26/1914, he criticizes Indian freedom fighters and commented on the activities of Madan Lal Dhingra: "I will give you my estimate and you can take it for what it is worth. He was a morbid, melancholy and indolent man; very susceptible to personal influence and very unbalanced; very vain; and unwilling to exert himself for a successful career. This is my idea of him." This was a change of his state of mind since he had described Dhingra as a hero in a July 1909 editorial in *Bande Matram*.

His criticism of India's freedom movement and those involved in it is a clear indication that he was not a wholehearted supporter of it. He may have originally sought to join the ranks of the movement either to get financial benefit or to use it to further his own agenda through its offices and supporters.

While trying to work for his freedom and fight deportation, he received communication from his female friend, Frieda Hauswirth, who was looking for help with her flight from Switzerland to the US in the case of her divorce. Har Dayal made arrangements to send her $200 to help her make arrangements for her fare to the US.

This happened during the days while he was facing deportation and he was living on financial assistance provided from funds collected for the Ghadr Lehar. It is evident that he was using money received from community funds for a cover up and assist Ms. Frieda Hauswirth, with whom he had developed an unexplainable relationship even while still legally married to Sundar Rani of Barnala and had a daughter named Shanti Devi born in 1908.

Phase 2:

In April 1914, he left the United States and began a new phase of life that mostly consisted of his failures and inability to work with other nationalists based in Europe. He arrived in Sweden and was provided a German passport. While visiting Turkey, he connected with other revolutionaries fighting for India's freedom. In late 1914, he broke away with Indian National Committee in Berlin and criticized its work for freedom of India. INC was set up to get help from the Germans for the revolutionary freedom fighters.

From 1915 to 1918, he stayed in Germany but criticized not only INC but also the Germans for not being dedicated to a free India. His correspondence critical of German intentions was intercepted by the authorities and he lived practically under house arrest.

Meanwhile Ghadr uprising planned for February 19, 1915, that was supposed to be the beginning of a revolution in India ended with disaster, and all leaders of the movement in India were either killed, detained, or went into hiding. This ended the dream of a revolution as envisioned by the leaders of Ghadr.

Har Dayal moved around from Switzerland, Germany, Turkey, and finally settling in Sweden in October 1918. He met his future wife, Agda, in 1926 and for practical purposes, remained inactive in all community affairs. His only superficial and limited involvement was confined to an occasional letter addressed to either fellow Indians or British diplomats. The decade in Sweden appears to be the time of his soul searching and coming to terms with the reality of the situation that he was a defeated man who turned to the study of Buddhism to find inner peace from the world torn apart around him.

In 1918, he published an article in San Francisco and criticized Germans and Nationalist Indians who were involved in freedom movement, including members of the Ghadr Movement. This was his attempt to distance himself from the Ghadr party as the conspiracy trial began in San Francisco on November 20, 1917, for 34 people, including 17 members of the Ghadr party and the rest Germans or German Americans. As he had been associated with Ghadr Party, he sought to distance himself to avoid his name being included as a defendant in the trial.

In March 1919, just a month before the massacre at Jallianwala Bagh, his letter under the heading of "Mr Har Dayal's Confession of Faith" was published by a journal based in London named *India*. In this, he publically avowed his "conversion to the principle of Imperial unity and progressive self-government for all civilized nations," but advocated that "they remain within the Empire."

A June 8, 1919, edition of *New York Times* headline read that he no longer believed in freedom for India but sought autonomy within the British Empire because he saw "the Indolent Oriental Unable to stand alone at present."

While writing in the *New Statesman* of London, he wrote, "I now believe that the consolidation of the British Empire in the East is necessary in the best interests of the people of India, Burma, Egypt, and Mesopotamia." While describing the people and history of India, he further writes, "Their history is indeed noble and interesting, but it is rather moldy with age and lack the inspiring power of recent achievement." He believed that "it is foolish for Southern races to imagine that they can, in the long run, hold their own against the Northerners if it comes to a trial of strength between them."

He announced his support for the British Empire publically in a book published in 1920 from London. In this book, he exhorts all Indians to support British rule as this is the only way to save India as a nation. He writes, "England has much to give us besides protection and orgnisation." He further asks Indians to help expand the ideal humanistic rule, the English Empire, and predicts, "If we help to realize this ideal, generations yet unborn will bless our names. The future keeps its secret but we must do our duty in this spirit, looking forward to the advent of the time."

In 1925, he published his "Political Statement" in the *Partap*, a prominent newspaper from Lahore. This was also carried by the widely distributed daily *Times of India*. In the introduction of his statement, he wrote, ". . . in the future this testament will be embodied in school texts for the boys and girls of free India and free Punjab." Interestingly enough, he considers "Free India" and "Free Punjab" as separate identities.

In the statement, he writes, "I declare the future of Hindu race of Hindustan and Punjab rests on 4 pillars." Then he describes these four pillars in detail. Again, it is interesting to note that he considers "Hindustan" and "Punjab" separate and distinct from each other.

His four pillars of saving "Hindu race of Hindustan and Punjab" consisted of (1) Hindu Sangathan—a united Hindu community with solidarity among its various branches and casts; (2) Hindu Raj—establishment of an Empire with Hindus as the ruling class to further the cause of Hinduism; (3) Shuddhi of Moslems—Purification of Moslems—bringing all Moslems back to Hinduism since originally they were all Hindus; (4) Conquest and Shuddhi of Afghanistan and Frontiers—he considers all people of Afghanistan to have been converted by force.

He writes that unless these four tasks are accomplished without delay, future generations of Hindus will be in danger. He believed that it would be impossible to save Hinduism and provide for its safety unless an action plan were devised to implement his ideology.

It is amply clear that someone so devoted to the cause of Hinduism cannot expected to be wholeheartedly devoted to a secular movement like Ghadr Lehar. His sole goal, as he has documented himself, was to further the cause of Hinduism and not that of the nation of India and all its people.

In 1926, he married Agda in Sweden and was given a temporary British passport for travel to the UK only. His wives in the UK and India did not know of each other's existence, but in his will, he left his house to his Indian wife, while, actually, his wife in the UK took care of him for rest of his life, right up to his last days. He married Agda while still legally married to Sunder Rani and never divorced her but abandoned her and their daughter, Shanti Devi.

Phase 3:

In February 1919, he initiated communication with India Office in London regarding the possibility of amnesty for him and to be given an opportunity to travel and live in the UK. His initial request was denied. Again in March 1924, he applied for amnesty and requested to be provided with a UK passport. His request was again denied.

After publishing several papers and a book about his ideology of denouncement of revolution and superiority of English society, he applied for amnesty to India Office in London in March 1927. He requested an amnesty for himself and a British passport to travel to the UK and permission to live in the UK as a resident.

In 1927, the British Government granted blanket amnesty to all the political refugees, and Har Dayal was able to return to England. In England, he lived in Edgware in a small house with his wife, Agda. On December 30, 1935, once again he requested amnesty from the British Government on the grounds that he had lived in the UK for almost a decade and had received his Ph.D. and published his book titled *Hints*, which he described as his *tour de force*.

His stay in England to complete his studies appears to have transformed his ideological leanings from a protagonist of free India to a disgruntled nationalist who saw struggle for freedom as a lost battle. He concentrated on his studies and turned introvert to matters spiritual. He exhorted to public opposition to the freedom movement and criticized all those waging the struggle, including Ghadr Lehar.

Phase 4:

He publically advocated the necessity of a strong British Empire. He went to the extent of not only accepting the British as the future of India but also urging all Indians to support and ensure survival and success of the Empire. He saw the Empire as the only viable solution to India's ill wills based upon the caste-ridden society divided amongst itself.

This change in attitude, or at least public expression of it, helped him stay in England completely undisturbed and unchallenged. This also helped him in completing his education and he was awarded Degree of Doctor of Philosophy by the University of London in 1932. His thesis for the doctorate, "The Bodhisattva Doctrine in Buddhist Sanskrit Literature," was published in book form. This helped in getting accepted for various lecture tours in England and United States.

It was during one of these tours that took him to various cities of the US, that he suffered a heart attack after delivering a speech in Philadelphia. It was reported to the media by his brother-in-law, Gobind Bihari Lal, that Har Dayal was poisoned to death by Sikhs. This was unfounded as Sikhs had no contact with him, and he did not contact any of his old friends and coworkers from the Ghadr Lehar. No one in the Sikh community or old Ghadr party workers was aware of his presence in the country.

The fact that Har Dayal made no contacts with Sikhs in California or any other non-Sikhs related to the Ghadr Lehar clearly indicates that he had no desire to connect with his own past or the movement he once is said to have associated with. This once again provides weight to our argument that he was never a devoted soldier of the Ghadr Lehar and only joined it as an opportunist to help advance his own agenda of self-promotion.

He died on March 4, 1939, at the age of 54. Shunned by Indians, whom he betrayed, forgotten by family he left in India, and mistrusted by British who saw him as a confused and defeated enemy. He lived his life as a wanderer and was cremated in Philadelphia not by his family or friends but by the members of the Philadelphia Ethical Society.

5. Ideology - In His Own Words

Looking briefly at his ideology in his own words reveals an unbalanced personality that was confused and torn apart by ideological conflicts and spiritual starvation. On the one hand, he wanders around the world looking for a quiet and serine place for meditation, and on the other hand, he claims to be leading a revolutionary movement. On one hand, he preaches inner peace and spiritualism, while on the other hand abandons his family and establishes relationships that would meet the definition of immorality.

He had delivered many lectures during his post-Ghadr life, but many of these remain unpublished and are lost. Much that is known about his unbalanced mental state and ideological confusion is based on his own writings that he had published either in newspapers in Europe, America, or Punjab, or had published in book form from Europe.

From what was written by him and survived the wrath of time, his personality as a confused and defeated soldier becomes clear? He himself had, on several occasions throughout his writings, admitted that he was a changed man who had finally come to terms with the reality of the world and did not support his earlier views on revolution and the freedom movement; in fact, he went out of his way to declare that he did not associate with any revolutionary movement fighting for freedom of India.

His important ideological statements/write ups provide insight into his mind as a staunch Hindu who was obsessed with the creation of a Hinduism-based state that would ensure supremacy of Hinduism, protect the cow as a sacred animal, bring back those inhabitants of Afghanistan who are supposed to have been converted forcefully, and would absorb all faiths of South Asia back into the Hindu fold since they were all seen by Har Dayal as offshoots and branches of Hinduism.

He appears to be following the teachings of Hinduism even when he had questioned the Hindu community's inability to gain the freedom it lost due to century-old ideas that are irrelevant in the modern scientific age. He even went to a great length and outlined his plan to preserve cows of Punjab from an unknown threat. He documented his plan and published it in newspaper intentionally for a wider audience than in a book that would be limited to only few readers.

In 1908, his essay on sacredness of the cow appeared in Lahore newspapers. He recommended that each city in Punjab should implement a 4-point program to save sacredness of cows: 1) Start a monthly magazine called "Gau Raksha" (Cow protection), 2) create a center for training of preachers who would spread the gospel of sacredness and protection of cows, 3) establishment of cow shelters to take care of abandoned cows, and 4) teach Sadhus (holy men) to accept no compensation for inspection of cow shelters.

His writings also highlight his concern about growing Christian influence on the Hindu mind. He was suspicious of Christian missionaries and their inroad into the land of Hindus and blamed these missionaries for all ills and deteriorations facing Hindu thought and people of India. Rather than acknowledging the morally deteriorated condition of Hinduism, he blames Christianity for the decay of Hindu philosophy.

In 1909, after he moved to Paris, he published article about his political views in *Modern Review* in Calcutta. He attacked Christianity and blamed it on the decaying state of Hinduism. He wrote that Christians are busy "not only in destroying Hinduism from the outside by Christian missionary activities, but trying to control it from inside in the guise of sympathy for the religion."

Even though his philosophical outlook on life drastically differed from Sikhs, he could not but praise Sikhs after spending some time with the Sikh community on the West Coast of the US. He admired their patriotism and interest in public affairs. He also observed and documented their willingness to donate large sums of money to the community's cause.

In 1911, in the July issue of *The Modern Review*, he wrote a lengthy article describing his opinions about Indians in the United States. He titled it "India in America," and he praised Sikhs with high regards. This is somewhat surprising as he had considered Sikhs "timid, shabby, and ignorant" prior to living among them. He had completely changed his opinion about Sikhs following his close encounter with them while living in California. He was of the opinion now that Sikhs have a "keen sense of patriotism, which manifests itself in deeds of kindly service to their fellow countrymen here, in quickened interest in public affairs, in the revival of religious consciousness, in preference for an independent career on their return to India, and in constant readiness to subscribe large sums of money for the corporate welfare."

It is evident from his writings that he did not believe in the institution of marriage and family life. He was forced to resign from his teaching position at Stanford after he published his theory of "Free Love" and had developed an unexplainable relationship with his student, Frieda Hauswirth. He defended this relationship by advocating the "Free Love" ideology and maintained contact with Frieda even after leaving the US.

In 1912, he wrote an article in one of the San Francisco newspapers and advocated his theory of "Free Love" after his friend entered into a "Free Love" contract prior to marriage. He considered the bride of this contract as a pioneer of women's freedom. He wholeheartedly supported the couple's courage to oppose the conventional marriage custom. He wrote that he himself has been a "consistent and convinced opponent of the entire fabric of slavery and hypocrisy that is called the marriage system." He considers the decision of the couple to enter into the free love contract as a noble idea of life and hoped that others would follow the example of this couple.

In the June 8, 1919, edition of *New York Times* appeared a lengthy write up on Har Dayal. The paper provides an insight into his ideological and mental state by extensively quoting from his earlier writings and paints a picture of a man who has lost all sense of direction in life and accepted his defeat and the fate of his people as the subject of the British. He believed that all people of the South would be unable to stand up to the aggression of the North and "it is foolish for Southern races to imagine that they can, in the long run, hold their own against the Northerners if it comes to a trial of strength between them."

He had surrendered to the circumstances and advised Indians not to fight the "iron imperialism" and recommended that "It is part of wisdom for us not to tempt fate, but to stay under the protection of the British fleet and army in our quiet, sunny home of Hindustan, and make the best of our position in the Empire. We are not equipped for the deadly rivalries and fierce struggles of this age of iron imperialism." He considered Indians unable to rule and as poor administrators, and thus recommended that "The majority of the higher officials of the Police Department, and all officers and generals in the army should be English-men or Europeans."

In 1920, he published his most ideologically comprehensive work titled *Forty-four Months in Germany and Turkey: February 1915 to October 1918 – a Record of Personal Impressions*. It was published in London and dealt with all aspect of his thinking on matters of politics and international relations as well as social fabric of East and West.

In this work, he defended the British Empire, its existence, and its right to rule India and other Asian nations. He declared, "We must now learn that England has a moral and historical mission in Asia." He considered Empire more stable now than before WWI and found that "the stability of the British Empire is a salient fact that emerges from the dust and smoke of the war" and for this reason he predicted the eternity of the Empire and declared that "The British Empire is an institution that has come to stay."

He supported British rule over India since Indians "cannot establish or maintain free national States in this era of armed imperialism. They must live and die as friends and protégés of the great Powers." He did, however, admit that "English and French imperialism is a thousand times preferable to German or Japanese imperialism." He believed that Asian and African "feeble people should work with the great nations which have already organized the vast empires in Asia and Africa." He warned Indians that they would be worse off with self-rule and that struggle for freedom was bound to fail and that British rule should not be disturbed as "Disruption can only expose them to much greater evils than those from which they suffer under the present system. The policy of separation and intrigue is futile and fallacious."

In 1925, he published his "Political Statement" in a prominent newspaper from Lahore and other major newspapers of India. He introduced to his fellow Indians his testament for the future and felt that ". . . in the future this testament will be embodied in school texts for the boys and girls of free India and free Punjab." In this testament, he declared that "the future of Hindu race of Hindustan and Punjab rests on 4 pillars." He described the four pillars as "Hindu Sangathan, Hindu Raj, Shuddhi of Moslems and Conquest and Shuddhi of Afghanistan and Frontiers." He promised that "so long as the Hindu nation does not accomplish these four things, the safety of our children and great-grandchildren will be ever in danger. And the safety of the Hindu race will be impossible."

He believed that humans are fundamentally pacifist and peaceful by nature, and he called this human trait the "universal law." Since Ghadr party consisted basically of Sikhs and by nature Sikhs believe in the principal of Dynamic Optimism (Chardi Kala) as envisioned and expounded by Sikh Gurus, even while being publically executed, it is difficult to expect that Sikhs would have accepted a leader with such a negative and pacifist outlook on life.

In December 1938, he published an article in *New History* entitled "The Inevitability of Pacifism." His inner self speaks loudly through it and his belief in Pacifism is outlined in detail. He wrote that "Biology clearly demonstrates that human nature is radically and fundamentally pacifist." He goes on to write that "Pacifism is broad-based and solidly grounded on this biological and psychological verity: Human nature is peaceful." This contradicts with Sikh belief of *Dynamic Optimism*, and such pacifist ideology would not have been acceptable to Sikhs, especially in a leader.

6. Conclusions

1. In most writings in India or by an Indian, he is often referred to as a freedom fighter who devoted his life for Freedom of India. However, facts paint a picture of an opportunist who betrayed not only a revolutionary movement but an entire community and country—for self-interest. Special-interest historians like to put him in the category of "freedom fighters," while the British did not even list him as a member of Gadar Movement in the secret British Gadar Directory either in the 1917 or 1934 editions (despite the fact that he was still alive at the time of publication of these editions). During the hearing of the special tribunal that began on April 26, 1915, several of the leading figures of the Gadar were tried. A total of 291 persons were tried and many of them in absentia as these leaders were either in hiding in Punjab countryside or out of the country. Har Dayal was not one of those tried during these hearings. His name did not figure in the list as he was considered neither a leading soldier nor an officer of the Gadar Lehar.

2. "Har Dayal decisively rejected his earlier revolutionary viewpoint. He abandoned his Anglophobia, advocated the mixed British and Indian administration of his country, and became a firm admirer of Western culture and values." This is how *Encyclopedia Britannica* describes Har Dayal. "Har Dayal was arrested on the pretext of a speech delivered by him three years earlier. The party got him out on bail and managed to send him away to Switzerland. Thereafter he took no part in the Gadar movement." This is how the *Encyclopedia of Sikhism* describes Har Dayal's arrest as being not for involvement in Ghadr but for a speech he made prior to the establishment of the Gadar Party. It also supports our opinion that he did not take any part in the activities of the Gadar Lehar.

3. Har Dayal was not a revolutionary, either in thoughts or actions. His writings do not reflect any revolutionary ideology. He either misunderstood global revolutionary movements or did not subscribe to the ideology of "freedom for all." His interests lay in starting a new religion rather than starting a revolution. He moved from one place to another in search for a peaceful environment for meditation and lived a life of

isolation from community in general and specifically out of touch with the Indian community settled abroad. His interest lay more in protection of Sacred Cows and Hindu superiority rather than freedom of the country and its people.

4. "He asks his countrymen to act up to his advice and not to follow his example, which shows that he knows absolutely nothing of human nature. It is a gross mistake on his part to prohibit Indians from going to England"—this is how Hindustan newspapers commented in 1908 after his articles appeared in several newspapers asking young men of India not to go to England and "not to pollute themselves in that country of *malechhas* (foreigners)." This clearly shows his confused mental state as he is having trouble understanding the benefit that an education will bring to his countrymen.

5. Gadar party was formally launched on June 2, 1913, and Har Dayal associated with it from November 1913 after he had set up the Hindi Association of America and when first edition of the organization's newspaper *Gadar* was issued. He left the US in March 1914. This shows his association with Gadar Lehar was less than 6 months. Clearly, it was not a sufficiently long enough association to influence an organization, develop a strategy, or establish strong footings for future actions.

6. Before leaving the US, he handpicked and appointed Ram Chandra, a Brahmin from Peshawar, as head of the Gadar Party. This was a wrong choice as Ram Chandra was a corrupt man who misappropriated funds collected by party workers. Ram Chandra was shot dead by Bhai Ram Singh, a Sikh member of the Gadar Party on April 23, 1918. He was killed at the end of the trial that began on November 20, 1917, and during the trial, it became public knowledge that Ram Chandra had taken possession of the building that housed the headquarters of the Gadar, the newspaper, and all the accounts of the Ghadr Party. Har Dayal should have left the appointment of Gadar leadership up to the working members of the party rather than impose a leadership on them with his own personal choice.

7. He left Turkey in October 1914 without informing anyone of his associates. Many members of the Indian National Committee were taken by his surprise move out of Turkey and his criticism of Germany that had financed his stay in Europe and supported INC. He not only betrayed German but also INC. His decision to leave Turkey and the

revolutionary movement was seen by many as an action that suggested an acceptance of defeat by Har Dayal. He never took active part in any nationalist or revolutionary movement after this.

8. After leaving the freedom movement, he did not just lie down quietly; he, in fact, actively defended the British rule and urged Indians to help maintain it at all costs. He broke not only from his family, but also the community he was supposedly fighting for. He lived in isolation while in Europe and even upon his return to England. He applied for amnesty to British, not once but four separate times; it shows that he lived his life as a defeated soul, unlike the Gadari Babas who continued to fight against odds, all their lives. He had given up his struggle and accepted his defeat and intended to live his life as close to a normal subject of the British Empire as he could. He had no revolutionary spirit that could keep him fighting any longer.

9. His concern was protecting and expanding Hinduism and not freedom for Hindustan; thus he cannot be placed in the same category of fighters as the members of the Ghadr Lehar. It was not an agenda of the Lehar to protect and project any one community but to free India from British rule. All communities that reside in India were seen as equally deserving of freedom and equal rights.

10. Betrayal of those around him were hallmark of his personality, and right up to the end, he lived by this trait. Even after his death, the news was circulated that he was poisoned by Sikhs because of the animosity he earned by disowning the ideal of the Ghadr Movement. It was proved beyond doubt that he died due to heart attack, but the idea that rumor was circulated about his animosity with Sikhs simply proves that he was not held in high esteem by the members of the Ghadr Lehar.

11. During his tour of the United States in 1939, he made no attempt to contact any members of the Ghadr Lehar. This was despite the fact that many original members of the Gadar and his fellow workers involved with the original organization were still alive and had established families in California. His total neglect of the remaining members of the original organization indicates he was not dedicated to the organization and its goal.

12. It was due to betrayal by men like Har Dayal that, despite high degree of devotion for the cause and willingness for ultimate sacrifice, the Gadar Movement could not achieve success as envisioned by faithful foot

soldiers that returned to India to fight for India's freedom and paid the ultimate price with their lives.
13. He was not a Gadari, but a Safari (wanderer), who just wandered in and out of the Gadar Lehar, as a mute spectator and left no mark on the history of the movement and played absolutely no role in its development and its actions. He sought meditation rather than revolution as the sole goal of his life. He never possessed a revolutionary spirit to head a revolutionary movement.

7. References:

Opinions expressed and conclusions drawn are solely of the author; however, earlier research works are duly acknowledged for providing one or more of the data, facts, figures, and quotes used in this paper. While not referenced separately in the body, collectively following works were used to research and correlate facts provided in this article. Information about historical dates and activities were taken from, derived from, and correlated from the works listed below.

English:
1. Emily C. Brown, 1975, *Har Dayal: Hindu Revolutionary and Rationalist*, University of Arizona Tucson Arizona USA, 0-8165-0422-9, pp 321. South Asian edition published by Manohar Books Delhi India, 1976.
2. Emily C. Brown, 1996, *Ghadr Movement* in Encyclopedia of Sikhism Vol II, Punjabi University Patiala Punjab India, 81-7380-204-1, p60
3. Har Dayal, 1920, *Forty-Four Months in Germany and Turkey: February 1915 to October 1918, A Record of Personal Impressions*, P. S. King & Sons Ltd Orchard House Westminster England, pp 104
4. Dharmavira, 1970, *Lala Har Dayal and Revolutionary Movements of his Times*, India Book Company New Delhi India, pp 363
5. Editorial Staff, 1997, *Ghadr Directory: Containing Names of persons who have taken part in Ghadr*, Punjabi University Patiala Punjab India, 81-7380-415-X, pp 298
6. Harold S. Jacoby, 2007, *History of East Indians in America*, Chattar Singh Jiwan Singh Amritsar Punjab India, 81-7601-863-5, pp 280
7. Jaiwant Paul etal., 2003, *Har Dayal: The Great Revolutionary*, Roli Books Pvt Ltd New Delhi India, 81-7436-287-8, pp 184

8. Harish K. Puri, 1983, *Ghadr Movement: Ideology Organisation and Strategy*, Guru Nanak Dev University Amritsar Punjab India, pp 218
9. Maia Ramnath, 2011, *Haj to Utopia: How the Ghadr Movement Charted Global Radicalism*, University of California Press Berkeley California USA, 978-0-520-26955-2, pp 328
10. Malwinderjit Singh etal. Ed., 2001, *War Against King Emperor: Ghadr of 1914-1915, Verdict by Special Tribunal*, Bhai Sahib Randhir Singh Trust Ludhiana Punjab India, pp 541
11. Nahar Singh etal. Ed., 1986, *Struggle for Free Hindustan Volume 1: 1905-1916 Ghadr*, Atlantic Publishers New Delhi India, pp 339
12. Nahar Singh etal. Ed., 1996, *Struggle for Free Hindustan: Ghadr Directory*, Gobind Sadan Institute New Delhi India, pp 230
13. Wadhawa Singh, 1983, *Introduction to Sikh Temple Stockton and Gadar Party*, Sikh Temple Stockton California USA, pp 258
14. Ved Prakash Vatuk editor, 1999, *The Gadarite No. 1*, Gadar Heritage Foundation Berkeley California USA, pp 37
15. Ved Prakash Vatuk editor, No DOP, *The Gadarite No. 2*, Gadar Heritage Foundation Berkeley California USA, pp 60

Gurmukhi:

16. Gurdev Singh Deol, 1970, *Ghadr Party te Bharat da Quomi Andolan* (Ghadr Party and India's National Revolution), Sikh Itihas Research Board Amritsar Punjab India, pp 346
17. Giani Kesar Singh ed, 2008, *Ghadr Lehar Di Wartak* (Prose of the Ghadr Movement), Punjabi University Patiala Punjab India, 81-302-0095-3, pp756
18. Giani Kesar Singh ed, 1995, *Ghadr Lehar di Kavita* (Poetry of the Ghadr Movement), Punjabi University Patiala Punjab India, 81-7380-013-8, pp 502
19. Jagjit Singh, 1979, *Ghadr Party Lehar* (Ghadr Party Movement), Navyug Publishers Delhi India, pp 183

On Line Sources:

20. http://www.advancedcentrepunjabi.org/eos/, Accessed on February 12, 2013. See entry under Ghadr Movement.
21. http://www.britannica.com/EBchecked/topic/254783/Lala-Har-Dayal, Accessed on January 29, 2013.

22. http://diplomat.anandweb.com/2009/10/fwd-lala-har-dayal-enigma-of.html, Accessed on February 25, 2013. This article first appeared in the online publication *South Asia Post*, Issue 97 Vol IV, October 15, 2009.
23. http://punjabfreedomfighter.blogspot.com/2011/01/lala-har-dayal.html , Accessed on February 12, 2013. This blog site also has articles with brief but factual information about other Ghadr Lehar activists as well.

Fresh Look at Ram Chandra Bhardwaj and Vinayak Damodar Savarkar

Jasbir Singh Mann MD, California

The Gadar Movement of 1907–1918 cannot be discussed outside of the Sikh paradigm. All leaders of the movement—initially Hindus, Muslims, and Sikhs—appealed to Sikh archetype of a soldier while fighting and embracing martyrdom. Everyone was appealing to this archetype but all had different goals. The British wanted to reduce German and German-American influence and sought to induce the US into World War I. Leaders of Arya Samaj background had larger goals of securing the Indian subcontinent for themselves. Ghadrites' real value lay in creating danger for the British and increasing their bargaining power with the British. Most Sikhs who jumped in the Gadar movement were primarily inspired by socialistic, secular, and democratic human ideals of Sikhism as enshrined in *Guru Granth Sahib* compiled in 1604 and Nash doctrine of the Khalsa Revolution 1699 AD. This paper presents, from the Sikh perspective, a fresh look at three important personalities who played significant roles in the century-old movement. Jatinder Singh Hundal has provided details in his paper about Lala Hardayal, "Gadar Lehar and Lala Har Dayal: Life, Activities & Ideology." Present paper briefly reviews the life and activities of Ram Chandra Bhardwaj and Vinayak Damodar Savarkar.

Ram Chandra Bharadwaj

Germans always wanted to strike against the British for colonial supremacy. German agents were in touch with Indian revolutionaries and pan-Islamic Groups since 1909 in Europe. In 1911, Bernhardi, a German General, in his book *Germany and the Next War* indicates that the Hindu Population of Bengal, having nationalist and revolutionary tendency, along with Pan-islamists might create very grave danger that would be capable of shaking the foundation of England's high position in the world. Germans wanted promotion "Of German doctrine that Fatherland would strike against England." In December 1914, Graff Thurn, German consulate in Calcutta, confirms Germans' interest by his report as "It concludes that an India which has disintegrated into splinter states could offer its German (and Austrian) advisers the mineral and industrial wealth of the richest land in the world." Germans assisted in funding for publishing anti-British Literature and its distribution worldwide, collection of arms and ammunition, and getting passports for free mobility through their consulates. Since 1909, Germans were in touch with Indian revolutionaries in Britain. As admitted by V. D. Savarkar that "His warning to leave England in 1909 after assassination of Sir Curzon Wyllie had actually come from a German Agent" (Emile C Brown page 149). Gustav Steinhart of the German Intelligence Service had made considerable efforts before the war to place agents in Britain.

On November 15, 1913, the Gadhar spokesman writes, "The Germans have a great sympathy with our movement and liberty because they and ourselves have a common enemy. In future Germany can draw assistance from us and they can render a great assistance also."

On December 31, 1913, in a meeting in Sacramento, German Consulate Franz Bopp was sitting on stage when Lala Hardyal declared, "If I am turned out of this country, I can make preparation for the mutiny in another country . . . I shall have to go to Germany to make arrangements for the approaching Gadhar."

On December 31, 1913, during the Sacramento meeting, "Finally lala hardyal told the audience that German was preparing to Go to war with England and that it was time to get ready to go to India for coming revolution."

A large number of sign boards were seen posted in Ashram in San Francisco and sent to other places in the world which read, "Do not oppose the Germans."

> "March 6th 1914 'Berliner Tageblatt' published article on 'England's Indian trouble' depicting gloomy Situation in India and representing that secret societies flourished and spread and were helped from outside. In California especially, it was said there appeared to be an organized enterprise for the purpose of providing India with arms and explosives."

Early 1915 – Raja Mahindra Pratap Singh, son in law of Jind state (wife, Maharani Balbir Kaur), leaves India, goes to Germany, and meets with Kaiser Wilhelm II, along with vice minister of foreign affairs Mr. Zimmerman, at the imperial palace in the Tiergarten. They talked twenty minutes. The Kaiser speaks English and says that the English rule must come to an end in India during these years. Kaiser was well prepared for the interview; in spite of his very heavy duties as the ruler and the Commander-in-Chief, he had found time to remember something about his relation with the Phulkian States of Punjab. He spoke of Jind, Patiala, and Nabha and of their strategic position in case of a military move from the side of Afghanistan. He told Mahindra Pratap, "Don't forget to give my greetings to the Amir of Afghanistan."

Later, German Ambassador Bernstorff referred to the Hindu plot in his memoirs as "an absolute wild-goose chase." German military attaché Von Pappen years later wrote in his own memoirs that "he never really expected Germany to successfully export revolution to India, but rather create a diversion of British effort."

SIKH GADAR LEHAR 1907-1918

Ram Chandra Bharadwaj, also known as Pandit Ram Chandra, was the in charge of the Ghadar Party from August 1914 onwards, when all Gadhrites left for India. As a member of the Ghadar Party, Ram Chandra was also one of the founding editors of the *Hindustan Ghadar* (very good writer) and a key leader of the party in its role in the Indo-German Conspiracy. Ram Chandra promised the Ghadrites in August 1914 that on their arrival in India they would receive the arms. Hari Singh Usman was the in charge on the ship *Mavrick* that left Los Angles, USA, on April 23, 1915. In his diary, Hari Singh reports that Pandit Ram Chandra became a British spy and told all secret plans to British Council about Hari Singh being the leader on the ship and transfering the load of arms from the *Annie Larson* schooner to the *Maverick* ship. British Ambassador Spring Rice notified the US Secretary of State and orders were given to blow up the ship *Maverick*. But, the German consulate notified Hari Singh Usman and his group about it. Therefore, Hari Singh Usman's route for the *Maverick* was changed through New Guenia. Hari Singh Usman's story is confirmed by British Ambassador correspondence to US State Secretary Larson, which shows "During 1915 British Ambassador Cecil Spring-Rice asked that a shipment of arms the Germans had purchased in New York for shipment to Mexico on the Annie Larsen be investigated. British undercover agents knew the Germans planned to transfer the arms to the Maverick in Mexico and to ship them to Batavia for distribution to Indian revolutionaries . . ." (Joan M. Larsen: "The Hindu Conspiracy: A reassessment"). This was the end of Ram Chandra for the Gadar party. Please note Gadar failed in Panjab on February 19, 1915. Gadarites in Panjab received no money or arms as promised by their leader Ram Chandra. The young North American Sikh generation may not visit India in the future, but they may see portraits of their great grandparents with turbans in their drawing rooms and may have some quarries: What exactly happened? Why did they go back to India in 1914 with no money and no arms to fight an armed revolution? Did Gadarites fail in their inspiration, or did their leaders fail? It is clear that Gadarites were pushed into this armed revolution without supply of arms or money by their leaders.

Ram Chandra assumed the role of president of the party following Lala Har Dayal's departure for Switzerland in 1914. He, along with Bhagwan Singh and Maulvi Mohammed Barkatullah, was key in rallying the support of the South Asian community in the Pacific Coast in the wake of the *Komagata Maru* incident for the planned February mutiny. More than $15,000 in cash was reportedly deposited in banks in the name of Pundit's wife. Properties were purchased in the name of Pandit's personal friends. It is reported that two plots on Wood Street were put in the name of Mr. Reed. Harish Chandra took $8,000 out of party funds and absconded. Ram Chandra was assassinated on April 24, 1918, on the last day of the Hindu–German Conspiracy Trial by Ram Singh, probably on accusation by his group of Ram Chandra misappropriating party funds and misusing his position/power. Ram Singh himself was big donor for Gadar party and participated in Sikh Gadar. It is reported that Ram Singh owned poperty worth $125,000 in Vancouver at that time. Ram Singh in turn was shot by the US Marshal on duty. Ajit Singh, who was leader of Gadar since 1907 and left India, writes that the British Government took several other measures to crush the movement: "The old policy of 'divide and rule' was used. Hindus were encouraged and cajoled to leave the party. Similarly Dr. Syed Hussain and Shaukat Ali toured the State and started a Moslem league to wean away the Mohammedans. Some prominent Sikh members were also deceived in heading a dissident movement."

VINAYAK DAMODAR SAVARKAR

"A major source of movement's Inspiration was V.D. Savarkar's exciting history of the rebellion The Indian war of independence 1857. Experts and chapters from that Book were published in various issues of Gadhar" (Harish K. Puri, 2011, Introduction, Page XII). On the contrary, Dr. Ganda Singh (1969) wrote his paper on Sikhs and the Sepoy Mutiny of 1857 based on evidence by historians like Dr. Surendra Nath Sen, Dr. Romesh C. Majumdar, Maulana Abul Kalam Azad, and S. Acharya Kriplani, which places before its readers a number of historical facts based on the research of India's leading historians of international fame and unapproachable integrity, and their impartial verdict is that "it would be a travesty of truth to describe the revolt of 1857 as a national war of independence." If one reads Sarvakar's book, one finds it has very strong anti-Sikh bias as it completely suppresses the 18th century glorious period of Sikh history. He blamed the Sikhs for supporting the British in the 1857 Mutiny, which wanted to bring back the Mughal raj who massacred the Sikhs in 17th and 18th centuries. But in his personal and political life, V.D. Savarkar in turn did what he blamed the Sikhs for, serving the British in 1857. He himself surrendered to Britshers from 1911 to 1947. **Bahadur Shah issued the Hindus and Muslims but not Sikhs the** following decree, a *Shahi Firman* (King's decree), on May 12, 1857: "To all the Hindus and Muslims of India, taking my duty by the people into consideration at this hour, I have decided to stand by my people. Whoever shows cowardice at this delicate hour, or whoever in innocence will help the cunning English, believing in their promises, he would stand disillusioned very soon. He should remember that the English will pay him for his faithfulness to them in the same manner as they have paid the rulers of Oudh. It is the imperative duty of Hindus and *Mussalmans* (Muslims) to join the revolt against the English. They should work and be guided by their leaders in their towns and should take steps to restore order in the country. It is the bounden duty of all people that they should, as far as possible, copy out this *Firman* and display it at all important places in the towns. But before doing so, they should get themselves armed and declare war on the English."

As asserted by historian John Harris, Sikhs participated in 1857:

1. Sikhs wanted to avenge the annexation of the Sikh Empire eight years earlier by the Company with the help of *Purabias* ("Easterners"): Biharis and those from the United Provinces of Agra and Oudh who had formed part of the East India Company's armies in the First and Second Anglo-Sikh Wars. (These *Purabias* ["Easterners"] used to throw smoke fumes on faces of Sikhs when they entered Punjab.)
2. He has also suggested that Sikhs felt insulted by the attitude of sepoys who (in their view) had only beaten the Khalsa with British help; they resented and despised them far more than they did the British.
3. It is also believed that the Sikhs were not willing to help reinstate the Mughal rule in India. Who ordered total elimination of Sikhs in the 18th century?

Readers must know that only the Sikh armies of Patiala, Nabha, and Jind helped the British, and these states had had an alliance with the British since 1809 AD.

A.G. Noorani exposes Savarkar's alliance with British for which he blamed the Sikhs in his book *Indian War of Independence 1857* written in 1909. Savarkar met the arch imperialist Viceroy of India, Lord Linlithgow, in Bombay on October 9, 1939—the month Congress asked its Ministers in the provinces to resign—and pledged his enthusiastic cooperation to the British. Linlithgow reported to Lord Zetland, the Secretary of State for India: "The situation, he [Savarkar] said, was that His Majesty's Government must now turn to the Hindus and work with their support. After all, though we and the Hindus have had a good deal of difficulty with one another in the past that was equally true of the relations between Great Britain and the French and, as recent events had shown, of relations between Russia and Germany. *Our interests were now the same and we must therefore work together.* Even though now the most moderate of men, he had himself been in the past an adherent of a revolutionary party, as possibly, I might be aware. (I confirmed that I was.) But now that our interests were so closely bound together the essential thing was for Hinduism and Great Britain to be friends, and the old antagonism was no longer necessary." It was a clear offer of collaboration with the British to suppress the Congress' movement. Savarkar's colleague in the Hindu Mahasabha and founder of the Jan Sangh, Shyama Prasad Mookerjee, was Finance Minister in the Bengal Ministry headed by Fazlul Haq. Mahasabhites were members of the Muslim League Ministry in Sindh. On July 26, 1949, Mookerjee wrote to Governor John Herbert renewing this offer in these explicit terms: "I have been thinking over the questions which we discussed at some length at the last Cabinet Meeting, specially arising out of the threatened Congress movement. It is of utmost importance that there should be complete understanding between you, as Governor, and your colleagues during the present critical period. . . . Let me now refer to the situation that may be created in the province as a result of any widespread movement launched by the Congress. Anybody who, during the war, plans to stir up mass feelings, resulting in internal disturbances or insecurity, must be resisted by any government that may function for the time being."

Savarkar was president of Hindu Mahansabha in 1937 and 1942. And his book *Hindu Rashtra Darshan*, a collection of his presidential speeches from 1937 to 1942, goes into detail about the Hindutva/Hindu nationalism/communal nationalism to be enforced upon all Indians as compared to the secular nationalism as envisioned by the Indian National Congress, Nehru, and Gandhi. The British and the Mahansava in 1945 had very closed relations. When Indian National Congress passed the of Quit India resolution, the Hindu Mahansava supported the Britishers by not joining such movement in Bengal. In September 1942, Savarkar issued an edict which reads, "I issue this definite instruction to Hindu Sabhaites in particular and all Hindu Sangathanists in general . . . holding any post or position of vantage in the Government services should stick to them and continue to perform their regular duties." The Hindu Mahansabha was in a coalition Government with the Muslim League in Sindh. Though the Sindh Assembly passed a resolution endorsing the demand for Pakistan, the Mahansabha Ministers did not resign from the government but contented themselves with a protest, for the record. He, on record, supports the British against the Quit India movement in 1942 and for the Second World War.

Born on May 28, 1883, Bhagur, Maharashtra, India. Recieved Bachelor of Arts from Fergusson College, Pune, Maharashtra (India); HE CAME TO ENGLAND IN 1906. Barrister from the "Honorable Society of Gray's Inn London" (England). Savarkar's revolutionary activities began when studying in India and England, where he was associated with the India House and founded student societies including Abhinav Bharat Society and the Free India Society, as well as publications espousing the cause of complete Indian independence by revolutionary means.[7] Savarkar published *The Indian War of Independence* about the Indian rebellion of 1857 that was banned by British authorities. He was arrested in 1910 for his connections with the revolutionary group India House. Following a failed attempt to escape while being transported from Marseilles, Savarkar was sentenced to two life terms amounting to 50 years' imprisonment and moved to the Cellular Jail in the Andaman and Nicobar Islands. But evidence shows SAVARKAR appealed for clemency, first in 1911 and then again in 1913, the latter during the visit of Sir Reginald Craddock. In a letter dated November 14, 1913, Savarkar (convict no. 32778) wrote to the Home Minister of the Government of India: "I hereby acknowledge that I had a fair trial and just sentence. I heartily abhor methods of violence resorted to in days gone by and I feel myself duty bound to *uphold law and constitution* [British] to the best of my powers and am willing to *make the reform* [i.e., the Montague-Chelmsford reforms of 1919 which did not satisfy the demands of the nationalist movement] *a success* in so far as I may be allowed to do so in future." We read again: "If the government in their manifold beneficence and mercy release me, I for one cannot but be the *staunchest advocate* of constitutional progress and *loyalty to the English government* which is the foremost condition of that progress [. . .] Moreover, my *conversion* to the constitutional line would bring back all those mislead young men in India and abroad who were once looking up to me as their guide [. . .] The Mighty alone can afford to be merciful and therefore where else can the *prodigal son* return but to the parental doors of the government." He was a prolific writer and wrote the following books: *Saha*

Soneri Paane (translation: Six Glorious Epochs of Indian History), *1857 che Svatantrya Samar, Hindupadpaatshahi, Hindutva, Jatyochhedak Nibandha, Moplyanche Banda, Maazi Janmathep* (translation: My life imprisonment), *Kale Pani, Shatruchya Shibirat, Londonchi batamipatre* (translation: London Newsletters), *Andamanchya Andheritun, Vidnyan nishtha Nibandha, Joseph Mazzini* (on Giuseppe Mazzini), *Hindurashtra Darshan, Hindutvache Panchapran, Kamala, Savarkaranchya Kavita* (translation: Poems by Savarkar), *Sanyasta Khadg.*

From 1923 onwards, he wrote and started the "Hindutva" concept, which means Hindustan is only for Hindus, and started Shhudi movement from Andaman jail from 1923 onwards. He became president of Hindu Mahan Sabha from 1937 to 1942, which, on record, supported the British against Quit India movement in 1942 and in the Second World War.

Savarkar's Apologies and Assurances to the Government, 1911-1950, Pages 140-147. Savarkar and Hindutva by AG Noorani, 2002, Published by Leftward Books.

Appendix 1: 1911, 1913

Savarkar arrived in the Andamans in June 1911. Before the year was out, he submitted to the Government of India a "petition for clemency." The text of this petition, however, is not available. Savarkar referred to it in his next petition sent on November 14, 1913. The bulk of the letter concerned facilities in jail and a request for transfer to an "Indian Jail for there I would earn (a) remission; (b) would have a visit from my people . . ."

The last and revealing paragraph of the petition is set out below:

In the end may I remind your honor to be so good as to go through the petition for clemency that I had sent in 1911 and to sanction it for being forwarded to the Indian Government? The latest development of the Indian Politics and the conciliating policy of the Government have thrown open the constitutional line once more. Now no man having the good of India and Humanity at heart will blindly step on the thorny paths which in the excited and hopeless situation of India in 1906-1907 beguiled us from the path of peace and progress. Therefore if the Government in their manifold beneficence and merely release me I for one cannot but be the staunchest advocate of constitutional progress and loyalty to the English Government which is the foremost condition of that progress. As long as we are in jails, there cannot be real happiness and joy in hundreds and thousands of homes of His Majesty's loyal subjects in India, for blood is thicker than water; but if we be released the people will instinctively raise a shout of joy and gratitude to the Government, who knows how to forgive and correct, more than how to chastise and avenge. Moreover my conversation to the constitutional line would bring back all those misled young men in India and abroad who were once looking up to me as their guide, I am ready to serve the Government in any capacity they like, for as my conversion is conscientious so I hope my future conduct would be. By keeping me in jail nothing can be got in comparison to what would be otherwise. The mighty alone can afford to be merciful and therefore where else can the prodigal son return but to the parental doors of the Government? Hoping your honor will kindly take into notion these points.

Appendix 2: 1924, 1925

Documents published in *Frontline*, April 7, 1995.

With compliments from the Director of Information of Bombay p.2/5-1-24.

The Government of Bombay has decided on the release of Vinayak Damodar Savarkar and the following government resolution has been issued by the Home Department.

1. 'In exercise of the power conferred by Section 401 of the Code of Criminal Procedure, 1898, the Governor in Council hereby remits conditionally the unexpired portion of the sentences of transportation for life passed up on Vinayak Damodar Savarkar.
2. The order for the conditional release for the convict should be sent to the Superintendent, Yeravada Central Prison, who should take an agreement from the convict accepting the conditions specified in the order, and forward it to the Government, through the Inspector General of Prisons, with the report that the convict has been released in the pursuance of the Order.'

The conditions attached to the release of releases are these:

1. 'That the said Vinayak Damodar Savarkar will reside within the territories administered by the Governor of Bombay in Council and within the Ratnagiri District within the said territories, and will not go beyond the limits of that district without the permission of the Government, or in case of urgency of that District Magistrate.
2. That he will not engage publicly or privately in any manner of political activities without the consent of the Government for a period of five years, such restriction being renewable at the discretion of Government at the expiry of the said term.

Mr. Savarkar has already indicated his – acceptance of these terms. He has also, thought it was explained to him that it was in no way made condition of his release, submitted the following statement: - 'I hereby acknowledge that I had a fair trial and just sentence. I heartily abhor – methods of violence resorted to in days gone by, and I feel myself duty bound to uphold Law and the constitution to the best of my powers and am willing to make the Reform a success in so far as I may be allowed to do in the future.'

True Copy,

        For Superintendent
**

Shirgaon, 9 May, 1925

To
D. O' Flynn, Esquire,
Acting Deputy Secretary to the Government of
Bombay, Home Department.

Sir,

I have received yesterday your letter dated 6 May regarding the article in the 'Maratha' on the subject of the riots at Kohat.

This letter makes me revise the meaning I put on the terms of my conditions which to my mind meant refraining from discussing or dealing with any question of current policies i.e. any matter that refer to the nature of activity of the Government directly bearing on its political aspect internal or international. In the light of this interpretation I had honestly striven to guide my public activities. But this order had forced me to understand the condition in a narrower sense.

While I am trying to define to myself my position in view of this new order I most humbly beg to request in as much as this order came to my hand on the 8th of May, all my writings and speeches prior to that date should be subjected to that interpretation as they were guided by the first and direct interpretation I naturally put on the meaning of terms of my conditions of release. Of course all my actions subsequent to the date of the receipt of your letter would be subjected to this interpretation.

I have the honor to be,
Sir,
Your most obedient servant,
Sd. V.D. Savarkar.
True Copy.

**

Extract from an article in *Frontline*, dated April 7, 1995:

In February 1925, serious communal trouble broke out in Kohat town of the North-West Frontier Province (NWFP). Jivan Das of Kohat had written a booklet, Rangila Rasool, portraying Prophet Mohammed in bad light. This caused communal riots in Kohat, in the other town in the NWFP and in the western parts of then Punjab. As rumors spread throughout the country, Savarkar felt so agitated he wrote an article in the Mahratta of Pune on Mar 1, 1925.

The Government did not take to this kindly. He was warned that 'any future writings of a similar character will be regarded by Government a sufficient justification for reconsidering the question of his release. Post haste despite his having very strong views on the Kohat incidents, Savarkar sent a longish explanation at the end of which he thanked the Government for having given him an opportunity to explain himself and hoped that in future too they would be pleased to be as kindly disposed towards him. In this letter, dated April 6, he made it clear he would have no truck with the idea of Swaraj; 'The only place where the word Swaraj occurs is at the end of the third paragraph and there it is obvious that a reference is not at all to show or indicate what I or other people think of Swaraj but in what exaggerated terms Mr. Gandhi thinks of Khilafat.

The Government was not mollified even by this. It told him curtly on May 6, 1925 it considered his explanation far from satisfactory. ".. it should have been obvious to you that an article of the nature which you published in the issue of Mahratta of the March 1, 1925 was bound to inflame the feelings and increase the tension between Hindus and Muhammadans and was contrary to your undertaking not to engage in any manner in political activities without the consent of the Government.

This letter was received by Savarkar on May 8 through the District Magistrate. It was so unnerved him that the very next day he wrote back to D. O Flynn, Acting Deputy Secretary to the Government of Bombay, Home Department, thus ". . . I most Humbly beg to request in as much as this order came to my had on the May 8, all my writings and speeches prior to that date should not be subjected to that interpretation as they were guided by the first or direct interpretation I naturally put on the meaning of terms of my conditions of release'.

Savarkar took fright that the Government might resort to some severe action against him for some of the writings and speeches made between March and May 8. One warning from the Government and his concerns for the so called welfare of Hindus had disappeared into thin air.

Appendix 3: 1948

Arthur Road Prison,
Bombay.

Dated 22-2-1948

To
The Commissioner of Police,
Bombay,

Sir,

Your notice No. 1202 of 1948 was served on me day before yesterday.

(I) My submission to the charges is that I never promoted hatred and incited Hindus to hate or to commit acts of violence against the Mohammedans as Mohammedans. I have been an advocate throughout my life of Genuine Indian Nationalism. I always emphasized that all citizens who owned loyalty to the Indian state must be loved as fellow citizens and treated with equality of rights and obligations to the state irrespective of caste, creed or religion without the least distinction being made as Hindu or a Mohammedan or a Parsee or a Jew. One man one vote and services to go by merit alone, these two principals will be found endlessly repeated in all my writings and speeches made throughout my political career for some 50 years in the past.

But it is this admitted fact that I have been exhorting the Hindus to defend themselves in virtue of the logic of self-defense was I believe misunderstood or misinterpreted as an incitement to the Hindus to commit violence against all Muslims alike. I submit that this interpretation is wrong and unwarranted. Sardar Patel himself in replying to provoking speeches of some Muslim leaders retorted 'sword shall be met with sword'. But that does not surely mean that he hated all Muslims alike or incited violence.

(II) To substantiate the fact I need not quote one of my latest, statements issued just before my arrest and published in the 'Times' in the course of which after denouncing the gruesome crime of the assassination of Mahatma Gandhi the fratricidal crimes committed by the mob fury, I implored every patriotic citizen to bear in mind that a successful national revolution and a newly born National State could have no worse enemy than a fratricidal civil war specially so when it was surrounded from outside by alien hospitality.

(III) In the end I beg to submit that I am now some 65 years old. For the last three years I have been every now and then confined to bed owing to attacks of heart-ache and debility. On the August of 15, last I accepted and raised on my house our new National Flag even to the embarrassment of some of my followers.

Consequently, in order to disarm all suspicion and to back up the above heart representation I wish to express my willingness to give an undertaking to the Government that I shall refrain from the taking part in any communal or political public activity for any period the Government may require in case I am released on that condition.

Sd/-V.D. Savarkar

**

For Savarkar's undertaking of 1950, see chapter 6 "The Aftermath."

A summary of the book *Savarkar and Hindutva* by A.G. NOORANI reads, "though delayed, justice has finally been done to the man. After years of prevarication, the Bharatiya Janata Party has at last publicly and explicitly owned up Vinayak Damodar Savarkar as its cult figure. The BJP seeks to displace Gandhi from his position as the pre-eminent symbol of Indian nationalism and project, in his stead. Savarkar as a national hero. This is an enterprise, however, that is fraught with risk. The risk of the truth coming out in the open. This book investigates the figure of Savarkar, the author of the term Hindutva?. What it finds does not add up to a flattering portrait. Savarkar rejected the inclusive, secular concept of ?territorial nationalism? and advocated the exclusivist, communal concept of ?cultural nationalism?. He repeatedly apologized and gave written undertakings to the government. He was directly connected to more than one murder. And most damagingly, as the book demonstrates in great detail, it was Savarkar who led the conspiracy to assassinate Mahatma Gandhi on that fateful winter evening of 1948. Inimitably forthright and hard-hitting, A.G. Noorani builds a devastating case against Savarkar. With a wealth of information and historical detail, this book is a must for all those interested in modern Indian politics and the history of communalism in India."

CONCLUSION:

Savarkar wrote an exciting history of the 1857 rebellion entitled, *The Indian War of Independence*. Excerpts and chapters from that book were published in various issues of *The Gadhar*. But from the Sikh perspective, this book completely suppressed the glorious 18th century period of Sikh history. This book also ignores the Values of Equality, Goodness, Civil liberties, Social reforms, Universal human freedom, Independence and Religious freedom as ingrained in *Shri Guru Granth Sahib* which was known to the Sikhs from 1604 AD to Khalsa Revolution of 1699 AD. The Sikh participants in the Gadar Lehar of 1907–1918 were loyal for the independent movement of India as well as they were Loyal Sikhs. Savarkar blames the Sikhs for supporting the British in the 1857 Mutiny which had as its goal to bring back the Mughal

SIKH GADAR LEHAR 1907-1918

raj who massacred the Sikhs in 18th century. Although he blames the Sikhs for their role to help the British in 1857, <u>in his own political life, he surrendered to the British himself from 1911 onwards as noted above from his apologies as documented by A.G. Noorani</u>. From 1923 onwards, he wrote and started the propagation of the Hindutva concept, which means Hindustan is only for Hindus, and started the Shhudi movement from Andaman Jail. He became president of Hindu Mahan Sabha from 1937 to 1942 and records his support of the British during World War II and against the Quit India movement in 1942. His concept that Sikhs, Bodhi, and Jainism are part of Hinduism ultimately was enshrined in Article 25b explanation of Indian constitution and was the end of Savarkar for minorities. History shows Savarkar's nationalism was Hindutva for which BJP government honored him. But in spite of all above historical facts, all Credit of Gadar movement has been given to him as noted below.

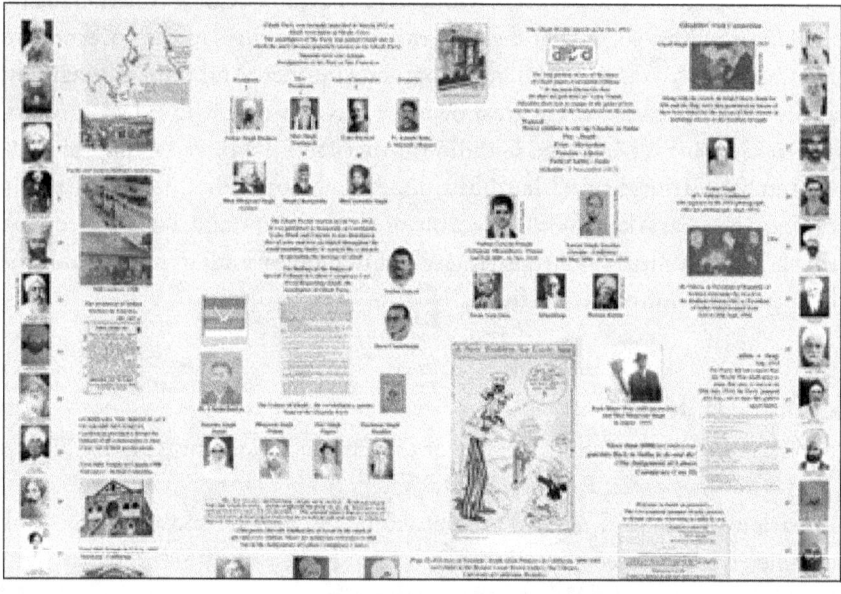

Above Poster by Prof. Malwinderjit Singh Warriach shows majorities of Gadrites who were hanged or suffered in 1914–1915 in Andaman Jails were Sikhs as noted from turbans in the above poster. But all Credit has been given to VINAYAK DAMODAR SAVARKAR as noted below:

Below Feb 26, 2003, Portrait of Savarkar installed in Parliament House New Delhi.

Below. May 4, 2002, Deputy Prime Minister, L.K. Advani, Renames the Port Blair Airport in Andaman Islands as the Veer Savarkar Airport.

BIBLIGRAHY & REFERENCES for V.D. Savarkar

1. "Why blame Jinnah and the congress when even Savarkar supported partition?" http://in.answers.yahoo.com/question/index?qid=20100418042115AALUURL
2. VINAYAK DAMODAR SAVARKAR AS A NARROW VISIONARY AND A HINDUTVA HARDLINER By Dr. J. Kuruvachira http://www.donboscoindia.com/english/resourcedownload.php?pno=1&secid=256
3. INDIA War Of Independence B Sarvkar,V.D. http://www.scribd.com/doc/3250543/the-indian-war-of-independence-1857-by-veer-sarvarkar
4. *Savarkar and Hindutva: The Godse Connection* by A.G.Noorani, published by Left Word, New Delhi, 2002. http://www.swb.co.in/store/book/savarkar-and-hindutva
5. GANDA SINGH; THE INDIAN MUTINY OF 1857 AND THE SIKHS, 1969. GURDWARA PARBANDHAK COMMITTEE SISGANJ, CHANDNI CHOWK, DELHI
6. ***Sarvakar and Hindutva* by AG Noorani, 2002, Leftward Books.** A.G. NOORANI, a lawyer, constitutional expert, and political commentator. His columns appear regularly in *Hindustan Times, Frontline, Economic and Political Weekly* and *Dainik Bhaskar*. He is the author of *The Kashmir Question, Badruddin Tyabji Ministers' Misconduct, Brezhnev's Plan for Asian Security, The Presidential System, The Trial of Bhagat Singh,* and *Constitutional Questions in India*.

Bibliography & References for Ram Chander Bhardwaj

1. Echoes of Freedom: South Asian pioneers in California 1899-1965. University of California, Berkley. Bancroft Library.
2. [www.aicc.org.in/role_of_press_in_india's_struggle_for_freedom.php Role of Press in India's Struggle for Freedom]. The Indian National Congress. Accessed 22 November 2007.
3. Saga of indomitable courage. Ivninderpal Singh. The Tribune, India. Accessed 22 November 2007.
4. Gadar Memorial Center, San Francisco.
5. Hoover, Karl. (1985), *The Hindu Conspiracy in California, 1913-1918. German Studies Review, Vol. 8, No. 2.* (May, 1985), pp. 245-261, German Studies Association, ISBN 01497952.

6. Brown, Giles (1948), *The Hindu Conspiracy, 1914-1917.The Pacific Historical Review, Vol. 17, No. 3. (Aug., 1948), pp. 299-310*, University of California Press, ISSN 0030-8684.
7. Puri, Harish K (1980), *Revolutionary Organization: A Study of the Ghadar Movement. Social Scientist, Vol. 9, No. 2/3. (Sep. - Oct., 1980), pp. 53-66*, Social Scientist, ISSN: 09700293.
8. G.S.Deol "The Role of gadhar party In The national Movement" sterling publication, Jalandhar 1969.
9. Joan M.Larsen, "The Hindu Conspiracy: A reassessment" Pacific historical review 1979 page 73 Spring-Rice to Bryan May 12, 1915; Spring-Rice to Lansing June 14, 1915; Johann von Berstorff to Lansing, July 2, 1915and Spring-Rice to Robert Lansing, Dec. 21, 1916; T. W. Gregory to Robert Lansing, Feb. 26, 1917, file 9-10-3, NA, RG 60
10. The Ghadr Rebellion by Khushwant Singh. Printed in Illustrated Weekly of India Feb 26, 1961. Pp 34-35; March 5, 1961 P. 45; March 12, 1961 P.41
11. "German hindu Cospiracy in California" By Carl Douglas Hoover. Unpublished PHD thesis UC Santa Barbara Ca. 1998.
12. S. Ajit Singh's Autobiography (BURIED ALIVE) http://www.shahidbhagatsingh.org/index.asp?link=about_ajit

It Takes a Massacre: The Sikhs are Really Americans Now

Harold A. Gould

When the news came out that an unidentified gunman had murdered five members of the Sikh faith within the confines of their temple in a Milwaukee suburb, most Americans, and even most members of the press, had no accurate idea of who and what the Sikhs are. Media reporters could not pronounce the community's name properly, calling them Siks rather than Sikhs (pronounced *seeks*). Because Sikh men traditionally wear turbans and beards, and their women traditionally wear *saris* or other native garments (like the *salwar kameez*), most ordinary Americans assumed that Sikhs are some kind of Muslims, which means they had not the slightest clue as to what their customs and religious beliefs actually are. At most, they probably knew that Sikhs are originally from some part of India, who came to this country, god knows how and when, as immigrants of some kind. Presidential candidate Mitt Romney called them *sheiks* (a Muslim term) instead of *Sikhs* (the name of their non-Muslim cultural community).

However, now that Sikhs have died at the hands of a psychopathic racist bigot displaying a Nazi Swastika and using a gun, which the NRA and the Gun Lobby are implicitly responsible for putting in his hand, the American press and general public now can finally pronounce their name correctly and are learning that Sikhs, like so many other immigrant communities, are in actuality a national treasure who are respectable, industrious, educated contributors to the American Dream, who practice a religion which, albeit originated in India, promotes peace, tolerance, integrity, and love; and under normal circumstances there is not an ounce of fanaticism or extremism in their doctrinal bones.

Yes, it took a massacre to make it clear that the Sikhs are one of us. This is something that has happened repeatedly among the ethnic communities who have come to our shores and been gradually woven into the fabric of American life. Think of the violence that was inflicted upon African Americans, the Irish, the Italians, the Chinese, the Japanese, *etc., etc.*, before they took their place in the mainstream of society. Because in the end, the cruelty and violence perpetrated by the ignorant bigots in our midst eventually produced a public backlash which resulted in the victims receiving the welcome, respect, understanding, and social justice that our Constitution guarantees and inspires.

In short, it seems that ultimately it took a massacre or two to awaken the mainstream public to the fact that an injustice had been done here; that one more immigrant group had been knocking at our cultural door for a long time and deserved admission to the main event, access to the American Dream.

This has now happened in the case of the Sikh community who has languished in comparative anonymity for more than a century, quietly enduring the prejudice and indignities that go with ignorance-driven minority status.

The longevity of their wait is actually being commemorated in Stockton, California, on September 22nd even as we speak. This is when the Sikh community gathers under the auspices of the *Pacific Coast Khalsa Diwan Society* and the *University of the Pacific* to commemorate the 100th anniversary of this society and, of course, the migration and assimilation of Sikhs as well as other South Asians into North American society.

This was a process which began at the turn of the century after a smattering of the Sikhs who were serving throughout East Asia in the British imperial armed forces discovered Canada and the United States. The smattering of demobilized soldiers who formed the vanguard came mainly from farming backgrounds in the region of India known as the Punjab; they saw the opportunities which the fertile land and the bustling economies of the Pacific coast offered, and soon their numbers grew; and with this, of course, came the racism, as resistance to their presence emanating from the already established White communities intensified. Confrontations mounted, such as the 1907 riots in Bellingham, Washington, the *Komagata Maru* incident (the refusal to allow a shipload of Sikhs to disembark in Vancouver in 1913–14), the founding of the *Ghadr* Party in the US in 1913, the San Francisco conspiracy trial in 1917 (which sent Taraknath Das to prison), until in the end the combined mobilization efforts of South Asian Indians in the US led to immigration and citizenship rights by 1946.

But despite these achievements, Sikhs have never been recognized fully as equals in the the American civil community. That is why Wisconsin happened. Their lot has been compounded by the terrorism frenzies which have flowed from 9/11 and the backlash from the Afghan war and the myriad manifestation of Islamic extremism emanating from the Middle East. But the racist prejudice has always been there, as has been true of other ethnic communities. According to an article in the *Palm Beach Post* by Toni-Ann Miller, the New York-based Sikh Coalition has reported more than 700 hate crimes in the United States since Sept. 11th, plus thousands of complaints from Sikhs about workplace discrimination and racial profiling.

My point, however, is that the Wisconsin massacre will, indeed has already, injected a higher measure of public consciousness and contemplation into the presence and nature of the Sikh community in this country. The murder of innocents on a significant scale is different than an individual killing, much as the latter is in its fundamentals no less tragic and heartbreaking than the former. Put another way, it takes a massacre, i.e., collective suffering, to focus the mind, and this is the case for the American Sikh community. **The public is now conscious of them as never before, aware of their majesty, their magnanimity, their civility, and their worthiness to be an accepted and honored part of mainstream American society. The public will know them more and better because they have suffered and sacrificed more.**

Indeed, sad to say, it takes a massacre! Henceforth, as one Sikh has put it, We want this opportunity to pretty much educate everyone around us ... We are not al Qaida or Taliban because some of us wear turbans ... We are other Americans just like you.

I would welcome any comments. halgould22554@gmail.com

Editor's note: Recommend to readers an important book By Dr. Harold A. Gould on the same subject titled ***Sikhs, Swamis, Students, and Spies*, published by sage publications 2006. This book deals with the Indian Lobby in the United States, 1900–1946.** Dr. Gould mentions the prominent role played by the Sikh community. On page 149, he writes, "The most important groups in the period leading up to World War I that consummated in the Ghadr Party obviously were the grassroots Sikh communities scattered across California, Oregon, Washington, and British Columbia." Then again in final chapter page 433, he writes, "The Sikhs were an agrarian peasantry who sank deep roots into the soil of their adopted land. Against all odds, applying technological and organizational models they brought with them from the Punjab, they gradually created the material and fiscal wherewithal needed to expand their patrimonies. To accomplish this they were compelled to challenge the legal and political obstacles that were hurled in their path by White society. With great tenacity, they built the institutions required to do so. *Gurdwaras* sprang up in many places on both sides of the border, and became not only foci for their cultural and religious life but also headquarters for the promulgation of political action. They found lawyers who would represent their interests in the American and Canadian courts and, as their fortunes improved, eventually produced their own lawyers. They created agro-businesses and mercantile enterprises which funded education and political action."

Ghadar Movement: Role of Media and Literature

Gurmel S. Sidhu, Professor

*California State University,
Fresno, California.*

Abstract:

Regardless of the nature of activities, the survival and success of a movement is dependent on its aims and objects and their dissemination through media and literature. Ghadar Movement launched for the Independence of India against the British rule relied heavily on journalism and literature. It is well known that the social and political movement of this scope and nature needs mass media attention to disseminate its message and achievements. Realizing the importance of media and press, Ghadar Movement published about 22 news papers in Punjabi, Urdu, Gujarati and English from America and Canada. They established the most effective centers for conducting their activities in these countries and brought out a number of news papers and pamphlets. Among them the *Ghadar* news paper played a significant role in preaching and nurturing the message of the mutiny. Its title page always contained the heading, "The exposure of the British Government" and followed with fourteen counts of injustices meted by the British Government towards the Indian nation. One of them was , "56 years have elapsed since the last mutiny of 1857, another one is due". The language of the paper was bitter , pungent and vitriolic.

Whereas social and political media played a pivotal role in focusing the cause and response of the movement, Poetry was an integral part of Ghadar movement and played a frontal role in conveying the message of the revolt. The message was vehemently preached through popular versification by employing images and motifs relating to heroes and martyrs of the movement. Its dominant theme was exposure of exploitation of natural resources of lands under the colonial rule, and oppression and suppression of the people with the force of guns and the threat of gallows. Profoundly patriotic nature of Ghadar poetry became a crucial source and force of inspiration for extreme sacrifices. There is no doubt that this corpus in verse held out a great appeal to activists of the movement and the public, in general. Its patriotic theme inspired a dream of future democratic Indian Republic based on liberty, equality and fraternity; free from corruption and discrimination of any caste, creed, and religion.

This article seeks to discuss how the Ghadar movement was characterized by the media coverage, how it helped framing the issues and goals of the struggle for national freedom, and what kind of response it received from the general public. The structural part of the analysis will focus on the power and reliability of media, and the emotional part will be presented as communicated by the Ghadar poets. My formulations is meant to hold how the presentation of independent struggle through the press affected the outcome and how the strategy adopted by the leadership succeeded in framing the cause and effect of the Ghadar movement.

Introduction

Early nineteenth century witnessed an economic downturn in India which lead to a high level of emigration to North American. Many Punjabis as well as a few people from other parts of India landed in Canada during the first decade of 20th century. A greater number of immigrants were Sikhs who were either retirees from the British army or farmers rendered poor by the selfish land laws of the British government. The Sikhs being a crucial loyal force for the British Empire, expected equal treatment and Human rights from the British and Commonwealth governments as extended to British and white immigrants. But the white Canadian community took it as an invasion on their "color conscious culture". The Canadian government decided to delimit this influx and enacted laws primarily aimed at the entry of new

Indian immigrants and curtailing the political rights of those already in the country. These laws lead to a discontent, therefore, protests and anti-colonial sentiments within the Indian community. Facing this unwanted and unlawful discrimination and communal attitude, the community started organizing political groups. Facing the discriminatory situation in Canada, many Punjabis moved to the United States, unaware of the fact that they might face a similar situation in another country ruled by white people. Initially, they experienced relatively less discriminating in US. But as the jobs became scarce, they were labeled as unwanted "job snatcher" Hindu minority. This resulted in communal hatred and, of times, lead to scuffles and physical harms.

When the social and political environment became harsh and unbearable in North America, survival for Indian migrants became a serious problem. To survive in such an environment, three things are important: organize, politicize and publicize. That is exactly what the Ghadrites did, established a Ghadar party with head quarter at San Francisco, initiated publications of newspapers, pamphlets, and propagated their message through literature, especially poetry. Verse is a powerful medium of expression of thoughts and emotions. Some members of Ghadar movement were natural born poets and others cultivated poetic art for expressions of their experiences they faced in real life. They wrote patriotic poems and songs emotionally charged and embedded with the message of obtaining independence of India from the British Rule. This paper deals with the role played by media and literature in the independence movement of Ghadrites against the British Rule in India.

Media: Historical Background

The people of Indian origin founded a party namely, "The Ghadar Party", in 1913 in the state of Oregon, USA. Initially called the *Pacific Coast Hindustan Association*, was formed under the leadership of Sohan Singh Bhakna as its president and Lala Har Dayal as its general secretary. The members of the party were largely from Punjab and some of them were students at the University of California, Berkeley, including Kartar Singh Sarabha, Har Dayal, Tarak Nath Das, Maulavi Barkatullah, and V.G. Pingle. The party quickly gained support from Indian expatriates, especially in the United States, Canada and Asia mainly through news papers and pamphlets published from America, Canada and some other countries (Darshan Singh

Tatla, 2003). A chronological list of newspaper with necessary information is given below. (Table 1).

Publication	Script	Editor	Year	Place
1.Circular-i-Azadi	Urdu	Ram Nath Puri	1907	America
2.Free Hindustan	English	Tarakh Nath	1908	America
3.Pardesi Khalsa	Punjabi	Hira Singh	1010	Canada
4. Sudesh Sewak	Punjabi	Guru Datt Kumar, Babu Harnam Singh	1909	Canada
5.Khalsa Herald	English	Kartar Singh	1911	Canada
6.The Aryan	English	Sundar Singh	1911	Canada
7. Sansaar	Punjabi	Kartar Singh Hundal, Dr. Sundar Singh	1912	Canada
8. Gaddar	Indian langs.	Hardyal, Ram Chandra	1913	America
9.Hindustan Ghadar-1	Indian langs.	Bhagwan S. Pritam	1914	America
10.Hindustani Ghadar-2	Indian Langs.	Ram Chandar Pashauria	1917	America
11.Yugantar	Punjabi/ Urdu	Ratan Singh etc.	1917	America
12.Independant Hindustan	English	Gadar Party	1920	America
13. United States of India	English	Gadar Party	1923	America
14.Hindustan Ghadar	Punjabi	Gadar Party	1925	America
15.Hindustan, San Francisco	Indian (Gandhian)	Dissident Group	1927	America
16.Ghadar Dhandora	Punjabi/ Chinese	Gadar Party	1930	America/China
17.Sansar	Punjabi/ Sangh	Gadar Party Urdu	1932	America/China
18.India and Canada	Punjabi/ English	Kartar S. Hundal	1930	Canada
19.Social Sudhar	Punjabi	Gadar Party	1942	Canada
20.India's Voice	English	Gadar Party	1943	America
21.Nawan Yug	Punjabi	Giani Bhagwan Singh	1950	America
22.The Gadarite	English	Ved Parkash Vatuk	1988	America

Table-1: Newspapers published by the Ghadar Party from America and Canada.

Among them **"Ghadar"** (mutiny, rebellion, revolt, uprising) was the first prominent newspaper published under the leadership of official Ghadar Party from San Francisco. It was a weekly newspaper initiated from the official head quarter of the party, "Yugantar Ashram". The name "Yugantar" was borrowed from a revolutionary Bengali paper. The first issue was in Urdu released on November 1, 1913 (See picture) followed by Punjabi issue in December, 9, 1913 (See picture) and Gujrati version in May 10, 1914. It is stated that 2,200 and 2,500 copies of Ghadar were printed weekly in Urdu and Punjabi languages , respectively. Former Professor, Ved Vatuk, of Berkley, has collected all the original issue of " Ghadar" published in Punjabi published during 1913-1914, and Xeroxed them as such and put them together in a book form (Ved Vatuk, 2010).

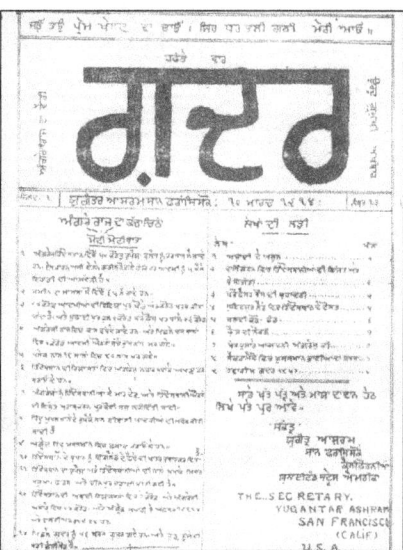

Urdu Newspaper   *Punjabi Newspaper-1*

On the top of the title page of the Punjabi version of "Ghadar", a line from Guru Nanak's Shabad, ਜਉ ਤਉ ਪ੍ਰੇਮ ਖੇਲਣ ਕਾ ਚਾਉ, ਸਿਰੁ ਧਰਿ ਤਲੀ ਗਲੀ ਮੇਰੀ ਆਉ॥ (Should thou seek to play the game of love, step into my path with thy head on thy palm). ਜਉ ਤਉ was modified to ਜੇ ਚਿਤ in first few issues and was corrected in the 12th. issue of the 1st. volume . Table of contents starts with: ਅੰਗਰੇਜੀ ਰਾਜ ਦਾ ਕੱਚਾ ਚਿੱਠਾ (A balance sheet of English Rule) followed by a list of 14 topics on the left side of the paper depicting the "Ills" that were brought upon the Indians. These points refer to sending of Indian wealth to England thereby, making Indians poor. Average per capita daily income of Indians, including farmers, is only 5 pais, whereas, land tax is 65 percent. Spending only 97.5 million rupees on 240 million people and 290 million on military. 800,000 people died of plague and 20 million died of famine during the last 10 years. The English are never punished for murder of Indians, and insulting women. Many years have elapsed since the Mutiny of 1857, now there is an urgent need for a new one.

On the right side of the page under the heading, " Our Work, Our Name, " it was declared:

'Today on November 1, 1913, a new calendar is launched in the history of India. From now onward, a war against the British Rule is initiated from a foreign land in our native languages. It is an auspicious occasion that a paper in Urdu and Gurumukhi is launched to uproot the British evils from India.'

In the editorial section challenging questions were raised and answered therein:

- What is our name? Mutiny.
- What is our work? Mutiny
- Where will the mutiny take place? In India
- When? In a few years
- Why? Because the people can no longer bear the tyranny and oppression of the British rule and are anxious to fight and die for freedom.

"Ghadar" newspaper, from time to time, printed the following advertisement in its "wanted Columns"

- Wanted -- Heroic and enthusiastic soldiers for mutiny
- Remuneration -- Death
- Reward -- Martyrdom
- Pension -- Freedom
- Field of work -- Hindustan

The first issue of Ghadar newspaper was released in Shattuck hotel in Berkley in the presence of a large audience which included Punjabi farmers, students, laborers and intellectuals. Some American politicians, economic professors, writers and editors of English newspapers also attended the meeting. Lala Hardyal was the editor of the first issue and the Urdu translation was done by Vishveshwar Parsad of U.P. In his inaugural Address, Har Dyal said:

'In the history of today's India, a new era is set in motion. The power of 'PEN' will explode like a ball of cannon. This newspaper is the stanch enemy of the English Empire, and a bugle of challenge for the Indian youth. Wake up, take up the arms and fight for the independence of India.'

Right from the beginning the paper was violently ant-British in nature expressing views that were pungent and revolutionary every which way. It carried articles, notes, news and especially poems openly expressing discontent against the British Rule in India. Every sentence of articles and lines of verse preached mutiny and open revolt and urged all Indians to go back with the intention of committing murders, if need be. Inciting revolution and dislodging the British Government by any means possible, and holding responsible every seditionist and murderers who had attained notoriety (Isemonger and Slattery, 1998).

The **Ghadar** newspaper became a needle in the butt for the British Government, therefore, it became an integral part of judgments pronounced against the Ghadarite by the Special Tribunal in the "Lahore Conspiracy Case" of September 13, 1915. The judgment included that:

"We have not only pursued the portions of this newspaper marked as exhibits but we have taken a survey of all issues from the first one of 1st November, 1913 to that of the 15th September, 1914. The day of its issue was changed in December 1913 to Tuesday, the *Mangal* of the Hindus, the name of Mars, the proverbial god of war, with a remark that some of the readers know the reason why. Below the name of the paper appears the word 'Ghadr, enemy of the British Government-a weekly Urdu and Gurumukhi newspaper. The first page opens with the heading ' The exposure of the British Government' and fourteen counts of calumnies, needless to detail, are recited, the last count being '56 years have elapsed since the last mutiny of 1857', another one is urgently needed."

"Its salient features are:--

1. Perversion of figures and statistics on various subjects, e.g., settlements, railways, canals, exportations of wheat, epidemics, &c., &c., calculations to bring into disrepute and contempt the British Government of India.
2. Accounts of revolts, revolutions, past and present in various countries of the world, to serve as models for emulation by Indian subjects.
3. Translation in Urdu of Savarkar's history of the Indian Mutiny issued in installments in every issue.
4. Appreciative notes ref Tilak, Arbindo Ghosh, Ajit Singh &c., the so called 'martyrs'.
5. Appreciative notes of political murders and political dacoities in India.
6. Sympathy and admiration for Germans.

7. Incitement to Indian subjects to rebel as promptly as possible; and exhortations to Indians in America to return to India quickly for revolution.
8. Wholesale condemnation in the foulest language of every paper, every institution and every individual that has, or had, the misfortune to differ from the views of the Ghadr party.
9. The language employed throughout is either vitriolic or disgustingly abusive, and, looking to the class of people for whose consumption it is meant, perhaps it is designedly so.
10. Announcements of members of the Ghadr Party, and accounts of proceedings thereof from time to time. In short, its exclusive *raison d'être* is to bring about a rebellion in India. No stone is left unturned to achieve the object. Its columns are the best of its power, imputing all the basest motives to the English, even to ascribing plague and famine to them. They are described as drainers of the wealth of India, desecrations of religious places and bent upon extirpating Indians like aborigines in other countries." (Isemonger and Slattery, 1998).

The judgment also referred to particular issues of the paper which carried special appreciations of the events that happened in India against the British Government. e.g. political dacoities in Bengal (November 13, 1913), throwing of bombs and looting for revolution (December, 23, 1913), Incitement of Indian soldiers (February 17, 1914), letter of Ajit Singh urging 'patriots' to rise against British during the war between Germany and Britain (July 28, 19140). In the issue of the 15th November, 1913 it is expressed that, " The Germans have great sympathy with our movement for liberty because they and ourselves have a common enemy (the English).

The Sedition Committee noted that ... a newspaper called Ghadr... was printed in more than one Indian languages. It was widely distributed among Indians in America and was forwarded to India. It was of a violent anti-British nature, playing on every sentence, and urging all Indians to go to India with the express object of committing murders, causing revolution and expelling the British Government by any and every means. (Sedition Committee Report, 1918).

Ghadar Movement: Role of Media and Literature

In addition to regular papers, many pamphlets in Punjabi and Urdu languages were also published from time to time from the San Francisco office. A list of these is given below.

Pamphlets
1. Shabash (Urdu, 1913): Written by Har Dyal, the title means " Bravo!" . On the front page it says, " a present on the anniversary of the Bomb". Then it has a picture of " the tree of liberty", and below the tree is written, "price per copy the head of an Englishman."
2. Nim Hakim Khatra Jan, Navan Zamana de Naveen Adarsha (Punjabi, 1914): It includes five assays written by Lala Har Dyal translated from his English articles.
3. Zulam Zulam! Gore Shahi Zulam (Punjabi, 1914): It depicts and strongly condemns the deportation of Bhagwan Singh from Canada and urges Indian to bear arms to kill the 'white people.'
4. Ailan-i-jung (Urdu/Punjabi,1915) : It contained an appeal for Indian to revolt against the British rule.
5. Angan di gavahi, angrezi raj vich praja de dukh di kahani (Punjabi, 1915): This is the issue number 3 of Ghadar party books.
6. Rusi Ghadrian de Samachar, arthaat Rus di Ghadar Parti de Bir te Birnian dein Kahanian (Punjabi, 1916): It contains the heroic deeds of Russian revolutionaries. It evaluate the impact of the Russian revolution and narrates the dramatic events of Bloody Sunday when men and women overthrew the century-old Russian monarchy.
7. Gulami da zahir: Ik tavarikhi lekh (Punjabi, 1918): It is a translation of Har Dyal's article , 'The Poison of Slavery.'
8. Gulami da zahar: Ik tavarikhi lekh (Punjabi/Urdu, 1918): It was originally written in English by Har Dayal and translated in Punjabi/Urdu. It blames religion associated traditions in India that fostered values of a feudalistic society that predispose for easy acceptance of enslavement under colonial rule.
9. Wartman Zamana (Urdu, 1919): It depicts an account of imperialist atrocities of Jallianwala Bagh tragedy and strongly urges Indians to gain freedom at any cost.
10. Hindusatan Ghadar Parti da Kansatitushan-1 (Punjabi, 1920): This pamphlet contains a charter list of thirty three 'by-laws' and one amendment.

11. Hind Vich Ghadar (Punjabi, 1920): This contains anti-imperialist tract which praises the Russian revolution with an appeal to Indians for a similar uprising against the foreign rule.
12. Inqilab-i-Hind: Hindustan mein Angrezi Raj ka Khaka aur Duniya kya kar rahi hai (Urdu, 1920): It contain two essays describing miserable economic, social and political conditions in India due to British Rule.
13. Pahli Navambar: Ghadar da Janam Din (Punjabi/Urdu, 1920): This is a commemorative pamphlet celebrating the anniversary of the Ghadar Party and the first issue of Ghadar magazine published on November 1, 1913.
14. Hindustan Ghadar Parti da Kansatitushan-2 (Punjabi, 1928): A reorganized Ghadar party evolved with modified charter of its functions. It notes that there were 1500 members out of total Indian population of 6,000 in California. The aim of the party was reexamined and set goals such as, (a) To encourage the establishment of a system of government in India which shall be free from all foreign control, and which shall have its aim in the greatest good for the greatest number, and which shall guarantee freedom of thought, speech, press and organization, and ensure the minimum necessities of life to all. (b) To publish a periodical review of political, economic, social and intellectual conditions in India by voluntary contributions and without sale.
15. Khudgarzi Phasaad Khare Kardi Hae (Punjabi,1930): It was written by J.K. Basi who extends his analysis to include colonialism and war, and notes with irony that selfishness divided subjugated people and make them fight among themselves rather than against their exploiters.
16. Ghadari Ailan (Urdu, 1930): Ghadar party announces to prepare for impending revolution in India. It invites the brave and fearless Ghadrites to prepare for training to fly airplane and other methods of revolution.
17. Brabri da Arth (Punjabi,1931): It is translated from English and explains the values of equality in a caste ridden society.
18. Hamari Khana Jangi: Is ka Sabbab aur Ilaj (Urdu, ?): It brings out the state of division among Indians, based on religion, class and castes. It calls for unity for the sake of combined struggle against the British Rule.
19. Hindustanion ke Naam Khulli Chitti: Hindustan ke mazhabi jhagron kaa sabbab (Urdu, ?): This was an open letter to all Indians making a strong appeal for unity for the sake of freedom-fight. It condemns the

divisions on the basis of religion and asks to rise above the narrow sectarian goals.
20. Pardesi Hidustanion ki Bharat Nivasion ke Nam par Khulli Chitti (Urdu, ?): An open letter from foreign Indians to their Indian counterparts with an appeal to join the struggle for freedom. It assure them that the Ghadar Party is fully committed to the cause of freedom of India from foreign rule.
21. Rajsi Mantar Yad Rakhan Valian Batan (Punjabi/Urdu,?): This pamphlet takes a critical look at the political situation in British India. It lists 110 unacceptable conditions and calls upon Indian patriots to remember and recite them daily like a prayer so that you feel the agony of British Rule.
22. Angon ki Gawahi Angrezi Raj Mein Praja ke Dukh ki Kahani-Angrezi Rapoton ki Zabani: (Hindi, 191?): It gives an account of the story of the suffering of subjects under British Rule based on figures collected from various books and official records.

Some reports in English published by the San Francisco Office of Ghadar party.

1. British Rule in India by Bryan, William Jennings (1906): Mr. Bryan was a secretary to American President, Woodrow Wilson. He visited India in 1906 and gave a lecture namely, "The British Rule in India" after his return. Based on his observations he denounced the policy of British Rule toward India. Its translation was published in the **Ghadar** newspaper.
2. India in America (1911): This pamphlet contains Lala Har Dyal's first article after coming to US. In this he discusses the first meeting with California Ghadrites. He explores the possibility of Indian students with nationalistic feeling to become spies. But decides against it because Indians are too out spoken and would easily become the target of British intelligence agency. Nevertheless, he himself became the target of Mr. Hopkins , a Canadian agent working for British Government. Mr. Hopkins was eventually killed by Sardar Mewa Singh in Vancouver.
3. Yugantar Circular (1913): The subject of this pamphlet is the attempted murder of Lord Harding on December 23, 1912. About the murder attempt it proclaims that "One may say that it is one of the sweetest and loveliest bomb that has exploded in India ...Who can describe the moral

power of the bomb? It is a concentrated moral dynamite. When the strong and the cunning in the pride of their power parade their glory before their helpless victims, when the rich and the haughty set themselves on a pedestal and ask their slaves to fall down before them and worship them, when the wicked ones of the earth seem exalted to the sky and nothing appears to withstand their might, then, in that dark hour, for the glory of humanity, comes the bomb, which lays the tyrant in the dust..."

4. Publication of Indian National Party. (1914): Indian National Party was established by C. Pillai in Berlin whose members were Har Dyal, Taraknath Das, M. Barkatulla, Chandra Chakarborty, Heramba Lal Gupta. A similar organization was floated by Taraknath Das in New York. The aim was to write petitions/ letters to various governments, organizations and officials seeking assurance for Indians who were under threat of deportation after the conclusion of San Francisco trial of 1917.. Agnes Smedley, an American journalist, offered to post hundreds of these letters.

Agnes Smedley (1832-1950)

5. Manifesto of the Indian National Party. (1915): It denounced the British imperialism and declared state of war until the freedom is achieved.
6. The method of Indian Police in the 20th Century (1915): Fredrick Mackarness of US wrote letters in support of Indian freedom struggle against British Rule which were published in 1910. They were reprinted by the office of Ghadar party in 1915. The letters tell stories of police brutality in India and their repression by an indifferent British judiciary and administration.

7. Why India is in revolt against British Rule? (1916): This pamphlet predicts that Britain will lose the first world war against Germany and hopes that Indian nationalist and Ghadrites will inevitably gain freedom
8. Exclusion of Hindus from America due to British influence. 1916: This booklet contains newspaper articles, letters and other materials put together by Ram Chandra, then editor of **Ghadar**. The letters were mainly written by Ram Chandra to various American newspapers against the proposed new legislation directed towards the exclusion of Hindu immigrants. He argues that the American policies were guided by the British government. In one letter written to New York Times dated August 13, 1916 Ram Chandra wrote:

> "Congress is planning to pass a new Oriental exclusion law in which the Hindus are included. The Japanese Ambassador protested vigorously against the terms of the sect concerning Japanese and secured important changes, satisfactory to the Japanese Government. There is no hope that the British Ambassador will make any protest on behalf of the Hindus, because the British Government itself does not want Hindus to come here. They might become imbued with pestiferous ideas of political freedom!"

> "It is claimed that the Hindu is an undesirable immigrant, I would like to ask what kind of immigrant American legislators would consider to be desirable (Immigrant)? The Hindus who have come to this country have certainly proved themselves to be law- abiding and faithful workers. .."

> "Is it on account of color? I would reply that the Hindus have the same color as the Spaniards, Mexicans, or Southern Italians. Their features are not inferior to high -class Europeans. So far as color is concerned all physicians who have dissected the human body agree that under the skin all look alike."

Ram Chandra wrote many letters, some in Hindustan Ghadar newspaper namely, "The Appeal of India to the President of the United States (1917), The Balance Sheet of British Rule in India,

India Against Britain. A reply to Austin Chamberlain, Lord Harding, Lord Islington and Others 9116)."
9. An open letter to His Excellency, Woodrow Wilson. (1917): It contains an appeal to President of USA for supporting the Indian National Movement against British Rule in India.
10. British Terror in India (1920): This pamphlet is written by Surendra Karr and condemns the callous behavior of British administrator while narrating the tragic circumstances relating to Jallianwala Bagh massacre in April, 1919. It points out towards the sacrifices made by Indians in First World War for the British and how the British Rulers overlooked them . I alleges that the British rulers has no regard for the feelings of Indian people.
11. Collection of Pamphlets on India written for the Hindustan Ghadar Party (1920): These pamphlets are put together by Ed, Gammons and they contain a mixture of news and comments about the plight of India under the British Rule. It contains Gammon's commentary on Punjab events such as imposing martial law in Punjab, Jallianwala Bagh massacre and as a result renunciation of knighthood by Ravinder Nath Tagore. Gammons also wrote the following pamphlets:
    a. The Tragedy of India (1919): It discusses the aftermath of San Francisco trial of Ghadrites and their German associates held in 1917. Gammons argues and appeals on behalf of Indians against their deportation . It contains statements of people hostile towards the British Rule in India.
    b. India in Revolt (1920): It condemns the firing by police in Amritsar and the findings of Hunter Commission set to look into the tragedy of Jallianwala Bagh.
12. Resolutions of the League against Imperialism in India. (1929): This pamphlet condemns British imperialism, England's Independent Labor Party and Right-wing Indian Nationalist Leaders for undermining efforts to organize workers and peasants and preventing their participation in the international labor movement.
13. India is America's Business, A lecture by Louis Fischer (1943): Mr. Fisher made a speech at the Town Hall Session In San Francisco in which he openly condemned the British oppression in India and defended Indian's right for freedom.

14. India's voice at last: India's reply to British propagandists and Christian missionaries (192?): This pamphlet rebuts some misconceptions about India which are deliberately fed to the media by the British Rulers in order to subjugate Indians.

Literature and Ghadar Movement

Poetry written by Ghadrites, immensely contributed to the independence movement against the British Rule in India. Poems were mainly composed in Punjabi language primarily by Sikh poets. Each issue of the "Ghadar" and other newspapers devoted a sizable portion to poetry. The poems were recited at local meetings and distributed to public through newspapers. Later, *Yugantar Ashsram* produced them in booklet or pamphlet forms and distributed in other countries. Some of them were printed in Urdu and a few in Hindi languages. Anthologies of these poems were named as Ghadar De Goonj (Thunder of Revolution). They were also published in series under the name, Ghadar deaN PustakaN dee Lari No. 1-3 and 4-6 (Punjabi, Urdu and Hindi). Number 5 has not been found and number 7 was published in 1932. Poems became so impressive that they were greatly in demand in Punjabi/Indian Diaspora and in India. Desh Bhagat Yadgaar Commttee, Jullandhar, reproduced the poems under the title of "Desh BhagtaN de Bani :Ghadar dee Goonj" from Lari numbers 1-3 (see picture below).

The impact of these poems was so enormous that the Special Tribunal at Lahore (1915), cited them in their report as "seditious literature especially used to incite Sikh soldiers and peasants to revolt against the British rule in India". The tribunal used the poems against Ghadrites as an evidence of revolt and therefore, imposed rigorous sentences upon them.

Ghadar Leha r dee Kavita (Poetry of Ghadar movement)

The poems of Ghadarite poets were scattered all over in various Ghadar party newspapers and pamphlets. Kesar Singh Noblest of Canada collected them with great labor and effort from various sources and published them in a voluminous book called "Ghadar Lehar dee Kavita" (Poetry of Ghadar Movement: ਗ਼ਦਰ ਲਹਿਰ ਦੀ ਕਵਿਤਾ-). The collection has a long introduction by professor Kesar Singh Kesar of Punjab University and was published by the Punjabi University, Patiala (Kesar Singh and Kesar Sigh,1995). The book has twelve sections and each section represents the newspaper(s) in which the poems were originally published. For example section-I has poems from monthly newspaper, Swadesh Sewak; section-II has poems from bi-weekly newspaper, *Sansar*; section-III (the longest of all) collected poems from *Ghadar* and *Hindustan Ghadar* and so on. Most of the poems bear no names but some names were identified with the help of Kesar Singh of Canada and Giani Heera Singh Dard. According to them the Poems were mostly written by Munsha Singh Dukhi, Bhai Bishan Singh, Harnam Singh Tundilat, Wasakha Singh, Bhagwan Singh, Mula Singh, Hari Singh Usman, Sohan Lal Pathak, Kartar Singh Sarabha, Kartar Singh Hundal, Kesar Singh Thathgarh , Karam Singh Daulatpur, Sant Singh Nidharak, Banta Singh Sewak etc. Apparently, the message was important, not the names of the poets. This shows the spirit of a unified effort by the Ghadar poets without any consideration of caste , creed, religion and individualism.

The Spirit of the Ghadar Poetry

The spirit of any genre of literature is inherent in the personal experiences of the writer gathered under various set of conditions. Poverty, atrocities of life, ethnicity, sociopolitical atmosphere, religious intolerance, and above all the slavery are the greatest stimuli for a creative mind. India was motherland of

Indians ruled by British. To feel like a slave in your own country is an unbearable mental and moral torture. The Ghadar poetry portrays the themes that evolved as a result of continuous struggle for freedom of India from the British Rule. Though a clear-cut demarcation of these themes is not possible, however, the spirit of poetry can be categorized into five phases, such as:

1. Ethnic hatred and Nostalgia.
2. Awakening against the British Rule.
3. Divide and rule policy.
4. Sounds of mutiny.
5. Sikh ideology and Ghadar poetry.

1. Ethnic hatred and Nostalgia

In a foreign land the first shock one experiences is the feeling of alienation and ethnic hatred in the foreign land. Especially when you are unwanted, you are like a 'weed' and the indigenous people try to weed you out with sickles of religious hatred and social slurs. This aspect is vividly expressed in many poems. A sample is quoted here.

ਘਰ ਤੋਂ ਵਗੈਰ ਅਸੀਂ ਨਹੀਓਂ ਸੱਜਦੇ, (We have no prestige without our motherland)

ਕੁਲੀ ਕੁਲੀ ਅਸੀਂ ਸਾਰੇ ਜੱਗ ਵੱਜਦੇ। (Over the whole world coolie we are called)

****

ਘਰ ਸੌਹਰਿਆਂ ਦੇ ਨਹੀਂ ਢੋਈ ਮਿਲਦੀ, (We are not horned in alien land)

ਨਹੀਂ ਪੇਕਿਆਂ ਦੇ ਸਾਨ ਬਾਨ ਕਿਧਰੇ। (No place for us in the mother land)

ਦੇਸੋਂ ਪੈਣ ਧੱਕੇ ਬਾਹਰ ਮਿਲੇ ਢੋਈ ਨਾ, (Driven out from motherland and shunned from the alien land)

ਸਾਡਾ ਪਰਦੇਸੀਆਂ ਦਾ ਦੇਸ ਕੋਈ ਨਾ। (We the aliens have no place to live)

Word 'ਸੋਹਰੇ' means foreign country and the 'ਪੇਕੇ' means motherland. Implicit in these couplets are the feelings of a rejected and disgusted individual who has no land to live and no hut to hide. The essence of the poems do not portray a 'cry' but a 'mutter' that have the potential to explode into an uncontrolled anger and rage infused with patriotism. Especially, these couplets paint the thematic tension of freedom-slavery milieu.

In North America, Indians became the most undesirable class of laborers, therefore, victims of racial hatred and pungent slurs. They were made to live under unhygienic conditions with no facilities for bathing and bashing, and for answering the 'call of nature'. The most deplorable situation was that they have no place to cremate their dead. The overall daily environment became so hateful and venomous that it became unbearable for them to exist. Under such conditions, one either commits suicide or becomes a rebel. Laborers, who were mostly Sikhs with valiant spirit, refused to yield to undue, unreasonable and uncalled for atrocities. A spirit of honor sprung up to stand against the prevailing undue circumstances. A poem depicting this spirit in an ironical manner is given below.

ਅਜ ਰਹਿ ਗਏ ਅਸੀਂ ਬੇਅਣਖ ਕਾਇਰ, (We are taken as cowards without respect)

ਗਏ ਸੂਰਮੇਂ ਹਿੰਦ ਦੀ ਜਾਨ ਕਿੱਥੇ। (No where are to be seen men of honor)

ਕਾਲਾ ਲੋਕ ਡਰਟੀ ਅੱਜ ਕਹਿਣ ਸਾਨੂੰ, (We are labeled dirty slaves)

ਗਏ ਹਿੰਦ ਦੇ ਉਹ ਅਦਬੋ-ਸ਼ਾਨ ਕਿੱਥੇ। (Gone are glory and prestige of India)

ਆਓ ਬੀਜ ਪੈਲੀ ਝੁੱਗੀ ਪਾ ਲਈਏ, (Let's assert and claim her as our own..)

ਕਰਕੇ ਟਾਕਰੇ ਸੱਚ ਸੁਣਾ ਦੇਈਏ। (and through fight show our mettle)

Ghadrites experienced the same fate in Canada and America. Pangs of strenuous labor, scolds of white people, agony of ethnic hatred, taunts of black color and disgrace of slavery are the most fertile field for a poetic mind.

Poetry provides solace for releasing mantle tension and is a great medium of relaxation, as is depicted in the following poem.

ਪੈਸੇ ਜੁੜੇ ਨਾ ਨਾਲ ਮਜ਼ਦੂਰੀਆਂ ਦੇ, (nothing to gain through labor)

ਝਿੜਕਾਂ ਖਾਂਦਿਆਂ ਨੂੰ ਕਈ ਸਾਲ ਹੋ ਗਏ। (for years we have suffered rebukes)

ਕੀ ਕੁਝ ਖੱਟਿਆ ਜੋ ਮਿਰਕਣ ਵਿੱਚ ਆ ਕੇ, (We have earned nothing in America?)

ਦੇਸ ਛੱਡਿਆਂ ਨੂੰ ਕਈ ਸਾਲ ਹੋ ਗਏ। (Though years have passed since we left mother land)

ਕੁਲੀ ਕੁਲੀ ਕਹਿ ਕੇ ਦੁਨੀਆਂ ਨੱਕ ਚਾਹੜੇ, (World over we are snubbed as coolies)

ਵੀਰੋ ਅਸੀਂ ਬੇਸ਼ਰਮ ਕਮਾਲ ਹੋ ਗਏ। (O brothers! shameless we have become.)

ਹੋਵੇ ਅੜਖ ਤੇ ਸਮਝੀਏ ਝੱਟ ਸੈਨਤ, (Only by taking its notice can we regain honor.)

ਡੰਡੇ ਖਾਂਦਿਆਂ ਦੇ ਚੁੱਡਰ ਲਾਲ ਹੋ ਗਏ। (Beatings have turned our backs read)

2. Awakening against the British Rule
When the Ghadrites saw the plundering of their motherland, a sense of awakening sprung up against the British Rule. A few couplets depicting this sense are given below.

ਜਦ ਨੀਂਦ ਹਿੰਦ ਨੂੰ ਘੇਰਾਂ ਦੀ, ਤਦ ਫੇਰੀ ਪੈ ਗਈ ਚੋਰਾਂ ਦੀ।
(India was in deep slumber, thieves came in large number)

ਲੁੱਟ ਦੌਲਤ ਕਈ ਕਰੋੜਾਂ ਦੀ, ਹਿੰਦ ਸਮਝੇ ਵਾਂਗਰ ਢੋਰਾਂ ਦੀ।
Looting millions from the motherland, they took us as stupid beings)

ਆ ਜ਼ਾਲਮ ਪਾੜ ਲਗਾਆ ਹੈ, ਹੁਣ ਨਵਾਂ ਜ਼ਮਾਨਾ ਆਇਆ ਹੈ।
Foreigners looted us, but present is the new age)

ਜਦ ਡਿੱਠਾ ਹਿੰਦ ਨਕਾਰੀ ਹੈ, ਵੜੇ ਚੋਰ ਖੋਲ੍ਹ ਕੇ ਬਾਰੀ ਹੈ।
Finding India as helpless, thieves have broken into the house)

ਸੱਭ ਖਾਲੀ ਕਰੀ ਪਟਾਰੀ ਹੈ, ਧਨ ਵਿਚ ਵਲੈਤ ਪੋਚਾਇਆ ਹੈ।
Emptied our treasury, the wealth is taken to England)

****

ਹਿੰਦ ਦੇ ਸਪੁੱਤਰੋ ਕਰੋ ਧਿਆਨ ਜੀ, ਲੁੱਟ ਕੇ ਤੇ ਹਿੰਦ ਕੀਤਾ ਹੈ ਵੈਰਾਨ ਜੀ।
Listen O! the sons of the motherland, they have left her in desolate stage)

ਤੁਸਾਂ ਵਿਚ ਪਾਕੇ ਵੀਰੇ ਖਾਨਾ ਜੰਗੀਆਂ, ਖਾ ਲਿਆ ਮੁਲਕ ਲੁੱਟ ਕੇ ਫਰੰਗੀਆਂ।
Made you to engaged in mutual strife, and the White have looted our land)

ਹਿੰਦੂ ਮੁਸਲਮਾਨ ਅਤੇ ਸਿੰਘ ਸੂਰਮੇ, ਕੁੱਟ ਕੇ ਬਨਾਓ ਵੈਰੀਆਂ ਦੇ ਚੂਰਮੇ।
O Hindu, Muslim and Sikhs heroes, thrash the enemy into pulp)

ਫੜ ਲਓ ਸ਼ਤਾਬੀ ਹੱਥੀਂ ਤੇਗਾਂ ਨੰਗੀਆਂ, ਖਾ ਲਿਆ ਮੁਲਕ ਲੁੱਟ ਕੇ ਫਰੰਗੀਆਂ।
Draw your swords at once, the Whites have looted our country)

ਕਿਉਂ ਨਾ ਸਿੰਘ ਸੂਰਮੇ ਮੈਦਾਨੀ ਗਜਦੇ, ਕਿਉਂ ਨਾ ਪੀਕੇ ਰੱਤ ਗੋਰਿਆਂ ਦੀ ਰਜਦੇ।
Let the brave roar in the battle field, quench your thirst upon the White's blood)

ਗੱਡ ਦਿਓ ਲੜਾਈਆਂ ਦੀਆਂ ਲਾਲ ਝੰਡੀਆਂ, ਖਾ ਲਿਆ ਮੁਲਕ ਲੁੱਟ ਕੇ ਫਰੰਗੀਆਂ।
(Declare the war open, the White have looted our land)

3. Divide and rule policy

Where ever the British ruled, they adopted the policy of 'divide and rule'. Basically, it means that you divide the population into manageable chunks so that it becomes impossible for people to join together and revolt against the foreign ruler. British exactly used this policy. A Poems beautifully depicting this aspect is given below.

ਆਪਸ ਵਿਚ ਲੜਾਕੇ ਸਭ ਲੋਕੀ ਮਾਰੇ, ਮੱਲੇ ਮੁਲਕ ਫਰੰਗੀਆਂ ਅਜ ਕਹਿਣ ਹਮਾਰੇ।
Incited people to kill each other, and the English claimed the countries)

ਅਜ ਤਕ ਸਭ ਮਾਨੀਆਂ ਮੌਜਾਂ ਯੁੱਗ ਚਾਰੇ, ਕੀਤੇ ਸ਼ੁਗਲ ਕਲੋਲ ਬਹੁ ਧਰ ਤੇਜ ਕਰਾਰੇ।
Had a good time worldwide, had pastime and frolicked with sharp sword)

ਪਹਿਲੇ ਵਕਤੀਂ ਨਿਕਲ ਕੇ ਪਰਦੇਸ ਸਧਾਏ, ਲੋਕੀ ਸੁੱਤੇ ਘਰਾਂ ਵਿਚ ਸਭ ਆਣ ਜਗਾਏ।
Entered India in early days, invaded people in their own homes)

4. Sounds of mutiny

The primary purpose to form a Ghadar party in North America was to dislodge the British Rule from India. This would require mutiny at a large scale The apparent signs of rebellion against the British rule in India are obvious in Ghadar poetry.

ਹਿੰਦੋਸਤਾਨ ਦੇ ਬੱਚਿਓ ਕਰੋ ਛੇਤੀ, ਚਲੋ ਦੇਸ਼ ਨੂੰ ਗਦਰ ਮਚਾਨ ਬਦਲੇ।
(O, the children of India, let us go back to stage mutiny)

ਹੀਰਾ ਹਿੰਦ ਬੇ-ਕੀਮਤੀ ਪਿਆ ਰੁਲਦਾ, ਸਸਤਾ ਬੌਹਤ ਜੇ ਮਿਲੇ ਭੀ ਜਾ'ਨ ਬਦਲੇ।
(Priceless jewel of India is neglected, it will be worth buying with life)

ਦੱਸਾਂ ਗੱਲ ਮੈਂ ਗ਼ਦਰ ਦੇ ਪਿਆਰਿਆਂ ਨੂੰ, ਜੇਹੜੇ ਤਿਯਾਰ ਹਨ ਗ਼ਦਰ ਮਚੌਣ ਬਦਲੇ।
(let me advise who love mutiny, who are ready to incite mutiny)

ਵੇਲਾ ਫੇਰ ਨਾ ਆਵਣਾ ਹੱਥ ਯਾਰੋ, ਚੰਗਾ ਵਕਤ ਹੈ ਜੰਗ ਮਚਾਣ ਬਦਲੇ।
(The time will never wait again, time is ripe to wage a war)

****

ਸੁਣੋ ਨੋਜਵਾਨੋ ਕਾਹਨੂੰ ਨੀਵੀਂ ਸੁੱਟੀ ਗੋਡਿਆਂ ਤੇ, ਕਦੋਂ ਫੜ ਤੇਗ ਨੂੰ ਮਦਾਨ ਵਿਚ ਆਓਗੇ।
(Listen o young people, why are you sitting idle, when will you come to battle field with sword)

ਸ਼ੇਰ ਬੁਆਡਾ ਨਾਂਓ ਤੇ ਲੁਕੋਂਦੇ ਫਰੇ ਜਾਨ ਕਾਨੂੰ, ਦੱਸੋ ਕਦੋਂ ਸ਼ੇਰ ਵਾਲੀ ਬਾ'ਣ ਉਪਰ ਆਓਗੇ।
(Lion you are called, why are you hiding, when are you going to act like a lion)

ਤਬ ਤਕ ਸੁਖ ਨਾਂਹੀ ਹੋਵਨਾ ਕਦੰਤ ਭਾਈਓ, ਜਿੰਨਾ ਚਿਰ ਜ਼ਾਲਮਾਂ ਨੂੰ ਮਾਰ ਨਾ ਮੁਕਾਓਗੇ।
(O brothers, no peace will prevail, until you teach a lesson to the tyrants)

ਬੈਠੇ ਚੁੱਪ ਕੀਤੀ ਅੱਖਾਂ ਮੀਟੀ ਜਿਵੇਂ ਭੰਗ ਪੀਤੀ, ਕਰਕੇ ਗ਼ਦਰ ਕਦੋਂ ਹਿੰਦ ਨੂੰ ਛੁੜਾਓਗੇ।
(Quietly sitting like an opium addict with eyes closed, when will you wage mutiny to free India)

5. Sikh philosophy and Ghadar poetry

Sikh philosophy is vividly portrayed in Ghadar Poetry. Poems relating to the heroic deeds of Guru Gobind Singh and other martyrs like Banda Bahadar, Dip Singh, Hari Singh Naluwa, Akali Phoola Singh are composed to induce spirit of bravery among Indians. Such poems played a definitive role to reinforce the nature of bravery that Sikhs are known for in the history. Some examples of poems reinforcing the Sikh philosophy are give below.

The heading of one of the poem is 'An appeal to Panth' (ਪੰਥ ਅੱਗੇ ਪੁਕਾਰ) starts with Baba Kabir's Salok, ਸੂਰਾ ਸੋ ਪਹਿਚਾਨੀਐ ਜੁ ਲਰੇ ਦੀਨ ਕੇ ਹੇਤ॥ ਪੁਰਜਾ ਪੁਰਜਾ ਕਟਿ ਮਰੈ ਕਬਹੂ ਨ ਛਾਡੈ ਖੇਤੁ,॥ (He alone is known to be a warrior, who fights for the sake of his religion). Following the Salok, poems depicting the act of valor of Gurus and their Sikhs in the battle fields are, given below.

ਪਰ ਉਪਕਾਰ ਕੀਤਾ ਗੁਰਾਂ ਸਾਜਿਆ ਸੀ, ਹੱਥੀਂ ਕੀਤੇ ਸੀ ਜੰਗ ਕ੍ਰਮਾਲ ਸਿੰਘੋ॥
(With guru's blessing we were created, fighting valiantly for the people)

ਭਾਰਤ ਵਰਸ਼ ਤੋਂ ਜ਼ੁਲਮ ਹਟਾਇਆ ਸੀ, ਬਹੁਤ ਕਰਕੇ ਜੰਗੋ ਜਮਾਲ ਸਿੰਘੋ॥
(Terror vanished away from India, due to the miraculous fight they gave

ਏਸ ਹਿੰਦ ਦੀ ਰੱਖਿਆ ਕਰਨ ਖਾਤਰ, ਵਾਰ ਦਿੱਤੇ ਸੀ ਜਿਗਰ ਦੇ ਲਾਲ ਸਿੰਘੋ॥
(It was to defend the motherland, that he sacrificed his loving sons)

ਜੰਗ ਵਿੱਚ ਪਾ ਗਏ ਸ਼ਹੀਦੀਆਂ ਨੂੰ, ਜਦੋਂ ਸੱਦਿਆ ਆਪ ਅਕਾਲ ਸਿੰਘੋ।
(They laid down their lives in the battle field, on the call of almighty)

ਸਿੰਘ ਨਾਮ ਧਰੀਕ ਦੀ ਲਾਜ ਰੱਖੋ, ਭਾਰਤ ਵਰਸ਼ ਤੇ ਖੇਡੋ ਗੁਲਾਲ ਸਿੰਘੋ॥
(Keep up the prestige of being a Singh, and shed your blood for your motherland)

ਛੇਤੀਂ ਗ਼ਦਰ ਮਚੌਣ ਦੀ ਕਰੋ ਤਿਆਰੀ, ਫਤੇਹ ਦੇਵਸੀ ਤੁਸਾਂ ਅਕਾਲ ਸਿੰਘੋ॥
(Make no delay to cause uprising, and the almighty shall bless you with triumph)

****

ਗੁਲਾਮੀ ਦਾ ਅੰਧੇਰਾ ਜੇਹੜਾ ਛਾਇਆ ਥੋਡੇ ਸੀਸ ਉੱਤੇ, ਕਰੋ ਜਲਦ ਤੇ ਭੜਾਓ ਗ਼ਦਰ ਭਾਨ ਨੂੰ।

The dark that hangs over your head, make no delay in waging war)

ਇਕ ਦੂਜੇ ਓਹਲੇ ਲੁਕ ਬੈਠੇ ਹੋ ਕਿਉਂ ਖਾਲਸਾ ਜੀ, ਦੱਸੋ ਲੜਨ ਜਾਉ ਕੋਣ ਜੰਗ ਦੇ ਮੈਦਾਨ ਨੂੰ।
(If you take refuse in each other's arm, who will go to the battle field to fight)

ਆਓ ਜੰਗ ਦੇ ਮੈਦਾਨ ਨਾਹੀਂ ਛੋਡੇ ਸਿੰਘੀ ਨਾਮ ਐਵੇਂ, ਲਾਜ ਕਿਉਂ ਲਗੌਂਦੇ ਹੋ ਗੁਬਿੰਦ ਸਿੰਘ ਦੇ ਨਾਮ ਨੂੰ।
(Let's wage war and justify our faith, and shouldn't bring bad name to the Tenth Master)

ਸਿੰਘ ਨਾਮ ਰੱਖ ਕਿਉਂ ਗੁਲਾਮੀ ਵਾਲੀ ਛਟ ਚੁਕੀ,ਗਿੱਦੜਾਂ ਦੇ ਵਾਂਗ ਕਿਉਂ ਲੁਕੋਂਦੇ ਫਿਰੋ ਜਾਨ ਨੂੰ।
(With Singh aligned to your name, why to waver, and hide like jackals to save your skin)

Bibliography

1. Darshan Singh Tatla. 2003. Ghadar movement : A guide to Sources. Guru Nanak Dev University, Amritsar. Pages 283.
2. Ved Vatuk. 2010. Ghadar Party da Saptahik Parcha (Bhag pehla, 1913-1914. Folklore Institute, Berkley, California. Pages 354
3. Isemonger, F. C. and Slattery, J. (1998). An account of the Ghadar conspiracy. Folklore Institute, Berkley, California. 173 (with appendices).
4. Sedition Committee Report. 1918. Superintendent Government Printing, Calcutta, India.
5. Kesar Singh and Kesar Singh. 1995. Poetry of Ghadar Movement (Punjabi). Punjabi University, Patiala.

Appendices

Majority of the Sikh pioneers in North America
worked in railways and Lumber mills
WITH Courtesy from *http://www.sikhs.org/100th/part1.html*

Sikhs outside the Mill

Sikhs standing on a train engine

Sikhs working in the lumber industry Abbotsford, Canada 1911

Hardial Singh Atwal was the first Sikh born in Canada on August 28, 1912.

The printing press used by Kartar Singh Sarabha was moved from the Kesar Singh Dhillon Ghadar Memorial Trust in Emeryville, CA in September 2011. Preserved at the Ghadri Baba Museum at Gurdwara Sahib Stockton.

Appendices

In 1929, Stockton Gurdwara honored Sarojini Naidu with gold medal. A marching band led the procession from the railway station to the Gurdwara. Sarojini Naidu, also known as Sarojini Chattopadhyaya, was a famous Indian poet and a major freedom fighter who became the first Indian woman appointed the president of the Indian National Congress and also the Governor of a state in India.

President Woodrow Wilson and his friend, Professor Bliss Perry helped Professor Teja Singh intellectually, morally and financially.

President Woodrow Wilson   Professor Bliss Perry

SIKH GADAR LEHAR 1907–1918

GADAR PARTY FLAG

Conference speakers and organizers

Appendices

Dr. Gurmel Singh, Dr. Amrik Singh, and Dr. Jasbir Singh Mann

Dr. Hugh Johnston, Dr. Paul Englesberg, and Johanna Ogden

SIKH GADAR LEHAR 1907–1918

Members of Society Amarjit, Kashmir, Satwinder, and Satnam with Dr. Amrik Singh

Moderator Dr. Jagjit K. Khaira

Appendices

Moderator Dilipreet K. Ghtaura

Principal Dilip Singh honoring Dr. Englesberg

SIKH GADAR LEHAR 1907–1918

Joint Proclamation

WHEREAS, the City of Bellingham and Whatcom County are committed to promoting harmony between people of all races, creeds and denominations; and

WHEREAS, cultural and religious diversity is one of our community's greatest endeavors; and

WHEREAS, numerous individuals and organizations in our community are joining together to raise awareness of the importance of reconciliation between people of different backgrounds; and

WHEREAS, September 4, 2007 is the 100-year anniversary of the anti-Sikh and anti-East Indian riots that took place in Bellingham; and

WHEREAS, the purpose for a Day of Healing and Reconciliation is to celebrate a positive, collective healing and reconciliation movement within our families, communities, churches and government and to educate ourselves and others about our collective history of government policies which impacted Native communities and other ethnic groups; and

WHEREAS, a Day of Healing and Reconciliation can promote racial reconciliation and bring all community members together through the celebration of our common bond of freedom; and

WHEREAS, when we are judged by history and by our children, let it be said that we overcame our differences for the sake of our children and that we shared a common dream for the future; and

WHEREAS, our community continues to reaffirm our fundamental belief in human dignity and our unchanging reverence for human rights;

NOW, THEREFORE, DO WE, Tim Douglas, Mayor of the City of Bellingham, and Pete Kremen, Whatcom County Executive, proclaim Tuesday, September 4, 2007 to be a

DAY OF HEALING AND RECONCILIATION

in the City of Bellingham and Whatcom County, Washington.

Signed this 14th day of August 2007

Tim Douglas, Mayor
City of Bellingham

Pete Kremen, County Executive
County of Whatcom

Appendices

PROCLAMATION

WHEREAS: Astoria, Oregon is the oldest American settlement west of the Rocky Mountains, founded in 1811; and

WHEREAS: By 1911 Astoria had a working waterfront that included fishing, canneries, and lumber mills that contributed to the economic vibrancy of the city; and

WHEREAS: Workers in these industries included in large part immigrant laborers from China, India, and Finland; and

WHEREAS: The Hammond lumber mill in Alderbrook listed about 100 Punjabi Sikh Indians working alongside Finnish immigrants from 1910-1922; and

WHEREAS: The Punjabi Sikhs were inspired by the success of the American Revolution against Great Britain, and by Finland's struggle for independence from Russian occupation; and

WHEREAS: The Punjabi Sikhs met at the Finnish Socialist Hall in 1913 and formed the Ghadar (mutiny) Party; and

WHEREAS: Supporters of Ghadar, thousands of whom living in the United States and Canada, returned to India, and inspired their countrymen to fight for their independence from Great Britain, which was achieved in 1947; and

WHEREAS: The Ghadarites fought and died not only for the freedom of their home country, but also for the innate rights of the immigrant worker to lead a dignified and discrimination-free life; and

WHEREAS: 2013 is the 100-year anniversary of this historic meeting that recognizes the universal right of sovereign nations to independence and self-rule.

NOW, THEREFORE, I, Willis L. Van Dusen, Mayor of Astoria, do hereby proclaim 2013 as a celebration of the

CENTENARY OF THE FOUNDING OF THE GHADAR PARTY IN ASTORIA, OREGON

IN WITNESS WHEREOF, I have herewith set my hand and caused the Seal of the City of Astoria to be affixed this 18th day of March, 2013.

Mayor

SIKH GADAR LEHAR 1907–1918

Greetings from the President of the United States of America

THE WHITE HOUSE
WASHINGTON

October 2, 2012

I send greetings to all those attending the Centennial Celebration of the Stockton Gurdwara Sahib.

Throughout our Nation's history, houses of worship have been cornerstones of our communities. They are places where neighbors can come together to celebrate faith and to seek inspiration and guidance.

The Stockton Gurdwara Sahib reminds us that our religious sanctuaries are also reflections of the diversity and pluralism that are central to the American experience. It stands as a testament to the trials and triumphs Sikh Americans have experienced; serves as a center for civic, political, and social life; and displays the principles of equality, service, interfaith cooperation, and respect that Sikh Americans share with people across our Nation.

As you mark this historic milestone, I wish you all the best.

Brief Bio with Photos of Contributors

 **1. Dr. Hugh Johnston is** a professor emeritus in history at Simon Fraser University, where he taught full-time from 1968 and continues to teach in the Seniors Program. He is author of several books, including *The Voyage of the Komagata Maru: The Sikh Challenge to Canada's Colour Bar* (1989), *The Four Quarters of the Night: the Life Story of an Emigrant Sikh* (1995), *Radical Campus: Making Simon Fraser University* (2005), and *Jewels of the Qila: The Remarkable Story of an Indo-Canadian Family* (2011). He is currently working on a biography of Kapoor Singh, a Sikh pioneer, mill owner and philanthropist.

 **2. Dr. Paul Englesberg is** professor of education at Walden University, specializing in adult and higher education, and educational research. Previously he was on the education faculty at Western Washington University where he initiated the Asian American Curriculum and Research Project. He has also taught in several universities in Taiwan and China. He has conducted research on the history of Asian Americans in the Pacific northwest of the US, focusing especially on the 1907 riots and expulsion of the majority-Sikh population from Bellingham and Everett in Washington State.

3. **Dr. Gurmel Singh Sidhu is** a Professor of Biology at California State University, Fresno. He is also a Director of Research and Development for Greek and Turkish biotech companies. Dr. Sidhu has written several scientific books, including *Genetics of Pathogenic Fungi* (1986), *AIDS: A Miserable Disease* (2003), *Life and Cloning* (2004), and *DNA: The Language of Life* (2006). He has also authored over 150 scientific papers for a range of scientific journals. Dr. Sidhu is also a renowned and highly accomplished literary critic who has authored nine books of poetry, edited another nine, and written over 100 literary articles and reviews.

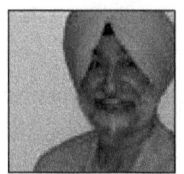

4. **Dr. Amrik Singh is** a Professor of Punjabi and ethnic studies at California State University, Sacramento. He holds a Ph.D. in English. Formerly president for two years of the Punjabi Literary Society of California, he is also active in the Punjabi American Heritage Society. A journalist for *The Ambedkar Times* and *The Sacramento Examiner*, Dr. Singh pursues study of Sikh-Americans, globalization, the history and socio-politics of India, and a range of other issues.

5. **Dr. Jasbir Singh Mann is** an orthopedic surgeon, practicing in California since 1980. He is a Medical Graduate from Punjab Uni. and received his Post Graduate degree from PGI Chandigarh and Columbia Uni. New York. He is a Sikh community activist, a scholar and writer on Sikh Academic issues. His articles have appeared in a range of journals, including *Nishaan*, *The Sikh Review*, and *Abstracts of Sikh Studies*, and in several books. He has co-edited five books on Sikhism and arranged many international Sikh Studies conferences, including in 1988, 1990, 1993, 1994, 1995, 1996, 2000, 2004, 2012, and 2013. In 2001, he received a D.Lit. (Honoris causa) from Punjabi University, Patiala, for his contributions to Sikh studies. He is also a Fellow of the American Academy of Orthopedic Surgeons, a Fellow of the International College of Surgeons, and a Fellow of the American College of International Physicians.

Brief Bio with Photos of Contributors

6. Prof. Sohan Singh Pooni lives in Vancouver and is an expert on the Gadar history. Formerly a history professor in Punjab, he is author of *Canada De Gadri Yodhay* (2011), a book about how the Ghadar combatants from Canada played a part in the formation of the Ghadar Party movement.

7. Jatinder Singh Hundal is an Electronics Engineer by profession. He graduated from Oregon State in 1985. He is currently based in Sacramento as a professional with the State of California. His field of study deals with Sikh Numismatics and the history of the community's struggle for survival. His articles on technical and community issues have appeared in international technical and academic publications. He is actively involved in tracing the roots of Sikh sovereignty through linking the history of Sikh Numismatics to current under waves within the community for a homeland. He has been an active participant in community events since 1984 and is involved/aligned with organization dedicated to bringing justice to the community's ill treatment.

8. Rajwinder Singh Rahi is a writer and journalist from India whose many literary achievements include writing for *Daily Ajit* and *Aj Di Awaz* and authoring *Ghadar Lehar Di Asli Gatha (The Real Story of Ghadar Movement)* Volumes I–III (2012), *Meri Ram Kahani (The Story of My Life)* (2012), *Jithe Pash Rehnda Hai (Critique of Poet Pash's Life and Ideology)* (2007), *Punjab Di Pug – Jaswant Singh Kanwal* (2010), and *Chaunh Killian Te Usriya Tibba* (short stories) (1987). In addition to the above, he has also published numerous articles on literary and contemporary historical issues have been published in various newspapers and reputed magazines, as well as presented literary papers at academic conferences in the UK.

9. Dr. Baljeet S. Sahi is a practicing veterinarian in California and President of Sikhs for Preservation of Sikhism and Sikh Heritage, a watchdog organization for Sikh and Punjabi Studies and Sikh politico-religious affairs in Diaspora. He is also the spokesperson for Coalition of Gurdwaras of California and a correspondent with World Sikh News. He has been actively involved in Sikh affairs of the past twenty years with special interests in "Sociopolitical impact of Sikh religious studies in western nations," and "Societal understanding of Sikh religion and politics in Diaspora." He has lectured on various subjects related to Sikh Studies, sociopolitical affairs, and Sikhism at Yuba City (2005), Chaffy College Rancho Cucamonga (2006), Chandler School Pasadena (2008), University of California Riverside (2008), and Stockton California (2012). His current focus is post-Guru history of Sikhs, particularly their armed resistance to suppression in pre- and post-independent India, and is keenly working on a book.

10. **Dr. Pooran Singh Gill,** Ph.D. in History, M.A. History & Political Science, Bachelor of Library Science & Diploma in Religious study; Editor of *Sikh Marg*, Retired as Cataloguer from Asian Library of UBC, Served as a lecturer (Political science), and Librarian 1974–1976. Served as an Editor of a monthly magazine *The Western Sikh Samachar*. He is author of *Kiv Sachiara Hoi (The Art of Living)*, *Sikh Darshan di Vilakhanta (The Uniqueness of Sikh Philosophy)*, *Dharmak Sanskaran Naal Jure Veham te Bharm (Myths of Superstitions in Religious Rites)*, *Sikh Nawan da Kosh (The Dictionary of Sikh Personal Names)*, *Komagata Maru da Dukhant (The Tragedy of Komagata Maru – 1914)*, *Parja andi Gian Bin*, *Punjabi sabhiachaar wich Trairaran*. Besides books, he has also published many articles in various monthly magazines and newspapers.

11. **Johanna Ogden is** a long-time community activist and independent, regional historian based in Portland, Oregon. Her recent work focuses on Punjabi, and largely Sikh, settlers in the Columbia River Basin, their involvement in the formation of the Ghadar Party in Astoria, Oregon, and the historical erasure of their presence and contributions. Her previous research has centered on domestic wartime issues in the Pacific Northwest, including WWII war resisters and the arrival of Mexican contract laborers coincident with Japanese internment. Her work has been supported by various Canadian and US grants, appeared in the *Oregon Historical Quarterly* and Michigan State University Press, and included in professional Western historical conferences and popular venues. She received her M.A. (History) at UBC and her B.A., *Summa cum laude,* at Portland State University, Oregon.

Brief Bio with Photos of Contributors

12. **Dr. Bruce La Brack is** Professor Emeritus at the School of International Studies, University of the Pacific in Stockton, CA. He is a cultural anthropologist who has conducted over 35 years of research on the impact of the South Asian Diaspora outside Punjab, primarily in North America, but also in East Africa, England, and India. He has held an American Institute of Indian Studies (New Delhi) Language Fellowship and was awarded a Fulbright Scholarship to study in India. Dr. La Brack has published extensively on the South Asian diaspora, particularly Sikhs and Punjabis in the US and Canada. He authored the ethnographic study, *The Sikhs of Northern California: 1904-1975*, which is being revised and updated for republication by American Migration Series Press, New York.

13. **Dr. Harold Gould is**, since 1991, a visiting scholar in the Center for South Asian Studies at University of Virginia, Charlottesville. From 1968 to 1991, he served as a Professor of Anthropology and Asian Studies at the University of Illinois, where he specialized in study of India and South Asia. Author of hundreds of articles, Dr. Gould has also written six books, including *The Hindu Caste System* Volumes I–III (1988, 1988, and 1991), *Grass-Roots Politics in India: A Century of Political Evolution in Faizabad District* (1994), *Sikhs, Swamis, Students and Spies: The India Lobby in the United States, 1900–1946* (2006), and *The South Asia Story: The First Sixty Years of U.S. Relations with India and Pakistan* (2010).

15. **Dr. Gurdarshan Singh Dhillon is** an expert on Sikh social, political, and religious history and is a Ph.D. recipient from and former professor of history at Punjab University. He has published scores of articles in reputable national and international journals, as well as academic pieces in newspapers including *The Tribune* (Chandigarh), *The Indian Express* (New Delhi), *The Illustrated Weekly of India*, *The Washington Times*, *The Globe and Mail*, and the *Punjabi Tribune*. He is author of several books, including *Researches in Sikh Religion and History* (1989), *Insights into Sikh Religion and History* (1991), *India Commits Suicide* (1992), *Truth About Punjab: SGPC White Paper* (1996), and *Perspectives on Sikh Religion and History* (1996).

17. Dr. Nirmal Singh Mann is a Professor of Medicine & Gastroenterology and Senior Consultant on Gastroenterology and Hepatology at University of California, Davis Medical Center. A graduate of Christian Medical College, Ludhiana, he later also earned a Ph.D. in nutrition and a D.Sc. in gastroenterology. Dr. Mann is also certified as a Fellow by the Royal College of Physicians of Canada in Internal Medicine and Gastroenterology. He has served on the medical school faculty boards of University of Alberta, University of Louisville, Texas A&M University College, and University of California, Davis. Author of two books and 350 papers relating to his specialty, he has also published a biography of Sikh pioneer Pakher Singh Gill. An avid follower of Urdu poetry, he has additionally published 3 collections of his own Urdu poems.

18. Dr. Sukhmandar Singh is a Professor of Civil Engineering and a holder of Nicholson Family Chair in Engineering at Santa Clara University. He is also a visiting faculty at Cambridge University, UK. He earned his Ph.D. from U. C. Berkeley. Dr. Singh served as the first president of The Sikh Council of North America. He is a long-time organizer and participant in conferences related to Sikh affairs and studies within that field.

20. Dr. Tarlochan Singh Nahal (b. 1953) received an M.A. degree in English from Guru Nanak Dev University Amritsar in 1977 and Ph.D. in Political Science from Senior University International (USA) in 1999 under the supervision of Dr Noel Q. King, Professor Emeritus, University of California, Santa Cruz. He is a keen student of Sikh history and observer of political developments. He has been working as a Sr. Technical Writer in the computer industry for the last 27 years. He organized many international Sikh conferences in past. He has authored many articles published in various journals and newspapers. He is the author of the book *Religion and Politics in Sikhism: The Khalsa Perspective*, published by the Singh Brothers, Amristar, 2011.

Brief Bio with Photos of Contributors

21. Prof. Gurcharan Singh Aulakh is a former professor and the author of 60 books, including 55 in Punjabi and five in English. Among these books are *History of Babbar Akali Lehar, Sikh Generals and Gallant Warriors* (2006), *History of Sikhs: Men and Movements, 1469-2009* (2009).

22. Dr. Balwant Singh Dhillon, Director, Centre for Studies on Sri Guru Granth Sahib, Guru Nanak Dev University, Amritsar. He has been Professor and Head, Department of Guru Nanak Studies, Dean of Faculty of Humanities and Religious Studies, and has also served on the Senate and Syndicate of Guru Nanak Dev University, Amritsar. Author of *The Sikh Gurus and the Mughal State*; *Parmukh Sikh te Sikh Panth*, an exhaustive account of the expansion of Sikh Panth during the early 17th century; *Early Sikh Scriptural Tradition: Myth and Reality*; critical text of *Sri Gur Panth Parkash* (by Rattan Singh Bhangoo); *Eighteenth Century Persian Historiography on Banda Singh Bahadur*. He is Editor of two research journals: *Journal of Sikh Studies* and *Perspectives on Guru Granth Sahib*, both published by GNDU. Presently, he is working on two projects—*Rajasthani Sources of the Sikh History* and *Persian Sources on the Sikh Gurus*.

23. Jagtar Singh Grewal, a former Professor and Vice Chancellor, Guru Nanak Dev University, Amritsar, and Director and later Chairman, Indian Institute of Advanced Study, Shimla, has written extensively on historiography, medieval India, and the Punjab and Sikh history. His books by the Oxford University Press are *Muslim Rule in India: The Assessments of British Historians* (1972), *The State and Society in Medieval India* (e.d. 2005), *Religious Movements and Institutions in Medieval India* (ed. 2006) and *The Sikhs: Ideology, Institutions, and Identity* (2009), *Guru Nanak in History* (1969), *Sikh Ideology, Polity, and Social Order* (1996), *Historical Perspectives on Sikh Identity* (1997), and *Contesting Interpretations of the Sikh Tradition* (1998).

 **24. Pritam Singh Aulakh** received an M.A. in Mathematics from Punjab University in 1962 and UBC in 1970. He then entered the field of Computer Science/Information Technology and worked in the private sector for 8 years before working with the Government of Canada as Regional Manager for 23 years. He was President Akali Singh Sikh Society in 1978 and Vice President, Federation of Sikh Societies of Canada, Western Region, for 7 years, from 1981 to 1987. He organized and celebrated the anniversary of *Kamagata Maru* in 1989 at KDS Vancouver. He was a member of Sikh Centennial Committee in 1997. He was also President of the Federation of Sikh Societies of Canada for 6 years, from 2004 to 2009, during which time he re-activated the Federation of Sikh Societies of Canada to deal with the issue of Vacant Chair and publications made by the chair holders. Presently, he is a member of the working Committee with UBC Faculty and helps community youth education in Punjabi/Gurmukhi and Gurbani.

Coordinators for Conference

Satnam Singh Johal
Home: 604-520-0161 Cell: 604-307-3800
Fax: 604-520-9568 Email: sjohal@telus.net

Dr. Jasbir Singh Mann
Off: 714-895-1774 Res: 714-526-5349 Fax: 714-758-1485
Email: jasbirmann@aol.com

Canadian Sikh Study & Teaching Society
#108-1083 East Kent Ave., Vancouver, B. C. Canada. V5X 4V9.
Phone: (604) 327-4142 E-mail : cssts25@yahoo.com

Shri Guru Granth Sahib Foundation
1771 W. Romneya Drive, Suite E, Anaheim, 92801
Tel 714-758-8553 Fax 714-758-1485
Email: sggsfca@gmail.com
Web page www.globalsikhstudies.net

Index

A
Abdulla, Syed 31
Advani, L.K. 515
Agda 480, 485, 487
Ajnala, Rattan Singh 6, 114
Anand Marriage Act 7
Andaman jail 56, 95, 507
Anglo Sikh War 54
Army 17, 25, 28, 31, 32, 35, 91, 98, 123, 164, 180, 211, 217, 258, 354, 368, 370, 378, 401, 405, 428, 431, 465
Article 25 7, 98, 121
ARYAN 79
Arya Samaj 5, 55, 77, 94, 161, 163, 170, 172, 175, 178, 181, 186, 193, 207, 210, 218, 391, 499
Asiatic Exclusion League 61, 71, 73, 214, 230, 332, 341
Astoria 11, 50, 79, 82, 84, 236, 274, 278, 279, 280, 282, 283, 284, 285, 286, 287, 288, 289, 294, 295, 300, 301, 342, 357, 368, 382, 388, 400, 419, 420, 421, 422, 423, 449, 479, 560
atrocities 34, 127, 128, 207, 211, 360, 383, 463, 464, 531, 538, 540
Azad, Maulana Abul Kalam 16, 22, 27, 53, 503
Aziz, Qutubuddin 464

B
Baba Bohar 132
Babar Akali Lehar 115
Babbar Akali Dal 219
Babbar Akali Movement 122, 165, 411, 412, 425, 428, 429, 430, 431, 432, 433
Banda Singh Bahadur 129, 171, 399, 563
Bandi Jiwan 107, 121
Barkatullah 251, 502, 525
Behari Lal Verma 254, 255
Bellingham Herald 62, 215, 216, 306, 311, 315, 320, 321, 322, 323, 324, 326, 327, 328, 334, 337
Bellingham Riots 54, 214, 303
Bengal Army 28
Bernstorff 5, 94, 119, 501
Besant, Annie 178, 179, 184, 185
Bhakna, Sohan Singh 80, 82, 84, 88, 89, 109, 110, 124, 147, 154, 172, 173, 174, 259, 293, 294, 300, 340, 343, 344, 345, 346, 350, 355, 381, 382, 383, 385, 388, 415, 417, 419, 420, 421, 422, 423, 441, 448, 449, 483, 525
Bharat, Abhinava 4, 5, 53, 54, 95, 114
Bibi Gulab Kaur 145, 146, 423
Black Tom Island terminal 93
Blavatsky, Madam Helene 177
Bopp, Franz 4, 83, 92, 245, 501
Bose, Sudhindra 203, 212
British Embassy 205, 242
Brown, Emily C 116, 117, 119, 120, 167
Budge Budge 100, 107, 157, 200, 250, 252, 261, 262, 349, 350, 394

C

Chakravarty 92, 94, 115, 200, 245
Chaliah, Justice Venkata 8
Chand, Amir 193, 219
Chandra, Harish 92, 503
Chandra, Ram 5, 8, 50, 82, 85, 92, 94,
    106, 114, 200, 204, 423, 494, 499,
    500, 502, 526, 535
Chankayan politics 195
Chatarji 193
Chattopadhyaya, Virendranath 77
Cleveland, C. R. 235
Colonial terrorism 107
Colonization Act 54, 58, 60, 61, 113
Columbia University 39, 40, 41, 47
Communist 6, 113, 389
Conspiracy 87
Continuous Journey Law 68

D

Das, Taraknath 66, 114, 229, 232, 240,
    245, 258, 259, 290, 291, 293, 294,
    318, 320, 521, 534
Dayal, Lala Har 5, 186, 190, 199, 200,
    201, 203, 205, 232, 448, 449, 450,
    451, 471, 496, 499, 502, 525
Dayananda, Swami 186
Dhingra, Madan Lal 73, 77, 219, 477,
    479, 484
Digan, Don K. 6, 119
Directory 55, 116, 223, 249, 252, 254,
    255, 260, 280, 282, 493, 496, 497
'divide and rule' 503, 543
Doab Bari Act 54, 57, 58, 60, 61, 113
Dwarkanath Tagore 182, 184, 207, 210
Dyer, General 170, 426, 454, 460, 462,
    463

E

East India Company 19, 26, 183, 210, 504
Edgware 487
Everett Herald 217

F

failure 26, 27, 36, 134, 144, 218, 316,
    344, 345, 380, 424, 425
Finns 288, 289, 299
Foucault, Michel 102
Fowler, A. E. 305, 332
French Revolution 6

G

Gallagher, Mary Anne 334
Gandhi, Mahatma 34, 384, 427, 455, 512,
    513
Gargaj, Kishan Singh 428, 431
Germans 4, 5, 55, 56, 79, 83, 84, 85, 91,
    92, 93, 94, 113, 115, 160, 190,
    194, 200, 240, 245, 453, 454, 480,
    484, 485, 500, 501, 502, 529, 530
Gill, Parkher Singh 398
Gokhale, Gopal K. 193
Goonj, Ghadar De 537
Gurdwara in Shanghai 146
Gurdwara of Bangkok 147
Gurdwara of Hongkong 146
Gurdwara of Penang 147
Guru Arjan Dev Ji 145, 148
Guru Granth Sahib 4, 1, 3, 4, 9, 13, 53,
    76, 96, 100, 101, 105, 107, 108,
    131, 139, 144, 148, 149, 345, 364,
    377, 391, 392, 393, 441, 499, 513,
    563, 564
Guru Ka Bagh 107, 110, 427, 466
Guttenberg, Von 224

H

Haig, H. G. 442
Hall, L.W. 46
Hammond Mill 280, 286, 288
Harkin 41, 70, 224, 225, 228, 341
Harper 248
Harvard University 48, 176, 203, 478, 481
Highgate 77
Hindi Association of Pacific 82
Hindu–German conspiracy trial 91
Hindu Maha Sabha 161, 163
Hindustan Association 73, 154, 155, 381,
    416, 418, 419, 420, 421, 446, 448,
    449, 525
Hindustan Ghadar 103, 125, 502, 532,

Index

535, 536, 538
Hindustani Association of Vancouver 78
Hobson, J.B. 59
Honduras 12, 41, 52, 70, 97, 201, 218, 224, 341, 347, 351, 354, 357, 369, 389, 413, 439
Hoover, Karl Douglas 116, 119
Hopkinson 69, 70, 71, 72, 74, 78, 84, 95, 99, 157, 158, 203, 222, 223, 224, 226, 227, 228, 229, 230, 231, 232, 233, 234, 235, 236, 237, 238, 240, 241, 242, 244, 245, 255, 259, 260, 291, 341, 353, 355, 356, 357, 358, 359, 360, 361, 362, 363, 364, 372, 376

I

India Home League 190
India Independence League 79
Indian Home Rule 185
Indian Nationalism 98, 175, 177, 178, 180, 187, 195, 197, 512
Inspiration 1, 3, 4, 6, 7, 37, 51, 53, 54, 95, 100, 101, 102, 105, 113, 138, 155, 171, 342, 345, 425, 502, 503, 524

J

Jallianwala 87, 98, 164, 184, 187, 188, 189, 426, 437, 442, 455, 456, 457, 458, 460, 462, 485, 531, 536
Jallianwala Bagh 98, 164, 187, 188, 189, 437, 442, 455, 456, 457, 458, 460, 462, 485, 531, 536
jehad 23
Jenson, Jon M. 119
Josh, Sohan Singh 6, 103, 104, 114, 121, 206, 208, 260, 382, 448

K

Khalsa Diwan Society 5, 3, 45, 46, 73, 81, 84, 99, 105, 137, 138, 143, 155, 175, 193, 203, 204, 222, 237, 268, 275, 291, 340, 341, 342, 348, 349, 356, 365, 368, 371, 372, 394, 417, 418, 422, 429, 432, 433, 439, 443, 468, 469, 473, 476, 483, 520
Khalsa Herald 79
Khalsa pamphlet 75, 118
Khalsa Revolution 6, 499, 513
Khan, Khan Bahadur 24, 30
Kingsland fire 93
Koje, Khan 79
Kolkata 260, 261
Komagata Maru 84, 218, 222, 236, 238, 247, 248, 249, 250, 251, 252, 253, 254, 255, 256, 257, 258, 259, 260, 261, 262, 303, 339, 347, 348, 349, 350, 351, 355, 357, 371, 372, 375, 379, 383, 394, 400, 423, 432, 440, 441, 466, 502, 520, 557, 560
Kumar, G.D. 73, 74, 78

L

Lalton, Gurmukh Singh 206, 249, 350
Larson, Annie 85, 94, 502
letter carrier 233

M

MacGill 225, 227, 231
mahants 170
Majumdar 16, 25, 27, 30, 36, 53, 56, 167, 168, 503
Manela, Erez 184, 185, 205
Martyrdom 13, 97, 113, 166, 167, 422, 528
Maverick 85, 91, 502
McGarrity, John 334
Mehli, Kartar Singh 250
Meri Ram Kahani 173, 174, 559
Mexican Revolution 6
Minto, Lord 60, 61, 107, 115, 117, 121
Montesquieu 102
Morley, John 66, 73
Mozumdar 176, 202, 203, 318, 320, 321
mutiny 4, 18, 19, 20, 21, 22, 23, 24, 25, 26, 27, 30, 35, 53, 66, 67, 83, 95, 123, 146, 147, 148, 194, 200, 206, 218, 219, 357, 368, 376, 377, 384, 385, 386, 387, 389, 424, 451, 501, 502, 523, 526, 528, 529, 539, 543, 544

N

Nagar Keertan 51
Namdhari Movement 123, 381
Nankana 427, 428
Natal Act 61, 67
newspaper 5, 42, 50, 53, 67, 69, 71, 72, 79, 80, 82, 100, 104, 121, 127, 136, 143, 146, 147, 148, 212, 235, 236, 238, 260, 273, 292, 295, 305, 307, 308, 310, 312, 314, 319, 320, 344, 351, 375, 378, 382, 384, 388, 417, 443, 450, 451, 483, 486, 489, 492, 494, 526, 528, 529, 530, 533, 535, 538
Noorani, A.G. 56, 117, 504, 513, 514
Nya Varlden 325, 337

O

O'Dwyer, Michael 4, 81, 87, 89, 243, 373, 374, 386, 414, 424, 426, 428, 442, 451, 456, 461, 462, 463, 464, 466
Oregon 11, 44, 50, 61, 62, 79, 80, 82, 138, 217, 236, 273, 274, 277, 278, 279, 280, 281, 282, 284, 285, 286, 288, 289, 291, 292, 294, 295, 297, 299, 300, 301, 302, 313, 330, 333, 336, 342, 379, 381, 382, 400, 402, 416, 417, 448, 449, 476, 479, 483, 525, 559, 560

P

Pacific Coast Khalsa Diwan Society 5, 45, 483
Panama Maru 255, 347
Panth Aggey Pukar 129
Papen, Von 5, 94
Parmanand 149, 351, 384, 481
Pingley, Vishnu Ganesh 198, 385, 388
Plague 60
plunderers 20, 31
Poorbia soldiers 19, 24, 29, 35
Port Blair Airport 8, 515
Proclamation 12, 56, 57, 85
Puri, Harish K. 53, 55, 56, 74, 95, 116, 117, 118, 153, 169, 170, 171, 172, 173, 260, 279, 497, 503

Q

Queen Victoria's 12, 62, 411

R

Rai, Lala Lajpat 60, 86, 107, 158, 184, 185, 186, 187, 188, 190, 191, 201, 219, 374, 412, 419
Ram, Kanshi 79, 80, 82, 114, 293, 294, 342, 346, 382, 400, 419, 420, 421, 423
Rani of Jhansi 22, 24
Reid, Malcolm 231, 240, 245, 348, 355, 356, 359
Ricouer, Paul 102
Ripon, Lord of 426
Rousseau, Jean-Jacques 102
Rowlatt Act 164, 438, 456
Roy, Ram Mohan 182, 207

S

Sahri, Harnam Singh 71, 74, 147, 356, 375, 378, 381
SANSAAR 80
Sanyal, Sachinder Nath 107, 148, 150, 385
Sarabha, Kartar Singh 39, 89, 107, 120, 124, 125, 128, 131, 155, 157, 172, 198, 344, 350, 384, 385, 386, 387, 388, 394, 418, 419, 420, 421, 422, 423, 424, 451, 455, 525, 538
Sarkar, Jadunath 26, 27
Savarkar 4, 5, 6, 8, 53, 54, 56, 77, 95, 106, 114, 117, 120, 155, 161, 162, 168, 452, 499, 500, 503, 504, 505, 506, 507, 508, 509, 510, 511, 512, 513, 514, 515, 516, 529
Scheffauer, Herman 318
Sen, Surendranath 27, 34, 36
Sepoy 16, 26, 36, 53, 194, 463, 503
Shanti 477, 484, 487
Shiromani Akali Dal 108, 426
Sidhu, Satpal 334
Singh, Ajit 58, 61, 66, 98, 107, 117, 184, 191, 193, 219, 412, 419, 503, 517, 529, 530
Singh Arora, Harnam 78

Index

Singh, Balwant 9, 71, 73, 81, 96, 110, 151, 152, 228, 244, 251, 252, 258, 259, 342, 347, 349, 353, 355, 356, 359, 364, 368, 369, 370, 371, 372, 373, 374, 375, 376, 377, 379, 391, 414, 418, 563
Singh, Bela 84, 242, 244, 356, 357, 359, 361, 362, 364, 376, 428
Singh, Bhag 73, 84, 96, 109, 115, 151, 206, 207, 228, 258, 291, 342, 343, 348, 353, 355, 356, 357, 359, 360, 361, 362, 363, 369, 372, 375, 376, 379, 418, 428
Singh, Bhagwan 82, 96, 125, 146, 151, 201, 216, 225, 251, 252, 256, 258, 262, 290, 342, 346, 350, 357, 418, 423, 502, 526, 531, 538
Singh, Bhai Mewa 99, 353, 354, 355, 356, 357, 358, 359, 360, 361, 363, 364, 365, 376, 379
Singh, Bhai Randhir 55, 121, 149, 157, 164, 391, 392, 393, 394, 395, 454
Singh, Dip 171, 544
Singh, Dr. Ragunath 244
Singh, Gajjan 108, 386, 387
Singh, Ganda 15, 18, 115, 516
Singh, Giani Harnam 151, 432, 443
Singh, Gurdit 96, 110, 157, 251, 252, 253, 254, 255, 256, 257, 260, 261, 262, 342, 347, 348, 349, 432, 441, 466
Singh, Guru Gobind 4, 44, 67, 72, 75, 96, 97, 99, 102, 139, 140, 145, 171, 172, 186, 204, 370, 392, 399, 419, 438, 458, 459, 483, 544
Singh, Hari 8, 38, 85, 86, 96, 110, 115, 119, 129, 130, 141, 151, 171, 377, 416, 417, 421, 428, 502, 538, 544
Singh, Jawala 37, 48, 49, 50, 82, 109, 124, 138, 144, 147, 148, 186, 198, 232, 346, 418, 419, 422, 423, 431
Singh, Karam 82, 107, 111, 112, 115, 152, 428, 429, 431, 538
Singh, Phula 171
Singh, Prof. Puran 140
Singh, Randhir 87, 112, 119, 392, 393, 394, 455, 497
Singh Sabha Movement 137, 164, 166, 170, 171, 172, 391
Singh, Santokh 82, 98, 100, 101, 103, 104, 110, 121, 125, 138, 144, 147, 148, 345, 346, 380, 382, 422
Singh, Sunder 46, 97, 99, 113, 151, 342, 428, 430
Singh, Tara 45, 49, 81, 173, 401
Singh, Teja 3, 37, 38, 39, 40, 41, 42, 44, 45, 46, 47, 48, 49, 50, 51, 52, 70, 80, 81, 96, 97, 103, 113, 120, 138, 170, 175, 201, 218, 228, 229, 342, 347, 369, 415, 416, 417, 419, 424, 425, 426, 430, 475, 478, 481, 483
Singh, Vasakha 37, 48, 49, 51, 141, 148, 157
Smedley, Agnes 186, 187, 201, 202, 534
Smith, Colonel John 67
St. Johns 280, 291, 292, 293, 294, 297, 300
Sudesh Sevak 74, 378
Surveillance 116, 118, 221, 222, 291, 298, 301

T

The Daily Province 59, 60, 62, 69, 70, 71, 74, 79
Theosophical Society 177, 178, 180, 185, 187, 188, 200, 201, 207, 211, 218
The Sangat of Victoria 51
Tilk 106, 184, 185, 187, 188, 189
Tantya Tope 22, 23
travesty 9, 17, 53, 503
Swami Trigunatita 72, 95

U

United India League 46, 73, 155, 291, 293, 341, 394, 418
Usman, Hari Singh 8, 85, 86, 119, 502, 538

V

Vande Mataram 106
Vedanta center 72, 113
Voltaire, Francois 102
voting rights 54, 66, 368, 378, 397

W

Wadi, Mahimaji 24
Wallinger, J. A. 233, 240
War Against the King 7
Wark, Reverend 323, 324
Wasco 281, 282, 302
Welland Canal 93
Wilson, Woodrow 184, 186, 189, 190, 205, 212, 533, 536
World War One 183, 270

Y

Yat-Sen, Sun 289

JASBIR SINGH MANN MD

Dr. Jasbir Singh Mann is an orthopedic surgeon, practicing in California since 1980. Medical Graduate from Punjab uni, Post Graduate from PGI Chandigarh and Columbia Uni. New York. Sikh community activist, a scholar and writer on Sikh Academic issues. His articles have appeared in a range of journals, including Nishaan, The Sikh Review, Abstracts of Sikh Studies, others and in several books. He has co-edited five books on Sikhism and arranged many international Sikh Studies conferences including in 1988, 1990, 1993, 1994, 1995, 1996, 2000, 2004, 2012 and 2013. Recipient of 2001 of D.Lit. (Honoris causa) from Punjabi University, Patiala for his contributions to Sikh studies. President Shri Guru Granth Sahib Foundation Anaheim, CA. & Editor web page www.globalsikhstudies.net. He is also a Fellow of the American Academy of Orthopedic Surgeons, a Fellow of the International College of Surgeons and a Fellow of the American College of International Physicians.

SATNAM SINGH JOHAL

Born and raised in India with Master's degree in Geography, moved to Canada in 1978. Former General Secretary of the Khalsa Diwan Society Vancouver & Vice President of the Burnaby Multicultural Society. Currently President of the Federation of Sikh Societies of Canada, President of the Canadian Sikh Study &Teaching Society Vancouver and Burnaby Library Trustee. Written many articles and organized numerous seminars and conferences on Sikh issues including religion, culture and history. Additionally holds Extensive leadership and management experience in Insurance, construction and Real Estate Sector.

www.ingramcontent.com/pod-product-compliance
Lightning Source LLC
Chambersburg PA
CBHW071956150426
43194CB00008B/899